THE JEWS OF THE OTTOMAN EMPIRE AND THE TURKISH REPUBLIC

Also by Stanford J. Shaw

BETWEEN OLD AND NEW: THE OTTOMAN EMPIRE UNDER
SULTAN SELIM III, 1789–1807

THE BUDGET OF OTTOMAN EGYPT
(*editor and translator*)

THE FINANCIAL AND ADMINISTRATIVE ORGANIZATION AND
DEVELOPMENT OF OTTOMAN EGYPT, 1517–1798

HISTORY OF THE OTTOMAN EMPIRE AND MODERN TURKEY
Volume 1: Empire of the Gazis: The Rise and Decline of
the Ottoman Empire, 1280–1808
Volume 2: Reform, Revolution and Republic: The Rise of Modern
Turkey, 1808–1975 (*with Ezel Kural Shaw*)

OTTOMAN EGYPT IN THE AGE OF THE FRENCH REVOLUTION
(*editor and translator*)

OTTOMAN EGYPT IN THE EIGHTEENTH CENTURY:
THE NIZAMNAME-I MISIR OF AHMED CEZZAR PASHA
(*editor and translator*)

STUDIES ON THE CIVILIZATION OF ISLAM
(*co-editor with William Polk*)

L'IMPERO OTTOMANO DALLA FINE DEL CONQUECENTO
ALLA CADUTA
Vol. 6: L'Impero Byzantino, L'Islamismo, e l'impero Ottomano
(*with Allesio Bombacci*)

OSMANLI IMPARATORLUĞU VE TÜRKIYE CUMHURIYETI TARIHI

The Jews of the Ottoman Empire and the Turkish Republic

STANFORD J. SHAW

Professor of Turkish and Near Eastern History
University of California, Los Angeles

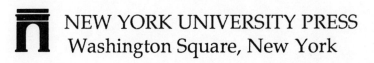

NEW YORK UNIVERSITY PRESS
Washington Square, New York

NEW YORK UNIVERSITY PRESS
Washington Square, New York

Library of Congress Cataloging-in-Publication Data
Shaw, Stanford J. (Stanford J.), 1930–
The Jews of the Ottoman Empire and the Turkish Republic /
Stanford J. Shaw
p. cm.
Includes bibliographical references and index.
ISBN 0-8147-7924-7 ISBN 0-8147-7958-1 pbk.
1. Jews—Turkey—History. 2. Turkey—
Ethnic relations.
I. Title.
DS135.T8S46 1991
956.1'015—dc20   91-6927
CIP

New York University Press books are printed on acid-free paper,
and their binding materials are chosen for strength and durability.

Manufactured in the United States of America

c 10 9 8 7 6 5 4 3 2
p 10 9 8 7 6 5 4 3 2 1

Mustafa Kemal Atatürk to the Jews of Turkey
2 February 1923

There are some of our faithful people whose destiny has been united with that of the Turks ruling them, in particular the Jews, who because their loyalty to this nation and this motherland has been confirmed, have passed their lives in comfort and prosperity until now, and will continue to live thus hereafter in comfort and happiness.[1]

This book is dedicated to the
Muslim and Jewish Turks of the Republic of Turkey,
in celebration of five hundred years of brotherhood and friendship.

1492–1992

Contents

Acknowledgements

This study is the product of some thirty five years of research on Ottoman history in the libraries and archives of Turkey, Great Britain, the United States and France. It could not have been undertaken or completed without the assistance and contributions of many people throughout the world.

I would like to thank in particular Rabbi Haim Nahum Efendi, last Grand Rabbi of the Ottoman Empire, whose comments to me during several meetings in Cairo in January and March, 1956, where he had been Chief Rabbi since 1925, inspired me to begin this work and provided me with the first inklings as to the actual nature of the relationship among the different religious communities in the Ottoman Empire; Rabbi David Asseo, Chief Rabbi of Turkey since 1961, who kindly allowed me to consult the library and archives of the Chief Rabbinate in Istanbul and to visit and photograph many of the synagogues under his jurisdiction; the pioneering historian of Ottoman Jewry, Avram Galante, who during our meeting on Kınalıada, Istanbul in May, 1957 gave me the initial direction as to how I should approach the subject of Ottoman and Turkish Jewry; Naim Güleryüz, Historian and Counsellor to the Grand Rabbinate, who opened many doors for me in Istanbul; and to many others whom I interviewed regarding the situation of Jews in the Turkish Republic, including Mr. Jak Kamhi and Mr. Elie Acıman, of Istanbul, Stella and David Candioti, of Jerusalem, Istanbul, and Rome, and Nedim Yahya of Istanbul.

I would also like to thank Professor Ismet Miroğlu, General Director of the *Başbakanlık Arşivi* (Prime Minister's Archives) and Professor Yusuf Halaçoğlu, Director of the Ottoman Archives section of the *Başbakanlık Arşivi* in Istanbul; Professor Georges Weill, Director of the Archives and Library of the *Alliance Israélite Universelle* in Paris; and to the directors and staffs of the major libraries and archives used in this study: the *Archives de la Guerre*, Chateau de Vincennes, and the *Bibliothèque Nationale* in Paris; the Municipal Library, Bayezit General Library, and Istanbul University Library in Istanbul; the Historical Archives of the Turkish General Staff, the library and archives of the Turkish Historical Society (*Türk Tarih Kurumu*) and the Turkish National Library (*Milli Kütüphane*) in Ankara; the University Research Library at the University of California, Los Angeles; the Harry Elkins Widener Library and Houghton Library at Harvard University; and the Library of Congress and National Archives in Washington, D.C.

Particular gratitude must be paid to the pioneers in the study of Ottoman and Turkish Jewry: Avram Galante, whose many works provide an essential source of reference; Joseph Nehama, one of the few Salonica Jews to survive Nazi concentration camps to complete his masterful history of Salonica Jewry; Moise Franco, of Istanbul; Professor Bernard Lewis, of the Walter Annenberg Institute for Judaic and Near Eastern Studies, Philadelphia, Pa.; Professor Salo Baron, of Columbia University; Professor Uriel Heyd and Professor Jacob Landau, of the Hebrew University, Jerusalem; Rabbi Mark Angel of New York City; Solomon Rozanes; Cecil Roth; Gershom Scholem; and Israel Zinberg; and among the brilliant young contemporary scholars whose works have been used extensively for this study: Yaakov Barnai (Israel), Esther Benbassa (Paris), Benjamin Braude (Boston), Amnon Cohen (Jerusalem), Paul Dumont (Strasbourg), Haim Gerber (Tel Aviv), Joseph Hacker (Jerusalem), Haim Hirschberg, David Kushner (Haifa), Neville Mandel (Israel), Moshe Ma'oz (Jerusalem), Robert Olson (Kentucky), Mim Kemal Öke (Bosporus University, Istanbul), Aron Rodrigue (Indiana), Mark Epstein, David Farhi, and Aryeh Shmuelevitz (Tel Aviv).

My gratitude to the following publishers for granting permission to include quotations from their works: The Cambridge University Press for the first quotation by Rabbi Tzarfati, taken from Philip Argenti, *The Religious Minorities of Chios: Jews and Roman Catholics* (Cambridge, 1970), pp. 150–152; the Hebrew Union College, for permission to publish the second quotation by Rabbi Tzarfati, taken from Israel Zinberg, *A History of Jewish Literature, vol. V, The Jewish Center of Culture in the Ottoman Empire* (New York, 1974), pp. 5–6; the Jewish Theological Seminary of America, for permission to quote from Israel M. Goldman, *The Life and Times of Rabbi David Ibn Abi Zimra* (New York, 1970), pp. 88–91, regarding the powers and duties of the Ottoman Rabbi; the Herzl Press of New York for permission to publish Kaiser Wilhelm II's statement supporting Zionist settlement in Palestine, from the *Herzl Yearbook*, ed. Ralph Patai (New York, 1961–62) IV, 236–68, and Sultan Abdülhamid II's purported statement to Newlinsky opposing Jewish settlement in Palestine, from Theodor Herzl, *The Complete Diaries of Theodor Herzl*, ed. Raphael Patai (5 vols, New York and London, 1960), I, 378.

Rabbi Jacob Ott, Rabbi Perry Netter, and Cantor Isaac Behar, of the Sephardic Temple Tifereth Israel, Los Angeles, California, inspired me to bring all my research materials together into this study by inviting me to give three public lectures on Ottoman and Turkish Jewry during April 1989, while the warm welcome provided by their congregation gave me the courage to publish the results.

Finally, my special appreciation to my wife, Ezel Kural Shaw, Professor of History, California State University, Northridge.

STANFORD J. SHAW

List of Plates

List of Abbreviations

AAS	*Asian and African Studies.*
AE	*Archives des Affaires Etrangères,* Quai d'Orsay, Paris.
AHR	*American Historical Review.*
AIU	*Alliance Israélite Universelle,* Paris.
BA or BAA	*Başbakanlık Arşivi,* Prime Minister's Archives, Istanbul.
BAIU	*Bulletin de l'Alliance Israélite Universelle: Deuxième Serie* (Paris).
BAO	*Babı Ali Evrak Odası,* Archives of the Ottoman Prime Minister's Office, Prime Minister's Archives, Istanbul.
BS	*Balkan Studies.*
BSOAS	*Bulletin of the School of Oriental and African Studies* (London).
BTTD	*Belgelerle Türk Tarih Dergisi.*
EB	*Etudes Balkaniques.*
EI	*Encyclopaedia of Islam: New Edition.*
EJ	*Encyclopaedia Judaica* (17 volumes and supplements, Jerusalem, 1972).
HTA	Historical Archives of the Turkish General Staff, Ankara (*Genelkurmay Harp Tarih Arşivi*).
HUCA	*Hebrew Union College Annual.*
IA	*Istanbul Ansiklopedisi.*
IJMES	*International Journal of Middle East Studies,* ed. S. J. Shaw, 1970–81.
IJTS	*International Journal of Turkish Studies.*
JA	*Journal Asiatique.*
JEH	*Journal of Economic History.*
JESHO	*Journal of the Economic and Social History of the Orient* (Leiden).
JO	*Journal d'Orient.*
JQR	*Jewish Quarterly Review.*
JSS	*Jewish Social Studies.*
MES	*Middle East Studies.*
MVM	*Meclisi Vükelâ Mazbataları.* Minutes of the Ottoman Council of Ministers, at Prime Minister's Archives, Istanbul.
REB	*Revue des Etudes Byzantines.*
REJ	*Revue des Etudes Juives.*
RH	*Revue Historique.*
ROMM	*Revue de l'Occident Musulman et de la Mediterranée*

TED	*Tarih Enstitüsü Dergisi.*
TK	*Tapu ve Kadastro Genel Müdürlüğü.* Directorate of Cadastres, Ankara.
TKS	*Topkapı Sarayı* Archives, Palace of the Ottoman Sultans, Istanbul
TM	*Türkiyat Mecmuası.*
TOEM	*Tarih-i Osmani Encümeni Mecmuası.*
TV	*Takvim-i Vekayi.*
WI	*Die Welt des Islams.*

1

Ingathering of the Jews

This study encompasses the Jews of the Ottoman Empire, those who lived in the areas now known as Southeastern Europe, Turkey, and the Middle East, from about 1300, when the empire was established under the leadership of Osman I, until its dissolution at the end of World War I. It then carries on the story of the Jews in the principal Ottoman successor state in modern times, the Republic of Turkey.

THE STUDY OF OTTOMAN AND TURKISH JEWRY

What was especially significant about Ottoman Jewry? Why should its experience in particular be studied? Perhaps the most important reason of all is that the Ottoman Turks provided a principal refuge for Jews driven out of western Europe by massacres and persecution between the fourteenth and twentieth centuries, particularly from blood libel massacres in western and central Europe, pogroms in Russia, and from the Holocaust. While many Ashkenazi Jews from western Europe took refuge in Bohemia, Poland and Lithuania in earlier times, many more found shelter in the Ottoman dominions of Southeastern Europe and the Middle East, where their reception was far more congenial and long-lasting. In addition, the Ottoman Empire also incorporated Romaniote Greek-speaking Jews who survived persecution in late Roman and Byzantine times and Sephardic Jews driven from the Iberian Peninsula by the Spanish reconquest and the Inquisition, as well as those who had remained in the Middle East following their dispersion from the Holy Land in Roman times and who had prospered during the centuries of the Islamic caliphate of Baghdad, the so-called *Musta'rab*, or 'Arabized' Jews. The Ottomans thus brought together for the first time since the destruction of the Temple and exile of Jews from the Holy Land those who had been dispersed to all parts of the western world. This confluence can truly be taken as an ingathering of the Jewish people, particularly since it took place in the Empire which now ruled the Holy Land, thus providing the first opportunity for their long-awaited return to their homeland.

Another important reason for studying the Jews of the Ottoman Empire

1

is that for two centuries they constituted the largest and most prosperous Jewish community in the world and a major center of Jewish religious, cultural, and intellectual life. From Jewish communities concentrated in Istanbul, Salonica and the Holy Land itself, the Ottoman Empire nourished some of the greatest Jewish intellectual and religious thinkers of their time, many of whom have remained influential in Jewish life thought and culture to the present day.

We study Ottoman Jewry, moreover, because while the Christian subjects of the sultans were constantly attempting to undermine and destroy this Muslim empire so as to restore the supremacy which they had exercised in late Roman and Byzantine times, the Sultan's Jewish subjects remained content with Ottoman rule, contributing significantly to the Empire's economic development and benefiting from toleration and protection in return. They therefore resisted all efforts to get them to join revolts and movements against it, particularly during its last century of existence. A comparison of the different Jewish and Christian experiences under and responses to Ottoman rule provides important insights into both.

And, finally, we study the Jews of the Ottoman Empire because in their ways of organizing themselves and dealing with each other we find out how Jews long separated into different cultures and traditions managed to come and live together once again, partly maintaining their adopted traditions and ways of life while forming a new and united community, very much as has been taking place in modern Israel during the twentieth century.

But why did the Jews flee from Europe? How did they come to the Ottoman Empire in its era of greatness, from its foundation in 1300 until about 1600, and why did they go there rather than elsewhere? We must examine these questions before looking into the manner in which Ottoman Jews were organized, how they related to the Ottoman state and ruling class, and how they achieved prosperity and accomplishment.

As one sifts through the centuries, it becomes apparent that the fortunes of Ottoman Jews directly paralleled those of the Ottoman Empire. While it expanded and prospered, they prospered. As the Empire began to disintegrate and weaken in the seventeenth and eighteenth centuries, its Christian subjects replaced and suppressed its Jews with the help of the great powers of Europe, where anti-Semitism was once again on the rise, causing them to lose their political influence and economic prosperity. The Ottoman Empire continued to receive new waves of Jewish refugees from various parts of Europe who were fleeing the political and religious reaction that followed the Napoleonic era early in the nineteenth century, the conservative reaction to the revolutions of 1848, persecution and pogroms in Central Europe and Russia starting in the 1880s and 1890s, the Bolshevik revolution and Russian Civil War during and after World

War I, and, finally, during the time of the Turkish Republic after 1923, Jews who fled from the greatest persecution of them all, the Holocaust, in the 1930s and during World War II.

In the nineteenth century the Ottoman Jewish community was revived and reinvigorated as part of Ottoman renewal, due both to the Ottoman reform movement, or *Tanzimat*, and to the stimulus and assistance given by Jews who had finally begun to achieve prosperity and wealth in western Europe and America. This continued into the Young Turk Constitutional era before and during World War I. The relationship between the Ottoman Jewish community and the world Zionist movement, the contribution of Ottoman Jews during World War I and their help to the Turkish national movement during the Turkish War for Independence which followed, and then the role of the Jewish community in the Turkish Republic today, are all key issues which must be explored in evaluating the Jewish experience under Turkish rule over the centuries.

SITUATION OF THE JEWS IN EUROPE

The stimulus for this study is the five-hundredth anniversary of the massive expulsion of the Jews from the Iberian Peninsula and their refuge in the Ottoman Empire starting in 1492. In fact, however, this date marked not just the beginning of a great exile wave but also the culmination of Christian persecution and Jewish movement to the East which had begun almost three centuries before. Just as the Turks began moving into the Middle East and Anatolia from Central Asia at the end of the eleventh century, beginning the process by which they would take over the area two centuries later, the Jews of Europe began to experience new waves of persecution. Church theologians condemned what they considered to be Jewish influence over the Christian masses, so legislation was issued by high religious leaders and councils to bring such contacts to an end. In 1078, the Pope decreed that Jews should not occupy important positions in Christian countries and that no Jew could be superior to any Christian. Jews who had settled in France and Germany subsequently found their occupations increasingly narrowed by economic and religious prejudice to trades associated with banking and money changing, which in turn exacerbated long-held religious prejudices and converted them into political and economic persecutions based on racial and religious anti-Semitism.

Jews had long been accused of being Christ killers, the people who had caused the Crucifixion because of their anguish over his departure from the religion of his fathers. Added to this, however, were new accusations, of which the most pernicious were the popular myths known as 'blood libel', or 'ritual murder' accusations, first circulated by the Greek church.

This was the idea that Jews kidnapped and murdered Christian children and drained their bodies of blood for use in religious ceremonies, especially those associated with wine and the making of unleavened bread, or 'matzoh' during Passover. Added to this was the myth of 'desecration of the Host', which alleged that Jews profaned the wafer consecrated in the Catholic ceremony of the Eucharist by stabbing, tormenting or burning it in order to subject Christ once again to the agonies of the Cross. Added to the ritual murder theme, which pervaded all of western culture at the time, 'the Jew' was represented as an inhuman and grotesque character equated with immorality, magic, and complete Evil.

It stretches the imagination to believe that such strange notions could stir people into frenzies of emotion. But they were powerful influences on the Christian masses of the time, impelling them to repeated attacks, even on aged and crippled Jews and on children, not only stoning them and pulling their beards and hair but massacring them and destroying their shops and homes, particularly during the week preceding Easter when Christian religious passions were at their peak. Such incidents took place repeatedly in Europe for seven centuries, starting first at Norwich, England in 1144, and continuing into the late nineteenth century. They also occurred in the Middle East, with even more vehemence and violence, perpetrated by Christians whose ancestors had infected their European co-religionists with these prejudices in the first place. Of course in many cases those who spread these myths and thus stimulated these attacks, as well as many who carried them out, had motives which were far from religious, using them to avoid payment of debts, to eliminate competitors, or particularly in the Middle East after 1800, to transfer to Jews Muslim hatred of Christians resulting from Christian attacks on Muslims in the newly independent states of Southeastern Europe.

The religious fervor and greed which permeated the Crusades during the twelfth and thirteenth centuries added fuel to these passions and resulting attacks. It all started on 27 November, 1095 when Pope Urban II went to Clermont-Ferrand in southern France and delivered a speech which started almost half a millennium of Crusades against the Islamic world. With great emotion he said the Christians of the East, and particularly in the Holy Land, were suffering terrible agonies at the hands of the Muslims, formerly the Arabs and now the advancing Turks. He went on to state that Jerusalem already had been profaned by the anti-Christs and that Christian Constantinople now was under threat, and he appealed to all of Christian Europe to send out an army to save Byzantium and rescue the Holy Land from the unbelievers, offering remission from all sins, past and future, for those who shared in this endeavor. Peter the Venerable (1090–1156) followed with advice to King Louis VII of France to adopt harsh measures against the Jews, producing an anti-Jewish tract, *Adversus Judaeorum inveteratum duritam* (1140), which had substantial influence in spreading and deepening anti-Semitic attacks throughout western Europe.

All of Christian Europe was driven to frenzy by such religious and political leaders who spread the idea of freeing the Holy Land and Byzantium, though again, as with the blood libel and desecration of host accusations, for many economic motives were probably as important as religious ones. And Christians who were stirred to believe that Muslims were the embodiment of all evil soon found it convenient to include the Jews, whose co-religionists were prospering in the Muslim lands and therefore supporting the Muslims against the Crusader attacks in fear of renewed spread of anti-Semitism into the Middle East. The Crusaders were led to believe that they were servants of God, with all sins forgiven in advance for what they were going to do in the Holy Land, so they were in no way inhibited from attacking and plundering Jewish communities as they went along, particularly when the monks who accompanied them suggested that it would add to their favor with God if they forced the Jews they found along the way to convert to Christianity. So as the Crusaders marched along the Rhine through Germany and Austria southward toward the Islamic Middle East, they sacked and often destroyed the Jewish communities found along their paths, massacring hundreds in each place as they went and ravaging their homes and shops. Moreover they left in their wake new 'blood libel' and 'desecration of host' passions which in turn led to subsequent attacks on the surviving Jewish communities wherever there was even the slightest rumor which provided a pretext and rallying cry. Needless to say, on their arrival in the Holy Land, and particularly at Jerusalem, where the Latin Kingdom lasted from 1099 to 1291, the Crusaders were even more harsh in their treatment of its Jews than they were of the Muslims whom they were originally sent to exterminate.

The spread of the Black Death throughout Western Europe, particularly between 1348 and 1350, provided a new pretext to blame Jews for catastrophe. In this case the story was spread widely that they poisoned water supplies to cause the plague and wipe out Christianity, even though in fact the plague seems to have reached Europe through sailors coming in ships from the Far East. Christian Europe began to feel that by persecuting and eliminating the Jews the spread of the plague would come to an end. Jews throughout Europe were therefore subjected to new waves of massacres. Anti-Jewish attacks were particularly virulent in Germany. Many Jews were tortured until confessions were extracted, which then were used to attack and kill others. Similar hysteria soon spread to France, the Christian parts of Spain and to Poland-Lithuania, to which Jews had earlier fled as a result of persecution in the West, with passions so great that many Jews were torn apart even before the plague reached their localities. In many places the Jews fought back to defend themselves, but they were overwhelmed. Many Jews who survived were ultimately allowed to resettle in their old homes, but invariably on worse terms than before. The Black Death and the resulting pogroms not only caused deaths and destruction of homes and shops of thousands of Jews, thus, but also intensified the popular Christian stereotypes of the Jew which have remained the basis for Christian anti-Semitism in modern times.

Christendom, thus, could not tolerate the presence of the Jews in its midst. Insofar as the Church and its followers were concerned, the only tolerable Jew was a Jewish convert to Christianity. The rest had to be eliminated or at least isolated from all true believers. The resulting discrimination against Jews was institutionalized by a series of regulations enacted throughout Christendom attempting to force them to convert and requiring them to wear distinctive badges and hats if they did not. In most parts of Christian Europe Jews were compelled to hear sermons intended to convert them to the 'true faith'. The kings of France ordered Jews to wear a special circular badge on the breast and a second one on the back, with insult compounded on injury by the collection of heavy taxes in return for the 'privilege'. Spanish Jews were ordered to wear the 'Badge of Shame', though the requirement was not constantly enforced due to fierce Jewish resistance, including threats to leave Christian Spain for the areas that remained under Muslim control. It was only during the early years of the fifteenth century, when Muslim resistance in Spain was almost at an end that this requirement was rigidly enforced. There were additional stipulations that Jews allow their hair and beards to grow long, with fines and whipping stipulated for violators. Similar stipulations were enforced in England, with Jews required to wear a piece of yellow taffeta, six fingers long and three broad over their hearts, normally in the shape of the Tablets of the Law. In Italy the badge took various forms, in Rome a circular yellow patch worn on the outer garments of men or on the veils of women, and in the Papal states a yellow hat for men, a yellow kerchief for women. Such stipulations spread through much of Christendom in later years. In Germany, church councils required Jews to wear a pointed hat, with the badge introduced later. One German church council in 1418 ordered Jewish women to attach bells to their dresses. Even in the eighteenth century the Jews of Prague had to wear yellow collars over their coats.

Though the Reformation ultimately benefited Jews by stimulating a trend toward religious liberty, in the short run it proved disastrous for those still remaining in Christian Europe. Luther's first call for toleration of the Jews was given in the hope of their conversion to Christianity. When missionary activity failed to secure conversion, they were treated with fear, hatred and loathing.

Luther believed and preached that the Jews committed public blasphemy by slandering Christ and everything Christian. He urged that action be taken against them so as to curtail this blasphemous activity and to avoid the complicity of Christians in their conduct. Of course, this insistence on action against the Jews was entirely consistent with his dealings with other opponents, whether they be papists, Turks and other Muslims, Anabaptists, or Sacramentarians. But for Luther the Jews were the most important example of opposition to the Gospel, which he felt encouraged Christians to blaspheme.

Once he became certain that he could not convert them, then, Luther displayed even greater hostility to the Jews than that expressed regarding the Prophet Muhammad and Muslims, who, after all, were not in daily contact with his followers. Luther complained about the Jews' insistence on retaining their old beliefs in the face of his message. Because of his strong aversion to usury he called them 'venomous and virulent', 'thieves and brigands', and 'disgusting vermin'. Most other German religious reformers of the time were equally anti-Jewish. Among them were Martin Bucer, whose sermons and writings emphasized in particular the losses caused to Christian merchants by the economic aptitude of Jews. John Calvin (1509–64) and his collaborators often accused Jews of blaspheming against the Christian religion while accusing their opponents of Jewish interpretations of scripture. This mentality led to a determined policy of eliminating Jews in Christian lands, an important background to the horrors inflicted on European Jewry by Nazi Germany.

The Jews suffered even more as a result of the Catholic Counter-Reformation, whose leaders often claimed that European Jews were responsible for the 'Judaizing' tendencies of the Reformation. Papal persecution of the Jews in Rome set the pattern for the rest of Christian Europe. In 1542 an Inquisition court was established in Rome to pursue the same policies which had driven the Jews out of Spain. On Rosh Hashanah, 4 September 1553, many Hebrew books, including the Talmud, were condemned and burned by the government of Rome. A Franciscan Friar who had converted to Judaism was burned alive, after which a ban was issued against the presence and use of all Talmudic literature in the city. Even worse was to come when Cardinal Caraffa, leader of the Counter Reformation in Rome, became Pope Paul IV in 1555 and issued a bull which revived all the restrictive religious legislation against Jews which previously had been enforced only intermittently. Jews now were confined to a special quarter of the city, called the *ghetto*, located on a humid low site on the left bank of the Tiber which was regularly subject to flooding, causing the spread of serious illnesses even among the healthiest members of the community. Jews were forced to wear the yellow Jewish badge, either a yellow hat for men or a yellow neckerchief for women. They could no longer own real estate or most other property. They could not act as physicians for Christians, could not deal in food stuffs or anything other than old clothes and second hand goods of various sorts, and they could not be called by any title of respect such as *signor*. While these regulations were relaxed for a time by his immediate successors, they were enforced again by Pope Gregory XIII (1572–85), who in 1577 revived the thirteenth-century 'Sermons to the Jews', requiring a certain percentage of each Jewish community to attend local churches in order to hear the sermons of priests, visiting friars, or even converted Jews who were sent to open their eyes to the 'true faith' and if possible convert them, a practice which was to inflame Catholic-Jewish relations in many parts of Europe for centuries thereafter.

On the whole, political and religious leaders in Western Europe were not anxious to eliminate or destroy their Jewish communities. Particularly in their role as bankers and money lenders, Jews performed important economic services which Christians could not do because the Catholic church maintained its prohibition against Christians charging interest in return for lending money. They were aware that the presence of Jews contributed greatly to their prosperity, so they often protected them against persecution whenever they could, since their incomes in many cases were managed and enhanced by Jewish advisers. But such protection went only so far in the face of popular religious passions, and it was largely dissipated and ineffective when the political and religious leaders were themselves threatened unless they went along with the demands of the bigots. So the periodic persecutions and blood libels and massacres went on, sometimes extending to forced conversions of Jews to Christianity upon penalty of death.

The plight of the Jews in sixteenth-century Europe was not new. There had often been massacres, as for example in Frankfurt in 1241, Munich in 1285–86, and Amleder in 1336–37. Expulsions had been carried out in earlier centuries, but they always had been limited both in time and area. But as royal authority extended more widely in each kingdom, so also had the expulsions become more extensive and permanent. They began in, England, starting with the decree of banishment issued by King Edward I on 18 July 1290 and enforced for the next four centuries, until 1650. In France, Louis IX (1226–70) ordered the expulsion of all Jews from his kingdom as he left for his first Crusade in 1249. The decree was only imperfectly carried out, and many of those who left were able to return later, but Philip the Fair (1285–1314) ordered all French Jews to be arrested (22 July 1306). He followed this up with a decree condemning them to expulsion and confiscation of their property, but this was revoked by his successor. Charles IV expelled the Jews again in 1322, and it was only due to a financial crisis in 1359 that they were admitted to France once again a few years later. In 1380 and 1382 there were riots against the Jews in Paris, and starting in 1394 they were expelled again, this time not to return for centuries, in some areas not until the start of the

French Revolution at the end of the eighteenth century. In 1495 Jews were expelled from Lithuania, where they had only recently taken refuge from western persecution, unless they converted to Christianity. While they were restored in 1503, the Christian merchants of Kiev secured from King Sigismund III a prohibition against permanent Jewish settlement or purchase of real property in their city, a prohibition which became permanent when Kiev was annexed to Russia in 1667. As a result of the virulent anti-Semitic hatred spread by the Russian Orthodox church, Jews were excluded from Russia itself from the fifteenth century until 1772, when they were included as a result of the Russian annexation of Poland and Lithuania. They were banned from Hungary after 1376, from Naples in 1510–11, and sporadically from almost everywhere in Germany in the fourteenth and fifteenth centuries. Because of German lack of unity, however, these deportations were temporary and local. Jews simply went from one locality to another and then ultimately returned to their original homes as time passed and the deportation decrees were annulled or forgotten by political and religious leaders who saw their own incomes falling in the absence of their Jewish advisers.

Many more, however, fled to more distant lands in search of safety. Some went to the lands still ruled by Muslims, particularly to Egypt, North Africa, Cyprus, Rhodes and other islands in the Aegean and eastern Mediterranean, as well as to Spain and Iraq, where Jews had always found far more toleration and prosperity than had been the case in Christian lands. Some, however, went to Byzantine Constantinople and Alexandria, during the early Crusades in the eleventh and twelfth centuries, particularly from France and England. Other Jewish refugees who arrived in Salonica before the Ottoman conquest were expelled from Italy by Charles II in 1290, from Hungary in 1375 and from Spain in 1391 following the anti Semitic speeches of Vicente Ferrar, but in all these places they found their lives little better than they had been in Christian Europe.

THE JEWS OF ISLAM

The situation in Spain was different than that in the rest of Western Europe because of the influence of Islam, which ruled all or part of the Iberian Peninsula from the seventh through the fifteenth centuries while making its Jews a tolerated and extremely prosperous and productive minority.

There were two parallel traditions in Islam regarding Jews. On one hand Muslims shared and strengthened the pre-Islamic Arab feeling of friendship with their Jewish neighbors, both in northern and southern Arabia, who were praised in the Arabic literature of the time for their loyalty, hospitality and generosity. Islam considered that Jews, like Christians, worshipped the same one God as did the Muslims, that they used the same books sent down by God, the Old and New Testaments, Holy Books proclaiming the word of the one God which he revealed to the Prophet Muhammed, as later set down in the Koran. This was emphasized by the fact that the great figures of the Old and New Testaments, Moses, Isaac, Abraham, and Jesus Christ were included in the Koran, with the familiar biblical stories appearing in only slightly altered form in the holy book of Islam. To Muslims, Moses was a Prophet just like Muhammad. Moses was the man that God chose to speak to the Jews just as he later chose Muhammad the Prophet to speak to the Muslims and Jesus Christ to speak to those who became Christians. To Muslims, therefore, Jews, like Christians, were considered to be believers in the same God; they were to be accepted and protected in whatever Muslim community they lived.

At the same time there was another less favorable tradition about Jews in Islam. Since Jews and Christians worshipped the same God as did Muslims, since Moses and Jesus Christ were considered by Muslims to be earlier recipients of the message of God, and since the Prophet Muhammad brought a later version of the same message, there was no real reason, insofar as the Prophet and later Muslims were concerned, why Jews and Christians should not accept his message and themselves become Muslims. The fact that they did not, even when the twenty Jewish clans who lived in Medina were invited to do so by the Prophet himself, brought a certain irritation, and at times attacks as a result of Muhammad's belief that Islam rather than Judaism was the true religion of Abraham, that Abraham himself was not a Jew, and that differences between Islam and Judaism were due to the latter's corruption or distortion of the truth. When the Jewish tribes in Arabia refused to support the Prophet's attack on Mecca in AD 625, he attacked and defeated them, but subsequently allowed them to live in peace under Muslim rule in return for paying a proportion of their produce as tax, a tradition that survived well into the Ottoman period. Cases of persecution of Jews were, however, very few and far between in the great Islamic empires, except in Shi'a Iran and the parts of Iraq which it at times ruled, where religious fanaticism led to persecution, not only of Jews but also of Muslims who followed Orthodox Sunni Islam, the more prevalent view which dominated most of the Muslim world. Except in Iran there were hardly ever any cases of the kind of forced conversion or open attacks on Jews that were all-too common in Christian lands. For the most part, then, Jews and Christians, considered to be 'people of the book' (*ahl al-kitâb*), lived as protected minorities, or *dhimmis* (*zimmis* in Ottoman Turkish), in the classical Islamic empires of the Umayyads of Damascus and Spain and the Abbasids of Baghdad. They preserved their religions and freedom within their own religiously-based communities and paid a special poll tax called *harac* or *cizye* in return for protection of their lives, properties, and religious practices and beliefs by the Muslim rulers, exemption from military service, and the right to maintain their own forms of government and justice in their own communities. While they lived in great comfort and prosperity, there were limitations, some marks of discrimination, so that one could say that Jews and Christians were not as equal as Muslims. The testimony of Jews was given less weight in Muslim courts than that of Muslim witnesses, they could not marry Muslim women or keep Muslims as slaves, they could not bear arms, and the like, but compared to the active persecution to which Jews were subjected in the Christian lands of Europe, the world of Islam was paradise for them.

Nowhere in the centuries of exile following the destruction of the Second Temple did the Jews reach greater heights than in Spain, to which they fled in large numbers following the Muslim conquest of Cordova in 711. But Muslim Spain began to disappear with the start of the Christian reconquest in 1100, which continued steadily through Leon, Asturias, Aragon, Navarro, Catalonia and Castille until the elimination of the last Muslim states at Seville, Saragossa, and finally Granada in 1492. The Christian reconquest of Spain did not mark a sudden change for its Jews. The new Christian rulers of Spain found it convenient to retain Jews for a time, not only as bankers but in many other high court positions, so many Spanish Jews prospered for quite some time under Christian rule. Alfonso VI (1072–1109) and his grandson Alfonso VII (1126–1157) of Castille in fact offered refuge to Jews fleeing from persecution in North Africa, taking them into their courts as interpreters, bankers, advisers and even tax farmers. Jews were granted large estates, and they were encouraged to engage in trade and commerce in the major cities. Jewish men of letters made significant contributions to the development of Castillian literature in the early centuries of the reconquest. James I of Valencia allowed Jews to have lawsuits between them judged by Jewish law, with the king's law applying only in criminal cases. A special Jewish oath was established to take into account their religious beliefs. Jews had the right to acquire land, even from noblemen and clergymen. Jewish prisoners even were given furloughs so they would be on their homes on the Sabbath.

But as time went on and Christians grew confident in the wake of victories over Muslims, the Jews of Christian Spain faced more and more restrictions and difficulties. As Christian rule became solidified, there was less need for Jews, so starting in Saragossa in 1250, the Spanish Jews came to be subjected to the same persecutions by Christians as had taken place elsewhere in Western Europe. The old blood libel and desecration of host attacks now became more and more common in Spain. Restrictions began to be imposed against the appointment of

Jews to high places where they would be in a position to direct the activities of Christians. Jews were gathered into ghettos, they were not allowed to leave their homes at night or on Christian holidays, they were subjected to special tax impositions which drove many to poverty, and various clothing restrictions were imposed from time to time. Crusaders attacked Jews in Toledo in 1212 and again just a century later. All the Jews in Castille were arrested and imprisoned in 1281, and they were released only after the payment of a huge ransom. Under the influence of itinerant preachers from France, a whole series of popular disturbances almost exterminated the Jewish communities of Navarre in 1328. In 1340 King Alfonso XI restricted Jewish participation in trade and commerce. The Jews of Castille, Aragon and Valencia suffered during the Black Death that spread through most of Spain in 1348, but they still were blamed for it, as was the case elsewhere in Europe at the time, and were subjected to severe persecutions in subsequent years as a result. The Jewish community of Toledo was sacked in 1355. In 1391 Bishop St. Vincent Ferrer issued a series of hostile accusations against the Jews, causing the spread of violent attacks throughout the Iberian peninsula and the extermination of many Jewish communities and destruction of their synagogues, including those at Madrid, Burgos, Cordova, Barcelona, and Toledo and throughout Castille and Valencia. Only those of Granada remained untouched because of its continued rule by the Muslim Nasirids. Christian soldiers and sailors went by ship from one port to another in Spain, inciting the local Christian populations to attack their Jewish communities, raping, plundering and murdering as they went. Many Jews who survived were forced to flee elsewhere in Europe and many others were forced to convert to Christianity, particularly in mass conversions carried out in 1391. In the fourteenth and fifteenth centuries, those of these 'new Christians' called *marranos*, who remained crypto-Jews and secretly continued to practice Judaism, were at times persecuted and burned at the stake, while the *conversos*, those 'new Christians' who converted and practiced their new faith wholeheartedly and sincerely, were often involved in 'guilt by association', and subjected to the same fate.

Repression increased during the early years of the fifteenth century. Under the influence of the *converso* Bishop of Burgos, in 1408 Jews were forbidden to be given positions in Castille which would enable them to have any authority over Christians. In 1412 they were forbidden to leave their quarters, to practice the professions or crafts, to employ Christians, carry arms, go into public without beards, or even to levy community taxes or have cases judged in Jewish community courts. About the same time, mobs inspired by Dominican monks forced thousands of Jews in Castille and Aragon to convert to Christianity. Despite these problems, the New Christians still did amazingly well for a time, rising rapidly and becoming extremely prosperous and important in the government, the army and the universities. It did not take long, however, for the more fanatic Catholic clergy to inspire the masses to jealousy at their success, accusing them of secretly remaining Jews and causing attacks on them as well during the later years of the century.

As a result of these two centuries of anti-Semitic persecutions, then, thousands of Jews had already fled from Spain long before the final expulsion took place in 1492. By the time that Ferdinand II took the throne of Aragon (1479–1516) and Isabella I that of Castille (1474–1504), the once flourishing Jewish communities of Barcelona and Valencia had already disappeared. Even Castille, which once had the most densely-settled Jewish quarter in Europe, had no more than 30,000 Jewish families, though many more had become *conversos*, seeking to prove their loyalty by persecuting their former co-religionists even more fiercely than their Christian colleagues.

In the end, it was the marriage of Isabella with Ferdinand that doomed Spanish Jewry, even though it had been arranged by Jewish and *converso* courtiers. At first, they continued the policy of tolerance followed by their predecessors in Christian Spain, protecting Jewish communities whenever they were attacked by mobs instigated by fanatical monks and employing Jewish administrators in the government. Their advisers, however, convinced them that the only way to solve the kingdom's many problems was to unify it religiously, particularly by eradicating the sin of heresy and by confiscating the wealth possessed by the Jews. In 1480, as a result, a special court called the Spanish Inquisition was introduced, with the job of hunting out and punishing all heretics, particularly those like the *conversos* who were accused of remaining Jews in secret and thus corrupting not only the Church but also the Kingdom. *Converso* families accused of Jewish activities were imprisoned and tortured and some were publicly burned at the stake. During the 1480s, the Inquisition discovered that not only were the *conversos* returning to Judaism but that Jews were helping them to do so, leading to the inevitable conclusion that because of the close relations of *conversos* with Spanish Jews, the former would persist in their heresy unless the latter were eliminated, either by conversion, execution or expulsion. Heresy among the *conversos* thus was inevitable unless the Jews were no longer available to corrupt and mislead them.

The Inquisition worked as a double-edged sword, turning first on the *conversos* who survived the Inquisition's questioning, and then on all Jews who refused to convert despite persecution. Starting about 1481 Christian mobs inspired by Inquisition monks ran through the Jewish quarters of the major Spanish cities, pillaging, beating and murdering Jews of all ages and desecrating synagogues, often while religious services were in process. In 1483 alone, thirteen thousand Jews were executed by order of the Chief Inquisitor, Fray Thomas de Torquemada, who himself is said to have been of Jewish origin. During the next decade thousands more suffered the agonies of torture and death while resisting his agents.

The defeat of the last Muslim dynasty in Spain, with the Christian capture of Granada on 20 January 1492, brought to an end 781 years of Muslim rule and doomed Spanish Jewry. The final expulsion of Jews from Spain and Sicily, decreed by Ferdinand and Isabella at the Alhambra on 31 of March 1492, and their forced conversion and subsequent expulsion from Portugal starting with the decree of 5 December 1496, thus were only culminations of what had been going on for at least three centuries. While the *marranos* remained longer, their persecution by the Inquisition intensified, particularly in the seventeenth century, forcing many of them to emigrate as well. Similarly the conversion of the *moriscos*, their Muslim counterparts, remained equally suspect by the Inquisition. After their use of Arabic as well as their traditional customs and costumes were forbidden by Philip II in 1566, they also were deported between 1609 and 1614.

The expulsions from Spain were particularly brutal, with as many as 150,000 Jews being forced to leave in just four months between the end of April and 2 August 1492, the final day stipulated by the expulsion order. It is difficult to determine how many Jews actually left Spain and how many remained as converts to Christianity. Estimates of the exiles vary from as few as 100,000 to as many as almost one million. Generally, however, it is now accepted that approximately 300,000 Jews left the Iberian peninsula during the fifteenth and early sixteenth centuries. Most simply abandoned their properties or sold them to Christians at mere fractions of their actual values. Many departed with nothing but their knowledge and skills in seeking out new homelands.

But where to go? Where could they go? Some managed to survive for a time in Germany and Italy where, despite the many persecutions, massacres and expulsions, their very lack of unity made refuge possible in neighboring districts at least for a time. But these were temporary and uncertain solutions in view of the popular prejudices and passions, particularly in Germany, which often were stirred up as a result of the arrival of more than a few Jews at once. As a result, few Iberian refugees stayed in western or central Europe for any length of time.

Some took the relatively easy road eastward into Poland and Lithuania where they founded the great Jewish communities of Eastern Europe which flourished for centuries before being destroyed, first by the great nineteenth-century Russian pogroms and then by the Holocaust. But already in the fourteenth century the Jewish immigrants to Eastern Europe were being subjected to persecution, not only by native Polish Christians who resented the influx of so many non-Christian strangers, but also by Germans emigrating eastwards who brought with them the same prejudices which had driven the Jews out of their Central European homes not long before. John of Capistrano, who had spread a blood libel in Germany which had caused the massacre of most of the Jews of Breslau and the expulsion of the rest early in the fifteenth century, was brought to Poland by its Roman Catholic religious leaders. His preaching led to the Edict of Nieszawa in 1454, which annulled all the charters of freedom which the Jews had obtained from earlier rulers, and to the Jews' temporary expulsion from Lithuania in 1495. In 1527 the notables of Vilna secured from King Sigismund I of Poland the right to prohibit further Jewish settlement there. These edicts ultimately were annulled and the charters restored, but a feeling of incipient persecution remained, so not nearly as many Jews went to Eastern Europe at that time as might otherwise have been the case.

Some refugees instead joined the Arab *moriscos* going across the Straits of Gibraltar to the seaports of Morocco, Algeria and Tunisia, the latter two to come under Ottoman rule a half century later. But most followed the bulk of their Jewish brothers from the rest of Europe eastward through the lands bordering the Mediterranean into the territory of the greatest Muslim power of the time, the Empire of the Ottoman sultans, in the hope of regaining the power and prosperity they had achieved in Islamic Spain.

THE JEWS OF ROME AND BYZANTIUM

The Middle East itself did not seem that inviting in the early centuries of European persecution of Jews. The last of the great Islamic Caliphates, that of the Abbasids of Baghdad, had started to crumble in the eleventh century. It had disappeared entirely with the Mongol conquest of Baghdad in 1258 which, along with the invasions of the Holy Land by the Crusaders from the West, had left considerable political, economic and social anarchy throughout the Middle East and little haven for refugees. Until early in the fourteenth century, moreover, the remaining lands of the Middle East and much of Southeastern Europe were ruled by the heirs of the same empire that had driven the Jews out of the Holy Land in the first place, the East Roman Empire of Byzantium from its capital at Constantinople.

Jews had emigrated from the Holy Land to the Aegean shores of Roman Anatolia as early as the fourth century BC. They had reached the Pontic shores of the Black Sea at present-day Trabzon, no later than the second century BC. They came *en masse* and settled in the thousands around Bursa and Konya and in central and southeastern Anatolia after the destruction of the Second Temple in AD 70, long before the foundation of Byzantium. Pagan Rome had been reasonably tolerant to Jews once their revolt in the Holy Land had been put down. Jews constituted about twelve percent of the empire's population, and were allowed to live and to engage in whatever occupations they wished without any limitations by the state. At times, moreover, they were given special exemptions from civil obligations required of all other citizens, to enable them to fulfill their religious duties.

In Roman Egypt and Syria there were difficulties caused by the long-standing Greek antipathy for Jews. Hellenic authors depicted Jews as a contaminated rabble of unclean lepers, whom the Egyptians had thrown out of their country in the time of Moses in order to purge themselves of defilement. Already at this time the Greeks were inventing the blood libel and desecration of host fantasies which were to cause so much suffering in later times, affirming that Jews sacrificed human beings at the Temple in Jerusalem, using their blood for religious rituals. Many Greeks used the destruction of the Temple as proof that God hated the Jews and was punishing them for their 'evil acts'. As a result, even as Rome continued to treat the Jews well, in the East there were numerous Greek attacks against Jewish settlements.

After the Edict of Milan (AD 312) began the Roman Empire's gradual conversion to Christianity by providing equal rights for all religions and recognition and some degree of toleration to Christians, however, the Empire became increasingly intolerant toward Jews. The Hellenistic anti-Semitic images of the Jews as a people whom God hated were revived. Roman Jews therefore were gradually deprived of their rights and made into second-class citizens. They were excluded from administrative and military positions. Jewish missionary activities among Christians along with Christian conversions to Judaism were forbidden. Jews were no longer allowed to have any relations with Christian women, and the masses increasingly attacked them in the streets as well as in their homes and shops. In 387–388 Christian mobs followed the destruction of all the heathen temples in Rome by going on to destroy synagogues as well. Under Theodoric (493–526), after some Christian slaves were punished for murdering their Jewish master, mobs attacked Jews throughout Rome, burning their homes and synagogues. Soon afterwards, the Jews were accused of causing an earthquake in Rome by mocking a crucifix, and many were tortured to death as a result.

This intolerance and persecution was even worse in the East Roman Empire, founded in AD 330, when Emperor Constantine dedicated the old town of Byzantium as the site for his new capital and gave it his name, Constantinople. Imperial edicts starting with those of Emperor Arcadius in 395 and continuing until the Ottoman conquest of Constantinople in 1453, subjected Byzantine Jewry to over a millenium of oppression and persecution. Thousands of Jews who had flooded into Asia Minor following their exile from the Holy Land and their descendants were forcibly converted, murdered, or driven out as a result of sporadic purges.

The Jews of Byzantium, like other subjects of the emperors, engaged in only a few occupations. They had practiced law and medicine in Rome and in the early days of the East Roman Empire, but in later times they were prohibited from such activities. Instead they concentrated on trades that Christians abhorred the most, serving as leather tanners and executioners in particular. Wealthier Jews handled the importation of spices, perfumes and pearls from India, silks from China, and precious stones and oils from Iran. Jews also were artisans, manufacturing and selling copper wares, glassware, and leather goods and monopolizing carpentry and textile dying.

The Jewish settlements in Byzantine cities such as Constantinople and Thessaloniki were concentrated in a few 'ghettos', which were moved from time to time according to the caprices of the reigning emperors of the time. In fourth and fifth century Constantinople they initially seem to have been concentrated around a synagogue in the *Chalkoprateia* (coppersmiths) section of the city, located near modern Bayezit square, but their synagogue then was transformed into a church and in AD 422 the Jews living in the vicinity were moved away by East Roman Emperor Theodosius II, who wanted to get them out of Constantinople proper altogether. While the Italian, German and Spanish merchants were allowed to remain in the center of the city, the Jews were moved to the southern shore of the Golden Horn, across to *Stenum/Stanyere*, on the slopes of modern Galata facing the Bosporus, and to what are now Ortaköy and Arnavutköy, on the European shores of the Bosporus toward the Black Sea. The Jews seem to have returned to Constantinople in the ninth century, settling along the southern shores of the Golden Horn eastward around the modern Topkapı Sarayı point from Ottoman Bahçekapı to the area beneath the palace and extending to the shores of the Sea of Marmara, with one of the gates in the Byzantine sea walls in that area coming to be called *Porta Iudece* (the Jewish gate) as a result. These Jews were once again moved out of the city in the late eleventh century, across the Golden Horn to the modern Galata/Beyoğlu area, with others moving along the northern shores of the Golden Horn to *Picridion*, where they remained in Ottoman Hasköy until the twentieth century. In the twelfth century, some Jews again moved across to the southern shores of the Golden Horn in Constantinople. There they settled beneath the Byzantine palace heights in the areas known in Ottoman times as *Bahçekapı* and *Balıkpazarı*, immediately north and west of their former settlement, while those on the northern shores moved up the hill from Galata to the base of the Genoese tower and to the heights of modern Beyoğlu.

When the Latin crusaders occupied Constantinople starting in 1204, the Jewish synagogue and quarter in *Bahçekapı* was destroyed by a widespread fire which spread all the way to the Hagia Sophia church, but the adjacent Jewish quarter and synagogue seem to have remained intact. After the departure of the Latins, the Jewish settlements along the northern shores of the Golden Horn extended into the area between Galata and Hasköy, particularly to the Ottoman Kasımpaşa quarter. From 1275 to the Ottoman conquest in 1453, the Venetian and Genoese colonies in Constantinople were able to settle wherever they wished due to the strong support of their governments, while the Byzantines compelled the Jews, who lacked such protection, to move to areas in which no-one else wanted to live. The Venetians thus settled along the southern shores of the Golden Horn in the area of Fener, which later became the center of the Greek Patriarchate, while Jews engaged in the odipherous occupation of curing and selling leather moved around to *Langa*, on the northern shores of the Sea of Marmara, where the odors of their trade would not disturb others, remaining there until the Ottoman conquest. Other Jews engaged in sea transport moved from Galata to the shores of the Bosporus, the areas of present-day Kabataş and Ortaköy, where there emerged new Jewish settlements and synagogues which have remained until modern times.

Byzantine Jews were nominally free to follow their own faith, but just as the Romans had reduced Jews to no more than subject status, so also starting with the edicts of Emperor Arkadius issued in 395, the Byzantine emperors excluded Jews from rights of full citizenship and restricted the locations of their settlements and synagogues as well as their rights to engage in trade and the professions. The motives of Romans were mainly political; but Byzantines were moved also by religious bigotry. From their strong conviction that the Jews were condemned by God for rejecting his Word and for the crime of killing Jesus Christ, it was logical to them to conclude that the Jews ought to be punished by God's new chosen people, the Christians, by being subjected to restrictions and persecutions. To the Greek Church, Jews were absolute filth, whose touch was considered contaminating. Christians who had any contact with Jews had to be excommunicated. As a result, once Christianity was declared to be the religion of the state by Theodosius II (408–450), those Jews who lived in the Byzantine Empire were subjected to severe legal restrictions, substantially limiting even minor details of their secular and religious lives, excluding them from most of the privileges of citizenship while imposing all sorts of intolerable burdens. Theodosius himself excluded Jews from all offices of honor and prohibited them from building new synagogues, though he did allow them to repair old ones. Soon afterwards, during a battle between parties in the chariot races at Rome, many Jews were murdered, their synagogues burned and their bodies thrown into the fire. Theodosius went on to prohibit the celebration of Purim on the pretext that it symbolized repudiation of Christians and Christianity.

In 415 he outlawed the construction of new synagogues and ordered the destruction of those already in existence, driving out all Jews who had acted as advisers to previous emperors. He subsequently rescinded these orders in 423 and actually ordered the construction of new synagogues, on condition that Jews make no effort to convert Christians. In 438, however, Jews were officially declared to be enemies of Roman law. As a result the performance of Jewish religious rituals was prohibited, and once again the previous restrictions against the construction of synagogues was re-imposed, and old ones were ordered to be destroyed.

The *Corpus Juris Civilis* as well as the *novellae*, or additional new edicts, issued by Emperor Justinian (527–565), added to the restrictions and disabilities imposed on the Jews. Some of the measures were directly related to religion and aimed at curbing Jews and the spread of Judaism. Though synagogues could be repaired, no new ones were to be built. Justinian went on to prohibit the sale of religious property to Jews and ordered the confiscation of synagogues built on land later proven to have originated as religious property. Jews were allowed to circumcise their own children, but if they circumcized those of another religion, they were to be punished by decapitation and confiscation of property. Any attempt by Jews to convert a Christian was punishable by confiscation of property and death. A Jew could not purchase a Christian slave. If a Jew circumcized a slave who was a Christian, he had to be punished by decapitation. Any Christian who converted to Judaism was subjected to confiscation of property. Any Jew seeking conversion to Christianity with the ulterior motive of escaping some obligation was not to be received into the Church. A Jew who threw stones at a convert to Christianity or disturbed him in any other way had to be burned at the stake.

In legal matters, Jews were not allowed to testify in cases involving Christians on either side. Cases between Jewish litigants involving religious matters had to be adjudicated according to Roman law in Roman courts. And if there was a quarrel between a Christian and a Jew, it was to be judged by a Christian magistrate and not by Jewish priests. Regarding marriage, Jews could not be guided by their own laws in contracting marriages, nor were they allowed to continue the practice of polygamy. Intermarriage between Jews and Christians was subjected to the same penalty as adultery, that is death by stoning. Finally, under the precept that 'Jews must never enjoy the fruits of office but only suffer its pains and penalties', they were prohibited from holding offices higher than those of Christians or from securing exemption from the heavy financial burdens caused by service on local municipal organizations or from corporal punishment for crimes.

In line with the Caesaropapistic inclination to render judgment in Christian theological issues, Justinian was the first emperor to set a precedent for interference with the social and religious practices of

Judaism. In 553 he even went so far as to dictate that Greek and Latin translations of the Old Testament should be used in Jewish religious services in the hope that this would convince some Jews to convert. He forbad the use of the phrase 'our God is the one and only God' in Jewish services because he considered this to be blasphemy against the Christian Holy Trinity, and he outlawed the reading of sayings by Isaiah promising consolidation for the downtrodden people of Judaism. He also forbad the observance of religious services during Passover, forbad the celebrating of Passover at the same time as Easter, and ordered an end to the baking of unleavened bread. He even placed spies in synagogues during services to watch out for any violations of his rules, though he soon found they could not prevent secret praying of the disputed passages at other times of day when the spies were not present. These measures, added to the restrictions imposed on Jews in civic and legal matters, caused them to work against the Byzantines in their effort to conquer Italy. When Justinian's armies attacked Naples, its Jews gave up their property and even their lives joining in defense of the city against the Byzantines. As a result, in the late sixth century and throughout the seventh, relations between Christians and Jews in Byzantium became worse, and ever more stringent laws against the latter were issued by the emperors in response to popular demands.

The policy of changing synagogues into churches, practiced previously under Justin II, was resumed under Emperor Maurice, who in 592 ordered all Jews to be removed from Antioch because of a false rumor that they had destroyed a Christian school in the area. Jews throughout the empire were ordered to be converted forcibly to Christianity. Heraclius (610–641) ordered that Byzantine Jews be converted to Christianity by force, establishing a precedent followed by most other emperors between the eighth and tenth centuries. Justinianus II prohibited Jews and Christians from bathing in the same public baths because of the popular fear that the former would corrupt the latter either by touch or smell.

The Quinisext Council of 692 declared that:

> Whatever remnant of pagan or Jewish perversity is mixed with the ripe fruit of the truth must be uprooted like a weed . . . . Neither clergyman nor layman may partake of the unleavened bread of the Jews, associate with them, accept medical treatment from them, or bathe with them. Should anyone attempt to do it, he shall, if a clergyman, be defrocked, if a layman excommunicated.[1]

Many Byzantine Greeks demanded on numerous occasions that Jews be removed from Constantinople and the Empire altogether, and several expulsion orders were issued. Judaism actually was outlawed and Jews ordered forceably converted at least five times, by Emperor Heraclius I

(610–641) in 632, in 680 in an effort to secure unity against Islamic attacks, by Leo III (717–741) in 721–723, by Basil I (867–886), particularly in 873–874, and by Romanos I Lecapenus (919–944) in 930. Jews were allowed to seek salvation through conversion, but even those who did convert were suspected of potential acts of blasphemy and were therefore subjected to periodic persecution, as was later the case in Spain. Legends of Jewish moneylenders took on the negative dimensions of the later Shylock tradition in Europe. In church services Jews were normally referred to as 'the accursed', but they still were allowed to benefit from divine guidance through baptism. Passion plays also exploited popular prejudice. Religious traditions and folklore accounts influenced the Christian neighbors of Byzantine Jews, causing intermittent persecution and conflict.

After the Vandals destroyed a Jewish synagogue in the late fifth century, the Byzantines refused to allow it to be restored. Soon after Heraclius died, the Church prevented the survivers of previous persecutions and newly-arriving Jewish immigrants from building new synagogues to meet their religious needs. The Byzantine emperors of the Iconoclast period were even more restrictive. Emperor Leo III, who himself had been born and raised in Syria and who believed the Muslims and Jews were plotting together to destroy Christianity, in 721 ordered that all Jews be converted to Christianity in order to achieve the religious unity that he felt was necessary to beat back the foreign invaders which then were threatening to destroy the empire. To the same end in 723 he forbad holiday celebrations and the performance of most Jewish religious rituals. Theofilis (829–842) reissued most of the old laws restricting the Jews. Basil I (867–886), founder of the Macedonian dynasty, first tried to convert the Jews by persuasion, inviting rabbis to debate to defend their faith and offering them benefits if they accepted defeat. He then resorted to bribery, providing gifts to those who agreed to convert. After that failed, in 884 he ordered all Jews converted to Christianity. Though this was abandoned under his immediate successors, the pressure continued, and most Byzantine theologians and church leaders protested vigorously when those who had converted under pressure during the preceding regime were allowed to return to Judaism. Leo VI (886–912) 'the Wise' at first allowed Jews who had been forcibly converted to return to the religion of their ancestors, but in 894 he ordered that all Jews 'not dare to live in any other manner than in accordance with the pure and salutary Christian faith, and if any of them should be found disregarding the ceremonies of the Christian religion and to have returned to his Jewish practices and beliefs, he shall suffer the penalties prescribed for apostates'.[2]

Emperor Romanus I Lecapenus, in about 935, again ordered the forcible conversion of all the Jews of Byzantium, leading to the murder of hundreds of Jews and the desecration of many synagogues throughout the Empire. All the while Jews came under increasingly savage attack by Byzantine popular preachers and writers as well as by officials trying to stir the populace in support of the Crusading knights coming from the West to wrest the Holy Land from the 'infidel Muslims'. As a result, Emperor Andronicus I Comnenus (1183–85) again attempted to convert the Jews to Christianity, though by persuasion and argument rather than force. When Crusaders passed through Constantinople on their way to the Holy Land, they invariably were assigned to camp next to the Jewish quarters, particularly that adjacent to the Galata tower, and usually spent most of their spare time attacking and killing Jews and stealing their properties. At the same time they stirred the local populace to similar activities. It was at this time, also, that Constantinople's Armenians joined the Greeks in attacking Judaism for the first time.[3]

Things became even worse for the Jews during the time of the Latin Kingdom (1204–1261) established by the Fourth Crusade, when the presence in Constantinople of thousands of Latins, whose anti-Semitic prejudices compounded by their Crusading fervor, stimulated further persecution. The Jewish quarter of Salonica was burned several times by the Latins, while the Jews of Constantinople and the other major cities were subjected to a series of attacks.

After the departure of the Latins in 1261 and the restoration of the Byzantine Empire within reduced boundaries under the rule of the Paleologi, the rise of the Muslim Turkomans and Ilhanids in Anatolia and the Great Seljuk Empire of Baghdad added to the fear, with considerable justification, that the surviving Jews were sympathetic to the Muslim drive to take over the Byzantine world. Frequent Byzantine outbursts against the Jews and efforts to suppress Judaism followed during the thirteenth and fourteenth centuries.

The Orthodox church theologian Matthew Blastares seemed especially concerned that barriers might crumble, so in 1335 he wrote that one should not have any communion with the Jews under any circumstances. According to him, the 70th Christian canon stipulated that 'fasting with Jews, either celebrating with them or accepting festival gifts from them, either the feast of the unleavened bread or anything else . . . ' was cause for excommunication, with the cleric involved having to be defrocked. The 71st canon was about the 'Christian who offers oil in pagan temples or in synagogues of the Jews, or the Christian who lights oil in the evenings' and extends excommunication to him for giving the impression of honoring these Jewish rites. The 11th canon of the Vito Synod suggests through its wording that in spite of repeated warnings, there was association and intermingling of Jews and Christians. 'In the case of one who does not stop eating the unleavened bread of the Jews; who does not stop esteeming their friendship worthy; who does not stop from summoning them for medical aid when sick; who does not stop bathing together with them in the communal bath; if a cleric he must be defrocked, if a non-cleric he must be excommunicated . . . '

As the Byzantine empire declined further, with its economy increasingly reflecting the decline, the state repeatedly attempted to outlaw Judaism as means of restoring religious unity within the embattled empire. Emperors pressured Jews even more through secular laws which restricted their social and economic activity. Old legal restrictions which had fallen into disuse were reissued and confirmed. Those who happened to favor Jews were condemned for allowing them to live and work beside Christians so that they might contaminate or even influence them. Thus Patriarch Athanasius I complained to the Emperor Andronicus II Palaeologues (1282–1328) early in the fourteenth century about the presence of a Jewish synagogue in Constantinople:

> . . . the Byzantines simply tolerate that one should erect in public view of the Orthodox city a synagogue of the deicide people who ridicule that (city's) religion, its faith in Jesus Christ, its sacraments, and its worship of images . . . . The masses have not only been allowed to live in ignorance, but have also been contaminated by the admission of Jews . . . . [4]

Conditions for the Jews were no better in the Christian lands which threw off Byzantine rule. Following the establishment of the Second Bulgarian Kingdom at Tirnovo starting in 1186, the Bulgarian monarchs extended their realm from the Danube to the Aegean and the Black Sea to the Adriatic, including Albania, Serbia, Macedonia, Thessaly and Thrace, and attempted on several occasions to capture Constantinople. Not only did they acquire former Byzantine territory, but they also continued Byzantine persecution of the Jews, who were accused of 'preaching the religion of Israel among the Christian population in the capital itself', and 'undermining the foundations of the dominant Christian faith. By emulating the nobility, Jews endeavor to penetrate the ruling classes in order to create the necessary conditions for the triumph of their religion'.[5] Jews were accused of

> . . . . conducting themselves arrogantly toward the priests, cursed the icons, and denied the sanctity of Christ and the Virgin . . . . Three advocates of Judaism were sentenced to death, but subsequently, by order of the king the sentence was commuted to expulsion. One of the Jews renounced his faith and embraced Christianity. But the other two stubbornly resisted. Then irate Turnovo citizens attacked them, beating one to death, while the other was taken away and his tongue was cut out. The pious were overwhelmed with joy, whereas the theophobe

Jews, now threatened with complete annihilation, were mortified and devastated.[6]

Jews were similarly persecuted on a large scale in Serbia and the other Balkan states in the two centuries before they were conquered by the Turks. In Crete, the Jews comprised a middle class between the mass of Greeks and the feudal nobles, acting as bankers, artisans, lawyers and physicians, with the right to maintain their own community organization. They were treated as serfs, however, forced to live in a ghetto (*Ciudecca*), and to affix the special Jewish badge to the fronts of their houses as well as on their clothing. After the island came under Venetian rule in 1204, local Greeks continued to harass, persecute, and attack their Jewish neighbors, particularly because of Jewish support for the periodic Muslim efforts to conquer the island. Stories that the Jews were driving Christians out of trade and supporting Ottoman ambitions for the island led to popular riots and massacres of Jews in 1364 and to regulations restricting their purchase of property in 1416 and 1423, while the blood libel and accusations of desecration of host led to similar treatment in 1449 and again in 1452. In 1433 they were forbidden to act as bankers or brokers. During the Venetian war with the Ottomans in 1538, the Jews were subjected to extortions to finance the military operations, and a rumor that the Jews of Crete were helping the Ottomans led local Greeks to massacre all the Jews they could find. Giacomo Foscari (1574–77) introduced harsh anti-Jewish laws intended to force them to convert or to live in isolated parts of the island.

In Corfu Jews were subjected to violent attacks and almost constant persecution by its Greek population. They had to row in the galleys even when they had committed no crime. They had to provide food and lodging for soldiers on demand, were required to go to Greek law courts on the Sabbath as well as during Jewish festivals, and as elsewhere in the Byzantine Empire they were compelled to act as public executioners, adding to the public wrath to which they were normally subjected. After Venice took control of the island in 1386, conditions became even worse. In 1406 its Jews were forbidden to acquire land and ordered to wear a special Jewish badge. The Venetian administrators often imposed extra heavy taxes on the Jews to finance the wars they were then carrying on against the Ottomans.

There had been thousands of Jews living in Byzantium following the exodus from the Holy Land, but in consequence of all this persecution many were forcibly converted or massacred, and most of the remainder fled north of the Black Sea to the Russian Principality of Kiev. There they soon experienced more persecution in the eleventh century when the Ukraine was converted to Orthodox Christianity, leading most of them to move onward to more friendly territory, to the Jewish-Turkish Khazar

Empire in the Caspian region and, as it was subsequently conquered by Muscovy, to Kafa and the Tatar Khanate of the Crimea in the thirteenth century. As a result by the time that the Ottomans conquered Anatolia during fourteenth and fifteenth centuries, hardly any Jews remained.

JEWISH ABSORPTION INTO THE EMERGING OTTOMAN EMPIRE

Byzantium, however, was breaking up, fortunately for the few Jews who remained under its dominion. As the Turkomans invaded Anatolia starting with their rout of the Byzantine army at the Battle of Manzikert (1071) and formed Turkoman principalities throughout the peninsula, and as the Seljuk Turks established a more settled state centered, first in defense of the Abbasid Empire of Baghdad, and later in Konya and central Anatolia starting in the twelfth century (the Seljuks of Rum, 1077–1246), Byzantine Jewry sprang rapidly to their assistance, welcoming the tolerance and prosperity which the rule of Islam was offering them once again, as it had done previously both in the Middle East and Spain, with thousands of Jews fleeing from Byzantine persecution to Seljuk protection even before the Ottoman state was born.

The Ottomans first established their principality in northeastern Anatolia about 1300 under the leadership of the founder of the dynasty, Osman (d. 1324?). Within a century, after taking over most of western Anatolia, they expanded through Southeastern Europe all the way to the Danube, conquering what are today Greece, Bulgaria, Rumania and Yugoslavia. For a time they bypassed Constantinople, which remained, though already depopulated and ravaged by the Latin Crusaders who occupied it early in the thirteenth century, isolated from the outside world, until it finally was conquered by Mehmed II the Conqueror in 1453. At the same time the Ottomans moved rapidly through Anatolia to the East, reaching the Tigris and Euphrates in the late fourteenth century. After a temporary check due to an invasion of Anatolia by the Tatar chief Tamerlane, they solidified their rule of eastern Anatolia by the end of the fifteenth century and then went on to conquer Syria and Egypt under the leadership of Selim I between 1512 and 1520. His successor, Süleyman the Magnificent (1520–66), called *Kanuni*, 'the lawgiver' by the Turks, completed the great Ottoman conquests in Europe, crossing the Danube and conquering Hungary in 1526. He then placed Vienna under siege in 1529, challenging the Habsburg Emperor, Charles V. In the East he conquered Iraq and much of the Caucasus in 1535, and then extended Ottoman rule across North Africa almost to the Atlantic before his reign came to an end in 1566.

These Ottoman conquests marked a very substantial change for the Jews of the Middle East and Europe. They meant instant liberation, not only from subjugation, persecution, and humiliation but often from actual slavery in Christian hands. As a result, Jews contributed significantly to the Ottoman conquests. The Jews of Bursa, Byzantine administrative center of northwestern Anatolia, actively helped Osman's son Orhan (1324–59) capture the city in 1324. As a reward, to repopulate the city and develop its economy, he brought in Jewish artisans and money changers from Damascus and Byzantine Adrianople (Edirne) so that it could become the first Ottoman capital, with the ancient *Etz ha-Haim* synagogue marking the center of the Jewish quarter (*Yahudi Mahallesi*), established to assure their autonomy in religious and secular matters. In complete contrast to their situation under the Byzantines, Jews entering the Ottoman dominions were allowed to practice whatever profession they wished, to engage in trade and commerce without restriction, and to own landed property and buildings in town and country alike, in return paying a percentage of their revenues to the state as head tax in the traditional Islamic manner, though the Chief Rabbi, the Cantor, and other servants of the synagogues were exempted. At first all the Jews of Bursa were Romaniotes, or Greek-speaking Jews who had escaped from the Byzantines, but later they were joined by Ashkenazis from France and Germany as well as Sephardic Jews from Spain and Portugal, making Bursa into an early model of what was to follow of Jewish life in Salonica and Istanbul.

The Ottoman conquests of Gallipoli (1354) by Orhan's son Süleyman Pasha, of Ankara (1360) in central Anatolia and of the Byzantine administrative capital of Southeastern Europe, Adrianople, in 1363 by Murad I, also were accomplished with support from the small and impoverished Jewish communities which had lived there under Byzantine persecution. Just as at Bursa, so also at Adrianople, now called Edirne, to restore it economically and make it into the capital of the Ottomans' European possessions as quickly as possible, the Turkish conquerors repopulated it with large numbers of Jews resettled from the newly conquered lands in Bosnia and Serbia as well as with Ashkenazi refugees from Hungary, southern Germany, Italy, France, Poland and Russia, providing them with substantial tax and other concessions. This transformed Ottoman Edirne quite suddenly into the largest Jewish community in Europe at the time. Its Chief Rabbi (*hahambaşı*) was appointed to lead all the Jews of Southeastern Europe as the Ottoman conquests continued, and Edirne itself became a major center of Jewish religion and culture.

When the Ottoman sultan Mehmed II *Fatih* (The Conqueror) captured Constantinople and brought the Byzantine Empire finally to an inglorious end in 1453, his armies broke into the city through one of the Jewish quarters and with the assistance of the local Jewish population who, as at Bursa and Edirne, were overjoyed at the opportunity to throw off their Greek oppressors. So also at Buda and Pest in 1526, on the island of Rhodes in 1522, at Belgrade (1526), in Azerbaijan (1534), Iraq and Iran (1534–35, 1638). Yemen (1628) and elsewhere, Jews welcomed the conquering forces of Süleyman the Magnificent, and in each case they were rewarded with tax exemptions, concessions for trade and exploitation of minerals, repair or expansion of old synagogues, and even free houses and shops to meet the needs of the increasing Jewish populations.

Mehmed II's conquest of Constantinople was not followed by killing and destruction, as Greek nationalists have claimed to the present day in efforts to depict Turks as barbarians, but rather by an effort to rebuild and repopulate the city so that it could become the center of the great multinational empire he was trying to create, extending far beyond the Roman Empire and incorporating all the people of the world as he knew it under the dominion of his Turkish dynasty. Therefore though by Muslim tradition Constantinople should have been looted since it had forcefully resisted Muslim conquest, Mehmed prevented his soldiers from taking any more than nominal revenge during a single day so as to fulfill Islamic tradition in theory while in fact sparing it from destruction so that it could become his capital as soon as possible.

Mehmed II initially established the center of his government on the heights of Old Istanbul, south of the Byzantine Tauri Forum, at what came to be known as the *Eski Saray* (Old Palace), now the site of Istanbul University and the Süleymaniye mosque complex, but he subsequently created an entirely new palace that became known as the *Topkapı Sarayı* overlooking the Sea of Marmara and the Golden Horn. During the remaining three decades of his reign (1451–81), he built one hundred ninety new mosques in the city in addition to seventeen converted churches, twenty-four Muslim elementary schools (*mektep*) and colleges (*medrese*), thirty-two public baths (*hamam*), and twelve major commercial and industrial establishments (*han*) and markets (*bazar*) centered around the Grand Bazaar (*bedestan*), which rapidly became the nucleus of the Empire's commercial activities. Old Istanbul was divided into twelve quarters (*nahiye*) each centered around a major Muslim mosque and related complexes of schools, hospitals and other charitable institutions supported by foundations (*vakıf*) endowed with substantial portions of the conquered properties so as to support them in perpetuity. The quarters in turn were divided into sub-districts (*mahalle*) based on smaller mosques, churches and synagogues as well as the tombs and monasteries of the mystic orders.

But how to repopulate this city? It had already been despoiled and depopulated by the Latin crusaders at the start of the thirteenth century, and there were few people and little wealth left by the time the Ottomans arrived. No more than between thirty and fifty thousand people lived in squalor among large gardens and the ruins of what once had been a great metropolis. Mehmed II could not have an empire if his capital lacked people and economic activity. So in imitation of what had been done earlier at Bursa and Edirne he undertook strenuous efforts to repopulate and rebuild the city as quickly as possible. Initially, he tried to get those Christians who had fled during and immediately preceding the conquest to return, allowing them to reoccupy their houses and practice their trades and religion without hindrance if they arrived within a certain amount of time. He also settled one-fifth of his Christian prisoners and their families along the Golden Horn, providing them with free houses and tax exemptions in return for joining the effort to rebuild the city and beginning to practice their trades, thus allowing them to use their earnings to pay their ransoms. He initiated an effort at forced migration (*sürgün*) of different elements of the empire, Muslims, Jews and Christians alike, from all the conquered lands to constitute the population of the new Ottoman capital of Istanbul. Sometimes they were brought by force, sometimes by inducements such as free land and tax-free incomes if they developed shops, trades, and commerce. As a further inducement Mehmed II allowed the members of the major religious groups to govern themselves in their own religiously-based communities, or *millets*,[7] first the Greeks, then the Armenians, and finally the Jews, meaning that they could live under their own leaders in their own way and follow their own religions and customs as they had in the past. This gave Mehmed II another great advantage in conquering and ruling his empire, namely the support of the religious leaders to whom he was giving secular as well as religious authority over their followers, an extent of power they never were able to achieve or exercise in states where they had to share it with temporal rulers. As a result of all these efforts, during the three decades following the Ottoman conquest, Istanbul's population increased by 1478 to 16,326 housholds (*hane*), perhaps as many as 114,248 people, including 5,162 Christian and 1,647 Jewish households respectively, establishing proportions of fifty-eight percent Muslim, thirty-two percent Christian and ten percent Jewish which remained relatively unchanged even as the city's population grew in later centuries.

But this still left the city relatively empty compared with its heyday half a millenium before at the height of Byzantine power. Mehmed could secure only so many people for his capitol from the conquered lands without depopulating them as well. And in any case he did not trust his new Christian subjects, since they remained strongly anti-Muslim as well as anti-Jewish and, still not reconciled to conquest and rule by Muslims and to the new freedoms given the Jews by the Sultan, were trying to stir Christian Europe to reconquer their lands from the Ottomans by new Crusades as soon as possible, continuing to do so well into the sixteenth century, though with little success.

While many Christian inhabitants of Constantinople had left the city before it was put under siege, and others had fled to Europe during and immediately after the conquest, the Jews, who welcomed the Turks, remained where they had lived in late Byzantine times, particularly on both sides of the Golden Horn and in what subsequently became Turkish Galata. It was therefore to Jews that Mehmed turned primarily to help revive trade, industry, and commerce in his capital. Not only did they offer the same sort of economic and financial skills which had attracted them to political and even religious leaders in Europe despite great religious prejudice, but they also had no liking for Christian Europe. They were in fact being driven out of Europe and were desperately seeking new homes where they could live and work and prosper. From the start, Mehmed assured the Jews remaining in the city that they would be allowed to practice their religion and occupations freely and without the hindrances to which they had been subjected by the Byzantines. In addition, just three days after the conquest, he sent messages to the Jews of Bursa and other places in Anatolia and to those living in Salonica and Edirne in Europe inviting them to come to Istanbul. As inducements he offered them free property in the northern areas of Balat (*Tekfurdağı*) and *Hasköy* as well as the *Bahçekapı* area where Jewish coppersmiths had lived since Byzantine times, adding exemptions from taxes on their incomes for substantial periods of time as well as permission to build synagogues as needed.

Mehmed II retained the old Islamic prohibition against allowing Christians to build new churches, but placed Jews in a special category above Christian *zimmis*, enabling them to use legal formalities in order to evade this and other prohibitions imposed on Christians, in this case by allowing them to build synagogues on the foundations of existing houses. This arrangement was preserved throughout Ottoman history by means of orders (*irade*) issued by later sultans on the basis of this precedent, and it was applied as well to other traditional Islamic clothing and building restrictions imposed on Christians, which for Jews became in fact no more than requirements to secure official permits before such nominally forbidden acts were carried out. Mehmed II moreover placed the Jews in a position where they could dominate his Christian subjects financially and economically in order to make certain that the latter would not use their wealth to undermine the Empire, as they probably intended to do. As a result of these inducements, large numbers of Jews emigrated to Istanbul from Bursa and Edirne in particular.

Even more than the Jews living in the expanding Ottoman Empire itself, Mehmed from the start attempted to encourage the emigration of Jews from Europe. Just as the Jews of England, France, Germany, Spain, and even Poland and Lithuania were being subjected to increasing persecution, blood libels, massacres, and deportations, the Turkish rulers of the expanding Ottoman state actively encouraged them to come and live in the Ottoman Empire under the same conditions of tolerance and freedom which had favored the lives of Jews in the empires of the Umayyads of Damascus and Abbasids of Baghdad, and more recently in Muslim Spain.

Mehmed himself is said to have issued a proclamation to all Jews:

> Who among you of all my people that is with me, may his God be with him, let him ascend to Istanbul the site of my imperial throne. Let him dwell in the best of the land, each beneath his vine and beneath his fig tree, with silver and with gold, with wealth and with cattle. Let him dwell in the land, trade in it, and take possession of it.[8]

The sixteenth-century Jewish historian Elijah Capsali wrote at the time:

> In the first year of the Sultan Mehmed, King of Turkey . . . , the Lord aroused the spirit of the king . . . , and his voice passed throughout his kingdom and also by proclamation saying: (from *Ezra* I, 1–3)
>
> 'This is the word of Mehmed King of Turkey, the Lord God of Heaven gave me a kingdom in the land and he commanded me to number his people the seed of Abraham his servant, the sons of Jacob his chosen ones, and to give them sustenance in the land and to provide a safe haven for them. (Based on verses in *Ezra* and *Genesis*) Let each one with his God come to Constantinople the seat of my kingdom and sit under his vine and under his fig tree with his gold and silver, property and cattle, settle in the land and trade and become part of it' (from *Genesis* 34:10).
>
> The Jews gathered together from all the cities of Turkey both near and far, each man came from his home; and the community gathered in the thousands and ten thousands and God assisted them from heaven while the king gave them good properties and houses full of goods. The Jews dwelled there according to their families and they multiplied exceedingly (*Exodus* 1:7). From that day hence, from every place that the king conquered wherein there were Jews, he immediately forced them to emigrate (paraphrasing *Isaiah* 22:17), taking them from there and sending them to Istanbul the seat of his kingdom. And he bore them and carried them all the days of old (*Isaiah* 63:9).
>
> Because the Jews feared the Lord, He gave them prosperity (based on *Exodus* I:21), and in the place wherein formerly in the days of the Byzantine king there were only two or three congregations, the Jews multiplied and increased and became greater in number than forty congregations, and the land did not let them settle together because their property was so great (*Genesis* 13:6). The congregations of Constantinople were praiseworthy. Torah and wealth and honor increased among the congregations. In the congregations they blessed the Lord, the fountain of Israel (*Psalms* 68:27), the doer of great

wonders. They opened their mouth in song to heaven and blessed the Lord, all the servants of the Lord who stand in the house of the Lord in the night seasons (*Psalms* 134:1).[9]

The Ottoman rulers actively propagandized throughout Europe to attract Jewish emigrants to their newly expanding state. The most famous example of this effort was the letter sent in the name of the Ashkenazi Rabbi Isaac Tzarfati,[10] who had come to the Ottoman dominions from Germany, apparently just before the conquest of Istanbul, became Chief Rabbi of the second Ottoman capital Edirne (Adrianople),[11] and who some time afterwards wrote his co-religionists in Central Europe, in particular in Swabia, the Rhineland, Steuermark, Moravia, northern France, and Hungary, informing them of the advantages of the sultanate and of its liberal attitude toward Jews.

Several versions of Tzarfati's letter have survived. The most famous expresses vividly the enthusiasm which he conveyed to the oppressed Jews of Central Europe:

> My brothers and my masters, having prayed to God to grant you peace, I wish to relate to you the circumstances under which the young Rabbi Zalman and his companion Rabbi David Cohen came to me. They recounted to me all the ordeals, harsher than death, which our brothers, the sons of Israel who live in Germany, have undergone and still endure; the decisions taken against them, the martyrs, the expulsions, which take place every day and compel them to wander from country to country, from town to town, endlessly, without any place accepting them; for when these unfortunates arrive in a town of refuge hoping to find repose there, they do not find it, and they have so much misfortune that they say: the first town was the most welcoming and the second is more harsh than the first. It is 'As if a man did flee from the lion and a bear met him; or went into the house and leaned his hand on the wall and a serpent bit him' (Amos v 19); also 'they shall not escape and their hope shall be as the giving up of the ghost' (Job xi 20) . . . Now a decree harsher than all the others has been enacted, and no Jew is permitted to embark, and they are lost in a country which has closed the sea routes to them; and they do not know where the wind of persecution will blow them, nor whither they can flee.
>
> These are the circumstances which Rabbi Zalman and Rabbi David recounted to me. When they arrived herein Turkey, a land on which the wrath of God has not weighed heavily, when they saw the peace, the tranquillity and the abundance which holds sway in these lands and when they saw that the distance between Turkey and Jerusalem is short, and may be traversed overland, they were overcome with great

joy and they said: without any doubt if the Jews who live in Germany knew a tenth of the blessings which God has bestowed on His people of Israel in this land, neither snow nor rain, neither day nor night, would be of consequence until they had journeyed here.

They have asked me to write to the exiles, to the Jewish communities which reside in Germany, in the towns of Swabia, of the Rhineland, of Styria, of Moravia and of Hungary, to inform them how agreeable is this country . . . . When I realized that their desires were disinterested, I decided to acquiesce in their entreaties, for I too would like to give Israel the opportunity of acquiring its just deserts . . . . [12]

Another version of Tzarfati's appeal was even more emotional:

Your cries and sobs have reached us. We have been told of all the troubles and persecutions which you have to suffer in the German lands . . . . I hear the lamentation of my brethren . . . . The barbarous and cruel nation ruthlessly oppresses the faithful children of the chosen people . . . . The priests and prelates of Rome have risen. They wish to root out the memory of Jacob and erase the name of Israel. They always devise new persecutions. They wish to bring you to the stake . . . . Listen my brethren, to the counsel I will give you. I too was born in Germany and studied Torah with the German rabbis. I was driven out of my native country and came to the Turkish land, which is blessed by God and filled with all good things. Here I found rest and happiness; Turkey can also become for you the land of peace . . . . If you who live in Germany knew even a tenth of what God has blessed us with in this land, you would not consider any difficulties; you would set out to come to us . . . . Here in the land of the Turks we have nothing to complain of. We possess great fortunes; much gold and silver are in our hands. We are not oppressed with heavy taxes, and our commerce is free and unhindered. Rich are the fruits of the earth. Everything is cheap, and every one of us lives in peace and freedom. Here the Jew is not compelled to wear a yellow hat as a badge of shame, as is the case in Germany, where even wealth and great fortune are a curse for a Jew because he therewith arouses jealousy among the Christians and they devise all kinds of slander against him to rob him of his gold. Arise my brethren, gird up your loins, collect your forces, and come to us. Here you will be free of your enemies, here you will find rest . . . . [13]

Rabbi Elija Capsali relates that Mehmed II's successor, Sultan Bayezid II (1481–1512), who ruled at the time of the expulsion of the Jews from Spain, made even more urgent efforts to attract the Jews of Europe into his empire:

Sultan Bayezid, monarch of Turkey, heard of all the evil that the king of Spain inflicted on the Jews and he heard that they were seeking a refuge and resting place. He took pity on them, wrote letters, and sent emissaries to proclaim throughout his kingdom that none of his city governors be wicked enough to refuse entry to Jews or to expel them. Instead, they were to be given a gracious welcome, and anyone who did not behave in this manner would be put to death . . . . Thousands and tens of thousands of the deported Jews came to the land of the Turks and filled the land. Then they constructed righteous communities without number in Turkey and generously provided money to ransom captives, and so the children returned to their own country . . . [14]

As a result of these and other such appeals, large numbers of Ashkenazi Jews who just then were being subjected to tortures, massacres, and expulsions from Bavaria and elsewhere in Central Europe, flooded into Mehmed's newly-conquered provinces in southeastern Europe, settling at Sofia, Vidin, Plevna, Nicopolis, Salonica and Istanbul, establishing Ashkenazi synagogues and communities which subsequently received hundreds of Jewish refugees from persecution in Hungary and eastern Europe.

Bayezid II is said to have remarked during a conversation in his court: 'you call Ferdinand a wise king, he who impoverishes his country and enriches our own . . . ' by expelling the Jews.[15] Despite considerable religious conservatism of his own, Bayezid went on to decree that all Jews fleeing from Spain and Portugal should be admitted to his dominions without restriction, and with the same inducements that had been offered during the reign of his predecessor. Ottoman officials were ordered to do everything they could to facilitate the entry of Iberian Jews into Ottoman territory, and strict punishments were provided against all those who mistreated the immigrants or caused them any sort of damage.

So it was not just in 1492, but already starting with the Ottoman conquest of Bursa in northwestern Anatolia in 1324, and particularly after Mehmed II's conquest of Constantinople in 1453, that Jews started flooding into the Ottoman Empire, Ashkenazi Jews from Germany, France, and Hungary, Italian Jews from Sicily, Otranto, and Calabria, Sephardic Jews from Spain and Portugal. And while most of them settled in the major Ottoman centers in Southeastern Europe where there were already flourishing communities of Ottoman Jews, such as Istanbul, Salonica and Edirne, others settled among their co-religionists in Anatolia as well as in the Arab provinces, at Cairo, Damascus, Beirut and Tripoli in particular, as well as in the Holy Land at Safed and Sidon more than at Jerusalem.

It is estimated that as many as 250,000 Jews came from the Iberian peninsula to the Ottoman Empire in the late fifteenth century, but the exact numbers will probably never be known. Jews at the time saw in the victorious Ottoman armies the punishing rod of God, his iron hand, predestined to carry through the righteous judgment of the Almighty against the enemies of his people and to destroy what they called the 'kingdom of Edom', steeped in blood and sin. They declared the Ottoman leaders to be scions of the 'righteous Cyrus', the 'anointed of God', and firmly believed that at the head of the warlike Ottoman hosts the angel Gabriel himself strode with sword in hand to bring near the 'end' and prepare the way for the glorious Messiah.[16]

Some of the new emigrants came directly by sea through the Mediterranean or overland from Central Europe. Some of them came indirectly, stopping off first across the Straits of Gibraltar in North Africa or going overland or by sea to Naples, Genoa or Venice in Italy or to the islands of the eastern Mediterranean and the Aegean, where they settled for a time before they were expelled and had to move on to the East. Some of them came in small boats with nothing but the clothes on their backs and had to be helped by the older Ottoman Jewish communities. Many of the wealthier Spanish and Portuguese Jews managed to survive in the West European dominions of the Spanish Habsburgs under Habsburg protection, in return for sizable gifts, before the Inquisition finally caught up with them and forced them onwards, though they still managed to bring a great deal of their wealth.

More Jews were included in the Empire by the Ottoman conquests during the sixteenth century. Selim I's (1512–20) conquest of the old Islamic provinces of the Middle East, Syria, Eretz Israel, and Egypt, brought with them the old-established Jewish communities of Jerusalem and Safed, Damascus and Antioch, Cairo and Alexandria, including many who had only recently fled from the Spain and Portugal, often coming through Cyprus on their way to the East. Selim continued the policy begun by Sultan Mehmed II the Conqueror of deporting (*sürgün*) segments of the conquered population to Istanbul to assure the obedience and good behavior of those left behind. In order to strengthen the economy of the Ottoman capital at the same time, most of these were chosen from among the most experienced Jewish craftsmen and merchants of Cairo and Alexandria, who went most willingly to join their co-religionists in the capital of this new and rapidly expanding empire. Insofar as those left in Egypt were concerned, Selim continued the late Mamluk practice of appointing a leading Jewish merchant, Abraham Castro, as *negid*, to lead the Jewish community of Egypt, but starting late in the sixteenth century this office was eliminated, and Egypt's Jews thereafter were led by Jewish representatives sent from Istanbul with the title of *Çelebi*, while Jewish bankers were appointed to direct Egypt's mint as well as to act as chief money changers (*Sarraf Başı*) and bankers for the Ottoman governors. Egyptian Jewry prospered so much that, within a short time, a substantial proportion of the emigrants to the Ottoman Empire from North Africa, the Iberian Peninsula and Central Europe, found their way to Cairo and Alexandria rather than to Istanbul, Salonica, or elsewhere in Southeastern Europe or Anatolia. *Kanuni* Süleyman's (1520–66) conquests of Serbia (1521) and Hungary (1526) rescued thousands of Jews who had been subjected to persecution under Habsburg influence, many of whom, at the invitation of the Sultan in his *Ferman de los Alemanes*,[17] immediately migrated southward to Edirne and Istanbul in particular, greatly expanding their Ashkenazi populations. At the same time Jews both from Central Europe and from Spain migrated to Bosnia starting in the middle of the sixteenth century, settling first in its major cities Sarajevo (Bosna Saray) and Travnik, and later spreading into the smaller towns, Tuzla, Banja Luka, and Zenica as well as to Mostar, capital of Herzegovina. Süleyman's subsequent conquest of Iraq and parts of the Caucasus added the ancient eastern Jewish colonies of Baghdad as well as many Jews who had fled from Byzantine persecution north of the Black Sea, only to be persecuted by the Shia Safavids who had conquered the eastern part of the province.

Nor were the anti-Semitic persecutions in Christian Europe and the resulting flood of emigration into Ottoman territory ended by the exile from Spain in 1492. The acquisition of Apulia by the Papacy in 1537 led to a new wave of Jewish emigration into Ottoman territory from Italy, while anti-Semitic riots and legislation enacted by the Diet of Bohemia in 1542 caused more Jewish emigration from Central Europe, partly to Poland but much more to the Ottoman possessions. In 1555 Papal demands for substantial new taxes from the Jews in return for continued possession of their synagogues, subsequent orders concentrating them in newly-formed ghettos along the Tiber in Rome, forbidding them any exit during nights and on Sundays and Christian holidays and requiring them to wear distinctive clothing, stimulated similar anti-Semitic legislation in much of Italy. As a result, thousands more Jews sailed eastward through the Mediterranean to Ottoman territory during the remainder of the century.

So whether in the fourteenth century or the sixteenth, Jews rich and poor continued to come into the Ottoman dominions in large numbers from all over Christian Europe, settling in all parts of the sultans' empire, in modern Hungary, Rumania, Bulgaria, Serbia, Greece, Egypt, and in Anatolia at Bursa, Gallipoli, Manisa, Izmir, Tokat, and Amasya. Some settled on the eastern Mediterranean islands of Cyprus, Patras and Corfu. But most frequently they settled in the places that became the centers of Jewish life in the Ottoman Empire, in the capital Istanbul, in eastern Thrace at Edirne, along the shores of the Aegean at Salonica, or Thessaloniki, and in the Holy Land, especially at Safed, in total numbers estimated anywhere from 100,000 to 250,000 people, compared to little more than 30,000 Jewish refugees in Poland and Lithuania at the end of the fifteenth century, and 75,000 in the mid-sixteenth. This made the Ottoman Jewish community not only the largest but also the most prosperous Jewish community in the world at the time, during the sixteenth and early seventeenth centuries, a period which constituted the Golden Age of Ottoman Jewry.

2

The Golden Age
of Ottoman Jewry

JEWISH COMMUNITY ORGANIZATION IN THE OTTOMAN EMPIRE

The Jewish Population of the Ottoman Empire

How many Jews gathered together in the dominions of the Sultans during the Golden Age? Exact figures lack, at least until the Ottomans themselves began to compile reasonably accurate census reports starting in the middle of the nineteenth century, but from early Ottoman cadastral records and poll tax registers along with the estimates of foreign visitors, approximations at least are possible.

The largest Jewish population in the Empire, not surprisingly, was at Istanbul, its administrative, financial, and economic center, though Jews here constituted a much smaller proportion of the total than that of Salonica, where they were in a majority. When Benjamin of Tudela passed through Byzantine Constantinople in AD 1160, he found some 2,500 Jewish families (about 17,500 individuals) in all. An early Ottoman census of the capital in 1477, a quarter century after the conquest , shows a population of 1,647 Jewish households (about 11,529 people), or eleven percent of the total 16,326 households (103,621), which also included 9,486 Muslim and 4,891 Christian households. By 1489, as a result of Mehmed II's intensive settlement efforts, this figure had risen to 2,491 Jewish households (17,437 people) out of a total of 10,685 non-Muslim households.

The later Jewish emigration from Spain (estimated at about 36,000 people to Istanbul alone) and from western and central Europe, along with forced resettlement of Jews from newly-conquered territories in Serbia, Greece and Iraq, brought this number to 8,070 households (56,490 people) in 1535, five percent of the total, which included 46,635 Muslim households and 25,292 Christian. The famous Ottoman traveler Evliya Çelebi stated in 1638 that the Jewish population of Istanbul, settled mostly in the Hasköy quarter of the city, numbered about 11,000 families (77,000 people), which he said was twice as large the Greek population at that time. Ottoman poll tax registers for 1690–91 state that there were 8,236 Jewish (57,652) and 45,112 (315,784) Christian heads of households in Istanbul, the latter suspiciously high since registers for the household tax (*avariz*) from the same year show 9,642 Jewish (67,494) and 14,231 (99,617) Christian households. The British traveler Richard Pococke estimated in 1771–73 that there were 100,000 Jews in Istanbul, but in view of the population figures compiled by the Ottoman census a century later, this number seems exaggerated.

The largest Jewish city in Southeastern Europe, Salonica, almost depopulated at the time of the final Ottoman conquest in 1430, had 2,509 Jewish households (about 17,563 people) enrolled in synagogues in 1530.[1] This rose to 23,001 in 1518, 23,942 people in 1589 and 22,767 in 1613. Although more refugees arrived during the next century, from Central Europe as well as Spain, numerous plagues and fires left the figure about the same until the end of the eighteenth century, still making it the only large city of the empire where the Jews constituted a majority of the population. Elsewhere in Macedonia, Monastir had 48 Jewish households (342 people including bachelors) in 1529 and 60 households (467 people including bachelors) in 1597. Skopje (Üsküp) had 32 Jewish households (224 people) in 1544, increasing to 228 people in 1597.

Among the other larger Jewish communities in the European part of the Ottoman Empire, there were 102 households (714 people) at Buda shortly after its conquest by Süleyman the Magnificent. Since most Buda Jews were sent to Istanbul soon afterwards, the number left fell to 72 households (504) in 1546, compared to 318 Christian households, but this rose to 122 Jewish households (854) in 1566.

In eastern Thrace, Edirne (Adrianople) had 231 Jewish households in 1519 (1,624 people including bachelors) shortly after most of its Jews had been transferred to Istanbul. This rose to 553 households (3,907 people with bachelors) in 1568, as the result of the arrival of new refugees from Central Europe, but fell to 341 (2,532 people with bachelors) in 1570 as the new residents moved to Salonica and Istanbul, which were rapidly becoming more important economic and political centers.

In Albania, the important trade center Valona had a large number of Jewish immigrants from the Iberian peninsula, rising from 97 households, as compared to 665 Christian housholds, in 1506–7, to 609 in 1519–20, though the subsequent Christian Albanian revolt against the Ottomans, led by Scanderbeg, massacred most of the area's Muslims and Jews and forced the remainder to flee, mostly to Istanbul or Italy. In Bulgaria, Nicopolis had 66 Jewish households during the reign of Süleyman the Magnificent (492 people including bachelors), rising to 186 households (1,389 people including bachelors) in 1579. There were only 21 Jewish households at Sofia (147) in 1544, falling to 126 individuals during the reign of Selim II, while Vidin had 31 Jewish households (217) in 1585,

Filibe (Plovdiv) had 32 (224) both in 1519 and 1530 and 41 (287) in 1570. Smaller groupings of Jews also were present in Rusçuk (Ruse), Şumla and Varna along the road northward to Belgrade and Vienna as well as in the west at Köstendil, Samakov, Vratsa and Lom. At Terhala (Trikkala) there were only 19 Jewish households (103 people) in 1506. Their number rose to 181 households (including bachelors and widows, 1310 people) in 1521 and fell back to 111 households (828 people including bachelors and widows) in 1601.

In the Aegean islands, Lepanto (Inebahti) had 84 households (605 people including bachelors and widows) in 1521, 120 households (896 people including bachelors), in 1571–72, and 188 households (1,383 people including bachelors) in 1597. Forty-two Jewish households (294 people) lived at Chios in 1566 and there were 144 Jewish households (1,008) on the island of Rhodes during the time of Süleyman the Magnificent. Patras (Balyabadra) had 168 households (1,213 people with bachelors and widows) in 1512, and 252 households (1,812 people with bachelors and widows) during the reign of Süleyman the Magnificent.

In Anatolia, there were nowhere as many Jewish communities as in either the eastern or western parts of the empire. The largest Jewish community was at Bursa, center of Anatolia's trade and administration, where there were 166 Jewish households (1,162 people) in 1540; but as the Ottomans brought large numbers of Jews to resettle the city, this rose to 265 households (1,855) in 1551, and 683 households (4,781) in 1571. Local Muslim judicial records indicate that there were 504 Jewish households (3,528 people) in Bursa in 1583, but this fell to 270 households (1,890) in 1618–19, and to 141 households (987) in 1696–97. Gallipoli had 15 households (107 people) in 1519, and 23 households (141) during the time of Suleyman the Magnificent, falling to 30 people in 1600. Ankara had only 33 Jewish households (231) in the 1520s and 61 (747) in the 1570s. At Mardin there were 92 households (644) in 1518, and 118 households (826) in 1540. There were 88 Jewish households (649 people with bachelors) at Manisa in 1530. Kaffa, on the north shore of the Black Sea, had 81 Jewish families (579 people with bachelors and others) in 1542 during the reign of Süleyman the Magnificent.

While Jews had lived in Izmir in ancient times, they had been entirely wiped out by Byzantine persecution by the time of the Ottoman conquest. It remained at best a minor Aegean port, not important enough to attract settlers for some time, though there some Jews settled in Tire and Manisa nearby late in the sixteenth century. It was only as a result of *marrano* emigration from Spain in the seventeenth century, and of Sephardic emigration from Salonica as a result of Greek persecution during the early years of the twentieth, that Izmir came to constitute a major Jewish community.

Turning to the eastern provinces, the Jewish population of Eretz Israel, divided into the *sancaks* of Jerusalem, Gaza, Nablus and Safed, increased substantially following the Ottoman conquest once orderly and tolerant rule for Jews was assured. According to the European travelers Meshullam da Volterra and Obadiah di Bertinoro the Jewish population of Jerusalem decreased from 250 in 1481 to only 76 in 1488 as a result of the chaos and anarchy in the final decades of Mamluk rule. There were 199 Jewish households (1,393 individuals), or about twenty percent of the total, at Jerusalem in 1525–26, compared to 119 Christian and 616 Muslim, 224 Jewish households (1,587 people including bachelors) in 1538–39, 324 (2,282 people, including bachelors and a widow) in 1553–54, but down to 237 households (1,671 with bachelors) in 1562–63, about equal with its Christian population for the first time but far less than that of the Muslims.

Safed had 233 Jewish households (1,671 people including bachelors) in 1525–26, 716 (5,012 people) in 1548, and 1,075 (7,525 people) in 1555–56, falling to 957 households (6,699 people) in 1567–68 and 976 (6,832 people) in 1596. Gaza, finally, had 95 Jewish households (665 people) in 1525–26, 98 (701 people including bachelors) in 1538–39, 115 (830 people including widows and bachelors) in 1548–49, decreasing to 81 (585 people including bachelors) in 1556–57, and 73 households (519 people including bachelors) in 1596–97.

In rest of the Near East, the travellers Meshullam da Volterra and Obadiah di Bertinoro found approximately five thousand Jews in Mamluk Cairo in 1481 and 1488 respectively. Quite a large number of Spanish Jews emigrated to Egypt in the early sixteenth century before the Ottoman conquest, but we have no exact figures. A Jewish traveler who visited Cairo in 1541, however, said it had 21 synagogues for the Rabbanate community alone, indicating a fairly substantial number of people, perhaps as many as ten thousand. In Lebanon, Tripoli had about one hundred Jewish households (about 700 people) in 1521, most of whom had been expelled from Sicily in 1492, according to the traveller Moshe Basola, who added that they were merchants and craftsmen and also had one permanent synagogue. Basola reported that the Jewish community at Beirut had only twelve Jewish households, all from Sicily, while Sidon had twenty five Jewish households, all *Musta'rabs*. Damascus had 503 Jewish households (4,040 people including bachelors and others) in 1548. At Musul there were only 31 Jewish households (180 people) in 1525, but this rose to 105 (650 people) in 1558. There were also said to have been approximately 25,000 Jews at Baghdad in the sixteenth century, but we have no exact figures.

Bringing together all these figures, one reaches a total of approximately 150,000 Jews in the Ottoman Empire as a whole at its height in the sixteenth century, approximately three percent of its population, compared to only 75,000 Jews in Poland and Lithuania at the same time.

Jewish Community Organization

Contrary to general belief in the west, the Ottomans were considerably more tolerant toward other peoples and faiths than were contemporary rulers in Christian Europe. The main problem insofar as the sultans were concerned was not to suppress or convert non-Muslim subjects but to organize and control them so that they would keep order, obey the law, and pay their taxes. The Ottoman sultans initially thought it would be easy to manage the Jews and Christians. They would follow the traditional patterns by which 'people of the book', or *zimmis*, were ruled in the classical Islamic empires, in their own religiously-based communities. Their immediate model for organization was, however, that surviving from Byzantine times. Initially Mehmed II hoped that Istanbul would be governed on his behalf by the principal Byzantine secular official remaining, Grand Duke Lukas Notaras, but he was executed soon after the conquest because of efforts to encourage a new European Crusade effort to retake the city. It was only some six months after the conquest, then, in January 1454, that the Sultan turned to the Greek Orthodox church as the only significant source of authority remaining. It had a Patriarch from Byzantine times. He commanded a hierarchy of priests who could be used to control his subjects, and in return for this power the Patriarch would be loyal to the Sultan and use his influence to keep his Greek subjects in line. Mehmed II therefore appointed Greek Orthodox Patriarch George Scholarius (Gennadios II) as secular as well as religious leader of the Greek Orthodox community.

Some maintain that Gennadios was appointed leader of the Jews and Armenians as well, but this is very doubtful. Nothing had changed from Byzantine times. To the Greek priests the Armenians were almost as heretical as were the Jews. For a sultan who wanted to restore order and who was inviting Jews to immigrate in order to build up his capital, moreover, it is highly unlikely that he would have placed them in a situation where the Greeks could continue to persecute them.

The Armenians followed the Greeks in getting their own community organization. Their Gregorian Apostolic church, while Orthodox like that of the Greeks, preserved national Armenian traditions and religious beliefs, language, and rituals. Its members therefore refused to accept subordination to the Greek church and pressured the sultan to recognize them as an independent community. In consequence, in 1461, Mehmed II authorized a separate Armenian Orthodox community under the chief Armenian bishop of Istanbul, appointed as Patriarch in preference to the older Armenian sees centered at Sis in Cilicia and Echmiadzin in the southern Caucasus which were not yet under Ottoman control.

Was Ottoman Jewry led by Grand Rabbis? What to do with the Jews, however, who so long as they lacked organization and protection were being persecuted by the Greek priests in apparent contradiction to all the promises that Mehmed II was making to attract them to his capital? The entire plan to rebuild the Empire's economy would come crashing down if they also were not protected. Historians have claimed that the leader of the Romaniote Byzantine Jewish community of Istanbul, Rabbi Moses Capsali (1420–95), offered the solution, agreeing to pay a special tax, the *Rav Akçesi*, or Rabbi Tax, in return for the Sultan's recognition as Grand Rabbi (*Hahambaşı*) of a separate Jewish community, which he is said to have led until his death in 1495, when he was succeeded by another distinguished Romaniote Rabbi, Elijah Mizrahi, who served as his successor in that position until his death in 1535. It is said that these Grand Rabbis directed all the rabbis and Jews throughout the Ottoman Empire in the same way that the Greek Patriarch led the Greeks and the Armenian Gregorian Patriarch dominated the Armenians. Both are said to have been granted membership in the Imperial Council with precedence over their Christian counterparts.

Neither the exact date of their appointments or even the extent of their powers, however, have ever been established with any precision from contemporary sources. The story regarding their membership on the Imperial Council, moreover, seems to have been a myth, since extant contemporary Ottoman records do not mention their presence in this august body. It seems more than likely, in fact, that no centralized position such as Grand Rabbi over all Ottoman Jews ever was authorized or carried out during the Golden Age since, unlike the Greek and Armenian churches, there is no religious hierarchy in Judaism, and even those who describe Capsali and Mizrahi as Grand Rabbis point out the difficulties they had in securing the co-operation, let alone obedience, of other rabbis around the Empire. It is more likely that they never claimed or received the title of Grand Rabbi for the empire, instead functioning mainly as collectors of the poll tax owed the Sultan by members of the Istanbul Jewish community and as its chief judges (*dayyan*).

Even if one accepts this limited role, moreover, one finds that Mizrahi in particular encountered considerable opposition from other Rabbinical leaders even in Istanbul because of his attempts to establish relations with the Karaites, unlike Capsali, who sternly opposed them, leading to constant quarrels with those who wanted to try to retain them within the Jewish community. Mizrahi also raised opposition because of attempts to impose the stricter Romaniote legal interpretations on members of the other groups, particularly on the far less-rigorous Sephardic Jews, condemning them for what he considered to be departures from Judaism as he knew it.

Whatever their exact titles or roles, then, neither Capsali nor Mizrahi seem to have exercised any extensive authority over Jews outside of the capital. Mizrahi in particular seems to have been so busy with his rabbinical and scholarly activities that he had no time left even for his minimum task of maintaining relations with the Ottoman government. Instead, he surrendered this function, as well as business management and collection of both community and government taxes, to the newly-created position of lieutenant (*kâhya*; Heb. *shtadlan*), which was given to Rabbi Shaltiel, who because of his close relations with high Ottoman officials as well as his knowledge of Ottoman Turkish acted as the community's principal representative (*cemaat temsilcisi*) with the officials of the Ottoman Ruling Class, supposedly the principal function of the Grand Rabbi. Following Mizrahi's death Ottomans and Jews alike seem to have been satisfied with the Jewish community functioning in this decentralized manner without any central authority, with the Jews of each major city led by Chief Rabbis (*hahambaşı*) of equal rank and with *kâhya*s acting as business managers and agents in charge of relations with Ottoman officials. Grand Rabbis with authority over all the Jews of the empire seem not to have been appointed, then, until the system was modernized and centralized during the nineteenth-century *Tanzimat* reform era.

The Ottoman Millet System. How were Ottoman Jews organized and led in their Golden Age, and what functions did their leaders exercise?

The community comprising Ottoman Jewry was one of several religiously-based communal organizations of subjects called, at various times, *tâ'ife, cema'at,* or most commonly in later times *millet*. This Ottoman institution constituted a self-governing organization based on religious affinity and directed by religious leaders possessing both secular and religious authority. The old-established Middle Eastern tradition developed long before Islam, but continued in the classical Islamic empires as well as that of the Ottomans, was that the small Ruling Class elite around the ruler existed only to defend and expand the state, to keep order and security, and to exploit the wealth of the empire to support itself and its members. Everything else was left to the subjects, Muslim, Jewish and Christian alike, to deal with as they wished in their own communities. Whether in religion or economic regulation, justice, education or social security, or cleaning and lighting the streets and putting out fires, the subjects managed these affairs through these self-governing entities directed by their religious leaders in all but the economic sphere, which was dominated by separate craft and merchant guilds. Within these communities, members of each major religious group thus were allowed to worship in their own way and to govern themselves according to their own laws and traditions, using their own language. The *millet* leaders were in charge of making certain that their followers did their duty to the Sultan and his Ruling Class, which meant they had to keep the peace and pay taxes. So long as they did they had very little contact with the government, which intervened only when these obligations were not met.

The system survived throughout Ottoman history until its break-up following World War I. In many ways it served a good purpose. It allowed peoples to maintain their own religions, traditions, cultures, customs and languages without interference. It enabled each to operate its own courts, schools, charitable institutions, hospitals, and even community governments. It isolated people of different religions from each other and thus attempted to prevent the kind of inter-communal conflicts which have become so common in the Middle East since the Ottoman Empire disappeared. But all of this was accomplished at a great price. People of different religions were kept so segregated from one another that they became more mutually hostile and contemptuous than ever, with their own concerns, religious prejudices, and, ultimately, political aspirations deepening into ever greater enmity as time went on. Though Jews, Turks, Armenians and Greeks lived in immediate proximity to one another, then, and in many ways shared a common Middle Eastern way of life which made them more like each other than like their cousins in other parts of the world, they remained strangers. They lived together within the same empire, the same city, sometimes in the same neighborhoods, yet they were separated by more than the walls of their quarters; they were separated even more by barriers of religion, language, customs, and political aspirations which in fact were nourished and deepened by the very Ottoman liberalism which made their separate existence possible. Nor did separation prevent conflict even in Ottoman times since, as we will see, the Sultan's Christian subjects attacked the Jews on numerous occasions. Centuries of living in close proximity to one another thus brought no common force of unity and no understanding so that when the Ottoman empire first weakened and then disappeared during the nineteenth and twentieth centuries, their conflicts and clashes became even more bitter and bloody than they might have been had the Ottomans done more to lessen their isolation and bring some sort of common appreciation and understanding over the centuries.

Divisions Within Ottoman Jewry

There were very good reasons for the absence of central Jewish authority throughout the first five centuries of Ottoman rule. Ottoman Jewry was very diverse, reflecting the different cultures in which Jews had lived in the centuries since their exile from the Holy Land.

There were, first of all, those who had remained under Roman and then Byzantine rule, the Greek-speaking Jews, called *Romaniotes* or *Griegos*, who continued to use Greek as their secular language. They had survived centuries of persecution but still were proud of their Greek heritage, and in consequence considered themselves the aristocracy of Judaism, looking down on the newcomers from Europe.

In the eastern provinces that had been under the Islamic caliphates there were the Arabized (*Musta'rab*) Jews, who spoke Arabic and were heirs of the great Islamic civilizations of the Umayyads of Damascus and the Abbasids of Baghdad. They therefore disdained both the Romaniotes and the European Jews, though they themselves were divided, between the true 'easterners', called *Mizrahiyyim* in Iraq, and 'westerners', or *Ma'raviyyim*, of Aleppo, Damascus and Cairo.

Entering the Ottoman empire in flight from Christian persecution in Europe were the *Ashkenazi* Jews from Western, Central and Northern Europe, who because of constant persecution had been desperately poor and isolated in ghettos, and who in consequence had fallen back on strict observance of all the old Jewish dietary laws and rituals, disdaining as irreligious the others who had modified their practices as they were assimilated to the cultures in which they lived.

Finally there were the *Sephardic* (*Sepharad*, or 'Spanish') Jews from Spain and Portugal as well as from the lands in which they had taken refuge following the great expulsions of the fifteenth century, in particular Italy and North Africa, who, unlike most of the others, had been wealthy nobles and businessmen and leading intellectuals and who in their assimilation to Spanish culture had greatly modified their Jewish practices, to the disgust of the Ashkenazis in particular. They never had known the limitations and scorn of the ghettos of Central Europe. They had mixed freely with their social equals in Muslim Spain, both Christians and Muslims, so once arrived in the Ottoman Empire they lacked the servility and even shyness toward superiors which characterized the other Jewish groups, in consequence looking down on the latter as ignorant and backward.

Each of these groups was proud of its own origin and past, though they often divided into sub-groups according to place and province of origin. Each was jealous of its traditions, customs and prejudices, and attributed sacred value to its own liturgy while disdaining those of the others. Each maintained its sovereignty, rejecting all encroachments. All, however, adhered to the generally-accepted Rabbanite form of Judaism based on the Torah, except for the Karaites, who, denying talmudic-rabbinical tradition, maintained their own traditions and practices in isolation, thus constituting another quite separate community.

It could not be expected that now when all these different groups had come together for the first time in over a thousand years they would suddenly all become as one. While Hebrew remained for all the language of religion, in their daily lives they spoke Greek, Arabic, German, French, or Spanish, and for those coming from eastern Europe Yiddish. Even more than in language, moreover, in their food, manners, and behavior they continued to reflect the cultures from which they came, in which they manifested great pride despite all the persecution from which they had suffered. These differences naturally enough led to rivalries and disputes.

They differed on almost everything. The Ashkenazi man could simply repudiate his first wife and return her dowry with the addition of an indemnity, though he could not marry a second wife without the first one's permission. On the other hand, the Sephardic Jews provided all sorts of rights for the first wife, whose co-operation played an important role in the granting of divorce. In the marriage contract the husband would solemnly agree to not marry again and to remain united with her so long as she lived and was faithful. If he violated the agreement and married a second wife, he could not live with her if the first wife opposed it, and in such cases he had to send the intruder back. Some Sephardic communities stipulated that a husband could not secure a divorce without the consent of his wife, providing severe punishments in case of violations, including corporal punishment and excommunication. Among the Ashkenazis, however, if the first wife was barren for ten years, or became insane, then he could marry again without her permission, whereas the more liberal Sephardic Jews did not allow such concessions. Sephardi girls were supposed to avoid marriage with Ashkenazi boys, and so on.

Liturgy in the synagogue was a constant source of dispute. There was hardly any prayer said on any occasion which did not differ between the two rites, and there were also substantial differences among the different groups within each. They also quarreled over rules regarding fasting, observance of the Sabbath and religious holidays and in their approach to the Bible, the Talmud, and most branches of science.

There were substantial differences regarding food. They disputed mightily on how the animal should be slaughtered, with the Ashkenazis far stricter than the Sephardis, disqualifying meat for eating as the result of even the slightest pulmonary lesion, though at times exceptions were allowed if the adhesion on the lung could be rubbed in such a way that it could be dissolved. Sephardis rejected meat which was rich in fat and tallow. For all practical purposes, Ashkenazis could not even eat meat prepared by Sephardic butchers. Such dietary differences were so great that the faithful of the two rites normally could not eat together.

No greater disputes arose than those regarding the treatment of the Crypto-Jews or *marranos*, who had converted to Christianity in Spain by the force of the Inquisition, and their descendants, many of whom had remained Christians willingly, sometimes for three generations, ignoring opportunities to leave and return voluntarily to Judaism until they were finally forced out by mounting persecution. Were *marranos* to be considered as Jews who had defected, whatever the reason, and who wanted to return to Judaism, or were they to be treated like other Christians wanting to convert for the first time? Much depended on their parents. It was relatively simple to find out if mother and wife were Jews and if marriage rites had been performed in accordance with Jewish law, but even here there were disputes, and for children of *marrano* marriages as well as second and third generation *marranos* who were themselves born as Christians, the issues became very complicated and the source of heated discussions among Ottoman rabbis. There were a few rabbis who favored a strict approach, considering all those born as Christians, together with those who had failed to escape when they had an opportunity to do so as Christians who wanted to convert to Judaism. But in view of the force and violence of the Inquisition, most Ottoman Rabbis tended to allow such people to 'return to Judaism' without too much consideration of their background, however complicated it might be, asking only that they accept circumcision with the proper blessings as an indication that they were 'leaving the impurity of the Gentiles for the purity of Israel'. Since Jewish law prohibited men from having sex relations with female slaves, however, the offsprings of such unions, which took place most frequently among the *marranos*, could not be accepted as Jews under any circumstances, and such people, while continuing to live in the Jewish quarters, formed a highly disputatious and divisive group demanding their rights and inspiring heated arguments in consequence.

The Karaites, finally, differed with everyone else. Insofar as they were concerned, the Bible was the only source of Jewish creed and law, and all of Rabbinical-Talmudic tradition had to be ignored except when it was indispensable for applying its ideas, clarifying ambiguities, or making up for matters simply not covered in Biblical texts. Law was determined by literal application of the biblical text, as supported by community consensus, by a limited application of knowledge based on human reason, and conclusions reached by applying logical analogy to Scripture. Their actual belief was close to that of Rabbinical Jews, that the unique and unitary God, who was not created, created the world out of nothing. He revealed himself through the Torah that he sent to Moses, which contains the truth which cannot be altered by any other law, and he will resurrect the dead on the day of judgment and will reward each man according to what he did during his own life. But Karaite religious law did not develop like that of Rabbinical Judaism, and it contained many differences which separated its followers from the latter and led to violent disputes, particularly involving the observance of holidays, reqirements of ritual purity, and regulations regarding marriage. The Karaites therefore lived among themselves, without contact with the other Jews, who in turn treated them with horror and repulsion. The Karaites were considered to be desecrators of the Sabbath since, because of differences in calendars, they worked on days and at times that other Jews considered sacred. Intermarriage of Rabbanite Jews with Karaites generally was forbidden, if for no other reason than because their women did not take the bath ritually required by the other sects before marriage was consummated. Karaite marriages and divorces also were considered not valid by the Rabbanites because of ritual differences, so that the former considered all the latter to be living in sin.

Jewish Community Organization and Operation

Division into kahals. The Ottoman Jewish community, whether called *ta'ife, cema'at* or *millet*, remained not as a single, unified organization headed by a single leader as were those of the Armenians and Greeks, then, but as many self-governing congregations. These were organized into communities called *kahals (kahal kadosh, kehilla,* pl. *kehillot),* created according to national, provincial and even city origins to carry out communal activities according to their individual customs and traditions, each entering into direct relations with the Ottoman Ruling Class authorities as required. Occasionally, however, and particularly in periods of decline starting in the seventeenth century, the local rabbis in certain towns and cities did select the most eminent of their number to serve as chief community rabbi, usually called *rav ha-kolel (rav kolel),* who usually headed a common rabbinical court as well as a community *yeshiva,* or higher school. In Izmir and a few other places, moreover, there were two chief rabbis, both called *ha rav ha-gadol,* one in charge of civil law and administration and the other of religious activities. In the smaller towns, or in cities where there were few Jews, there were only single *kahals,* but in Istanbul, Salonica, Izmir, Edirne and the other major cities where numerous Jews lived, there were many, each with its own Rabbi, synagogue, hospital, cemetery, schools and slaughterhouse, and each providing members with secular and religious leadership.

The rabbis of the time encouraged such arrangements to provide the kind of homogeneous group life which could enforce strict observance of religious requirements as well as the regular payment of tax obligations. Rabbi David Ibn Abi Zimra thus stated: ' . . . with the breaking away of groups from their fellow-townsmen and their common language, there is also a corresponding breaking up of devout hearts; nor are their prayers of praise to God united. But if they are of one city of origin and of one language, then will peace dwell among them, for each one will feel at home and know his status'.[2] Normally, as each *kahal* was formed, the founders attempted to insure its permanence by signing communal agreements forbidding current or future members from leaving to join another or even to subdivide. Such agreements were not often observed for very long, however, so additional divisions often followed.

Islamic law prohibited the construction of new synagogues, whether by old or new *kahals,* allowing only the repair and reconstruction of existing houses of prayer. Starting with Sultan Mehmed II, however, numerous exceptions were made for Jews through the issuance of imperial orders (*irade*) allowing even the smallest existing structures to be transformed into major religious establishments while the letter of the law continued to be observed. Each became the nucleus of a separate Jewish community.

Residential isolation and the major Jewish communities. Ottoman Jews lived in their own quarters (*mahalle*), or on occasion sections of quarters, from which they rarely emerged except to go to market. This sort of residential segregation was common to all religious groups, and by their own choice, so it cannot be considered discriminatory. It was dictated not only by the long-standing Middle Eastern tradition separating people of different religions, but also by simple convenience in preserving and observing the social and religious customs and rites unique to each group. Insofar as the leaders of Ottoman Jewry were concerned the best way of preventing conversion or backsliding was isolation of their followers from the adherents of other religions. Most Rabbis discouraged all contact between Jews and Muslims, because 'many evils can result from this, and Israel is a holy people'. One example will suffice. Milk taken from the cow by Muslims could not be drunk by Jews unless a Jew was present when the milking took place and witnesssed that no unclean animals were nearby at the time which might have contaminated it. It was better to keep everyone apart.

Like all the urban quarters in the Middle East, those of the Jews were veritable labyrinths of narrow streets and alleyways, with buildings of widely varying sizes and levels forming seemingly endless mazes penetrable only by those with the greatest familiarity.

Istanbul. In Istanbul, the earliest Jewish settlements occupied in Ottoman times by the Romaniote Jews surviving from Byzantium rule concentrated, on the one hand, in the area immediately beneath and to the west of the Topkapı Sarayı palace of the Sultans, today occupied by the Yeni Cami, as well as in the Ottoman quarters of Eminönü, Tahtakale, Bahçekapı and Yemişiskele and at Galata, on the opposite shore of the Golden Horn. They had also been resettled by the Byzantine emperors where other Romaniote Jews remained from olden times, at Hasköy (Byz: *Picridion*), on the northern side of the Golden Horn.

Most Jewish immigrants who came to the capital from Anatolia, Southeastern Europe and, particularly, from Spain during the reign of Bayezid II, were settled in the southern shores of the Golden Horn between the Greek quarter of Fener and the land walls of the city in the area known as Balat (Byz: *Balata*). Subsequent Jewish immigrants settled on both sides of the Golden Horn, with regular small-boat service providing direct communication between Balat and Hasköy, leaving them in virtual isolation from the remainder of the city. The Jewish communities living on the Golden Horn beneath the Topkapı palace were supplanted by the construction of the Yeni Cami and the Mısır Çarşı market during the seventeenth century, with the Karaites moving to Kağıthane and the

Romaniotes to Balat and Hasköy. These remained the dominant centers of Jewish life in Istanbul for another two hundred years. It was only in the nineteenth century that the Jewish revival as part of the *Tanzimat* reform movement led their more prosperous members to move into the 'European quarters' of Galata and Beyoğlu, the European Bosporus suburbs of Ortaköy and Arnavutköy, the Anatolian suburbs of Kadıköy and Kuzguncuk, and to the Marmara islands.

In Balat, the largest and most prosperous of the Jewish communities in Istanbul through most of the Ottoman centuries, there were subdivisions according to function and wealth, though the exact definitions and locations shifted over time. The Karabaş quarter, located adjacent to the Golden Horn outside the city's sea walls in the area known in Judeo-Spanish as *Balat Afuera* (external Balat), and occupied by the poorest elements of Balat's Jewish population, particularly street sellers and boatmen, was the location of the major Jewish ports. The *Skala de los kayikes de yemiş* was the quai for the boats which brought fruit and vegetables from the great markets of Eminönü. The adjacent *Skala de la lenya*, or quai for heating wood, gave its name to the street which for centuries led from it, called *Odun Iskele sokak* (Wood Quai Street). The *Skala de los kayikes*, directly opposite Hasköy, handled the small boats (*kayıks*) which sailed almost continuously between the two major Jewish quarters carrying not only produce and people but also corpses after the Balat Jewish cemetery was filled in the third quarter of the nineteenth century. The *Skala del estyerkol* cared for cargoes of trash and waste, while the *Skale de los vapores* was added in the nineteenth century to care for the steamers which sailed through the Golden Horn between the adjacent Muslim quarter of Eyüb and Galata. Among the major buildings of Karabaş located along its main street (today named Demirkapı Caddesi) were the *Gerush* and *Pul Yashan* synagogues, founded originally by the Romaniotes in Byzantine times, and toward the Sea of Marmara, in the sub-district known as *La Lonca*, the *Kal de Selanico* (or *Sigiri*) and *Eliaou* synagogues, whose surviving ruins indicate that they probably were established for the first immigrants who came to Istanbul during the time of Mehmed II. In modern times, though most of Karabaş was razed as part of a city renewal project around the Golden Horn during the late 1980s, the Jewish community *Or Ahayim* hospital (built in the late nineteenth century) has continued to dominate the area between this street and the Golden Horn.

Entrance to Balat proper (*Balat Aryentro*, or 'Balat within the sea walls' in Judeo-Spanish) was achieved through the Balat Gate (*La Puerta de Balat*), which led to the main commercial section (called *kavafhane*, or 'street of shoemakers', by the Turks and *kanfafana* in Judeo-Spanish), to the right leading into the *Eski Kasap caddesi* ('old butchers street'), and to the left the parallel *Leblebiciler* ('street of the chick pea sellers') and *Lapçinçiler* ('sandal-makers') streets, each with its own walls and gates, which continue to be occupied by both small manufacturers and commercial shops to the present day, though most are no longer Jewish. Where the two latter streets came together were the two major synagogues of Balat, the *Yanbol*, founded in Byzantine times by emigrants from Yanbolu, in Bulgaria, and a little further south, the *Ahrida*, founded by Jewish immigrants from Ohrid, in Macedonia. Next to the *Yanbol* synagogue was the principal public bath of Balat, *el banyo de Balat* (now called *Ferruh Kâhya Hamamı*), which had separate buildings for men and women, used for ritual washings for ceremonies involved with birth, marriage, and death.

The two Jewish quarters outside Balat on the north, *Kasturiye* and *Iştipol*, were separated from *Balat Aryentro* by quarters occupied by mixed populations, mainly Greeks spreading over from the Fener and Armenians from Kumkapı, on the northern shores of the Sea of Marmara. It was in this area in particular that conflicts among the groups took place, particularly when the Sultan's Christian subjects invaded the Jewish quarters and assaulted their Jewish neighbors as the result of the endemic ritual murder accusations.

Salonica. Whereas in Istanbul the Jewish communities dominated only certain parts of the city, in Salonica, Jews comprised a substantial majority of the population so they spread into most quarters, though they concentrated most completely in those nearest the seaport along the city wall, in the Frankish quarter, and in the quarter near the Hippodrome. The older Jewish residents formed three congregations, the original Greek-speaking Romaniotes (Griegos), to whom were added immigrants from Bulgaria, Ashkenazi emigrants who came from Bavaria and elsewhere in Central Europe in the mid fourteenth century and who comprised the largest Jewish community until the Spanish immigrants arrived, and the Italians, who dominated before the arrival of the Sephardim in the late fifteenth century.

At first the Spanish refugees, coming in disorder across the Mediterranean or overland via Italy, attached themselves to the Romaniotes, not only because they were the oldest Jewish group but also because of particular abhorrence of the Ashkenazis, who seemed to them crude and backward since the latter were far stricter in observing Jewish laws than were those who had been assimilated to Spanish life. As the Spanish immigrants became more numerous, however, they became too burdensome for the Romaniotes, who also were comparatively strict, so first the Catalans left to establish their own synagogue, then the Castillians, and finally the remaining Spanish immigrants formed single congregations under the name *Gerush-Sefarad* (exodus from Spain), taking people from all the Spanish provinces and hastily improvising a synagogue that they had to rebuild later.

Among the Italians in Salonica, the Sicilians were mostly humble artisans, forgers and fishermen, who lived together after their arrival in 1497 but did not have the means to build a synagogue, so for a long time they assembled in a private house for religious services before finally building a small synagogue in the middle of the fifteenth century. The Calabraise Jews, who had been banished from Naples along with some fugitives from Pouille who came in 1497, did not mix with the other Italian groups in Salonica but instead founded their own congregation at the start under the leadership of the famous Jacob ben Habib, who had just come from Portugal, forming a community which was far more pacific than the others.

The Portuguese Marrano fugitives, who came in large numbers starting in 1506, were originally assigned by lot to the seven original refugee synagogues, who thus got the right to collect large taxes from them. In 1510, however, now for the most part converted back to Judaism and fully familiarized with their new home, they organized a separate community called Lisbon, and built a beautiful synagogue which eclipsed most of the older ones by its size, splendor and decoration as well as by its large number of wealthy and important members.

All the Sephardic synagogues of Salonica were divided by discord during the sixteenth century, but the worst in this respect was the venerable *Gerush Sefarad*, since it had included all the exiles who first arrived from Spain regardless of their places of origin. The *Gerush Sefarad* held the record for turbulence. In the late fifteenth century about one hundred members separated and temporarily formed another temple, then returned, but maintained a separate administration within the reunified temple. Near the end of sixteenth century, moreover, another group became unhappy over matters of fiscal taxation and left to form a new congregation, with others joining them, leaving *Gerush Sefarad* divided for all practical purposes into three communities.

In 1510 the Catalan synagogue of Salonica divided into two, the Old Catalan and New Catalan, over the question of who should be appointed as *Marbitz Torah* for its *Talmud Torah*. Rabbi Samuel de Medina, most important member of the synagogue and one of the leaders of Salonica Jewry, managed to reconcile them in 1540, but the synagogue was destroyed during the disastrous Salonica fire of 1545. It was restored with the financial assistance of Barukh Almosnino, whose prestige managed to keep the congregation together for a time, but as soon as he died, conflict broke out again, leading it to divide again into Old and New Catalans, which remained separate for over two centuries.

The Italian Apulian synagogue divided into five separate synagogues in 1550, Pouille, Neve Shalom, Neve Tsedek, Otranto and Astruc, all so poor and weak that they could not pay either their judges or rabbis. After 1505, the Sicilian synagogue divided into two sections in the same building, each with its own Torah scrolls, celebrating its own religious services, and maintaining its own welfare institutions until 1562, when they moved into separate buildings. The Lisbon synagogue broke into the aristocratic Old Lisbon and the more democratic New Lisbon synagogues in 1536. The Old Lisbon manifested its wealth by constructing a magnificent new synagogue in 1560, but it then broke up in 1570 in a dispute over Rabbinical autocracy.

The Rabbis of all the Salonica communities attempted to stop these break-ups and divisions since they harmed their ability to enforce the observance of religious rituals as well as the more practical need to collect community taxes. At one point the community notables, assembled at the Salonica Talmud Torah, solemnly threatened with excommunication (*herem*) any members who formed a new community or temple, but this had little effect, and the divisions continued. As a result, by the middle of the sixteenth century there were as many as twenty-six *kahals* in Salonica as well as forty-four in Istanbul.

Sarajevo, capital of Ottoman Bosnia, was the major center of Jewish life in the Ottoman Danubian provinces. It included both Sephardic refugees from the Iberian Peninsula as well as Ashkenazis fleeing from persecution in Germany, Hungary and Poland. All of these started settling in what had been an entirely Muslim community in 1551, when Gazi Husrev Bey (later Pasha), its Sancak Bey at the time, built the extensive *Bursa Bezistan* (Bursa Cloth Market), in the vicinity of its major trading establishment, the *Baş Çarşiye* (Central Market), as a center for the silk trade with Bursa, which at the time was largely in the hands of Jewish merchants from western Anatolia. As a reward for Jewish assistance against the Habsburgs, in 1577 the Ottoman governors allowed Sarajevo's Jews to live in a particularly salubrious part of the city located nearby, which came to be known as the Jewish quarter (*mahalla judia*), or in honor of the governor who permitted it, the *Siyavuş Pasha Dairesi*.[3] Later Jewish quarters also remained clustered around the market, with most living in the *Pehlivan Oruç* and *Ferhad Pasha* quarters well into the nineteenth century. As elsewhere in the empire, Bosnian Jewry gained the favor of the Muslim masses by their work as physicians and pharmacists as well as merchants who could be trusted to maintain quality as well as reasonable prices. Jews also worked as artisans, dominating the trades as tailors, shoemakers, butchers and wood and metal workers as well as manufacturing glass and dyes of various sorts. Sarajevo's Jewish merchants traded westward across Bosnia to the Dalmatian coast and across the Adriatic to Italy as well as southward to Istanbul via Skopje and Salonica. Its rabbis and synagogues remained subordinate to those of Salonica, where most of them were trained, until the arrival in 1752 of Rabbi David Pardo, who as its Chief Rabbi expanded and reorganized its *Talmud Torah* and established a Rabbinical school, which not only trained all Sarajevo Rabbis, and so made them largely independent of

Salonica and able to become major legal scholars whose *responsa* had wide influence, but also became a major center for Rabbinical students coming from throughout the empire.

Izmir. While Jews had lived in Izmir in ancient times, they had been driven away by Byzantine persecutions so none were left by the time of the Ottoman conquest. The Ottoman Jewish community in Izmir was formed relatively late, only during the last quarter of the sixteenth century, when Jews who had been settled at Manisa and Tire after the Ottoman conquest of Syria fled to the coast as a result of the anarchy caused by nomadic tribal resistance to central authority which just was beginning to make itself felt in that part of Anatolia. They were joined in the early years of the seventeenth century by Sephardic Jews immigrating from Salonica as a result of the endemic fires, plagues and political anarchy that were beginning to infect not only that city, but much of Rumelia, and also by Portuguese and Spanish *marranos*, who were subjected to increasing persecution by the Inquisition despite the conversion of their ancestors to Catholicism more than a century earlier. These *marranos* formed their own congregation, originally called *Kahallat Kodesh Portugal Neve Shalom*, but it later divided into two, the *Portugal* and the *Neve Shalom*, with other Jews joining but the *marranos* continuing to dominate politically and culturally.

Palestine. Following the conquest of Eretz Israel by Selim I in 1516, the Ottoman governors divided it into four *sancaks*, Jerusalem (*nahiyes* of Jerusalem and Hebron), Gaza (Gaza, Ramla and Lydda), Nablus (Cebel Şami, Cebel Qibli, Qâqun, and Bani Sa'ab), and Safed (Safed, Tibnin, Tyre, Şaqif, Acre and Tiberias), while restoring security and order and developing agriculture and trade. The Jewish population grew rapidly due to immigration of Ashkenazis from Central Europe, Sephardim from the Iberian Peninsula, *Mağrebi*s from North Africa, and *Musta'rabs*, or 'Arabized Jews', both those who had lived there since Roman times and those who immigrated there from other Arab provinces once they were included in the Ottoman dominions. While all towns and cities of Eretz Israel benefited from this immigration, it was Safed which developed most, becoming a major industrial and trade center during the early years of *Kanuni* Süleyman's long reign (1520–66) and developing also into the Empire's most important center of Jewish mystic learning and contemplation. The most important source of wealth at Safed and Sidon came from a highly developed wool industry. Raw materials coming mainly from Salonica and Istanbul were woven into cloths which were sold throughout Eretz Israel and Syria as well as being exported to Anatolia and throughout the Mediterranean area through the port of Sidon. The Jews of Sidon also were very much involved with agriculture, either cultivating adjacent fields and vineyards directly or renting them to Arab cultivators while spending most of their time participating in the city's industrial and trade activities. Their prosperity seems to have been greatly assisted by the local Ottoman officials, who at times intervened forcefully to secure favorable decisions from the Safad rabbinical court.

Syria. Following the Ottoman conquest of Syria, the Jews of Damascus were very prosperous, producing a number of wealthy mercantile families, with cultural and religious activities flourishing. To the original Arabized Jews and Karaites, refugees from Spain and Portugal had begun to arrive already after 1492, but they came in floods after the Ottoman conquest, becoming merchants, artisans and traders and, in addition to their own flourishing religious and cultural institutions, developing close relations with their counterparts in the Holy Land. The new arrivals formed their own communities, often disputing not only with the older Jewish communities but also with refugees from Sicily, who formed their separate community as well. It was only in the seventeenth century that the three groups finally got together in response to Ottoman decline and its consequences.

Egypt. The status and prosperity of Egyptian Jewry increased greatly as rule passed from the hands of the Mamluks (1250–1517), many of whom were converted Christians, to the Ottomans following the conquest by Sultan Selim I in 1517. The Jews of Cairo were initially subjected to pillaging by converted Christians in Ottoman service, at first Mamluks who went over to the Ottomans after their empire was destroyed, and for two decades following the conquest by the Ottoman Janissaries. Jewish merchants subsequently were able to establish business relations with the latter, however, acting as agents for the sale or distribution of their booty, in return for which they compelled the Janissaries to stop pillaging the Jewish quarters. Since the Ottoman rulers in any case trusted Jews much more than they did their Arab Christian subjects, who were constantly resisting and revolting, or plotting to revolt, Jews were given all the important financial positions in both the central and provincial governments, collecting taxes and customs duties, which provided the basis for subsequent Jewish prosperity while the Ottomans remained dominant in Egypt well into the seventeenth century. Jews in Cairo prospered as money lenders and bankers as well as dealers in precious metals, goldsmiths and shopkeepers. Many Jews acted as tax farmers (*multezim*) for Ottoman officials, not only collecting taxes from cultivators, but also controlling the mint as Supervisor of Currency and levying and collecting customs duties in the ports of Alexandria and Damietta, by far the most important source of revenue in the province. In Alexandria, a far smaller and less important city in early Ottoman times, the Jews were a significant element of the population, acting as merchants as well as translators for the European diplomats, travellers and traders who passed through the city on their way to Cairo as well as to the eastern seas, with the Jews themselves subsequently participating in this international trade as well as that with the other major Ottoman centers.

Unification of Ottoman Jewish Communities. In the towers of babel that were the Ottoman Jewish communities during the century after the ingathering, it was Castillian Judeo-Spanish, commonly called Ladino, that above all else was the main force which gradually brought the national and regional groups together. Supple and comprehensive, it underwent Greek, French, German, Turkish and Arabic infiltration, but its force of adaptation enabled it to assimilate them all, helped considerably by the fact that its advocates dominated the community culturally and economically to a far greater extent than did their competitors, as well as because for later generations places of origin were less important than they had been to their ancestors. Its influence toward unity was supplemented and supported, moreover, by the fact that all Ottoman Jews now shared a common ruler and Middle Eastern civilization and way of life, while their separate legal interpretations were largely reconciled and brought together by the codification of Jewish laws, rules and regulations by Rabbi Joseph Caro (1488–1575) in the *Beyt Yosef* and its summary the *Shulhan Arukh*, which came to be accepted as authoritative by most congregations on Ottoman territory. Practical unity ultimately did come to Ottoman Jewry, therefore, though beneath the surface differences relating to ancestral origins still remained.

Jewish Housing. Most common among the Jewish residential plans, in Istanbul and Salonica at least, was the *cortijo* inherited from Spain, very much like the traditional Muslim *han* which had influenced the latter centuries earlier. This was a low building stretching around a central courtyard, one, two or even three stories high, normally with tiled roofs, with residences and shops intermixed in some, and constituting a veritable village in itself. Over the outside streets, balconies and terraces hung precariously as if they were ready to fall onto the people passing below. The residences themselves, of whatever size and shape, were intensely crowded, except for those of the most wealthy, as constant shortages of housing in the face of continued immigration of refugees from elsewhere in Europe led families to crowd on top of one another, with one or even two or three families crowded into each room until there was little space left to breathe. Most daily activities were therefore carried out in the open, on the terraces, or in the courtyards and streets beyond. There was little permanent furniture, not even more than the barest utensils needed for meals. Food was scarce even in times of prosperity, and meat and oil were consumed only on special occasions. In most of these buildings there was no running water and no ready drinking water, the latter being supplied by nearby public fountains. There was, moreover, little sanitation and no heat, with insects and animals running everywhere, so it did not take very much for small blazes to become great fires and for individual illnesses to become epidemics which quickly infected a substantial portion of the community. Most habitations were therefore no more than temporary bivouacs at best, with no particular reason for their inhabitants to remain any longer then necessary when better accomodations became available.

Community Organization and Functions. The Ottoman Jewish *millet*, comprising all the *kahals* organized by its members and gathered into quarters, provided them, above all else, with status and protection. In the absence of municipal government as such in Ottoman cities, each *kahal* was like a separate municipality. It was responsible for registering members, imposing and collecting taxes, making expenditures for community activities, maintaining religious, social and political institutions, punishing violations of its laws and sometimes of Ottoman laws, settling internal disputes when possible, and delivering to the Ottoman treasury those taxes intended for the Sultan and his ministers. It represented members with the government and with members of other *millets*. It provided religious, judicial and cultural leadership. And it helped to promote economic prosperity among members by organizing those in the small artisan groups unable to maintain craft guilds of their own, limiting competition among them in price and quality and attempting to preserve for them monopolies over certain occupations, not only against the competition of members of other *millets* but also against all those coming from outside, including other Jews.

The *kahal* shared functions and authority in certain areas with other bodies. Most important of these were the guilds organized by the more important crafts and mercantile activities, which were responsible for the quality of products, fairness of trade, fixing of prices, and internal order and discipline. In addition there were the Ottoman quarter (*mahalle*) chiefs, who commanded the urban police, and the market supervisors (*muhtesib*), who regulated the corporations and the market place, particularly in regard to price, weights and measures, and quality of goods. Finally there were the Muslim *kadis*, or judges, who regulated and registered all property transactions, leases, legal documents, money lending agreements, commercial transactions and tax payments; they also announced and carried out Imperial and local government orders, and supervised certain services such as the maintenance of public buildings, city walls, roads and bridges, town cleanliness and food supplies.

All the *kahals* of the major cities developed central community organizations and committees called *Bet Din Hagadol* or *Ha-Va'ad ha-Kolel shel ha-Kehillot*, composed of delegates from each *kahal*, but these usually met only rarely for particular matters of common interest, such as participating in city festivals, sending delegations to the Sultan to secure or maintain particular privileges, maintaining community *talmud torahs* and *bet din* courts, joining other groups in defending the city against outside attacks, and also appointing community officials called *kethudas* or *kâhyas* (in Hebrew *shtadlanim*), who were in charge of relations with the Ottoman officials. Their powers were limited both in time and scope and they had little authority to enforce decisions on recalcitrant communities. Only in Salonica was the central Jewish organization more powerful and influential than elsewhere, particularly in the age of decline. There it acted at first under the aegis of the city *Talmud Torah*, and then as the Federal Jewish Council, developing rules and regulations which were applied to all the *kahals* for the good of the entire community. Elsewhere, however, it was the *kahals* and synagogues rather than the collective bodies which dominated the system.

During the first century of the Golden Age, each *kahal* in the major cities maintained its own separate quarter (*mahalle*), usually separated from others by high walls and gates which were closed during the night and guarded at all times. In later centuries, however, when numerous fires and plagues broke down many of the old barriers, the walled quarters contained Muslims and Christians as well as Jews, each concentrating in one area without actual physical separation. The *kahal* itself maintained the streets and arranged for whatever street cleaning and lighting there was, though in many cases these services were provided by the house and shop owners themselves. Night watchmen patrolled between sunset and sunrise to provide security after dark, lighting and extinguishing street lamps, looking out for thieves and robbers, watching for fires, and calling out the appropriate alarms when necessary. Security against more serious threats such as Janissary raids and Christian mob attacks from outside usually was provided by regular bribes provided to the Janissaries and other military units and, more cautiously, by networks of secret tunnels which enabled residents to escape to neighboring houses or under the walls and outside the city entirely, as the occasion demanded.

A particularly important institution maintained by the *kahal* for the benefit of its members was the traditional Jewish property right known as *hazaka*, originally developed in Europe during the Middle Ages, which as applied by community legislation in the Ottoman dominions referred particularly to the right to follow certain occupations and to limit competition among Jews in the same occupation, and even more important at a time when large-scale immigration created severe housing shortages, the right of a Jewish tenant to maintain his rental tenancy in property owned by non-Jews as a permanent possession, without being subjected to dispossession or increased rentals as a result of pressure from other Jews seeking accommodation. No Jew could thus try to evict a co-religionist from his house, shop or *cortijo* if that building belonged to a Muslim. Every Jewish renter thus acquired a right of usufruct over the place that he rented. The right could be lost by three consecutive years of non usage, when the renter ceased to occupy the locale by his own will, and he would lose the right without waiting for three years if he left the town without expectation of returning. Conflicts came most often when Muslim property owners sold to Jews such buildings in which *hazaka* rights were held by Jews, with the new owners trying to annul the *hazakas* and take over the properties for their own use or to rent them out again at much higher rents by evicting the *hazaka*-holding tenants. On the whole, however, *hazaka* was enforced successfully over the centuries because of the spirit of solidarity and social discipline that existed in the *kahals*, based on the collective interest that predominated over that of the individual. While Muslim owners might have been expected to contest this arrangement among Jewish renters, they did not since the *hazaka* very much resembled the old Muslim practice of 'fair price', which dominated most aspects of the market place in Middle Eastern life.

The *kahal* trained, examined and licensed slaughterers (*shohet*, pl. *shohetim*) and cheese makers, making certain of their moral qualities as well as their knowledge of how to prepare their products in accordance with Kosher ritual requirements; for example, inspecting their knives to make sure of their sharpness so that members of the community could consume the resulting products in confidence of their ritual purity. Close inspection was carried out by special rabbis, and severe punishments were provided for violations.

The *kahal* had great powers over its members, whose rights were considered subordinate to those of the whole. Whenever there was a dispute between community and individual, the former was presumed to be in the right unless the latter could prove the contrary. The need to maintain sufficient current income to meet expenses led many communities to exercise strict control over members, not only to maintain regular payments but also to prevent them from leaving and joining another *kahal* because of the financial losses that such departures would cause. Social custom therefore forced the individual to remain within the *kahal* of his ancestors and to accept the decisions of its leaders and of the majority, regardless of his personal feelings.

Every *kahal* had its own synagogue, rabbis, teachers, elementary schools called *talmud torahs* when maintained by the community or *heders* if private, hospitals, cemeteries, and social and welfare institutions and societies. In most cases it also had a *bet din*, or supreme judicial body, composed of judges (*dayyans*), chosen among the most learned members of the community. On occasion, however, particularly in the centuries of decline, several *kahals* maintained and used common courts, hospitals and cemeteries.

The Rabbi. Each *kahal* was a legal administrative unit. Its members elected its Rabbi (Ott: *Haham*, Heb: *Rav*), who, in the absence of any state municipal authority, thus was mayor as well as spiritual leader of the quarter, with members of the community obligating themselves not to listen to any instruction in the *Torah* except from him and to obey his orders in all matters, both secular and religious. The Rabbi was of course the religious leader of the congregation, so he had to be learned, dignified, expert in all aspects of the religious law, as wise as Daniel, and above reproach in all matters. It was indispensable for him to be married, not only so his wife could lead the women of the congregation, but also so that the men of his congregation would be assured that he would maintain proper relations with their wives. At the synagogue he directed services as well as marriage, funeral and circumcision ceremonies, and gave sermons commenting on the law and deriving moral lessons for the education and edification of his congregation. He usually also was chief educator of the community schools, adding the position of *marbitz torah*, and as such directing the communal public elementary school (*Talmud Torah*) as well the university (*Yeshiva*) where older students as well as adults pursued Talmudic studies along with mathematics, astronomy, and natural sciences.

He was head of the *Bet Din*, or religious court, and as such he performed two major functions. First of all he was the chief propagator of the law, not only interpreting *responsa* written to settle legal questions but also when necessary exercising legislative power, issuing ordnances (*takkanot*), sometimes by himself and sometimes together with the community authorities and legal scholars. In addition, along with the judges (*dayyanim*), he settled differences and administered penalties to those who violated the law or failed to perform their community duties or pay community taxes. He signed marriage contracts and divorce papers and administered the inheritances of widows and orphans. He could inflict various degrees of punishment, including fines, usually for infractions of industrial or commercial rules, corporal punishment with the bastonnado (*malkut*), limited by Jewish law to no more than thirty-nine strokes, usually inflicted by the *shamash* or in his absence by one of the teachers of the *Talmud Torah*, or imprisonment in the community prison. For more serious crimes requiring more severe penalties, Muslim officials were brought in so that Jews would not violate their own Law. Thus the Muslim *çavuş* (sergeant) was sent by the Muslim judge at the request of the Rabbi to inflict more than forty blows of the bastonnado, with as many as two hundred being applied at times, to the great pain, not only of the criminal, but also to other members of the community who hated to see outsiders mix into its affairs even when requested by the Rabbi.

The greatest punishment which the Rabbi could inflict was excommunication (*herem*), complete exclusion of the believer from membership in and protection by the community, which was imposed on members who gave false testimony in court, gravely failed to carry out their religious duties, or who angered the Rabbi in any other way. This punishment was so extreme, however, that it was rarely applied. Strictly speaking *herem* meant that the communicant no longer could enter the temple or be counted as one of the ten Jews indispensable for the quorum (*minyan*) required for the performance of the daily prayers, particularly at mealtime. No Jew could eat with him since his bread and wine were accursed. No one could use his *mezuza* or phylactics, receive alms from him, or even read a book belonging to him. His children could not be circumcised or admitted to community schools. His relatives and servants could continue to contact him, but no other Jew was allowed to visit or even console him. He had to dress entirely in black and live like a hermit, and he was not allowed to cut his hair. If he died while still in a state of excommunication, he could not be buried with rabbinical rites, and while a large uncut stone could mark his grave, there could be no epitaphs on it, and it was the custom for the community to stone it. You can imagine what horror such punishment might have caused if it was strictly enforced. Normally, however, things never went that far. The procedure for absolution was very simple. After thirty days the excommunicated person could come before the rabbi and confess his sin. If he expressed repentance without reserve, the Rabbi would absolve him, saying 'I absolve you, may God pardon you', and he then would be admitted back into full membership in the community.

The legal opinions of the sixteenth century Rabbi David Ibn Abi Zimra give us an idea of some of the rights, duties and powers of Ottoman rabbis in the synagogues:

1. To escort the bridegroom, to escort the father of a new-born son, and to visit the family in which some happy event had occurred or the house of a mourner.
2. To perform marriage ceremonies and authorize divorces.
3. To act as judge between members of the congregation.
4. To preach in public in the Synagogue and at the Cemetery.
5. To be called up in the sanctuary to read to the congregation the Song of Moses and the Ten Commandments.
6. To excommunicate members of the community to maintain the dignity of the Rabbinate and the community.[4]

Members of the congregation in return had the following obligations to the Rabbi:

1. To show reverence to the Rabbi in and out of the Synagogue.
2. As manifestation of this, after the Service to wait and let the Rabbi leave the Synagogue first.
3. And to support his decisions, whatever they might be.

Some but not all Rabbis also were recognized as *Haber 'Ir* ('friend of the city'), which gave them authority over the charitable funds belonging to the congregation, to manage its property and in general everything contributed to the Synagogue, and to transfer the charitable funds within prescribed limits, but a rabbi was given these powers only if he fulfilled the following conditions, again according to Rabbi David Ibn Abi Zimra:[5]

1. That all the property and funds that were collected or contributed were given because of his leadership.
2. That he be recognized as 'leader of the generation'.
3. That he be well-established and permanently residing in the city or community.
4. That he be respected by the donors and that he enjoy their confidence that he will dispose of their benefactions properly.
5. That the poor of the city or the *kahal* should be regularly dependent on him.
6. That he himself be not a recipient of the charities of that community so that no one would suspect that he had taken anything for himself.

A Rabbi who was recognized as a *Haber 'Ir* also had the power to say, in the case of a congregational dispute, to which congregation sacred objects belonged, and to use charitable funds for other communal purposes after the poor had been adequately cared for and money was left over in the various charitable funds. But if the *Haber 'Ir* saved on the poor and failed to give them what was required, and instead used the money from charities to buy decorative objects for the Synagogue to find favor in the eyes of the community, such a man was to be called not a *Haber 'Ir* ('friend of the city') but *Gozel 'Ir* (robber of the city), for he robbed not only the poor but also the rich who had intended the contributions for the poor.

As we have seen, the Rabbi also was chief secular officer within his congregation's quarter and as such operated as an official of the central government, or at least its agent in his locality. In this respect, however, he had help. Secular leadership in each *kahal* under the supervision of the Rabbi was assumed by elected lay representatives (*parnassim*), who were chosen for administrative councils (*ma'mad*) by congregation members assembled in public meetings, with representatives of all groups and classes included so as to assure a democratic regime in which all were equal and all interests represented. In the early days, when no-one had too much money, and later during times of prosperity, this ideal was maintained and the entire community participated in governance, at least until well into the seventeenth century. Jewish community administration continued to be inspired by ideas of equality, justice and charity, and all efforts to establish the domination of one group over the rest were strenuously resisted. But when misery came, when the Ottoman empire declined, and the weight of taxes fell on a minority of rich people, and in times when the community was under attack and the need for authority was felt very strongly, then popular government functioned only in theory in most communities. The wealthy few were able to rule without consultation, even naming their own successors as necessary. As a result, by the eighteenth century communal government acquired the character of an aristocratic oligarchy, with the Rabbi commanding along with the leaders of a small number of wealthy families, and the mass of believers accepting the situation with little protest, since they had no alternative.

Despite all the laws and regulations as well as the nature of community organization, in no way was the Rabbi absolute. First of all, there was no pre-eminence among rabbis. Each had authority only in his own congregation and not within the jurisdictions of other rabbis except where his prestige convinced them to accept his judgments. While each of his own congregation members owed him respect and obedience, moreover, they usually had far too much of an independent and critical spirit to leave him to act without control and objection. The mantle of religion that covered him did not, for them, give him any sort of immunity or infallibility. Many congregation members, particularly the former *marranos*, had the same strong spirit of skepticism and defiance regarding their own rabbis as they had maintained previously with the priests and monks with whom they had to deal in Spain. There were therefore always people who would argue against the decision of a Rabbi no matter what it involved and no matter what it was. The taste for controversy and opposition and even obstruction was very strong among Ottoman Jews, as we have already seen in discussing divisions within congregations, so there was little peace for most Rabbis most of the time. Some members would attempt to prevent the Rabbis from continuing to preach and to carry out their duties, with outsiders sometimes brought in to decide disputes. The Ottoman authorities did contribute somewhat to increasing the prestige of rabbis by giving them official recognition and power, particularly the authority to give special permits to congregationers who wanted to travel or to violate Islamic prohibitions, as for example to ride on horseback, dress like a Muslim or to bear arms, but this was only of help during the limited times that the individuals in question needed the Rabbi's help. The rest of the time he was on his own. The Rabbis who were most successful were those who understood that they could not simply impose their will and who knew how to secure the respect of their followers through a combination of ability, tact and energy, and sometimes through liberal expenditure of their own money, thus enabling them to establish some order and discipline around them at least for a time.

Community Administrators and the Law. The elected lay *parnassim* who assisted the Rabbi in carrying out the *kahal*'s administrative and financial affairs, sometimes referred to modestly as the 'Great Men of the *kahal*', were by tradition limited to seven, though sometimes fewer actually served in the community council (*ma'mad*). While the community occasionally would allow them to nominate their successors, the latter had to be approved by a majority of the members in public meeting since, by tradition, 'he who is not acceptable to the community cannot be called its *parnas*'.[6] Though they had the right to administer the *kahal*, they were bound to listen to the advice of men of prominence in the community before decisions were made, though once these were determined by majority vote, dissenters had to go along or suffer severe penalties. The *parnassim* administered the *kahal*'s affairs according to the Jewish law (*halakhah*) and custom (*haggadah*), as well as old-established community regulations or ordinances (*takkana*, pl. *takkanot*) and agreements (*haskama*, or *askama* pl. *haskamot*, or *askamot*), the latter often based on the *takkanot* of Toledo (1305), Aragon (1335) and Castile (1432). For problems not covered in existing law or agreements or created by new conditions, the *parnassim* enacted new regulations, which gained the force of law equal to the dictates of the *halakhah* once they were accepted by the community and rabbis and confirmed by *halakhic* scholars who had to certify that they did not depart from the general principles of justice underlying the Judaic legal system. The Talmud, the *halakhah* laws and the *takkanot* regulations also were interpreted by the famous legal scholars of the time in *responsa*, or answers to legal questions, whose influence depended on the reputation and dignity of those who issued them, with the opinions and decisions of the most influential rabbis being published and followed almost as codes of law in themselves. These *responsa* provide us with substantial information on how Ottoman Jews lived, quarrels about property and personal relations, monopolies, insecurity on the roads, the value of currency, tax problems, and the like.

The laws, regulations and *responsa* concerned various matters, for example prohibition against leaving one *kahal* for another within the limits of the original membership agreements; appointment of rabbis and *talmud torah* teachers and conditions of their employment and activity; limitations on competition in price or quality among Jewish artisans or tax farmers; observance of the permanent *hazaka* rights for community members to rent property owned by non-Jews for homes and shops; prohibition against Jews taking legal cases to Muslim or Christian courts; enforcement of ritual butchery regulations against unlicensed slaughterers (*shohetim*) and butchers (*kassap*), and prohibition against wearing expensive clothing and jewels by women.

They established commercial standards for prices and quality as well as contract conditions relative to merchandise, particularly for those community members who had no guilds of their own to manage such affairs.

They regulated community taxation and particularly tax assessments for the capital levy which was the major source of community revenue, and they established the exact obligations of each member to contribute to the community's help to the poor. They regulated games, entertainments, and festivals. They determined the exact form and color of the clothing that people wore; the length and shape of their beards, mustaches and hair styles; the quantity and value of jewels and garments that a woman could wear in public or even in private; the number of people that had to be invited to banquets and entertainments; the number of witnesses that had to be present at weddings, circumcisions and other ceremonies; the size of graves and tombs and the form and wording on gravestones; the days and hours that had to be taken off for the Sabbath; the order of precedence, rank and etiquette that had to be observed by each member in public festivals and ceremonies; and the exact form of conversation and behavior in dealings with each other and with members of other *millet*s. They fixed the privilege of the dower in inheritance of deceased husband. They limited the importation of wines and other alcoholic drinks not only to provide secure markets for local producers but also to prevent Jews from angering Muslim religious officials by selling this product to Muslims, for whom it was absolutely forbidden. And they even imposed the Rabbi as the obligatory host at all celebrations so as to limit excesses by his presence. Each *takkana* or *haskama* described the problem along with the regulation supposed to solve it and provided a threat of excommunication and heavenly punishment in the hereafter for any who violated it. Members thus were under the tight control of the community in most activities and actions of their daily lives far more completely than they were of the sultan and his ruling class, who generally looked on from above with little interference so long as the system worked.

Together Jewish law and custom, community regulations and customs and judicial decisions constituted what amounted to a code of law and jurisprudence which regulated in great detail all religious, social and economic areas of life in each Jewish community as well as in the *millet* as a whole. The *kahal* enforced them with a kind of police surveillance to make certain that they were applied, whether in the temple, the school, the marketplace, or the home. Various penalties such as *herem* (excommunication) and *niddui* (bans) were imposed by the *bet din* courts and by the rabbis against those who violated the laws and regulations or their decisions and instructions. Prisons were maintained in the synagogue buildings, usually on the ground floors directly beneath the sanctuaries, to punish members who violated the community regulations and laws, while violators of the Sultan's laws and those requiring execution and more severe or lengthy punishments were turned over to Ottoman police and prisons.

Synagogue Congregations, Buildings, Organization, and Administration

Synagogue communities founded in the Ottoman Empire generally secured their names from one of the following characteristics:[7]

(1) *Place of origin.* Many were named after the locale from which the founders came, particularly during Byzantine and early Ottoman times, as for example the synagogues of the Macedonian immigrants: in Balat the *Ahrida* (from Ohrid), *Siroz* (from Serez), *Verya* (from Verya), *Inoz* (from Enez), *Demotika, Üsküb* (from Skopje), *Selaniko* (from Salonica) *Kasturiye* (from Castoria), and *Iştipol* (from Iştib, or Iştipol). The *Chana* (Ciana, from Tzyana) synagogue, used by the Romaniotes in Byzantine times, was taken over by the Sephardim in the seventeenth century and became the seat of the *Bet Din* (Chief Religious Court) after 1908. The synagogues in Balat founded by immigrants from Bulgaria included the *Yanbol* (from Yanbolu) and *Nikopoli* (from Nicopolis); while those from Serbia founded the *Belgrad* synagogue. The Spanish immigrants established the *Katalan* and *Aragon* synagogues at Hasköy and Edirne, the *Kordova* synagogue of Hasköy, and the *Toledo* synagogues of Edirne and Manisa. In the 1520s, refugees from Portugal formed separate *Lisbon*, *Portugal* and *Evora* communities in Istanbul and the *Portugal* synagogue of Edirne. Immigrants from Italy formed the *Italia* (Italy), *Calavres* (Calabria), *Sicilia* (Sicily), *Pulia* (Pouille) and *Messina* synagogues at Balat, and those from Majorca established the *Mayor* synagogues of Hasköy, Bursa and Izmir.

(2) *Method of arrival in Ottoman Empire.* Some bore a name indicating the means by which the founders came to the Ottoman Empire, as for example in Istanbul the *Kendi Gelen* synagogue, formed by those who came from Central Europe 'of their own free will', unlike the forced exile from Spain; the *Sürgünlü* (deported), formed by some of those compelled to resettle in Istanbul following its conquest by Sultan Mehmed II, and the *Gerush Sefarad* synagogues of Balat, Edirne and Bursa, founded by those who were 'forced to leave' the Iberian Peninsula.

(3) *Name of Ottoman locale.* Some named their synagogues after the locale where they settled or building where they were located, as for example in Istanbul, the Zeyrek, Yeni Mahalle (Hasköy), Kalaycı Bahçe (Hasköy), Yeniköy, Bakırköy, Sirkeci, Unkapanı, Cibalı, Balıkpazarı, and Çorapçı Han.

(4) *Profession of founders.* Some used the occupation of the principal founder or founders, as for example the *Tofre Begadim*, or Synagogue of the tailors, established in Galata by Ashkenazi Jews from Germany; the *Çakacı* (Turkish *Çuhacı*), or clothiers' synagogue, located in the Tahta Minare (Vodina) section of Balat; and the *Kal de los Kasapes* (Synagogue of the Butchers), *Kal de los Küfecis* (Synagogue of the basket

makers), and *Kal de los Hammales* (Synagogue of the Porters) synagogues in Edirne.

(5) *Names of founders or donors.* There were a few synagogues which were founded by wealthy individuals or families, and they usually bore the names of their donors, such as the *Hamon* synagogue in Hasköy, bearing the name of the famous doctors who served in the courts of *Kanuni* Süleyman and Selim II after emigrating from Granada; in Kuzguncuk, on the Anatolian side of the Bosporus, the *Midrash Azarya*; in Izmir, the *Sonsino, Algazi* (named after the seventeenth-century Rabbi Salamon Algazi), *Beth Hillel Palacci* (named after the famous nineteenth-century Izmir Grand Rabbi Hayim Palacci), *Beth ha-Levi* (named after Nesim ha-Levi Baryakeli), and *Beth Esther* (named after the aforementioned's wife, who died young) synagogues; in Tire the *Midrash Dünyas* (named after the local *muhtar* Çelebon Duenyas, who gave his house for the synagogue); and in Çanakkale, the *Halio* synagogue, named after Merkado Elie Halio, who gave his house to replace a burned out synagogue. Also the *Giveret* or *Seniora* synagogues founded especially for women in Istanbul and Izmir by Doña Gracia Mendes, and on the island of Rhodes the *Kahal Tikkun Hazzot*, also called *Keila de los Vicos* (the synagogue of the rich) and the *Kahal Kamondo*, founded in 1865 by the Istanbul Camondo banking family.

(6) *Distinguishing characteristics.* Some synagogue names emphasized a characteristic which differentiated them from others, as for example the *Kal Yashan* (Old Synagogue) and *Kal Hadash* (New Synagogue) in Çanakkale, the *Poli Yashan* (Old City) and *Poli Hadash*(New City Synagogue) in Istanbul, the *Kal Yashan-Kal de Abasho* (Old Synagogue or Lower Synagogue) and *Kal Hadash-Kal de Ariva* (New Synagogue or Upper Synagogue) in Tire, *Kal de Abasho* (Lower Synagogue), *Kal de Ariva* (Upper Synagogue) and *Kal den Medio* (Middle Synagogue) in Aydın, *Kal de Abasho* (Lower Synagogue, called *Beth Ya'akov*) and *Kal de Ariva* (Upper Synagogue, called *Virane*) in Kuzguncuk.

(7) *Aim or purpose of foundation.* A few synagogues were named after the special aim or ambition for which they were founded, as for example the *Etz ha Haim* (tree of life), given to numerous Ottoman synagogues including that founded by the Jews who helped Orhan conquer Bursa in 1324, given to them as reward, and those in Izmir, Manisa (from Byzantine times), Kasaba/Turgutlu, Ortaköy, and Kuzguncuk (the *Kal de Abasho*). Others of this sort included the *Sibhat Lev* (joy in my heart) synagogue in Manisa, the *Mekor Haim* (source of life) in Çanakkale, *Heset Leavra'am* (the goodness of Abraham) on Büyükada, the *Ginat Veradim* (flower garden) of Izmir, the *Or Hadash* (new light), the old Ashkenazi synagogue near Yüksek Kaldırım in Istanbul, *Hemdat Israel* (the compassion of Israel) in Haydarpaşa, the *Bikur Holim* in Izmir, the *Shalom* (peace) synagogues of the Aegean cities of Bursa, Manisa, Turgutlu, Milas, Rhodes (1593), and

Izmir, the *Neve Şalom* (house of peace) in Galata/Şişhane and Salonica, the latter from Byzantine times, the *Sha'ar Ashamayim* (gate of the heavens) in the Alsancak section of Izmir, and the *Kabel Rinat Hameha* ('my Lord, accept the goodness of the people'), founded in Foça in 1885.

(8) There were also synagogues in outlying localities which tended to group together Jews representing different backgrounds, as for example those along the Bosporus on the European side at Beşiktaş, Kuruçeşme, Büyükdere, Bebek, Ortaköy, Yeni Mahalle, Arnavutköy and Yeniköy, and on the Anatolian shores at Haydarpaşa, Kuzguncuk, and Beyköz.

All aspects of Jewish community and individual life in each quarter were reflected in its Synagogue (*havra*), which was at the center of the *kahal*'s activities, serving not only as a place of worship but also for education, public and group meetings, and other activities. The synagogue thus was the place where the *ma'mad* met and enacted and declared its regulations and where its *parnassim* were elected, where the Rabbinicial court (*bet din*) held its sessions and pronounced its sentences and bans, where gifts were made to communal charities, where marriages and circumcisions were performed and celebrated and where announcements of divorce or renunciation were proclaimed. Community schools were usually in the synagogue building or immediately adjacent. The basement of the synagogue usually was the location of the community prison.

Since there were many communities in the major Ottoman cities, most had relatively small memberships, in Istanbul none larger than 125 family heads in the *Gerush Sefarad*, and in Salonica the largest being that of Aragon, with 315. Their structures therefore were often very small and without pretension. In many cases the smaller congregations simply rented rooms to carry out their religious and secular activities. Most, however, managed to build their own quarters, some simple but some relatively large and elaborate.

Ottoman synagogues were usually rectangular buildings constructed of stone, plastered brick or wood, with wood ceilings, situated in the heart of the Jewish quarters, surrounded by houses connected by tortuous and twisting streets, far from the great arteries, and thus buried away from the world. They served as places of prayer (*Beth Tefilla*), study (*Beth Midrash*), and community meetings (*Beth Knesseth*). Most were hidden from the streets by high walls, shops and the like, but all had interior courtyards, with fountains and basins for ritual washing of hands before performing prayers, very much like those of the Muslims, with windows opening from the sanctuary to the skies so that it could be lit naturally and the worshipper could see the heavens, considered necessary to inspire devotion and reverence during prayer. The sanctuary itself was relatively simple, though some were decorated with carvings and paintings, and the stone floors usually were covered with thick Turkish carpets.

Ottoman Jews generally avoided external decoration to avoid attracting attention. Austerity of manners prohibited sumptuous decoration of the exteriors or even the interiors of synagogues, particularly in the Ashkenazi structures. From early times, however, the Gerush, Catalan and Lisbon congregations built magnificent architectural fantasies, souvenirs of the splendors that they had known in the houses of God in Toledo, Cordova and Lisbon. The Portuguese synagogues of the Lisbon, Portugal, Evora and Liviath Hen communities also had interior ornamentations with rich rugs and tapestries, remembering the Catholic churches in which the Marranos had worshipped.

The Holy Ark (Sephardic: *hekhal*, Ashkenazi: *aron kodesh*) which housed the scrolls of the Torah and was thus considered the holiest object in the synagogue aside from the scrolls themselves, usually was slightly elevated on the side that faced Jerusalem, with the entrance doors placed opposite. It was not supposed to be decorated with animal figures, for reasons taken from the decalogue. Only the Catalans, who were not very orthodox, ignored this prohibition, and on the walls of their synagogues engraved reptiles and lizards which were intensely disliked by the more rigorous orthodox Jews.

The pulpit from which the Torah was read, the *teva* (Ashkenazi *bema*), often the most elaborately decorated part of the sanctuary, and sometimes surrounded by columns supporting the domed ceiling, was located in its center so that all worshippers could see and hear, but in some synagogues, like the Ahrida of Balat and Beth Ya'akov of Kuzguncuk, it was located near the back wall. Most synagogues also had a smaller sanctuary nearby, usually within the courtyard, the *midrash*, which was used for daily study of the Torah as well as for secular purposes not considered proper in the main sanctuary itself. Women were not allowed to pray together with men, but were instead provided with separate though adjacent quarters, either in a rear room which had access to the sanctuary through small windows or slits in its wall, or in galleries above. The floors were often composed of stone or wood, with the worshippers spreading out carpets or straw mats while performing their prayers, very much like the Muslims in their mosques. There were many simple windows on all sides, but not much other decoration except for small hanging lamps. On most days, several ceremonies were celebrated at the same time in different corners of the synagogue and in the courtyard. Since there were so many worshippers doing so many different things, there was often considerable noise and even confusion as the services progressed. Rabbi David Ibn Abi Zimra complained that many of the worshippers followed 'the bad practice of speaking during the Reading of the Torah', and that they then repeated the words by heart after the reading so that 'with the multitude of worshippers there is also a multitude of confusion and no-one listens either to the prayers or to the Reading of the Torah'.

It was considered a great honor to sit near the *hekhal* so this was normally reserved for men who were particularly qualified by learning, wealth, contributions to the community, or age. Sometimes the auditoriums were divided into pews, which were sold to families who could afford them, thus becoming permanent property held as *hazaka*s and inherited by eldest sons. Rabbi David ibn abi Zimra, however, criticized this practice, declaring that such inheritances of favored locations should be allowed only if the sons were worthy of sitting ahead of older and more learned men; if not, the community had to force him to sell the pew, buying it out itself if no qualified buyer could be found. The community secured much of its income from the sale of the right to perform certain honored functions during the course of services, such as carrying the Sacred Scrolls, kindling the Sabbath candles in the synagogue, and the like, all of which were considered to be particularly honorable 'good deeds' (*mitzvahs*), which provided credit in the eyes of God as well as of the community.

The synagogue administrators (*gisbar*, pl. *gisbarim*) were collectively in charge of maintaining and cleaning the building. They authorized, supervised or carried out all temple services, including circumcisions, marriages and burials. Decisions were taken by majority vote, with the minority required to submit to the will of the majority without further discussion. The *gisbarim* included the Cantor (*hazzan*, pl. *hazzanim*), who chanted the prayers and read from the Torah as well as pronouncing marriage and burial prayers, while the Rabbi, who also served as Preacher and delivered the Sermon every Sabbath, read the Additional Service on *Rosh Hashanah* as well as the Ten Commandments and the Song of Moses. The *sofer*, or scribe, kept the record books of the community, and maintained its library when there was one.

In many ways the most important synagogue official of all, however, was the beadle (*shamash*), who undertook just about everything that the other officials did not do. He was the principal guardian of the temple, locking and opening the doors and maintaining general security. On Friday and holiday evenings when the sun went down he went around the Jewish markets and quarters, and told the artisans, shopkeepers and shoppers as well as men in their homes or on the streets to come to prayer, very much like the *muezzin* of the Muslim mosques who called out from the minaret. The *shamash* cleaned the Ark and changed its curtains on holidays. He lit the candles and lamps in the synagogue and supervised the chapels. While the synagogue services were being carried out, he kept people quiet and arranged the prayer services, going among the worshipers to choose those who would have the honor of participating in the service by opening the sacred Ark, taking out and carrying the Torah scrolls, reading selected sections, and the like. In many ways he, more than the Rabbi, thus, presided at synagogue ceremonies and celebrations and told even the Rabbi what to do. He also had to be a learned man, for he helped the rabbis in applying laws, making necessary preparations for ceremonies and at times acting as a teacher. In the smaller communities he also was repair man, supervisor of the soup kitchens and charity houses, and even the gravedigger. The *shamash* was the *kahal*'s messenger, carrying communications to members as well as to officials of the Ottoman government. He was community notary public, court clerk, and court recorder. He brought parties and witnesses to court and kept the audience quiet during court procedures. He was the synagogue policeman. He executed the sentences of the *Bet Din*, inflicting corporal punishments with whips or leather belts and incarcerating guilty members in the synagogue prison. He went out into the streets as public crier to announce new regulations enacted by the council or sentences issued by the *Bet Din*. He distributed invitations for communal ceremonies. He also was the community collector, acting to collect the taxes owed by members and admonishing them for failure to pay on time and in full when required.

The school rooms were next to the synagogue, the *talmud torah* for children, and for the adults the *yeshiva*, which also maintained the community library. An annex was reserved for secular gatherings, particularly for the *tandas*, gatherings of the more active community members following services, where they would drink fermented *raki* and eat hard eggs with fried onions while discussing Talmudic questions or edifying anecdotes from the Midrash.

Community Charity Activities. The Bible requires each practicing Jew to provide charity (*zedakah*) for the poor and those in need:

> 'If there be among you a needy man, one of your brethren, within thy gates, in thy land, which the Lord thy God giveth thee, thou shalt not harden thy heart nor shut thy hand from thy needy brother; but thou shalt surely open thy hand unto him and shalt surely lend him sufficent for his need in that which he wanteth . . . . ' (*Deut.* 15:7–10)

Each individual Jew therefore was obliged to contribute what he could to charity, even those who themselves received it, for there always was someone in even greater need. For those with means, at least one-tenth of their wealth was supposed to be given, but no more than one-fifth so as not to impoverish the giver. To avoid shaming the recipient or overly praising the giver, such charity was supposed to be distributed through the community. Each *kahal* therefore had the duty of carrying out the obligation of its members to provide charity through voluntary charitable societies (*hevra*), called *bikur holim* if they involved visiting and helping the sick, *hakhanasat kallah*, when they provided dowries for brides of the poor, *sandak*, which arranged for circumcisions, and *gemilut hasadim* or *halva'at hen*, which provided loans to businessmen and artisans. Other organizations made regular provisions of food and money and distribution of clothing to the poor, all paid by separate treasuries maintained by the community. During the first century of Ottoman Jewry, each *kahal* was able to provide its own hospital facilities since so many physicians were available among the refugees coming from the Iberian peninsula. Later on, as available physicians became scarce and individual and community finances more limited, city-wide community hospitals were established, often with the financial support of wealthy members, who usually also left foundations to provide for continued support, though additional fees also were collected for service from those able to pay. In the same way early separate *kahal* arrangements to care for orphans later were replaced by community and even city-wide orphanages, also maintained by foundations as well as regular contributions by community members.

Burial of the Poor. In many ways most important of all the synagogue's charitable activities, as it was one of the most important duties of all believing Jews, providing each participant with special merit in the eyes of the Law, was the task of providing help for the proper burial of the poor. This obligation was carried out by the special Funeral Society Brotherhoods (*hevra kaddisha*) attached to each synagogue throughout the Jewish world. These were composed of volunteers who assumed the macabre but honorable task of washing and burying the bodies of all deceased community members in accordance with the proper religious rituals, doing so without charge for the poor. Each synagogue jealously guarded its right to bury its own members and rejected all instances which threatened to deprive it of that right for anyone related to it in any way. Membership in the Society itself was considered to be one of the greatest honors which any member could have, and was supposed to be given as reward for those who had done the most in carrying out other community activities as well as meeting the highest standards of the community in other respects. Members (*rohatsim*) of the Burial Society included people from all classes of the community who came together without distinction of class or wealth and worked without any compensation except in the eyes of God. All contributions made by believers went into the special burial treasury which paid for all Society expenses. Normally the *rohatsim* met at the synagogue in a *tanda* every Saturday as well as on festival days, after the morning prayer, in order to discuss biblical or Talmudic subjects or current controversies as well as to hear an inspiring sermon and prayer from the Rabbi, at the same time drinking *uzo* (spirits) and eating a hard boiled egg (*ghevo enhaminado*) and a paté of cheese (*enkyusa*) before beginning their work. Once a year they held a special banquet at the home of their chief, and once every seven years a week-long festival, all at their own expense. Because of their special position of honor in the community, the *rohatsim* were much more active and had far more influence in the community than their title and nominal function alone would indicate, influencing synagogue management and policies. They usually were consulted by the *parnassim* regarding important problems, and constituted one of the few groups of the community whose members were exempted from all taxes, including the poll tax.

Jewish burial ceremonies themselves, whether carried out at the expense of the families of the deceased or for the poor at no charge, were regulated by the particular rites and customs of each synagogue, which prescribed minutely the rights and obligations of the family, the form and cloth of the shroud, the exact dimensions and material of the coffin, the fees to be charged, when required, and the commemorative prayers to be recited after a month and a year from the burial. They also provided solutions to complicated questions such as providing that a widow without children should be buried by the synagogue of her husband if the dowry had not been restored to her following the death of her husband, or by the synagogue of her father if it had. The bodies of members of the same family were supposed to be buried as close as possible to each other, except for those who had died from the plague, who normally were buried in special distant sections of the community cemetery. A stranger or visitor who died and was buried while in the town also had to be remembered in the prayers of its faithful after a month and a year.

Ransoming Captives and Slaves. A particularly important *mitzvah*, or good deed, expected of all good Jews, was the obligation to ransom Jewish captives or slaves to spare them from torture or dishonor. This tradition began in Roman times when the Jews were sent into exile from the Holy Land, many into slavery. In the twelfth and thirteenth centuries most Jewish slaves were those captured by marauding Crusaders on their way through central Europe to the Holy Land. In the mid-sixteenth century and after, Jews were enslaved by Christian and Muslim privateers in the Mediterranean, who imprisoned them at places like Algiers, Tunis, Naples, and Candia, selling them into slavery unless they were ransomed within a certain time. The Knights of Malta were particularly notorious in this respect after being established there by Habsburg Emperor Charles V and Pope Clement VII in 1530, maintaining a highly-developed pirate organization with the ostensible mission of fighting for Christianity against both Judaism and Islam. Their pirates operated throughout the Mediterranean, capturing ships, stealing their cargoes and enslaving their passengers, always being particularly harsh when they found Jews before even offering them for ransom. Whenever they descended on a port, their first act invariably was to sack the Jewish quarter, raping, robbing and killing, and carrying off those inhabitants who could be sold into slavery. They demanded exorbitant ransoms for their Jewish captives, treating them very badly while in captivity, continuing their marauding until

Bonaparte arrived in Malta in 1798 followed by the British who took over in 1800.

There were many other instances of this sort. The great fleet of the Holy League which came up against the Ottomans under the command of Andrea Doria between 1542 and 1544 took many Jewish captives who were imprisoned and sold into slavery at Coron, Patras and Zantha. In the late seventeenth century many Jews who were not massacred were captured and enslaved during the notorious Zaporogian Cossack rebellions led by Boghdan Chmielnicki in 1648–49 against the Polish nobles.

Jewish communities throughout Europe, including those of the Ottoman Empire, often worked together to ransom such Jewish slaves, taxing themselves very heavily for this purpose with the refugee tax (*Pidion Shevuyim*), originally raised to help the new emigrants to Ottoman territories from the Iberian Peninsula. The main ransom centers were maintained at Venice and Salonica. By Jewish law, women captives had to be given preference over men in providing ransom. Ransom prices differed according to the age and importance of the captive. Jews generally agreed to pay only the fair market value so as to avoid exorbitant ransom demands by their captors, a favorite tactic of the Knights of Malta in particular. Jews, however, always paid high ransoms, at times ten times more than the market value for non-Jewish captives, because of the community's sense of responsibility toward its members. The ransom price of virgins was much higher than that for other women, so the captors took care to guard their women captives in particular, avoiding sexual relations so as not to lessen their value. A Jew captured with both his father and teacher was allowed to ransom himself first so that he could go out and find the ransom for the others, but then he had to ransom his teacher before his father because of the former's importance for the community as a whole. The importance attached to such activities was shown by the regulation that the *kahal* could use the money set aside for charity or to build or expand a synagogue to ransom such captives. It was only when slavery itself was largely eliminated during the nineteenth century that this particular activity of the Jewish communities fell into abeyance, though occasionally individuals captured during ritual murder attacks still had to be ransomed by *ad hoc* committees organized for the purpose.

Jewish Education. Elementary education was considered to be the personal obligation of the father, who provided for it in a fee-paying *heder* conducted by a learned person of the community. The community cared only for the elementary education of the children of the poor who could not afford to pay, and for this purpose maintained a communally-supported *talmud torah*, both normally adjacent to or near the synagogue.

Both schools taught Hebrew reading and prayers, the Bible with its *ladino* translations and explanations, the cursive *rashi* Hebrew script used for the Judeo-Spanish of the Sephardic Jews, and the rudiments of arithmetic and calculus. Those students who appeared to have some intellectual promise were admitted to special Talmud classes and a kind of secondary education in the elements of juridical and religious sciences which prepared the select few for higher education in the great higher institutions, or *yeshivas*, of the time. These were organized and maintained both by the local rabbis and by other learned men, sometimes with at least partial support from the community, from wealthy members, and from the students themselves. The crowning glory of the educational system of Ottoman Jewry, many illustrious *yeshivas* were organized throughout the empire, particularly in Salonica, Istanbul and Safed, providing a firm basis for the strong intellectual development which enriched Ottoman Judaism until the later years of the seventeenth century.

Taxation and Finance. Members of the Jewish *millet* paid two kinds of taxes, those owed to the Ottoman treasury and those for the community. Of the former the most important was the poll tax, or *cizye*, which was levied annually in three amounts, high, middle and low, according to the income of each head of household. In addition there were various excise taxes, such as customs duties, the household *avariz* tax levied to finance army expenses, the *harac* tax on agricultural produce, the *rav akçesi* (rabbi tax) originally promised on behalf of the community by Moses Capsali and paid long after Grand Rabbis ceased to be appointed, the *ordu akçesi* paid to maintain the army, the *resm-i kismet* share of inheritances, and the *celb akçesi*, to maintain the imperial flocks. These all were assessed and collected by the *millet* leaders on behalf of the Treasury, with Ottoman officials intervening only if individuals failed to pay and the community neglected to make up the difference. In addition, the Ottomans required the community to provide a certain number of men for labor (*corvée*) for the construction of forts (*hısar yapmacı*), digging trenches, leveling hills, guarding government offices and courts, and to house new recruits for the army. Individual Jewish notables, particularly physicians and diplomats who performed important services to the Sultan, often were given exemptions from such taxes, not only for themselves but also for their descendants. Jews who held tax farms (*iltizam*) assigned by the Treasury also owed portions of their profits to it as part of the conditions of their appointments, but these were individual obligations for which the community was not concerned or obligated.

Most permanent *millet* community institutions, like synagogues, *talmud torahs*, *yeshivas*, hospitals and orphanages, just like those of the Muslims and Christians, were financed by income from permanent foundations, called *vakifs* or *evkaf* by Muslims and *ekdeshe (ekdeshot)* in Hebrew. To finance current community activities, however, regular taxes were levied on all community members. The most important of these was the annual tax on capital, called *pesha* in Salonica and *aritha* in Istanbul and elsewhere in the empire, which was assessed and collected by community commissions composed of officials called *meharehim* (estimators) appointed by the community council *(ma'mad)* from among members known for their honesty and fairness. They were supposed to make detailed accounts of all the possessions of each member to assure a fair and accurate assessment of the tax. Their decisions were enforced when necessary by the community policeman *(shohet,* pl. *shohetim)*, the latter often of foreign nationality so as not to be accused of favoritism for relatives in the community. Most of the *aritha* collections were set aside to provide for the collective community payment of the poll tax due from its members, with the remainder going for current expenses. Every time the government modified the poll tax obligations of the community according to the estimated number of its members, usually every ten years, the community accordi1gly sent out the *meharehim* to make new estimates of its members' wealth, and their *aritha* obligations were adjusted accordingly. In addition there was the *kisbe,* a proportional annual tax on income.

In general, the length of the individual's residence within the boundaries of the *kahal,* as well as his wealth and ability to pay, determined his liability to financial participation in its communal and charitable activities. An individual who just arrived in the community at the time a particular tax payment was due was exempted only for the following month. Residence of thirty days brought the obligation to contribute to the communal soup kitchen. Three months residence added the obligation to contribute to the general community charity fund. Six months added payment of one's share of the costs of providing free clothing to the poor. Nine months added contributions to the community fund to meet funeral costs for the poor, while continuous residence for one year, or purchase of a home at any time, changed the individual's status to permanent inhabitant, subjecting him to all the communal taxes, contributions, and other obligations. If an individual left the community he still was considered liable for payment of his full obligation for the preceding year even if the payment date came after his departure. Since each *kahal* was responsible for caring for its own poor, members were not free to provide individual charity or to help the charities of other *kahals,* except on the rare occasions when several communities banded together for specific purposes. They were subjected to penalties ranging from fines and imprisonment in synagogue jails to excommunication if they failed to meet their obligations.

Most other taxes imposed by the community were indirect excise charges. Among these the most important and permanent was the *gabilah* tax (Ottoman: *qabâla),* or *gabelle,* in modern Turkey called *gabella,* imposed on certain goods like Kosher meat, wine, cheese and textiles, to provide for special services like charity, ransoming of prisoners, and gifts for

Ottoman tax collectors and local administrative and legal officials. Physicians, rabbis, synagogue officials, and all those who lived and worked in the *yeshivas* were exempt from all tax obligations, since they devoted most of their time to study and religion. They shared these exemptions with members of families whose ancestors had been given permanent exemptions by past sultans in return for unusual or meritorious services and by members of the community burial societies. Only regular residents who were members of the community were required to pay, with all visitors, travelers, and the like being exempted since it was assumed that they were subjected to taxes by their own communities.

In addition to regular community impositions, moreover, Ottoman Jewry considered itself to be 'treasurer for Eretz Israel', collecting and sending not only its own contributions but also those of the Jewish communities of much of Europe, adding an additional obligation to pay the debts owed by the Jews of Jerusalem, for which an extra imposition of one *para* weekly was assessed on every Jew in the Empire as well as in western Europe.

JEWS IN OTTOMAN SOCIETY

While in Islam Jews, like Christians, were classified as 'unbelievers', or *kâfirs*, and as 'protected subjects', or *zimmis*, the Ottomans for the most part applied the term only to Christians. It was rarely used for Jews, who were kept in the higher and relatively privileged position provided them by Sultan Mehmed II. This gave them far greater freedom of action and relieved them of many of the restrictions imposed on Christians in fact if not in law, while making certain that they maintained the financial and economic domination over Christians given them by the Conqueror, a situation which remained until it was overturned with the help of Christian European diplomats and merchants starting in the late seventeenth century. Despite traditions to the contrary, Jews regularly served as witnesses in Ottoman Muslim courts without any discrimination or discounting of their testimony. Jews paid their Ottoman tax obligations to their own *millet* leaders rather than to government tax collectors so that they had very little of the negative contact with members of the Ruling Class which has so stimulated Christian hatred over the centuries. The Ottomans in fact anulled most of the really discriminatory sumptuary laws which had been imposed on Jews by the Byzantines, and those that were left were relatively minor, and enforced more in theory than practice.

Conversion to Islam. Anyone with ability and luck could rise into the Ruling Class, but to do so one had first to be a Muslim. Conversion was possible only for non Muslims; once in the Muslim *millet*, one had to stay there. Even in conversion, however, Jews were given a superior position to that of Christian converts. Whereas the latter had to replace their Christian names with Muslim ones and to substitute the name *Abdullah* ('slave of God') for that of their Christian fathers, thus becoming, for example, Ahmed ibn Abdullah, Jewish converts were allowed to retain their own and their fathers' names, as Isak ibn Abram, in the process making it easier for historians to follow their careers in the Ruling Class. But aside from the opportunities offered for those who went on to become members of the Ruling Class and for non-Muslim women marrying Muslim men, there was little pressure to convert. Conversion was in fact discouraged on all sides. For Jewish religious leaders it had to be prevented, if for no other reason than it cost the *kahal* treasuries the revenues they needed to finance community services. Nor, for the most part, were Ottomans themselves any more anxious to secure conversion, since it cost the Treasury the substantial income it received from the Poll Tax (*cizye*) and caused considerable hard feelings among members of the *millets* involved, particularly since it took place most often when a women from one *millet* married a man from the other. She was compelled to convert and join her husband's community due to the intense hostility and resentment of her former co-religionists more than anything else. If the Ottoman government intervened in such matters, it was to discourage such conversions because of their disturbing effect on social tranquility, and when they did take place to rush the offending parties to far distant parts of the Empire in order to stifle the resentments that followed. It was for social peace above all else that the *millet* system was maintained throughout the Ottoman centuries, then, not for discrimination but, rather, for the kind of separation of irreconcilable and hostile groups which was sorely needed to prevent religious and social differences from breaking into the kind of conflict with which the modern Middle East has been so frequently cursed.

Clothing Regulations and Practices. Ottoman clothing regulations often have been called discriminatory, and they were, but only in the sense that they identified the position and status of each individual in the Ottoman system, an arrangement borrowed from the Byzantines. They applied, moreover, not to one particular religion or group but to all members of the Ruling Class and Subject Class alike, followers of all religions and members of all religiously-based communities. All members of Ottoman society had to wear garments of certain materials and colors depending on their class, *millet* and position, with the shape and color of the headgear and shoes being of particular importance in order to show the status of each person and enable all others to treat him accordingly. Clothing thus was not simply a matter of individual preference or taste; it was, rather, an essential element in Ottoman society's rules of proper behavior.

Clothing even differed among members of the Ruling Class according to which institution an individual belonged to, how high was his rank, and how close he was to the Sultan. Enforcement, however, for the most part was far more lax for Jews than for Christians, since abusive enforcement against them was strictly punished by the sultans.

Dress regulations for individuals and groups varied so widely in different places and times that it is difficult to specify what was required of Jews or any other group. In general, however, the color green was reserved for Muslims since it was considered particularly sacred by Islamic tradition. Muslims also wore bright, multi-colored costumes on numerous occasions. Muslim turbans also usually were colored white and their shoes yellow. Muslims generally were allowed to include more material in their costumes and turbans than were others. Muslims also wore the finer fabrics, while Jews wore courser materials, but most of these practices resulted more from the desire of the *millet* leaders to avoid ostentatious display and also to distinguish their followers from members of other *millets* than they did from any regulations imposed or enforced by the Ruling Class.

It is almost impossible to state that there was a specifically Jewish costume at any time, but in general the colors reserved for Jews were darker than those for Muslims, with black or dark red garments and shoes dominating. Jewish men often wore a dark coat with wide sleeves over a plain or striped gown or wide *şalvar* trousers attached with a wide folded sash. On their heads were cylindrical hats widening at the top with a colored turban (*boneta*) over the lower part. Jewish women on the street wore simple long dark cloaks with wide shawls covering their heads, but within their own homes they wore robes, shirts and long trousers similar to the men, differing mainly in their head coverings.[8]

On the other hand, these traditions were often ignored, as Jews sometimes were observed wearing white turbans and red shoes in different places. The Jewish immigrants from Spain attempted to preserve their old local dress customs, particularly to emphasize their superior intellectual, cultural and economic level relative to the other Ottoman Jewish communities, so instead of the long cloak often worn by the other non-Muslim subjects of the Sultan when they first arrived during the fifteenth century, they wore the Spanish *caperone*, a woolen topcoat, while refusing to put on the yellow cap supposedly required of all Jews at the time. Jewish groups from Central Europe, Italy and France also preserved the costumes that were customarily worn in the lands from which they came. Others adopted variations of the officially required dress or even wore clothing reserved for members of the Ruling Class as well as the other *millets*.

Various imperial orders issued in the late sixteenth century specified that as a result of Jewish complaints that they were being required to wear clothing which differed markedly from their traditional costumes, and of the complaints of others that Jews were wearing the costumes of

Muslim and Christian subjects as well as cavalrymen, all Jewish men were required to wear cloaks (*ferace*) or overcoats (*yaşamak*) of black cloth, with skirts of calico or cloth rather than silk and belts of mixed cotton and silk material not costing more than 40 *akçes* and not-too-large hats of green-blue cloth, with no silks to be used in any part of their costumes. Their turbans had to be blue and relatively small, nor could they resemble those used by Muslims or Christians. Later Christians and Jews alike were prohibited from wearing turbans at all and required instead to wear hats – red or blue green for Jews, black for Christians. At this point the shoes of Jews had to be black and relatively wide, and without the interior linings used by Muslims, but later this was changed to a requirement of white or red sandals. Their trousers had to be green or blue, and if they wore collars they had to be made of satin and cotton. Jewish women were not allowed to wear cloaks at all outside their houses, but, apparently in accordance with Jewish law, they were supposed to wear robes (*jupe*) made of cotton. Their slacks could be only blue, and they were not allowed to wear shoes but, again in conformance with old Jewish law, only sandals, nor could they wear the brocaded collars worn by Muslim women, though if they did they had to be of cotton and not silk or other material.

During much of the sixteenth century, regardless of these regulations, Istanbul Romaniote Jewish men usually wore yellow turbans, while only the newly-arrived Sephardic Jews who abandoned their Spanish costumes wore officially-assigned red hats shaped like sugar loaves. Jews generally were required to wear dark garments, with lighter colored ones permitted only on the Sabbath and on religious holidays, and then only within their own quarters. Green was reserved for Muslims. Many Jews continued to wear costumes intended for Muslims, including the *kalpak*, a kind of bonnet bordered with furs, or a *kavuk* (*chapeo*), a round bonnet fitted with a cotton base and muslin trim and of different colors, including green. Rabbis wore the dark religious costumes they had become accustomed to wear in Europe. Regulations were often issued and re-issued, both by the Jewish community and by the Ottoman authorities, to clearly distinguish among the costumes worn by different groups, but these were honored more in the breach than anything else, so they were regularly repeated, but with little effect.

In eighteenth-century Istanbul, since the different Jewish groups were far closer to each other than they had been earlier, most Jewish men wore violet turbans, black or violet suits and violet slippers. Jewish women wore long, dark red sleeveless *pelisse* coats lined with fur except in Istanbul where short loose jackets were substituted, though again orders were frequently issued requiring them to discard Muslim costumes and adhere only to the cloths, styles and colors assigned to them at the time, including outer garments colored in blue or 'other somber colors', and short *kalpaks*.

The clothing regulations imposed on Jews by their *millet* and *kahals* were in fact far more severe and pervasive than anything the Ottomans imposed. The Jewish communities themselves discouraged outward displays of wealth or luxury both in their houses and on the street, not only to discourage jealousy on the part of other elements of the population, particularly the Christians, but also to distinguish Jews from members of the Christian *millets*, who were considered inferior. Rabbinical regulations thus often were issued prohibiting Jewish women from wearing any garment colored green or embellished with metal threads or the more expensive furs. Those who violated these community admonitions were subjected to severe punishment by their Rabbis.

Other Social Restrictions in Ottoman Society. In the Ottoman legal system, there were innumerable laws and regulations which prohibited various acts. But whereas in other societies prohibition signified that an act could not be performed, and if performed would cause the application of a severe penalty, in Ottoman society the equivalent term *yasak* in fact signified only that it could be performed if only an established fee was paid. In Ottoman society, as in other Islamic empires before, it was the tradition that non-Muslims could not bear arms and thus could not serve in the army. This was hardly considered a burden or a mark of discrimination by most young Jews and Christians, however, since they were far happier entering their life careers than fighting on the battlefield, and they willingly paid the poll tax collected in return for this exemption.

There were regulations limiting the height and repair of houses and synagogues and the construction of new ones, but, as we have already noted, Jews were allowed to evade this requirement for the most part by repairing, expanding or even replacing old houses that were already in existence and paying the relevant fee to the *kadi* of the quarter in which the building was located. Every subject of the sultan, moreover, regardless of religion, was subjected to building regulations of some sort, which limited not only the height and composition of houses but also their distance from one another so as to lessen the damages caused by fire and other calamities. Though mosques and Muslim houses were allowed to be somewhat higher than those of Jews and Christians, such limitations could be and were evaded by securing official permits, oiled by a system of bribes which was so pervasive and regularly applied that for all practical purposes they were legally established fees, thus leaving the limitations and restrictions in force only in theory. Even the prohibitions against building Jewish and Christian houses and shops near mosques were matched by the practice of preventing construction of Muslim houses and shops near synagogues or churches. As a result, despite the official regulations, many synagogues were in fact built during the Ottoman centuries. It was the same with restrictions intermittently imposed on burial processions and burial of the dead.

There were regulations dictating how people of different classes and ranks should treat each other as they passed in the streets, but again these applied to all in order to prevent insults and clashes among members of different groups, and cannot be considered to have been discrimination unless one considers one group superior to another. For long periods of time non-Muslims were forbidden from riding on horseback in urban areas or from using barques with more than three sets of oars, but Jews were allowed to evade these by provisions allowing them to use and ride pack horses (*bârgir*) on one hand and to consider oars above the limitations as steering implements.

Jews were subjected to restrictions in Turkish baths (*hammam*s), for example by the custom that the large towel used to cover the body after entering and leaving the bath as well as other objects used by non-Muslims could not also be subsequently used by Muslims and that to distinguish between Muslims and non-Muslims in the bath, the latter could wear only wooden sandals. Once again, however, as with other such restrictions, these seem to have been only formal and theoretical, honored more in the breach than anything else, as shown by the frequent re-issuing of the relevant orders.

Non-Muslims were prohibited from selling coffee in Istanbul and to practice certain trades reserved for members of the other *millet*s, but this was part of a general system in which members of each *millet* monopolized certain occupations, with, for example, Armenians and Greeks having the sole right to sell *pastırma*, the Jews monopolizing gold making and the jewelry trade as well as tailoring and the manufacture of parchment and turbans, the Armenians the manufacture of tissues and engraving on gold, and the Greeks dominating as marine carpenters, gold workers, tailors and manufacturers of bonnets. These also changed over time.

The purchase and holding of Muslim slaves by non-Muslims was pro-hibited in principle, but special permits could and did make exceptions, particularly for the *marranos* who brought slaves with them from Spain. There was nothing to prevent Jews from holding non-Muslim slaves or, for that matter, for Muslims and Christians from holding Jewish slaves. Jews and Christians who did possess slaves were required to pay an additional poll tax for them, thus legalizing the illegal, which for the most part was often neglected by tax officials in return for the payment of special fees and bribes. In any case, however, Jews preferred hired servants, since the institution of slavery was basically incompatible with the sentiment of human dignity which was inherent in Judaism, and the freeing of slaves was considered to be a special good deed so long as the repudiation was accomplished ritually and in front of witnesses.

When there were court cases involving Muslims, they were dealt with in Muslim courts. Those involving Jews were dealt with in the Rabbinicial *Bet Din* courts, and so on. When cases arose involving members of different *millets*, they had to be settled in the Muslim courts unless the parties concerned agreed on presenting them elsewhere, in Muslim or non-Muslim courts. As a matter of fact, however, insofar as the Ottomans were concerned, parties were free to choose the courts that would give them the best deal. Because of the strictness of the Rabbinical courts in certain matters, moreover, there often were cases where even though all the parties were Jews they chose to have their cases settled in the Muslim courts or to apply the Muslim *Sharia* religious law in economic as well as social matters, including inheritence, marriage and divorce and disputes within the Jewish communities, much to the disgust of the Rabbis, who constantly issued decrees threatening excommunication for Jews who avoided the Rabbinical courts in this manner. Even in cases that did go to the Muslim courts, while nominally at least the testimony of Muslims and men was supposed to be given greater weight than that of non-Muslims and women, examination of the court records indicates that testimony was accepted without consideration of the religion of the witnesses and that judgments were for the most part quite fair and without the kind of discrimination that often has been cited in the West.

For the most part, then, all these marks of discrimination were relatively minor, they applied to all groups, and they were dictated more to preventing conflict among individuals and groups than they were to manifest feelings of superiority or inferiority. That is the way they were accepted by most subjects of the sultan, who adjusted to them with little difficulty or complaint. What real misrule there was in the Ottoman system in the Golden Age took place within the *millets* by religious leaders whose powers over their followers were far more absolute than that of members of the Ottoman Ruling Class over the subjects, and where there was little remedy from abuse, either from Ottoman or *millet* laws.

Christian Persecution of Ottoman Jews. Ottoman Jews were quite aware of a community of interest between them and Muslims, in relation to Christians in particular, for if there was persecution of Jews in the Ottoman Empire at its height, it came not from the Ottoman rulers and their Muslim subjects but, rather, from the Christian subjects, bitter not only at the imposition of Muslim rule in lands which had for centuries been Christian, but also at the imposition in urban life, particularly in the spheres of finance, industry and trade, of domination by Jews, whom most Christians continued to consider beneath contempt. This feeling was heightened by the knowledge that Jews had contributed significantly to the Ottoman conquests of the centers of Christian civilization, that Jewish artisans, particularly *marranos*, were assisting in the development of new muskets, cannons and other armaments which made the possibility of a successful Christian crusade to drive the Turks out extremely unlikely, and that Jews strongly supported continuation of Ottoman rule because of the certainty that they would be subjected to renewed persecution if the Empire came to an end.

Christian religious leaders constantly agitated with the Sultan and his ministers to advance their rights and privileges at the expense of the Jewish community which, without a Grand Rabbi to represent it, was at a disadvantage in resisting their advances. The patriarchs insisted with great vehemence, for example, that they, rather than the Chief Rabbis of Istanbul, should have precedence in official Ottoman ceremonies, finally achieving this objective in 1697 as a result of French and English pressure in the Ottoman court.

As the Jewish community in the Ottoman Empire rose in numbers, influence and prosperity during the sixteenth century, moreover, there followed a long series of ritual murder assaults and persecutions by Christians, who dragged Muslims along whenever they could, though with nowhere the sustained vigor and effect as in Europe because here the ruling Ottomans suppressed them as quickly and completely as possible. Ritual murder accusations and attacks were made against Jews by Ottoman Christian subjects of the Sultan starting in the early years of the sixteenth century. The earliest and most famous of these came in the central Anatolian town of Amasya, probably in 1530, when an accusation was spread by local Armenian priests and notables who said that an Armenian woman had seen Jews slaughter a young Armenian boy and use his blood at the Passover feast. Several days of rioting and pillaging and attacks on Jews followed, with Armenian mobs devastating the Jewish quarter of the city, beating men, women and children alike. The Armenian notables convinced the local Ottoman governor to imprison several Jewish leaders, including Rabbi Yakub Avayu, who was accused of having supervised the blood letting. They were said, after underoing severe torture, to have confessed to their crimes and were hanged. Later, however, the Armenian boy who supposedly had been murdered was found and a new Ottoman governor punished the accusers, though nothing could be done about the Jews who had suffered in the process.

Soon afterwards a similar ritual murder attack took place at Tokat, where the Jewish quarter was ravaged in the week before Easter, this time by Greeks. At this point, however, the Sultan's personal physician, Moshe Hamon, convinced him to issue a *ferman* prohibiting provincial and local officials and judges from being involved in any such cases in future, and in particular from punishing Jews accused of ritual murder crimes, requiring that all such cases be brought before the Sultan and his Imperial Council in Istanbul so that real justice could be provided outside the highly emotional atmosphere produced by hysterical provincial Christian populations.

During the centuries that followed, whenever Christians resumed their attacks on Jews, or for that matter when Muslims showed prejudice, the Ottoman government intervened strongly, for economic reasons if for none other, so that Jews continued to live in a security far more permanent than that provided those of their co-religionists who remained in Europe. Ritual murder incidents in Anatolia and Rumelia were not as frequent as they became later, in the nineteenth century, but there were attacks from time to time, mainly by Christian subjects or Christians who had converted to Islam to become members of the Ottoman armed forces. Thus in 1633 two Janissaries, recently converted from Greek Orthodoxy, accused Jews of having killed a Christian child six days before Easter, and it was only due to the intervention of Sultan Murad IV himself that the resulting attacks on Jews in the capital and in many parts of Anatolia were finally put down. There were also a number of ritual murder cases in Jerusalem, where the presence of Jews and Muslims in positions of power and influence was considered particularly offensive by the local Christian priests and populations. While the local officials usually restored order fairly quickly, Jews there felt insecure enough that most concentrated outside the city, particularly at Safed and Tiberias.

The only place in Ottoman Muslim society where discrimination was regularly practiced against Jews was in the Kurdish areas of eastern Anatolia, where Kurdish tribes controlled by feudal leaders regularly ravaged the settled areas, Muslim, Christian and Jewish alike. As a result, the situation of Jews, like other settled people in the area, was very poor, and while a few urban Jews engaged in trade and industry and there were a number of Jewish farmers, banking was controlled by the tribal leaders rather than Jews, and most of the latter lived in considerable poverty.

Plagues and Fires. If anything brought the different Jewish communities together in Ottoman times, it was the fires and plagues which decimated these closely packed urban settlements on numerous occasions, affecting people of all classes and religions regardless of where they lived. Entire sections of the great cities of the Empire were periodically destroyed by vast fires which spread quickly among buildings which, for the most part, were built of wood. Typhus, cholera, and other such diseases easily developed into city-wide epidemics against which even the wealthy had little defense. All sorts of precautions were taken, isolation in houses or abandonment of the cities for refuge in the countryside or mountains for months on end, and citywide organization of the removal and burial of bodies, but with little effect so long as the real essentials of quarantine and infection were not yet known, and thousands of people of all religions were carried off on each occasion. Needless to say, moreover, it did not take much for the same communities who spread 'ritual murder' rumors to accuse Jews of starting the fires and causing plague and other epidemics by poisoning water supplies, leading inevitably to new mass attacks, sometimes by Muslims egged on by the Christians, just as soon as the immediate dangers had passed.

JEWISH SOCIAL AND ECONOMIC LIFE IN OTTOMAN TIMES

Jews played a tremendous role in the economic life of the Ottoman Empire in its Golden Age, a contribution all the more remarkable considering their small number in comparison with the other non-Muslim religious groups among the subjects of the Sultan.

Jewish Physicians and Bankers

First of all there were those Jews who through their wealth or knowledge made themselves indispensable to the sultans and leaders of the Ruling Class as physicians, financiers and political and diplomatic advisers, while at the same time using their influence to help and protect their less influential Jewish co-religionists, in many cases far more than the official leaders could do.

Among the influential physicians who served early in the Ottoman court were Ishak Pasha, chief physician for Murad II (1421–51), who gave him the title *Galeon* (Galen), and the Venetian Yakub Efendi (Maestro Jacobo), physician to Mehmed II the Conqueror, who resisted Venetian efforts to get him to murder the Sultan or at least persuade him to attack Rome in order to increase Venetian influence in the Italian peninsula.

Most influential of all the physicians in Ottoman service were members of the Hamon (Amon) family, who dominated both the Ottoman court and Istanbul's Jewish community during much of the sixteenth century. The family dynasty originated with Joseph Hamon, born in Granada about 1450, who emigrated to Istanbul during the reign of Mehmed II and served as physician to Sultan Bayezid II and Selim I. The dynasty reached its peak with his son Moshe Hamon (1490–1567), physician to Selim I and *Kanuni* Suleyman the Magnificent between 1490 and 1554, who following the ritual murder attacks on Jews at Amasya and Tokat in 1530, secured a *ferman* from the Sultan providing governmental protection against such excesses in future. He also patronized the schools and published many of the works of a number of important Jewish cultural figures and Talmudic scholars of the time, including Joseph ben Solomon Taitazak and Samuel ha-Levi ibni Hakim, while himself writing a number of books on drugs and medicines. Moshe Hamon exercised considerable influence in the major Jewish communities in the Empire at the time, using his connections with members of the Ottoman Ruling Class to secure the arrest and bringing to Istanbul of some corrupt Jewish officials from Salonica in an effort to end the disputes plaguing that community. He served the Sultan as diplomatic agent with many of the important European ambassadors in Istanbul, arranging peace with Venice in 1540, from which in 1552 he also intervened successfully to secure permission to send on to Istanbul much of the wealth of the newly emigrating Portuguese Marrano Jewish bankers, Doña Gracia Mendes and her nephew Don Joseph Nasi, thus making possible their rise in court during the subsequent reign of Selim II.

Moshe Hamon ultimately fell from power due to court intrigues, but his son, Joseph Hamon, probably with the help of Don Joseph Nasi, gained considerable influence at the court of Selim II, though probably not to the extent of that of his father. In 1568 he secured the renewal of the privileges originally granted to the Jews of Salonica by Bayezid II, at the same time gaining a permanent exception from all Ottoman taxes for himself and his descendants, who were given the name *Evlad Musa* (sons of Moses). He also was a member of a Hebrew cultural group then active in Salonica and Istanbul, joining poets such as Sa'adia Longo, Yuda Zarko and Absalon Almozlinos, and publishing some of their works.

In addition to these physicians made famous by their association with the Ottoman imperial court and influence on Ottoman policy, many others came from the medical schools at Salamanica and Lisbon to Salonica, Istanbul, and elsewhere in the empire, where they introduced the latest advances made in medical treatment in the West. At the same time, without having to limit and conceal their researches as they had been forced to do in the West due to fears of accusations of heresy, and often with the patronage of the Ottoman court, they developed the sciences of anatomy and surgery far beyond what was practiced in western Europe at the time, making the Ottoman Empire a leader in the medical sciences while providing Ottoman's subjects of all religions with a superior level of medical treatment to that provided in contemporary Europe. Few Ottoman families of any substance did not have Jewish doctors, and their skillful practice, along with their willingness to go to treat patients at their homes even during plagues, brought them and the Jewish community praise and respect from Muslims at least.

Quite a number of Jewish bankers managed to bring most of their capital into the Ottoman Empire from Spain and Portugal. They went on to engage in all sorts of profitable and far reaching financial enterprises, not only in the Empire but throughout Europe, with the *marranos* in particular making major contributions to the growth of Ottoman banking, capital investment, and trade. Jews monopolized the Ottoman mint and customs houses and served as money lenders and tax farmers, gaining tremendous wealth while largely controlling the Ottoman financial and economic system, though in the process they fitted themselves into the existing Ottoman economic systems rather than bringing mercantilist tendencies with them from Europe.

Doña Gracia Mendes and Don Joseph Nasi. Probably the most prominent Jewish banking family in Ottoman service during the sixteenth century, that of Mendes (originally Benbanaste), was founded by a *marrano converso* refugee from Portugal, Doña Gracia Mendes (1510–68), known as *La Señora*, or *Giveret*, who after the death of her husband Francisco Mendes (Nasi) in 1537 had become a major banker on her own right in Portugal, making loans to such important monarchs as the Habsburg Emperor Charles V and Francis I of France before and after being exiled from her homeland by the Inquisition. After long sojourns in Belgium and Italy by special arrangement with the Spanish king, she publicly renounced her Christian conversion and name and openly resumed the practice of Judaism. She reached Istanbul in 1553, transferring much of her wealth from Venice through the influence of the physician Moshe Hamon.

Doña Gracia gained economic power in the Ottoman Empire very quickly by building a consortium of Jews and Muslims which traded wheat, pepper and raw wool for European goods. She gained political influence in the Ottoman court, getting *Kanuni* Süleyman to intervene in 1556 with Pope Paul IV on behalf of her fellow *marranos* who had just been imprisoned in Ancona, securing their release by getting the Ottomans to boycott its Mediterranean trade, lifeblood of its prosperity, until the Jews were freed.

It was about this time that Doña Gracia was joined by her nephew, Don Joseph Nasi (1524–79), with whom she worked closely until her death. Born in Lisbon as Joao, son of Agostinho (Samuel) Miquez (Mendes), a *marrano* Professor of Medicine at the University, Joseph had been raised by Doña Gracia because of his father's death in 1525 when he was only one year old. He emigrated with her to Antwerp in 1537, married her daughter Reyna, graduated from the University of Louvain, and then entered the Mendes family bank, in whose service he became close friends with Charles V and Emperor Maximilian of Holland. In 1547 he joined many other Portuguese *marranos* who fled from the Inquisition to Venice, and then to Istanbul, where he arrived in the company of some 500 other *marranos* in 1554, soon afterwards joining his aunt, only then openly throwing off Catholicism and resuming his Jewish heritage.

Soon afterwards, Doña Gracia and Don Joseph gained even greater influence by financing the rise to power of Sultan Selim II in 1566, with the support of his mother, Süleyman's wife, Queen Mother Roxelana. This was accomplished against the opposition of Grand Vezir Mehmed Sokullu, who supported a rival Greek party led by Michael Cantacuzene, which he hoped to install in place of the Jews to cement his influence in the Ottoman court, unsuccessfully supporting the candidacy for the throne of Selim's half-brother and rival, Prince Bayezid.

Together Doña Gracia and Don Joseph developed vast wealth through a network of international enterprises. They used much of it to help many Ottoman Jewish communities, housing and feeding newly-arrived refugees and developing major new centers of Jewish settlement and learning at Tiberias and Safed in the Holy Land, making silk culture, fishing and agriculture the bases of their economy. Tiberias in particular became a new center for Jewish settlement and cultural activity, with a new *yeshiva* being established by Doña Gracia to support students and scholars from all over the Jewish world. Don Joseph also encouraged the Ottoman conquest of Cyprus, achieved in 1570, at least partly with the idea of making it into a place of refuge for Jews arriving from Europe, though after its conquest Jewish reluctance to leave the Holy Land led it to be used instead to settle Turkoman and Kurdish tribesmen from eastern Anatolia.

In gratitude for his services to the Ottoman court, Selim II appointed Don Joseph as Duke of the island of Naxos and the Cycliad islands (Andros, Paris, Antiparos, Milo, Sira and Santorin), with control of all their tax farms, and gave him a monopoly over trade in wine between Crete and Moldavia and Wallachia and of beeswax with Poland, where Ashkenazi Jews became his agents. With the resulting profits, he was able to fight off the challenges of Greek and Armenian competitors for the favors of the Sultan for themselves and their peoples. Don Joseph at his peak built a luxurious palace for himself and his family at *Belvedere*, on the shores of the Bosporus near modern Ortaköy, where he entertained lavishly, styling himself as *Josephus Nasi Dei Gratia Dux Aegi Pelegi, Domunis Andri.*

After Doña Gracia's death, Don Joseph developed even greater fortune and political and economic influence throughout Europe as well as in the Ottoman Empire. Like Moshe Hamon a century earlier, he became diplomatic agent for the Sultan, acting for all practical purposes as his Foreign Minister in negotiations with the major monarchs of Europe. In 1550 he was involved in the Ottoman efforts to rescue *marranos* then being persecuted in Venice. In 1562 he was the principal negotiator in the negotiations between the Ottoman Empire and Poland. In 1569 he used Ottoman influence to help the notables of Holland, who revolted against the Spanish Habsburg King Philip II under the leadership of William of Orange, at least partly to keep the Inquisition from disrupting their society and economy as it had done in Spain and the other Habsburg possessions. He also mediated the agreement signed in October of the same year between Selim II and the King of France, Charles IX.

Solomon ben Nathan Ashkenazi. Later on in the sixteenth century, Solomon ben Nathan Ashkenazi (1520–1602), succeeded Don Joseph as principal adviser to the sultans, first to Selim II, and later to his successor Murad III (1574–95). Born at Udine, Italy, in 1520, Soloman received his medical education at Padova before entering the service of the Polish King Sigismund II at Cracow, after which he moved on to Istanbul in 1564. There he first entered the service of the Venetian Ambassador Marcantonio Barbaro as physician and translator, in the latter role gaining the favor of Grand Vezir Mehmed Sokullu during the Ottoman capture of Cyprus from Venice in 1570. Later he became physician and advisor to Selim II, thus succeeding to the role previously exercised by the Mendes family. In 1574 he arranged the Ottoman-Venetian peace treaty which ended the war begun with the Ottoman conquest of Cyprus, and he subsequently served for several years as Ottoman Ambassador at Venice, where he successfully helped the local Jews against proposals made to deport them as had been done elsewhere in Italy. In 1583 he mediated in a quarrel between the British and Venetian representatives in Istanbul, and in 1586 he used his contacts in Europe to arrange peace between the Ottoman Empire and Spain, himself signing the peace treaty on behalf of the Sultan. In 1591 he intervened in Moldavia to secure the election of Emanuel Aron as its native *Voyvoda*, apparently in return for quite substantial bribes.

Ashkenazi's influence at court continued while he served as physician and advisor to the new Grand Vezir Ferhad Pasha even after the death of Mehmed Sokullu and Selim II and well into the reign of Murad III (1574–95). While continuing to practice medicine at court, he followed in Don Joseph's footsteps by using his Ottoman connections to develop vast commercial dealings throughout Europe, at the same time reinvigorating the Jewish settlement at Tiberias and leaving a huge fortune to his descendants. Ultimately, his wealth and influence built up such a coterie of enemies that while he was travelling in Transylvania in 1593 he was imprisoned by its Prince at their instigation. He was freed through the intervention of the British Ambassador in Istanbul, but he died soon afterwards in 1602. His son Nathan Ashkenazi engaged in private medical practice in Istanbul and undertook some diplomatic missions for the Porte in Venice in 1605, but never achieved the wealth and influence of his father.

Esther Kyra. A number of Jewish ladies also achieved considerable influence in the Ottoman court late in the sixteenth century, when as the quality of sultans declined and the *devşirme* parties at court fought for power, the women of the Harem became particularly powerful in an age known as the 'Sultanate of the Women'. Most famous of these was Esther Kyra Handali, widow of the Istanbul merchant Ribbi Elie Handeli, who originally entered the palace as one of the *kiras*, or female agents of harem women with the outside world who also acted as merchants of silks, garments, and precious stones in the Imperial Palace. She gained great influence over official appointments and tax farm concessions during the time of sultans Murad III (1574–95) and Mehmed III (1595–1603) due to her close connections with Murad's mother, Nur Banu Sultan, and his favorite wife, Safiye Sultan, a Venetian woman from the Baffo family, who became Queen Mother on Mehmed III's accession. Both relied on her, not only for garments and precious stones, but also for diplomatic advice and connections, using her to enter into relations with the European embassies in Istanbul, to the great profit of all concerned. As a result for many years she had the power to assign Ottoman fiefs to whomever she wished, for the most part to those who promised the most to her rather than service or money to the Treasury, while her son gained substantial wealth through control of the Istanbul customs. She finally fell from power and was killed by the Janissaries in 1600 due to the influence of the *Ulema*, as well as the hatred of several recently-converted Christian *devşirme* men, who were particularly unhappy at such Jewish influence in the court.

Solomon Aben Yaesh. There were many other Jews who rose to eminence in the sixteenth and seventeenth centuries. Perhaps most important and influential of these was Don Alvaro Mendes, a *marrano* from Portugal. He travelled to India in 1545, where he gained great wealth in a decade through exploiting the Narsingra diamond mines. Returning to Portugal in 1555, he became a confident of King Joao III, who made him a *Chevalier* and entered him into the Portuguese nobility. As Don Alvaro he lived in Madrid for seven years, but in response to the increasing pressure of the Inquisition against *marranos*, he went on to Florence (1564), Paris (1569), Antwerp, London and finally Venice, establishing close business relationships with leading European statesmen and monarchs, including Queen Elizabeth I of England, Henri III of France, and Catherine de Medicis. Due to the influence of his second cousin Don Joseph Nasi, he was invited to come to the Ottoman Empire by Selim II. After arriving in Salonica in the spring of 1585, like other *marranos* he immediately threw off off his Christian cover and returned to Judaism as Soloman Aben Yaesh (Abanaes/Ibn Yaiş/Ben Yaesh). He soon won the favor of Sultan Murad III (1574–1595), and became Duke of the island of Mytelene (Midilli). He assumed Don Joseph's rule as principal sponsor of the Jewish community of Tiberias, there acting through his son Jacob, who, however, was not too successful in restoring the prosperity of the Jewish colony. Like Don Joseph, Solomon Yaesh used his European contacts and a string of agents throughout Europe to develop a network of trade and communication, gaining substantial wealth for himself while keeping his Ottoman masters informed of the latest developments on the continent. Yaesh's most important service came when he established close diplomatic and economic relations for the Porte with England, first sending the *marrano* couriers Solomon Kormano and Judah Sarfati to Queen Elizabeth's private doctor Rodrogo Lopez and subsequently arranging for her representative William Harbourne to come as Ambassador to the Porte in 1583. He thus ended the French domination of Ottoman foreign economic and political relations which had lasted since the time of *Kanuni* Süleyman and secured British support in the Ottoman wars with the Habsburgs at the end of the sixteenth century in return for the award of Capitulations privileges to England on the model of those earlier awarded to French merchants in the empire, putting the sultans in a position where they could play these two competing Powers off in subsequent centuries.

Solomon Ashkenazi's widow Bula Ikshati, gained great influence in the court during the reign of Sultan Ahmed I (1603–17) after she successfully treated the Sultan for an illness for which none of the court doctors had been able to prescribe a cure. There was a whole group of Jewish physicians serving in the Ottoman palace during the seventeenth century, particularly during the reign of Murad IV and Mehmed IV (1648–87) and the reforming Köprülü Grand Vezirs, all making such major contributions to the Ottoman Ruling Class that they were felt to be indispensable. They, along with the Jewish community were awarded handsomely in return.

Jewish Artisans

There were many active Jewish artisans in all the major Ottoman cities. Very industrious and extremely diligent, they were expert in all the trades now that they were living where they could exercise their initiative and ingenuity without being limited by laws, restrictions, and guild exclusivity or by religious restrictions, as had been the case in Europe. They themselves, however, had their own Jewish guilds, many of which were closely associated with their Muslim counterparts, and all of which applied typical guild regulations limiting production, the number of artisans, and the free sale of products.

Jews were especially good as iron forgers, smiths, wheelwrights, coach builders, sail makers, and rope makers. Some were expert sailors and fishermen. There were also Jewish painters, shoemakers, hide processors, workers in precious metals such as gold and silver, locksmiths, lime burners, masons and the like in all the major Ottoman cities. Within the Jewish quarters there were also ambulant merchants and small shops selling all sorts of things. There were small holes-in-wall shops of spice merchants and wine merchants. One Jewish family in Salonica, the Venezia, had the right to collect the tax on weights, held since the town belonged to Venice in 1423–30, and it continued to hold it as a professional *hazaka* until modern times.

Ottoman Jews were without equal in the trades of weaving and dying, particularly at Salonica. It was only after the arrival of the Spanish Jews, particularly those from Toledo and Segovia, that it became the most important clothing and weaving center in the East. Jews made stuffs of all kinds, cloths, silks and rugs. The products of the Salonica Jewish textile industry were appreciated for their refined quality compared to local goods, which were short, dry, and mixed with odd materials. Salonica became a kind of vast cloth factory, with most of the families participating as units, working long hours at home, day and night – men, women and children alike, on their terraces, even in the streets, producing the finest and softest quality stuffs. The constant noise of the weaving machines was an immediate reminder of what the city was doing. The waters used to wash the woolens joined in rivers with the dye liquids, running through the streets and forming permanent pestilential lakes in the lower areas of Salonica. Many people thus lived in quite unhealthy conditions, but tolerated the situation, accepting life as it was without complaint because of personal and community needs.

Almost all the artisans on Sicily were Jews, so when the Spanish government decreed that they be expelled, most of the Christian inhabitants of Sicily intervened on their behalf, either to end the expulsion or at least delay it, but were unsuccessful due to the strength of the Inquisition. These Sicilian Jewish immigrants went mainly to Salonica where they had numerous shops and workshops where they worked as cauldron makers, tinners, woodworkers, furriers, dyers, tailors, shoe makers, gold makers, weavers, butchers, millers, and oil pitchers. They also were fishermen, boatmen, salt makers, and burden bearers along the docks.

Jews in International and Domestic Trade

Participation by Ottoman Jews in the Empire's international trade reached a peak in the sixteenth century, with the Ottomans relying heavily on the Jews, in trade as in diplomacy and banking, since they were the only subjects who combined the necessary aptitudes and connections without developing treasonable relations with the Christian Powers of Europe. Since the Ottoman Empire spread over three continents, it provided extraordinary means for merchants to trade throughout the world. Jewish knowledge of European banking methods and the main European languages and their contacts with fellow Jews in most European trade centers helped them develop intense commercial relations with the west which brought substantial benefit both to themselves and to the Empire. Ottoman Jewish traders knew how to keep accounts and write commercial letters and contracts. They had considerable geographic, financial and administrative knowledge as well as expertise in foreign languages. Having travelled from country to country, while regularly corresponding with Jews everywhere, they knew first hand the needs and products of each. The presence in most countries of relatives and friends in whom they could have full confidence gave them an economic cosmopolitanism that enabled them to undertake imports and exports with a minimum of risk.

Particularly important in assuring the continuity and prosperity of Jewish trade and commerce was the family partnership, dominant form of Jewish business organization in Ottoman times. Throughout the Empire, as well as in foreign countries, branches were managed by brothers, sons and even brothers-in-law of the dominant partners. As a result they were able to carry out an very profitable system of exchanges, in particular using a sophisticated system of bills of exchange honored by Jewish bankers and merchants in different countries to transfer funds in a manner that their Muslim and Christian competitors were not able to do. They were audacious speculators. As a result, they developed a virtual monopoly over colonial trade. Contrary to medieval custom, they did not confine themselves to one article or another. They knew all the articles, traded in merchandises of all kind without being limited by state barriers or corporation limits. They made themselves indispensable on the world markets and became the arbiters of the great exchange goods – sugar, coffee, and spices. Jews generally did not emulate the Greek and Armenian subjects of the Sultan who assumed foreign citizenship to take advantage of the Capitulations, thus adding to Muslim suspicion of them and their motives. Instead, Jewish family members who were European nationals often were brought to the Empire to manage the family businesses so they could take advantage of the Capitulations privileges without betraying the long-standing Jewish loyalty to an empire which had rescued them from persecutions in Europe.

Jews from Istanbul and Salonica maintained widespread commercial relations through Thrace to Southeastern Europe and up the Danube into Hungary, Austria, and Central Europe as far east as Poland and Russia. Ottoman Jewish merchants went to France and England, and even a few to Spain, though normally in disguise to avoid persecution. Spanish Jews who had settled in Corfu under Venetian rule since the twelfth century traded particularly with Jews who settled in Ottoman Albania, particularly at Avlonya (Valona), while the latter traded widely through Ragusa (Dubrovnik) and across the Adriatic to Naples and Genoa and through Dalmatia to Venice and Central Europe.

Jewish merchants settled in Izmir only starting in the last quarter of the sixteenth century, when they came from neighboring Tire and Manisa and in flight from persecution by the Shia Safavids in Iran. In the early years of the seventeenth century, many also came from Salonica as a result of its persistent earthquakes, fires and disorders as well as increasing persecution by its Greek population, and they were soon joined by thousands of *marranos* from Portugal and Castille, who were being subjected to increasing persecution by the Inquisition despite their conversion to Catholicism over a century earlier. It was just at this time, most likely no coincidence, that Izmir finally began to grow in economic importance, becoming an entrepôt for international trade from the Mediterranean and the Aegean and overland through Anatolia to the north and east, with the *marranos* in particular using their close contacts with relatives in Livorno and Amsterdam to great advantage.

Jews also participated in the international silk trade centered in Bursa in Anatolia, sending their ships through the Aegean and Adriatic to Venice and through the Red Sea and Persian Gulf to the Indian Ocean, to India and China and beyond. They created major markets for Ottoman goods and raw materials both in Europe and the East. They exported articles like drugs, the woolens of Ankara, dried fruits from Anatolia, silk from Bursa and Iran, beeswax, rugs, hides, cement, cotton, corals, and important articles like camelots, alun, porcelain, linens, canvases and they traded in construction wood, nails, tin and the like. When the popes of Rome tried to shut Jews out of the international trade in Italy, they convinced the Ottoman sultan to boycott the prinicipal Italian ports until the popes relented, under the pressure of Italian merchants who were losing their share of international trade as a result of the shutting out of the Jews.

Ottoman Jews from Istanbul, Salonica, Safed, and Izmir were greatly helped by the communities of long-established *Musta'rab* Jewish merchants to develop trade in Middle Eastern centers like Cairo and Alexandria, Baghdad, Damascus and Basra, and in North Africa at Algiers, all of which became centers for the import of goods from the East as well as the export of Ottoman manufactures and raw materials.

In Egypt, most aspects of governmental financial administration, including the collection of taxes and customs duties and the operation of the mint, were delegated to Jews, who used these positions to help not only themselves and their families but also relatives and friends in their commercial activities. Jews controlled the commercial routes, and ships carrying their goods passed through the ports of the Mediterranean, the Black Sea and the Indian Ocean to all parts of the world.

As a final support to their role in Ottoman international trade, Jews held most tax farms over the quais of Istanbul and the provinces of the Empire. They were absolute masters of the customs, and levied such high customs duties on non-Jews that many hated them, leading to government intervention at times, though the Ottomans did not dare remove them entirely or permanently due to their unrivalled knowledge of the value of goods and how much people could and would pay.

Ottoman Jews also played important roles in trade within the Ottoman Empire. Jewish merchants were less numerous than artisans when the Jews first came but their number increased rapidly as refugees arrived. All across Macedonia and Thrace in Europe, and Anatolia and the Arab provinces of the east, Jews set up branch banks and hostels which were managed by other Jews. They visited even the smallest towns, went into the mountains and deserts, and offered coffee, sugar, indigo, cloths and a thousand other objects manufactured by industries of the world to the subjects of the sultan. They made loans to cultivators, bought animals, tobacco, and the like. They developed new tastes and needs among the people and taught farmers how to meet the resulting demands. The Jews knew how to develop and finance products as well as to transport and sell them where they could get the highest prices. They were willing to take loans and develop enterprises. They thus speculated on future developments and benefited enormously when they were right. Jews always were very punctual and scrupulous in carrying out their contracts and engagements, and for this they were universally respected. They also knew how to maintain an affability in relations with outsiders to gain the confidence needed in transacting business. They did not use written documents very much in the market or in the shops of the large merchants and bankers; most affairs were settled by word of mouth without witnesses. In foreign commercial relations, a simple letter concluded and certified even the most important transactions. Anyone who did not live up to his word would be discredited and boycotted in future business activities. When there did have to be a written document, the parties would use a Rabbi to draw it up, according to solemn formulations, with the parties affixing their seals in order to confirm its authenticity. Even business associations were usually arranged by oral agreement and not by written contract. Sometimes contracts were used, but often, even large associations, where parties put all goods and possessions and profits in common, between members of the same family, were arranged by conventions that were tacit and not explicit, though this often led to quarrels which the Rabbis had to settle. In agreements with merchants in foreign ports, a treaty would be used to stipulate arrival of the goods within 30, 60 or 90 days, with the treaty itself then becoming the instrument of payment.

Right from the time of their first arrivals in the Ottoman Empire, Jews participated actively in trade fairs, which they often organized in order to meet their religious and commercial needs, for example arranging that they should not take place on Saturdays and the days of the other major Jewish holidays. To avoid attacks on the roads, they went in groups with heavy escorts, and they knew well how to use their arms. While travelling to trade in Europe, they usually wore heavy turbans and Muslim cloaks to avoid arrest by the Inquisition. Trade with Italy was open to them. There they used facilities provided by the Jewish bankers who controlled the Adriatic basin and whose agents covered all of southern Europe. At Venice and in all the Italian ports they had secure correspondents. When Christian governments and merchants attempted to squeeze Jews out of international trade, the latter were able to secure Ottoman support for boycotts and other such actions which effectively defeated these efforts.

Jews in Agriculture, Food Production, and Sales

While the greatest wealth came to Ottoman Jews from trade and commerce, they also played important roles in agriculture. In most countries of Europe, prohibitions against Jewish ownership of landed property and old-established systems of feudal tenure excluded Jews from farming, but, as with the trades, this was not the case in Ottoman Empire. As a result, there were Jewish *timar* fief holders as well as owners of fields and vineyards which they cultivated through tenant farmers or occasionally themselves. In the countryside there were Jews working as vine growers, winemakers and market gardeners, renting their fields from Muslim owners to whom they paid what they owed in cash or kind after the harvest. Other Jews knew how to look for minerals and to refine copper, lead and pewter and to manufacture vitriol, seeking them out in the areas of Macedonia and elsewhere. Jewish merchants and traders also imported rice, grains, fruits and vegetables where they were not grown locally.

Sheep products often were exploited directly by Jewish specialists who knew how to prepare excellent cheeses, which were, for ritual purposes, submitted to close Rabbinical surveillance so that no suspect ingredient or prohibited contact would damage their purity and make it impossible for pious observers of Jewish law to consume them. There were Jewish vineyards and wine makers who produced wine which could be used for ritual purposes as well as for the general Jewish public, though the product was strictly forbidden for Muslims. Jews were very active in milling and baking. There were Jewish butchers and ritual slaughterers (*shohetim*), whose activities and products were subjected to careful and severe regulation by the rabbinical establishment so they could be accepted as *kosher* and consumed by the Jewish community.

As in international trade, moreover, Jews assured their position in Ottoman agriculture by monopolizing the very profitable tax farms established over many of the necessities of life as well as most agricultural products, collecting the taxes owed the Sultan by the producers, paying the treasury what had been promised in advance, and keeping most of the collections as profit for themselves.

THE EFFLORESCENCE OF OTTOMAN JEWISH CULTURE

Jewish culture and intellectual life flourished as brightly in Ottoman times as in the greatest days of Islamic Spain. Every refugee arriving from the Iberian Peninsula or Italy brought with bags of books and manuscripts. All kept in close touch with relatives and colleagues throughout Europe, keeping the Ottoman Jewish community in close touch with intellectual life throughout the world as they knew it and adding to the rich Ottoman intellectual mosaic which produced so much creative activity in the fifteenth and sixteenth centuries. The *talmud torah*s and *yeshiva*s of Istanbul, Salonica, Safed and Jerusalem replaced those of Barcelona, Cordova and Toledo as centers of religious and secular thought. Istanbul was called by scholars 'a large city of scholars and scribes'. The poet Samuel Usque called Salonica 'a metropolis of Israel, city of righteousness, loyal town, mother of the Jewish nation like Jerusalem in its time'.

The Ottoman Empire now exercised an irresistible attraction to the intellectual elite among the Jewish exiles from Spain, who developed a true aristocracy of spirit and knowledge. Talmudists, philosophers, jurists, doctors, poets, and writers came to live in the domain of the sultans. At first they intended to remain only temporarily on their way to somewhere else, most likely the Holy Land. But when they found it to be an asylum of quiet and security away from the prejudices, struggles and noise of the world, with resources which would enable them to carry out their studies without diversion, most remained. In each of the cities and towns of the empire of the Sultans, the Jewish communities and wealthy individual Jewish bankers and doctors gathered magnificent libraries and supported the work of hundreds of rabbinical scholars, producing rabbis who served synagogues not only within the Empire but also the communities left in Europe, and leaving a rich literature which influences Jewish thought throughout the world to the present day.

Centering this intellectual life was the Ottoman synagogue, which constituted not only a center of religious devotion and community social activity, but also a *yeshiva*, a school of high knowledge, a seminary, a place of study for all Jews. It became a library, center for manuscripts and books, and a refuge for all wishing to study them in their moments of leisure. Sometimes the studies took place within the sanctuary itself, sometimes in a separate annex, where students and curious alike gathered under the direction and supervision of the *marbitz torah*, who taught them the essential elements of the Talmud in a systematic fashion.

Libraries and *yeshiva*s alike often were subsidized by wealthy Jewish bankers, merchants and traders. Doña Gracia Mendes and Don Joseph Nasi, for example, subsidized the *yeshiva* led by Elijah ha-Levi, pupil of the second Grand Rabbi, Elijah Mizrahi. In Salonica Don Señor Benveniste, whose father once had been Minister of Finance in Christian Spain, and who had managed to bring along most of his family fortune, founded a myriad of libraries as well as schools providing instruction in astronomy, philosophy and mathematics as well as the religious sciences. Most of the famous rabbis and professors opened their own *yeshiva*s with the support of wealthy members of local congregations, located adjacent to but usually outside the synagogues and libraries, enlarging their instruction beyond strictly religious and philosophical subjects to include logic, astronomy, medicine, poetry, and the like, and attracting students from throughout the world of Judaism. There were, for example, the *yeshiva*s of Rabbi Elijah Mizrahi in Istanbul, of Joseph Passy, Jacob ben Habib, Joseph Taitazak and Samuel de Medina in Salonica, of Jacob Berab and Joseph Caro in Safed, and of Levi ben Habib and David ibn Abi Zimra in Jerusalem. Children of rich or well-off families attended the *yeshiva*s for substantial periods of time, developing their knowledge of humanities in the Hebrew style in preparation for lives outside the world of knowledge. A few of the best students specialized more in jurisprudence and procedures so they themselves could become rabbis. But most of them studied simply to know, without intending to pursue rabbinical or religious careers. In addition to the regular students, there were also auditors of all ages and occupations, retired merchants, foreigners passing through, convalescent persons to weak to resume their daily occupations, and even beggars.

The *yeshiva*s were characterized by free expression of ideas as well as fraternal and egalitarian relations among Jews of all classes. The most humble and least learned person could ask for clarification, state his objections, and propose solutions to the problems under discussions. The *marbitz torah* encouraged such interventions, and explained, corrected and criticized. All persons present collaborated actively in the process of understanding and learning. The *yeshiva*s were full of animation, controversy and disputes, often passionate, with people arguing with energy amidst those who were reading and studying. Often the discussions would continue into the streets, and for all adults there was no more interesting distraction than to inform themselves of the debates going on among the apprentice Talmudists and their teachers in the great *yeshiva*s of the time.

Hebrew furnished the religious and juridical terminology and texts from the Bible and Talmud, but scholars and students, like the common people, conversed and taught in Castillian. It was in Castillian that the elementary school teacher (*melamed*) gave instructions and explanations and it was in Castillian that the *marbitz* conducted discussions in his *yeshiva*. At first the Jewish savants made a point of using Castillian with the same purity and elegance that they had learned in Spain. The second generation of emigrées also tried to preserve this elegance, but as they lost contact with Spain they gradually abandoned classical clarity or forgot the rules of elegant composition and use of the good language. As Castillian thus decayed, they continued to use it, but increasingly mixed it with Hebraisms along with local Turkish, Arabic, and Greek words and phrases, thus producing the dialect which came to be known as Judeo-Spanish or Ladino, in most of the empire, and as Judeo-Arabic in the eastern provinces.

Salonica, often then called 'Little Jerusalem' because of its Jewish majority as well as the large numbers of synagogues and schools, and Safed in Gallilee, became major centers for the Jewish mystic thought of the Kabbalists during the Golden Age. Immigration from Spain brought not only the positive sciences but also the obscurantism of mysticism. Many of those who escaped the Inquisition had endured such terrible suffering that they began to believe that they were being punished by God for their sins and those of their ancestors who had converted to Christianity in the face of death. They sought to repent by concentrating on the coming of the Messiah to save the Jewish people, thus bringing together mystic ideas with long-standing Messianic dreams and spreading their ideas among the mass of Jews along with the idea that the arrival of the Messiah could be speeded up if they devoted their lives to meditation and asceticism. To build their courage, Don Isaac Abravanel used calculations based on the Book of Daniel and legends of Guemara to announce in three different works that the deliverance of Israel would be accomplished during the fifty years following 1503.

As a result, many Jewish communities began to devote themselves entirely to fasts and flagellations to prepare for the imminent arrival of the Messiah. The Kabbalah developed rapidly among Salonica thinkers. Kabbalism was for philosophers an object of science and meditation, permitting one to attain transcendent spheres of speculative thought and high theology; it was a sort of pantheistic cosmology, near to neo-Platonian and Alexandrian concepts. It was considered to be a superior synthesis based on mysticism, with roots in the philosophy of Philo and neo Platonism of Alexandria. It had gained an allure in Spain at the end of the thirteenth century with the work of Moses Semtov of Lebon, who most likely compiled the *Zohar*, the Bible of the Kabbalists, a mass of allegorical commentaries on the Pentateuch, full of descriptions of Heaven, Hell, messianic times, furnishing combinations of numbers and letters, of revelations, and of mystic titles of astrology and magic. Kabbalism began to be studied with a frenzy at Salonica. Its adherents asked it for the means of purifying themselves and of disengaging themselves from matter to accelerate the coming of the Redeemer of Israel. In the *yeshivas* as well as outside they discussed the *Zohar* and developed mystic tendencies which as time went on gained influence over most of the Rabbanites. Among the leading Kabbalists were Joseph Taitazak of Salonica, his disciple Solomon Molho, who settled in Safed before travelling to Italy, and Meir ben Ezekiel ibn Gabay, who linked the older Kabbalistic traditions of Spain with the newly developing mystic schools of Salonica and Safed.

While orthodox Rabbinical Judaism flourished in Jerusalem under the Chief Sephardic Rabbi of Eretz Israel, called *Rishon le-Zion* or 'first of Zion', starting in the seventeenth century with Rabbi Moses ben Jonathan

Galante (1620–1689), Kabbalism flourished even earlier in Safed starting with Rabbi Ya'akov (Jacob) Berab (Beirav) (1474–1538), who settled there after years of wandering in Morocco and Egypt following his expulsion from Spain. He founded his own *yeshiva*, which became a major center of Jewish intellectual life. Relying on some ideas of Maimonides, Berab developed the concept that the ancient *sanhedrin* of Judaism, its central religious and legal council that had been abolished by the Romans, should be restored, so it could resume the old practice of ordinating rabbis (*semikhah*), who could provide authoritative interpretations of the law. His school trained most of the next generation of Kabbalists, including Joseph Caro, Solomon ben Moses Alkabetz, Elijah ben Moses de Vidas, and Jacob Cordovero, though the proposal for a restored *sanhedrin* ultimately was abandoned due to the powerful opposition of the Chief Rabbi of Jerusalem, Rabbi Levi ben Habib, who accused Berab of planning to be president of the *sanhedrin*. But Kabbalism in Safed continued and strengthened during the sixteenth century and after.

There were many original and influential Jewish scholars active in the Ottoman Empire during the Golden Age, but we can mention only but a few of the most important here.

Elijah ben Abraham Mizrahi (1437–1526), also known as *Reem* and *Ribi Eliau ha-Parnass*, was born in Istanbul of a Romaniote family shortly before the Ottoman conquest in 1453. He produced a substantial body of works on medicine, mathematics, astronomy, geography, the Talmud and Jewish law, many of his works being subsequently translated into Latin, before he became preoccupied with administrative positions, becoming the head of a Romaniote synagogue in Istanbul in 1475, and subsequently being appointed second Grand Rabbi of the Ottoman Empire in 1495 following the death of its first occupant, Moshe Capsali. Mizrahi spent a great deal of his time trying to educate the Karaites so they would return to the Orthodox fold, while defending himself against those who criticized this activity on the grounds that the Karaites were beyond redemption. He was the first Ottoman geographer since the Exile to produce a map of the Holy Land. He wrote a detailed commentary on Rashi's criticism of Maimonides, strongly defending the latter in a work which became a major source for Rabbinical commentaries in later centuries. He also produced a textbook on mathematics, *Sefer ha-Misbat*, which later was published by his son in Istanbul in 1534 and subsequently was translated into Latin.

Mordehai ben Eliezer Comtino (1420–87), a Romaniote Jew who lived in Istanbul in the early years of Ottoman rule in the fifteenth century, was inspired by the great twelfth-century Spanish Jewish scholar Abraham Ibn Ezra (Benezra), called the wandering scholar of Toledo, as well as by his teacher in Catalonia, Manok Saporta, one of the great Rabbanites of his time, and he wrote many commentaries on Ibn Ezra's works. As Ibn

Ezra was in his time, so also Comtino set as his major task the spreading of culture and making accessible to the masses basic knowledge in logic, philosophy, mathematics, and the natural sciences. His *Sefer ha-Heshbon ve ha-Middot* taught the basics of arthmetic and geometry. *Perush Luhot Paras* described the instruments of astonomy. *Tikkun Keli ha-Zefihah* taught people how to build a sun dial to tell the time. His *Sefer ha-Tekunah* was on astronomy, *Ma'mar al Likkui ha-levanah* studed philosophy and other sciences. *Millot ha-Higgayon* constituted a commentary on Maimonides's works on Logic.

Comtino did more than teach the people about the Torah. He tried to reconcile traditional Jewish Rabbinical thought with the Karaites, considered heretical by most of his colleagues. Whereas most Jewish religious leaders of his time refused to have anything to do with them, Comtino tried to teach some of their young leaders, including Eliyahu Başyazı and Kalef Afendopulo, and with some success, though bitterly opposed by most of his Rabbinical contemporaries. Nonetheless he did more than anyone else to create an intellectual rapprochement between Rabbinicial and Karaite scholars in Istanbul. In this he was defended by Grand Rabbi Elijah Mizrahi, though the disputes that followed were a major reason that the office of Grand Rabbi was left vacant for three centuries afterwards.

Ya'akov ben David Tam ibn Yahya (1475–1640) came with his father from Lisbon to Istanbul in 1496. His deep religious learning soon brought him to the attention of Grand Rabbi Mizrahi, who made him a member of the Istanbul *Bet Din* and left him the spiritual leader of Istanbul Jews after Mizrahi's death left them without a Grand Rabbi. Like Mizrahi he refused to accept the opinions of most Jewish leaders that the Karaites were no longer Jews, maintaining that they had remained among the people of Moses even though they had strayed. He had the mental openness to study the ideas of the Kabbalists, even though he opposed them, and to learn Turkish, Arabic and Islamic law to widen his horizons. Most of his works were destroyed in a great fire in Istanbul in 1541, but his *Responsa* were published as *Oholei Tam* by his daughter in 1642, and were widely used, not only in the Ottoman Empire but also in France and Germany.

Joseph Taitazak (1487–1545) was one of the leading Talmudists and Kabbalah scholars of his time after emigrating from Spain to Salonica with his father in about 1510. Though we know little about early his life and career until he became well known as a *halakhic* authority in Salonica in 1520, we do know that among his students were Isaac Ardabi, Samuel de Medina, Isaac Aroya, Eliezer Ashkenazi and Solomon Alkabez, all major figures in Ottoman Jewish life. Taitazak himself lived an ascentic life and can be considered one of the founders of the great Kabbalist schools that flourished at Safed as well as Salonica. The most important of his published works was *Porat Yosef*, a commentary on the philosophical system of Thomas Aquinas, while his *Responsa* were published in the works of his contemporaries, including the *Avkat Rokhel* and *Beit Yosef* of Joseph Caro and the *She'erit Yehudah* published by his brother Judah.

Joseph ben Ephraim Caro (1488–1575) was most likely born in Toledo (Castille), Spain, though it is possible that since his family emigrated to Portugal some time before the Spanish expulsion he might therefore have been born in Lisbon. After being expelled from Portugal in 1497, he went first to Nicopolis, on the Danube, then to Plevna, where he became a Rabbi. For some years he wandered through Europe, suffering various tribulations along with Jews whom he met. Finally in 1521 he came to the Ottoman Empire, settling first at Edirne, where he began to teach and gather disciples, then at Salonica, where he studied with Solomon Shlomo Molho, Joseph Taitazak, and Shlomo Alkabez, and finally at Safed, joining Berab's *yeshiva*. As he travelled within the Empire between 1522 and 1542 he compiled his monumental *Beyt Yosef* (published first in 1555), an immense collection and systematic arrangement of all the laws and religious precepts of Judaism from their origins in the Bible to his own time, as interpreted mainly by the Sephardic authorities (*rishonim*) that preceeded him. He also arranged a condensation of this work in the *Shulhan Arukh*, a codified collection with clear, simple statements without all the discussion and citations, but in definitive form, giving all the laws and rules in the same order as they were found in the larger original work. It was the latter work, printed in 1550–59, and republished in Venice in 1564–65, that played a major role in later Jewish legal studies, becoming the cornerstone of later rabbinic Judaism, the focus around which the intellectual creativity of major rabbinic authorities of later Sephardic generations was concentrated, though it did lead to a negative reaction among the Ashkenazi authorities (*aharonim*) of Germany and Poland, who criticized Caro's failure to take into consideration their decisions and those of their predecessors. Caro went on to publish *Keshef Mishneh*, a commentary on eight of the fourteen books of Maimonides's *Mishneh Torah* (Venice, 1574–75), adding the sources or alternative opinions that Maimonides had failed to give in his own work. Parts of Caro's own *Responsa* written in Safed and Nicopolis, the former in particular showing disputes with Moses di Trani and David ben Solomon ibn Abi Zimra, were published in Salonica after his death in 1598 by his son Judah as *Even ha-Ezer*. Like most other leading rabbinic scholars at the time, Caro also was a kabbalist, believing that he was visited during the night by his divine teacher (*maggid*), who transmitted the ideals of mystic theology and asceticism, which he practiced until the end of his life. His accounts of his experiences as *Maggid Mesharim* were published also after his death (Lublin, 1646, Venice, 1649).

Isaac Luria Ashkenazi (1534–72), born in Syria of Spanish exiles but educated in Cairo by his uncle, the famous Rabbi Besalel Ashkenazi, mastered both the Talmud and the *Zohar* in six years, spending his days at the *yeshiva* and his nights along the Nile, returning home to his uncle only on holidays and weekends. Afterwards, he returned to Safed where he originated practical Kabbalism in opposition to the theoretical Kabbalists. He died of the plague, however, after only a few years of intellectual activity (1569–72), so much of his work was published by his disciple and successor, Hayim ben Joseph Vital (1542–1620), who used his notebooks and notes together with his own to write a series of works reporting on Luria's Kabbalist system in great detail, though in the process he put many of his own ideas into the mouth of his master. Luria's Kabbalistic ideas as amplified by Vital spread throughout the world of Judaism in subsequent centuries, first orally and then, starting in the seventeenth century, in print, influencing in particular those expelled from Spain whose traumatic experiences made them particularly susceptible to ideas of mysticism and asceticism. Luria's inner circle and followers developed a strong musical element to their mystic call right from the start. Their inner visions and their expression encouraged an oral type of inner experience and mystic expression, with singing and playing, even in prayer, coming to symbolize fulfillment of God's command and thus being required of all believers.

Moshe ben Baruh Almosnino (1510–80), born in Salonica of a Jewish family from Aragon, was a major philosopher, whose *Penei Mosheh*, commenting on Aristotelian ethics (1556), his commentaries on the Islamic philospher al-Ghazzali, and his Ladino poems and philosophical works were of major importance. His *Regimento de la Vida* (Salonica, 1566) commented on the major Arabic, Hebrew, Greek and Roman philosophers, while his *Extremos ya Grandezas de Constantinopla* provides important source material on the political and social situation in Istanbul during the time of Sultan Süleyman the Magnificent in the mid-16th century.

Samuel ben Moses de Medina (1506–89) was born in Salonica of a family that had come from Spain during the great exile. He became a principal Jewish community leader in Salonica and an influential *Halakhah* authority, not only for Ottoman Jewry but for communities throughout western Europe. His decisions generally prevailed because of his prestige even though many scholars disagreed with him. He gave decisions according to his judgment when he found no *Halakhah* precedent and insisted on implementing customs which were in force in Spain, striving to make them accord with the *Halakhah*. He dealt with the various socio-economic problems that emerged in Salonica during his time, though in controversies between rich and poor he maintained the right of the wealthy members of the community to direct and regulate communal affairs, stating that leadership of the community had to be held by those who bore its financial burden so long as they were loyal to religious principles. He earned a living as a tradesman and served as rabbi and communal leader of several Iberian congregations in his home town, including the Gerush and Lisbon. He suffered much misfortune and illness and some poverty in his life but found consolation in study, communal leadership, and trade.

Poetry also had an honorable place in Ottoman Jewish intellectual activity, particularly at Salonica where an entire poetic institute was founded and maintained by Moses ben Gedaliah Ibn Yahya at his opulent villa in the outskirts of the city. The two leading poets here were Abraham Lebeth Hazan and Salomon Alcabets ha-Levi, who reached a peak of poetic expression with their profound emotion and purity, equalling the great Sephardic copies of the Arab epic style and distinguishing themselves in particular with their liturgical odes.

Among the most creative Ottoman Jewish poets were Solomon ben Mazal-Tov, who came to Istanbul from Spain in 1505, and Israel ben Moses Najara (1530–1625), one of the most important members of the Salonica school, who after coming under the influence of the Kabbalist Hayim Vital and Rabbi Menaham Lonzano, published a series of melodic and simple, but striking, poetic works in Safed, including *Mesaheket ha-Tevel* and *Zemirot Yisrael* in 1587, and a collection of the poems of his youth, *Meimei Yisrael*.

Mazal-Tov and Najara also combined religious Hebrew songs and Spanish secular melodies with Turkish classical music, adapting the Turkish and Hebrew singing melodies to Jewish songs and uniting word and tone to inspire the masses through a unique Ottoman Jewish musical language. In the process they absorbed the complex Ottoman musical forms and techniques and arranged their religious poems according to the Turkish *makamat*, with their complicated instrumental forms. The Ottoman framework of twelve *makamat*, each representing a certain mood, was imposed on most synagogue songs as well as secular tunes. Thus the majestic *Siga* mode of the *makamat* was used to read the Torah and related texts. The happy *Ajam-Nawruz* was adapted for the *Shabbat Shira*, *Simhat Torah* and for wedding music, the mournful *Hijjaz* for funerals and songs mentioning death, and the *Sabba*, developed by Turkish musicians for poems of chaste love and filial affection, was used for texts connected with circumcisions. Each verse began with an introduction (*petihah*) in which the name of its *makam* was mentioned in a phonetically similar Hebrew word or rhyme before the actual melody and song followed. Under this Turkish musical inspiration, the popular and profane melodies brought from Spain soon infiltrated the hymns and prayers of synagogues throughout the Ottoman Empire, with Turkish melodies and styles being used more and more as time went on. As a result, for example, the collection of Mazal-Tov's songs published in Istanbul in 1545 had six of his poems sung to Spanish music, thirty to Turkish ones, and twenty-nine to older Jewish ones. Following Najara,

Menahem de Lonzano composed hymns primarily with Turkish melodies because their ascent to the tenth note over the note D in the Islamic scale was considered to be the 'utmost range of the human voice'.

These religious songs meant both for the synagogue and the outside secular world influenced and deepened the piety of believers. The work of these Ottoman Jewish poet musicians added to and enriched the liturgy of Sephardic and Ashkenazi Jewry, not only in the Ottoman Empire but throughout the world. Singing these melodies, moreover, became an important *mitzvah*, or 'good deed' for believers so that religious musical brotherhoods were organized as orchestras and choirs to play and sing their hymns and songs at gatherings in the synagogue before prayer and in public. Groups such as the *Maftirim* of Istanbul, Izmir and Salonica, the *Mezammerei Barukh she-Amar* ('Singers of the *Barukh she-Amar*') of Germany, and the *Shomerim la-Boker* ('Watchers of the Dawn') of Italy and the like became important parts of Jewish communities in Europe and the Ottoman Empire, in some places as important as the burial societies. The fact that singing and playing these melodies was a *mitzvah* and that it was for the masses, moreover, encouraged large-scale and rapid composition free of the rules of the traditional synagogue songs, in consequence leaving Jewry throughout the world with a mass of rich melody which never can be exhausted even if no more are composed.

Bringing together, distributing and preserving much of the Ottoman Jewish heritage of the Golden Age was the Empire's Hebrew-language press which, only a short while after the first Latin printing press produced its first book at Gutenberg in 1436 and the first Hebrew language book was printed in Avignon in 1475, inaugurated two centuries of activity in the dominions of the Sultan. Long before the Arabic/Ottoman printing press was brought to Istanbul by Ibrahim Müteferrika early in the eighteenth century, in 1493, two exiles from Spain, David and Samuel ibn Nahmias, established the first Hebrew press in Istanbul, printing Ya'kov ben Asher's *Arba'alı Turum*. While printing in Christian Europe was being subjected to severe restrictions due to religious influences, the freedom of religion and expression provided by the sultans enabled the Hebrew press to develop and expand widely. Dr Israel Nathan Sonsino and his son Yeshua Sonsino, also Spanish exiles, established their Hebrew press in northern Italy in 1483, soon afterwards printing the Talmud and then setting up other presses throughout Italy, in Naples, Rimini, Fano, Pisaro, Brescia, to meet the demands of exiles who, freed from the restrictions under which they had suffered in Spain, demanded and received more books of all sorts. In 1526 Israel Sonsino's grandson Gershon ben Moshe Sonsino left Italy with his son Eliezer and settled in Salonica in 1527. In 1530 they started a Hebrew press there, and soon after went to Istanbul where they established a new press, while Solomon Sonsino continued to operate the press in Salonica. Between

1530 and 1547 the Sonsino presses in Salonica published some forty works in Hebrew, including several works of Maimonides, a Hebrew translation of Yaa'kov Alkabes's Spanish romantic novel *Amadis de Gaula*, and the *Bible Polyglotte*, providing on the same page the text of the Torah in Hebrew, Aramaic, Arabic and Persian. After the death of Gershon Sonsino in 1534 and of Eliezer in 1547, their work was carried on by one of their apprentices, Moise ben Eliezer Parnas, while a fourth generation of Sonsinos operated a Hebrew press in Cairo, producing books in 1557 and 1562.

While the Sonsino establishment was the most famous Ottoman Hebrew press, and produced the most printed books, there were others. Between 1551 and 1553, a Hebrew language press was operated in Istanbul by the Halicz brothers, who had been forced to convert to Christianity in Crakow (Poland) before fleeing to the Ottoman dominions, where they returned to Judaism, and by the Spanish exiles Solomon and Joseph Jabes, who after a short stay in Edirne operated presses in both Salonica and Istanbul, printing a series of philosophical, rabbinical and Karaite works, including two editions of the Talmud. Don Joseph Nasi himself operated a Hebrew press at his Belvedere mansion at Ortaköy as well as at other places around Istanbul, and its operations were continued after his death by his wife Reyna between 1578 and 1600. Eliezer ben Isaac printed several Hebrew works at Safed between 1577 and 1587. The Bat-Sheva family from Italy settled in Salonica in about 1590 and operated a Hebrew printing press there well into the seventeenth century. During the remaining years of the sixteenth century, moreover, other Hebrew presses were maintained in the Ottoman dominions for various lengths of time by people such as Judah Sason, Moshe ben Smel Psilino, Solomon ben Mazal-Tov, Hayim Kasarno, Joseph Israel Sarfati, Ya'akov ber Rafael Zihri, Esaac Elhakem, Joseph ha-Levi, Solomon Ushki, Samuel ben Yusef ha-Koren, Eliezer ben Izak Ashkenazi and David ben Eliezer Kashti.

Few Hebrew books were produced in the Empire during the early years of the seventeenth century until Solomon Franco established a press in Istanbul in 1638, which was operated by his son until 1683. In Salonica, there was some Hebrew publishing during the last half of the seventeenth century, but it resumed on a large scale only in 1709 with a press established by Abraham ben David and Yomtov Canpillas, who printed rabbinic novellae, respons and homiletics well into the eighteenth century. A Hebrew press established in Istanbul by Jonah b. Jacob of Zalocze, who fled from the Chmielnicki massacres in Galicia, published books in Istanbul from 1710 to 1743. Jedidiah Gabay's Hebrew press established at Leghorn in the early seventeenth century was transferred to Izmir by his son Abrahim in 1657, where Jonah b. Jacob also printed books between 1729 and 1741. And, finally, Istanbul's first Karaite press was maintained in Istanbul between 1734 and 1741.

The Golden Age of Ottoman Jewry lasted for about two hundred years, until about 1700, and then, almost overnight, it was gone, just as the Ottoman Golden Age had vanished. The powerful Jewish bankers and international traders were replaced by more energetic and knowledgeable Armenians and Greeks. Large-scale Christian anti-Semitism, supported by European diplomats and merchants, drove the Jews out of the privileged position which had been given them by Mehmed II and retained by his successors during the next century. No more were there influential Jews at court. The mass of Jews, moreover, never as prosperous as their leaders even in the Golden Age, now settled into a poverty and ignorance which lasted well into the nineteenth century.

3

Decline of Ottoman Jewry in the Seventeenth and Eighteenth Centuries

DECLINE AND DISINTEGRATION OF THE OTTOMAN EMPIRE

All the prosperity, power and influence gained by Ottoman Jewry during the Golden Age of the fifteenth and sixteenth centuries largely disappeared during the next two hundred years. Much of this change was the result of the simultaneous disintegration of the Ottoman Empire as a whole. Starting late in the reign of Süleyman the Magnificent, the empire began a slow process of decay which affected all elements of the population. It started with decline at the top of the Ruling Class. Ottoman greatness had been secured by the successive reigns of ten powerful and capable sultans who achieved a judicious Ruling Class mixture of Turks and other Muslims with elements of the conquered non-Muslim peoples, who were for the most part recruited and trained through the *devşirme* system, which converted young Christians to Islam and brought them into the service of the Sultan in high positions in both the administration and the army. The great sultans of the fifteenth and sixteenth centuries balanced these two groups off so as to control and use both for the benefit of the state without abusing the people through misrule or excessive taxation. Insofar as the Ottoman Jews were concerned, this meant that whenever any member of the Ruling Class subjected them to misrule, or whenever Christian subjects tried to attack them with accusations of ritual murder, they were suppressed and punished, this providing them with the stability and security needed for successful undertakings in trade, industry and commerce, with the influential Jewish physicians and bankers at court making very certain that such cases were dealt with expeditiously and properly.

Starting late in Süleyman's reign in the middle of the sixteenth century, however, one of the two major groups in the Ottoman Ruling Class came to dominate the system, not the Turkish aristocracy, descendants of the Turkomans of eleventh-century Anatolia who had led during

109

the Ottomans' centuries of greatness but, rather, the *devşirme* men, Christian converts and their descendants, who had begun to contribute in a significant way only a century later. Starting with Grand Vezir Damad Ibrahim Pasha (1523–36) midway during *Kanuni* Süleyman's reign, the *devşirme* seized control of the system and drove the Turkish aristocracy out of the Ruling Class and back to the Anatolian estates inherited from their ancestors. Once the *devşirme* no longer had to face competition in the struggle for power in Istanbul, they were able to dominate the sultans and take over the administration and army for their own benefit. At the same time, however, they broke into competing political factions and assigned positions in the government not according to honesty or ability, as had been done previously by the great sultans, but simply according to which party the applicants belonged to and how much they were willing to pay as bribes in return. Sultans themselves now were chosen according to which group of *devşirme* men supported them and how powerful their mothers were in the Palace, which usually meant that the weakest and least capable princes came to power while those who had minds of their own were eliminated along the way.

Decline in the quality of sultans and their ability to curb misrule soon spread through the entire system. *Devşirme* men who gained positions of power as investments used them to recoup what they had paid and to add profits. Without the restraining hand of the Sultan and without the competition of the Turkish aristocracy, they could and did impose on the hapless subjects far more than the legal taxes, adding extra illegal impositions to such an extent that, as they went on year after year, these became *de facto* legal, while new means were found to levy additional extra-legal taxes and charges of all sorts. Frequent Janissary revolts and consequent rapid changes of Grand Vezirs and other high officials at the top were matched throughout the system, with each new official working to recoup his costs as rapidly as possible in the certain knowledge that he would soon be replaced by someone offering greater bribes in return.

With this sort of anarchy in the central government, the cycle of abuse spread throughout the Ottoman system, and provincial and district authorities abused their authority for personal profit. Whether Ottoman governors and their officials, who constantly invented new taxes and other charges, or Janissary garrisons led by their *aghas*, who periodically ravaged and raped, or the judges who were supposed to administer and enforce the Sultan's laws but often sold their decisions to the parties who paid the most, oppression was pervasive, with individual subjects securing only the limited protection which their own communities could provide, unless they had access to protection from outside the system, from European diplomats and consuls, who had special extraterritorial status due to the Capitulations privileges granted their governments during the course of the sixteenth century.

Venality and misrule on the part of members of the Ruling Class combined with the resulting chaos led to resentment and revolt on the part of an ever more burdened populace, Muslim and non-Muslim alike. Members of the Turkish aristocracy, forced out of the imperial service by the *devşirme* men, returned to their ancestral estates in Anatolia, where they took advantage of popular discontent to launch increasingly serious and widespread popular revolts against their rivals in Istanbul, depriving it of much of its control over the provinces and the tax revenues which were so important to Ottoman greatness.

In Southeastern Europe, depredations of the *devşirme* were multiplied by hundreds of local Christian robber bands, called *klephts, hayduks*, and the like, in modern times idealized as forerunners of modern national movements but in fact no more than brutal bandits seeking to gain their fortunes from their less powerful neighbors. In Anatolia the absence of strong central government led to the rise of bandits as well, to whom the general name *celali* was applied during the early years of the seventeenth century after the the name of the strongest of their number, driving out thousands of cultivators and town dwellers of all religions. In many places also rule was seized by local notables, called *derebeys*, who provided far more secure government in the areas of their control than the Ottoman government was able to do. In the Arab provinces, it was the *mamluk* slaves of the Ottoman governors and other officials who seized power in most places, leaving their masters as little more than puppets, and misruling and oppressing all their subjects, Muslim and non-Muslim alike.

Anarchy ruled everywhere. There was brigandage on land, not only along the public roads but even within towns. Janissary and other Ottoman garrisons stationed throughout the empire to enforce security spent most of their time adding to the disorder, raiding and ravaging at will in town and village alike and spreading fear and horror wherever they went. It became almost impossible to travel along the roads without being robbed. Merchants going to trade fairs as well as ordinary travelers and cultivators attempting to take their crops to market had to hire and arm their own guards to have even a chance of reaching their destinations. Jews were afflicted more than others because many of the attackers were either Christians or Christian converts in the Janissary corps and, in any case, it was general knowledge that only the Jews had an organized system of ransoming hostages.

Town and countryside alike were devastated. The great aqueducts which had brought water to Istanbul and the other cities since Roman times fell into ruins, leaving the urban populations with polluted water supplies at best. The vast forests which had existed in many parts of Thrace and Anatolia were cut down. Ancient tombs were robbed and their contents either destroyed or sent to the great museums of Europe.

Roads decayed.

As revenues coming to the central Treasury from the provinces declined in consequence of these uprisings and revolts, the government attempted to meet its financial obligations by debasing and depreciating the currency, calling in gold and silver coins and re-minting them with substantial additions of base metals, but this only drove good gold and silver coins from the marketplace and led to wild inflation and financial disorder, adding to all the pressures and difficulties.

In the face of misrule, not only by agents of the central government but also by those revolting against it, thousands of cultivators who were being turned into serfs without benefit from their labor fled from the lands, which soon dried up and fell out of cultivation, substantially reducing the amount of food available for the cities. Many formed robber bands of their own to secure sustenance from raiding the lands that remained under cultivation or by attacking caravans and villages and towns alike, with the cultivators and villagers having to organize their own protection since the security forces organized by the government were joining in the attacks. In consequence, even more cultivators fled into the cities in the hope of finding work and sustenance. Finding none, to a great extent because of the monopolistic labor restrictions and economic controls imposed by the craft guilds, they formed restless mobs ever ready to riot in the streets and attack, not only the officials of the Sultan, but anyone who showed the slightest indication of having money or food or both, leaving most cities in virtual anarchy and decay, with streets going uncleaned, sewage piling up, houses and shops falling into ruins, and people hardly daring to go into the streets, even to the marketplaces.

With cultivation falling drastically and with disrupted systems of transportation making it extremely difficult for the food that was still produced to find its way into the cities on a regular basis, severe shortages of food as well as all the other necessities of life resulted. All of this in turn led to great natural disasters, famine, plague, and great fires which often destroyed entire towns or large sections of the great cities, with the government doing little to alleviate either the causes or results. All the urban conglomerates of the empire in consequence turned into the anarchical collections of poverty-stricken inhabitants which were described by so many European travelers during the eighteenth century.

Ottoman cities and towns in the age of decline were extremely crowded. The buildings were often of several stories, with little light or ventilation, leaving putrid and fetid air, often very humid and dank. There was no running water or sewage facilities, and garbage and excrement deposited in the streets outside added to the stench. There usually were wells, but the water was badly polluted. The streets were filled with dogs and other animals which added to the filth. Stagnant lakes and ponds as well as pestilent swamps provided convenient sources of contagion. Merchant ships coming from far places to Salonica, Istanbul, Izmir and the other Ottoman ports often brought diseases with them from the Far East or Europe, since no sanitary service or quarantine existed to prevent their crews from entering the city without restriction. Hunger and famine, which were the natural results of the anarchy in the countryside, of course weakened the mass of the people and made them easy prey to the spreading infections. Illnesses such as the plague, typhus, scurvy, diphtheria, malaria, leprosy, and ringworm were therefore quite common, and often developed into mass epidemics because of ignorance of their causes as well as of the systematic quarantine measures needed to isolate those stricken and so prevent their spread. Common sense at times prevailed among those wealthy enough to do something about it, who at the first sign of the plague, would go into the provinces, or at least isolate themselves in their houses, though by sending their servants out to secure food and other supplies, they continued to expose themselves without realizing it. So epidemics were common, if not of one terrible disease then of another.

As byproducts of the political chaos and struggles between various armed forces along with the lack of municipal controls over building and a municipal fire-fighting system, moreover, the major urban communities also were decimated by large fires which, together with the spread of disease, effectively disrupted and destroyed what few areas of life that human hands had not left alone. In Istanbul alone between 1606 and 1698 there were 26 major fires which burned large portions of the city, often those inhabited by Jews. The great Istanbul fire that started on the night of 20 May 1606 largely destroyed the ancient Jewish center of coppersmiths near Bahçekapı, causing more than eleven thousand Jews in twenty congregations to move to Hasköy. A conflagration which destroyed the central *Bedestan* of the Covered Market in 1618 decimated the remaining Jewish quarters in the old city. Most of its inhabitants moved out along the Bosporus to Ortaköy, which now became one of the major Jewish centers for the first time, leading to the reconstruction of its synagogue. In the same year a massive fire in Galata caused many of its Jews to move across the Bosporus to the Anatolian suburbs of Üsküdar and Kadıköy, which became important Jewish centers. City wide fireworks celebrations following the birth of a crown prince the night of 7 August 1633 destroyed most of the Jewish quarters of Cibalı, whose inhabitants moved to Balat and Hasköy. Much of Balat in turn was destroyed by a fire which broke out at a candle factory (*mumhane*) just outside the Balat gate on the night of 30 August 1640. During the great Istanbul fire of 24 July 1660 which destroyed some 80,000 homes in old Istanbul and Galata, the *Giveret Yeshiva* constructed by Doña Gracia Mendes was destroyed along with thousands of Jewish homes and shops.

During the eighteenth century there were no less than sixty major fires in Istanbul alone. A fire near the Yeni Cami in 1715 caused hundreds of Jews to move to the Piri Pasha section of Hasköy. In 1729 a fire which began in the Greek quarter of Fener destroyed one-eighth of old Istanbul during a single day, including much of Balat. After the fire which destroyed much of Istanbul in 1740, Jews were permitted to construct new buildings and synagogues without permits in Galata, Ortaköy, and Üsküdar, to which they moved in such large numbers that in 1744 a new *ferman* was issued limiting this privilege. The Cibalı fire in 1756 destroyed more than eight hundred Jewish homes, whose inhabitants mostly moved to both sides of the Bosporus, particularly to Kuzguncuk on the Anatolian shores opposite Ortaköy. Numerous earthquakes, floods and other natural disasters similarly disturbed the settled population on numerous occasions, with the absence of governmental regulations and organization exacerbating the results.

Travel by sea was no safer than that by land. It was bad enough that most ships were small and poorly built, capsizing or sinking at the least provocation. But more than this was the constant threat of pirates and corsairs, particularly in the Aegean, through which passed all shipping between Istanbul, Salonica, Egypt and Syria, involving not only pilgrims but also shipments of grains, gold and slaves from Africa and the Near East. Many of the pirates were organized by Christian Crusading orders established specifically to attack the lands of Islam and to drive the Turks out of the Holy Land. Most feared of all were those maintained by the Knights of Malta, who terrorized ship and shore alike, killing, raping, ravaging and stealing without mercy, all in the name of Christian civilization. Other pirates were sent out by Venice, Austria and Russia during their wars with the Ottomans. There also were Spanish, Italian, Albanian, Greek, and Tunisian pirates, and even some Dutch and Scandinavian adventurers operating regularly in the Aegean and the Eastern Mediterranean. Muslim pirates came from Algeria and elsewhere in North Africa, with a few organized locally along the shores of the Aegean and Eastern Mediterranean. Sometimes these pirates took over entire islands and small cities, raping the women and holding the men for ransom or forcing those without means to secure payment to join them at sea. At times they even entered the major ports and sacked warehouses near the shores. Salonica was raided on the night of 25 November 1718, Chios in February 1742. Algerian pirates raided the Aegean coasts in 1747. Ships from Dalmatian Ragusa raided Salonica in 1756. Sea transportation became even more dangerous and uncertain in the last half of the eighteenth century, particularly during the wars between the Ottomans and Russia (1768–74, 1787–92) and the long wars between Napoleon and England. Even though the British navy joined that of the Ottomans in the fight to free the seas from such attacks, they achieved only limited success against the pirates.

It did not take long before the developing nation states of Europe became aware of the extent of Ottoman decay, once the constant Ottoman advances which had so alarmed Central Europe in the middle years of the sixteenth century came largely to an end following Süleyman's reign. European colonialism and imperialism were now in their first bloom. The Ottoman Empire and its subjects increasingly came under the economic domination of the great states of Europe which were able to take advantage of the Capitulations treaties, which were provided by the powerful sultans as concessions to the relatively small European merchant communities so as to enable them to live within their own quarters under their own laws as administered by their own consuls, very much like the different religiously-based communities of Ottoman subjects in their *millets*. These were now used to exploit the Empire and its non-Christian subjects by ignoring its laws and the authority of its officials. These concessions had been granted first in 1455, when Mehmed II, just two years after conquering Istanbul, recognized the autonomy of the Genoese and Venetian merchants living in Galata under conditions similar to the privileges they had received from the Byzantine emperors previous to the conquest, thus allowing them to form their own small autonomous communities, led by their consuls under overall Ottoman authority. The first formal Capitulations agreement had been signed in 1535 between Francis I of France and Süleyman the Magnificent as part of their military alliance against the Habsburg Emperor Charles V. By the terms of this treaty, the all-conquering Sultan extended the privileges previously given the Italian merchants to all subjects of the French king. French subjects, and as they were added, those of other nations, as well as their employees and local protegés, who were enabled to live under their own laws, as enforced by their own consuls, without being subject to Ottoman laws or officials in any way. These concessions included exemptions from most excise taxes and special lower rates for others, such as the customs duties charged, not only for trade in and out of the empire, but also for internal shipments of goods, normally three per-cent levies instead of the five per-cent charged Ottoman subjects, thus giving foreign traders substantial advantages over the latter.

France moreover was given the right to represent and control all other Europeans wishing to travel, live and trade in the Ottoman dominions, who thus were required to accept the protection of the French flag as well as the authority of the French consuls if they wished to enter the lands of the Sultan. These privileges were subsequently renewed and extended so that French agents were given the right to protect, not only persons directly subject to the King of France and other European monarchs, but also all Catholics, Catholic monasteries and monastic orders and other charitable organizations in the Ottoman Empire. This assured French predominance in the Levant even after Great Britain and

Holland received similar Capitulations concessions for their own subjects in 1583, with other nations following during the seventeenth century. In consequence of the resulting French predominance in the Levant, the Ottomans themselves referred to all Europeans, regardless of country, as *Franks*. The French language, culture and manners dominated all foreigners and many non-Muslim natives in Ottoman territories until modern times, and France's Mediterranean port, Marseilles, supplanted Venice, Malta and Livorno as Queen of the Eastern Seas and principal trading partner of the Ottomans.

By the seventeenth and eighteenth centuries, the Capitulations rights of each nation in Istanbul were watched over by their consuls. In other major Ottoman trading centers and ports, such as Salonica, Izmir, and Alexandria, they were handled during the seventeenth century by wealthy merchants, some even non-Muslim Ottoman subjects, sometimes by sea captains who wanted some sort of official appointment to maintain themselves in retirement. It was not long before the positions became so important and complicated, however, that by the eighteenth century consuls were appointed to handle these tasks and lead their communities there as well. In addition to making certain that the Capitulations privileges were observed by Ottoman officials, these consuls also acted as agents to facilitate the sale of cargoes arriving from their home ports as well as the dispatch of trans-shipped goods and Ottoman raw materials on returning ships. More and more also they began to arbitrate commercial differences among their subjects and sometimes to judge cases in which their own or Ottoman law had been violated. Most also carried on their own private business activities, with their official positions contributing significantly to their profits and wealth as well as those of their friends.

So long as the Ottoman government was strong enough to defend its own interests, and so long as few of the sultans' subjects were protected by the Capitulations, these Frankish colonies and their privileges had little impact on the empire. But as anarchy spread and the government weakened, the situation changed drastically. Those who benefited from the Capitulations became major exploiters of the Ottoman economy and people, and particularly of those who had profited most from Ottoman trade and commerce in the past, the sultans' Muslim and Jewish subjects. The same anarchical conditions which oppressed local merchants and traders also disrupted the activities of the European and native Christian merchants operating in the Empire. But they had a defense. Each of the consuls now formally organized their subjects into regular communities, whose privileges they protected with vigor. As the Ottoman government in desperation increased its taxes and customs levies, and as these were multiplied on all sides by dishonest officials, the European merchants and their consuls were able to successfully insist on maintenance of the official rates and exemptions for them, as specified in the Capitulations, and even on the refund by the government of excess payments and bribes collected by the malefactors. In consequence, foreign subjects now paid far less taxes than did their Ottoman counterparts, not only customs duties but all taxes. By living under extraterritorial conditions, entirely under their own laws, as loosely enforced by their consular leaders, they were able to evade the increasingly onerous laws and taxes imposed by the government of the Sultan and to ignore the authority of the local Ottoman governors and police. This situation enabled them to develop their businesses and prosper while largely driving their native competitors out of business, both in trade and industry, while the Ottoman Treasury not only was unable to receive most of the collections kept by its dishonest agents, but also was forced to make good on all excess collections taken from foreign merchants.

Nor was this all. When other European merchants began to comprehend what profits could be made, hundreds and even thousands entered Ottoman territory to take advantage of the situation, transforming what had been relatively small protected Frankish communities into major states within the state, which increasingly took over the Ottoman economy. In addition, as Ottoman subjects were driven out by the competition of their privileged European competitors, it did not take much encouragement for the more imaginative of them, for the most part Christians since most European consuls did not wish to deal with Jews or Muslims, to purchase European citizenship or to secure various forms of employment such as translators (*dragomans*), agents, or domestics. Starting in the early years of the eighteenth century this gave them the status of protegés and entitled them as well to Ottoman orders (*berats*) which gave them the protection and Capitulations privileges of their employers, including exemption from most Ottoman laws and taxes, with greedy consuls multiplying such positions and guarantees far beyond their needs in order to secure additional profits. As time went on a few Jews also were able to benefit from such foreign protection, particularly those coming from outside the Empire, most notably from the port of Livorno in Italy, but also some Ottoman Jews. Together the protected foreigners and their local protegés, called *beratlıs*, gathering around their churches and consulates, developed into large and wealthy colonies, living off the fat of the land, with huge houses and many servants, guarded by fierce Albanian *kavas* guards as well as by hired Janissaries, living lives of luxury and plenty, with vast entertainments, balls and parties. These constituted islands of plenty in the midst of misery, with those benefiting from the Capitulations looking down on the poor helpless native subjects of the Sultan – Muslim, Jew and Christian alike, who continued to live in increasing poverty, subjected to all sorts of abuses. Even among the *beratlıs*, there was a marked distinction between the real subjects of the great kings of Europe and their native protegés, with the latter considered at best to be second-class subjects, sharing much of the scorn felt by most Europeans for Jews and Muslims, with their only saving grace being their Christian religion, thus enabling them to at least share partly in scraps of the privileges which were fully reserved for those involved more completely in the benefits of European civilization.

At times foreign consuls also sold their protection to those who ravaged the most, sea pirates, bandits, and revolting Janissaries. As such, they acted more or less as 'fences', sending the booty for sale outside the Empire in return for a share, thus covering many of the abuses and scandals with their protection, with the Ottoman government far too weak and powerless to complain about such blatant misapplication of the original Capitulations agreements.

Under such conditions and in such chaos, one wonders why the Ottoman Empire did not break apart entirely. That it did not was due to two important factors. First of all, Europe was diverted by its own internal quarrels and wars, many of which involved disagreement on how the Ottoman spoils should be divided if the Empire was in fact conquered. It was only at the end of the seventeenth century, following the failure of the Ottomans' second effort to capture Vienna in 1683, that the Holy League moved to the attack, capturing important parts of Ottoman territory including Hungary, Serbia, Bosnia, Wallachia and Dalmatia, with the Janissaries and other Ottoman forces doing little more than moving to and from the fronts, ruthlessly imposing their care on friend and foe alike with little distinction, while only occasionally achieving success against the enemy. Even in such a situation, however, the Holy League push came to an end and the Ottoman Empire was allowed to survive because of continued conflicts elsewhere in Europe.

In addition, Ottoman leaders themselves began to recognize that something was wrong and to move to correct the situation before it was too late and the empire was lost. When foreign attacks and internal anarchy became too threatening the Ottomans mounted their own efforts at reform, not so much to modernize the system but, rather, to restore its basic administrative and military institutions to the manner in which they had operated successfully before the decline began, and with considerable success during the seventeenth century, at least to the extent that the immediate problems were alleviated, the anarchy and corruption brought to an end and the empire enabled to survive and continue. This 'traditionalistic reform' was modified and added to during the eighteenth century by efforts to introduce European military weapons and techniques, during the 'Tulip Period' (1718–30) and the reigns of sultans Abdül Hamid I (1774–89) and Selim III (1789–1807), though invariably as soon as the reformers achieved sufficient success to defeat the immediate dangers and preserve the empire a little longer, they were driven out of power and the old abuses were allowed to return.

THE EFFECTS OF DECLINE ON OTTOMAN JEWRY

While the Ottoman Empire survived during these years of anarchy, it is not surprising to learn that Ottoman Jewry suffered even more than other major communities because of added problems caused by the importation of Christian anti-Semitism back from Europe.

All sorts of conditions adversely affected Ottoman Jews. First of all, without the security and stability which had characterized the Empire in its age of greatness, it was inevitable that the trade, industry and commerce on which most of them depended for their livelihood should decline, with depreciation of the currency and inflation adding to the difficulties.

In addition, as the ability of the Ottoman sultans and Ruling Class to protect their subjects from misrule lessened, as rule fell into the hands of converted *devşirme* Christians who retained much of the anti-Semitism which dominated the lands of their origins, as Christian European diplomats and merchants came into the Empire to take advantage of its weakness for their own profit, as Catholic Marseilles replaced Venice and Livorno, in which many Jews at least shared trade opportunities, as the principal European port for the Levant trade, while Greek-dominated Izmir replaced Jewish-dominated Salonica in the East starting in the 1740s, and as the expansion of Christian rule into the Ukraine and Hungary after 1683 shut Ottoman merchants out of the rich markets which lay beyond them in Central and Eastern Europe, it was inevitable that the participation of Ottoman Jewry in international trade should largely cease, while the same anti-Semitic prejudice which had driven so many Jews out of western Europe gained increasing influence within the empire.

Devşirme men and European diplomats and merchants actively worked to drive Jews out of positions of importance in the Ottoman palace and to replace them with native Christians, both Armenians and Greeks. In many cases they simply told the sultans and their officials that they would not deal with Jews as interpreters or agents, forcing the Ottomans to hire Christians if they wanted to negotiate on diplomatic, political or economic matters. Greeks and Armenians as a result mostly replaced Jews as the dominant advisers and bankers to the Ottoman court, though at times Jews continued to act on diplomatic missions for the Sultans, Dr Israel Konegliano, physician to Grand Vezir Kara Mustafa Pasha, acting as adviser in the negotiations which led to the Treaty of Karlowitz in 1699, and Moise ben Judah Beberi being assigned by Grand Vezir Köprülü

Mehmed Pasha to discuss an alliance against Russia with agents sent
to Istanbul by the Swedish king Charles XII. Jews also continued to
serve as physicians at court during much of the century, occasionally
intervening in support of Jewish communities elsewhere in the empire,
though with nowhere the influence that they had in the Golden Age
due to the competition of Armenian and Greek physicians who were
supported by their European protectors.

Jewish merchants now often were not allowed to import or export
goods, as the Europeans used the Capitulations agreements signed
between their nations and the Ottoman government to favor the
local Christians, who were thereby given legal, financial and trade
privileges and tax exemptions not available to their Jewish counterparts.

The *devşirme* men in control of the Istanbul government, moreover,
in active cooperation with the Janissary infantry, most of whom were
themselves converted Christians who continued to nourish hatred for
Jews, directed the misrule, overtaxation, and robbery and ravaging of
homes and shops against Jews and Muslims more than the Christian
elements of the population, particularly since the latter were able to
rely on the protection of the European diplomats and consuls against
the worst abuses, while the Jews and Muslims had no outside protectors.
Janissary attacks against Jews had begun shortly after the Ottoman
conquest of Egypt as soon as Sultan Selim had gone back to Istanbul
and left control of the province in the hands of Mamluk leaders who
had professed loyalty to him and to the Ottoman way, only to revolt
against him as soon as he returned to Anatolia. These attacks spread
throughout the empire and became far worse once the Sultans were
too weak to control them altogether. In the seventeenth century, thus,
Jews often were subjected to the *corvée*, or forced labor, on roads as well
as farms owned by members of the Janissary corps. Jewish corporations
were charged double the fees demanded of Christian corporations, which
themselves were excessive. Agents of the Treasury collected far more
than the official taxes from Jews. Special war taxes, moreover, were
charged on businessmen and merchants as well as wealthy householders
whenever the army marched through or even near various cities and
towns. At the accession of each new Sultan, whether the result of a
revolt by the Janissaries or natural causes, each community had to
pay him an accession tax, contribute to the 'gift' which he customarily
gave to the Janissary garrison of Istanbul in return for allowing him
to ascend the throne, and then also provide substantial 'gifts' to the
local Janissary garrisons in the European provinces and to the *mamluks*
who supplanted their Ottoman masters in most of the Arab provinces,
particularly in Egypt and Iraq. Sometimes even this failed to protect
them.

The pillaging of Jewish homes and shops in particular went on everywhere, by the Janissaries throughout the empire along with local Christian bands in Macedonia and Thrace and converted Christian *mamluks* in the Arab provinces leading the way and with the Sultan having little power or ability to protect anyone. Everyone suffered, but the Jews and Muslims suffered far more, particularly in the Sultan's European provinces where Christian subjects joined in the attacks.

Attacks on Jews directly paralleled the decline of central Ottoman control and the rise of provincial and local rebels against the Sultan. In Cairo as the *mamluk* slaves of Ottoman officials assumed control over the latter, most Jews moved into the Citadel itself, building their houses and synagogues within the shelter of its high walls in order to avoid the depredations of the *mamluk* gangs that ravaged throughout the city. At times, when peace seemed to be returning to the capital, they left the Citadel and began to once again live in the town, but these periods of peace were short and for the most part they continued to stay close to what protection it could offer until direct Ottoman rule was ended by the arrival of Bonaparte's expedition to Egypt in 1798. Not only were Egyptian Jews subject to attacks by the *mamluks*, but since Jews remained as tax collectors, it was natural for the local population to blame them for the ever-increasing *mamluk* depredations, often as a result of stories spread by local Christians in order to divert Muslim attention from them. Jewish merchants continued to prosper despite the increasing anarchy, due to their business acumen and energy. There was increasing jealousy and resentment against them by the mass of Egyptians, which in turn made them easy prey to extortion and misrule by the same officials whose misconduct was causing the problems in the first place. The *mamluk* rebel, Ali Bey ul-Kebir, who established almost complete independence from the Sultan at the end of the eighteenth century, ordered Egyptian Jews and Christians to change the names of their prophets as well as to free all their slaves, cancelling the orders only after large bribes were paid.

In Palestine and Syria, particularly at Sidon and Damascus, Jews continued to prosper as artisans, merchants and traders until well into the eighteenth century, often in collaboration and with the help of the French merchants who were flooding into Syria at the time, with the Asseo and Farhi families in particular dominating. This prosperity came to an end with the rise of local *mamluk* despots, such as Zahir ul-Umar and later Ahmed Jezzar Pasha based at Acre, who not only attacked and ravaged local Jews as part of their revolt against local Ottoman officials, but also forcefully shifted Syrian imports and exports from Sidon to Acre. The combination of ravaging and impoverishment caused the rapid decline of Sidon Jewry, with the final blow administered by the devastating plague of 1759–60, which left only ten Jews remaining in the city. The remainder immigrated to Mount Lebanon and Beirut, which under Emir Bashir II

(1788–1840) flourished with the active participation of a revived Jewish community.

Back in Southeastern Europe, in July 1703 the Janissary rebellion which dethroned Sultan Mustafa II in Istanbul was followed by large-scale sacking of Salonica's Jewish quarter by the Janissary garrison as well as the local Greek population. After the death of Osman III in October 1757, Jews as well as Greeks and Muslims were the objects of exactions on the part of the military garrisons in most Ottoman cities and towns in Europe. It is an oddity of history that, for the most part, the same Janissaries who gained much of their wealth by pillaging Jews in particular disposed of their ill-gotten gains and, when they invested their wealth in lands and tax farms, worked their holdings and collected their taxes through Jewish agents for the most part.

All the wars that the Ottomans had to fight with Russia, Austria and other enemies during the eighteenth century, whether successful or unsuccessful, were paid for by the levy of new and higher taxes on those still able to pay, as well as by the various illegal taxes which continued to be collected. Süleyman III (1687–91) charged an extra high war tax to pay for the costs of the war with Venice then in progress. After Venice seized the Morea in April 1715, Grand Vezir Damad Ali Pasha brought an army of 120,000 men as well as a powerful fleet to Salonica, remaining there for a month in preparation for the campaign to regain the lost territories. Even though cultivation that year had been very limited due to lack of sufficient rainfall as well as the usual anarchy and food was in very short supply, he confiscated almost all the food and money that could be found, leaving the inhabitants even worse off than usual. On his return from the Morea, the Janissaries sacked Salonica's Jewish quarter once again, adding to the booty which they had secured from the Venetians. In 1721 the Janissary garrison of Salonica revolted against the governor because their salary had not been paid in time. Once again their ravaging soon spread into the Jewish quarter, pillaging, burning and demolishing houses and shops and mercilessly killing all those who tried to resist. Again in the spring of 1727 the Ottoman forces gathered in Salonica to resist an Albanian revolt in eastern Macedonia imposed their keep on the Jewish quarter, seizing goods and massacring people without mercy during April and May. Even after the Albanian revolt was put down the troops returned to the attack while passing through Salonica on their way home, causing unusually terrible suffering and deaths throughout 1728. The Patrona Halil revolt which ended the modernizing 'Tulip Period' in Istanbul in 1730 was followed by new Janissary exactions and massacres of Jews in Istanbul, Salonica, Izmir, and Bursa as well as throughout Macedonia. There were numerous appeals for protection to the Sultan and the Imperial Council, and the attacks relented for a time, perhaps less because of imperial action than the fact that there were no wars during and the Imperial Council, and the attacks relented for a time, perhaps less because of imperial action than the fact that there were no wars during these years and, thus, no occasion to bring the army together and send it on its destructive campaigns. On 30 July 1752, however, the Janissaries again revolted in Salonica and sacked the Jewish quarter in reaction to an earthquake, with neither their own officers or the local governor able to stop them. Similar attacks took place in 1758 and 1763. In 1770 after the Russian fleet commanded by Admiral Orlov sailed from the Baltic through the Mediterranean into the Aegean and armed Greek rebels, the latter preceded to massacre large numbers of Turks and Jews in southern Greece and the Morea, and then went on to massacre the same peoples on many of the Aegean islands. In revenge the Janissaries in Salonica rose up and massacred not only Greeks but also local Jews. In the summer of 1774 one of Admiral Orlov's Russian squadrons captured an Ottoman ship carrying a number of wealthy Jews, freeing one of their number in the expectation that he would be able to deliver substantial ransoms for the remainder from Salonica. After he failed to return in time with the ransom money, however, the Russian sailors put the remaining Jews to the sword. After the Muslims of Salonica revolted against the central government in 1808, the Janissaries put down the revolt and then charged local Greek and Jewish merchants huge extra taxes to meet their expenses and leave a substantial profit.

Added to the internal pressures throughout the Empire were changing patterns of Jewish immigration into the Ottoman Empire, which, evidently, was nowhere as inviting as it had been two centuries earlier. No longer did the continued flow of *marranos* fleeing from Spain come to Salonica and Istanbul. Not that the Jewish converts to Catholicism who had remained on the Iberian Peninsula had ceased to be persecuted by the Inquisition despite their conversion. Its interrogations and persecutions continued and in fact intensified early in the seventeenth century, leading to their final expulsion starting in 1609 from Spain and 1612 from Portugal. But it was no longer to the Ottoman dominions that most of them fled. Now they were finding refuge in western Europe, at Amsterdam and Antwerp, where they developed an important diamond industry, at Venice, Ferrara, and Livorno in Italy, and at Marseilles and Bordeaux in southern France, where they were building the same sort of international trading businesses that earlier Iberian immigrants had established at Salonica and Istanbul, with the resulting competition seriously effecting their Ottoman co-religionists just at the time when conditions in the empire were making business more difficult than ever. Some *marranos* from Spain and Italy did find their way into the Ottoman Empire during the late seventeenth and eighteenth centuries, but these had been Christians for several generations, and they were so far removed from the Jewish communities into which they entered that their arrival only added to the internal disputes and divisions, instead of mixing into and strengthening the community as had their ancestors a century earlier, making the Jewish response to Ottoman anarchy that much weaker.

Other Jewish refugees continued to enter the Ottoman Empire during the seventeenth century, but these were for the most part the far less cultured and economically developed Ashkenazi Jews of central and eastern Europe fleeing from Hungary as a result of persecution following Hungarian revolts against the Ottomans in 1617, from Poland and the Ukraine as the result of the savage torture, robbing and massacres of Jews during the Cossack and peasant uprisings led by Bogdan Chmielnicki (1595–1657) in 1648–1649, and from continued ritual murder massacres and persecutions throughout France and Central Europe. These immigrants mostly settled at Sofia, Stara Zagora and Kazanlık in Bulgaria and, because of Salonica's decline, at Izmir, on southwestern Aegean shores of Anatolia. They were not the well educated and industrious Sephardic immigrants of the fifteenth and sixteenth centuries. Instead they were quite backward and withdrawn, coming from long centuries of persecution and isolation in ghettos, so instead of promoting the economic prosperity of the Ottoman Empire and its Jewish community by developing their own enterprises, they instead for the most part depended on the generosity of the older Jewish communities, adding to their burdens.

Jewish communities throughout the Empire fell into serious debt as a result of these new conditions. Economic chaos reduced the value of the capital possessions and businesses of most of their members, considerably lessening the *aritha* tax revenues just as the communities were obliged to undertake new burdens, particularly caring for the increasing number of poor members and refugees, ransoming those kidnapped by bandits, pirates and others, and paying the collective poll-tax obligation to the central treasury, which remained the same regardless of the lessening incomes of its members. In Salonica, moreover, the *dönme* apostasy to Islam in the late seventeenth century cost its community a large amount of revenue, particularly since many came from old-established members of the community in addition to those who had come to the city with Shabbatai Tzvi. Added to its difficulties, finally, was the so-called 'clothing tax', by which the Jewish community of Salonica collectively agreed to provide a fixed amount of cloth each year to the Janissary corps, with inflation of the currency making the cloths so valuable after the seventeenth century that the community almost went bankrupt until the establishment of a centralized organization of the weaving industry made possible some alleviation of the burden.

As deficits mounted, and to fulfill current community obligations, Jewish community leaders throughout the empire tried to sell the sacred objects and tapestries in their synagogues, particularly those embroidered in gold and silver, but the rabbis usually refused permission for them to do so, so in desperation wealthy members were forced to make special contributions by sacrificing their own jewels and other valuables. Even this was not enough in most cases, however, so members who still had wealth were subjected to special emergency taxes, far beyond those normally charged, at times amounting to virtual confiscation, with all the penalties at the disposal of community leaders being applied in full to secure obedience. Efforts also were made to end tax exemptions traditionally given to rabbis, physicians and synagogue servants, but they absolutely refused to pay, declaring that God had given them the exemptions and excommunicating all those who violated their rights, even refusing admission to the synagogues to those who dared to try to tax them. In the end, the men of religion continued to be exempted from taxation, leading the rich at times to react by refusing to pay even their regular *aritha* obligations, and leaving the communities virtually bankrupt.

Efforts then were made to apply community taxes to resident Jewish foreigners, particularly to Ottoman subjects who had taken up foreign citizenship or who accepted employment in the foreign embassies and consulates to benefit from the Capitulations, thus removing themselves from the authority and tax obligations both of the Ottoman government and of their own communities. In 1690 Grand Vezir Mustafa Köprülü, soon after the disastrous retreat from the second Ottoman failure to take Vienna and the Holy League capture of Hungary, ordered that foreigners living in the Ottoman Empire and devoting themselves to profitable employment should pay taxes, but the foreign consuls absolutely refused to allow such taxation, relying on their Capitulations rights. Ultimately they prevailed, now going into business on a large scale and deriving substantial profits from selling paper citizenships and employments to Ottoman subjects, thus damaging even more the *millet* treasuries as well as that of the Sultan. A few Jews who had taken up French citizenship tried to mollify the Jewish communities of Salonica and Istanbul by making voluntary payments to help their charitable activities at least, but in view of the mounting deficits these irregular payments were far too little to make any significant difference, and the community treasuries fell further into debt. The poll tax obligation to the government had to be paid before everything else, and by 1740 it absorbed almost all the revenues still coming to the communities, leaving almost nothing for the regular community services. As a result, schools, orphanages, and hospitals closed or operated on such reduced budgets that the poor were unable to secure any appreciable benefit from them.

In the middle of the eighteenth century, new efforts were made to meet community needs by levying a special one percent annual capital tax in addition to the normal amounts. The Janissaries were hired to punish those who failed to pay their taxes, but they usually deducted a substantial portion of their collections for their own profit, even farming out various community taxes to tax farmers who used far more ruthless means to make their collections and secure their profits than the community itself had ever dared to do. The butchers then began to collect heavy *gabelle* taxes for the community from sales of meat, the wine sellers from wine, and the grocers from other foods, with the poor suffering the most since the tax remained the same regardless of income. Even then revenues were not sufficient, but the communities survived, largely because of free-will gifts by wealthy individuals who, in the end, respected their obligation to the community and to God by providing for those less fortunate than themselves, and also because the poor did not complain appreciably, though the community's services for them became less and less, because of fear of excommunication.

Ottoman Jews suffered along with other members of society in many other ways during the years of decline. As part of the traditionalistic efforts to restore the institutions and practices of the past, the reforming Sultans and their ministers attempted to apply the old restrictions to all the *millet*s, including the Jews, who had been relieved of most of them and placed on a higher plane than other *zimmis* since the time of Mehmed II, reviving the old clothing and building regulations and enforcing them far more strictly than ever had been the case in the past, though here at least the Jews were not particularly singled out, since these regulations applied to all groups. In 1702, in reaction against the disastrous wars against the Holy League and the forced signature of the Treaty of Karlowitz (1699), the Grand Vezir prohibited Christians and Jews from wearing yellow shoes and red headgear, demanding that they wear only black. In desperate efforts to appease the Istanbul mobs who were reacting violently against the lavish parties, gardens and palaces and other excesses which characterized the so-called 'reforms' of the Tulip Period (1718–30), Sultan Ahmed III in 1726 restored the regulation that the height of Jewish houses should be limited to six meters, as opposed to the eight meters allowed to Muslims; and in April 1730, shortly before his deposition by the mobs, he prohibited Jews from wearing the turbans which were supposed to be limited to Muslims, decreeing that they should once again wear the old conical hats (*külak*). As part of the reaction that followed Ahmed III's deposition and the end of the Tulip Period in 1730, his successor Mahmud I ordered an end to the import and sale of wines by Jews as part of his effort to limit their use to foreign embassies, though soon afterwards, in response to Jewish complaints, in January 1733 he permitted Jews to import and use a certain amount of wine for religious ceremonial purposes. And Sultan Mustafa III in 1758 decreed that Jews and Christians should not wear any garments which resembled those of Muslims, limiting them to blue or dark-colored textiles and *kalpak* head coverings, restricting their use of furs, and prohibiting their riding of horses without special permission. These efforts, moreover, had little effect, since as always the prohibition (*yasak*) in fact signified no more than the need to pay a fee to secure permission, which was invariably granted. They did not last too long, moreover, since as soon as the immediate dangers which had caused them had passed, the old abuses returned along with abandonment of all efforts to apply the traditional restrictions.

Far more serious for Ottoman Jewry was the effect of European military victories and conquests of Ottoman possessions. Starting with the Austrian conquest of Hungary after 1683, whenever a piece of Ottoman territory was occupied by European armies, invariably their first act was to join the local Christian population in massacring or driving out its Jewish population and seizing its property. Christian subjects of the Sultan, moreover, were thus encouraged to imitate their European brothers, and the ritual murder attacks, particularly by Greeks, Armenians and Bulgars, which had largely ceased as the Jews had fallen into poverty during the seventeenth century, resumed early in the eighteenth. As a result of all these problems, then, a Jewish community which reached a peak of some 200,000 people by the end of the sixteenth century, fell by more than half during the next two hundred years as part of a general decline of Ottoman population.

In reaction to increasing internal anarchy, misrule, oppression, financial difficulties and economic depression, members of the Ottoman Jewish community reacted in several ways. The most important result of all was that they began to unite. The first generation of immigrants, who had vigorously preserved the customs and traditions of the lands from which they came, died out and were replaced by new generations born in the empire of the Sultans, who had much less connection with the land of their ancestors and, thus, with their rivalries. At the same time, as Sephardic cultural and religious domination was achieved, with the common use of Judeo-Spanish, the Spanish brought by the Jewish exiles mixed with Ottoman Turkish, Hebrew and French to form the living language of all members of the Ottoman Jewish community regardless of origins,[1] and as all groups accepted the compromise rituals specified in the *Shulhan Arukh* of Joseph Caro, it became inevitable that the once fiercely isolated synagogues and *kahals* should accept central community leadership far more extensively than in the previous century. In Istanbul, Edirne, Jerusalem and other cities, the communities accepted the authority of chief rabbis (*hahambaşı*), with the central councils gaining considerably more authority over all than they had in the past. In Salonica a whole series of desperate crises, including a disastrous fire in 1620, increased fiscal oppression by Ottoman officials, the need of organizing a monopoly over the manufacture of military cloths to meet the Janissary demands, and the deep divisions created by the Sabbatean crises between

1657 and 1666, led the Federal Council to create a Triumvirate of rabbis. It acted as a central Directorate, a communal government led by one of its members as *Rav ha-Kolel*, which ruled the community with an iron hand, restoring order and stability and securing at least a partial restoration of foreign trade, with the leaders of the *kahals* and synagogues as well as the various interest groups voluntarily abdicating most of their powers in the face of the community crisis so as to avoid anarchy and ruin, and the French consul provided needed protection from the worst effects of anarchy. The synagogues continued to run their internal affairs with intense individuality and vitality, acting not merely as places of worship but also as social, educational and cultural centers, each with its own distinct customs, traditions, legends and secular festivals, and often with its own nickname. The Aragon synagogue of Salonica, for example, where the Gattegno family dominated, was called *Kal del Gato* (the cat); the Evora was called *Kal del Arroz* (rice); that of Provence was *Kal de Proves* (poor people), the Ashkenazi synagogue, founded by refugees from Russia, was *Kal de la Mosca*; the *Etz ha-Haim*, where the Agi family dominated, became *Kal del Ajo*, that of Pulia became *Kal del Macarron*, the Mallorca synagogue was called *Kal de los Ladrones* (thieves), and so forth. Now, however, all were placed under the strict supervision of the Federal Council to prevent the deep divisions which had arisen so often in the past, and with the individual *bet din* courts being superseded by a community court. For the most part, then, unity was achieved, with the minorities accepting majority decisions, but at times bitter internal struggles continued to break out, with one side bringing in the authorities to suppress the other, thus resuming the turbulence and usually bringing new forms of oppression on the community as a whole.

In Izmir it was Chief Rabbi Joseph Escapa who brought community administration together in the early years of the seventeenth century in response, not only to anarchy, but also to the arrival of large numbers of Jewish refugees from even greater crises in Salonica as well as persecution in western and central Europe. Escapa created a united communal admin-istration which survived with little change into the twentieth century. It was composed of two councils, the religious council (*bet din*), composed of five rabbis headed by the Chief Rabbi, who chose a sub-committee to direct religious education, and the lay council composed of the twelve (later seven) annually elected *memunim* (also called *truvé ha-ir*) who actually administered the community under his direction, with their most important duties being involved with finance, assessing and collecting community income taxes (*aritha*) and the *gabelle* excise tax on meat and wine, making expenditures, and drawing up annual budgets for the approval of the Chief Rabbi.

Those Jews in Istanbul who were wealthy enough emulated their co-religionists in Cairo in seeking protection both from attacks and conflagrations by living among powerful and wealthy Muslim Ottoman officials who had the means to protect themselves and those around them. Jews tended more and more to move away from the old city beneath the walls of the Topkapı Palace due not only to a series of fires and earthquakes during the first half of the seventeenth century, but also to the construction between 1597 and 1660 of the Yeni Cami in the middle of the old Jewish quarters at Eminönü by order of Mehmed III's wife Safiye Sultan, causing so many Jewish buildings to be destroyed that, at the time, the mosque was known by the community as the *zülmiye*, or 'tyrannical' building. For the most part, the displaced Sephardic and Romaniote Jews moved along both sides of the Golden Horn to the old settlements at Hasköy, on the Golden Horn, where Evliya Çelebi at the end of the seventeenth century found about three thousand luxury houses, with gardens full of oranges and lemons, and with Jews dominating in all but one of the quarters, the only part of Istanbul where Jews were in an absolute majority. They also moved out the Bosporus to Ortaköy and Arnavutköy, where many wealthy Jews had *yalıs* on the shore side by side with Muslim notables, and where, according to Evliya, they felt secure enough to fully display their wealth with no effort to hide it from the public. On the Asiatic side of the Bosporus they moved to Kuzguncuk, Üsküdar and Kadıköy, while the Karaite Jews, in order to keep to themselves, moved first to Hasköy and then, because of their desire to avoid contact with other Jews, to the ends of the Golden Horn, carefully stationing themselves between Balat and Hasköy, for the most part at Kâğıthane. At the same time, destruction of the old quarters forced the Jews who had emigrated from Italy and initially established their own synagogues as *Pulia, Messina, Kalabra, Sicilia, Italia* and the like, to live among the Spanish Jews and so to become an integral part of the Sephardic communities. In all these areas, however, the mass of Jews, sharing the poverty of their Muslim brothers, were crowded into poorly built tenement buildings called *yahudhânes* (Jewish houses), whose lack of fresh air and running water and primitive sewage arrangements facilitated the rapid spread of all shorts of diseases and illnesses which further debilitated their inhabitants and made it that much more difficult for them to participate actively in the economic life of the time.

Some Ottoman Jews reacted to the misrule and anarchy, and in particular to the increase of Christian blood-libel attacks and the depredations of Janissaries and robber bands, by abandoning their original settlements at Salonica, Edirne and other places in Southeastern Europe where these difficulties were most severe, as well as Bursa and Manisa in Anatolia, going to areas less subject to the prevailing anarchy, either to Istanbul or to the increasingly important Aegean port of Izmir, which became a major center of Jewish life at this time. Izmir had no Jews at all when the Ottomans conquered it because massacres and persecutions in Byzantine times had entirely removed the Jews who had come there in Roman times, but it became a major Jewish center at the end of the seventeenth century. The first mention of a Jewish community in Izmir comes in 1604–20, when a series of fires and attacks in Salonica caused many Jews to move across the Aegean. By 1631 there were 7,000 Jews, and by 1675 there were 15,000, though Greeks continued to dominate the economy, doing all they could to prevent the Jews from achieving the success they had reached elsewhere, and accomplishing this to a great extent with the help of the Christian merchants from its principal trading partner, Marseilles. By this time, however, there were several synagogues and communities in Izmir, the *Etz ha-Haim, Portugal* (used later in the century by Shabbatai Tzvi), and *Gerush* founded by emigrants from Salonica and headed by Rabbi Joseph Escapa, a Castillian who died in 1662 at the age of 93. Three more synagogues were founded by emigrants from Istanbul and Southeastern Europe and headed by an Istanbul Rabbi, Isaac ben Meir Levi, replaced after his death by the Salonica Rabbi Azarya Yeshua Ashkenazi. It was not long before a controversy broke out between Escapa and Ashkenazi over liturgical differences, causing the community to split into two factions soon after it was formed. After Ashkenazi died in 1648, however, both factions accepted Escapa's leadership and the division came to an end, with Escapa establishing regular community councils and taxes for the first time. Other communities subsequently established were the *Mahazike Torah, Shalom* (also called *Kal de Abasho*), and the *Talmud Torah*. Several synagogues built in Izmir later in the century took the names of their founding families, the *Pinto, Bakısh*, and *Galante*, the latter founded by Rabbi Moise Galante, who declared Shabbatai Tzvi to be the real Messiah and took the lead in spreading his doctrine throughout the empire. The Jewish community of Izmir remained deeply divided between these two groups until a twenty-six man *Bet Din* was created with members elected according to a complicated formula to assure that all congregations and economic groups were represented.

Izmir Jewry generally prospered during the seventeenth century, engaging in the production of textiles, silk, cloths, carpets, candles, figs, grapes and wine, and trading not only with other parts of the Empire but also through the Aegean and Mediterranean to Africa and the Far East. Jews in Izmir also engaged in banking, money changing, brokerage and translation work for the many foreign merchants and consuls in the city, though in this they faced severe competition from the local Greeks, who previously had dominated. The Jewish quarter of Izmir developed around two major commercial streets, *Mezarlıkbaşı*, and *Havra Sokağı*, located in between the Armenian (Basmane) and Muslim (Namazgâh, Keçeciler, Başturak, and Ikiçeşmelik) quarters. The physical limitations of these quarters, however, caused a great deal of crowding, with two or three families living in each *yahudhâne* and the families therefore spilling out into the streets during the summer months. Most of the more prosperous Jews, therefore, moved into the suburbs, concentrating in the Karataş quarter near the Jewish cemetery and in the Alsancak quarter as time went on.

Jewish cultural activity flourished in Izmir under the leadership of rabbis Aaron Lapapa, Salamon Algazi and Chief Rabbi Haim Benveniste, and many schools and *yeshivas* were built during the seventeenth century. Hebrew printing presses were established there in 1658 by Abraham ben Yididya Gabay, who first printed Escapa's *Rosh Yosef,* and also two Judeo-Spanish books, Menashe ben Israel's *Esperanza de Yisrael,* and Eduardo Nicholas's *Apologia para la noble nacion de los cudios,* the latter translated from English by R. Menashe.

Despite this progress, Izmir Jews still also were assaulted by many of the same problems that afflicted Jews elsewhere in the Empire. Local Greeks and Armenians bitterly resented their presence, let alone their success, and constantly harassed them with the assistance of European consuls. There were numerous fires and many earthquakes. Plagues were endemic, particularly since the city was a major port without any organized system of quarantine and the Jewish quarters were overcrowded. In 1616 the plague swept the city for three months, forcing many Jews to move out to the new *Güzel Hisar* quarter, which was relatively free of the disease. Another plague epidemic in 1663 caused most Izmir Jews, including Chief Rabbi Haim Benveniste, to move their homes to the *Pınarbaşı* suburb, though this was resisted by the Greeks, who wanted to settle there themselves. A violent earthquake and numerous after-shocks which hit the city for four months during the summer of 1688 destroyed three-quarters of the city's buildings, with more than four hundred Jews killed by the initial shocks, including the Chief Rabbi Aaron ben Haim, and many more losing their lives out of the 15,000 who were killed in all.

Mysticism, the Kabbalah, and Shabbatai Tzvi. Economic decline and political anarchy stifled much of the intellectual curiosity of the past and ended contacts between most Ottoman Jews and those outside the Empire. Europe now was beginning to enter onto the path of rationalism and enlightenment, but Ottoman Judaism remained dominated by religion. While the Jews of Germany and France emancipated themselves under the influence of Mendelsohn and the *Encyclopédie,* the overpowering and depressing combination of Ottoman disintegration and abuses, violent community strife, economic decline and poverty, and the domination of life by rabbinical authorities led most Ottoman Jews to withdraw away from active participation in society altogether. The schools which had long perpetuated the culture and progressive thought brought from Spain declined and for the most part closed. Ignorance and superstition replaced knowledge and thought.

Prayer and religious contemplation absorbed all of life and left no place for more secular activities. The innumerable religious prescriptions for food, dress, hygiene and social activity determined all family, economic and moral considerations, leaving no opportunity for change to meet the needs of the time. Pietism dominated mind and body alike. Obscurantism prevailed, while Rabbinical tradition itself was deformed under the mantle of *Kabbalah* mysticism. The *Zohar* of the Kabbalists replaced the Talmud and dominated life automatically and autocratically, without discussion, commentary, or understanding. People spent all their time in the *yeshivas*, no longer studying and discussing problems but memorizing and repeating the *Zohar*, whose every word dominated their lives. Kabbalistic symbolism determined all acts of daily life, morality, sexual and hygienic behavior, housing, clothing, food, education, the shape and length of hair and beards, the furniture used in houses, all that had once been influenced by the Talmud.

The Shamanism of the ancient nomadic tribes now greatly influenced Jewish society. The world was considered to be full of demons, phantoms and spirits which had to be satisfied. Superstition replaced science. Amulets, charms, and magical *Kabbalah* formulas were used to heal wounds and remedy illnesses and became panaceas for every problem. And while all of this went on all work was suspended. All the once-bustling Jewish shops, factories and counting houses in the great cities of the empire were closed for hours and sometimes days on end while their occupants busied themselves with religion. Every act came to be determined by the stars. When plagues and fires spread, Jews prayed to God to produce instant miracles to stop them, fervently blaming God when he did not, praying to Saints in his place, for all practical purposes making Judaism polythesic instead of monotheistic.

This tendency was manifested most vividly in the development of the Kabbalistic Messianic movement inspired by Shabbatai Tzvi (1625–76), also called Shabbatai Sevi, who claimed to be the Messiah sent by God to prepare his Chosen People for the imminent coming of the last day and of the Redemption, which he predicted would take place in the year 1666. Born in Izmir in 1626 during the reign of Murad IV, to Ashkenazi parents that had emigrated from the Morea along with most of their village due to frequent attacks by their Greek neighbors, he was the youngest of the three sons of Mordechai Tzvi, called Kara Menteş, who from origins as a dealer in chickens became a commissioner and agent for the Dutch and British merchants then thronging into Izmir to take advantage of Ottoman weakness in the early years of the seventeenth century. Young Shabbatai pursued traditional Jewish legal studies at first under the direction of Joseph Escapa, concentrating on the works of Lurianic Kabbalism with such precocity, memorizing both the Torah and the Talmud and mastering the *Zohar*, that even in his teens he was said to be 'teaching instead of being taught'. Ascetic from an early age, he married young according to the Jewish custom of the time but remained distant from his wife in order to preserve his purity, divorcing her after a time and marrying again, though maintaining the same relations with his second wife as he had with his first.

It was in reaction to the news of the Chmielnitski massacres of Jews in the Ukraine and Poland in 1648 that he began to go out into the streets, proclaiming to his fellow Jews that he was the Messiah who had been sent by God to recall his people from exile. In this, however, he clashed with the local *millet* leaders, including his teacher Joseph Escapa, who in 1654 forced him to leave because of his disturbing influence on the community. He first travelled to his family's original home in Greece, reacting to hostile receptions by moving north into Macedonia. He attempted to settle among the Kabbalists in Salonica, declaring that he would never marry a woman because he was already married to the Torah, only to be expelled after nine months by the Jewish Federal Council due to the divisions he was causing within a community which, as we have seen, was suffering from all sorts of economic and social problems compounded by the old sectarian divisions. After wandering through the empire propagating his beliefs and securing followers, he returned to his father's home in Izmir where he spent several years in a deep state of melancholy and depression.

In 1662 he went to Rhodes, and for a time he settled in Egypt, gaining the support of the Cairo Jewish leader Rafael Joseph Çelebi. In 1662 he made his first visit to Jerusalem, gaining new confidence by visiting the holy places and synagogues with which he was so familiar by reputation, securing many supporters among the poor whom he encountered in the streets. In 1663 he returned to Cairo, where with the support of Joseph Çelebi he secured a wide following as well as substantial funds for further prosyletization and development of what now was becoming a major movement. It was at this time that he heard of a Polish woman living at Livorno, daughter of a Rabbi, who, it was said, would marry the Messiah before too much time had passed. Feeling that this was a sign from God, Tzvi had her brought to Cairo, where he married her on 31 March 1664 in a lavish ceremony and celebration held in the house of Joseph Çelebi, paying the expenses of both her trip and the celebrations from the contributions of his many followers. In April 1665 he went to Gaza, where he came into contact with Nathan b. Elisha ha-Ashkenazi (1644–80), usually called Nathan of Gaza, who had been following similar lines, engaging in asceticism and exercises in moral purification while concentrating on the *Zohar* and the disciplines of Luria. Soon afterwards, on 31 May 1665, under the influence of Nathan's enthusiastic encouragement, Tzvi openly proclaimed himself to be the Messiah, and his apostle Nathan began energetically propagandizing on his behalf throughout the Holy Land, creating excitement and support among the Jewish masses.

It was at this point that Shabbatai Tzvi's influence really began to rise. He went to Jerusalem, going around the city's circumference seven times on horseback. He was received with adoration by the populace and a few rabbis, including Samuel Primo and Moise Galante, but he was met with considerable reserve by the leading rabbis of the city, who sent messages to the chief rabbis of Istanbul and Salonica warning them of his effect on their followers.

While Nathan returned to Gaza to carry on his propaganda, Shabbatai Tzvi went via Safed and Aleppo and then back to Izmir in October 1665, there gaining substantial financial support as well as a mass of followers to the point where the entire Jewish community was involved, either in support or opposition. Though admonished by the Chief Rabbi of Istanbul to suppress Tzvi's movement, the Chief Rabbi of Izmir did nothing, feeling that he had the situation under control and would only make matters worse by actively moving to suppress the self-proclaimed Messiah. Tzvi and his followers, however, were emboldened by this inaction. On Friday, 11 December 1665, his supporters broke down the door of the house of his principal opponent in the city, Rabbi Haim Peña, and the next day they did the same to the latter's Portugal Synagogue. Tzvi began to act as if he was a monarch as well as Messiah, holding court and insisting that he be approached with the kind of ceremony usually reserved for the Sultan. Perhaps in reaction to rabbinical condemnation, he went out of his way to violate Jewish laws, desecrating the Sabbath, developing his own liturgy, and eating food forbidden to Jews, in the process attracting many followers away from the *millet* leaders.

As more and more local rabbis began to support the movement, on 23 December 1665 he got them to depose Chief Rabbi Aaron Lapapa and to replace him with Hayim Benveniste, now one of Tzvi's supporters, who immediately ordered that Tzvi's name be mentioned instead of that of the Sultan in the Friday prayers performed in Izmir's synagogues, a clear sign of revolt against the Empire's Ottoman as well as Jewish establishments. Tzvi now ordered his followers to abandon the traditional reading of the Torah and mentioning of the name of God in religious services, and he replaced the ancient Jewish dietary laws with his own regulations, declaring that the final day of Judgement would come on 18 June 1666. Just as the Jews in Spain had responded to persecution by devotion to Kabbalism, now also in consequence of the enthusiasm and devotion inspired by the Shabbatean movement, thousands of Ottoman Jews responded to their miseries by leaving their shops and businesses and giving up trade, commerce and industry altogether, marching in processions shouting 'Long Live the King Messiah, Long live Sultan Tzvi', while devoting themselves entirely to contemplation and prayer in almost hysterical preparation for the great day which they were convinced would come in the not-too-distant future.

Though Tzvi's actions and claims continued to be met with considerable hostility by Ottoman rabbinical leaders, his fame and following spread widely among Jews throughout the East and Europe, in particular at Amsterdam and Hamburg, where Jews for the first time in centuries began to hope for liberation from the long-standing persecution to which they had been subjected in Christian lands, at the same time considering themselves freed of the long-standing restrictions imposed by Jewish orthodoxy on matters such as marriage, diet, and activity on the Sabbath. Those Jews who refused to accept his message and insisted on observing the regulations and traditions of the past were now considered by him and his followers as 'unbelievers', who could be and were attacked forcefully in order to compel them to accept him as Messiah, resulting in deep divisions in Jewish communities throughout Europe as well as the Ottoman Empire. His cause in Europe, moreover, was taken up by the *marrano* physician Abraham Miguel Cardozo (1627–1706) of Livorno, who became the leading theoretician of what was now becoming the Shabbatean version of Kabbalism.

Shabbatai Tzvi's fall was even more sudden than his rise. On 30 December 1665 he decided that the time had come for him to go to Istanbul to fulfill his self-appointed role as king of the Empire. With a number of followers he left Izmir, travelling to the capital by sea. In the meantime, however, reports had come to the Sultan of what was going on in Izmir. These were compounded by the complaints of the Istanbul Chief Rabbi Yomtov ben Hanaya Benyakar that the movement was causing unrest and disturbance among his followers, many of whom were responding to his message by abandoning their shops and work as well as their observance of community and religious regulations.

Orders therefore had been sent to the governor of Izmir to arrest Tzvi, but they arrived after his departure and were carried out only after his ship landed near Istanbul and the Messiah and his followers approached the city gates on 6 February 1666. They were arrested and sent in chains to the Ottoman court, then being held at Edirne, second capital of the Empire. Since Shabbatai Tzvi did not speak Turkish well enough to converse easily, the Jewish convert and physician Moshe ben Rafael Abravanel (Hayatizade Mustafa Fevzi Efendi) acted as translator. At first Grand Vezir Fazıl Ahmed Pasha felt that the only solution to the troubles being caused by Tzvi was his execution, but the court banker, Mordehai Cohen, convinced him that this would only create a martyr which would expand instead of destroying the movement. Instead, therefore, Tzvi and his followers were offered the alternative of conversion to Islam, with Shabbatai Tzvi accepting on 15 September 1666, taking the name Mehmed Efendi, his wife Sara becoming Fatma Hanım, his two brothers taking the names Ahmed and Abdullah, and his son becoming Ismail. Tzvi and his followers were sent to imprisonment at the fortress of Kumkapı (Aydos) at Gallipoli, on the Dardanelles, while the Grand Vezir decided what to do with them to quiet the disturbances which the movement had caused in Ottoman society. Even there, however, he managed to live relatively freely, receiving followers and continuing to spread his message throughout the Empire and Europe despite the disappointment of many that the Day of Judgement which he had presaged did not in fact come during the year 1666.

The orthodox Jewish establishment was shocked by Tzvi's surprising conversion to Islam, fearing that it would lead many other Jews as well, not only Tzvi's followers, to do the same. While some of his followers were puzzled by his action, most rationalized it as a new means of offering penitence for past sins and suffering so as to speed up the final redemption under the leadership of Tzvi as Messiah, so many but not all followed him in conversion, creating new divisions and arguments among his own supporters as well as in the Rabbinical community. Tzvi himself was later allowed to stay in Edirne, and later Istanbul, where he settled first on the Bosporus at Kuruçeşme and later at the end of the Golden Horn at Kâğıthane. It is said that sometimes he lived as a Muslim and sometimes as a Jew, reading Psalms with Jews who came to his house or at the Ahrida synagogue. Wherever he was, however, his home became such a center of pilgrimage that in 1673 the Grand Vezir finally had him exiled to Berat, along the Dalmatian coast in Albania, with the costs of his travel being paid by Istanbul's Jewish community to get him out of the way once and for all. In 1674 his wife Sara (Fatma Hanım) died, after which he married one of his followers, Esther (Ayşe Hanım), daughter of one of his Salonica followers who had converted, Rabbi Joseph Pilosof (Abdülgaffar Efendi). Shabbatai Tzvi died at Berat on 17 September 1676, though some of his followers developed the idea that he had not in fact died but rather had disappeared and would remain away until the world was finally ready to receive him as Messiah.

Many of his followers did not imitate his conversion but remained as Jews, though secretly continuing to practice the rituals which had brought so much opposition from the Orthodox establishment in his own lifetime, in many cases coming to be treated very much like the *marranos*, whose conversion to Christianity in Spain led to permanent suspicians of them by the orthodox even after they had ostensibly returned to Judaism. Those of his followers in Salonica who joined him in converting to Islam in 1687 and their descendants developed their own sect there, continuing to openly act as Muslims but secretly practicing the Shabbatean mystic form of Judaism to such an extent that they were recognized neither by Orthodox Muslims nor Jews, with the former calling them *dönmes*, or 'turncoats', by their apostacy creating a new source of very deep division in both the Muslim and Jewish communities, though by their ability and energy developing mercantile fortunes which enabled them to resist pressures from all sides and maintain their independent existence until well into the twentieth century. Gradually replacing Judeo-Spanish with Turkish in everyday life as a result of their conversion, they continued to use Hebrew for their esoteric religious practices, carried out in great secrecy in concealed synagogues, but themselves divided into three distinct sects differing in traditions and ideas, often rivaling one another and rarely intermarrying. True Muslims avoided them, correctly suspecting them of non-Muslim leanings and practices, as did Jews, who considered them to be heretics. It is related that until the very last day of Ottoman rule in Salonica in 1912 they sent a daily delegation of seven to the city gates each morning to see if Shabbatai Tzvi was finally returning.

Community Despotism During the Age of Decline. The Shabbatean movement deepened and extended the tendencies toward tyranny which anarchy and poverty had caused within the Ottoman Jewish community. Not only intellectual curiosity but also individual freedom were largely extinguished during the centuries of decline. Rabbis and legal scholars multiplied their sermons, admonitions and edifying prescriptions designed to moralize the masses, enclosing members of the congregations in a myriad of regulations which were now bound with a Kabbalistic rigor and asceticism that had not existed before. The kind of public democracy which had existed in the early *kahal*s was ended. Chief Rabbi Judah ben Samuel Rosanes (1657–1727), excommunicated all those who refused to abandon the study of the Kabbalah and Shabbatean beliefs though at times when he agreed to lift the bans for those who recanted he himself was attacked for his leniency by the community zealots of the time. Community policy was determined from on high without discussion or contradiction. The masses simply had to obey the leaders, the rabbis and notables, without having a voice and without even understanding the reasons for what was being done.

For all practical purposes, the Jewish communities were now subjected to the rule of highly theocratic plutocracies, which tried to establish discipline and order to remedy all the difficulties of the time. All games and entertainments were now considered to be immoral because they limited the time the faithful for prayer and to study the law. There could be no relationship between men and women before marriage, which was, of course, arranged without participation of either the man or woman. Women could no longer show themselves to men except under the most complete of veiled costumes, and without any jewels or sign of luxury of any sort which might attract attention. They were not supposed to walk along the sea or in public places, particularly where non-Jews might be present. Women were not supposed to go into the streets to buy food, and if they had no servants who could do this for them and had to go to shops, they were supposed to conduct their purchases from outside, through the door, not to enter at any time. Women were not allowed to work outside the home because of the presence of other men. When in the presence of men, they had to maintain themselves in subordinate and respectful positions without speaking unless spoken to. When guests were present in the house, they were supposed to remain in the background. Normally they were not even supposed to eat with their families. They were there only to serve, eating what was left after the meal was over. Women were admonished to maintain strict chastity at all times, even in relation with their husbands, except on the rare occasions when the marriage was to be consummated so that male children in particular could be produced.

Not that men were particularly free either. The form and length of their beards and mustaches as well as their headgear and clothing were rigorously regulated, far more by the community than by the state. Alcoholic beverages were not supposed to approach their mouths except in the course of the *kaddish* ritual. All were supposed to be in a permanent state of repentence for past and future sins, and no better sign of piety could be demonstrated than voluntary submission to flagellation to mortify oneself by suffering in the eyes of God.

Real prayer could be accomplished only before the Tabernacle of the Ark in the synagogue, so men were required to come, and when necessary their employers had to allow them to leave their jobs, in order to perform their prayers at the required time. Every morning, criers went through the Jewish quarters calling the faithful to perform their ablutions and go to prayer, lamenting the destruction of the Temple and the dispersion of the people of Israel. Even after the prayers were over, they still could not go to their places of work, for the psalms had to be read, and pity the believer who dared hurry off before these were finished in order to get to his daily tasks. Nor could they absent themselves from the required prayers on the Sabbath, on festival days, and on every Monday and Thursday, when the Torah was read in public lecture. They had to arrive on time, they had to bring with and use their *tefillim* in performing the prayers, and they had to pray properly if they wished to avoid strict punishment.

The Sabbath was particularly regulated with rigorous precision. All members of the congregation had to cease work as soon as the sun began to set on Friday evening. Rabbis, beadles and others would go around the streets to remind shop keepers and artisans to close up and send their customers home in time so all could reach their homes before the sun had completely set. At home, of course, the women had to busy themselves all day making final preparations which had to be completed by sunset. When the men reached home, they were required to inspect what their women had done and to severely punish any failures and inadequacies or inability to finish on time. Nothing could be done on Saturday. On the Sabbath the believer was not allowed to go more than two hundred meters from his home for any reason, though by tradition the entire quarter was interpreted to be the home of all Jews so that people could in fact go through the streets in order to proceed to the synagogue, since only before the Tabernacle of the Ark could real prayers be said to God.

Jewish community organizations now became the watchdogs of morality and suppressors of all signs of luxury. *Memunim* walked around each quarter and street entering homes, shops and synagogues alike, helping the poor and the sick to be sure, but at the same time watching out for even the smallest violation of public or individual morality and notifying the community leaders so that the proper punishment could be inflicted. Whenever the Jewish community was ravaged by an earthquake or fire or by another Janissary attack, the *memunim* would attribute the suffering to impiety and to appease divine anger would increase the severity of their supervision and punishments. Even the slightest mistake during religious services or infraction of the most complex *takkanot* would lead to severe chastisement and punishment, with corporal punishment most common.

Jewish schools limited themselves to training their pupils for lives of prayer and contemplation and little else. Elementary schools largely were reserved for the children of the rich or for those preparing for the *yeshivas* and for rabbinical careers. Temporal studies were now gone, and instead the rabbis concentrated entirely on prayer, hardly teaching their students how to read Hebrew let alone the other languages of the empire in which they lived. As the *kahals* became too poor to support public education in the *talmud torahs*, the mass of children did not have access to any school, and so were left in complete ignorance, unable to read or write. As they grew up, they labored in the most humble occupations, without any of the spirit of learning or intellectual argument which had infected all classes in past centuries. The *yeshivas* continued to survive on the basis of foundation revenues left from more prosperous times, with those of the Ottoman Empire attracting students from all over southern and central Europe, but these also were products of their time, hostile to all instruction beyond the accepted religious norms, without any efforts to go into the sciences and liberal ideas which were freeing minds in Western Europe, and were in any case largely isolated from the communities around them and thus contributing little to Jewish intellectual development.

Economic Pursuits. For the most part young Jews no longer learned or followed the trades of their father, leaving the more productive occupations requiring fine skills, such as gold and silver making and banking, to their Muslim, Greek and Armenian counterparts, and falling into poverty and misery emphasizing prayer and religious contemplation while practicing only simple occupations, requiring only limited knowledge and intelligence, like peddling the foods and goods produced by others, and acting as fishermen or cultivators producing fruits and vegetables. Those Jews who did have more intelligence and training now were limited for the most part to service as scribes (*soferim*), reproducing the great Holy Books or writing letters and keeping accounts for others, or as typesetters, usually now for Greek or Armenian masters. Jews also continued to operate small shops in town and country, selling spices, meat, stuffs, drugs, oils and wines or to practice trades such as dying, tailoring, weaving, binding, and the like. They largely abandoned international trade to Christians, however, if for no other reason than the Judeo-Spanish which they spoke no longer enabled them to communicate with their brothers in Europe, but they did continue to trade within the empire, between Bosnia and Üsküp in the Balkans to Salonica and Istanbul, and beyond them, across the seas to Alexandria, and on a smaller scale going into the countryside to sell manufactured products and buy the products of the land, particularly tobacco, wines and cheeses, bringing them to market in the cities, but the great profits from international trade were gone.

Weaving remained the most important trade for the Jews of Salonica in particular, and there still were many Jewish cloth merchants, but the entire industry fell into depression due to the internal anarchy, the loss of foreign markets to European cloth manufactures, and also the cloth tax which had to be paid regularly to the army and the Treasury. As a result, much less than before was left to divide among the workers, and poverty and suffering among the mass of Jews increased substantially. The Jewish Federal Council of Salonica tried to revive the industry after 1680 by replacing the home factories which had produced most of the work earlier with a vast cloth factory, called the *Beylik*, situated only a short distance from the White Tower and the Maritime Wall of the city. Masters and workers were grouped into their own corporation for the first time, not so much to protect their interests as to make certain of their willingness to work at low wages so the community could meet its obligations. Even then, however, production was insufficient to meet the community's tax payments to the government, which as a result were increasingly made in cash rather than kind, leaving even less for the workers to do. Wages therefore became so small and available jobs in the *Beylik* so few that the community had to allow individuals once again to produce their own cloths at home, especially in the *cortejos*, to provide sufficient money for their daily expenses once their obligation to the community was completed. At the same time, the Jewish quarters of Istanbul and the other major cities of the empire emulated the Muslim quarters by deteriorating into little more than slums, with Jews crowded together into tenement-like *yahudhânes*, whose lack of fresh air and water as well as sewage facilitated the rapid spread of diseases of all sorts, adding to the misery. While the government at times tried to help revive Jewish industries and to relieve crowded living conditions, its efforts were of little help so long as new markets could not be found. These efforts also were countered during the later years of the eighteenth century as well as in the nineteenth when Salonica was flooded with thousands of formerly-nomadic Turkish *yöruk*s who were being settled in an effort to control anarchy and banditry in eastern Anatolia and were willing to accept even less than the Jews for working in the weaving factories. Between their competition and the deterioration of the industry, few Jewish weavers were left by the start of the nineteenth century, with poverty increasing enormously as a result.

As Armenians and Greeks took over most of the more profitable businesses, a few Jews increasingly developed a new sort of profitable occupation, as agents (*loez*, pl. *loazim*) for foreign merchants and traders in the Ottoman lands. In the eighteenth century Ottoman Empire, the new masters of international trade were European Christians coming from ports like Marseilles, Venice, Ragusa, Ancone, Livorno, Genoa, Hamburg, Antwerp, Bordeaux and London. These people lived in the empire for several months at a time, selling European manufactured goods such as cloths and stuffs as well as spices and drugs from the East, and with the product of these sales purchasing Ottoman wheat, wool, skins, cotton and tobacco, which they sent back to Europe, gaining substantial profits in the process. It was not long before Jews became their agents in most of the ports of the Levant, buying and selling on their behalf, securing lucrative contracts to build houses, shops and depots and furnishing them with food, furniture, tapistries and the like, often at huge profits for themselves. These Jewish agents became in reality the masters of their patrons. They arranged for their homes and furnishings, bargained on their behalf for food and other commodities in the market places as well as with customers and sources of raw materials, kept their accounts, watched over payments, and cared for their problems in the local courts, leaving their masters with little do and also with little knowledge of what was being done in their name, and thus making themselves indispensable. Whether the actual traders were Greeks, Armenians or Europeans, it was said that in Macedonia, Thrace, Anatolia and the East nothing was bought, sold or exchanged without the participation of the Jews, who were the only persons who could deal with the local people of all religions as well as the increasingly corrupt officials.

Jews remained as bankers, money changers, and customs agents as well as the doctors and druggists within the Empire. Only the Jews continued to know the quality and prices of goods, what prices should be paid or charged in purchases and sales, what customs duties should be charged, and the like, so few Muslim or European merchants or officials did not have their Jewish agents for these and other purposes. Jews continued to secure valuable tax farms over many of the products of the empire due to their unique ability to manage them for the profit of all.

Jews were not able to benefit from the protection of European consuls to the same extent as did native Christians in the early part of the eighteenth century since France led the way in ordering its agents not to protect Jews because of their competing with Christian merchants, with Britain and Holland following.[2] But there were other ways to secure European protection. Some Ottoman Jews began to invest in countries such as Prussia, Denmark, Ragusa and Holland in particular, gaining their citizenship and protection during the course of the century, at times becoming their honorary consuls back in Istanbul, making it relatively easy for them not only to secure protection for their own families but also for relatives and members of their own *kahals*. During the later years of the century also, as European prejudices began to break down, Ottoman Jews also secured *berats* of protection or employment as translators and domestics for the consuls of France, England, Sweden and Austria while using their influence to become rich merchants, bankers and traders by sharing the privileges of their masters. The sale by European consuls of paper positions as translators, domestics and the like became so blatant that in 1729 the Ottoman government tried to end the subterfuge by limiting such appointments to two for each consul, but strict insistence on the application of the Capitulations to the letter defeated this, as all other efforts.

Jews continued at times to use their skills as physicians to gain influence among foreign consuls and ambassadors as well as in the Ottoman councils of state, though now not so much among members of the Ottoman dynasty as, rather, for their ministers.

Tovia ha-Cohen served as physician and adviser to Sultan Mustafa II (1693–1703) Grand Vezir Rami Pasha, and later to Ahmed III's (1703–30) Grand Vezir Baltacı Mehmed Pasha, advising the latter during his campaign which forced Peter the Great to surrender at the Battle of the Pruth (1710).

Daniel de Fonseca (1672–1740) was born a *marrano* in Portugal. His grandfather was burned at the stake by the Inquisition; his father fled to escape the same fate. Daniel as a result was raised as a priest, but secretly continued to practice Judaism. When the Inquisition finally found out about this he fled to France, first to Bordeaux and then Paris, where he studied medicine, and finally to Istanbul, where he settled as a practicing physician in 1702 while openly embracing Judaism for the first time. Very much like the Jewish physicians who gained power and influence during the previous century, de Fonseca's medical skills gained him wide esteem among leading Ottoman statesmen of the time as well as with the foreign diplomats and merchants then crowding into Istanbul. He soon became physician to the French Ambassador, and at the same time used his contacts to represent France with Ottoman officials against Austria, gaining such prestige in France that when the Ambassador died, he was consulted by the Foreign Minister as to his successor, leading to his retirement in France, where he became a member of high society, Voltaire referring to him as 'the only philosopher of his people'.

Judah Baruh served as banker (*sarrafbaşı*) to Sultan Mahmud I (1730–54), using his position to get the Sultan to send agents to Vienna to dissuade Maria Teresa from her plan to deport all the Jews of Austria as a result of the entreaties of the Chief Bishop of Madrid.

It was particularly when the European merchants were Jews that Ottoman Jews were able to benefit from the Capitulations by acting as their local commercial agents and intermediaries, in return receiving *berat*s which provided European protection from the application of Ottoman laws and regulations and also with the same tax exemptions as those granted to their employers. Throughout the eighteenth century and into the nineteenth, the large colonies of European Jews who settled in Damascus, Aleppo and Eretz Israel worked so closely with its Jewish community that together they came to be called *Francos*, often adopting the surname for themselves, and dominated local commerce and international trade by using the Capitulations rights derived from their home countries, extending their prosperity and protection by sending agents to places like Jerusalem, Acre, Jaffa and Safed, where local Jews benefited in the same way. In Damascus, it was the Farhi family that dominated as bankers and tax collectors as well as in foreign trade, largely because of its ability to maintain good relations with European protectors. In Egypt and the North African provinces, on the other hand, leading Jewish families managed to benefit from the Capitulations by having one member take up foreign citizenship, usually that of Austria or France, and then using such relationships to gain the desired privileges.

These Jewish agents, honorary consuls, translators and the like, became the new dominant element in the Jewish community because of their relations with Europeans, gaining so much power that they were able to acquire *hazaka* legal rights of tenure to their positions, thus preventing other Jews from attempting to displace them by offering their services at lower prices to their masters. As time went on, however, they adopted themselves to the European languages and cultures of their patrons and largely cut themselves off, not just from the Muslims, but also from the masses and leaders of their own communities. This development left the latter in turn to become assimilated even more to a Sephardic culture which became increasingly Middle Eastern and even Islamic in its outlook and customs, separating them far more from Europe than had been the case in the past while they continued to descend into the pious poverty which characterized most of the Ottoman Jewish community as it entered the nineteenth century.

Culture and Intellectual Development. The partial revival of Jewish economic fortunes starting in the late seventeenth century led to an intellectual and cultural revival, particularly during the eighteenth. Hebrew now was limited to the role as language of religion, while the living Judeo-Spanish developed into the language of culture and communication among all elements of Ottoman Jewry.

This movement started with the work of Jacob ben Meir Culi (1690–1732), who had emigrated to Istanbul from the Holy Land in 1714 and studied with Chief Rabbi Judah Rosanes (d. 1727), who appointed him *dayyan* and chief teacher for the entire community. Culi felt that after the anarchy in the Jewish community resulting from the Shabbatai Tzvi affair as well as the chaos then prevalent in the Empire, it was necessary for him to re-educate the Jewish masses in their own religious and cultural traditions. Since most of them knew very little Hebrew, he saw that such education and popularization would have to be carried out in the only language they knew, Judeo-Spanish, which combined the Spanish that their ancestors had brought with them in the fifteenth century with some Hebrew as well as Turkish, language of the country. In 1730 he published the first volume, covering the Book of Genesis and part of the Book of Exodus, of a massive series which he planned of Old Testament commentaries and called the *Me'am Lo'ez*, after the original Hebrew of the biblical phrase 'the house of Jacob'. Written in a simple and popular Judeo-Spanish understandable to most Jews of the time, the series, as planned by Culi and carried out by his successors, became an encyclopedia of all aspects of eastern Jewish life and culture, presented so the people could easily understand and appreciate the principles of their faith and culture.

All the great works of Jewish culture were to be elaborated on and explained – the Torah, the Talmud, the Mishna, the Midrash and the Zohar, along with the other great works of Rabbinical learning, bringing in Jewish traditions, history and folklore and clarifying the prescriptions of the Law. Culi himself died only two years later, while still working on the second volume of his work, which discussed the rest of the Book of Exodus. He left extensive notes and plans for the remaining volumes, however, and these were taken up by his colleague, Isaac ben Moses Magriso, who completed and published the volume on the Exodus (Istanbul, 2 vols, 1733, 1746), followed by Leviticus (Istanbul, 1753) and Numbers (Istanbul, 1764), with later volumes published periodically during the nineteenth century. The *Me'am Lo'ez* has remained the principal reader in Judeo-Spanish until modern times, for all practical purposes an encyclopedia of Sephardic knowledge. In its time, moreover, it was a major stimulus to the development of Judeo-Spanish literature, with numerous works being published. Among these were Abraham de Toledo's popular Judeo-Spanish poem *Las Coplas de Josef ha-Zaddik* (the couplets of the biblical Jacob's son Joseph) (Istanbul, 1732), which had some 400 quatrains with its own peculiar melody and is often sung during the Purum festival; *Meshivat Nefesh* (1743), a translation and commentary by Shabbatai Vitas of the poems of Solomon ibn Gabrol; the anonymous *Ma'assioth del Senyor de Ya'akov Avinu*(1748); and moralistic poems by Yomtov Maggala, *Tohakkat Magula* (1756). Benjamin Perez published numerous translations for the masses, including the letters of Ribi Akiba (1729). The 'father of Judeo-Spanish literature', Abraham ben Isaac Assa (1710–68), published numerous original works and translations of historical, scientific and religious studies during the middle years of the eighteenth century, including the Old Testament(Istanbul, 1739–45), a manual of religious ritual and prayer called *Zorkhei Zibbur* (Istanbul, 1739), the *Shulhan Arukh* of Joseph Caro, and even a history of the Ottoman dynasty. One of the great Jewish poets and composers, Rabbi Moshe Faro (d. 1776), also was active at this time, producing his memorable *Suzikâr Peshrevi* and *Shadarban Peshrevi*, which brought him fame among Muslims and Jews alike during much of the next century. The Jewish musician Isaac Fresco Romano, known as *Tanburi Izak*, also was so famous that he became the instructor for Selim III in playing the *tanbur*.

The Hebrew-language presses which had flourished a century earlier were largely closed from 1590 through the first three decades of the seventeenth century. They were revived, however, by Rabbi Solomon Franco in 1638, with the help of several refugees from the Chmielnicki massacres, and continued by his son Abraham Franco and son in law Soloman Gabay, who continued to publish until 1695, for the most part, however, printing religious tracts including those of Shabbatai Tzvi. Jedidiah Gabay's son Abraham transferred his father's press from Leghorn to Izmir in 1657.

Jewish printing in the Ottoman Empire revived early in the eighteenth century as part of the literary revival in Judeo-Spanish. Ribi Jonah ben Jacob Ashkenazi (d. 1745), a refugee from Galicia, emigrated to Istanbul soon after the Chmielnicki massacres, establishing a new press there in 1710, at first in partnership with another emigrant, Ribi Naftali ben Azrial of Vilna, and then on his own a year later in Ortaköy, which remained in operation with some fifty workers well into the century. In 1720 a shipment of his books was lost at sea, while a dishonest agent fled to Poland without paying him. Ashkenazi followed in an unsuccessful effort to recover his funds, and though unsuccessful he stopped in Amsterdam on the way back, there printing several books which he had brought with from Istanbul. On his return, he printed the *responsa* and other works of Ottoman rabbis, including some which he secured during a trip to Egypt. In 1728 he opened another press in Izmir in partnership with Rabbi David Hazzan, though this was closed in 1739 when the latter moved to Jerusalem. Although his press was destroyed by fire in 1741, it was restored with the help of Istanbul Chief Rabbi Abraham Rosanes, and it continued in operation by his sons and grandsons, printing some 188 works in all, including the *Zohar* and *Hemdat Yamin* as well as a Judeo-Spanish translation of the Old Testament, *Josippon,* and the first volume of *Me'Am Lo'ez,* before it was finally closed in 1778. In Salonica, printing was revived by Abraham ben David and Yomtov Canpillas in 1709, the latter going on to operate his own press after 1729, for the most part printing rabbinic novellae, homiletics, and responsa. Printing remained largely a Jewish trade in the Empire during the remainder of the century so that when Ibrahim Müteferrika established the first Ottoman Turkish press beneath the walls of the Topkapı Saray in 1727, it was the Jewish master Ribi Yonah ben Yakov Ashkenazi who designed and cast the Arabic letters and advised him on how the press should be operated. Presses also were set up in Istanbul by Izak Valero in 1755 and by Haim Eli Pardo in 1782, by Yonah Ashkenazi, David Hazzan, Barzilay Yaves, Samuel Danon and Judah Hazzan in Izmir, and by David Nahmias, Besallei Levi Ashkenazi and Raphael Kalay in Salonica, all printing Hebrew religious works as well as literary works and translations in Judeo-Spanish, contributing significantly to the latter's development in place of Hebrew as the major language of culture as well as communication among the Sephardic Jews of the Ottoman Empire.

4

The Revival of Ottoman Jewry in the Nineteenth and Twentieth Centuries

OTTOMAN JEWRY AND THE NINETEENTH-CENTURY OTTOMAN REFORM MOVEMENT, 1800–76

The Tanzimat Reform Movement. The situation of Ottoman Jewry and of the Ottoman Empire as a whole changed dramatically during the nineteenth century. For one thing, the Ottomans finally became aware of the extent of their weakness in comparison to the rising nation states of Europe and decided that the only way to remedy their problems and save the empire from destruction was to abandon efforts to restore the institutions and ways of the past and to replace them with new and modern ones which better met the needs of the time. The reform movement that followed, known as the *Tanzimat*, or 're-orderings', was planned during the reign of Sultan Mahmud II (1808–39), and carried out under his two sons Abdül Mecid (1839–61) and Abdül Aziz (1861–76) and a group of modernist bureaucrats led by Grand Vezir Mustafa Reşid Pasha. Their work was largely completed during the controversial reign of Sultan Abdül Hamid II (1876–1909), who through his autocracy brought the empire into the modern world though at the price of suppressing a gradual evolution toward representative government which had been begun during the previous quarter century. Ottoman modernization culminated during what has come to be known as the Young Turk period, from 1908 to the end of World War I, when efforts to democratize the system through Constitutional government led to an intense but very short period of political, social, and economic democracy between 1908 and 1912, only to be replaced in consequence of foreign attacks and domestic nationalist revolts and massacres by the Young Turk autocracy which brought the empire into World War I on the side of the Central Powers, whose defeat led to its final disintegration and to the emergence of a number of national states led by the Republic of Turkey.

Execution of Jewish Community Leaders. The nineteenth-century Ottoman

147

reform movement had a major impact on Ottoman Jewry. It really began on 15 June 1826 when Sultan Mahmud II destroyed the Janissary corps, composed of Christian converts and their descendants, which during the years of disintegration had constituted the principal military arm of misrule, abuse and reaction, including repeated ravaging of Jewish homes and shops in the major cities of the empire. The principal leaders of the Jewish community at the time, however, the Baghdad banker Ezekiel ben Joseph Gabay, Janissary paymaster Isaiah Acıman and money changer, court banker and chief tax collector Çelebi Behor Isaac David Carmona (1773–1826), were executed in 1826 by order of the Sultan, ostensibly because of their involvement with Janissary finances. In fact, however, this event was only one more illustration of the long-standing rivalry between Jews and their Christian rivals, in this case the Armenian bankers who had monopolized Ottoman court finances since the decline of the Jewish bankers in the late seventeenth century. For some time there had been considerable competition in the Palace between these Armenian bankers, now led by Allahverdioğlu and his two brothers, and the leader of the Jewish bankers, Ezekiel Gabay, who in 1811 had been appointed banker (*sarrafbaşı*) for the Sultan as a reward for his assistance in putting down the revolt of the Mamluk leader Küçük Süleyman Pasha in his home town of Baghdad. Gabay for some time had maintained his position amidst the Byzantine intrigues then current in the Sultan's entourage largely through the support of Selim III's favorite, Halet Efendi, and the Queen Mother (*Valide Sultan*). In response to Armenian pressure to get the Jews out of the Palace once again, Gabay got the Queen Mother to arrange for the execution of the three Armenian bankers, leaving Gabay and his associates in control for the moment. This in turn led the Armenian Director of the Mint (*Darbhane Müdürü*), Kazaz Artun Haratyun, to spread accusations that Gabay, Acıman and Carmona were supporting the Janissaries against the Sultan's efforts to reform them because of bribes as well as the very substantial profits they were securing from their long-standing association. At first Gabay was able to counter these accusations by going to the Sultan in turn and, with Halet Efendi's help, accusing Artun Kazaz of irregularities in purchasing gold for the Mint, in fact a long-standing prerogative of its directors during the centuries of decline. Kazaz Artun in consequence was removed from the Mint and exiled to Rhodes, but he had his own friends in the Palace who intervened on his behalf. After a short exile, therefore, he was pardoned, returned to Istanbul, regained his Directorate of the Mint, and then intrigued successfully to get the Sultan to disgrace Halet Efendi and exile him to Konya, where he was executed. This left Gabay without his principal protector in the Palace, so Kazaz Artun and his Armenian colleagues once again spread rumors that the three Jewish bankers were trying to protect the Janissaries, intriguing to get rid of them as the best means of restoring the Armenians control of Palace finances. Gabay was the first to go as a result. In 1826 Artun Kazaz got the Sultan to imprison him, and although the Queen Mother was able to secure a pardon for him as soon as she heard what had happened, Kazaz Artun moved quickly to get him executed before the order arrived. Now the Armenian bankers were free to do what they wanted. Kazaz Artun went on to secure the dismissal and murder in his Cyprus exile of Isaiah Acıman, and of Behor Carmona, who was arrested at his *yalı* at Arnavutköy, also on the pretext of his Janissary sympathies, thus restoring Armenian supremacy in Palace finances, at least for the moment.

That this incident was entirely a product of Armenian palace intrigues and did not manifest any policy of anti-Semitism or abuse toward Jews on the part of the sultan is shown by the fact that soon afterwards Mahmud took the first step toward abolishing differences among subjects of different religions to achieve equality for all by ordering government and army officials to abandon wearing the turban and flowing robes of the past, whose various shapes and colors marked the religion as well as status of each person, replacing them with the simple fez and frock coat, which had to be worn by all regardless of their status in life.

Restoration of the Grand Rabbinate. Initial Reorganization of the Jewish community. Mahmud went on to institute major reforms in the Jewish *millet* to enable it to share in the reforms he was introducing. In 1835, soon after he had destroyed the Janissary corps and begun his efforts at modern reform, the Jewish community of Istanbul got him to resume appointing Grand Rabbis for the entire Ottoman Jewish community, largely so they could have political rank and influence in Ottoman governmental affairs equal to those of the Armenians and Greeks, who long had used their Patriarchs as influential protectors in the Ottoman court. Jews had not felt the need for such protection during the century following the death of Grand Rabbi Elijah Mizrahi in 1535 because of the protection provided them in court during the sixteenth century by the influential Jewish physicians and bankers, so none had been appointed for some three hundred years. But by the nineteenth century the latter no longer had influence in court, and the triumph of Kazaz Artun had shown quite clearly how much the presence in court of an official like the Grand Rabbi was needed to protect the Jewish community from the intrigues of its rivals. Grand Rabbi Abraham ha-Levi thus became the first Jewish Grand Rabbi for the empire since Elijah Mizrahi had supposedly served, beginning a new line of official Jewish community leaders who have continued right to the present day. Ha-Levi's appointment was greeted with joy by the Jews of Istanbul, who set out lanterns throughout the Jewish quarters of the city while praying for the continued good health of the Sultan.

The new Grand Rabbi was far more powerful than his predecessors three centuries earlier had been. His *berat* of appointment indicated that he was to perform three basic functions.

First of all he was an Ottoman official, the chief governmental representative in the Jewish community, responsible for collecting government taxes from community members and seeing to it that they obeyed all the laws of the Sultan, delivering the collections to officials of the treasury, and turning violators over to the Sultan's police and courts for punishment according to the law. He also was the principal community representative with the government, replacing the old *Kâhya*, and as such he transmitted community complaints and requests to the relevant officials and departments and secured imperial orders and regulations to meet its needs. In all of these duties, as well as in his appointment and removal, the Grand Rabbi was under the supervision of the Ministry of Foreign Affairs until 1877, after which, as part of the Constitutional reforms then introduced by Sultan Abdül Hamid II, supervision was transferred to the Ministry of Justice and Sects.

Secondly, he was administrative leader of the Jewish community, not only in Istanbul but throughout the Empire, in charge of levying and collecting community taxes and administering and financing community functions such as organizing, maintaining and staffing schools, orphanages, hospitals, and charitable institutions. Synagogues and other religious buildings were officially supported by foundations, very much like those *vakıfs* which supported mosques and churches, but while these were placed under the supervision of the government as part of the *Tanzimat* reforms, the Grand Rabbi was in charge of appointing their administrators, and thus, for all practical purposes, operating them in the same way he operated the other community institutions. In these functions he received assistance when necessary from the Ottoman police and local officials as well as the local chief rabbis and their committees and administrators, but he also maintained his own bureaucrats to exercise his authority so as to rely on the government as little as possible.

Finally, he was religious leader. He was in charge of all rabbis and community heads. He was leader of the Jewish court system and alone had the right to administer the extreme penalties of ban and excommunication against those who seriously violated the religious law. Disputes among rabbis also could be settled in his presence, but while his functions as government agent and administrative leader gave him considerable prestige, his ability to convince the other rabbis regarding interpretation of the law depended even more on his personal prestige, which varied considerably according to the individuals who held the position, though in general their ability to lead tended to increase during the terms of the last three Grand Rabbis who occupied the post before and during World War I.

In the years following restoration of the Grand Rabbi and the appointment of Abraham ha-Levi, the Ottoman government specified and elaborated his authority in a whole series of regulations and *berats* which gave him power over the other rabbis of the empire and enabled him to help them enforce their communal regulations over their members and to force the latter to accept the authority of the rabbinical courts. By the terms of these regulations, the principal functions and powers of the Grand Rabbi were as follows.

Power Over Other Rabbis. The appointment or dismissal of city and provincial chief rabbis and rabbis throughout the Empire was valid only if approved by the Grand Rabbi. A Rabbi could not be arrested by civil authorities without the approval of the Grand Rabbi. The Grand Rabbi could get the Ottoman police to intervene and punish or jail rabbis who failed to obey his orders. If a rabbi died without heirs, his property could be taken for the public treasury, as was done for all Ottoman subjects in such circumstances, only after the affirmation of the Grand Rabbi that there were in fact no such heirs.

Power to Enforce Communal Regulations. The Grand Rabbi, chief rabbis and individual rabbis were given legal authority by the government to force Jews to obey communal regulations regarding all matters, including Kosher food regulations, with those failing to follow the Jewish dietary precepts being subjected to imprisonment in the city jails rather than those of the synagogues or the Grand Rabbinate. Marriages among Jews could be consummated only with the consent of the Grand Rabbi or his representatives in the provinces, the chief rabbis, even if they involved second marriages or marriages performed outside the empire. No-one could require a Rabbi to celebrate a marriage or approve a divorce which he felt was contrary to Jewish religious law, and no-one could yet get married or divorced without religious approval. Transfers of property required approval of the religious authorities before they could be completed. And in the absence of heirs to the property of deceased Jews, transfer of the property to the Public Treasury, as was done for all subjects without heirs, could be accomplished only after certification by the Rabbi rather than by the local *Kadi*, whose approval was required of other subjects.

Power Relating to Court Cases in Religious Courts. If any Ottoman rabbi was involved in a legal case involving Muslims or Jews which was heard in Muslim religious courts, he had to be judged before the Istanbul courts, where the Grand Rabbi had the right to station a representative to defend his interests. If the Rabbi or other Jews were involved in Muslim court cases, they were not required to give testimony under Muslim oaths, but instead the Grand Rabbi or his representative could take their testimony under oath in a synagogue for transmission to the *kadi*, so that their testimony could be given the same weight as that of Muslims in the *kadi*'s court.

Power in Relation to Government Authorities. Nothing belonging to a synagogue or school could be confiscated or seized to settle debts to individuals or to the government without the approval of the Grand Rabbi, and if this regulation was violated the Grand Rabbi had the right to demand that the property be restored with compensation. No-one could enter a Jewish school under pretext of investigation without advance permission of the Grand Rabbi. Police officials or treasury employees had to be punished if they sought to extort illegal payments or gifts. The Government provided special facilities to the Grand Rabbi and other rabbis when they or their agents travelled in the Empire, permitting them to go in disguise when necessary, particularly when they were going around to collect taxes on behalf of the Treasury, since the knowledge that they were conveying large amounts of gold and silver inevitably subjected them to the threat of robbery. Grand Rabbis and other rabbis were also given exemptions from most Ottoman as well as Jewish community taxes, as well as from the requirement imposed on subjects in time of mobilization to allow their homes to be used as barracks for soldiers.

The Sultan's official appointment letter (*berat*) of 26 July 1854 given Grand Rabbi Hayim ha-Cohen (1854–60), whose principal provisions were repeated in appointment letters given to the subsequent Grand Rabbis, gives a good idea of what the Grand Rabbis could and did do at this time:

> Following the necessary dismissal of Rabbi Yako (Jacob Behar David), Rabbi of the nation of Jews of Istanbul and its environs, my imperial *irade* has named in his place Rabbi Hayim (Hayim ha-Cohen), elected by the Jewish nation and possessor of this *Berat*. Hayim, as usual, has requested by petition that he be given the glorious *Berat*. The relevant registers have been examined, and it has been confirmed that for the post of Grand Rabbi Yako the sum of 60,000 *akçes* was provided (to the Sultan) as *pişkeş* (gift), and another fixed sum of 338,999 *akçes* was deposited into the Imperial Treasury from March of each year, sums which are included in the accounting books to the end of the year.
>
> Having been notified that the *pişkeş* of 60,000 *akçes* was paid into the Imperial Treasury, I have delivered this *Berat*, and have ordered that the above-named Rabbi Hayim be Grand Rabbi of the nation of Jews of Istanbul and its environs, and that all Rabbis of the Jewish nation and chiefs of communities, large and small, of my empire, recognize him as Grand Rabbi, that they address themselves to him regarding all affairs concerning the Rabbinate, that they not disobey his word when it is reasonable, and that they do not lack submission and obedience to him in matters regarding their religion. Since it is not contrary to their religion to read the Torah in the house of that Grand Rabbi and

in other houses, we order that no policeman commit any excesses or molest them or extort money from them, or mix into their cult in any way, which would be in violation of Muslim religious law and the (civil) laws in force, nor should they say to them 'You should organize your religion in your houses, and when you read the Torah, you should turn down the curtains and the lamps.' (We further order) that the synagogues and schools, which for many years have belonged to that (Jewish) nation, should not be the object of any descent under the pretext of inspection; that no-one should interfere with their restorations and repairs, which can take place without permission, nor should any barrier be made to their repairs; that no seizure should be made of objects in the schools and synagogues for debts or other reason; and that whatever has been taken by tricks should be restored through the intervention of the Muslim courts.

In matters concerning marriage and divorce of Jews as well as differences between two Jews, it is the aforementioned Grand Rabbi or his representatives who should settle them, if the two parties are content, in accordance with their own law. In matters concerning making peace or opening an inquiry, they can carry this out according to their law in their own synagogues. If, according to their law, guilty persons should be banished, according to their old custom, neither the Muslim judges nor anyone else should interfere; they should not seize their papers, and should not prevent the penalty of excommunication when it takes place.

The Rabbis or their representatives under the orders of the Grand Rabbi cannot contract marriages which are not permitted by their religion without the authorization of the Grand Rabbi or his representatives. If someone of the Jewish community (*taife*) wants to marry, divorce, or take a second wife without divorcing the first one, or wants to go somewhere else to get married, he can do so only after having secured the authorization of the Grand Rabbi. Thus even influential persons cannot force the Rabbis by saying to them, contrary to the law, 'Marry this woman with this Jew . . . . '

If, in accordance with their law, the Rabbis do not bury Jews who died and who are known to have acted against the law, the Muslim judges and police and other influential officials cannot force the Rabbis (to do so) by saying 'bury him'.

To prevent molestation of Rabbis in different places under the authority of the aforementioned Grand Rabbi who are appointed by imperial *Berat* and who go to collect taxes, the conditions to avoid such molestations are detailed in their *berats* (of appointment). Thus there will be delivered *berats*, stating privileges, to the Rabbis of the provinces, whose nomination is requested by sealed petition by the aforementioned Grand Rabbi. No-one has the right to solicit the appointment of a Rabbi for such or such place, nor to apply pressure to achieve such an appointment, or to request that such and such synagogue be given to such and such Rabbi.

Regarding clean or unclean (*kosher* or *taref*) foods and drinks, no-one can interfere and say such and such a thing is *kosher* or such and such a thing is *taref*.

If as a result of the bad conduct of a Rabbi, a *Pasha*, a *Kadi*, or a *Naib* makes complaints against him, requests his dismissal and the nomination of another in one of the places included in the provinces under the authority of the Grand Rabbi, nothing will be done about that complaint until the Grand Rabbi has testified as to the veracity of the information. In the same way, if in one way or another a *berat* has been given to a Rabbi in the absence of a sealed request by the Grand Rabbi, it will not be taken into consideration by the local authorities where the rabbi wishes to have a position.

When some Rabbis from outside come for some matter to my Istanbul, no policeman (*zabit*) can interfere with the appointment of their representatives. It is necessary to give guides to these representatives and to persons whom the Grand Rabbi sends to collect taxes owed to the Government. Moreover, since these persons, in order to go on the roads in security, must disguise themselves and carry arms against bandits, the policemen, treasury officials and other officials should not interfere with them or pressure them or request a gift or other income, which is contrary to the glorious Muslim Holy Law (*Şeriat*).

In any case when the Grand Rabbi, other Rabbis, their representatives or men are involved in a case under the authority of the glorious Holy Law of Islam, this case can be dealt with only by my Porte of Felicity in Istanbul. If there is a case where a Jewish Rabbi must be arrested by authorization of the Muslim Holy Law, it can be done only through authorization of the above mentioned Grand Rabbi.

A Jew cannot be forced to convert to Islam without his consent.

No-one can interfere with the foundations of synagogues and schools, which have been, from ancient times, the property of the places included under the authority of the Grand Rabbis. These foundations are their properties, as they have been in the past.

No-one should seek excuses or hesitate to pay the taxes of the Government, and community taxes, the *gabelle* taxes, and the Grand Rabbinate revenues the Jews must pay every year.

The properties, money, and horses, and all possessions of Rabbis who die without heirs, are to be taken for the government Treasury by representatives designated by the Grand Rabbi. No agent of the Public Treasury (*Beyt ul-Mal*) can interfere; these properties remain for the profit of the Treasury. No-one else can seize the money and property of those who die without leaving any heirs. The wills of Rabbis who die and who, in accordance with their law, leave (property and income) to their synagogues, their poor people, and to the Grand Rabbis are valid and can be extended by the Muslim (*Şeriat*) courts in accordance with their (Jewish) law and customs, and by witnesses of their own nation. If during their lifetimes, Jews leave by will something to their Grand Rabbi, their Rabbis, their synagogues and their poor people, the things that they have left will be, after the death of the testators, turned over to the heirs by intervention of the Muslim courts.

When transgressions are committed contrary to the religion of this nation and which merit being punished, the government policemen (*zabits*) and others cannot prevent the deputy (*faraş*) accompanying a delinquent accused by a declaration (*tezkere*) signed by the Rabbis and community chiefs from taking him to the prison at the Grand Rabbinate (*hahamhane*).

The police, the army and the mail men cannot interfere with the walking stick that this Grand Rabbi customarily uses, or with the horse that he rides, his employees and his clothing, and the mounts and mules used by Rabbis from other places.

The army should not attempt to force Rabbis and community chiefs to allow their houses to serve as barracks (*konaks*) to lodge soldiers and other guests. Nor should they demand that the Executive Secretary (*Kapı Kethudası*) or other (fifteen) persons in the service of the Grand Rabbi pay poll tax (*cizye*), household tax (*avariz*) or other customary taxes (required from the public).

Customs duties should not be collected at the quais or city gates for effects destined for their (Jewish) rabbinates, synagogues and schools.

If the Rabbis collect any sort of tax for visits of pilgrims, whether to Istanbul or places in the provinces, no-one has the right to interfere with what they do. Neither the police nor anyone else can interfere saying 'bury the dead here, read their fate'.

Everything that the Grand Rabbi requests of the Government with his official seal concerning religion will be permitted.

No-one can interfere with the Grand Rabbi by saying to him 'take us into your service'.

And no-one can, in any case or matter, act against the conditions mentioned in the register in relation to his power.[1]

Equal Treatment for Subjects of all Religions. The *Tanzimat* Imperial rescripts which declared the objectives and programs of modern reform, issued on 3 September 1839 and again on 18 May 1856, promised full legal equality for all subjects of the sultan regardless of religion, beginning a policy by which all the legal limitations imposed on members of society according to religion were brought to an end.[2] Mahmud II's son, Sultan Abdül Mecid (1839–61) stated to Albert Cohn, a Rothschild agent, during his visit to Istanbul in 1854 that 'My heart knows no difference among the *rayas* of my empire; all rights and privileges will be given to all *rayas* without any distinction.' In subsequent years he showed that these expressions were not empty words. Jews, Christians, and Muslims were admitted on an equal basis to government schools and positions in the Ottoman administration. The traditional clothing regulations distinguishing members of the different *millets*, classes and occupations were allowed to fall into disuse, along with restrictions on the construction and repair of synagogues and other buildings, though not without considerable opposition on the part of the Muslim religious leaders and public in the Arab provinces. The Ottoman government now provided assistance when needed to the Jewish communities in carrying out their functions, particularly in collecting the *gabelle* tax levied on cheese, wine, and meat. Security of life and property was guaranteed. Equal taxation was assured by gradually eliminating the old indirect tax farm collection system and the emphasis on indirect, excise taxes and their replacement with new impositions based only on income, though this process was completed only in the early years of the twentieth century. Freedom of worship and religious practice were confirmed on numerous occasions. Non-Muslims were given the right to hold public offices and authorized to be members of the representative assemblies then being formed on the municipal and provincial levels, so Jews as well as members of the other major minorities began to secure important positions in the government including those of directors of departments, as well as becoming teachers, doctors, ambassadors and consuls, and even judges in the secular courts. All of this was taking place at a time when in the western Europe that the Ottomans were nominally at least imitating Jews still were being subjected to substantial political and economic discrimination.

The traditional poll tax, which had been levied on non-Muslims in return for exemption from military service, was replaced in 1855 by a military substitution tax, *bedel-i askeriye* ('the military price'), levied on Muslims and non-Muslims alike who wished to be exempted from military service requirements which now were supposed to be applied to all, regardless of religion. In fact, however, Jewish and Christian youths continued to wish to avoid military service in preference for the greater opportunities offered in civilian life, and the Muslims were not anxious to have them, so all non-Muslim youths of military age paid the *bedel-i askeriye* and none served in the army. It was only in 1910, as a result of pressure from Grand Rabbi Haim Nahum Efendi in particular to show the Jewish *millet*'s loyalty to the Ottoman state, that this tax was abolished and non-Muslims were in fact conscripted into the armed forces along with Muslims despite the continued opposition of the Christian patriarchs to such military service for their young men.[3]

The Jewish *millet* and the other *millets* thus were not abolished, since this would have been misconstrued by the Ottoman enemies in Europe as an attack on religion as such. In fact their authority was strengthened in certain respects and new *millets* were created for Catholics and for Serbian and Bulgarian orthodox groups as a result of foreign pressure. But as first steps toward ending their monopolistic control over the lives of their followers, secular institutions of education, law and justice were created side by side with the old-established religious schools and courts, greatly lessening their power. Equal justice now was provided through enactment of new secular legal codes based on European models and enforced by new *Nizamiye* secular courts available to all subjects regardless of religion, which were opened throughout the empire during the century. All the new law codes and governmental regulations were translated into Judeo-Spanish so that those members of the Jewish community who did not yet know Ottoman Turkish would understand them and be in a position to take advantage of them. Secular schools were established on all levels to teach the sciences and languages needed for Ottoman youth to enter the modern world, but which long had been ignored for the most part in the *millet* schools, and they were opened to all subjects, Muslim and non-Muslim alike, regardless of religion and status.

The work of the modern state schools, moreover, was supplemented by the introduction of large numbers of foreign schools. Christian missionaries from England, Austria, France and the United States established schools all over the empire, with the intention, not only of educating young Ottomans, but also converting them to their brand of Christianity, both Protestant and Catholic. These schools were intended for Muslims and Jews as well as Christians. For the most part, however, Muslims were forbidden to attend, so that only Christian Greeks and Armenians took advantage of them. Many as a result converted to Protestantism and Catholicism as part of an effort to escape the control of their old religious leaders, and in many cases went on to develop violent, revolutionary activities against the Ottoman government, using the missionary schools as bases for their planning and storing of arms, sometimes going so far as to preach a 'crusade against the Turk' to their converts and friends. While Ottoman subjects were not prohibited from using their *millet* schools and courts, the advantages which the new secular alternative institutions provided attracted so many that the hold which their religious leaders long had exercised over their lives within the *millets* was necessarily weakened as a result.

Jewish Reaction to Ottoman reforms. The reaction of the Jewish community in most parts of the empire to Ottoman modernization was mixed, but for many years it was far less favorable than that of the Christians. As a result Jews took much less advantage of the new opportunities than did the latter, at least until after the Crimean War.

Only in Ottoman Egypt did Jews participate fully in the reform movement, largely under the stimulus of its autocratic governor, Mehmed Ali Pasha (1805–48), who after seizing power following the defeat of the French Expedition to Egypt begun by Napoleon Bonaparte, rapidly modernized state and army, not merely to establish a dynasty but also to conquer the rest of the Empire. Already in 1840 major European Jews like Moses Montefiore, Adolphe Crémieux and Solomon Munk had visited Cairo and founded modern schools in which Jewish youths were educated in modern standards. In the next two decades, Mehmed Ali emulated the pattern of the fifteenth and sixteenth-century sultans in attracting both Sephardic and Ashkenazi Jews, the latter from Eastern Europe, as well as many other Europeans to come to Egypt in order to participate in rapid economic development, enabling them to prosper and, in the process, further influence the modernization of Egyptian Jewry. Now it was families such as the Suares, Cicurel and Mosseris who led the way in banking and commerce, at the same time abandoning the traditional Jewish quarters of Cairo and moving into modern suburbs such as Zamalik, Helopolis and Garden City, where they mixed with equally wealthy members of other religious groups and, in particular, with foreigners. Jews entered the legislative assemblies created by Mehmed Ali's successors. Members of the wealthy Cattawi family became the governor's private bankers as well as chief revenue officers for the country. As a result, the number of Egyptian Jews increased from no more than four thousand in mid century to as many as 25,000 by World War I, most of whom were quite prosperous and very liberal.

The situation was quite different in Istanbul and elsewhere in the Ottoman Empire, where a substantial number of Jewish leaders had a vested interest in the preserving the old ways and defeated most efforts for Jews to participate, at least until later in the 19th century. Most Jewish religious leaders around the Grand Rabbi for the most part vigorously opposed all efforts to weaken their control over their followers by ending their monopoly over justice and education, and for some time they were much more successful than the Christian leaders in limiting the access of their followers to the new institutions. They bitterly opposed substitution of the fez in place of the turbans which long had distinguished the members of each community. They strenuously opposed the use by Jews of the new secular courts as well as traditional Muslim ones, at times excommunicating those who violated their injunctions in this respect, and occasionally securing government decrees prohibiting Jews from using non-Rabbinical courts without their permission. They did everything they could to discourage or prevent parents from sending their children to the new secular schools, at times excommunicating both parents and children as well as any other Jews that were involved, usually on the pretext that even the modern state schools, as well as the missionary institutions, would cause young Jews to convert to Christianity, particularly if they learned European languages. As a result, few in the Jewish community dared to take advantage of them, while the traditional Jewish schools remained as conservative and limited as they had been after the sixteenth century, due not only to the preferences of the religious leaders but also to the lack of sufficient funds for anything else.

As a result of the efforts of the Orthodox rabbis, moreover, very few Jews entered the new Military Medical School in Istanbul for years after it was established, even after Sultan Abdül Mecid installed a *kosher* kitchen at the school along with regulations allowing Jewish students to observe their religious and dietary rituals without penalty and for rabbis to be established at the school to supervise them in reaction to the criticism of the conservatives. In consequence, Ottoman Jews, who had for centuries led the way in Ottoman medicine, remained out of the mainstream of modern medicine in Istanbul and elsewhere, enabling Armenian and Greek physicians to dominate the profession until late in the century.

Under such conditions, moreover, it took many years and considerable effort before modern medical facilities were built to care for members of the Jewish community. As early as 27 August 1839 the Sultan had issued a *ferman* authorizing the Jewish and the Karaite communities each to build a hospital at Karabaş, on Balat's shores along the Golden Horn, but while a Jewish hospital was built in Izmir in 1874 with funds provided by Nesim Levi Bayraklı, a wealthy Jewish businessman, nothing yet was done in Istanbul, due not only to shortages of funds but also to the lack of Jewish doctors and nurses trained in the new medical sciences and to continued Rabbinical insistance on provisions which would have made such a facility impossible. As long before as 18 March 1858 Sultan Abdül Mecid issued a decree authorizing the Jews of Balat to erect a new hospital in the Karabaş quarter, but continued lack of funds as well as community disputes and opposition caused its postponement until 1897, when the *Or Ahayim* hospital finally was opened on land provided by the Sultan, largely due to the efforts of Dr Rafael Dalmedico and Grand Rabbi Moshe Levi. This hospital remains to the present day as the Jewish community's principal medical facility in Istanbul.

Secular Education in the Jewish Community. The conservative rabbis were not any happier when, in the light of their refusal to allow Jews to go to the secular state or missionary schools, wealthy members of the Jewish communities established their own Jewish secular schools in the major cities so as to assure that no conversions would take place in the process of modern education. Permission to establish a modern school for Jewish children in Istanbul was first secured in 1854 by the Rothschilds agent in Istanbul, Albert Cohn, to whom the Sultan had promised equal treatment for all subjects regardless of religion. Some time passed before anything was done to take advantage of this permission, since it was difficult to find any members of the local community willing to test the wrath of the rabbis.

It was only after the Crimean War was concluded that the task of organizing and opening the new secular school was assumed by the wealthy Jewish banker who had provided secular leadership for the Jewish community since the three Jewish bankers were executed by Mahmud II in 1826, Abraham de Camondo. Born in Ortaköy, in 1785, Abraham with his brother Isaac had built the Banque Camondo by acting as Istanbul and Middle Eastern agents for many wealthy Jewish bankers who emerged in Europe following the French Revolution, such as the Rothschilds and the railroad builder Baron de Hirsch. With branches in London, Paris and Vienna, Banque Camondo played a major role in securing European loans to meet the heavy expenses incurred by the Ottoman government in financing the operations of the British and French troops during the Crimean War as well as for the Ottoman *Tanzimat* reforms. As a result, he had become a close friend of the Father of the *Tanzimat*, Mustafa Reşid Pasha, as well as of his protegés and successors following the Crimean War, Grand Vezir Ali Pasha and Finance Minister Fuad Pasha, giving the modernists in the Jewish community a kind of entrée into the Ottoman court which Jews had not benefited from since the Golden Age. It was as a result of this friendship that Camondo felt he had the support needed for him to take the initiative in opening and operating the school despite the violent community objections which he knew would follow.

Camondo's banking operations had given him an opportunity to keep a close watch on developments in Europe as well as in Egypt and the rest of the Empire, making him more determined than ever that Ottoman Jewish youths should be given an opportunity for the same sort of modern education in French and Turkish, as well as Hebrew and in the modern sciences, that already was being provided to most subjects in the *Tanzimat* state schools as well as many of those operated by the Armenian and Greek *millets* and by Christian missionaries. A building was set aside for what came to be known as the *Escuela* in the Piri Pasha section of Hasköy, the French teachers Bernard Brunswick and Jules Dalem were hired, and instruction began on 23 November 1854. After the first week, however, the hysterical protests of the more fanatic rabbis as well as other members of the community got the Grand Rabbi to order the Jewish students not to attend the lessons any longer on the grounds that the school was turning them into Christians, so instruction was suspended. Finally in 1859, in order to secure permission for the students to return, Camondo agreed to several conditions proposed by the Grand Rabbi to satisfy the fanatics: that the Rothschilds and Camondo also finance the traditional *talmud torahs* and *heders* of Istanbul, thus limiting the funds available to the modern school, that rabbis be appointed to the *Escuela* to teach Jewish law and religion in the traditional manner, that the Grand Rabbi name four rabbis to make certain that the new school did not provide any teaching which could be considered contrary to the Jewish religion, and that history books used in the school would be examined and censored by the Grand Rabbinate to make certain that they would not pollute the minds of the young Jews in attendance. As a result, instruction began once again early in 1860 and this time it continued for some time.

The fanatics however were not appeased. Even with such restrictions, once the school began operations, its sponsors, teachers and students, as well as their parents, were persecuted by the rabbis who opposed any sort of modern education and condemned the Grand Rabbi for permitting Jews to attend. Rabbis Yitzhak Akrish and Shlomo Kamhi worked to suppress the school entirely, demanding that the parents withdraw their children on the grounds that Christian propaganda was being carried out and threatening excommunication if they did not. When this did not work, Akrish and several colleagues assaulted Camondo's home in Yeniköy, on the Bosporus, excommunicating him after he once again refused to close the school. Camondo responded by organizing the *Va'ad Pekidim* (*Meclisi cismi*, or 'Committee of Functionaries') composed of leading Jewish intellectuals and wealthy bankers and businessmen in Istanbul who shared his liberal views and were willing to help defend them, but it could do little against the constant agitation of the reactionary rabbis and the mobs of Jewish students and citizens whom they inflamed against Camondo and his associates.

At this point, the Ottoman government stepped in, for Camondo was essential to the continued financial stability of the government and the success of the *Tanzimat* reforms. Fuad Pasha ordered Akrish to be imprisoned at the *Iplikhane* of Eyüb, Istanbul's principal political prison at the time, ostensibly on his own volition but in fact at the request of Grand Rabbi Yakub Avigdor (1860–63), who himself wanted the Jewish religious schools to be modernized as well, but was unable to act openly due to violent opposition among his rabbis and followers. Avigdor had been modernizing community administration, reforming the assessment and collection of the *aritha* capital tax to increase revenues and establishing a new religious superior court, the *Bet-Din ha-Gadol* to exercise authority over the old *bet dins* of Balat and Hasköy, not only to assure more uniform administration of justice within the community but also to prevent men like Akrish from excommunicating anyone they did not like. He established a councils of notables (*meclisi pekadim*; Heb. *Tube ha-Ir*) composed of representatives elected by the people in each district (*mahalle*) of the Jewish quarters of Istanbul and he joined its meetings twice weekly in Galata to have some idea of what the people wanted and how the reforms were effecting them, and he now worked through them to get community support against Akrish.

The mobs carried the day, however. Akrish's arrest and imprisonment only excited his followers to even more direct action to save him. Within a few days they mounted a series of violent and noisy public demonstrations, marching through the Gülhane park beneath the Topkapı Saray and virtually assaulting the Grand Vezir's offices at the Porte. A climax was reached when Sultan Abdül Aziz was sailing through the Golden Horn to the Eyüb mosque to pray one Friday evening. As the Sultan sailed by the adjacent quai at Balat, thousands of Akrish's followers thronged along both banks of the stream, shouting and cursing and demanding his immediate release. When the Imperial barque passed Hasköy on its return from Eyüb, they loudly chanted sacred songs until the Sultan finally gave in and ordered Akrish's release in the face of what seemed to him to be popular demand from the Jewish community. This emboldened Akrish to demand, not only that Camondo's school be closed, but also that Grand Rabbi Avigdor be dismissed.

Avigdor attempted to settle the dispute as well as the evident divisions in the community which it had exposed by organizing a special rabbinical court composed of the Chief Rabbis of Serez, Edirne and Izmir to hear the claims of both sides, including the demand that he be dismissed due to his support for Camondo. The court finally exonerated Camondo and the Grand Rabbi in 1862, but Avigdor was deposed the following year as a result of the continuing intrigues and agitation of his reactionary opponents. Camondo, disgusted with the Sultan's surrender to the fanatics and anguished by the death from the plague of his only son, subsequently moved his home and headquarters to Europe, at first taking up Austrian citizenship and settling in Vienna and then in 1866 moving to Italy, endowing a school for Italians in Istanbul and receiving the title Count from King Victor Emmanuel in return. In 1872 Camondo moved to Paris, where he died a year later. His body was removed back to Istanbul, where it was buried at the Hasköy cemetery in a prominent mausoleum which still dominates the skyline in that part of the city.

Camondo's departure from Istanbul and Avigdor's dismissal from the Grand Rabbinate greatly encouraged Istanbul's conservative rabbis to increase their opposition to Jewish participation in the new institutions and convinced the the new Grand Rabbi Yakir Geron not to interfere for some time, so they continued to use excommunication and other religious penalties against Jews who dared to take advantage of the new courts or to open new schools, greatly limiting their influence on the Jewish community.

There were other attempts outside Istanbul, but with not much more success. As early as 1856 the Lemel School for boys and the Eveline De Rothschild school for girls were established in Jerusalem. The same year in Salonica a modern school founded by an Ashkenazi rabbi from Strasburg named Lipmann in an annex to the local *talmud torah* managed to provide education in the new sciences to about two hundred fifty Jewish children from wealthy families while at the same time attempting to infuse the neighboring *talmud torah* with new ideas. In the face of bitter rabbinical opposition led by Salonica Chief Rabbi Asher Covo, however, it was only partly successful, and closed in 1861. Some of Lipmann's students opened another modern private school in Salonica in 1866 and it lasted, though somewhat perilously, until 1904. Modern Jewish schools were founded in Sarajevo and Belgrade starting in the 1870s. Edirne had a secular Jewish school through much of the century, but only a few young Jews attended until some time after 1876. Under the very strong conservative influence of religious leaders, then, Ottoman Jews failed to take much advantage of the secular reforms during the first three quarters of the nineteenth century, and the advantages which Greeks and Armenians had held in government service became even greater as the century wore on. Those few Jewish families which did dare send their children to modern schools sent them not to those established and run by Jews, then, but, rather, either to the state schools or to the missionary schools, where many came under considerable Christian influence and efforts at conversion, just as the rabbis had feared.

The Alliance Israélite Universelle. Rescue came for Ottoman Jewry not so much from its own community, therefore, but from European Jews who were gaining wealth and power under the new conditions which came to Europe during and after the era of the French Revolution. Jews in England and Germany, and particularly in France, who themselves had been part of the Jewish Enlightenment movement and ideology (*haskalah*) which had begun in the 1770s, were stung when they learned of the poverty and degradation into which their brothers in the Ottoman Empire had fallen, and particularly by reports that Jewish children were being converted to Christianity as the price they had to pay for education in the modern schools being established throughout the Ottoman Empire by the foreign missionaries. In reaction, in France the *Alliance Israélite Universelle* (henceforth referred to as *AIU*) was formed in 1860 by prosperous Jewish professionals and businessmen led by Isidore Cahan, Narcisse Leven, Charles Netter and Eugene Manuel, largely as the result of a public campaign begun a few years earlier by the author Simon Bloch. Within a year it had eight hundred fifty contributing members, and by 1866 there were 4,610 members determined to raise Jews out of poverty and ignorance throughout the East. The principal aim of the *Alliance*'s educational work was to 'regenerate' and transform Eastern Jewries into the image of their emancipated Western, especially French, co-religionists. While some thought was given to reforming the traditional *talmud torah* schools operated by the Jewish religious establishment, rabbinical insistance to maintaining control quickly convinced the *Alliance* that this approach was hopeless. European-style schooling conducted in the French language, and in new independent schools, was therefore considered a better approach.[4]

To this end, it first established modern schools for Ottoman Jews at Damascus and Baghdad, where the most serious ritual murder attacks had taken place two decades before, going on to operate over one hundred schools for men and women at most Ottoman cities, including in Europe at Istanbul starting in 1874, Monastir, Demotica, Edirne, Skopje, Kavala, and Salonica, and in Anatolia and the east at Izmir, Jerusalem, Haifa, Jaffa, Tiberias, Safed and Basra among others. Many of the *AIU* schools were general elementary and high schools. Others provided special skills including training as craftsmen and farmers. There were modern religious seminaries and schools to teach women the skills they needed to be successful housewives in the traditional Jewish family. The *AIU* also developed a system of apprentice training to help Jews enter all the trades and crafts and compete once again with their Christian counterparts, though not without considerable opposition from the latter and their friends among the foreign diplomats and merchants living in the major Ottoman cities. While these schools were intended primarily for Jews, many Muslim Turks also attended, some of whom achieved considerable fame in subsequent years, including Celal Bayar, subsequently Finance Minister in the Turkish Republic led by Mustafa Kemal Atatürk, and President of Turkey between 1950 and 1960.

Similar schools were founded later in the century by the *Anglo Jewish Association* of Great Britain starting in 1871 and by the non-Zionist German *Hilfsverein des Deutschen Juden*, founded in 1901 to free Ottoman Jewry from the influence of the French-dominated *AIU* and to spearhead the formation of German-language educational institutions around the Empire. The *Hilfsverein* built a small-scale educational network in Jerusalem in particular, with kindergardens, primary schools, a teacher's college, a commercial high school, a kindergarden teachers' seminar and a rabbinical college providing comprehensive education to the Jewish community so that by World War I, over half the Jewish children in Palestine who attended modern as opposed to traditional religious schools went to those sponsored by the *Hilfsverein*.

Individual European Jews also played important roles in establishing schools in important Ottoman Jewish centers, particularly in Istanbul and Jerusalem. In 1906 the Bezal'el art school was established in Jerusalem by Professor Boris Schatz, providing training for painters and craftsmen, including gold and silver smiths and weavers, most of whose graduates became the pioneers of Jewish arts and crafts in Palestine during the era of the British mandate following World War I. Eliezer Ben Yehuda established a Language Committee in Jerusalem which centered efforts to revive and use the Hebrew language among all members of the Jewish community in Palestine. In 1907 a site on Mount Scopus in Jerusalem was purchased to provide room for a Hebrew University in Palestine. The eleventh Zionist Congress that met in Vienna in September 1913 endorsed the project, leading the the purchase of a neighboring plot during the war in 1916 and to the laying of the cornerstone for the Hebrew University in July 1918, shortly before the British occupation of the city. As a result of such activities, then, in the early years of the twentieth century, young Ottoman Jews finally were being given the same opportunities to enter modern life as had been provided earlier for Ottoman Muslims, Greeks, and Armenians. These schools were largely left alone by the Ottoman Ministry of Public Education, developing their own curricula and systems of teaching with almost no interference by the authorities, who actually provided indirect financial assistance by sending Ottoman professors paid by the state to supplement the work of the teachers brought from outside the country. As a result of these efforts the community barriers against modern education broke down on all levels. During the last half century of the Empire, not only did Jewish students attend the *AIU* and other such schools but they also flooded into the Ottoman technical schools, the school of Medicine and the University of Istanbul. Jews doctors once again led the profession, while Jews became teachers and professors alongside their Muslim and Christian colleagues in all the state schools.

The *AIU* schools were not without shortcomings, however, particularly insofar as they educated young Jews to be part of Ottoman society. Since they were founded and operated by French Jews for the most part, French was the primary language of instruction, and while Hebrew was also taught as part of religious lessons, the Turkish language and Ottoman and Islamic history were only rarely made parts of the curriculum, leaving most of the students entirely ignorant of the empire, its history and people. An *AIU* teacher thus reported to Paris later in the century that out of some 300,000 Jews then in the empire, as many as 100,000 knew French and only 1,000 understood Turkish. So just as the traditional Jewish schools had cut young Jews off from Ottoman society by teaching only Hebrew, now the modern *AIU* schools were doing the same thing by emphasizing French, with Turkish, if it was taught at all, being in a very subordinate position, and with many Jewish youths coming to share the feelings of contempt for their Muslim brothers that had long been products of the education provided in the Christian *millet* and foreign missionary schools. As a result, only a small minority of Ottoman Jews knew and used Turkish well into the twentieth century, causing a kind tension with Ottoman Muslims that had not really existed earlier when Jews were much more completely parts of Ottoman society. This tendency was vigorously fought by many within the Jewish community, led by the great Jewish-Turkish historian Avram (Abraham) Galante as well as by foreign Jews such as Sir Moses Montefiore when he came to

Istanbul. Their pressure finally led the *AIU* to alter its curriculum to include subjects which would indeed prepare their students to participate more fully in Ottoman and Turkish society than they had in the past, though Jewish women in particular, isolated as they were in their homes, continued to know Judeo-Spanish and French rather than the Turkish and Hebrew which they rarely had chances to use.

Modernization of the Jewish Millet: The Organic Statute of 1864. Restoration of the Grand Rabbinate and elaboration of its authority to represent and supervise other Jewish communities around the empire greatly strengthened the ability of Ottoman Jewry to maintain and expand its position during the last century of Ottoman rule. But for the moment, the *millet* organization itself continued to be run by religious leaders in accordance with religious law and, as we have seen, they were little more sympathetic with modern schools and courts than they had been earlier. The Grand Rabbinate essentially represented the rabbinical community in insisting that Jewish children go only to *millet* schools in preference to the new state and missionary schools and that Jews use only the *millet* courts. With the encouragement of the Grand Rabbinate, then, rabbis constantly intervened with the Government to suppress actions by Jews and others which they considered to be in violation of Jewish law and tradition.

It was only with the modernization of the Jewish *millet* structure imposed by the *Tanzimat* reformers themselves that this situation was altered and the Jewish community itself was made able to fully participate in the Ottoman reform movement. Ali and Fuad Pasha had become convinced by the events surrounding the attacks on Camondo's school that modernization of the community organization itself was the only solution. In 1860, in response to orders from Grand Vezir Fuad Pasha, a committee of Jewish notables was formed under the leadership of Abraham de Camondo for the purpose of advising the Sultan on how the Imperial Rescript of 1856 should be applied to the Jewish community in accord with the times. After Grand Rabbi Yakub Avigdor was deposed, moreover, in 1863 the modernist Chief Rabbi of Edirne since 1835, Yakir Geron, who already had won the favor of the Sultan as well as of most Ottoman Jews as a result of his successful efforts to rebuild his community following the disastrous Edirne fire of 1846, was brought to Istanbul as *locum tenens* (*Kaymakam*) of the Grand Rabbinate. He maintained this position until 1871, though without ever being appointed actual Grand Rabbi due to the opposition of the conservatives in the Jewish community. On the basis of the committee's recommendations and in imitation of earlier reorganization of the Greek and Armenian *millets* introduced in 1862 and 1863 respectively, Geron obeyed the Grand Vezir's order of 20 July 1863[5] that the Grand Rabbinate be reorganized, initially holding a general community meeting on 10 August 1863 at which he urged everyone to work together to institute necessary reforms, and promised severe punishment for those who failed to agree.

Soon afterwards, he organized a committee of fourteen representatives of the various Jewish electoral districts in Istanbul under the chairmanship of Abraham de Camondo for the purpose of initiating the reform process. It in turn chose a committee of twelve lay administrators and four rabbis who on 1 April 1864 presented him with the text of a new Organic Statute for the Ottoman Jewish community, which was approved without change by *Irade* of the Sultan on 21 March 1865 and put into force on 3 May 1865.[6] The rapid progress of reform of the Jewish *millet* so pleased the Sultan that he immediately awarded Geron the huge sum of 75,000 *kuruş* along with a monthly pension of 5,000 *kuruş*, and presented him with the *Mecidiye* medal of honor, the highest award ever presented to a Rabbi.

The new Organic Regulation regulation consisted of four main sections dealing with the selection and duties of Chief Rabbis, the General Council (*Meclisi Umumi*), the Lay Committee (*Meclisi Cismani*), and the Religious Committee (*Meclisi Ruhani*). It was put into force only gradually at first, and only in Istanbul, only much later elsewhere in the empire. The seat of the Grand Rabbinate was located at Cibalı (article 11), on the Golden Horn between Balat and Eminönü, where it remained until 1876, when it was transferred to the location in Beyoğlu where it remains to the present day.

The Grand Rabbi (*Hahambaşı*) was recognized as the administrative leader of the Jewish *millet* throughout the empire but as spiritual leader only of the Istanbul community, with the other major Jewish centers subsequently receiving their own supplementary regulations during the next two decades, particularly in the *berats* by which the provincial chief rabbis were appointed. Only his administrative duties were specified, with his religious and community duties being left to custom and tradition as before. He was defined as chief of the entire Ottoman Jewish community, with the duty of carrying out the orders of the government as well as the regulations of the Organic Statute and of the Jewish community, but in fact his powers were greatly limited compared to what they had been formerly in that he was subjected to the advice and direction of the lay element of the community.

The latter exercised its power through a general council (*meclisi umumi*), composed of sixty laymen, elected in seventeen districts (*hashgahot*) by the Jews of Istanbul and its suburbs, with 5,141 voters aged 20 and above who participated in the 1865 elections. The bulk of the voters, 2,312, came from Hasköy, the principal Jewish quarter at that time, which by itself elected twenty members of the council. Other important centers were Piri Pasha, with 322 voters, who elected 5 representatives; Ortaköy, on the Bosporus, from which 554 voters elected four representatives, and Kuzguncuk, from which 393 voters elected six representatives. After they got together, they appointed the general committee's twenty rabbinical members. It in turn elected seven rabbis who formed the religious council (*meclisi ruhâni*) and nine lay members of the executive secular council (*meclisi cismâni*), in addition to the Rabbinical Court (*Bet Din*), which was composed of three to five rabbis.

The religious council (*meclisi ruhâni*), required to meet two or three times weekly, was in charge of protecting religious interests, choosing and supervising the rabbis who administered each *hashgaha* district as *mare de atra*, and assuring that no rabbi or preacher opposed the opinions or will of the government or governmental and religious laws and regulations. It was charged with looking into religious questions, but only those submitted to it by the Grand Rabbi or the general committee, and it was specifically prohibited from preventing the publication of books or the diffusion of modern sciences and arts within the Jewish community, though with the significant exception of those which might be 'harmful to the Government, the community and the Jewish religion'. The Grand Rabbi now needed the approval of the president and vice-presidents of the religious council for inflicting excommunication or other major religious punishments on community members.

The secular council (*meclisi cismani*) was charged with regulating and supervising all other matters concerning the Jewish community as well as carrying out government and community laws, orders, and regulations. It had the right to assess and collect community taxes, to supervise the administration of the properties of community funds, foundations and orphans and of the administration of all the Jewish community organizations and institutions around the empire. Ottoman officials were prohibited from interfering in its affairs and operations, but provisions were made for the dismissal of all or individual members for violating the laws or the 'national interest'.

Ottoman Jewry was now divided into eight rabbinical districts outside Istanbul,[7] at Bursa,[8] Baghdad, Edirne, Izmir, Salonica, Cairo, Alexandria and Jerusalem, for each of which Chief Rabbis also were subsequently appointed along with general, secular and religious committees, all with powers, responsibilities and duties similar to those of their counterparts in Istanbul. At least in theory and insofar as the government was concerned, they were supposed to act under the general authority of the Grand Rabbi of Istanbul, but the exact relationship between them and the Grand Rabbi, among them, and with government officials, never was exactly defined, causing many disputes and quarrels later in the century. Additional chief rabbinical districts were created later in the nineteenth century at Sofia, Sarajevo, Damascus, Janina, Musul, Trablusgarb (Tripoli of Libya), Beirut, and Aleppo.

For the election of new Grand Rabbis, who could be no younger than thirty nor older than seventy, the general council was enlarged to include forty representatives of the eight major provincial Grand Rabbis, with the elections decided by majority vote.[9]

Ottoman Jewry Enters the Modern World. With Jews finally attending the modern state and *Alliance* schools in increasing numbers, and the new community structure no longer serving to block Jewish participation in the *Tanzimat* reform movement in all its facets, Ottoman Jewry moved rapidly to catch up with the other *millets*. Jewish graduates of the new schools entered the bureaucracy and occupied important positions in most of the government departments with the exception of the military. Jewish merchants and traders, often with the financial support of the great Jewish bankers of Europe, gained an ever-increasing share of the Ottoman marketplace and participated widely in international trade. With the lay element increasingly dominating the community machinery, many of the old restrictions and regulations were often ignored, or at least neglected. Nowhere was this more evidently manifested than in dress, where the old traditions and regulations differentiating the dress of members of different classes and *millets* were very quickly abandoned, particularly in the years during and after the Crimean War when a large-scale influx of foreign soldiers, merchants, diplomats and travellers spread European ways and dress among all elements of the population. Already under Sultan Mahmud II (1808–39), a fez common to all replaced the turban whose size, shape, and colors had marked social distinctions more than any other element of costume. In 1829 he followed this up by a decree ordering all his bureaucrats except those in the religious class to wear European clothing, leading all to replace the cloak with a European frock coat and their turbans or hats with the fez, though often many Jews and others began to use combinations of the long, dark *şalvar* trousers, colored navy blue or black, tied with sashes (*kuşak*) or cords at the waist and the ankles, with the traditional *entari* robe, with its long sleeves and narrow colors gradually being replaced by European frock coats of various sorts and the traditional cylindrical *bonetas*, with turbans around their lower parts, continuing to dominate until well into the century when they were supplanted by hats. Mahmud's successor Sultan Abdül Mecid (1839–61) began to wear the frock coat, setting an example which other members of the Ruling Class and *millets* soon followed, thus eliminating the last major element of differentiation, at least insofar as clothing was concerned.

Women changed their clothing more slowly, often using imported European cloths to manufacture clothing cut in Ottoman styles, with the addition of European cuffs and accessories like gloves and umbrellas. On the street, the long *ferace* cloak with its long wide sleeves and long rectangular collar continued to dominate until the 1890s, though with less attention paid to the distinctive colors previously assigned to the members of the different *millets*. On their heads, Muslim women wore the *yaşmak*, two cloths which covered the head and face and left only a narrow slit for the eyes, while Jewish and Christian women wore the *marama* shawl over both their heads and necks. Jewish women in Istanbul wore on their yeads the *yemeni*, a cotton printed floral kerchief with lace trimming, a silk *entari* robe with long sleeves, and a short *hirka* jacket lined with fur before they too changed to European costumes. This is not to say, however, that the transition took place without opposition from members of all the communities. At the end of the century, Sultan Abdül Hamid II tried to turn the clock back, at least insofar as Muslim women were concerned. And among the Jews, the influential leaders of Salonica and Izmir Jewry, Rabbi Raphael Asher Covo and Rabbi Haim Palacci, respectively, also appealed to Jewish women to return to their former modesty, stating that their wearing of European clothing and exposing parts of the body such as their hair was leading them away from their religion.[10]

Community Divisions. The Jewish community thus remained badly divided, principally between the traditionalists who wanted to retain the old Orthodox customs intact and the modernists, who wanted to transform Jewish life with the infusion of new schools and ways of doing things, largely from Europe. This quarrel was not really resolved until the last quarter of the century, largely as the result of the establishment of modern Jewish schools in the Empire by European Jewish organizations. Later on, there were community divisions over their relationship with the Zionist movement in particular.

Nor were disputes over national origins entirely neglected. In 1865, the wealthy Franco family led a separation from the Sephardic community of many Jews of Italian origin, forming a new 'Synagogue of Foreigners' (*Yabancılar Cemaatı*) which subsequently called itself the 'Italian Jewish Community' (*Italyan Musevi Cemaatı*) after it received official recognition and support from the King of Italy.

In addition, while Ottoman Ashkenazis earlier had been assimilated to Sephardic culture and recognized the authority of the Grand Rabbi as established under the Organic Statute of 1864, they remained autonomous, chosing their own deputies to the *meclisi umumi* to participate in community affairs. As their numbers increased substantially, moreover, as the result of the arrival of hundreds of new refugees in flight from persecution in Germany as well as from the Russian pogroms in Central Asia after the 1850s and in the Pale after 1881, they increasingly began once again to manage their own affairs without reference to the Grand Rabbinate. Since since the Ashkenazis prospered substantially in the trades, commerce, finance and professions, they increasingly built and maintained their own synagogues and rituals separate from those of the Sephardim, emphasizing the use of Yiddish rather than Judeo-Spanish as the primary secular community language. This separation was accomplished primarily under the leadership of the Ukrainian-born Dr David Marcus (1870–1944), who served as Rabbi of the Ashkenazi community and after 1912 *mare de atra* (district leader) of the Ashkenazi *hashgaha* from 1900 until 1940, founding and directing the Jewish Goldschmidt Lycée in Galata for Jews of all communities after the withdrawal of the *AIU* during World War I. The Ashkenazim maintained three synagogues in late Ottoman times. The ancient *Budin* (Buda) and the *Aleman* (German) in Balat, founded by refugees from Central Europe who had arrived during the sixteenth century reign of *Kanuni* Suleyman, were now gone since the original Ashkenazim had long since moved to other parts of Istanbul, mainly to Galata, but there they maintained the German synagogue on Yüksek Kaldırım, the *Tofre Begadim* (synagogue of tailors) synagogue, and the *Or Hadash* synagogue, at the Kemer Altı area. They also organized their own charitable societies to care for and house the indigent poor and to arrange for their funerals when necessary. They had their *Israelitischer Bruder-Verein*, gymnastic and social society and society of tailors and maintained their own *Talmud Torah*, founded with the help of the President of the *AIU* at that time, S. H. Goldschmidt, which for that reason bore his name until well into the twentieth century. They used the Sephardic cemetery, however, paying a special fee to the Grand Rabbi for this privilege. There were divisions among the Ashkenazim between the German and Austrian Jews, who were well educated and prosperous, and the Russian Jews, who came as peasants and preferred to maintain their own way of life, which often was closer to that of the poorer Sephardim than it was to their wealther Ashkenazi cousins from Central Europe. There also were emotional quarrels with the Sephardim over the rituals by which meat was made ritually clean (*kosher*) by the slaughterers (*shohetim*), most of whom were Ashkenazis, as well as over the taxes (*shahit*) which the butchers were supposed to, but often did not, pay to the Grand Rabbinate.

Nor were these the only divisions within Ottoman Jewry. Not all Jews recognized the authority of the Grand Rabbi. The Karaite community remained, as always, entirely separate, with its distinct rituals and customs constantly leading to disputes with the majority. Living mainly in the poorer sections of Galata and later Hasköy and Kâğıthane, on the northern shores of the Golden Horn, they had their own chief rabbi, officially referred to as the *Hazzan*, their *Bet Din*, synagogue, *Talmud Torah*, cemetery, located in the nineteenth century at the Yazıcı section of Hasköy, next to the Boton Han, and council of *memunim* administering communal affairs, all recognized by a separate imperial *ferman* issued directly to them. They did not maintain their own court system, preferring to apply when necessary to the Muslim courts and to accept Muslim law rather than using those of the rabbinites, referring to the latter only as a last resort, leading to almost constant campaigns against them carried on by one of Rabbi Isaac Akrish's followers, Rabbi Shlomo Kamhi, who in 1866 published *Melehet Şelomo*, which vigorously attacked the Karaites.

Grand Rabbi Yakir Geron. As a result of these and other divisions within the community, therefore, though the three governing committees of the Grand Rabbinate were elected in 1866 in accordance with the new Organic Statute, it was impossible to secure a majority to elect a Grand Rabbi in place of *Kaymakam* Yakir Geron, who therefore continued to administer the community as acting leader until finally resigning in disgust in 1872.

Despite these difficulties, however, Geron moved with vigor in his early years to implement the Organic Statute and reform the community. In every quarter of the major cities local rabbis were appointed as district leaders, or *mare de atras*, who became administrative as well as religious heads of their communities, in charge not only of leading the local synagogues and related institutions but also of acting as government agents with their members, collecting the *cizye* and other taxes and turning them over to the Treasury. Finances for the Grand Rabbinate as well as the provincial local rabbinates were provided by energetic collection of the *gabelle* excise taxes on meat, wines and spirits, the Capital Tax (*aritha*) on personal property and businesses, special taxes collected for circumcisions, weddings, and other ceremonies, and by community lotteries established at the same time as the Imperial Ottoman Lottery was begun to provide funds for governmental expenses as well as to finance the Red Crescent Society and the construction of new warships. To meet temporary expenses until the new revenues came in, Geron in January 1865 secured Fuad Pasha's permission to incur a loan from the Camondo Bank of 150,000 *kuruş*, which subsequently was repaid out of *aritha* revenues. Geron went so far as to review and eliminate traditional payments to certain rabbis who no longer performed any community service, something which shocked and angered quite a number of his colleagues, who added their hungry voices to the opposition. When he discovered lax enforcement of religious regulations, moreover, he decreed that all circumcisions, weddings and divorces previously per-formed and confirmed by his predecessors were invalid unless it could be proven that proper procedures were followed in each case. He also worked vigorously to combat the Christian propaganda being spread in Hasköy by Protestant missionaries in 1868, encouraging the publication of Jewish newspapers and handbills to counter their claims, finally getting the government to prohibit their activities altogether, at least in the Jewish quarters of the city.

Under the new Organic Statute, the Grand Rabbi was once again assisted in governmental relations by a *kâhya*, who reported births, deaths, marriages and divorces to the authorities and generally handled community relations with state officials. There were now only three Jewish courts (*bet din*) in Istanbul, but they were allowed to deal only with matters of marriage and divorce while most other cases were handled by the new secular *Tanzimat* courts which enforced the new secular law codes for all regardless of religion. Synagogue prisons were abandoned in favor of a single Rabbinical prison located at the Grand Rabbinate so long as it was in Cibalı and then at the Chana synagogue in Balat. For all practical purposes, thus, the *Tanzimat* was successful in limiting the power of Jewish as well as other religious leaders. The rabbis lost their monopoly of power within the Jewish community. They were forced to share power with the new generation of lay leaders, while the community itself lost considerable authority to the new secular state institutions in both legal and educational affairs. The rabbis still could protest, and some did, but they no longer had the power to impose their will over their followers and to punish modernizers.

Geron led the way in adapting to the new situation. He was the first Jewish chief rabbi since the sixteenth century to develop good relations with the principal officials of state as well as with the leaders of the new bureaucracy created by the *Tanzimat*, visiting the ministries regularly to keep key bureaucrats informed about the problems of his *millet* as well as to secure their permission for the changes he was introducing. He also made a point of contacting foreign dignitaries visiting Istanbul to secure their support as the Armenian and Greek patriarchs had done for generations, meeting the visiting Serbian Prince Michael III Obrenovich in April 1867, Austrian Emperor Franz Joseph in October of the same year, and Empress Eugenie, wife of French Emperor Napoleon III, during her visit to Istanbul on 7 October 1869.

Geron, however, became increasingly distant and autocratic in dealing with subordinates and handling community problems, causing a great deal of opposition and criticism in his later years. Just as had been the case during Elijah Mizrahi's term as Grand Rabbi in the early years of the sixteenth century, the Karaites remained a major irritant within the Jewish community. In an effort to stop divisions and disputes caused by Rabbi Kamhi's virulent attacks on the Karaites, Geron ordered that all copies of the latter's book on the subject be confiscated and destroyed, while Kamhi himself was subjected to religious punishments culminating in imprisonment. This action, however, deeply offended those who supported Kamhi's insistence that the Karaites were not Jews and that Jews should not be punished for attacking them, leading to several mass demonstrations outside the Grand Rabbinate as well as frequent demands that Geron be replaced with someone who was more in harmony with the demonstrators' feelings on the subject.

The Haim Palacci Dispute. Even greater difficulties came as a result of the Organic Statute's failure to define clearly the relationship between the

Grand Rabbi of Istanbul and the Chief Rabbis of the different provinces, as well as that between these Rabbis and their administrative councils. Izmir, for example, had maintained its own religious and administrative lay councils long before the *Tanzimat* had required them, since they had been created by Rabbi Joseph Escapa in the early years of the seventeenth century. It now had its own *Meclisi Cismani* composed of deputies elected by its thirteen synagogues,[11] but as a result of a century of experience in self-government they were rarely willing to concede their authority to the newly established Chief Rabbi of Izmir, let alone to the Grand Rabbi of Istanbul, leading to violent conflicts when the latter tried to exercise the authority which the Organic Statute had given him.

For several years, therefore, Geron constantly quarrelled over a whole series of problems with the Izmir's *rav kolel* (chief of Rabbis) since 1855 and Chief Rabbi (*Hahambaşı*) as established by the Organic Statute in 1865, Rabbi Haim Palacci (Palache/Palaggi; 1788–1869). Palacci like Geron was active and vigorous and preferred to go ahead without consultation, either with his local followers or with his superiors in Istanbul. He also was far more conservative than most other leaders of the community, in Istanbul as well as Izmir, stating that the distinctive Jewish food, clothing and religious practices were the main difference between them and Gentiles and that to abandon them in favor of the modern ways followed by Muslims and Christians alike would prevent Jews from being recognized as Jews and would therefore bring the wrath of God on all of them.[12] At the same time the members of the executive committee tried to take advantage of his advanced age and administer the community without consulting him, as had been done in Izmir since Escapa's time. His initial efforts to increase community revenues by raising the *gabelle* tax on foodstuffs led to so many complaints that in November 1865, in the midst of a violent epidemic of cholera which decimated Izmir's Jewish population, the administrative council ordered him not to make any decisions or to sign any documents in future without securing its prior authorization.

Several council members then got together and purchased a tax farm for the *gabelle* tax on wine, alcohol and salt at a price far below its market value, securing substantial profits by raising the impositions on Izmir's Jewish residents. When popular representatives came to the Chief Rabbinate and demanded an accounting they refused to comply. Palacci responded to the situation by unilaterally anulling the tax farm award, but this caused the council to accuse him of corruption and ask the Grand Rabbi to remove him. Geron responded in December 1866 by sending his secretary, Rabbi Samuel Danon, to Izmir to investigate the situation and try to resolve the dispute. Danon's intervention, however, only made things worse and led to open battles in the streets among the different factions. Danon recommended to Geron that the only way to resolve the complicated dispute was to dismiss Palacci as Chief Rabbi and appoint Danon in his place, and at Geron's request both the dismissal and new appointment were ordered by the government. Most members of the Izmir Jewish community, however, strongly resented the intervention from Istanbul, both by the Grand Rabbi and by the government, particularly since it involved dismissal of a Chief Rabbi who had been defending them against exploitation by members of the executive council, and convinced the city's governor (*vali*) to ignore the order and allow Palacci to remain in his post while he consulted his superiors in Istanbul. As a result, the governor was ordered to delay carrying out the dismissal while a further investigation was undertaken. In the meantime, Palacci's followers demonstrated violently in both Izmir and Istanbul and Palacci himself intrigued against Geron in Istanbul, stimulating the latter's opponents to attack him on this and other matters. Finally, in October, 1867 Palacci was officially restored as Izmir's Chief Rabbi for life. Instead of trying to gain revenge, however, he made peace with the council in return for their agreeing to fully apply the Organic Statute of 1864 in Izmir for the first time so as to define clearly the powers and responsibilities of all the different elements in the community organization. Palacci died, however, on 9 February 1868 before the new system could be organized, and the resulting conflicts over authority within the community and with Istanbul continued until a new Organic Statute specifically for Izmir was promulgated in 1911.[13]

The Palacci affair in particular greatly harmed Geron's ability to lead his community in his latter years as *kaymakam*. Finally, though he was respected and beloved by the mass of Ottoman Jewry, the increasing arguments and disputes to which he was subjected in the *Meclisi Cismani* and his own relative impotence due to his continued status as *Kaymakam* and not Grand Rabbi, led him to resign and move to Jerusalem, where he established his own *yeshiva* shortly before his death on 11 February 1874.

Revival of Ottoman Jewry and Christian Resistance. The revival of Ottoman Jewry was not limited to community institutions. Jewish capitalists from western Europe now played a major role in restoring Jewish economic and financial prominence as they help revive the empire's economy following the Crimean War. The *Tanzimat* reformers now were encouraging foreign investment in banking as well as in industry and commerce. Foreign banks, railroad, steamship and insurance companies and foreign mineral developers with mining concessions, often owned and managed by wealthy European Jews, now operated throughout the empire, and for the most part employed Ottoman Jews as their agents, helping the latter to re-enter the Ottoman market in their own right. Just as the Armenians and Greeks had been helped by European Christian merchants and diplomats in the seventeenth and eighteenth centuries, now

Ottoman Jewish bankers and merchants were encouraged, supported and protected by the great Jewish financiers of Europe, the Rothschilds and Baron Maurice de Hirsch to name only the most prominent examples. Once the Rabbinical reservations had been overcome, moreover, Jewish doctors emerged from the Ottoman medical schools to play leading roles in the development of modern medical treatment, serving in the army as well as in private practice, developing clinics and hospitals and as professors at the medical faculties and at the University of Istanbul. Other Ottoman Jews also stirred out of their lethargy, entering government and business in increasing numbers, particularly during the reign of Sultan Abdül Hamid II (1876–1909). The renewed Jewish competition was felt by Ottoman Christians, not only in the old centers of Jewish life in the empire, but particularly in Edirne, where the Jewish community increased from 12,000 in 1873 to 28,000 at the start of World War I largely as the result of flight from persecution in the newly independent states of Rumania and Bulgaria. Those Jews who prospered in trade and commerce gathered in the Kale İçi section of the city, while the artisans lived at Çukurmahalle-Bostan Pazarı and the laborers and hammals at Tabağna, with each section maintaining its own community organization, synagogue, and Bet Din under the general direction of the city's Chief Rabbi. The latter was prospering to such an extent that in 1905 it constructed the Great Synagogue in imitation of that of Vienna as well as a beautiful Yeshiva. Unfortunately, however, occupation of the city by Bulgarians and Greeks during the Balkan Wars so decimated its Jewish population that it fell to 13,000 by the end of World War I. The decline has continued since Thrace was the only part of the Turkish Republic to experience any sort of anti-Semitism in the 1930s, leading most of Edirne's Jews to move to Istanbul, and leaving the Great Synagogue to fall into ruins.

The Greek and Armenian minorities who had monopolized business and government service in the Empire since they had pushed the Jews out during the late seventeenth century strongly resisted this restoration of Jewish competition with the assistance of European diplomats and consuls in the empire through the continued use of the Capitulations agreements whose privileges were extended, not only to the hundreds of European merchants coming to the Ottoman Empire to benefit from the profits that could be secured, but also to hundreds of Ottoman non-Muslims, mainly Christians, who purchased either foreign citizenship as such, or at least the brevets of exemption (*berats*) originally authorized for the native translators (*tercuman* or *dragoman*) and other servants hired by the foreign embassies and consulates, who needed immunity from Ottoman laws in order to carry out their jobs. At the start of the nineteenth century, Sultan Selim III had attempted to limit the sale of these privileges, but without success due to the energetic opposition of the foreign ambassadors, so finally he had legalized them in return for substantial payments to his treasury. Mahmud II had tried to encourage Muslims to enter trade and commerce once again, but he had little success for the same reason. Despite all the equality granted to non-Muslim subjects by the *Tanzimat*, then, Greek and Armenian merchants continued to acquire foreign protection and often foreign nationality in this manner, enabling them to squeeze out Muslim and Jewish subjects alike as the century progressed.

Jewish subjects, however, did not take this sort of opposition without resistance as they had during the previous two centuries. With capital provided by the foreign Jewish bankers and merchants who had initially employed them as agents, they took the initiative in seeking out and investing in new urban industries where needs were perceived and not yet met by their Christian competitors, like cigarette-paper factories, spinning mills, brick-making establishments and tobacco-packing factories. Those Jews who engaged in commerce prospered substantially from the growing Ottoman trade with Europe, also with the help of their European co-religionists, with those of Izmir now coming to equal the older Jewish communities of Salonica and Istanbul in prosperity and power. In Izmir, *Havra Sokak* centered the activities of over one hundred Jewish artisans and merchants, to the extent that it was known during the century as the 'Jewish market' (*Musevi Çarşı*) until its shops were largely destroyed and its artisans driven out during the Greek occupation of the city during the Turkish War for Independence, from 1919 to 1922.

Dönme Prosperity in Salonica. The revival of Ottoman Jewry was shared by members of the *dönme* sect which, since the death of Shabbatai Tzvi in 1676, had concentrated its activities at Salonica. While many of his followers had remained Jews, some interpreted his conversion to Islam as a secret mission assigned to him by God for a particular mystic purpose, and emulated his conversion, calling themselves *ma'aminim* ('believers'), though continuing to practice their own form of Judaism in secret, based on what they called the 'eighteen precepts' left by Tzvi, which involved their own version of the Ten Commandments. In order to preserve their community, they prohibited marriage with real Muslims as well as Jews. To counteract the resulting limited marriage possibilites, they maintained a particularly liberal interpretation of the prohibition of adultery, allowing religious ceremonies involving the exchanges of wives and engaging in other practices which led some to accuse them of sexual deviations of various sorts. They engaged in virtual orgiastic ceremonies during their 'Festival of the Lamb' which celebrated the beginning of spring, and they celebrated other festivals, not recognized by Orthodox Judaism, involved with the events surrounding the life of Tzvi and his apostasy. Like the Karaites they abandoned the traditional Torah, which they called the *Torah di-Beri'ah*, or 'Torah of Creation', considering it to have been replaced by their own *Torah de-Azilut*, or 'Torah of Emanation', which they felt to be far more spiritual and sublime. Unlike the Karaites, however, in many areas they did follow the Torah, leading many rabbis to believe that they could still be won back into the fold, so that there was much less of violent public opposition to them than there was to the Karaites. There was in fact very little difference between their religious beliefs and those of the Shabbateans who openly remained Jews. They developed the idea that Tzvi was divine and emphasized what they called the 'three bonds of faith' as the upper forces of emanation.

Internal disputes caused a major split in the *dönme* community early in the seventeenth century, with Shabbatai Tzvi's original followers coming to be called *Izmirim*, or the 'people from Izmir', while those who followed the claim of Tzvi's last wife Jochebed, daughter of a Salonica Rabbi (who took the name A'isha after her conversion to Islam), that her brother Jacob Querido ('the beloved') was the reincarnation of her husband, came to be known as the *Ya'akoviyim* (in Turkish *Yakoblar*), or 'followers of Jacob'. Early in the eighteenth century the claims of one of Tzvi's early disciples, Baruchiah Russo, that he was the reincarnation of Tzvi, led to the formation of a third sect, called *Konyosos* in Judeo-Spanish and *Karakaşlar* in Turkish, which was far more extreme than the others, expanding rapidly through missionary activity among Jews throughout Europe, particularly in Poland, Germany and Austria. It was at this time that the Turks discovered that all these groups had not really become sincere practicing Muslims and so began to call them *dönmes*, meaning 'converts' or 'apostates', while the rabbis of Salonica called them *minim*, or 'sectarians'.

The *dönme*s settled in their own quarters of Salonica and came into close association with Muslim mystic orders, particularly the Bektaşis, who long had served as the spiritual leaders of the Janissary corps that had caused the Jewish community so much trouble, and with the Shabbateans who remained Jewish. By the early years of the nineteenth century, the three *dönme* divisions in Salonica constituted substantially different social groups, each organized as its own *kahal* with its own synagogue, but using the common *dönme* cemetery. The *Izmirli*s became quite wealthy in trade and commerce, constituting the aristocracy as well as the intelligentsia of *dönme* society under the name *Cavalleros* in Judeo-Spanish and *Kapancilar* in Turkish. For the most part they were assimilated to Ottoman Turkish society by the middle of the century, using Turkish as their primary language with Judeo-Spanish looked down on as the language of the masses. The *Ya'akoviyim* now consisted mostly of lower and middle-class *dönme*s, who for the most part earned their livelihoods in the lesser offices of the Ottoman bureaucracy. The third and by far the largest group, The *Konyosos*, were the poorest of the *dönme*s, consisting mainly of artisans and common workers, who

1. Rabbi Hayim Nahum Efendi, Grand Rabbi of the Ottoman Empire, 1909–20 and Chief Rabbi of Egypt, 1925–60.

2. (*left*) Rabbi Hayim Bejerano, Chief Rabbi of Turkey, 1920–31. Courtesy of Chief Rabbi David Asseo.

3. (*right*) Rabbi Rafael David Saban, Chief Rabbi of Turkey, 1953–60. Courtesy of Chief Rabbi David Asseo.

4. (*above*) Rabbi David Asseo (*right*), Chief Rabbi of Turkey since 1961, with the author.

5. (*below*) Yanbol Synagogue, Balat, Istanbul.

6. (*above*) Ahrida Synagogue in Balat, Istanbul (front gate).

7. (*below*) Ahrida Synagogue in Balat, Istanbul (interior).

8. (*left*) Bohçaci: wealthy Jewish woman pedlar by Jean Baptiste van Moor (1719).

9. (*right*) Istanbul: wealthy Jewish woman by Jean Baptiste van Moor (1719).

10. (*left*) Jerusalem Jews, 1873 from
Osman Hamdi *Les Costumes
Populaires de la Turquie en 1873.*

11. (*right*) Bursa Jews, 1873 from
Osman Hamdi *Les Costumes
Populaires de la Turquie en 1873.*

(*right*) Salonica Jew, 1873 from Osman Hamdi *Les Costumes Populaires de la Turquie en 1873*.

13. (*left*) Aleppo Jew, 1873 from Osman Hamdi *Les Costumes Populaires de la Turquie en 1873*.

14. (*left*) Sultan Abdül Hamid II, Ottoman ruler from 1876–1909 (*Illustrated London News*, 23 May 1877).

15. (*below*) 'Prayers offered at the Jewish Synagogue, Constantinople, for the success of Turkish arms in the Russo-Turkish war, 1877' (*Illustrated London News*, 9 June 1877).

remained far closer to older Sephardic traditions and the Judeo-Spanish language than did the others.

Jewish Cultural Revival and the Jewish Press. The nineteenth and twentieth centuries until the start of World War I witnessed a substantial Jewish cultural revival, not so much in the traditional Hebrew and Ladino religious and related legal learning which had prevailed in the Golden Age but, rather, in the popular Jewish literature expressed in Judeo-Spanish or *Judezmo*, developed by the constant use in periodic *meldares*, or community meetings, in which parts of the *Me'am Lo'ez* folk encyclopaedia were read and discussed, which with strong Turkish and Hebrew intermixtures in verbal and morphological usages and formations by now was accepted by all elements of the community as its *lingua franca*, and to a lesser extent in French, the common language of the minorities as well as of the foreign colonies living in the Empire. This Golden Age of Judeo-Spanish literature was expressed in an outpouring of secular newspapers and periodicals containing serialized *romansos*, or romantic novels, as well as poems, stories, essays and articles of popular interest and books and pamphlets on subjects ranging from Jewish popular traditions, folk songs and festivals to history, many translated from the Hebrew which most members of the Ottoman Jewish community could no longer read with any facility. Salonica and Istanbul continued to lead in learning and publishing by virtue of their political and economic leadership, with Edirne and Jerusalem also participating, but Judeo-Spanish publications flourished particularly brightly in Izmir because of the emerging prosperity and relative liberalism of its new community.

Very much as was the case in developing secular Turkish-language literature at that time, a few *romansos* were original, but more often they were Judeo-Spanish translations or adaptations from original Hebrew or French works, often without direct reference to the original. Most of the authors were not professionals but, rather, were merchants, government officials, or physicians, or even publishers or printers, who spent only small portions of their time writing. Only a few journalists devoted themselves entirely to writing, though even with them fictional composition absorbed only a very small part of their working lives. Some of their works were published as books right from the start, but for the most part they were serialized in newspapers and periodicals, with only those which proved to be most popular subsequently being issued in single volumes if sufficient demand was anticipated. Quite a number were published in individual fascicules, called *separates*, usually of sixteen pages, which were either sold by subscription or by sales in bulk to distributors such as Benyamin ben Yosef in Istanbul or Solomon Israel Cheresli in Jerusalem, who then placed them in local book stores or sold them directly to the reading public. Because they were for the most part published serially and intended for the poorly-educated Jewish masses, most of the *romansos* were crude and simple in structure, emphasizing adventure and melodrama with little attention to characterization or plot, and with the fine syntax and style of the Castillian brought from Spain deteriorated and greatly intermixed with the French taught in the *AIU* schools as well as with Italian, Turkish and Hebrew jargon, producing a *mélange* quite distant from the original.

Since most Jews at the time knew only Judeo-Spanish and Hebrew, and only the wealthy or educated knew French and Ottoman Turkish and read the developing Ottoman newspapers of the time, the Judeo-Spanish popular press played a vital role in bringing together and maintaining the Jewish community as well as in entertaining, informing its readers of events within and outside the Empire, and often leading the opposition to unpopular policies of the rabbis and the *millet* and community leaders, particularly in the years following enactment of the Organic Statute in 1864. A few publishers – like the pioneering publisher David Fresco (1850–1933), the most important Jewish newspaperman of the late 19th and early 20th century who published numerous newspapers and magazines – attempted to use their newspapers to educate and uplift their readers, most simply gave the latter the kind of entertainment and diversion that they wanted, with only miniscule space devoted to education or morality. While all Ottoman newspapers were subjected to government censorship following the Crimean War, the officials of the sultans paid little attention to the non-Ottoman press because of its limited readership, becoming involved with its journalists only when invited by Grand Rabbis or local Chief Rabbis, thus giving the latter considerable authority over the Jewish press, though this did not entirely prevent the latter from engaging in vigorous campaigns against the *millet* establishment from time to time. So it was, for example, that David Fresco was not only excommunicated by the Grand Rabbi but also sent into exile at his request by the government after he attacked the latter's corrupt financial administration. Since Egypt under British rule after 1882 was far more liberal in its treatment of the press, many leading Jewish and Ottoman writers concentrated their activities there, including Avram Galante, who was so vigorously suppressed because of his attacks against Grand Rabbi Moshe Levi, against the tyrannical rule of Chief Rabbi Haim Palacci in Izmir, and against the *AIU* schools because of their concentration on teaching in French to the exclusion of Turkish, that he went to Cairo where he carried on his attacks in his own newspaper, *La Vara* (The Stick), in 1907–8, while the leading Judeo-Spanish novelist Elia Carmona published most of his works in Egypt between 1902 and 1908. Both returned to Istanbul following the Young Turk Revolution because of the more liberal conditions promised by the newly-appointed Grand Rabbi Haim Nahum Efendi (1909–20) as well as a result of the new Constitutional regime established in Istanbul at the same time.

Two-thirds of the Jewish newspapers published in the Ottoman Empire during the nineteenth century appeared in four cities, Salonica, Istanbul, Sofia and Izmir, while others appeared in lesser numbers in Egypt, Palestine, and Rumania. While most of the Judeo-Spanish periodicals were published in the *Rashi* Hebrew script, a very few, starting with the bi-monthly *El Lucero de la Paciencia*, published in Turno Severin, Rumania, by Elia Crespin from 1855 to 1890, were published in Latin characters due to the deterioration of the language, which led *Rashi* to spell words of different meaning in exactly the same way, causing considerable confusion among readers.

The first major Jewish newspaper to appear in Istanbul was the French-language *Journal Israélite* (1841–60), edited by Ezekial Gabay. It was followed by the first Ottoman Judeo-Spanish paper, *La Luz de Israel* (*Or Israel*/The Light of Israel), edited by Leon de Hayyim Castro starting in 1853, which achieved its early success from its detailed reporting on the Crimean War; *El Manadero* (the Source) (1855–58), an illustrated journal with Christian propaganda spread by Scottish missionaries based in Hasköy who were trying to convert Istanbul's Jews; *El Jurnal Israelit* (1860–71), published weekly (later three times weekly) by Ezekial Gabay (1825–96), Secretary of the Jewish *Millet* council and long a high official in the Ottoman Ministry of Education, who used the paper to propound the new ideas so vigorously opposed by the fantic rabbis led by Akrish; and *Sefath Emeth* (The True Word)/*El Luzero* (The Luminaire), edited by Moise Elie starting in 1867.

El Nacional (1871–90), edited successively by Ezekiel Gabay's son-in-law, Ottoman provincial official Moise Dalmedico (1848–1937) and David Fresco replaced *El Jurnal Israelit* as the principal advocate of modernism in 1871, subsequently changing its name to *El Telegraf* and *El Telegrafo*, and continuing publication under the editorship of Ezekial Gabay's son Isaac Gabay until his death in 1920. *El Progreso* (Progress) was published in Istanbul after 1871 by Behor Molho, while *El Tiempo* (1871–1930), edited initially by Isaac Haim Carmona, and later, successively by Mercado Fresco, Sami Alkabez, Moise Dalmedico and finally by David Fresco, continued as the principal serious Jewish community newspaper in the capital until the departure of the latter's son in 1930. *La Patria* appeared in 1908–09 under the editorship of Victor Levi and David Elnécavé. The weekly *La Boz* (The Voice) was published and edited between 1908 and 1910 by Victor Levi, who subsequently changed it's name to *El Correo* in 1911, while the twice-weekly *El Relampago* was edited by Elia Kohen after 1909; among all Jewish newspapers, its run was exceeded only by *El Tiempo*. Politically, it was a strong supporter of Haim Nahum in his battle to become Grand Rabbi in 1908 and 1909, only to turn against him almost immediately due to his tyrannical conduct once in office. Its principal importance lay in its bringing together of many Judeo-Spanish folk traditions and stories in the popular language which placed Spanish archaisms and popular neologisms side by side while adding numerous Turkish, Hebrew, Greek and French words which were finding their way into the popular vocabulary. The only major Hebrew Language Jewish newspaper published in Istanbul was *Ha Mevasir*, put out by Nahum Sokoloff between 1909 and 1911.

The major French language newspapers that covered the Ottoman Jewish community were the weekly *L'Aurore*, published in Istanbul by the Salonica-born journalist Lucien Sciuto (1858–1947) following restoration of the Constitution in 1908, subsequently continued in Cairo until 1922; *Le Jeune Turc*, published by Sami Hochberg from 1908 to 1918; the daily *Le Journal d'Orient*, published starting in 1917 by the Swiss-educated Salonica political scientist Albert Carasso (Karasu) (1885–1982), with the help of Albert Benaroya (1889–1955), Lea Zolotarevsky and others, which lasted until 1971; and *La Nasion*, edited weekly by Jak Loria from October 1919 until 17 September 1922.

Newspapers published in Istanbul in the Ottoman Turkish language, but in Hebrew characters, included *Şarkiye* (the East), starting in 1867; and *Zaman* (Time), published in 1872 – both edited anonymously. *Ceridei Tercüme* (Translation Journal), edited by Jozef Niego started printing in 1876.

And starting in 1899, the *Ceride-i Lisan* (Language Journal), edited in both Judeo-Spanish and Turkish by Avram Leyon and the poet and writer Avram Ibrahim Naon (1878–1947), and encouraged by Avram Galante and his supporters, with the stated purpose of making Turkish a 'living language among the Jews', began publication. Despite efforts, these publications met with only limited success.

In Izmir, *La Esperanza* (Hope), later *La Buena Esperanza* (Good Hope), a weekly edited originally by Rafael Aaron Uziel Pincherle and later by the Turkish teacher in *AIU* schools, Aaron de Joseph Hazan (1848–1931), an Izmir-born Jew with Italian citizenship, appeared from 1842 until 1912, when Hazan had to leave due to the Italian invasion of Tripoli. A whole flood of periodicals followed, including, most prominently, *Sha'are ha Mizrah* (Gate of the East), edited by R. Pincherle starting in 1846, which emphasized religious and economic news, including stock reports, but lasted only for a few months. *La Verdad* (The Truth), edited by Behor Alexander Benghiotti (Benghiat), David Ben Ezra and Rafael Kori, appeared first in 1884 and continued for several years. *La Novelliste* (*El Novelista*) (1889–1922) was published both in French and Judeo-Spanish by Yaakov Algrante, first once a week and later much more often, sometimes daily. *El Ustad* (The Teacher) (1888–91) was published by Moise Fresco in Turkish, but in Rashi Hebrew characters. It later became *El Commercial*, founded in 1906 by Hizkia Franco and his cousin Gad Franco (1881–1954), which after *El Tiempo* of Istanbul was the most serious Jewish newspaper in the Ottoman Empire, propagating modernist ideas among the provincial intellengtsia. It was replaced in 1908 by the bi-weekly *La Boz del Pueblo* (Voice of the People), edited by Joseph Romano, who formerly had participated in publishing Judeo-Spanish newspapers in Salonica as well as Istanbul, leading modernist Jews in opposition to the Palacci party, which had him exiled to Bodrum, and to the dictatorial conduct of Grand Rabbi Haim Nahum. The weekly *El-Messeret* (Joy) (1897–1908) was edited in Izmir by Alexander Benghiotti (Benghiat), whose articles, both in Judeo-Spanish and Turkish, displayed a strong Ottoman nationalist tendency, while trying to teach Turkish to the Jewish community and teaching Turks about Jewish life and customs. After 1891, however, it published only in Judeo-Spanish and so limited its message entirely to its Jewish readers. *El Pregonero* was published weekly by Rabeno Kuriel starting in 1908. The weekly *La Boz de Izmir* (The Voice of Izmir) (1910–22), edited by Behor Hana and Jacques Ben Senior, was suppressed and its editors and writers arrested during the Greek occupation of Izmir in 1919 because of its continued strong support for Ottoman rule. The monthly *El Guion* (1912) was the organ of the former pupils of the *AIU* schools. *Bayram* (Holiday) was published weekly by Yomtov (Bayram) Abuaf starting in 1910. *Les Annales* was published weekly by Graziella Benguiat for six months during 1914. *Shalom* was put out by Joseph Romano during the Greek occupation of Izmir in 1919 and 1920. After the Greek army closed it, its work was taken up by the Hebrew language weekly *Haverenu*, published in 1921 and 1922 by Mois David Gaon.

In Salonica, the first Judeo-Spanish periodical was *El Lunar*, a monthly journal published by the historian and religious leader Juda Nehama (1825–99) between 1864 and 1867. The Ottoman provincial government published the monthly *Selanik* (Salonica) in Turkish, Judeo-Spanish, Greek and Bulgar under the editorship of Jacob Uziel from 1869 to 1874. The first real daily Judeo-Spanish newspaper in Salonica was the weekly *La Epoca*, founded by Sa'adi ha-Levi under the inspiration of Jewish socialist and labor leaders in the city, which lasted from 1874 until the Greek army which occupied Salonica in 1912 destroyed its building and presses when it ravaged the Jewish quarters of the city. The Zionist weeklies *La Esperanza* (Hope) appeared in Salonica between 1916 and 1920 as the official organ of the Zionist Federation of Greece, and *Lema'an Yisrael/Pro Israel* was published between 1917 and 1929 by Abraham Recanti, who subsequently emigrated to Israel. Other important Jewish newspapers published in Salonica were the weekly *El Avenir* (The Future), edited by Moise Aaron Mallah from 1897 to 1918, the bi-weekly *El Nuevo Avenir* (The New Future), edited by David Isaac Florentin from 1900 to 1918, the daily *El Liberal* (The Liberal), edited by Albert Matarasso from 1913 to 1918, the bi-weekly *La Boz del Pueblo* (Voice of the People), edited by David Isaac Florentin from 1914 to 1920, the weekly *La Nation* (The Nation), edited by Yehuda Asseo as the organ of the Cercle des Intimes (1900–13), *La Tribuna Libera* (The Free Tribune), organ of the *Nouveau Club* (1910–14), *Avante*, also called *La Solidaridad Ovradera*, a Socialist bi-weekly, becoming a daily in 1912–14 under the editorship of Alberto Arditi, lasting until 1935 under the editorship of Jak Ventura as the principal organ of the Jewish communists in Greece, whom he represented for some time in the Greek parliament. There also were the daily *El Pueblo*, edited by M. Ben Sandji (1915–30), the daily *El Imparsial*, published by Menahem Molho and Albert Matarasso from 1909 to 1915, the daily *La Verdad* (The Truth), edited by Abraham Yahiel Levi (1917–23), the daily *La Libertad* (Liberty), edited by Elie Semtov Arditi (1918–25), and the Zionist weekly *La Renecenvia Judia* (Jewish Rebirth) published in 1918.

In Edirne, the first Jewish newspaper was the bi-monthly *Yosef ha-Da'at*, also called *El Progresso* (the Progressive), edited in both Hebrew and Judeo-Spanish by the Edirne-born educator Rabbi Abraham Danon (1857–1925) after 1888, which published articles and documents on the history of Ottoman Jewry in both Hebrew and Judeo-Spanish. The bi-weekly (later daily) *La Boz de la Verdad* (The Voice of Truth), a political-literary journal, was edited in 1910–11 by Joseph Barishak, while the weekly *L'Echo d'Adrinopolis*, edited by Nissim Bahar, provided social, economic and political news in 1921–22 . The first entirely Hebrew newspaper published in Edirne was *Karmi Shelli* (*Bag'im*/My Vineyard), published first in 1882 under the editorship of David Mitrani, which also provided translations into Judeo-Spanish.

In Sofia, *El Amigo del Puevlo* (Friend of the People) was published in Judeo-Spanish from 1890 to 1899. Baruh Ben Isaac Mitrani published the monthly Hebrew-Judeo-Spanish *Be Mishol Ha Keramim* in the 1890s. *La Boz de Israel* was put out in Bulgarian and Judeo-Spanish by Yeoshua Kalev after 1896. *El Progreso* appeared twice weekly starting in 1897. *La Verdad* (The Truth) was published by Avram Tajir from 1898 to 1910. The Zionist weekly *El Judio*, which started originally in Istanbul, edited by David Elnécavé, one of the principal Zionist leaders in Southeastern Europe, continued to appear in Varna and then Sofia until 1931, when Elnécavé emigrated to Argentina. *Ha Mishpat* appeared irregularly starting in 1906 under the editorship of Aaron Amar, while *La Luz* was published weekly starting in 1917. In Filibe, Marco Romano and Yaakov Kalev put out *El Dia* from 1897 to 1901 and *Shofar* from 1901 until the Bulgarian police closed its offices and destroyed its presses four years later.

In Jerusalem, the Jewish press began with the first provincial Jewish newspaper in the Empire, called *Ha Lebanon*, a Hebrew language paper published in 1864. The bi-monthly *Havazelet*, edited by Ezra Benveniste, was published initially in Hebrew but thereafter in Judeo-Spanish, starting in 1870. *Shaare Tzion* was the first Yiddish newspaper published in

Palestine, appearing weekly from 1876 to 1884. *Ha Tzvi*, also called *Ha Or*, was published weekly from 1884 to 1915, becoming the forerunner of the modern Israeli press. *Mevaseret Tzion* was published for a short time by the famous Hebrew philologist Eliezer Ben Yehuda in 1884. The weekly Hebrew-Spanish *El Prospero* was edited by Baruh Mitrani from 1894 to 1896. *La Guerta de Flores* was published by Joseph Ben Rahamin and Nathan Meyohas starting in 1894. The monthly literary revue *La Guerta de Yerushalaim* was edited by Bension Taragon and Salomon Israel Cheresli starting in 1902, and *El Tresoro de Yerushalaim* (1902–3) was edited with similar contents by Moise A. Azrial. In 1907 a Hebrew literary journal called *Ha-'Omer* (the Sheaf) was begun, and at the same time the newspaper *Hapo'el Haza'ir* (The Young Worker) began publication as the organ of the Jewish Socialist labor movement. The political-literary bi-weekly *El Liberal* was issued immediately after restoration of the Ottoman Constitution in 1908, operated by Moise Azrial with first the *AIU*-trained journalist and secretary to Grand Rabbi Haim Nahum, Abraham Elmaleh (1885–1967), and later Haim Benatar acting as editors. And Solomon Israel Cheresli published the political literary bi-weekly *El Paradiso* starting in 1909. The second Hebrew socialist newspaper in Jerusalem, *Ha'akhdut* (Unity) began publication in 1910, under the editorship of David Ben Gurion, Yizhak Ben-Zvi and others. The principal Jewish publishing houses were directed by Moshe Azrial, who published a series of *romansos* concerning all aspects of Jewish life and Solomon Israel Cheresli, who also himself wrote, translated and published a large number of *romansos* and other discussing religious and social topics.

In Egypt, there were five Hebrew-language printing presses by the end of the nineteenth century. Starting in 1904 a weekly newspaper, *El Mizrayim* (Egypt), was published by Isak Carmona in Judeo-Spanish. Avram Galante published the bi-weekly *La Vara* for a short time in 1907. The publishing house of *Carmona y Zara* published many *romansos* as well as a number of newspapers. *La Tribuna* appeared starting in 1906 under the editorship of Isaac Sesana, and *La Luz* was put out by Moise Benguit on a weekly basis starting in 1907. In 1907 the Yiddish monthly *Die Zeit*, and in 1908 the French weekly *L'Aurore* appeared, both reflecting the views of Zionist agents, who were quite active in Cairo and Alexandria at the time.

In addition to the newspapers, in all the cities where there were sizeable Jewish communities there were Judeo-Spanish literary, theatrical, and humorous journals of all sorts, for example in Istanbul *El Sol* (The Sun), a bi-monthly scientific and literary journal, and *El Instructor*, a weekly geographic, historic and literary journal, both edited by David Fresco starting in 1888; *El Radio de Luz* (The Ray of Light), a weekly edited by Victor Levi on scientific and literary subjects starting in 1886;

El Amigo de la Familla (Friend of the Family), with emphasis on history and geography under the editorship of David Fresco and Moise Dalmedico starting in 1886; *La Edicion de Jueves del Telegrafo* (The Thursday edition of *Telegrafo*), a weekly literary, scientific and historical journal edited by Isaac Gabay after 1894; *El Judio* (The Jew), a Zionist weekly published in Hebrew and Judeo-Spanish, edited by David Elnécavé, first in Istanbul (1909–22), and later at Varna; the weekly humor and folklore magazine *El-Djugeton* (The Clown) (1908–31), founded and edited by Elia Carmona, which was suspended for a time by the government at the request of Grand Rabbi Haim Nahum due to its satires against him; the take-off on the stories of Nasruddin Hoca, *Djuha e Djuhayico*, put out by *Journal Israelite* starting in 1860; the weekly *El Burlon*, edited by Hayim Mitrani and Nissim Behar starring in 1908; and *Haménora*, organ of the Bnai Brith (1922–38), published quarterly in both in Hebrew and Judeo-Spanish, which presented numerous articles on the history of Ottoman Jewry.

In Salonica *La Revista Popular* (People's Journal) was published monthly by the Société Cadima (1900–1903). The Mizrahi organization published the daily *Haschahar* in Hebrew and Judeo-Spanish in 1921–22. Humorous weeklies included *El Kirbatch* (The Whip), edited by Moise Levi (1910–14), *El Culevro*, edited by Isaac Matarasso (1916–22), *El Punchon*, edited by Isaac David Florentin (1916–19), *El Chamar*, edited by Leon Boton (1917–20), *El Burlon*, edited by Baruh David Beses (1918–20), *La Vara*, edited by Isaac David Florentin (1918–20), *Charlo*, edited by Alexandro Peres (1919–24), *El Nuevo Kirbatch*, edited by Joseph Carasso (1918–23), and *La Trompeta*, edited by Hayim Samuel Alvo (1920–25).

Nor was literature the only area in which Jews participated actively during these years. Istanbul, Edirne and Izmir in particular were cosmopolitan musically, with European musicians, opera companies and music hall troups, mostly from Italy and France, playing for months at the local theatres, many of which were built and patronized by Muslims and Armenians as well as Jews. The major emphasis, however, remained on the development of Jewish songs to their highest form in the tradition of the Turkish *makamât*, often under the stimulous and with the help of the leading Muslim dervishes of the time, who in turn were influenced by the Jewish musicians with whom they worked. The *Maftirim* choir maintained by the Edirne Sephardic community reached the highest pinnacles in developing Turkish classical music among Ottoman Jewry as they met every Saturday morning before the morning service at the Portugal Synagogue to sing the Sephardic religious songs which had been written by Najara in the early seventeenth century as well as those written by Ottoman Jewish poets of their own time, subsequently departing for services at whichever congregation they were attached to. Other such choirs were organized by most other major Jewish communities in the Empire, including the *Hevrat Ha-Paytanim* (The Singers Society) of Salonica. The Jewish community of Izmir maintained its own brass band and orchestra, manned principally by *AIU* school students who had learned about Western music, and it played at public occasions to raise money for community charities and educational activities. All followed the long-standing tradition of arranging Jewish songs according to the classical Turkish *Makamât* style as it had developed in the Golden Age of Ottoman Jewry. It was out of this milieu that arose the greatest Sephardic musician of the twentieth century, Rabbi Isaac Algazi, whose fame spread widely among Muslim and Jewish Turks alike during the first decade of the Turkish Republic.

As a result of progress in all these areas and the resulting advancement of most members of the Jewish community, even the most traditional Ottoman Jews abandoned the intellectual lethargy of the previous two centuries and moved ahead into the new age, just a century after European Jewry had undergone a similar experience during and after the era of the French Revolution. Under the leadership of enlightened Grand Rabbis and members of lay community councils, the rigors of the past were forgotten, and in addition to the secular schools, traditional Jewish religious schools finally caught up with their foreign counterparts as well as those of the other *millets*, restoring Ottoman Jewry to a state of progressive enlightenment by the start of the twentieth century.

THE EFFECTS OF CHRISTIAN NATIONALISM ON OTTOMAN JEWRY

Despite all the advances made by the *Tanzimat*, however, the disintegration of the Ottoman Empire which had been going on for a century was disastrous for Ottoman Jewry. This was the age of nationalism among the Christian subjects of the Sultan, starting with the Greek Revolution early in the nineteenth century, which, based on the *Megali Idea*, or Great Idea, sought to add to the Greek kingdom Istanbul and large portions of Anatolia, union of which with Greece was felt to be the 'dream and hope of all'. The success of the Greek national movement, provided more in fact by the intervention of the Great Powers than by the efforts of the Greeks themselves, stimulated similar uprisings among the other subjects in Southeastern Europe who had long been oppressed, not so much by the Ottomans but, rather, by the Greek religious hierarchy which dominated the Orthodox *millet*, leading first to pressure for religious independence, granted to the Bulgarian Orthdox Exarchate in 1870, to the Serbian Church in 1879, and to the Rumanian Church in 1885, with subsequent aspirations for, and achievement of, political independence following. These national uprisings were unintentionally helped by the *Tanzimat* reform policies which undermined the authority of the traditional *millet* leaders, who preferred continuance of Ottoman rule as a vehicle for their absolute domination of their communities, just at the time that they had to face the challenge of new modernist and nationalist leaders who were able to use the lay participation in *millet* affairs imposed by the Ottomans to exite the passions and allegiance of their followers. They were greatly assisted in their campaigns against the Ottomans both by the diplomatic and consular representatives of the major Powers of Europe and also by Christian missionaries, who emphasized feelings of Christian superiority and hatred for Muslims and Jews which fortified the religious as well as ethnic bases of their pursuit of independence.

Christian nationalism, based as much on religious as on ethnic identity, soon resurrected the medieval bigotries which had devastated both Jews and Muslims and consequently had driven them together in the past. Vicious anti-Muslim and anti-Semitic movements developed, involving large-scale persecutions and massacres carried out by invading armies, by the independent states that resulted, and also by the Christian subjects who remained within the Empire, particularly because of Jewish and Muslim support for Ottoman integrity in fear of their fate in the emergent nationalist states of Southeastern Europe. The results were explosive and damaging.

Attacks on Ottoman Jews During European Invasions and Nationalist Revolts and Uprisings

The invading armies of Russia and Austria as well as the revolting nationalists and, later, successfully established independent Christian states, committed systematic genocide against Jews and Muslims throughout the nineteenth century, despite Great Power admonitions to the contrary in the treaties of Paris (1858) and Berlin (1878), reviving the old 'ritual murders' which had largely been laid to rest as Ottoman Jewry had fallen into decline. As the peoples of Southeastern Europe achieved their independence, their Muslim and Jewish minorities were systematically persecuted and massacred, and those who survived were driven beyond the ever-shrinking boundaries of the retreating Ottoman Empire in a kind of slaughter which had not been seen since the dispersal of the Jews from Palestine centuries earlier.

This sort of genocide had begun as long before as the late sixteenth century, with the Rumanian Principalities taking the lead, as united Rumania did subsequently during the later years of the nineteenth century. In 1579 the ruler of Moldavia, Peter the Lame, banished its Jews because of their competition with its Christian merchants. When Prince Michael the Brave revolted against the Ottomans in the Rumanian principalities of Wallachia and Moldavia in 1593, he ordered the massacre of all the Jews as well as Turks in Bucharest. Many Jews immigrated to Rumania in the late seventeenth century as a result of the Chmielnicki massacres in Poland and the Ukraine, but this added to Rumanian popular anti-Semitism, with the encouragement of the Cossacks, who at times invaded the Principalities and murdered Jews and Muslims alike. Greek Orthodox churches in Rumania declared all Jews to be heretics, forbad all relations with them on pain of excommunication, and refused to allow their testimony to be accepted in courts. After the Ottomans regained control and turned the Principalities over to the Istanbul-based Greek Phanariotes, Jews were re-admitted with special charters, exempting them from taxes and providing special places for temples, cemeteries and the like, but this enraged the Rumanian masses even more. They became particularly hostile to the Jews because of their defense of the Ottomans who had protected them. Ritual murder charges and anti-Semitic tracts led to anti Jewish riots in Bucharest in 1801. When Russian forces occupied the Principalities in 1806–12, therefore, Jews again were subjected to intense persecution. The Jews of Rusçuk fled across the Danube after the Russian 'liberators' had burned their synagogue and the rest of the Jewish quarter to the ground. After the Russians left, most of the refugees returned, only to be subjected to similar violence both by Russian troups and the local Rumanian population in 1811, and again in 1828.

The slaughter continued well into the nineteenth century. When the Greeks revolted against Ottoman rule many Greek volunteers coming from Russia and the Principalities to join in the effort slaughtered and plundered the Jewish communities along their paths as they went through Moldavia and Wallachia toward Greece. During the Russian occupation of the Principalities between 1835 and 1856, Jews were actively persecuted on the Russian model, with laws denying them citizenship, forbidding them from settling in the countryside, leasing land, or establishing factories in the urban communities, all because of the prevailing belief that they had exploited the Rumanians during the centuries of Ottoman rule.

Things were no better in Hungary as it was conquered by the Habsburgs after 1683. After Austria captured Buda in 1688, most of its Jews were slaughtered by the conquering army because they had sided with the Turks in defending the city. Austrian soldiers burned, looted and killed both the Turkish and Jewish population. The Jewish quarter was pillaged and the Torah scrolls were burned. A few Jews managed to flee, but most were imprisoned and sold as slaves in Vienna or offered to other Jewish communities for ransom. Emperor Charles III later allowed the survivors to return, but Maria Teresa (1717–80) exiled them again in 1746, though a protest by the Ottoman government subsequently caused this order to be annulled. When the Austrian Prince Eugene of Savoy besieged and captured Sarajevo in 1679, the Jewish quarter, including its synagogue, was completely destroyed by the conquerors despite the opposition of the local Bosnian Muslim population. While the city subsequently was returned to Ottoman rule, the arrival of Christian settlers from Serbia, Bulgaria and Italy during the occupation substantially altered the make-up of the city, leaving its Jews far more subject to persecution than they had been earlier. The Austrian occupations of Belgrade and Vidin in 1689 similarly were followed by massacres of their Jewish inhabitants, with many sold into slavery or offered for ransom by Jewish communities in the remaining portions of the Ottoman Empire. About a century later when the revolting governor of Vidin, Osman Pasvanoğlu, suddenly died, his Jewish physician was blamed by his bandit supporters, who subsequently ravaged the Jewish quarter of the city and killed most of its inhabitants, though some managed to flee on the Danube to Rusçuk. One unforeseen, but perhaps appropriate, result of the Habsburg persecution of Hungary's Jews during the later years of the seventeenth century was the rapid spread of the plague during the subsequent years because of the removal of most of the Jewish doctors who had cared for the population of Buda and Pest in particular since medieval times.

When Venice occupied the island of Chios in 1694, its Jewish population was either massacred or deported and all Jewish communal and personal property was stolen by the native Greek population, leaving those Jews who returned in utter poverty and reduced to begging, no longer able to compete with the Greeks in trade or commerce.

Jews living in Greece and the Rumanian principalities suffered terribly because of their continued support for Ottoman rule. When the Greek nationalist movement *Philike Etairia* started its uprising in Wallachia and Moldavia during the spring of 1821, hundreds of Jews and Muslims were killed by the Greeks who lived there as well as by native Wallachs.[14] During the height of the Greek revolution, five thousand Jews were massacred in the Morea along with most of the Muslim population, numbering about twenty thousand in all.[15] In Tripolizza alone 1,200 Jews were massacred along with uncounted Turks.[16] Reverend John Hartley, after describing the carnage, concluded 'Thus did Jewish blood, mingled with Turkish, flow down the streets of the captured city. The sons of Isaac and the sons of Ishmael, on this as well as on every occasion during the Greek Revolution, met with a common fate. Their corpses were cast out of the city, and, like the ancient sovereign of Judah, they received no burial superior to that of an ass.'[17] Jewish communities on the islands of Sparta, Patras, Corinthos, Mistra, and Argos were wiped out by bands of Greek rebels along with those of Thebes, Vrachori, Attica and Epirus.[18] The surviving Jews fled to the island of Corfu, where Jews who had fled from Italy, and the Iberian Peninsula had lived in peace and prosperity under Venetian rule since the twelfth century, though divided into rival Greek and Italian communities. It was not long, however, before it too fell victim to the Greek Revolution, leading to savage repression and massacre of Jews, forcing the surviving members of the two communities to come together for self-defense for the first time. Throughout the years of the Greek revolution, Greek nationalists went from torn to town on the mainland and from island to island in the Aegean, exterminating all the Jews and Muslims they could find, many along the roads as they desperately fled to safety in what was left of the Ottoman Empire. Contemporary accounts relate that the Greeks left the murdered Jews and Muslims lying exposed so their bodies could be torn apart by the buzzards.[19] Most of the Jews who surived these massacres fled across the Aegean in small boats to Izmir, thus starting its rise as one of the leading centers of Ottoman Jewish life during the nineteenth century. Only in northern Greece, particularly in the areas of Janina and Salonica, were the Jews and Turks able to successfully resist the Greek assaults, thus saving their populations from massacre as well.[20] During the remainder of the 19th century, particularly during the Greek-Turkish war in 1897, those Jews who remained in Greece in the areas of Athens, Chalkis, Larissa, Corfu and Crete suffered severe persecution and massacre, forcing thousands more to emigrate into Ottoman territory, particularly to Salonica and Izmir.[21]

Serbian nationalist uprisings against the Ottomans also severely affected their Jewish community. In 1804 and again in 1807 the Serbs who were revolting against the Janissary garrison of Belgrade (*dahis*) expelled all its Jews and Turks, most of whom fled into the Serbian hinterland. Some subsequently returned when Serbia gained autonomy, but its Prince Alexander Karageorgevich (1842–58) enacted a series of restrictions on Jewish residence, acquisition of property and participation in the professions. Jews were accused of competing unfairly with their Serbian counterparts and so were prohibited from settling in the countryside and instead concentrated in a dank ghetto in Belgrade, immediately beneath the great Ottoman fortress at Kalemeydan, where they could be constantly watched by the army. The independent Serbian press was virulently anti-Semitic, accusing Jews of robbing the peasants and debauching them with drink as well as of being Ottoman agents because of their continued support for Ottoman rule. Anti-Semitism also spread into neighboring Bosnia, particularly during the governorship of Ruzhdi Pasha in 1819, when he was also organizing opposition to the reforms then being planned in Istanbul by Sultan Mahmud II. Things were little better for the Jews in Dalmatia.

Persecution of Jews was most virulent during the later years of the nineteenth century in Rumania, which had a population of 134,168 Jews in 1871, in a predominantly Orthodox country. Jews as well as Muslims were massacred, persecuted and driven out as part of the process by which independence was achieved.[22] Jews were forbidden to own property and to acquire nationality, though they were at times able to get around these rules through bribery and the use of third parties.

Jews unable to find work were often expelled from one town after the other until they finally were huddled together into dirty and insanitary ghettos in the larger towns and cities, where they were despised by the Rumanians as dirty and unsanitary menaces to public health. In 1866, during the course of anti-Semitic demonstrations organized by the police, the principal Jewish synagogue in Bucharest was demolished and the Jewish quarter plundered by Rumanian nationalist mobs. The new Rumanian constitution restricted citizenship to Christians. Thousands of Jews were expelled from the villages, and Jews who were not citizens were expelled from the country. Large numbers of Jewish refugees from Russia, and particularly from the southern provinces and Crimea, came to Rumania in 1865 as a result of persecutions resulting from the Crimean War. In 1867, as a result of this new Jewish emigration, local police arrested Jews in the streets, dragging them off to prison in chains. Self-organized popular courts organized house to house searches, tried and sentenced their Jewish captives and deported them. The anti-Semitic press, for the most part operated by unemployed Rumanian teachers, incited the Orthodox masses against the Jews, saying that the latter had stolen their property, with British protests against these outrages being rejected by Prince Carol and the government, which stated blandly that there were no such persecutions.

During the Russian invasion of Bulgaria in 1876–78 in support of the Bulgarian national movement, Jews were officially declared to be a hostile element supporting the Turks, so they were subjected to intense persecution. Cossacks and Bulgarians plundered the shops of Muslims and Jews in Sofia and Vidin for four days, raping and killing all non-Christians they could find and leaving the bodies along the road to be eaten by the dogs, very much in the manner of the Greek rebels a half century earlier.[23] The Jewish communities of Kazanlık, Svishtov, Stara Zagora, Vidin and Nicopolis were ravaged and many were murdered by Bulgarian mobs with the help of the occupying Russian troops. Russian canons destroyed the newly-built Vidin synagogue and completely destroyed the Jewish community of Nicopolis, one of the oldest in Bulgaria. Assaults, robberies and murders engulfed Jews all over the country. Thousands of Bulgarian Jews followed the fleeing Muslims out of Bulgaria into the shrinking territories of the Ottomans, taking refuge for the most part in Istanbul and Edirne, where they were helped, not only by the Ottoman government and the local Jewish community, but also by a special fund set up in London by Baron Maurice de Hirsch.

Large numbers of Jews were persecuted at the same time in Serbia, but they were allowed to take refuge in Ottoman territory by terms of the Ottoman-Serbian peace treaty of 27 February 1877. Once again, following the war, large numbers of Russian Jews as well as others from all the Balkan nations were given refuge on Ottoman territory from mounting persecution of all sorts. The sufferings of Serbian and Rumanian Jews in particular were described in a memorandum drawn up by the *AIU* and, with the strong support of the Ottoman Jewish community, presented to the representatives of the Great Powers who met in Istanbul late in 1876.[24]

The Treaty of San Stephano (3 March 1878) imposed on the Ottomans by the victorious Russian army left the Balkan Jews in the same state as their brothers in the Russian Pale, without any sort of equality, freedom of religion, or representation in parliaments of the newly-independent states. However at the subsequent Congress of Berlin (1878) the position of the Jews in Rumania, Serbia and Bulgaria was placed on the agenda as result of the political pressure of the *AIU*, Baron Maurice de Hirsch and Sir Moses Montefiore, as well as many other European Jewish organizations, whose activities with their own governments got most of the Powers to instruct their delegates to demand the inclusion of equal rights for members of all religions in the countries of Southeastern Europe as part of the final agreement. This effort was strongly supported by the Jewish community of Istanbul as well as the Ottoman government, which pressured the British who were representing its interests in Berlin. The Congress responded by forming a special Commission to study the question, producing two memoranda which described the plight of the Balkan Jews and requested that people of all religions should be guaranteed equal rights in the peace treaty. As the negotiations went on in Berlin, Rumania pressured its Jews to withdraw their request to the Congress, threatening them with severe reprisals if any official declaration was issued. Finally it was agreed at Berlin that the Congress would include in the treaty provisions that the independence of Rumania, Bulgaria and Serbia would not be recognized unless they granted equal civil rights to citizens of all religions. Greece, Montenegro and the Ottoman Empire also were subjected to the same requirements as a result of outside political pressure, though the Jews in fact continued to praise the Sultan for his work in receiving refugees from pogroms in Russia as well as in the Balkans. The treaty of Berlin that finally was signed in July 1878, supplanting the Treaty of San Stephano, dictated that all the newly independent Balkan countries should provide equal rights and protection to those Jews and Muslims who remained under their rule, with full access to all public offices, equality for the minorities, and religious freedom for the Jews of Bulgaria, Rumania and Serbia in particular, despite the objections of the Russian delegate Gorchakov that the Balkan Jews constituted a veritable cancer to the local populace.

The inclusion in the Treaty of Berlin of stipulations providing protection for the Jewish and Muslim minorities in Southeastern Europe stimulated even more popular anti-Semitic and anti-Muslim hysteria in all the countries involved, with blood-libel accusations once again being used as pretexts for attacking and ravaging Jewish quarters as well as for new tactics of boycotting Jewish shopkeepers, merchants and professionals, a movement which was quickly adapted by the Christian *millets* in the major cities of the Ottoman Empire. Because the Bulgarians, Rumanians and Greeks correctly regarded the Jews as supporters of the Turks, both Jews and Turks were expelled from these countries in equally atrocious and brutal manners. Their property was plundered and their homes and shops taken over without compensation, while the survivors fled in desperation to Edirne and Istanbul. While official statements subsequently were issued granting equal rights to Jews, little was done in fact and they continued to be persecuted regularly well into the twentieth century.

During the years after the Treaty of Berlin, the Balkan Jews did best in Bulgaria, though not without problems. In 1878, its new Prince, Alexander of Battenberg, attempted to fulfill the provisions of the Treaty regarding Jews by telling the Grand Rabbi of Bulgaria, Gabriel Almosnino, that 'I shall love all my subjects, regardless of their creed. The law shall be applied to all without discrimination'. As a result, many Jews who had fled to exile to Istanbul returned with hope to their Bulgarian homes, resulting in increases in Sofia's Jewish population to 4,274 in 1881, 5,102 in 1888, 6,872 in 1893, and 12,862 in 1910. Jews began to participate actively in Bulgarian public life, entering the administration and the Parliament. However this enraged most Bulgarians, particularly since the newly-liberated Jews tended to emphasize their Judeo-Spanish heritage and French culture in their schools, leading to increasing anti-Semitism during subsequent years. Anti-Jewish laws were introduced in secret clauses and memoranda, Jews were increasingly barred from the Bulgarian military academy, the central bank, and most government positions. Anti-Semitic attacks appeared regularly in the press, and there were some mob attacks at times, but the Jewish community continued to maintain its legal position at least until World War I.

The Rumanian reaction to the Treaty of Berlin was far stronger, and its anti-Semitism far more severe and lasting. After 1885 Rumanian Jews were excluded from the professions. In 1893, Rumanian Jews were expelled from all public schools, and many Jewish political leaders and journalists were summarily expelled from the country, even those who had participated actively in the Rumanian War for Independence. They were not allowed to be lawyers, teachers, chemists, railroad officials, doctors in state hospitals, army officers or stock brokers and they were forbidden from selling commodities controlled by government monopolies, such as tobacco, salt and alcohol, causing 41,754 Jews, out of a total of 262,348, to emigrate between 1899 and 1905.[25]

Things were not much better elsewhere in Southeastern Europe or the Greek islands of the Aegean and the eastern Mediterranean. In 1891 the Jews on Corfu were subjected to severe persecution by local Greeks due to the revival of the old ritual murder accusations.[26] Many of those who survived found refuge in Ottoman territory with the help of a popular subscription drive carried out in Istanbul under the leadership of the Banque Camondo. In 1881 and 1884, and again in 1892 and 1903, thousands of Jews came to Ottoman territory as a result of pogroms in Russia which went on between 1881 and 1921 with only slight periods of respite. In 1899 Jewish families arrived in Istanbul in flight from persecution at Vidin, in independent Bulgaria.

The conquest of Ottoman Thrace and Macedonia by Greek and Bulgarian forces during the Balkan Wars (1912–13), including Salonica, Çorlu, and Edirne, was followed by general attacks on Jews, their synagogues, homes and shops, in both countries,[27] resulting in a renewed exodus toward Istanbul and beyond. Two reports from Salonica graphically described the situation caused by the invading armies:

> All the self-interested justifications of the newspapers of Europe, all the lies which they have used to cover up the truth, can never destroy the impression of the terrible anguish which has marked the entry of the Greeks into Salonica. A week of terror and horror one can never easily forget. The Hellenes now cruelly feel today all the damage that the explosion of hatred by the (Greek) population has done to their cause. The mob has shown itself odious and the government weak . . . . The incompetence of the Greek administration and the horrors inflicted by the soldiers has put them in a terrible situation. The consuls guaranteed the absolute safety of the Muslims, but sixty of them were massacred in a single night . . . . [28]
>
> It wasn't only the irregulars (*Comitacis*) who massacred, pillaged and burned. The soldiers of the Army, the Chief of Police, and the high civil officials took an active part in the events at Serres. Out of 6,000 houses, 4,000 were burned. Almost 1,200 shops were consumed by flames and destructive bombs. The (Jewish) population lost all, and without even anything to wear is in despair. Everyone wants to emigrate . . . [29]

The Bulgarian attacks on the Jews of Çorlu are described in the report of Saul Cohen to the Alliance in Paris:[30]

> The Bulgarian soldier does not bother to buy anything, paying whatever he wants. Under the pretext that the epicier does not understand his language, he pays half the price or nothing at all. And it is better not to protest since one risks being seized and struck . . . . After having pillaged the Turkish houses, the Bulgarian military authorities installed in our town designated the Muslim stores, shops and depots, emptying them methodically according to their needs. Having acquired what they needed, helped by the Greek population from here, they also despoiled of their properties those Jews who had associated

with the Muslims. Very greedy, they attacked closed shops. Why didn't they open them? If their owners were absent, it sufficed that they had left to consider them in agreement with the enemy Turk . . . This beautiful Thrace, true granary of Turkey, today the object of enemy depredations, will recover its prosperity only after long years . . . .

Isaac Catarivas, leader of the Jewish community of Silivri, wrote the President of the Alliance in Paris on 9 June 1912 describing a Greek boycott of Jewish shops at Silivri:[31]

> . . . for three months we have been boycotted by the Orthodox community because we voted for the Young Turk party. We do not engage in politics, but it appears that our conduct during the Parliamentary elections has indisposed against us the Greeks who have declared war against us. Our people live only from colportage in the villages around Silivri, all inhabited by Greeks. This boycott destroys all means of our existance. Our moral and material suffering is terrible. We do not even have the right of being ill. The doctors and pharmacists are all Greeks, and they create a thousand difficulties, a thousand miseries, doubling and tripling the prices of visits and prescriptions. Despite the demarches of the Grand Rabbi, despite a letter from the Ecumenical Patriarch, who sent an Archbishop, the Greeks pursue us with their hate . . . .

Grand Rabbi Haim Nahum on 14 March 1913 also sent the Alliance a detailed report [32] regarding Greek assaults on Jews in the areas occupied by the Balkan Allies.

As a result of these assaults, massacres, and forced deportations from the independent countries of Southeastern Europe, the Ottoman Empire received literally thousands of Jewish refugees who joined the Muslims who survived the persecution, flooding into the Empire where they provided their skills as well as capital, when they had any remaining, joining with its old-established Jewish community in contributing significantly to the modernization of Ottoman agriculture and industry.

Christian Persecution of Jews Within the Ottoman Empire

The revival of Ottoman Jewry during the last half of the nineteenth century produced ugly reactions among their rivals within Ottoman society. So long as the Jews were excluded from economic and financial life and remained in ignorance and poverty, the Ottoman Christians, secure in the protection they were getting from the Great Powers of Europe, left the Jews alone. But once Jewish competition rose once again, violence resumed, as the Christians sought to divert onto the Jews the increasing Muslim hatred resulting from assaults on Muslims throughout Southeastern Europe as well as North Africa and Russian Central Asia.[33] The virulent anti-Semitism, underpinned by long-standing anti-Muslim bigotry, that was propagated within the Ottoman Empire was spread back into Europe by Middle Eastern Christian churchmen seeking to secure European support for their causes, providing an important source for the hatred which culminated in the Holocaust little less than a century later.

Frequent Greek uprisings, particularly in Macedonia and during the Ottoman-Greek war over Crete that started in 1897, exacerbated relations in Istanbul, not only between Greeks and Muslims but also between the former and Jews, who invariably supported the Turks against their persecutors.[34] Muslims in the Arab provinces sometimes were convinced to join the Christians in the resulting attacks, but these were relatively minor and far between compared with the hatred nourished by both religious and economic factors, particularly since the Ottoman government regularly intervened to protect the Jews whenever possible.

In addition to the Greeks, 'The Jews were also hated by the Christian Syrians, the Christian Arabs, and the Armenians for religious reasons – a religious hatred which was deeply implanted in their hearts – and out of jealousy for the general competition of the Jews in the Ottoman Empire.' At each approach of the Eastern season, Jews in Istanbul, Salonica and Izmir in particular barracaded their shops and moved in the streets with great caution because of the fear that it would be they who would be set upon by Greek and Armenian mobs when no-one was around to defend them.

The American Presbyterian missionary H. H. Jessup, who spent some fifty-three years in the Middle East from his church at Beirut, said about the Jews:

They are hated intensely by all the sects, but more especially by the Greeks and Latins. In the gradations of Oriental cursing, it is tolerably reasonable to call a man a donkey, somewhat severe to call him a dog, contemptuous to call him a swine, but withering to the last degree to call him a Jew. The animosity of the nominal Christian sects against the Jews is most relentless and unreasoning. They believe that the Jews kill Christian children every year at the Passover and mingle their blood with the Passover bread. Almost every year in the spring, this senseless charge is brought against the Jews . . . the Jews of Beirut and Damascus are obliged to pay heavy blackmail every year to the Greek and Latin 'lewd fellows of the baser sort' who threaten to raise a mob against them for killing Christian children . . , and not only do they regard them as children of hell, but would rejoice to send them there if they could.[35]

The first modern pogrom within the Empire came early. In 1663 two Janissaries of Christian origin accused Istanbul Jews of killing the child of one, who had in fact been killed by his own father, who had thrown the body into the Jewish quarter on the night that Passover began in order to implicate Jews in the crime. In response to the complaint, local Greeks flooded into Balat from neighboring Fener, assaulting Jews as they were going to their synagogues and ravaging Balat's commercial quarter early the next morning. Subsequently, however, the Grand Vezir learned the facts of the case from his spies stationed in the Greek quarter, informed the Sultan, and the Janissaries in question were put to death, but only after the Greek mobs had killed almost twenty Jews and emptied out most of Balat's shops. In 1774 Greeks in Izmir reacted to the arrival of large numbers of Jews fleeing from Greek persecution in Salonica by mounting the first ritual murder accusation in modern times and in consequence attacking and sacking the Jewish quarters of the city.

In 1821 Greek rebels in the Archipelago captured a ship coming from Mecca and mistreated the Muslim pilgrims on board including the Molla of Mecca and his harem. The cruelties inflicted against the veiled women and a venerated old man excited the indignation of Muslims throughout the Empire. As a result on 27 April 1821, first day of Christian Easter, Grand Vezir Benderli Ali Pasha went to the Patriarchate of Fener with battalion of Janissaries who seized Patriarch Gregory V and hung him at the door of his palace in the presence of a large crowd. Those in attendance were mainly Greeks, but some Jews also had come from Balat, attracted by curiosity. The Grand Vezir is said to have remarked to them 'Welcome you Jews. Here is hung your enemy and mine. Take him to the sea, I order you.' Either because they wanted to or because of force, three Jews named Mutal, Bichachi and Levi took the body to the shore of the Golden Horn and dumped it into the water under the watchful gaze of the Janissaries. This led to an absurd rumor which spread rapidly through the Greek community that Jews had inspired the government to murder the Patriarch, leading to large-scale anti-Jewish riots in most of the major cities of the empire, with many deaths and considerable damage to Jewish houses and property. By the time the rumor reached Greece, then still in the process of revolting against the Ottomans, it was so exaggerated that it was the Jews of Istanbul who had hung the Patriarch. As a result, thousands more Jews as well as Muslims were besieged and massacred throughout mainland Greece and the Aegean islands, particularly at Rhodes and Chios as well as most of the smaller islands. Greek ritual murder attacks against local Jews followed at Safed in 1834 and 1838, largely decimating its Jewish population and ending its long standing economic and cultural prosperity.

During the remainder of the nineteenth century ritual murder accusations were spread hundreds of times to excite Christian mobs to attack and kill Jews and ravage their homes and shops, as reported in the weekly and monthly issues of the *Bulletin de l'Alliance Israélite Universelle* (Paris).

There was the famous Damascus Pogrom of 1840, in which hundreds of Damascus Jews, including their Rabbi and leader Haim Farhi, were attacked and killed as a result of the disappearance of an Italian Friar named Thomas and his Muslim servant. A rumor circulated by Capuchin monks was that they had been murdered by Jews in order to use their blood for the Passover service. This rumor had been spread with the support of the French Consul General, Ratti-Menton, who was working to counteract increasing British influence in the area following the failure of the French protégé, Egyptian governor Muhammad Ali's invasion of Syria and Anatolia and their evacuation which was carried out by an Allied force led by the British starting in September 1840. The French representatives in Alexandria and Damascus responded by attempting to increase their influence among the area's Muslims in addition to the local Christians by encouraging the spread of the ritual murder stories against the Jews, thus leading directly to the Damascus atrocities. The local French consuls used the coincidential release of the Jews imprisoned as a result of the ritual murder accusation at the same time as the restoration of Ottoman rule in Syria to blame the Jews for the latter, stimulating local Muslims and Christians alike to spread new ritual murder stories and attack Syrian and Palestinian Jews in subsequent years, often with the assistance and support of the local European consuls, and with devastating results.

Those Jewish merchants who managed to retain their positions did so for the most part by taking up European citizenship, usually of Britain, Austria or Tuscany, whose consuls accepted them, in return for substantial payments, to counteract the influence the French were gaining by bestowing French citizenship on local Armenians and Greeks. In the absence of a numerous native Protestant community, British Foreign Secretary Palmerston led the way in attempting to maintain British influence in the area and counteract the French efforts to restore their position by protecting Ottoman Jewry, informing his consuls throughout the Empire that the British government 'feels an interest in the welfare of the Jews in general and is anxious that they should be protected from oppression', and ordering them to inform every Ottoman official about British concern regarding the fate of Jews in the area. At the same time, of course, the British government began to send out numerous Anglican missionaries to the Middle East in the hope that a more congenial local community could be created which would, in the long run, better serve British interests in the area.

Palmerson's concern also stirred the increasingly wealthy and powerful British Jewish community to action. Leading European Jews led by Sir Moses Montefiore from England and Isaac Adolphe Crémieux

(1796–1880) from France interceded with Sultan Abdül Mecid, who declared to them in an interview on 27 October 1840:

> I have been moved by the events which have taken place in Damascus, but I have endeavoured to offer some satisfaction to the Jewish nation by giving orders that justice should be done in the affair of Rhodes. The Jewish nation shall always have from me the same protection and enjoy the same advantages as all other subjects of my Empire.

Sultan Abdül Mecid then issued his famous *ferman* of 6 November 1840 to the Chief *Kadi* of Istanbul specifically absolving Ottoman Jewry of guilt in these particular incidents and ordered that if such accusations were made anywhere in the Empire, they should be investigated and judged only by his own Imperial Council, where the Jews would be assured of justice:[36]

> An ancient prejudice has prevailed against the Jews. The ignorant believe that the Jews were accustomed to sacrifice a human being to make use of his blood at his feast of Passover. As a result of this opinion, the Jews of Damascus and Rhodes, subjects of our Empire, have been persecuted by other communities (*millets*). The calumnies which have been uttered against the Jews and the vexations to which they have been subjected have at last reached our Imperial Throne.
>
> Not long ago some Jews living on the Island of Rhodes were brought to Istanbul where they were tried and judged according to the new (*Tanzimat*) regulations, and their innocence of the accusations made against them fully proved. The justice and equity required thus was carried out on their behalf.
>
> In addition, the religious books of the Jews have been examined by learned Muslims, well versed in their theological literature, who found that Jews are strongly prohibited, not only from using human blood, but even that of animals. It therefore follows that the charges made against them and their religion are nothing but pure calumny.
>
> For this reason, and because of the love we bear our subjects, we cannot permit the Jewish nation, whose innocence of the crime alleged against them is evident, to be vexed and tormented on the basis of accusations which have not the least foundation in truth, so in conformity to the Hatti Sherif which has been proclaimed at Gulhane, the Jewish nation shall possess the same advantages and enjoy the same privileges as are granted to the numerous other nations who submit to our authority.
>
> The Jewish nation shall be protected and defended.
>
> To accomplish this objective, we have given the most positive orders that the Jewish nation dwelling in all parts of our empire shall be perfectly protected, as well as all other subjects of the Sublime Porte,

and that no person shall molest them in any manner whatever, except for a just cause, neither in the free exercise of their religion, nor in that which concerns their safety and tranquility. In consequence, the present ferman, which is ornamented at the head with our Imperial Signature, and emanates from our Imperial Chancellery, has been delivered to the Jewish nation.

You, the aforementioned judge, once you know the contents of this ferman, should endeavour to act with great care in the manner prescribed therein. And so that nothing may be done in contradiction to this ferman, you should register it in the Archives of your court. You will afterwards deliver it to the Jewish nation, and you will take great care to execute this order, this our sovereign will.

Issued at Istanbul, 12 Ramazan 1256 (6 November 1840).

Grand Vezir Rauf Pasha issued another declaration in 1843 ordering equality and protection for all subjects regardless of religion:

The Sultan, our master and father to us all, has come among us as in the midst of a family whose joys are his joys and sorrows are his sorrows. He knows all the obligations that divine Providence has imposed on him . . . you should not doubt for an instance his justice. Muslims, Christians and Jews, you are all subjects of the same emperor, children of the same father. If there are oppressed among you, it is the intention of His Majesty that the laws safeguarding life, honor and property of all subjects be strictly observed in the entire Empire . . . . Muslims or Christians, rich or poor, civil, military or religious officials, all Ottoman subjects should have full confidence in the sovereign who holds equal balance for all . . . [37].

In 1846 Grand Vezir Mustafa Reşid Pasha issued a similar statement to the non-Muslim religious leaders in Edirne:

His Majesty the Emperor, just as he wants the good fortune of his Muslim subjects, wants also that the Christians and Jews, who are equally his subjects, enjoy tranquility and protection. Differences in religion and sect do not concern him, nor do they hinder their rights; and as we all are subjects of the same government and citizens born in the same empire, we should not look on each other with a bad eye. Our sovereign is spreading his good works among all classes of his subjects, and they should live in good harmony among each other, and work together for national prosperity.[38]

As a result, then, of protection by the Ottoman government as well as of France's rivals in Europe, Syrian Jewry continued to prosper following the Damascus affair, at least until 1871, with wealthy families such as the Farhi, Harari, Lisabone, Stamboli, Pijotto, Angel and Amber living in large palaces with great luxury through much of the century.

This situation, however, only increased the envy and hostility of local Christians, and under their stimulus Muslims as well, constantly fanned and inflamed by French representatives determined to restore their influence in the Levant. The accusations continued and intensified, therefore, leading to pogroms all over the Ottoman Empire, occasionally mounted by Muslims but most often by Christians.

Relations among the different religious and ethnic groups in Damascus remained unusually difficult and complex after 1840 despite the admonitions of the Sultan. In 1860 many Christians in the city were massacred by the Druze and Muslims leading to accusations, not without some foundation in view of what had happened in 1840, that many Damascene Jews had been involved in the violence and had acquired some of the looted property. This led to nine more ritual murder attacks by Christians in Damascus between 1840 and 1900. Things were no better in Lebanon, which had a large population of Christians who hated their Jewish neighbors even more than they did the Muslims. In Dar al-Kamar, though there were only about one hundred Jews among some eight thousand Maronites, the latter regularly robbed Jewish homes and shops, culminating in a full-scale ritual murder attack by Christians in 1847 and again in 1849, which was stopped only after large ransoms were paid to the leaders of the Christian community, though the Jewish community itself finally was forced to move away to Beirut due to constant attacks during the Druze-Christian clashes during the 1860s. The latter events also decimated the Jewish community of Hazzbaya, many of whose members were slaughtered by the Druze in 1860 before wealthy Damascene Jews evacuated them, ultimately settling them in Beirut, Tripoli and Sidon, where Jewish communities continued to exist into the twentieth century, though increasingly impoverished and isolated as a result of constant pressure by local Christians. In 1865, immediately after enactment of the new Organic Statute for the Jewish community, and just as Jewish capital from Europe was beginning to have an effect in Istanbul, local Armenians and Greeks started a pogrom against Jews immediately across the sea of Marmara at Haydarpaşa, terminus of the Anatolia railroad, with three hundred Jews massacred and many more beaten and raped before the disturbance was stopped after the Sultan sent his personal guard across the bay to protect the Jews.[39]

In later years, ritual murder attacks against Jews, carried out mostly by native Greeks, Armenians, and, in the Arab provinces, by Maronites and other Arab Christians, often with the assistance of the local European consuls, took place throughout the empire. There were literally thousands of incidents almost continuously until World War I, in Southeastern Europe as far west and north as Monastir and Kavalla, in Istanbul, at Gallipoli and the Dardanelles, at Salonica, and in all the Arab provinces as far south as Damascus and Beirut and in Egypt at Cairo and Alexandria. These invariably resulted from accusations spread among Ottoman Christians by word of mouth, or published in their newspapers, often by Christian financiers and merchants anxious to get their Jewish competitors out of the way or to divert onto the Jews Muslim anger at reports of Christian massacres of Muslims in Southeastern Europe or Central Asia, resulting in individual and mob attacks on Jews, and the burning of their shops and homes.

Individual experiences were horrible. Jews constantly went in fear of Armenian or Greek attacks in the streets of most Ottoman cities. In Egypt and Syria, it was usually the Greeks who led the way, in many cases with the assistance of local Armenians and Syrian Christians, whose Greek, Arabic and French-language newspapers often printed all the rumors they could find regarding Jews, evidently with the desire of instigating violence. The Syrian Arab Christians in particular spread their long-standing anti-Semitic hatreds from Syria to Egypt, where their monopoly of the local press and their espousal of popular causes such as Egyptian nationalism and opposition to British rule, enabled them to spread their anti-Jewish message among the Muslim masses with little question or opposition.

On 20 June 1890, thus, Sir Evelyn Baring (later Lord Cromer), British High Commissioner in Egypt, received the following report from David and Nissim Ades, in Cairo:

> Sir,
> I beg sir to draw to your attention to the violent articles which has (sic) appeared in an Arabic paper called El Mahroussa which contained nothing but lies and false accusations against the Jews, especially those (the issues) of the 14th, 17th and 19th instant. Now, Sir, are we to have here an anti Semitic party amidst fanaticism Greeks, Armenians, etc, or is he to be allowed to continue to poison the people's minds with exaggeration and painted words? In an article he asserted that the Jews use Christian blood for Passover, of course this has caused a deal of excitement.[40]

Whenever Greek and other Orthodox religious authorities or prominent Greek business leaders or consuls were asked to help to stem the violence or reduce tension, they invariably indicated their cooperation and then failed to do anything to prevent attacks or punish those who stimulated or led them.[41]

The leader of the Ashkenazi community of Çorlu complained to the

204 History of the Jews of the Ottoman Empire and Turkish Republic

President of the *AIU* in 1902 about persistent Greek attacks against its
Jewish quarter:

> The fanatic Greeks of our city, as of other places in Thrace, have the
> habit of, contrary to the spirit of real Christianity, making a replica of
> Judas Iscariote and of burning it on the night of Holy Saturday. They
> construct a wooden figure, cover it with clothing which they claim
> is that of the ancient Jews, and they burn it publicly in the middle
> of a multitude of the ignorant and fanatic. It often happens that this
> multitude, already excited by the tales of the suffering of Christ that
> has been made to them at the Church, is exaulted at the appearance
> of the execution of he who is supposed to have betrayed Christ, and
> works up a great anger against the Jews . . . For a long time we have
> known that each year, on such a day, they will cut off the heads and
> arms of the corpses in our cemetery and will burn them with great
> solemnity. We make no complaint about this in order not to create
> differences between the two communities. But this audacious madness
> of these fanatics has increased. We ourselves see the flames and hear
> the cries of hatred and vengeance against the Jews.[42]

The great historian of Salonica Jewry, Joseph Nehama, reported to the *AIU*
in 1900 about the bad relations between Greeks and Jews in that city:

> The hatred between Jews and Christians living side by side has existed
> in all ages and all countries. Our city has not escaped this situation.
> Among us also these two hereditary enemies combat one another, and
> their hatred is translated in a very typical manner. The adversaries are
> not content with nourishing a reciprocal aversion among themselves.
> They manifest it often on all the corners of the streets in real battles,
> where bullets are replaced by large stones, the rifles and cannons by
> vigorous arms accustomed to battle . . . (*AIU* archives, Paris, II, 8).

Greeks and Armenians agitated widely to prevent Jews from constructing
new synagogues when needed in the Empire. The best example of
this came with Greek opposition to the construction of a new Jewish
synagogue at Haydarpaşa in 1899. Sultan Abdül Hamid II allowed the
synagogue to be built, and assured its opening despite Greek protests
by sending a contingent of soldiers from the nearby Selimiye barracks,
leading the congregation to adopt the name Hemdat Israel synagogue,
chosing the name not only because of its meaning, 'the mercy of Israel',
but also because the word Hemdat was close to the name of their benefac-
tor, Sultan Abdül Hamid.[43] Macedonia was a living hell for Muslims and
Jews alike, with terrorist bands organized by Greek, Bulgarian, Serbian

and even Rumanian nationalists slaughtering all those who failed to share their national passions.[44]

Avram Galante, who lived for many years among the Greeks on the island of Rhodes, where the Jewish community was numerous, but still a substantial minority compared to the Greeks and Muslims, relates how he tried desperately to secure assistance from the Greek religious authorities to end the pogroms, securing Patriarchal encyclicals in 1873, 1874, 1884, and 1898, but with only limited success as they felt pressure from their flocks to go along with the attacks, or at least not to object, while the lower priests actively encouraged the attacks against Jews, not only on the part of their own followers but also by Muslims.[45] Efforts of the Grand Rabbi and individual Jews within the empire to stop these pogroms were supported by leading European Jewish bankers such as Moses Montefiore and Baron Maurice de Hirsch (1831–96), principal builder of the Orient railroad between Vienna, Istanbul and the East, who as founder of the Jewish Colonization Association was the first Jewish philanthropist to help resettle Jews in the Holy Land, and by the *AIU*, whose educational efforts were also liberally subsidised by de Hirsch. Such interventions usually succeeded in getting the culprits imprisoned, but little could be done to remedy the damage done to Ottoman Jews during the course of the repeated attacks, and only the constant efforts at protection by the Ottoman government prevented things from becoming even worse as time went on.

Those Jews who survived these assaults in Southeastern Europe fled particularly to Salonica, whose Jewish population increased substantially as a result, from 28,000 in 1876 to 90,000 in 1908, more than half the total population, though even there increased persecution by local Greeks led many Jews to flee elsewhere in the Ottoman Empire, particularly to the great port of Izmir.

Despite all the pressure from Ottomans and foreign Jews alike, the ritual murders and other assaults by Christians on Jews went on and on. Greek efforts to decimate the Jewish population of Salonica culminated in 1912 and 1913, following the Greek conquest of Salonica during the First Balkan War, when many of its Jews, were either killed or terrorized into leaving so they could be replaced by Greek immigrants from Ottoman Thrace. The job of driving out Salonica's Jews was furthered by the great fire of 1917, which destroyed a good part of the city including the entire Jewish quarter, leaving 50,000 Jews homeless.[46] Since the Greek government was in any case trying to Hellenize the city, while it compensated those who had lost their homes, Jews and Greeks alike, the latter received substantially more than the former, who for the most part were not even allowed to return to their homes, forcing them instead to emigrate to the United States, France, Italy and Alexandria as well as to Turkey, while their places were taken by Greek refugees from Anatolia. The latter in turn were given substantial government assistance, including not only large amounts of cash but also grants of the lands and properties from which Jews had been forced out. Though Greece was obligated by the post World War I treaties to allow Jews and other minorities to use their own languages in education and to practice their religions without hindrance, a law was issued in 1923 which forbad all inhabitants from working on Sunday, stimulating a new Jewish exodus as it was intended to do. Between 1932 and 1934 there was a series of anti-Semitic riots in Salonica, with the Cambel quarter, where most of the remaining Jews lived, being burned to the ground. This was followed by regulations requiring the use of Greek and prohibiting the use of Hebrew and Judeo-Spanish in the Jewish schools. A start was made also on expropriating the land of the principal Jewish cemetery in Salonica for use by the new University in order to drive the Jews out.[47] By killing and driving out large numbers of Jews, the Greeks left a substantial Greek majority in the city for the first time, and starting Salonica Jewry on the way to its final decimation by the Nazis during their occupation of Greece starting in 1941.

Salonica and Izmir of course were not the only places of refuge for Jewish refugees entering the Empire during its last century of existence. Istanbul, Edirne, and other parts of Rumelia and Anatolia received thousands more. Nor were Jews the only refugees received and helped by the government of the Sultan. Thousands of Muslims accompanied them in flight from similar persecutions wherever Balkan Christian states gained their independence or expanded. The Russian conquest of the Crimea and the Caucasus starting in the late eighteenth century, and particularly during and after the Crimean War, combined with the same independence movements in Southeastern Europe that had caused so much suffering and flight among its Jews caused thousands of helpless, ill, and poverty-stricken Muslim refugees to accompany them into the ever shrinking boundaries of the Ottoman Empire, with the Istanbul government struggling mightly but vainly to house and feed them as best it could. From 1850 to 1864 as many as 800,000 Crimean Tatars, Circassians, and other Muslims from north and east of the Black Sea had entered Anatolia alone, as many as 200,000 more came during the next twenty years, while 474,389 refugees entered in 1876–77 as a result of the Ottoman wars with Russia and the Balkan states, with an equal number gaining refuge in the European portions of the Empire.

JEWISH PARTICIPATION IN OTTOMAN LIFE DURING THE LAST HALF CENTURY OF THE OTTOMAN EMPIRE, 1876–1923

The population of Istanbul almost tripled during the nineteenth century, increasing from approximately 331,647 in 1844 to 378,069 in 1856, 873,565 in 1883 and 909,978 in 1914, with the number of Muslims and Jews increasing respectively from 170,551 and 24,447 in 1844 to 560,434 and 52,126 in 1914.[48] In the Empire as a whole, the Jewish population varied between 253,435 and 256,003 according to the official censuses, while the *AIU* instructors counted some 439,000 Jews in the Empire in 1908, including Jews of foreign nationality who were not included by the official Ottoman census takers. While the increase of Christians came mainly from the arrival of foreign merchants seeking to take advantage of the Capitulations, most of the increase of Muslims and Jews came from the arrival of large numbers of refugees fleeing persecution in the newly autonomous or independent Christian states of Southeastern Europe as well as from Russian expansionism through Central Asia toward the Pacific. Foreigners and members of the Christian minorities tended to concentrate in the Sixth Municipal District, comprising Beyoğlu, Galata and Tophane, which at the end of the century had forty-seven percent foreign subjects and thirty-two percent non-Muslim Ottomans, while only twenty-one percent were Muslims. Foreigners also tended to live along the Bosporus in the Fourth District, from Tophane through Beşiktaş and Bebek to Rumelihisarı, where they constituted ten percent of the population, with Muslims having forty-three percent. The primary Muslim district remained Old Istanbul, while Jews concentrated along the edges of the Golden Horn, particularly at Balat, Kâğıthane and Hasköy. Some of the more prosperous Jews moved among the Christians in Galata, but most went up the Bosporus to Beşiktaş and Ortaköy, and some crossed to Anatolia, where they concentrated in the newer suburbs of Üsküdar, Kadıköy, and Kuzguncuk.

Jewish Prosperity under Sultan Abdül Hamid II. The long years in office of Yakir Geron's successor as *Kaymakam* of the Grand Rabbinate, Rabbi Moshe Levi (1872–1908), restored Ottoman Jewry's position as most favored minority community in the empire, particularly during the reign of Sultan Abdül Hamid II (1876–1909). With the Sultan's blessings and support, Levi actively carried on the work of modernization begun by his predecessor, cooperating with the *AIU*'s Istanbul committee in opening new elementary schools in Kuzguncuk and Piri Pasha, at least partly to counteract the efforts of Protestant missionaries to convert the Jewish children who went to their schools, and re-organizing and strengthening the various charity societies operated by community groups to help orphans, the aged and the poor. Levi's main difficulties came in raising sufficient funds to carry on community's activities. He was no more successful than Yakir Geron had been in collecting the annual *aritha* capital tax as well as the *gabelle* excise tax, in both of which he met insistent opposition from those who opposed his reforming policies, resulting in persistent deficits in the Grand Rabbinate's annual budgets which could only be met by pressuring wealthy Jews to make special contributions and by loans from Jewish bankers, which were not always repaid. The resulting arguments so disrupted the operations of the *Meclisi Cismani* that in 1874 an effort was made to reform it by giving it a new name, *Meclisi Idare* (Administrative committee), and electing new members, but this brought no permanent solution. Levi's years were therefore, very much like those of Geron, constantly troubled by internal political intrigues and disputes, resulting in relative inaction in resolving the community's many problems.

Perhaps the high point of Levi's years as Grand Rabbi came in 1892 with the celebration of the four hundredth anniversary of the exile of the Jews from Spain and their arrival in the Ottoman Empire. On the first day of Passover, special prayers of thanks were given in all the synagogues of the Empire, and special poems commemorating the occasion were published in the Jewish press. Telegrams of thanks came to the Sultan from most major Jewish organizations in Europe, while Moshe Levi himself went to the Yıldız Palace and presented a statement of gratitude along with copies of a special prayer for Abdül Hamid which was being read in all the synagogues of the empire.

Moshe Levi's years as Grand Rabbi saw an entire new generation of prosperous Jews arise in banking, industry, trade, medicine and government, resulting from the *Tanzimat* reforms and modernization programs, as brought to fruition by Abdül Hamid but also, particularly after 1885, because violent revolts by the Greek and Armenian minorities against Ottoman rule, their sympathy with outside assaults against the empire, and their evident efforts to secure European assistance for their own claims, so intensified in frequency and emotion that the Jews were left as the only minority community which was entirely trusted and respected by the government and the mass of Ottoman Muslims, very much like the situation following the Ottoman conquest of Constantinople in 1453. Ottoman Jewry once again prospered and gained influence in and out of the government. Grand Rabbi Moshe Levi had direct access to the Sultan, though he used this privilege with sensitivity and discretion so as not to excite the Sultan's suspicions. Both Ottoman and foreign Jews taught in the faculties of Letters, Medicine, Law and Sciences at the Istanbul University as well as in the imperial military and engineering academies. Jews joined the Ottoman bureaucracy in numbers far greater than their proportion of the population, and they often served as Ottoman consular representatives throughout Europe, particularly in the major Mediterranean ports. In all the major cities of the empire, Jewish merchants and industrialists greatly increased their share of the markets and Jewish traders more and more dominated Ottoman trade with the outside world.

There were more than 60,000 Jews living in Salonica at this time, still the largest single element of the population though no longer an absolute majority. Most were still craftsmen or unskilled workers, concentrating on the manufacture and trade in textiles and footstuffs, but the free professions and commercial capitalism were increasingly common. The community unity and social solidarity which had been built up during the centuries of crisis were, however, now weakened by renewed loyalties to their cities and provinces of origin in the distant past as well as with squabbles between the once-dominant Sephardim and the increasingly numerous Ashkenazim, the latter strengthened by renewed immigration from persecution in Central Europe. These quarrels were compounded by class divisions among notables, the rising middle class, and the workers, with unity achieved only in condemning the *dönmes*.

While the prosperity of the Jewish upper and middle classes spread to many other Jews, particularly because of the efforts of the *AIU* to develop Jewish artisanry, the continued reactionary spirit of some Jewish religious leaders, combined with the constant ritual murder assaults and persecution by Ottoman Christians and some Muslims, often with the encouragement of European businessmen, diplomats, travellers and consuls, pressure on the part of Armenians and Greeks to keep the Jews out of the more profitable occupations with the help of the Capitulations, and continued suffering from massive fires and epidemics of cholera and the plague which ravaged Ottoman cities kept many Jews in various degrees of poverty.

Most of Istanbul's Jewish population responded to prosperity by moving up the heights of Balat to Kasturiye or Iştipol, across the Golden Horn to Galata and Beyoğlu, and across the Bosporus to Kadıköy, Moda and Haydarpaşa, on the northern shores of the Sea of Marmara, where they lived in well-built houses of stone and marble, with streets all paved and well-maintained like those of the European and Christian quarters of Beyoğlu. Newly-arriving Jewish refugees from persecution in Southeastern Europe, coming mainly from Greece and Serbia, as well as from Russian Central Asia and the Caucasus, for the most part arrived by train at the Sirkeci terminal of the Orient Express and settled in its immediate vicinity, creating an entirely new Jewish quarter whose synagogue, at least, has remained active to the present day, long after its Jewish population has moved to the more modern suburbs.

With prosperity, wealth and influence, Istanbul's Jews repaired many of their ancient synagogues and built new ones in the areas to which they had moved. The Ortaköy *Etz ha-Haim* synagogue, originally constructed in 1628 was restored in 1825. The Zülfaris synagogue, located immediately below the 'Street of Banks' in Galata where so many Jewish bankers were active, was entirely rebuilt in 1890 with an interest free loan provided by the Camondo Bank in return for which it provided rooms for the Chief Rabbinate's Administrative Council. New synagogues were built for new Jewish communities along the Bosporus at Yeniköy and

Büyükdere, largely through contributions from the Camondo family. A new Ashkenazi synagogue was constructed by Austrian Jews on the Yüksek Kaldırım slope which connected Beyoğlu and Galata. The Italian community, which had separated from the Sephardim in 1866, constructed its new synagogue on Şair Ziya sokak in Galata in 1885, and the new Haydarpaşa synagogue was opened in 1899 to meet the needs of the Jews of Üsküdar and Kadıköy as well, despite the violent opposition of the local Greek community.

Christian revolts against the Ottomans with European help along with attacks on Muslims and Jews in the newly independent Christian nations as well as within the Ottoman Empire, particularly in Macedonia, and a common poverty among the masses created a feeling of brotherhood in suffering between Muslims and Jews within the shrinking boundaries of the Ottoman Empire which has lasted right through the Turkish Republic to the present day. It was the Jews and Muslims against the Christians, with the Jews extremely grateful for the protection provided by the Ottoman government. The *AIU* thus reported in 1893:

> There are but few countries, even among those which are considered the most enlightened and the most civilized, where Jews enjoy a more complete equality than in Turkey. H.M. the Sultan and the government of the Porte display towards Jews a spirit of largest toleration and liberalism. In every respect, Abdül-Hamid proves to be a generous sovereign and a protector of his Israelite subjects . . . . The unflinching attachment of Jews to His Person and to the Empire is the only way in which they can express their gratitude. Thus, the Sultan as well as his officials know that Jews are among the most obedient, faithful and devoted subjects of Turkey.[49]

Jewish resentment against the continued persecution and ritual murder attacks by Greeks and Armenians led to such hatred that, for example, many Jews actively assisted the attacks of Kurds and Lazzes on the Armenian quarters of Istanbul in 1896 and 1908, showing the Kurds where Armenians lived and where many of them were hiding and joining them in carrying away the booty. The result was even greater Armenian hatred for Jews than had been the case before, leading to further persecution and attacks in subsequent years.[50] It was therefore not just the modern education, not just the modernization of the Jewish *millet*, not just the help of the Jewish financiers of Europe, but also an increasing Muslim feeling of togetherness with the Jews against all other non-Muslims in the Empire which contributed to the revival of Ottoman Jewry in the nineteenth and early twentieth centuries. Ottoman Jewry therefore remained far more loyal to the Ottomans than any other minority.

Ottoman Jewry and Zionist Efforts in Palestine. There were repeated attempts to secure Ottoman approval for Jewish settlement in Palestine during the last quarter of the nineteenth century. The Ottomans repeatedly responded with encouragement for the continued flow of Jewish emigrants which had begun much earlier in the century in response to political repression all over Europe, but they specifically discouraged settlement in Palestine and attempted to divert it to other parts of the Empire, particularly to Anatolia, where Jewish settlers had done so much already to revive Ottoman agriculture and trade during the *Tanzimat* years. It has been suggested that Ottoman opposition stemmed at least partly from fears of creating a new minority problem in an empire already suffering from major nationalist revolts, of expanding the number of foreign subjects benefiting from the protection of foreign powers through the hated Capitulations, and, since most of the prospective immigrants were Jews fleeing pogroms in Russia, of helping spread Russian influence in the Empire. While these and other such factors may have been considered by the Sultan and those around them, since they continued to be more than willing to settle emigrant Jews elsewhere in the Empire, including areas of Eastern Anatolia where the Russian threat was even more imminent than in Palestine because of Russian support for Armenian national aspirations, these do not really seem to have been decisive factors in themselves.

In 1879, the well known British writer Laurence Oliphant proposed to the Ottoman government that Jews be placed in a utopian settlement on the River Jordan. Efforts of a group of British and German businessmen in 1881 to secure an Ottoman concession for building a railroad from Izmir to Baghdad with the help of Jews who would be settled along its route was met with a decision of the Ottoman Council of Ministers that Jews could, indeed, be 'settled as scattered groups throughout Turkey excluding Palestine . . . ' but they would have to 'submit to all the laws of the Empire and become Ottoman subjects',[51] and this was repeated during the next two years in official notices posted in Ottoman diplomatic and consular missions throughout Europe. Sultan Abdül Hamid II himself favored a plan proposed by Grand Rabbi Moshe Levi to rescue Russian Jews by settling them in agricultural colonies in Eastern Anatolia,[52] if only the Jewish community would agree to allow its men to be conscripted into the Ottoman army. The proposal was willingly accepted by the *Millet*'s Religious Council (*Meclisi Ruhani*) in 1893 but it was later abandoned by the government after the Greek and Armenian communities refused to join the effort.[53] Despite this failure, however, Abdül Hamid II admitted large numbers of Jewish refugees from Rumanian persecution[54] and Russian pogroms[55] almost as soon as the latter began on a large scale in 1881, and continued to admit them in large numbers during the remaining years of his reign, showing very clearly that whatever were his reasons for opposing

Jewish settlement in Palestine, anti-Semitism as such was not among them.

Shortly after Theodore Herzl published his famous *Der Judenstaat*, in which he suggested that the 'Jewish problem' could be solved only by establishing a Jewish state somewhere, hopefully in Palestine, he appointed the Viennese journalist Philipp Newlinski (1841–99) as his agent in Istanbul to lobby with Ottoman officials toward this goal. With Newlinski's help Herzl visited Istanbul for the first time in June, 1896, meeting with the Grand Vezir and other leading Ottoman officials and presenting a plan for the Sultan to allow the establishment of Palestine as a Jewish homeland in return for settlement of all the external debts of the Ottoman treasury by the wealthy Jewish bankers and investors of Europe.

Herzl also worked through Kaiser Wilhelm II, who was developing a close relationship with the Sultan as part of Germany's *Drang nach Osten*, stating when they met in Istanbul on 18 October 1898 that a reduction of Jews in Europe would weaken anti-Semitism as well as Socialism and the other revolutionary movements in which they had been active participants throughout the continent. At the same time the Ottoman Empire would gain enormously from the influx of an intelligent and energetic Jewish element into the Holy Land as well as from the injection of large amounts of money into her economy which would improve both her trade and her finances. The Jews would bring order and civilization to the Middle East, and by helping to build a railroad from the Mediterranean to the Gulf would assist Germany in establishing its position in the area. The Kaiser wrote to his uncle:

> I am convinced that the settlement of the Holy Land by the wealthy and industrious people of Israel will bring unexampled prosperity and blessings to the Holy Land, which may do much to revive and develop Asia Minor. Such a settlement would bring millions into the purse of the Turks . . . and so gradually help to save the 'Sick Man' from bankruptcy.[56]

The Kaiser went on to recommend Herzl's plans to the Sultan, but Abdül Hamid and his officials had for some time been struggling to lessen the powers of the Capitulatory powers over the Ottoman economy, and they were not at all willing to agree to the establishment of another protected community, this time that of the Jews in Palestine under German protection. In any case, as early as 1888 the Ottoman leaders had decided to allow Russian Jews to settle in Palestine as individual immigrants, though not in groups.[57] The Grand Vezir therefore replied both to Herzl and the Kaiser that the Sultan would be happy to have the support of European Jewry in paying off the Ottoman debts and building the empire, and that he was most anxious to continue to receive the Jewish refugees wishing to come to the Ottoman Empire from persecution in Central Europe and Russia who wished to help build its economy. He felt, however, that they should go to Anatolia and Iraq, where they were needed, not to Palestine, which, as Abdül Hamid said to Newlinsky, was as holy to Muslims as it was to Jews:

> If Mr. Herzl is as much your friend as you are mine, then advise him not to take another step in this matter. I cannot sell even a foot of land, for it does not belong to me but to my people. My people have won this empire by fighting for it with their blood and have fertilized it with their blood. We will again cover it with our blood before we allow it to be wrested away from us . . . The Turkish Empire belongs not to me but to the Turkish people. I cannot give away any part of it. Let the Jews save their billions. When my Empire is partitioned, they may get Palestine for nothing. But only our corpse will be divided. I will not agree to vivisection.[58]

Herzl attempted to modify his plans in order to mollify the Sultan. The terms 'Independent Jewish state', and 'republic', which were being used in presentations to Zionist congresses and supporters in Europe, were replaced by the idea of an 'autonomous vassal state . . . under the suzerainty of the Sultan', with Jewish colonists accepting Ottoman nationality and paying a substantial annual tribute to the Sultan in return for permission to establish an autonomous region in Palestine with the maintenance of a small army. With these proposals in mind Herzl managed to secure an audience with the Sultan himself for the first time, which took place on 17 May 1901.

The audience went on for over two hours. Herzl thanked the Sultan for his help to all the Jews then fleeing into Ottoman territory from persecution in Russia. Abdül Hamid replied that Jewish refugees were welcome to settle anywhere they wanted in his empire, since, as far as he was concerned, they were his only reliable non-Muslim subjects. The Empire needed the industrial and financial skills of the Jews and would most certainly benefit from their services. Abdül Hamid and his officials were, however, unconvinced that a Jewish state was necessary in order to achieve these benefits. Their opposition to a Jewish state in Palestine was supported not only by most of the Jewish bankers of Europe, who preferred to develop Jewish colonies in Eretz Israel under continued Ottoman rule, and who in any case had no desire to exhaust their resources by paying off the immense Ottoman foreign debt, but also by Rabbi Moshe Levi and the other leaders of the Ottoman Jewish community, who were very satisfied with their situation in the Ottoman empire and feared that such a Jewish state would undermine it. Abdül

Hamid was in fact surprised by the extent of Herzl's plan, and initially blamed the Grand Rabbi until the latter assured him that the Jewish community had nothing to do with it and strongly opposed the idea. Jewish immigrants in Palestine and some foreign diplomats in Istanbul at the time assumed that this opposition stemmed from Sephardic fears that they would be overwhelmed by a new Ashkenazi influx, but this does not seem to have played an important role in the *millet's* opposition to Zionism at this time.

A great deal of the Sultan's negative reaction to Herzl's plan came from the violent protests against Jewish immigration and settlement in Palestine which had been reaching his palace from its non-Jewish population. The Sephardic Jews of the traditional Jewish community that had lived in Palestine prior to the nineteenth-century emigration from Europe had nourished no political ambitions and had flourished as Ottoman subjects. The Ashkenazi settlers who had come to outnumber the Sephardim after 1877, however, generally shared European prejudices against the Ottomans (and even against their Sephardic cousins), were therefore reluctant to become subjects of the Sultan, preferring instead the protection of European consus in accordance with the provisions of the Capitulations treaties. These Ashkenazim refused to pay the special tax imposed by the Ottomans in return for the right to live in the Holy City, they avoided assimilation to the Ottoman way of life, and they continued to dress and behave like Europeans. It was, of course, against the latter that the Ottomans reacted on the imperial and local levels. The Porte correctly considered the Ashkenazim to constitute a danger to the empire, constituting a nucleus for a Jewish nationalist movement which might well resemble those of the Armenians and Greeks. Local Palestinian Arab notables, Christian and Muslim alike, correctly perceived the inherent dangers of such settlements to their own communities and persistently demanded that the immigrants be sent away. In Palestine itself local Arab Christians led the way in persecuting the settlers already there, reviving the old ritual murder accusations against Jews in fear that the new immigrants would compete successfully with them in agriculture, business and trade as well as in gaining the favor of the Muslim majority, as Jews had done so successfully elsewhere in the Empire. Opposition to Zionist plans even came from local Ashkenazi German and Russian Jews settled in Palestine who, so long as they did not take Ottoman citizenship, were able to join local Christians in benefiting from the Capitulations privileges and did not want to do anything which might limit or eliminate them or require any sort of sharing with the Ottoman Jews whom they were joining. Russia pressured Abdül Hamid II to limit or terminate this immigration because of fears that the rise of any new group would inevitably affect the status quo regarding the Holy Places which had been established following the Crimean War only a quarter century before, while England and France urged the Sultan in the same direction due to fears that increasing immigration of Russian Jews might well increase the Czar's power and influence throughout the Levant. Abdül Hamid II was particularly receptive to these pressures because of fears that large-scale Jewish immigration to Palestine would not only create a new nationialist problem in addition to those which he already faced with Armenians, Slavs, Greeks and others but also would also hinder his efforts to use Islamic nationalism and the idea of Pan-Islam to unite his Arab and Turkish Muslim subjects in order to revive and strengthen the Empire.

In response to all the protests and objections, then, the Sultan's government starting in 1882 issued orders prohibiting Jewish settlement in Palestine, requiring that those coming as visitors be required to leave after several months, and after 1892 adding limitations on the acquisition of landed property in Palestine by Jews and others who were not Ottoman subjects. In practice, however, local officials allowed these 'visitors' to remain long beyond the terms of their visas and to purchase land regardless of nationality, presumably as a result of bribes and other considerations. What is even more remarkable, however, is the fact that the Sultan's government in Istanbul did nothing substantial to stem the tide of Jewish emigration and settlement in Palestine aside from repeating its orders again and again in the face of numerous reports that they were being flouted, and it even authorized Ottoman and foreign Jews who were legally resident in Palestine to purchase property if they agreed not to allow illegal Jewish immigrants to settle on it and use it for agriculture, thus helping the Jewish settlements to become permanent and to expand despite all the orders issued to the contrary.

As a result, the first wave of Zionist immigration to the Holy Land continued unchecked, with the period from 1882 to 1904, known as the First Aliyah, seeing the establishment of twenty-three new Jewish agricultural settlements including as many as 30,000 settlers coming from Eastern Europe, though since most came from middle class backgrounds, without agricultural experience and with little financial support, a good number of the latter did not remain on a permanent basis, with the colonies surviving only in consequence of the large-scale financial assistance provided by members of the Rothschild family rather than from their own efforts. The 'Second Aliyah' that followed from 1904 until the start of World War I, brought in some 33,000 settlers including several thousand Jewish socialist workers led by David Ben Gurion who established the Eretz Israel workers' movement and led the immigrants into the communal *kibbutz* and *moshav* settlements. Jewish immigrants also began to settle in cities outside Jerusalem, with the Jewish population of Jaffa doubling to some 10,000 people and that of Haifa tripling to 3,000, while Tel Aviv was established as a separate settlement in 1909.

It was not long before the Jewish settlers established their own para-military organizations which were far better able to maintain and defend themselves than were the immigrants who came before 1904. Though they were concealed from the Ottoman authorities, they were known by the latter sufficiently for them to become even more hostile to the Jewish colonies than they had been at the start. The first such enterprise, was called *Bar-Giora* after a Jewish resistance leader to Roman rule in the time of the Second Temple, Two years later, members of *Bar-Giora* established the underground *Hashomer* (watchman) organization with considerably wider objectives, to constitute a political organization that would, in time, create an army which would be able to carry out 'national missions' as needed, including, perhaps, the establishment of an independent state. While the local Ottoman authorities were aware of *Hashomer* and other such groups, they did nothing about them, particularly since Israel Shochat felt that the organization's objectives could best be achieved within the Sultan's empire. In 1913, he proposed the formal establishment of a Jewish militia that would serve as a group in the Ottoman Army.

As a result of these activities, the Jewish population of Palestine rose dramatically in the late nineteenth and early twentieth centuries, from 24,000 in 1882 to 47,000 in 1890, 80,000 in 1908 and 85,000 in 1914, increasing their share of the total from five to over eleven percent during the same period. These immigrants (called *olim* in Hebrew) lived not only in the cities but also in twenty-six agricultural colonies. They operated with considerable success, developing out of their original settlements at Zichron Ya'akov, Rishon L'tzion, Petach Tikvah and Gedara along the coastal plain from Haifa to Jaffa, well into Judea and Upper Galilee, largely with the financial assistance of Baron Edmond de Rothschild of Paris, who also sent administrators, agricultural experts, physicians and teachers who helped the settlers at least until the end of the century. While modern Zionists tend to criticize the Ottoman government for restricting Jewish immigration and settlement, it must be remembered that the Ottomans were under considerable pressure from the Christian and Muslim inhabitants of Palestine to keep out new immigrants and to deport those who had come earlier, and that by issuing regulations to this effect without supplying the military and administrative cadres needed to carry them out, they were in fact helping the Jewish colonization and settlement, which could not have existed otherwise.

Abdül Hamid in fact knew exactly what the Zionists wanted. His ambassador in Washington, Ali Ferruh Bey, had grown up in Palestine while his father was governor of the *sancak* of Jerusalem, and was very much aware of what the Jewish colonists were doing there as well as the strong reaction on the part of the native Arabs. As a result he had taken care to study Zionist programs and activities while he served in various diplomatic posts in Paris (1888), London (1892), Petersburg

(1894) and Washington (1896), and it was from the latter that in April 1898 he informed the Sultan that their aim, clearly was 'to establish an independent government in Palestine', and that it was very likely that they constituted 'another advance guard of further political Western influence in the Ottoman Empire', concluding that Abdül Hamid should 'take certain measures to rectify the error committed by his forefathers in allowing non-Muslim communities to settle in Palestine'.[59] As a result, the Sultan concluded that Zionism was a threat to his Empire's position in Palestine. In consequence, Ottoman authorities greatly restricted Jewish settlement activity in Palestine by measures such as compelling Jewish visitors to leave cash deposits to guarantee they would leave and restricting the sale of land in Palestine to foreign Jews.

Despite these declarations and policies, however, the Sultan continued to want Jews to settle elsewhere in the Empire, so in his responses, which were as vague as Herzl's requests, he avoided closing the door, instead promising to provide the Zionist leader with a detailed account of the Empire's financial problems and to make a public proclamation favorable to Jews at a suitable opportunity. Herzl seems to have read much more than was intended into this, for while the Sultan subsequently lived up to what he thought he had promised by allowing thousands more Jewish refugees from Germany and Russia to settle in his possessions, not only in Anatolia but also in Istanbul and Izmir, when Herzl returned to Istanbul to hear these decisions, he felt betrayed because Palestine also was not included. Of course Herzl had not been able to live up to his promise to Abdül Hamid that he would interest wealthy European Jewish bankers in providing financial assistance to the Ottoman Empire, since while he had established the Zionist Bank (Jewish Colonial Trust) for this purpose in 1897, the Jewish bankers did not support it, so there was no reason for the Sultan to change his original proposal. In addition, moreover, if there was any deception involved, it came not from the Sultan, who from the start indicated that he wanted European Jews to settle in some other province than Palestine, but from Herzl himself, who in his *Judenstaat*, and later in the official Zionist program drawn up at the First Zionist Congress in Basle (1897), avoided openly declaring his real intention of establishing a 'Jewish state' in Palestine so as not to antagonize either the Sultan, from whom he wanted permission, or the wealthy Jewish bankers of Europe who were to finance the operation, using instead the term 'home' (*heimstaette*) for the kind of Jewish settlement he said he intended to establish. Abdül Hamid II, however, was fully aware of Herzl's real intentions, and acted accordingly.

Relations between Jews and Muslim Turks were improved by the role played by the Salonica *dönmes* in the Young Turk revolution of 1908 which overturned Abdül Hamid's autocracy. The Salonica attorney Emmanuel Carasso (d. 1934), who later took the name Karasu in the early years of the Turkish Republic, was close to many Young Turk leaders in his home town, particularly to Talat Pasha, and used his membership in the local Masonic Lodges to provide the Young Turks with places where they met to plan their revolutionary activities. He later served as unionist deputy in the Parliament and had great influence with Talat Pasha on economic policy. It is a matter of dispute among scholars, however, as to how much influence and importance should be attached to the role of Salonica Jewry in the success of the Young Turk movement. There can be no doubt, however, that Jewish communities throughout the empire strongly encouraged and supported the revolution and were very happy with its results.[60]

Grand Rabbi Haim Nahum Efendi. Leading the way in bringing the Jewish community into active participation in Ottoman life during the last two decades of the empire was its last, and in many ways most controversial, Grand Rabbi, Haim Nahum Efendi (1873–1960), who remained as leader of the community from 1909 until his resignation during the Allied occupation of Istanbul in 1920.[61] Right from the start, Nahum's upbringing and career reflected the desires of those who wanted to bring Ottoman Jewry into the mainstream of Ottoman life. Born of a poor Jewish family in Manisa, near Izmir, in 1873, he was first educated in traditional Islamic and Jewish studies, learning both the Talmud in Hebrew and the Koran in Arabic at a *yeshiva* in Tiberius (1881–1886), where he had been brought by his grandfather, before returning to complete his education at Manisa, where he learned both Turkish and French. Young Nahum so distinguished himself in these early studies that the governor of Manisa subsequently financed his education at the Ottoman *Sultani* lycée at Izmir and then at the Imperial School of Law in Istanbul, from which he graduated in 1891, thus gaining a fully rounded education in both traditional and secular subjects, rare among his Jewish contemporaries at the time.

Nor did his passion for a wide breadth of learning stop at the borders of the Empire. Once he had learned all that the *Tanzimat* educational system could provide, Nahum was determined to extend his knowledge in Europe. In 1891 he secured a fellowship from the *AIU*, which at the time was financing the religious education of a number of Ottoman Jewish rabbis in order to influence and direct their subsequent work. With this help, which incidentally tied him close to the *AIU* in subsequent years, Nahum continued his education in Paris, studying first at the Faculty of Law (1891–92) and then at the modern-style Rabbinical Seminary (1893–1897), which provided both secular and religious instruction to create a new-style Rabbi able to lead his community into the modern world, securing a law degree as well as ordination as a Rabbi in 1897. At the same time he studied Arabic and Persian at the *Ecole Speciale des Langues Orientales Vivantes* and the religion of Islam at the *Section des*

Sciences Religieuses de l'Ecole Pratique des Hautes Etudes and at the *College de France,* beginning a lifelong passion for Islamic studies, at the same time coming into contact with his Muslim Turkish contemporaries who as Young Turks were actively agitating against Sultan Abdül Hamid II's tyranny from exile in Paris.

Returning to Istanbul in 1897, Nahum started his career by teaching at the *AIU* school in Hasköy, one of the traditional centers of Jewish life, and also at Galata, to which newly-prosperous Jews had been moving since the Crimean War. At the same time, with the same energy and perspectivity which had marked the years of his education, he actively sought out acquaintances among his co-religionists, securing the admiration of the more progressive elements who felt stifled under the leadership of the old-style rabbis who continued to dominate the community at the time, all the while actively propagandizing on behalf of the *AIU* and its ideas. He also used his knowledge of Turkish, still rare among contemporary rabbis, to represent the *AIU* as well as the 'modernists' in the Jewish community in securing Ottoman government permission to transfer to Istanbul the Rabbinical Seminary established in Edirne in 1891 with *AIU* financing to train young Ottoman Rabbis in a more modern style than previously had been customary. Nahum joined its director, Abraham Danon, long leader of progressive Judaism in Edirne, in building the school in its new location, soon afterwards marrying Danon's daughter Sultana. Nahum's fame among the wealthier Jews of Istanbul spread even more widely in 1899 when he gave the Yom Kippur sermon at the synagogue of Haydarpaşa in the presence of the American millionaire philanthropist Oscar Strauss, then Ambassador to the Porte, as well as of Baron Edmund de Rothschild.

It was at this point that the rise of the Zionist movement, and the activities of its agents in Istanbul, effected Nahum's career and views in a manner which was to affect him during the remainder of his life. Nahum now represented those Jews who were prospering as part of the Ottoman Empire and resented the Zionist aspirations to establish a Jewish presence in Palestine, which they were sure would bring down the wrath of the Islamic world against all Jews. This led the Zionists in Sofia to secure rejection in 1898, and again in 1902, of the efforts of the *AIU* Secretary General, Jacques Bigart (1892–1934) to have him appointed as its Grand Rabbi.

Nahum then worked to advance his career in the Istanbul Grand Rabbinate, where in 1904 *AIU* influence secured his appointment as Secretary of the *Meclisi Cismani* and chief of the Chancery, acting more or less as the *AIU*'s agent to influence its policies as well as its inside informant. With the aged Acting Grand Rabbi Moshe Levi no longer able to actively carry on his post, a struggle for power ensued between the *Kaymakam*'s deputy, who represented the more conservative elements in the community while maintaining Levi's close connections with the Sultan and Palace, and the modernists, whom Nahum generally supported. With the conservative rabbis dominating the Council, however, Nahum could do little except to secure continued local support for the Rabbinical Seminar and the *AIU* schools.

Nahum added to his contacts by starting to teach French at the Imperial School of Engineering and Artillery in 1900, where he became acquainted with Selim Sırrı Bey, an *aide* to Sultan Abdül Hamid II and Vice-President of the Central Committee of Union and Progress, leaving at least the possibility that he might have even been involved in Young Turk activities at this time. Soon afterwards, he also became actively involved in the Jewish community at Galata, reorganizing and modernizing its administration while serving as its *mare de atra*. Strong public attacks made by the young Avram Galante against corruption and tyranny in the Grand Rabbinate under the leadership of Levi and his conservative supporters tended to tarnish Nahum's reputation, even though he was quietly opposing the conservatives. To get away from a problem that he could not resolve, therefore, in 1907–8 he went to Abyssinia to study the Falashas on behalf of the *AIU*. He therefore was absent from Istanbul at the time of the Young Turk Revolution (23/24 July 1908) when the Constitution of 1876 was restored, though he returned immediately thereafter in the hope of taking advantage of the Constitutional era to reform the community administration.

Led and stimulated by Haim Nahum and those around him, 'modernist' members of the Istanbul Jewish community maintained close relations with, and actively supported, the Young Turks and participated fervently and enthusiastically in the celebrations and manifestations of fraternity among the Empire's peoples which followed. At the same time they worked to use these changes made in the Empire's political structure to carry out the reforms in the Grand Rabbinate as well as in the Chief Rabbinates around the empire, which they had been advocating during the previous decade, with the Young Turks and Unionist party which they founded strongly supporting their efforts. The immediate instrument for reform had to be the *Meclisi Cismani*, which Levi had allowed to fall into disuse during the latter days of his service as *Kaymakam*. But only the Grand Rabbi or *Kaymakam* could convoke the *Meclisi Umumi*, which alone, under the Organic Statute, had the power to elect the members of the *Meclisi Cismani*, and Levi refused to do so in fear of the inevitable changes that would follow. Finally, however, the *Meclisi Umumi* met on 9 August 1908. Both Nahum and his father in law Abraham Danon of Edirne were appointed as religious members of the *Meclisi Cismani*, along with the equally progressive Ashkenazi leader Rabbi David Marcus, thus providing it with a strong modernist majority. While Nahum had been for some time the *Alliance*'s candidate to succeed Levi, at the last minute it recoiled from his strongly political activities, considering him 'a little too advanced . . . for the milieu of Istanbul . . .', and instead supported his father-in-law, the far less political but still modernist Danon, thus causing a split and bitter campaign. Levi finally resigned on 12 August 1908, leaving the modernists in complete control of the Grand Rabbinate, though divided as to who should succeed him. Within a few days, Haim Nahum was elected in Levi's place as *Kaymakam* despite the *Alliance*'s opposition, taking office on 7 March 1909, thus turning the Jewish community in an entirely new direction as part of the reforms of the Constitutional period, with the *Alliance* and its supporters supporting him as the only means through which the desired reforms could be accomplished.

Nahum's first task was to transform his appointment as *Kaymakam* into a regular appointment as Grand Rabbi, the first since Yakir Geron had taken office in 1863. For this to be accomplished he had to convoke the eighty Istanbul members of the *Meclisi Umumi*, to which, according to the Organic Statute, he had to assemble forty additional provincial delegates in order to carry out the election. But whereas modernists had dominated the *Meclisi Cismani*, conservatives and Orthodox still maintained a majority in the larger body, and they evidently opposed Nahum's election to any post of leadership, with the strong support of the *Hilfsverein der Deutschen Juden* (founded in 1901) and of the Zionist organization in Istanbul, both of which correctly feared that under Nahum the *Alliance* would dominate with a progressive but anti-Zionist policy. A political campaign therefore ensued within the Jewish community, with each group propagandizing widely in the Jewish press as well as securing help from allies in Europe. Nahum went on a campaign tour around the old Jewish centers of Istanbul Judaism, Hasköy as well as his own home, Balat, and also to the suburbs, even to Ortaköy on the Bosporus, where Levi lived and his support was especially strong. Nahum appealed for support to the Zionists against the conservatives, who opposed the establishment of a Jewish state in Palestine even more than he did, but in this he was unsuccessful because of his continued refusal to support the ultimate Zionist goal. The *AIU* itself provided Nahum with strong financial backing along with the support of its Jewish social and fraternal clubs, which long had advocated reforms, hoping as a result to itself gain control of the Jewish community.The conservatives reacted by getting the powerful guild of *kosher* butchers to go on strike, depriving the Grand Rabbinate of the *gabelle* revenues needed to conduct its normal activities, let alone to meet the expenditures which had to be made to convoke the councils required to elect the new Grand Rabbi. His opponents also stressed Nahum's close ties to the *AIU*, stating that his election would give foreign Jews control of Ottoman Jewry. The *AIU* and its clubs reacted by opening new butcher shops and selling *kosher* meat at prices far below those maintained by the guilds in what proved to be a successful effort to break the strike.

The struggle over the Grand Rabbinate became entangled in the Ottoman election campaign held during the winter of 1908–09 to chose deputies to the new Ottoman Parliament, with the divisions among Jewish modernists, conservatives and Zionists compounding the more traditional hostility among Sephardim, Ashkenazim and Karaites. Nahum led the modernists in supporting the successful Union and Progress candidates, themselves electing four members of the lower house (*Meclisi Mebusan*) and one of the Senate (*Meclisi Ayan*), while political combinations of Zionists and conservatives in opposition to the common enemy led by Nahum were largely unsuccessful. Under his leadership, members of the Jewish community continued to play an active political role in cooperation with the Unionists during the Constitutional period (1908–12).

Political success outside the community soon enabled Nahum to achieve appointment as Grand Rabbi. By terms of the Organic Statute, soon after the parliamentary elections, on 12 January 1909, five candidates for the position were named, out of whom one was to be chosen. The forty provincial electors assembled at the Grand Rabbinate along with the eighty Istanbul members, and after some protests from the deputies of Salonica, Edirne, Cairo and Alexandria over what they considered to be under-representation of their congregations in relation to those of Istanbul, Nahum finally was elected Grand Rabbi by majority vote on 24 January 1909.[62]

During his years as Grand Rabbi Nahum never really was able to achieve the modern reforms in the Jewish community that he had envisaged and advocated. Part of the reason was political: the community continued to be so fragmented, and the political formations and alignments so unstable, that, even after his election he rarely was able to secure a majority in the councils for any decisive action. Much of the difficulty was financial, due to a great extent to the long years in which *Kaymakam* Levi had allowed the reigns of leadership to loosen, including in particular his abandonment of the collection of the *gabelle*, the traditional tax on meat sales, and the *kisbe*, the proportional personal tax on income, which traditionally had formed the major bases of the Grand Rabbinate's revenues. Part of the reason for the strike of *kosher* butchers against Nahum's elections had been his declaration that he would impose the *gabelle* once again. Even after he was elected, they continued to successfully oppose its imposition, gaining the support of most community members who were happy to avoid payment of any taxes whenever possible. Only the Ottoman authorities had the strength necessary to force the butchers to collect and pay the tax, but even when Nahum finally got the Ministry of Justice to issue a new *tezkere* (27 June

1910) ordering the butchers guild to do so, it was not enforced, so that the tax continued in abayance to the end of his term. Nor was Nahum any more successful in collecting the *kisbe*, due in particular to the division of the community into districts (*hashgahot*) and the laxity of their authorities in collecting taxes from those around them, at best securing only a small percentage of what was owed, even by the wealther members of his community. Without real financial backing, then, he was able at best maintain the educational and social institutions of the community with the help of the *AIU* and other foreign philanthropic organizations and individuals. But his efforts to modernize community administration and to extend his authority over the provincial chief rabbis, a relationship mentioned only vaguely in the Organic Statute, were unsuccessful, due not only to natural local resistance to any extension of central authority but also to the spread of Zionist influence in the provinces even more than in the Capital.

Zionist activity in the Empire was, indeed, increasing, creating major new divisions within the Jewish community and increasing hostility without. The German Jewish gymnastic organizations (*Turnvereine*) began operations among the Jews of Balat (Istanbul) in 1895 and at Filibe (Plovdiv) three years later, subsequently transforming their local branches into agencies of the Zionist movement. The first official Zionist office in a Muslim country was established in Istanbul in 1908 by Victor Jacobson (1869–1935), with the help of such Zionist luminaries as Richard Lichtheim, Vladimir Jabotinsky and Arthur Ruppin, under the cover of the Anglo-Levantine Banking Company, which became very active in attracting and organizing those members of the Jewish community who opposed the domination of the 'modernists' led by Haim Nahum and the *AIU*.

With Ottoman Jewry prospering greatly during Abdül Hamid II's reign, these Zionists found little local Jewish support except among recent Ashkenazi immigrants from central and eastern Europe, and in Salonica, at least until its conquest by the Greeks in 1912, whose Jewish community was far more progressive socially and politically than that of Istanbul, with local Jews organizing and leading the Socialist labor organizations which greatly stimulated and disrupted Salonician society in the early years of the twentieth century.

The struggle between the Zionists and Ottoman Jewish community leaders took place on various stages. Haim Nahum was very much aware that, as a result of the rejection by minority nationalists of the initial Young Turk offer of equality for all subjects regardless of religion, the Young Turks had turned from Ottomanization to Turkish nationalism, and were now hoping to assimilate all the ethnic groups into what they hoped would become a Turkish state. Under these circumstances he knew that they would never accept the Zionist ideal of establishing a Jewish state in Palestine and that they would react very negatively if the Ottoman Jewish community supported the Zionists. He therefore strongly refused Zionist efforts to get him to influence the Young Turk leaders in their favor, avoiding any public stand regarding their activities and declarations, but privately working continuously against their efforts to get support from Jewish communities in Salonica and elsewhere around the Empire. At the same time he worked to assure the government of continued Jewish loyalty by urging the Young Turks to reject Zionist and other requests to allow additional Jewish settlements in Palestine and instead to settle in Anatolia or Iraq, as proposed by Israel Zangwill, or other sections of the Empire outside Palestine. The Zionists, however, insisted that Jewish settlements not be made outside Eretz Israel, and it was, in fact, only in Palestine that significant Jewish settlements were inaugurated in the years before World War I.

The Zionist organization did everything it could to oppose Nahum and his *Alliance* supporters, encouraging and helping the Orthodox groups who used their positions to frustrate the financial operations and activities of the Grand Rabbinate. In cooperation with the *Hilfsverein*, the Zionists established lodges of the *Bnai Brith* in 1911 in an effort to organize and direct popular support against the Grand Rabbi, in particular using the long-standing divisions between Sephardim and Ashkenazim to enlist the support of the latter because of their exclusion from the inner councils of the community.

Nahum's conflicts with the Zionists were strongly supported by the *AIU*'s local president, Isaac Fernandez, who stated that 'The movement led by Dr. Herzl is . . . harmful for the interests of the Jews of Turkey, for the work of the *AIU,* and for that of Palestinian colonization.'[63] With the support and help also of the Sultan and the Ottoman government, Nahum fought back by securing government approval for a new regulation for elections to the community councils which would dilute the strength of the quarters where Zionist support was the strongest.

The battle was reflected in the Ottoman Jewish press, with Jacobson subsidizing the French-language Istanbul newspaper *L'Aurore*, the Turkish-language *Ittihad*, and the *Journal de Salonique*, while the Grand Rabbinate with the *AIU* subsidized the Judeo-Spanish journal *El Tiempo* (edited by David Fresco), which also at times accepted support by the Zionists. Jacobson also purchased the French-language *Courrier d'Orient*, which he renamed *Jeune Turc* before turning it over to the editorship of Vladimir Jabotinsky. In Egypt, Iraq and Syria, Zionist agents published their own newspapers and agitated on a smaller scale among Jews who were much more willing to listen to their message because of the continued attacks mounted against them by Arab Christians.

In Balat, still the traditional center of Istanbul Jewry, the Zionist Maccabee organization, ostensibly established to encourage sports among

Jewish youths, established its locale in the *Ha Hemla* building on *Tahta Minare Sokak* (now called *Vodina*), holding rallies and meetings to encourage Jewish youth to go and settle in Palestine. At times it paraded its members in uniform though the streets of Balat flying the Zionist flag and singing the Zionist hymn, *Hatikvah*, much to the unhappiness of the Grand Rabbi, who continued to emphasize Jewish loyalty to the Empire. The old ethnic divisions between Ashkenazi and Sephardi now again came to the surface, with the former providing the most active supporters of the Zionists while the latter gathered in support around the person of the Grand Rabbi in repeatedly declaring their loyalty to the Sultan and to the Empire which had fostered and protected them for so many centuries. For a short time, Nahum and the Zionists cooperated, but after 1910, particularly after Zionism began to be criticized by the Unionists as well as others in the Muslim community because of what seemed to them to be a Jewish threat to take over Palestine, Nahum once again turned against them. Now, therefore, it was the Zionists who demanded democratization of the institutions of the Grand Rabbinate against what they called the autocracy of an oligarchy led by Haim Nahum.

Among the young Zionists who now came to the Ottoman Empire from Eretz Israel as agents of *Po'alei Zion*, first to Salonica and then after it was occupied by the Greeks in 1912 to Izmir and Istanbul, nominally to study law but in fact to spread their Zionist message, were later leaders of the *Yishuv* and the infant Jewish state of Israel formed after World War II, David Ben Gurion, Yitzhak Ben Zvi, and Moshe Sharett. At times they worked with some of the Unionist leaders, securing their support for Zionist aims. Riza Tevfik thus was quoted as saying that a Zionist could be an Ottoman as well as a Jewish patriot. The old Young Turk leader in Paris, now President of Parliament Ahmed Riza, joined Said Pasha's Foreign Minister Ahmed Tevfik in issuing public declarations in favor of Zionism. The Zionists, emboldened, began to extend their demands, asking for an end to Ottoman limitations on Jewish emigration to Palestine and advocating the establishment there of some sort of center for persecuted European and especially Russian and Polish Jews, though still under Ottoman sovereignty and without any open declaration of ambitions for independence or even autonomy.

All these Zionist activities and statements of purpose, both in Istanbul and Palestine, led to anti-Semitic statements by a few Muslim Ottoman politicians, led by Gümülcine Ismail Bey, leader of the People's ᵀarty (*Ahali Fırkası*), who voiced fears that a Jewish state would be established, not only in Eretz Israel, but also in Mesopotamia, seat of the ancient Jewish refuge in Babylon. There were some fears expressed that Zionism really was a plot to establish German hegemony in the Ottoman Middle East. Many Young Turks and Unionists themselves began to question how much support should be given to a Zionist movement which now clearly threatened to separate from the Empire one of the holiest places in Islam. At first, soon after the restoration of the Constitution in 1909, the Union and Progress party had publicly declared its support for Jewish immigration to all parts of the empire, but while its leaders favored Jewish entry into the empire in the face of continued Russian pogroms, they began to express the feeling that concentrations of Jews in particular places should be prevented so as not to create a new nationality problem in addition to those which had been plaguing it for the previous half century. After the Counter Revolution of 13 April 1909, therefore, the Unionists changed their previous position and opposed any changes in the limitations which Abdül Hamid had imposed on Jewish emigration to Palestine, though like him they continued to hope that Jews would settle in other parts of the Ottoman Empire.

Despite these changed attitudes among the ruling elite in Istanbul, for quite some time the Ottoman governor of Jerusalem continued to allow land sales to Jews to continue. To preclude anti-Semitic feelings from spreading among Turks in the face of continued Jewish settlement in Palestine, leading Ottoman Jews founded the Jewish Brotherhood Society (*Müsevi Uhuvvet Cemiyeti*) in 1909 to promote friendship and good feeling with Muslims. Jews also were involved in early Ottoman Social Democratic movements and labor organizations that developed in Istanbul and particularly in Salonica after 1908, with Avrom Benaroya bringing together various ethnic labor groups into the Salonica Socialist Club in October 1908 and publishing the *Amele Gazetesi* (Workers' Gazette) followed by the Judeo-Spanish *La Solidaridad Ovradera* (Workers Solidarity) before the movement broke up early in 1909 because of national divisions among its members. In 1911, Benaroya was sent into exile to Serbia and the Salonica Socialist movement was suppressed because of accusations of its involvement in an attempt to assassinate Sultan Mehmed V Reşad during his visit to Salonica the year before.

Problems regarding Zionism did not, however, effect the prosperity of Ottoman Jewry or its increasingly important involvement in Ottoman life during the Constitutional period before World War I. There were more Jewish bureaucrats in government than there ever had been under Abdül Hamid II, and they tended to do better than even Muslim officials both in compensation and promotions. Jews now served willingly in the Ottoman army, with special arrangements being made to provide for *kosher* food and observance of Sabbath and other religious rituals by Jewish soldiers. Relations between Jews and Muslim Turks improved even more as a result of the latter's increasing unhappiness with the violent activities of the Christian nationalist societies in Macedonia and Eastern Anatolia and, in particular, with the evident support of many of the Sultan's Christian subjects for the efforts of the Balkan states to drive the Ottomans out of Europe altogether during the first Balkan War (1912–13).[64] Jewish bankers, merchants and industrialists prospered due to all the reforms introduced during the Young Turk era, the improvement of Ottoman administration and the tax system, the freeing of trade and commerce from the restrictions imposed by Abdül Hamid, the continued development of Ottoman public education, of which young Jews now took full advantage in addition to the schools of the *AIU* and the more recent German *Hilfsverein der Deutschen Juden* and the Viennese *Allianz*, and the arrival in Istanbul of numerous wealthy Jewish bankers and businessmen from Europe, who more than ever 'took care of their own'. So for some time there was little support for Zionism among most Ottoman Jews and relations with their Muslim brothers continued to be excellent.

As more and more Jewish refugees flooded into the Empire from persecution in Greece, Serbia, Bulgaria, Rumania and Russia, however, Ottoman Jewry, (including Nahum himself) was forced to modify its opposition to Jewish settlement in Palestine in the face of the tremendous need to find homes and jobs for them. Most of the immigrants initially came to Istanbul, where they literally overwhelmed the community's ability to help, counteracting whatever improvement of economic conditions had provided the mass of Istanbul Jews, so they had to be sent on to the east as soon as possible, and Palestine seemed the best place at the moment since Jews there could be settled with the financial assistance of wealthy European Jews, without particularly burdening the Ottoman community. While still not sympathetic to the Zionist movement as such, the leaders of Ottoman Jewry, including Haim Nahum Efendi, now did everything they could to help and protect these immigrants, and in the process were compelled to support Jewish settlements in the Holy Land, though still advocating their maintenance under Ottoman rule so as not to stimulate a Muslim reaction which might well undermine the position of Jews elsewhere in the Empire. Nahum thus attempted to take the issue of Jewish immigration to Palestine away from the separatist Zionists and place it in his own hands, where it would serve to strengthen his own position and that of those who supported continued Jewish loyalty to the Ottoman Empire. In 1910 he toured Edirne, Salonica, Alexandria, Cairo, Jerusalem, Damascus, Beirut and Izmir to gain popular support for this program. Two influential Jewish parliamentary deputies, Nissim Rousseau and Nissim Mazliyah, and perhaps also Emmanuel Carasso (Karasu), now cooperated with Jabotinsky and the other Zionist leaders in Istanbul in support of the idea of settling the refugees in Palestine as well as Anatolia. Many were settled in Izmir and in southeastern Anatolia, very much as Sultan Abdül Hamid II had suggested, but most wanted to and did go on to Palestine, where they settled in agricultural colonies organized by the Zionists and others. Finally in September 1913 the Young Turks were convinced: the restrictions on immigration were limited, and new waves of Jewish colonists were allowed to go on to

Palestine without hindrance on the part of the Ottoman government.[65] This development contributed significantly to the development of agriculture on uncultivated lands in Palestine, and thus increased Ottoman food supplies as well as tax revenues. On the other hand Arab Christians as well as Muslims who lived there were bitterly hostile to the new immigrants, and in reaction developed new 'ritual murder' attacks on Jews, not only in Palestine but also in the other Arab provinces, with a vehemence and hatred that exceeded any of the attacks elsewhere in the Empire or in Europe. As time went on, moreover, Nahum himself modified his position regarding the Zionists, secretly interceding with the Ottoman government on their behalf whenever asked, but openly still retaining a hostile, or at least neutral, position, due not only to Ottoman sensibilities but also to the continued strong opposition to Zionism on the part of many of his supporters in the Istanbul community, led by the influential editor of *El Tiempo*, David Fresco.

While the battle between Haim Nahum and the Zionists went on, and then relented, Ottoman Jewry prospered as never before since the sixteenth century. And with the example of the massacres and persecutions of Jews then going on in the newly independent states of Southeastern Europe, the Jewish subjects of the Sultan were more loyal than ever. Young Jews now accepted conscription into the Ottoman army without paying the *bedel-i askeriye*, in contrast to the Sultan's Armenian and Greek subjects, whose continued avoidance of military service stirred considerable antagonism in the government as well as on the part of the general public, greatly increasing the tensions which were already rising as a result of increasingly violent independence movements in the Balkans and Eastern Anatolia. During the Balkan Wars the Jewish community's participation in the defense of Edirne and Salonica and refusal to welcome the Bulgarian and Greek armies as they entered these cities, resulting in their pillaging of Jewish houses, shops and synagogues and attacks on individual Jews, adding to the rush of Jewish refugees, enhanced Jewish determination to support the Ottomans in the World War that followed.

Just as economic prosperity and confidence in the government, combined with the mass influx of refugees, caused the Muslim population of the Ottoman Empire to increase substantially during the nineteenth century, despite severe losses from disease and war,[66] so also did the same factors cause its Jewish population to increase, from fewer than 100,000 in about 1800 to 184,139, or about 1.05 percent of the total in 1885, 215,425, or 1.13 percent, in 1895 and 256,003, or 1.122 percent in 1906 before the loss of territories in Macedonia and Thrace in consequence of the Balkan Wars in 1912–13 left 187,073 Jews, or exactly one percent of the total population at the start of World War I,[67] approximately the same percentage as it had been in the Golden Age of Ottoman Jewry.

OTTOMAN JEWRY DURING WORLD WAR I AND THE TURKISH WAR FOR INDEPENDENCE

World War I, 1914–18

Immediately preceding and during World War I, Ottoman Jews along with other subjects of the Sultan were staggered by a series of bold measures introduced by the Union and Progress government which largely completed the modernization and secularization policies of the Ottoman reformers while greatly lessening the power and authority of the *millet* leaders, thus in many ways anticipating the reforms introduced by the Turkish Republic after 1923. The Ottoman tax system was drastically modernized, with the traditional tax farms and tithes replaced by direct collection based on income. Municipal and provincial governments were rationalized and made far more efficient than they had been when first created during the *Tanzimat*, and urban and rural transportation systems were modernized, greatly enhancing internal markets as well as opportunities in both business and industry. The economic position of Jews improved in particular because of the Ottomans' unilateral abolition in 1914 of the Capitulations, which long had been the principal basis for the dominance of native Christian merchants and traders in the Ottoman market place with the help of the European diplomats and consuls.

Of even more immediate impact on the *millets* themselves were a series of major secular reforms. In 1913, judges in the *millet* religious courts were required for the first time to meet governmental standards of education and training in addition to whatever was required by their own communities. Their decisions also were for the first time subjected to review by the secular Ottoman supreme court (*mahkeme-i temyiz*) and other appeals courts. During the next two years, moreover, the religious courts were put under the direct authority and control of the Ministry of Justice, with the judges becoming salaried civil servants under direct government supervision, thus effectively removing them along with the courts from the control of the *millet* leaders.[68] Registration of property and contracts was taken away from the religious authorities and given to the Interior Ministry. Religious foundations were put under the control of the Ministry of Finance, which now managed their properties and kept most of their revenues for general purposes, greatly limiting the financial basis of *millet* independence. *Millet* schools were put under the direct control of the Ministry of Education, which began to control and standardize their faculties and curricula.

Emancipation also began for women, who now were admitted to high schools, trade schools and the University of Istanbul. Just as in Europe, moreover, the absence of a substantial portion of the male work force in army service during the Tripolitanian War (1911), the Balkan Wars

(1912–13), and World War I compelled women to take their places in factories, businesses, and stores, leading them to discard the veil and appear in European-style clothing long before such measures were decreed formally by the Turkish Republic. In 1916, women were for the first time allowed to secure divorces if their husbands were proved to be adulterers, took, or wanted to take, additional wives without the consent of the first wife, or violated the marriage contract in any other way, thus undermining long-held *millet* traditions based on religious law. And as the war came to a climax, on 7 November 1917, the Code of Family Law was promulgated which, though it included the basic regulations of the Muslim, Jewish and Christian religious laws regarding marriage, divorce and other family relationships, transformed these into secular contracts subject to the same state supervision as other contracts and thus, once again, greatly limiting the role of the *millet* officials in the process.

Members of the Ottoman Jewish community, led by Haim Nahum, who continued to distance himself from the Zionists though the *Alliance* had ceased all activities in the Empire, strongly supported the Ottoman war effort, and prospered greatly in industry, banking and trade as a result. This was in contrast to the Christian minorities, whose declared neutrality in the conflict and what appeared to most Ottomans to be apparent sympathy for the enemy in order to achieve national aims led to the deportation of many as the war progressed, leaving the Jews without serious competition for the first time in several centuries. Balat as a result now entered a new era of prosperity, which lasted with little break until the 1930s. Most of its streets were widened and given new, bright lighting and sewage facilities, while wealthy Jews built new brick houses near the Ahrida and Yanbol synagogues on Kürkçu Çeşme sokak, near the Chana synagogue, and up the hill toward Kasturiye and Iştipol. Whether rich or poor, the newer Jewish houses were built in similar styles and floor plans, the main difference being in the building materials and decorations, with the more expensive houses adding marble and fine woods to the brick which all used. Ground floor entrance halls and living and dining rooms were usually furnished in the traditional Ottoman style, with low sofas, buffets, and carpets as well as a great table where the members of the family dined. The kitchen, usually located in the rear but sometimes in the basement, had a water depot, coal oven, jar of drinking water, and a great copper cauldron for boiling. In the basement they kept the heating wood and coal, and usually the rooms where the servants lived. On the second floor was the great salon furnished and decorated in the European manner, but used only on special occasions. Next to it in the front of the house was the parents' bedroom, also richly furnished in the European style, while behind were the rooms of the children and a terrace looking out on the street. The more expensive houses usually had an additional upper floor which was used for storerooms as well as to house the servants. Middle-class Jews built their houses in the same way, but usually divided the floors into separate apartments, renting out the lower ones to secure additional income. Poorer Jews now lived only in the Sigri, Lonca and Karabaş districts immediately along the Golden Horn where their religious requirements were met by the ancient *El Kal de Sigiri* (or *Kal de Selaniko*) and *Eliaou* synagogues.

Jews had served actively in the Ottoman army during the Balkan Wars,[69] and they continued to serve with distinction during World War I, responding enthusiastically to the general mobilization decrees which called into service all male subjects between the ages of eighteen and forty-five who could not provide proof of foreign citizenship. Ottoman Jews also worked to demonstrate their loyalty to the government by getting young non-Ottoman Jewish volunteers to enlist in the army to demonstrate the community's determination to help the war effort. Jewish bankers in and out of the Empire provided a great deal of the financing needed for wartime expenditures and to pay the government's civil servants. Jewish agriculturalists throughout the Empire, and particularly those in Palestine, joined Muslim farmers in contributing animals, tools and carriages to local military units,[70] though this, like the conscription, severely curtailed agricultural production and led to problems of famine and disease in the later years of the war. Jewish charitable organizations organized campaigns to raise money to help the families of Ottoman soldiers, and the *Or Ahayim* hospital began treating people of all religions because of crowded conditions in the regular state hospitals. In the same way, the Bnai Brith lodge in Istanbul worked with Nahum in helping people of all religions in the face of wartime shortages food and clothing, with the Jews sharing what they received from American organizations with their Muslim and Christian fellow subjects, earning gratitude from all elements of the population as a result.

> The war itself, despite all the miseries, despite all the horrors that accompanied it, did not affect the harmony which continued among the Muslim and Jewish elements . . . . For the Turks, the Jew was the faithful subject par excellence, incapable of treason. The reason for the constant sympathy that the Turks nourished for us must be sought in the certainty that they had of themselves being the object of our sincere respect and our profound loyalty, of which we had given multiple proofs on innumerable occasions . . . . The Armenians and the Greeks, who held posts of confidence in almost all the important centers of the country at the start of the war, contributed no small part by their defection to precipitating the debacle.[71]

Jewish nationals of enemy countries were severely effected by the Ottomans' unilaterial cancellation of the Capitulations soon after the war began in Europe, on 4 October 1914. Following the Ottoman entry into the war on the side of Germany and Austria on 11 November 1914, the same wartime restrictions which were prevalent in other belligerent countries were introduced, including decrees forbidding the flying of foreign flags and the posting of letters written in foreign languages, including Hebrew and Yiddish, so as to ease the task of the censors. Starting in mid-December 1914, subjects of enemy countries, including Jews who had retained their Russian nationality, were required to close their stores and shops and to leave the empire, [72] with some two thousand colonists from Palestine going overland from Jaffa and Tel Aviv to northern Palestine and Damascus, and 11,277 who went by ship to Alexandria in sixteen groups between Chanukah of December 1914 and Passover of April 1915. Zionist pressure from Germany and America along with the protests of Haim Nahum, however, ultimately led the Ottoman government to allow such Jews, most of whom were Russian nationals living in Palestine, to remain so long as they adopted Ottoman citizenship and to do its best to protect the Jewish communities from the full effects of wartime shortages. German Foreign Minister Zimmermann, moreover, under the influence of the powerful Zionist lobby in Berlin, developed a plan to establish a Jewish state in Palestine under German influence, both to establish a German presence in the Levant and to win over world Zionists to support the Central Powers, but this plan was opposed by Haim Nahum and most Ottoman Jews in fear that it would significantly hurt their position as loyal Ottoman subjects.[73]

The Ottoman government made special efforts to allow foreign educational and charity institutions maintained by Jewish citizens of enemy countries to continue so long as they were managed by Ottoman Jews. After the *AIU* closed its schools despite this concession, the Ottomans arranged to substitute schools operated by German Jews, including an elementary school opened by the Ashkenazi leader David Marcus which in 1915 was transformed by the *Hilfsverein der Deutschen Juden* as well as local Jewish community organizations into the Beyoğlu Jewish Lycée (*Beyoğlu Özel Musevi Lisesi*) which has remained active to the present day as the only Jewish secondary school in Istanbul. Special state subsidies also were provided to the Grand Rabbi and the staff of the Grand Rabbinate to enable community operations to continue in the face of declining revenues from members, while they and the other religious chiefs continued to serve as members of municipal, provincial and other councils throughout the war.[74] Though the *Alliance* was gone, Haim Nahum in fact managed to solidify his support in the community by uniting all groups for the common war effort, and also by organizing the distribution of supplies of food and other goods sent into the empire by the *American Jewish Joint Distribution Committee*.

Palestinian Jews suffered considerably with the rest of the population during the early years of the war from famine, plague and other diseases when the area served as a base for Cemal Pasha's Fourth Corps offensive against the Suez Canal and Egypt, joining local Muslims and Christians in supplying forced labor on military roads and railroads built between Jerusalem and Gaza, Tiberias and Safed and Jaffa and Nablus, as well as supplying food, animals and equipment to the army. Since no less than fifty percent of the cultivated land was abandoned, food production in any case fell precipitously. This left little for the civilian population, which further suffered from a British naval blockade of the coast throughout the war, an invasion of locusts during 1915 and 1916, which destroyed most of the fields, vineyards and plantations maintained by the Jews throughout Palestine,[75] and the attack of the British from Egypt combined with devastating raids on the civilian population by Arab guerillas supplied by Şerif Hüseyn's Arab revolt. Starting in 1915, moreover, the entire population of Palestine suffered from a wave of epidemics, including typhus, varioloid and cholera, whose effect was compounded by the chaos among the Ottoman soldiers returning in disorder following the collapse of Cemal Pasha's campaign against the Suez canal. Thousands of people of all religions died as a result in Palestine, especially in Jerusalem and Safed. The Jewish settlements were better off than most, however, because of their ability to raise their own food at least as well as because of the receipt of food and money sent by American Jews as the result of the efforts of the American Ambassador to the Porte at the start of the war, Henry Morgenthau, and his Consul General in Jerusalem, Dr O. A. Glazebrook, and to a lesser extent of various German Jewish organizations, particularly the *Ezrah* or *Hilfsverein* of Frankfurt, with relief ships arriving periodically throughout the war.

The Jews suffered additionally, however, because of the efforts of Arab Christian leaders in Palestine, particularly the Greeks and Maronites, who had long resented the close Jewish-Muslim ties in the Ottoman Empire and mounted a series of violent ritual murder attacks in response. They now sought to use the Ottomans' need for support in the war as a means to satisfy their long-standing ambition to get the Jews out of the Holy Land. Almost as soon as the war began, the Greek Bishop of Jerusalem, Damiyanos, informed Minister of Navy Cemal Pasha, who had been appointed Commander of the Fourth Army and Governor of Syria, as well as his commanders and governors in Jaffa, that the Zionist colonists were planning to drive the Turks out of Palestine and that the only solution was to deport all foreign Jews (mostly colonists who had come from Russia as tourists), promising strong Christian support for the war effort in return. In 1917 he went so far as to propose to the Ecumenical Patriarch in Istanbul that the latter issue a public denial of allegations spread world-wide by the British that the Ottomans were mistreating the Sultan's Christian subjects if only this proposal was carried out. He went on to accuse Palestinian Jews of planning to help the Allied war effort in order to achieve the long-hoped-for Jewish homeland.[76]

These accusations seemed to be confirmed by Ottoman intelligence reports regarding the activities of some European Zionists and Palestinian Jews in support of the British war effort.[77] In the face of strong competition between the Central Powers and western Allies to gain the support of world Zionism, official British Zionist policy initially was to remain neutral because of fears regarding the fate of Ottoman Jewry should they openly support the Allied cause. In the same way, strong pressure by German Zionists to get their government to turn what had been strong sympathy for Zionist aims before the war into an open declaration of support were countered by the Kaiser's fears as to the effect such a policy would have, not only on his alliance with the Sultan, but also on the sensibilities of the Arabs.

The Zionist Executive in Britain, however, disagreed with its leaders' caution. Under the leadership of Chaim Weizmann and Vladimir (Ze'ev) Jabotinsky, it advocated a policy of supporting a British invasion to liberate Palestine by force, with the help of a 'Jewish Legion', as the first step toward breaking up the Ottoman Empire and getting it out of its alliance with Germany and Austria. Lord Kitchiner opposed the idea because of the fear that these Jewish radicals would then assume dominent control of the Zionist movement, which he preferred to keep under strong British influence. Following his sudden death, however, and with the assumption of the Prime Ministership by David Lloyd George, a much more activist British policy enabled Weizmann and Jabotinsky to secure issuance of the Balfour Declaration from the Lloyd George government and with it to gain support for their plans among young Jewish colonists in Palestine.

Even before this change of British policy, moreover, Jabotinsky had gone ahead, leading a group of Young Turkish Zionists from Palestine's agricultural colonies to Alexandria, Egypt. There, with the assistance of Yossef Trumpeldor, a Russian Jew who had gained considerable military experience through service in the Russian army, they established on 3 March 1915 the 'Zion Mule Transportation Corps', composed largely of Jewish exiles from Russia, which fought against the Ottomans during the early stages of the British invasion of Gallipoli.

Even while Zionists in Britain and Egypt were working to provide military support for the Allied war effort against the Ottomans, a few Jewish settlers in Palestine were working toward the same objective through the secret *NILI* society,[78] which starting in 1916 spied on the Ottoman army throughout Syria and Palestine, sending regular reports on its movements and dispositions. Late in 1917 *NILI* also joined with Armenian agents in Jerusalem to spread a rumor that Cemal Pasha was trying to negotiate with the British to overthrow the Istanbul government and make a separate peace which would leave him at the head of the Ottoman government, to make certain a British conquest to achieve complete fulfillment of the promises made by Balfour by dividing the Ottoman leaders.[79]

NILI was led by Aaron Aaronsohn, a well-known scientific agricultural agent who from his experimental stations at Zikhron Ya'akov and Atlit, south of Haifa, had been working among the Jewish settlements in Palestine for some years before the war. Aaronson became a leading advisor to the Ottoman governor in Damascus, Cemal Pasha, using his position to steal Istanbul's defense plans for the Arab provinces and send them off to the British in Cairo. He also used Cemal's influence to secure further information during a trip to Germany which he subsequently brought to the British authorities in London, remaining there until the end of the war while the organization's spying activities in Palestine were carried on by his sister Sara Aaronson, Na'aman Belkind from the Rishon Le-Tzion settlement, and Yossef Lishansky, former member of *Hashomer*, who established his own spy group in southern Palestine under the name *Hamagan* (Protector).[80] In 1916 *NILI* warned the British leaders in Cairo that the Ottomans were concentrating large forces for a second attack on the Suez Canal. Other information followed regarding the location of Ottoman defenses all over Palestine, and particularly around Beersheba, which was of considerable use once the joint British-Arab attack began in February 1917 under the command of Sir Edmond Allenby. *NILI* agents in Britain and the United States also worked to get support for American entry into the War on the side of Britain, spreading the anti-Turkish propaganda developed by Arnold Toynbee's propaganda unit in London while adding new stories of their own regarding the supposed Ottoman persecution of the *Yishuv* in Palestine.

In the face of Damiyanos's accusations that most Palestinian Jews supported the British and reports by Ottoman intelligence regarding *NILI*'s activities, and particularly about its spreading of Armenian rumors regarding him intended to split the Young Turk Triumverate, it is not surprising that Cemal Pasha became convinced that Zionism was anti-Turkish and that its representatives in Palestine had to be suppressed if the Ottoman war effort was to succeed. He quickly confiscated the arms of many Jewish colonists as well as those living in Tel Aviv during the late months of 1916. As Allenby's army marched through the Sinai peninsula on its way to Palestine in early March, 1917, the entire population of Gaza was suddenly evacuated by the Ottomans order to remove them from the impending battle.

As soon as Ottoman intelligence gave Cemal Pasha full details about what *NILI* was doing, he immediately moved to arrest Sara Aaronsohn along with other members who were known to Ottoman intelligence, but most of them fled successfully across the Sinai desert to Cairo. There they helped General Allenby plan his offensive into Palestine, which began with the help of hundreds of Jewish legion members, organized into the '38th Battalion of Royal Fusiliers' in England, later joined by the 39th (American) and 40th (Palestinian) battalions, all subsequently consolidated into the 'First Judean Regiment'.

Back in Palestine the crackdown continued. Displays of Zionist banners and flags were forbidden. A number of Zionist leaders were also arrested and deported, including David Ben Gurion and Yitzhak Ben Zvi, who earlier had been allowed to return to Palestine from Istanbul and who as a result had urged its Jewish community to take up Ottoman citizenship and to support the Ottoman war effort, but who were tarred with the actions of *NILI* and those local Zionists who did indeed support the British to gain fulfillment of the Balfour Declaration. On 28 March 1917, following the failure of the initial British effort to take Jaffa two days earlier, the entire populations of both Jaffa and Tel Aviv were ordered evacuated, Jewish, Muslim and Christian alike, causing considerable suffering, particularly since the evacuees were specifically prohibited from settling in the area of Jerusalem due to the expected British attack in that area. Orders were issued for the evacuation of Jerusalem, though this was not carried out, due at least partly to the intervention of the Ottomans' German allies as well as of Grand Rabbi Haim Nahum Efendi.[81] Half the Jewish evacuees went to the neighboring Jewish settlements at Petah-Tikva and Kfar-Saba, some found shelter in the older Jewish communities in the Galilee, particularly at Tiberias and Safed, some managed to reach Jerusalem and Damascus, while a few went on to Egypt, where they constituted a considerable burden on the local Jewish community.

These evacuations actually improved the lot of those who were affected, at least for the moment, since they were sent to colonies which had considerably more food and supplies than did the crowded cities. The general shortages which subsequently decimated the entire Empire ultimately hurt them as well, however, resulting in many deaths from starvation and disease during most of 1918 despite Ottoman efforts to allieviate their sufferings as well as those of other subjects remaining in Palestine at the time.[82] Subsequent charges, however, spread by the 'Secret War Propaganda Department' of the British Foreign Office in London under the direction of Lord Bryce and his young assistant, Arnold Toynbee, under the stimulus of the *NILI* agents who reached London, that Ottoman soldiers mistreated the deportees and looted Jewish synagogues, were denied in 1918 by Allenby's aide Clayton despite the efforts of War Council Secretary Mark Sykes in London to use them for propaganda purposes against the Central Powers.[83] After the failure of his intended expedition to capture the Suez Canal and the news that the Şerif Hüseyin was leading an Arab revolt against the Sultan,

Cemal Pasha became much more sympathetic to the Jews in Palestine, working with local community leaders, including some with close Zionist connections, to lessen the suffering of the remaining Jews.

The Swedish consul-general in Istanbul reported to the American government shortly before the British occupation of Jerusalem that:

> . . . the first reports of the evacuation of Jaffa by the civil population and ill-treatment of Jews in Palestine apparently reached the outside world via Egypt and were much exaggerated. All of the Jewish population of Jaffa was obliged to leave. Subjects of the Allied countries of Turkey were allowed to go to Jerusalem, but the bulk of the population had to go to the colonies and to the region of Tiberias. In the existing circumstances a general mass of evacuation of this sort within a short time was bound to cause much hardship and a great deal of sufferance . . . however reliable reports received in Constantinople indicate that apart from the difficulties and hardships inherent in the situation, there was no rioting nor systematic ill-treatment of the Jewish population, and above all that there was no such thing as massacres. As for Tel Aviv, a suburb of Jaffa, it was occupied by German military headquarters and was, therefore, relatively protected from devastation. The Jewish colonies in the vicinity of Jaffa, such as Richon-le-Sion and Petach-Tikvah, were not evacuated, and the Rabbi of Jaffa is now residing at Petach-Tikvah . . . . The greatest suffering among the Jewish population in Palestine is due to the very high cost of living there and a real scarcity of food for the population, combined with the cessation of practically all business of exportation, and also the cessation of the greater part of relief funds and charitable contributions which used to flow to Palestine from Jews all over the world . . . There never was a general measure of evacuation applied to the civil population of Jerusalem. Some 16 to 20 families of Ottoman Jews were sent away to various places in Asia Minor as an administrative measure, either because some of the heads of these families were accused of having dealt in gold illegally or for police reasons. A number of Zionistic leaders, both Ottoman and foreign, were also obliged to leave Jerusalem and a number of them are now residing in Constantinople.[84]

Jews throughout the empire suffered terribly, however, along with other elements of the population, from the badly mismanaged martial law administration, which kept the bulk of food, fuel and clothing for the army. These conditions were exacerbated by destructive communal fighting among the different ethnic groups, the arrival of thousands of Muslim and Jewish refugees from southeastern Europe as well as from the eastern Anatolian territories occupied by Russia, large and destructive urban fires in Istanbul, Izmir, Salonica and elsewhere, Russian naval bombardment of Ottoman towns and villages along the Black Sea coast, banditry, and foreign invasions, particularly those of Russia in eastern Anatolia and Britain in Iraq, all of which led to massacres and counter massacres, and famines and epidemics, particularly during the latter days of the war when dissolution of the Ottoman army and the disorganized flight of thousands of armed soldiers added to the chaos and anarchy. Adding even more to the misery was an Ottoman policy of deporting entire populations, Muslims, Christians and Jews alike, from the war zones of Eastern Anatolia, Thrace, Gallipoli, and later Palestine, movements which, given the critical shortages of food, disorganized administration, an almost complete lack of internal security in the face of large-scale bandit attacks, and widespread breakdowns of the railroad system, resulted in great suffering and heavy casualties. The result was an Ottoman catastrophe, the deaths of some two million people, twenty-five percent of the entire population, including as many as fifty percent in the eastern war zones, and the exodus of an equal number under brutal conditions.[85] Since most Jews lived outside the war zones and were helped by food shipments from American Jews, few died in comparison with other elements of the population.

The Turkish War for Independence, 1918–23

Following the war the situation became even worse for the Jews. The victorious western Allies restored the Capitulations almost immediately after occupying Istanbul, thus favoring the Christian minorities as well as their own economic interests at the expense of the Ottoman Jewish and Muslim subjects who had prospered during the war. The Allies proceeded to abolish the secular laws introduced by the Young Turks after 1912, re-establishing the authority of the *millet* leaders and laws in many areas, including education and justice, and in general strengthening the conservative elements in Ottoman politics as well as in the various communities as part of their effort to root out the Young Turks who had brought the empire into the war on the side of Germany.

Ottoman Jews were particularly discriminated against by the Allied authorities, who turned Jewish as well as Muslim properties over to Christians who claimed them, seriously disrupting trade and commerce as well as the import of food for the capital.[86] They went on to arrest some prominent Jewish leaders because of their support for the Young Turk movement[87] and the Ottoman war effort as well as because of the involvement of a few Russian Jewish refugees in Communist and Socialist activities in the Ottoman capital as well as at Baku. Several times the Allied High Commissioners rejected the Istanbul government's request to enlist Jewish and Muslim soldiers in its army so as to quell disturbances in Anatolia, fearing that they might cooperate against the occupation. While the Allied occupation forces assisted the emigration to Istanbul of thousands of Russian refugees from Bolshevism, they did little to stop the large-scale pogroms mounted against the Jews of southern Russia by the White forces led by General Denikin, who constituted their only hope to defeat the Bolsheviks, at times turning back those few Jews who managed to escape across the Black Sea to Ottoman territory, thus exposing them to almost certain death at the hands of the Whites, in whose territory they were deposited.[88]

While the Greek and Armenian community leaders in Istanbul and Paris pressured the Allies to drive the Turks out of Istanbul and much of Anatolia, the Empire's Jewish leaders, remembering very well the persecution their people had suffered as Ottoman territories had come under the rule of independent Christian states, not only refused to join their delegations but actively pressured the Allies to allow the Turks to remain in areas where they consisted a majority of the population, thus incurring further the wrath of the Christian leaders.

In Thrace and Southwestern Anatolia also the invading Greek army, which was attempting to provide the Paris Peace Conference with a *fait accompli* in the territories it wished to retain, armed the Christian minorities and encouraged them to attack Muslims, with the Jews suffering as well because of their support for the Turks during the war,[89] and with the once-flourishing Jewish community of Salonica in particular being permanently displaced by Greek refugees from Anatolia settled there after the Greek army evacuated Anatolia.

The Greek army that occupied much of southeastern Anatolia starting in May 1919 slaughtered thousands of Jews and Muslims in the course of its attack, not only during its initial landings at Izmir, but also in the interior during the subsequent two years, and particularly during its final retreat to Izmir, when it ravaged and burned Bursa and other towns and villages along the way. Albert Nabon, Principal of the *AIU* Boy's School in Izmir, reported to the *Alliance* on 6 July 1919: 'The city was put on fire and sacked, the people dispoiled of all they possessed. There is no food, putting the entire population in general, and our co-religionists in particular, in danger of suffering greatly from these privations', going on to describe how most Jews, not only from Izmir but also from Greek attacks at Aydın, Bergama and Manisa, took refuge in his school, where they were suffering from overcrowding, lack of food, and medicine.[90]

The Jews of Tire, led by Rabbi Ismail ha-Cohen, established close ties with the local Turkish resistance as well as with the Turkish national forces operating against the Greeks in the vicinity despite considerable pressure from the local Greek commanders.[91] In Ödemiş, Rabbi Isaac Franco refused the demands of the Greek military authorities for him to greet their army as it occupied the city.[92] In Aydın, Jews hid Turks in their homes as the Greeks ransacked the city following its occupation, and refused to join local Greeks and Armenians in welcoming the occupying army and flying Greek flags from their buildings.[93] As a result, the long-standing Greek religious prejudice against Jews as well as Muslims was manifested in numerous incidents that took place until Mustafa Kemal and the Turkish national army finally recaptured Southeastern Anatolia in 1922.[94] Jewish notables, like the Muslims, were beaten and executed, many Jewish homes and shops were ravaged and burned, and hundreds of Jews were deported to almost certain death in the countryside. As the Greek army retreated in panic late in the war, moreover, it burned the Jewish and Muslim quarters of Izmit, Manisa and Bergama, destroying synagogues, *yeshivas* and hospitals as well as homes and businesses while killing hundreds and forcing the remainder of the non-Christian population to flee in panic, while local Greeks retreated with the army in fear of the retribution which they would most certainly have suffered had they remained.[95] Though many Jews returned to Izmir following the restoration of Turkish rule and its inclusion in the Turkish Republic, the Jewish population of Izmir following the war reached no more than half its former size.

All these atrocities caused thousands more refugees to flee to Istanbul, with Muslims and Jews arriving from Greece and Bulgaria as well as the occupied territories in Thrace, Macedonia, and Anatolia. In addition, thousands more of all religions came across the Black Sea in flight from the Bolshevik Revolution and the Russian Civil War that followed, particularly from the Crimea and the Ukraine, with a resulting congestion of refugees in Istanbul in particular due to the refusal of neighboring states to take more than a pittance.

As a result, by 1922 Istanbul was packed with thousands of bedraggled, helpless and starving refugees, including some 50,000 Muslims, 65,000 Russian refugees of all religions, 15,000 Jews, 5,000 Greeks and 45,000 Armenians. An additional 70,000 refugees were concentrated across the Bosporus at Moda, on the Sea of Marmara, and 20,000 more were on the island of Lemnos, occupied by the French. The bulk of the refugees were soldiers, mostly from Wrangel's White army after it was routed by the Bolsheviks, but there also was a very substantial number of civilians.[96] The soldiers were housed in camps at Çatalca, outside the city walls of Istanbul, and at Gallipoli and Mondros, on both sides of the Dardanelles. Some nine thousand civilians were housed for the most part in wretched camps around the outskirts of Istanbul, while 3,600, mainly Armenians and Jews, were allowed to reside with relatives or friends within the city. They received only limited help from private organizations, while the Ottoman government was far too poor and helpless and the Allies too diverted with more pressing problems to do much to relieve their suffering. The Balkan states refused absolutely to provide any assistance at all. Help for the refugees was limited by the fact that Istanbul had suffered a series of large and destructive fires during the last year of the war, with over ten thousand houses burned, leaving thousands more city residents without permanent housing and with epidemics breaking out regularly. The Jewish, Greek and Armenian refugees were cared for in tent camps, synagogues, churches, and rented houses provided by their own communities as well as foreign relief organizations. The Muslims were housed largely in the great mosques of the city as well as the Selimiye army barracks in Üsküdar, and the mass of Russian refugees were housed on the islands of the Sea of Marmara as well as in Istanbul in portable barracks, tent camps, converted schools and hospitals, in most of the cheap lodging houses throughout the city and in private homes, with 7,000 actually housed in the old Russian embassy. But with only limited supplies of food and clothing available as a result of wartime damage and the blockade, starvation and epidemics were chronic, and soon spread to the regular Istanbul populace, with thousands more lost as a result.

At the same time in Anatolia, while the Allied occupying forces were too small and stationed in too few places to restore regular administration or put an end to the killings and suffering caused by the banditry and communal massacres and counter massacres as well as the constant guerrilla fighting going on between the Turkish resistance forces and various bandit and nationalist bands in Anatolia, they continued to refuse to allow the Istanbul government to maintain a sufficient army and gendarme force to do the job in fear, quite justified, that such forces might well join the Turkish resistance. At the same time the Allies added to the misery by maintaining a tight naval blockade of Anatolian ports in order to force the Ottomans to accept the harsh peace terms then being prepared in Paris, causing the wartime famine and disease and resulting deaths to accelerate in the postwar period, with the efforts of the Ottoman Red Crescent and Department for Settling Emigrants and Tribes as well as foreign relief efforts helping only somewhat to allieviate shortages in a few places.

Haim Nahum was sent to Europe by Grand Vezir Izzet Pasha on 30 October 1918, shortly after the Armistice was signed, to serve as an intermediary with the Allies in general and the United States in particular in an attempt to secure an honorable peace for the Empire on the basis of Wilson's Fourteen Points, a mission that was frustrated by the Allies' refusal to allow him to travel after he had reached Belgium. Because of his absence in the service of the Empire, moreover, his supporters lacked his leadership at a crucial time. All his opponents immediately took advantage of the situation to weaken and eliminate his leadership once and for all. Propaganda was circulated in the community to undermine his prestige and support by harping on accusations that he had left the Empire on a governmental mission without securing advanced approval of the communal authorities, that by continuing to support the Turks, he was placing the entire community in danger of punishment at the hands of the victorious *Entente* powers then occupying the capital as well as various parts of the empire, and that by his long-standing opposition to Zionism, he was endangering the Jewish people throughout the world.

In response to this appeal, a series of community meetings directed by the *Bene Brith* president M. Niégo, the Ashkenazi leader David Marcus, Nissim Rousseau, and the Istanbul representatives of the *Hilfsverein* and the *Maccabees* (Zionists) on 9 November 1918 revised the Jewish *millet* Organic Statute. Under the new regulation, the community structure was democratized, with the Grand Rabbinate and community executive more dependent than ever on elected lay representatives. The Jewish *Millet* of Istanbul as well as all Ottoman Jews were to be governed by the *Jewish National Assembly*, composed of members elected by universal suffrage for terms of four years. Its primary duties were to maintain the political and religious rights of Jews as well as the autonomy of the community, to deliberate and decide on matters submitted to it by the Central Communal Council, to propose suitable legislation to the government, and to provide for the material and cultural development of the people through a series of departments established to care for the maintenance and construction of synagogues, community properties and foundations, education and charity. It also had to draw up and approve the annual community budget, providing for both taxation of community members as well as expenditures; elect out of its own membership, supervise and, when necessary to dismiss the eleven men comprising its Executive Committee, called the Central Communal Council, in charge of carrying out its decisions; and to elect the Grand Rabbi of Turkey for a term of ten years, with the possibility of re-election. The Grand Rabbi's duties were little changed from those of the 1864 Organic Statute, serving as religious and secular head of the community, presiding over the rabbis of the empire as well as the *Bet Din*, or Religious Court. As before, the city's Jewish communities were divided into districts, each of which had its own committees which administered its own synagogues, schools, and charitable organizations as well as raising money through donations and collections as well as help from the central Grand Rabbinate.

This move was initiated and supported by the Zionist Jews in Istanbul, led by Emmanuel Carasso and Nesim Rousseau, who supported the Allied occupation in the hope that it would assure fulfillment of the Balfour Declaration and also substitute Ashkenazi for Sephardic leadership in the Jewish community. Nahum's mission on behalf of the Ottoman government was disavowed and steps were taken to secure his removal altogether, not merely to gain favor with the occupiers, but also to take advantage of the situation to make a major political change in the Jewish community.

In the meantime, Nahum's return to Istanbul was delayed by the Allies in order to give his enemies time to gain control of the community. He finally did return on 4 March 1919, initiating a violent struggle for power. Nahum's first step was to assemble the old *meclisi cismani* in order to explain the reasons for his trip outside the country, securing unanimous approval. After the *Jewish National Assembly* responded with a campaign of vilification, Nahum dissolved it against the opposition of the British High Commissioner as well as many local Jews seeking to curry favor with the occupiers because of his support for the Ottomans during and after the war. After failing in an effort to improve his relations with the Allies as well as with community members who had opposed him, Nahum began to strongly support the Turkish national movement then rising up in Anatolia under the leadership of Mustafa Kemal in commencement of the Turkish War for Independence, testifying in favor of the Turks to the American King-Crane Commission when it visited Istanbul and attempting to travel to the Paris Peace conference on behalf of the Turks. After the Zionists made substantial gains in the Jewish communal elections held in Istanbul early in 1920, however, Nahum finally gave in, resigning on 21 April 1920 and leaving the country shortly afterwards.

While Haim Nahum lost his battle and left the scene, a number of Istanbul Jews formed their own political party, the *Osmanlı Musevileri Intihab Cemiyeti* (Ottoman Jews Election Society) in order to participate in the last Ottoman Parliamentary elections in November 1919, electing Mishon Ventura Efendi as Jewish deputy. Even in occupied Istanbul, however, most Jews, led by men such as the historian, journalist, and educator Avram Galante and Behor Haim Bejerano, Chief Rabbi of Edirne since 1908 and first Chief Rabbi of the Turkish Republic (1920–31), rejected the Istanbul government's acceptance of Allied dictates. Instead they provided the Jewish cemetery in Izmir for the first popular Turkish protest against the brutal Greek occupation of the city in May 1919, and went on to continue to strongly support the Turkish resistance, many fleeing to Anatolia to join the Turkish national armies, which managed to drive out all the occupiers of Turkish territory. During this time Haim Nahum remained in contact with Mustafa Kemal and the Turkish nationalists, going to Paris on their behalf in September 1922, and then, starting in November 1922, advising the Turkish delegation at the Lausanne Conference, which sealed the success of the Turkish War for Independence against the onerous terms which the Allies had attempted to impose in the Treaty of Sèvres and made possible the foundation of the Turkish Republic in the years that followed.

5

The Jews of the Turkish Republic, since 1923

Chief Rabbi Haim Bejerano. Chief Rabbi Haim Bejerano led Turkish Jewry into the Republican age as a strong supporter of the Turkish national movement, rejecting the efforts of the Christian minorities to gain Jewish support to drive the Turks out of Istanbul and much of Anatolia. Born in Eski Zagora, Bulgaria in 1846 while it was still under Ottoman rule and trained in traditional *talmud torah*s and *yeshiva*s, he was a learned man in the broadest sense of the word. Unlike the reactionary rabbis who at the time were attacking members of the community turning toward the modern world, and particularly those who taught French to Jewish youth, he sought to broaden himself by mastering sixteen foreign languages, not only Hebrew and Judeo-Spanish but also Turkish, Arabic, Persian, French, German, English, Bulgarian, Italian, Latin, Rumanian, Sanscrit, Greek and Armenian. For thirty years he had served the Jewish community of Rusçuk, on the Danube, teaching among others the great historian of Ottoman Jewry, Solomon Rosanes. He then went to Vienna where he earned his rabbinate, subsequently settling in Bucharest as director of its Sephardic school. All the while he continued to expand his horizons through extensive correspondence with learned men throughout Europe, including Jules Simon and Ernest Renan, and made himself known to Ottoman Jews by publishing articles on a wide range of subjects in Istanbul's most important Judeo-Spanish newspaper, *El Tiempo*. Soon after the Young Turk revolution, on 8 December 1909, he was elected Chief Rabbi of Edirne, serving there during the dark days of the Balkan Wars, when the invading Bulgarian armies ravaged the Jewish quarters of the city, and continuing through World War I. After taking over Istanbul's Chief Rabbinate in 1920, he strongly supported the Turkish national movement's rejection of the peace settlement proposed in Paris. He refused to cooperate with the Greek and Armenian patriarchs who wanted to get Jewish support for their national aims and publicly denied their claims that Turkish Jewry was unhappy with the new regime. In this he set the pattern followed by all the leaders of Turkish Jewry to the present day.

Jewish Community Surrenders Special Status Guaranteed by Treaty of Lausanne. The Treaty of Lausanne guaranteed the legal status of the non-Muslim communities in Turkey as well as the special privileges and foreign protection which they had secured during the late years of the Ottoman Empire, including special seats for each community in the Turkish Grand National Assembly. Article 39 of the Treaty specified that non-Muslim Turkish nationals would enjoy the same civil and political rights as Muslims, with all inhabitants being equal before the law as well as in the enjoyment of civil and political rights with no restrictions being imposed on the use of languages other than Turkish in private conversations, trade, religion, publications, and the courts. Article 40 provided for legal equality for non-Muslim Turks along with their right to establish, manage and control at their own expense charitable, religious, social and educational institutions. Article 41 stated that the Turkish government would provide facilities for elementary education of nationals in the language of their choice, though teaching of Turkish would be obligatory for all. Article 42 provided that the laws and customs of non-Muslims would be used to settle legal questions involving these minorities, and that the Turkish government would provide full protection to non-Muslim religious and charitable institutions. Article 43 provided an assurance that non-Muslim Turkish nationals would not be required to act in violation of their religious principles, though this would not exempt them from such obligations imposed on all other Turkish nationals to assure public order. Article 44 put all these provisions under the guarantee of the League of Nation, and provided that they would not be modified without the assent of the signatories of the Treaty. Article 45 specified that Greece should provide the same privileges for the Muslim minorities on its territories.[1]

It quickly became clear to many Turks and Jews, however, that some of these provisions, and particularly those allowing them to live under separate legal systems, made it impossible for the new Republic to become a fully secular and independent state and for Jewish Turks to become fully integrated into the Republic on an equal basis with Muslim Turks. The special protections and privileges for minorities written into the Treaty, primarily because of the entreaties of Armenian and Greek nationalist delegations, created Muslim hostility not only against them but also against Turkey's Jews as well, something which had not existed before. The Constitution of the Republic established a secular nation state in which all citizens had equal rights regardless of religion; in return it was expected that all citizens would have primary loyalty to the state rather than to their communities and that, therefore, privileges based on religion as well as communal legal and cultural autonomy would come to an end. Soon after the treaty was signed and the new Constitution of the Turkish Republic put into force, therefore, on 15 September 1925

Chief Rabbi Haim Bejerano voluntarily renounced the Jewish *millet's* special legal status and rights deriving from Article 42 of the Treaty of Lausanne, leaving the Grand Rabbinate only as a center for Jewish religious, social and educational activities, while most other functions were turned over to the secular institutions created by the Republic for all its citizens. The Armenian and Greek communities soon made similar declarations, though with considerably greater reluctance because of their different wartime experiences and national expectations.[2]

This surrender of the special minority status guaranteed by the Treaty of Lausanne meant that the special Jewish seats in the Grand National Assembly were surrendered. The *millets*, thus, for all practical purposes were abolished as separate governments with separate laws, and non-Muslims were subjected to the same laws and regulations and administrative treatment as were all other Turkish citizens. Personal status now was under civil jurisdiction. The Jewish community lost the right to levy its own taxes, so communal institutions had to depend on voluntary contributions. Chief Rabbi Bejerano now led the Jewish community not by law and right, as had been the case for Grand Rabbis in Ottoman times since early in the nineteenth century but, rather, through the force of his own personality, which gained the deep respect, not only of Turkish Jewry, but of people of all religions in the Republic. Muslim and Christian as well as Jewish intellectuals and learned men gathered in his study at the Chief Rabbinate, located on Yemenici Sokak in Beyoğlu where it had been transferred from Cibali in 1876, for discussions of all sorts of subjects, from religion and morals to literature and history. Bejerano's mastery not just of the Old and New testaments but also of the Koran and of world history as well as that of the Turks and Jews, enabled him to continue publishing a wide range of articles as well as prepare a four-volume dictionary of Judeo-Spanish proverbs, all of which deepened the respect and admiration in which he was viewed by Muslim and Jewish Turks alike.

Jewish Life in Republican Turkey. In the first official census of the Turkish Republic, taken in 1927, there were 55,592 Jews in European Turkey and 26,280 in Anatolia, making a total of 81,872. The prosperity which Balat had experienced during World War I became even more dominant in the 1920s, when many substantial houses were built. Some of the wealthier Jewish families, however, moved across the Bosporus to Kuzguncuk, considered to be the most elegant Jewish quarter of Istanbul, and also to the adjacent towns of Üsküdar and Kadıköy, while many shopkeepers and unskilled Jewish workers moved to the less elegant slopes of Galata, where they mixed with the still-hostile Greek and Armenian communities. In 1932–33, the only year for which detailed records have been uncovered to date, of the 46,698 Jews living in Istanbul, 9,600 lived in the Istanbul-Fatih district, corresponding to old Istanbul, 32,277 lived in Beyoğlu-Hasköy-Şişli and the European Bosporus communities, 4,308 lived in the Anatolian suburbs, and 174 on the islands of Büyükada, Heybeliada, Burgaz and Kınalıada. These moves were encouraged not only by the shifts then taking place in the locations of Turkish commercial life, but also by the fact that the Alliance schools in Balat had been destroyed by fire in 1910, forcing its children to sail across the Golden Horn to the Alliance schools at Hasköy or Galata if they wanted to continue their education. Emigration from Balat to Galata continued, however, throughout the 1920s so that in the communal elections of 1935 only five deputies were elected from Balat and 28 from Galata, showing just how much Istanbul Jewry had shifted in the years since World War I.

For the most part, Jewish life in Turkey continued before World War II as it had for half a millenium under Ottoman rule. Despite the loss of many of its most enterprising families, Balat remained the largest and most active and vibrant Jewish center in the country, very much resembling the great Jewish communities which dominated the lower east side of Manhattan and the east end of London in the late nineteenth and early twentieth centuries. Here there lived and worked almost ten thousand Jews, freely carrying out their religious, cultural and social activities centered in seven ancient synagogues, the *Ahrida*, *Yanbol, Chana, Pul Yashan, Selaniko, Kasturiya* and *Iştipol*, all of which were packed to overflowing, particularly on holidays such as Rosh Hashanah and Yom Kippur. At the *Yanbol* synagogue, at least ten morning prayers (*tefilla*) were recited every day, each with forty to fifty worshippers in attendance. Most Jewish houses and shops in Balat had been rebuilt with brick or stucco, the streets were light and airy, and most Jews were quite prosperous and well dressed, with the exception of the relatively small number of laborers who lived along the shores of the Golden Horn in the Karabaş, La Lonca and Sigri. Many prosperous Jewish families had refrained from moving to the more modern sections of the city, though they moved their houses and shops inland and up the Balat hill away from the Golden Horn. Jewish glass makers were mostly located at Kasturiye and small textile manufacturers and exporters were centered along Tahta Minare boulevard.

The Zionist organization, which had been quite active in Balat and the rest of Istanbul during and after World War I, continued operations in secret, encouraging the poorer Jews to emigrate to Palestine, largely with financial assistance provided by Baron Edmond de Rothschild and some of the wealthier Istanbul Jews. Secret emigrations were organized, with Zionist societies furnishing passports, renting motor boats, and facilitating passage in other ways as well.

Though an increasing number of Jews lived outside Balat, it remained the center of Istanbul's Jewish life. There was one Jewish public school used by all groups in the community, the *Talmud Torah*, located immediately behind the *Ahrida* synagogue, which provided religious lessons to children. There was a *Mahaizeke Torah*, called *Korsos De La Tadre Del Ebreyo Kal Kadosh Yanbol*, founded by Bensiyon Bedelahmi in 1927, which provided evening classes in Hebrew for adult members of the Yanbol synagogue. At the peak of Balat's Jewish educational system was its *Yeshiva*, located on a small street behind the *Mahkemei Altı* street, whose members studied the Torah and debated religious issues every day under the leadership of Rabbi Moshe Benhabib. Both it and the *Ahrida* synagogue had their libraries of Jewish books. A few Balat residents also took small boats across the Golden Horn to attend synagogues and *yeshivas* and to do business in Hasköy and Galata. The secular community center, which served as a locale for community educational, cultural and recreational activities, providing rooms for dances and conferences as well as athletic events, was located at *La Hemla*, previously used by the Maccabee (Zionist) organization. It was located on Verya Sokak, so called, according to local Jewish tradition, because in Ottoman times when a Sultan was passing through Balat, the local Jews asked him for permission to build a synagogue there, and he replied with the words 'Ver ya', or 'let permission be given', to indicate his approval. Sunday evening entertainments at *La Hemla* often were attended by as many as two hundred members of all ages. It was closed during World War II when most Jewish men were conscripted into the Turkish army. Following the war, in 1952, it was transformed into a nursery school, which remained in operation for five years, by which time most Jews living in Balat moved elsewhere. The Maccabees were supplanted in the 1930's by the non-Zionist Bar Kohba sports society, which was located at the Şişhane section of Galata.

Sephardic Jewish culture continued to flourish during the 1920s and 1930s. The older Jewish daily Judeo-Spanish newspapers surviving from the nineteenth century, *El Tiempo* and *El Telegrafo*, published by the pioneering journalist David Fresco (1850–1933) and *El Djugeton*, published by the poet and author Elia Carmona (1870–1931) until the early 1930s, ended their long years of service not just because of the deaths of their editors but also because their younger readers came more and more to consider Turkish as their native language, and therefore preferred to read the more general Turkish newspapers. The Jewish news press revived in Turkey following World War II with a series of dailies, *La Boz de Oriente* (Voice of the East) (1931–39), founded by Isaac Algazi (1882–1964) and continued by Leon Israel, Moise Dalmedico, and Albert Kohen (1888–1949) with articles in both Judeo-Spanish and French, continued by the latter in Turkish and Judeo-Spanish as the bi-weekly *La Boz de Türkiye* (The Voice of Turkey) (1939–49), and in 1949–50 as the first Turkish-language Jewish newspaper, *Türkiyenin Sesi* (The Voice of Turkey), edited by Albert Kohen's son Sami Kohen (b. 1928), who subsequently became one of Turkey's leading journalists as foreign affairs editor for the national newspaper, *Milliyet*. During the same years, news of the Jewish community also received extensive coverage in the daily French-language newspaper *Le Journal d'Orient*, published by Albert Karasu (1885–1982) from 1917 to 1971, and in the weekly *L'Etoile du Levant*, published by Albert Benaroya from 1948 to 1958.

Music also played a vital role in preserving the vitality of Jewish cultural life while, at the same time, it provided a link between Turkish Jewry and the wider community of Turks among whom they lived. Hayim Efendi of Edirne and, even more particularly, Rabbi Isaac Algazi Efendi (1889–1950) were considered to have been the greatest Sephardic singers of their time. Muslim Turks considered the latter to be one of the greatest of their own musicians, honored him with Turkish titles such as *Efendi* and *Hoca*. Algazi thus preserved the tradition begun by Salomon ben Mazal Tov early in the sixteenth century and Rabbi Israel Najara a century later to combine Hebrew religious songs with classical Turkish music, adapting Turkish and Hebrew singing melodies to Jewish songs and even arranging religious poems according to the Turkish *makamât* style and its intricate instrumental arrangements. Algazi's recordings made in Istanbul between the foundation of the Republic and 1933, when he immigrated, first to Paris and then to Uruguay, remain major sources for appreciating the musical heritage of Ottoman Sephardic Jewry. Born in Izmir of an old family of Sephardic rabbis and cantors, he had been educated not only in an *Alliance* school and in the more traditional *Talmud Torah* and *Yeshiva* led by Izmir Chief Rabbi Abraham Palacci at a time when the established Jewish religious institutions and values were being challenged by modern ideas of free thought and behavior, but also, unlike most of his fellows, in one of the modern secular state schools established throughout the empire during the reign of Sultan Abdül Hamid II. During the last decades of the Empire, he had served after 1908 as Cantor of the new *Beth Israel* central synagogue in the Karataş quarter of Izmir and starting in 1914 as a teacher in the *Talmud Torah Mahazikei Anyim*, where he worked with the famous historian Moshe Gaon, and also at the local *Alliance* school, additionally serving on the Izmir Municipal Council. Thus he preserved his childhood connections with both new and old within Judaism as well as with the Muslim Turkish community around him.

All the while Algazi had studied not only Jewish religious music but also the Turkish classical music of the time and European music, both from his father, Salomon Algazi, called *Bulbuli Salomon* (Salomon the Nightengale) and the leading Jewish Sephardic composers, Shem Tov Shikâr (1840–1920) and Haim Alazraki (d. 1913), singing in the choir of Izmir's Portugal synagogue.

When the Greek army occupying Izmir during the Turkish War for

Independence attacked local Muslims and Jews, Algazi joined most other community leaders in moving to Istanbul with the encouragement of Chief Rabbi Haim Bejerano, who arranged for him to be appointed Cantor of the Italian synagogue at Galata, which for some time had emphasized musical activities. From then until 1933, when he left Turkey due to Atatürk's failure to appoint him to the Turkish Radio Commission, Algazi became a major figure in Turkish Jewish education, supporting Avram Galante and others in their efforts to spread the movement of European Enlightenment (*Haskala*) among Turkish Jews against the opposition of the rabbis and traditional teachers, while at the same time developing their role as part of Turkish society, supporting the reforms of Mustafa Kemal Atatürk and emphasizing good relations between Muslim and Jewish Turks. Algazi performed for Atatürk at the Çankaya presidential palace and later, during Atatürk's fatal illness, at the Dolmabahçe palace in Istanbul, often joining other Turkish musicians and intellectuals in spending hours with Atatürk to encourage and elaborate on his ideas.

Among other Turkish Jews who composed and/or performed Turkish music during the years of the Republic were Aaron Hamon (Yahudi Harun), Gelibolulu Ishak Varon, Mısırlı Ibrahim Levi Hayat, whose works continue to be performed regularly on Turkish radio as well as in concerts, Avram Mandil (Mandil Ağa), and from Izmir Santuri Eliya and Ishak Barki (Küçük Isak), and Santo Sikar (Hoca Santo).

In the 1920s/1930s, the Jewish community maintained eight elementary schools in the Istanbul area, at Balat, Galata, Hasköy, Haydarpaşa, Kuzguncuk and Ortaköy, all mixed schools for boys and girls, each with its own day-care center, enrolling some 1,500 students every year. It also supported the Beyoğlu Jewish Lycée (*Beyoğlu Musevi Lisesi*) and a middle school (*arta*), opened by Bnai Brith in 1911 and taken over by Ashkenazi leader David Marcus in 1915 to replace the *Alliance* schools which had been closed by the French government because of the war. Turkish was now the language of instruction in Jewish schools in place of French used in Alliance schools, but the latter was allowed for a time in the upper classes. Hebrew studies were de-emphasized as a result of the 1932 law which forbad religious instruction in all Turkish schools, with both language and bible classes now offered by lay teachers.

The rise of Turkish nationalism, and in particular its identification with Islam by some elements of the Turkish population, made some Jews fear for the future. In reaction, the Salonica Jew Moise Cohen (1883–1961), who had been in close touch with the Young Turks in his home town in the years preceding the restoration of the Constitution, took the old Turkish name Tekinalp and led a campaign among his fellow Jews to encourage them to speak only Turkish to integrate them fully into Turkish life declaring that 'Turkey is your home, so you should speak Turkish'. Tekinalp founded the *Türk Kültür Birliği* (Turkish Cultural Unity Society) and the *Türkçe Konuşturma Birliği* (Society to promote the Speaking of Turkish) emphasizing the use of Turkish in Jewish schools as well as daily conversations, the Turkification of Jewish names, and the attendance of Jewish children at Turkish government schools particularly on the elementary level, also distributing textbooks and holding adult Turkish classes.

The integration of Turkish Jews into the Republic's society was so successful that after Rabbi Bejerano died in 1931 no need was seen to appoint a new Chief Rabbi for two decades, since it appeared that the tasks assigned to the community easily were handled by the Chief Rabbinate's councils and staffs under the direction of Bejerano's last Secretary General, Samuel Altabev. The Jewish community continued to maintain a central administrative organization, and Jewish community institutions were supported, including synagogues, hospitals, old age homes, and schools. Jews had the same rights as non-Jews to enter public service, though for the most part, due to the rather poor conditions and salaries of civil servants, most preferred to remain in the private sector, where they were able to earn far more as bankers, industrialists, and businessmen.

This is not to say that the situation of Turkish Jewry was without its difficulties in the years before World War II. Atatürk's determination to introduce rapid, forced-draft secularization had great effect on the Jewish community as it did on all other Turks. Most of the secular measures introduced by the Young Turks before and during World War I, and abolished during the Allied occupation of Istanbul, were now restored and considerably expanded, though now only the Muslim foundations were taken over by the state, while Christian and Jewish foundations continued to be administered by their religious leaders, though under state supervision. Religious marriages were banned, though those who wished were allowed to have religious ceremonies after they were first married by civil officials. Jews, like other minorities and foreign organizations, were allowed to retain their own private schools, but they were not allowed to teach Hebrew or any sort of religious instruction and they were required to follow curricula drawn up by the Ministry of Education. Rabbis, like Muslim and Christian clerics, were no longer allowed to wear special religious clothing in public except on special occasions, such as funerals. But since all of this was to strengthen the Republic's secularizing programs, which Turkish Jewry strongly supported, they accepted this restriction, however reluctantly, for the good of the nation, in the same way that they accepted regulations forbidding affiliation with foreign bodies such as the World Zionist Organization and World Jewish Congress, introduced to prevent Muslim Turks from joining reactionary groups which were strongly opposing the secular reforms.

Among Turkish Jews who served in the area of eduction there were the famous historian Avram Galante, who was Professor of Ancient History at Istanbul University, and Moshe Ventura who was Professor of Roman Law. Others were assigned to Turkish high schools and elementary schools. Several hundred others contributed significantly to Turkish industry and medicine or entered business, mostly in Istanbul and Izmir. Yehuda Romano of Edirne acted as Istanbul representative of the Jewish Agency between 1940 and 1946, rescuing thousands of European Jews from the Nazis, with the Turkish government providing facilities to transfer many immigrants from Europe via Edirne and Istanbul to Palestine.

After the Nazis came to power in Germany and Austria, Turkey took in many Jewish and some non-Jewish refugees from persecution, including three hundred leading teachers, doctors, attorneys, artists and scientists as well as thousands more less well-known refugees. In most cases they were brought to Turkey and given positions within six months after their dismissals by the Nazis. Most were given major teaching positions as Ordinarius professors and professors in Turkish universities of Istanbul and Ankara, then being intensively reformed and modernized under the direction of Education Minister Hasan Ali Yücel, with many founding and directing major institutes in all branches of knowledge, where several generations of Turkish scholars were trained.

In the social sciences and humanities, the refugee scholars included the labor economist Alfred Isaac (Nurnberg), the economist and sociologist Alexander Rüstow, who tried to organize a last desperate resistance to Hitler before fleeing to Turkey in 1933, the Roman philologist Leo Spitzer (Cologne), who founded the School of Foreign Languages at the University of Istanbul, later taken over by Erich Auerbach (Marburg); Andreas Schwartz (Freiburg), who made important contributions to the adaption of western law in Turkey during the 1930s as well as training a whole generation of Turkish legal scholars at the Law Faculty of Istanbul University; Ernst Hirsch (Freiburg), who specialized in international trade law and legal philosophy; the sociologist and economist Gerard Kessler (Leipzig), who trained hundreds of Turkish students in labor economics at Istanbul University and who, with some of his students, helped found the first Turkish labor unions following World War II; the economist and financial expert Fritz Neumark (Frankfurt); the architect Gustav Oelsner (Hamburg), who in addition to teaching architecture and city planning played an important role in Turkey's municipal planning programs; and the French artist Leopold Levi, who helped develop the school of painting at the Academy of Fine Arts in Istanbul. At Ankara University there were the Assyriologist Benno Landsberger (Leipzig), the Hittitologist Hans Guterbock (Berlin), the Classical Philologist Georg Rohde (Marburg), who in addition to training a generation of philologists stimulated a major program of translation into Turkish of the major works of classical and European literature published by the Turkish Ministry of Education; the political scientist, Ernst Reuter, who after 1945 returned to Germany to become Mayor of Berlin, and the sinologist and sociologist Wolfram Eberhard. The renowned composer Paul Hindemith (Frankfurt) led the way in building the Turkish State conservatory in Ankara which included among its distinguished faculty the German theatrical producer Carl Ebert (Berlin), who founded the Turkish State Opera Company; and the conductor Dr Ernst Praetorius, who founded and led the President's Ankara Philharmonic Orchestra.

Among major Jewish scientists brought to Turkey in the 1930s were the botanists Leo Brauner (Jena) and Alfred Heilbronn (Munster), the geologist Wilhelm Salomon-Calvi (Heidelberg), and the chemist Otto Gerngross (Berlin). Jewish physicians invited to teach and direct University institutes included the microbiologist and epidemologist Hugo Braun (Frankfurt), the radiologist Friedrich Dessauer (Frankfurt), the internist Erich Frank (Breslau), the biochemist Felix Haurowitz (Prague), the hygenist Julius Hirsch (Berlin), the pediatrician Albert Eckstein (Dusseldorf), who made major contributions to the treatment of children's illnesses by creating a series of clinics throughout Turkey; the ophthamologist Joseph Ingersheimer (Frankfurt), the dental surgeon Alfred Kantorowicz (Bonn), the gynecologist Wilhelm Liepmann (Berlin), the pharmacologist Werner Lipschitz (Frankfurt), the histologist Karl Loewenthal (Frankfurt), the surgeons Edward Melchior (Breslau) and Rudolf Nissen (Berlin), and the physiologist Hans Winterstein (Breslau).

The arrival of these prominent Jewish refugees from Naziism was bitterly opposed by Istanbul's German community, which for the most part supported the efforts of Nazi ambassadors, merchants and spies to undermine Turkish faith in Jewish abilities and gratitude for their contributions, at times allying with Christian nationalist groups in efforts to drive the Jews out once and for all. At the same time, the Nazis encouraged some Turkish nationalists to revive the pan-Turkist movements of the nineteenth century in the hope of destabilizing the Soviet Empire by stirring up its large Turkic population in the Caucasus and Central Asia. They were not too successful in these efforts, however, not only because of public disinterest but also because of strong Turkish government curbs against such activities. As a by-product of these efforts, however, the Nazis did stimulate some anti-Semitic movements and newspaper articles as well as books by extreme right-wing and Islamist Turkish groups. The most virulent anti-Semitic newspaper was *Anadolu*, published in Izmir by C. R. Atılhan, but his press was suppressed by the Turkish government after only a few months. Atılhan went to Germany at the invitation of Julius Streicher, then returned to Turkey in May, 1934, where he established another anti-Semitic newspaper, *Milli Inkilâp*, which stimulated an anti-Semitic movement in western Thrace, already influenced by Greek anti-Semitism. The result was a series of attacks on Turkish Jews at Edirne, where hundreds of Jews had been coming across the border in flight from Nazi oppression. Prime Minister Ismet İnönü reacted with a powerful speech to the Grand National Assembly condemning anti-Semitism and defending the rights of all Jewish Turks, going on to close several anti-Semitic political groups and newspapers. Ferment in Thrace due both to Greek religious attacks and Nazi propaganda continued into World War II, however, and caused most of its Jews to resettle in the more tolerant and liberal atmosphere of Istanbul and Izmir. *Milli İnkilâp* was subsequently suppressed by the Turkish government. Atılhan was arrested and sent to jail along with his comrades in the anti-Semitic campaign, and the government openly declared to the Jewish community that it remained determined to protect Jews against all attacks and to treat them equally with all other Turkish citizens.

Starting in 1934, at least partly in reaction to the Nazi activities, Turkish Jews began to participate actively in politics, with Dr Abravaya Marmaralı being elected to the Grand National Assembly as a liberal independent, the first Jewish member of that body. Jews began also to depart from their previous emphasis on Judeo-Spanish and to engage in the wider stage of Turkish-language cultural activities as novelists, poets, playrights and artists. While the emergence of open clashes between Jews and Arabs in Palestine was widely published in the Turkish press, the government did nothing to hinder contacts between Turkish and Palestinian Jews, including participation of the former in the Maccabee games held in Palestine and the World Jewish Congresses held during the late 1930s. Efforts attempted in the Grand National Assembly during 1938 to limit Jewish immigration from central and western Europe in reaction to the arrival of hundreds of Jews because of increased anti-Semitic persecution in Poland, Hungary and Rumania were denounced in *Ulus*, official newspaper of Atatürk's Republican People's Party, and were defeated in the Grand National Assembly by overwhelming votes. Prime Minister Celal Bayar further declared: 'There is no Jewish problem in our country. There is no minorities problem at all. We do not intend to artifically create a Jewish problem because of external influences. We will not allow external currents to influence us.' Similar public remarks were made by other Turkish leaders.[3]

During the 1930s, in reaction to Nazi propaganda, as had been the case in the Ottoman Empire during the nineteenth and early twentieth centuries, it was not so much Turkish Muslims but, rather, Christians, who persisted in their anti-Semitic attitudes and activities. In 1938, when it appeared increasingly that the 'New Order' might dominate Europe, the Nazi flag was openly flown from the famous Armenian-owned Tokatliyan Hotel. The resulting Jewish-organized boycott of the hotel was supported by most Turks and condoned by the government, though opposed by Nazi sympathizer Yunus Nadi in his newspaper *Cumhuriyet*, causing it to be closed and turned into an office building.

Turkish Jewry during World War II. Turkey managed to remain neutral during World War II. The sympathies of President İsmet İnönü and most other Turkish leaders were clearly with the western Allies, with whom alliances were signed shortly before the war began. But the Allies' clear inability to provide assistance if an open war declaration had led to a German invasion from Greece caused the Turks to maintain an uneasy neutrality until Germany's impending defeat finally led it to join late in 1944. Thus Turkey emerged from the war among the victors, as Greece had been forced to do during World War I.

While the Nazis largely exterminated the remaining Jewish populations of the former Ottoman possessions of Greece during World War II, thus culminating the persecutions begun in these countries following their achievement of full independence during the nineteenth century, neutral Turkey defended its Jews and rejected Nazi demands for them to be deported for extermination in the death camps. In the face of constant German pressure, however, it did appear to try to satisfy them in some respects by limiting the entry of Turkish Jews into military schools and segregating them into separate units. In the darkest days of World War II, after German forces had occupied Greece and Bulgaria and pushed to the borders of Turkey in Thrace, moreover, rumors were spread by Balat's anxious Christian neighbors that as soon as the Nazis arrived in Istanbul they would use the ovens of the local Balat bakery, *Los Ornos de Balat*, to exterminate Turkish Jewry, creating considerable anxiety among the latter, though the story, apparently, was entirely without foundation.

In December 1942, in a desperate effort to resolve depressed economic conditions, inflation, shortages and budgetary difficulties caused by wartime mobilization measures, the Grand National Assembly enacted the disastrous *Varlık Vergisi*, or Capital Tax, program which in order to raise the equivalent of some $360 million to pay in part for the extremely large army being maintained against the possibility of a German invasion through Greece, taxed not only the depressed incomes of the mass of its citizens but also the capital of those who had property. This in itself was a fairly common practice in Europe at the time, but it was administered in such a way to bear most heavily on urban merchants, many of whom were Christians and Jews. Local commissions of Finance Ministry officials and Turkish merchants were organized to assess the taxes in their districts. Their decisions were not subject to appeal or change and the tax had to be paid in a very short time. Those unable to pay were subjected to hard labor at the Aşkale camp until their obligations were paid off. Those who lacked the financial liquidity needed to pay the tax had to sell everything or declare bankruptcy and even work on government projects in order to pay their debts, in the process losing most or all of their properties. In interviewing various Jewish survivors about the *Varlık Vergisi*, the author was told over and over again: 'We were Turkish patriots; we paid all we had gladly; everyone expected to suffer. But then they asked for more and we had nothing left to pay. On the other hand, the Nazis wanted them to turn us over or to kill us, and they didn't do that. We survived, unlike our brothers in Greece and most of Europe.' One interesting comment received from more than one source was that the *Varlık Vergisi* helped the Jews of Turkey by showing Turks that the Jews were suffering so much that they should not give in to the Nazi demands to deport their Jews to the death camps. The deprivation of their wealth by the government drained what resentment there might otherwise have been among Turks against Jewish wealth while the mass of the population was suffering because of the war.

Anti-Turkish political groups subsequently used the fact that many of those who suffered from the *Varlık Vergisi* were Christians and Jews to claim that the measure was directed primarily against the minorities. It cannot be denied that the centuries of Christian exploitation of Muslims through the Capitulation system had left their mark and that many of the local commissions did bear more heavily on non-Muslims, but both Muslims and non-Muslims did suffer. That the *Varlik Vergisi* was not directed primarily against the Jews, moreover, is shown by the fact that it never was accompanied by any sort of government-organized anti-Semitic propaganda and that Muslim Turks themselves never at any point showed any anti-Semitism either before, during, or after the program was in force. Turkish Jews not affected by the tax continued their lives normally. Jewish youths joined their Muslim fellow citizens in accepting conscription into the army, and Nazi-sponsored anti-Semitic publications were suppressed by the government.

Throughout the war, moreover, and despite continual Nazi pressure, the government of Turkey refused German demands that it turn over the Jewish refugees for internment in the death camps.[4] Instead it went out of its way to assist passage into its territory of Jews fleeing from Nazi persecution in Poland, Greece and Yugoslavia as well as in western and central Europe. Turkish soldiers in Thrace turned the other way when Jewish refugees managed to slip across the borders of Nazi-occupied Greece and Bulgaria, as related by a number of veterans of Turkey's Thracian border guards, including an officer in the Edirne district at the time, Emin Kural, father of the author's wife, Ezel Kural Shaw. Turkey condoned the presence in Istanbul starting in the summer of 1940 of fifteen Zionist *Aliyah* agents led by Hayim Barlas, including the subsequent mayor of Israeli Jerusalem, Teddy Kollek and Moshe Shertok (Sharret), who from their office in the Continental Hotel collected information about Nazi treatment of Jews all over southeastern Europe.[5]

With the passive approval of the Turkish government they mounted rescue operations, providing false passports as well as transportation to Turkey of thousands of Jewish refugees who managed to flee from Nazi horrors in Poland, Yugoslavia, Bulgaria, Greece, Hungary, Rumania, and Czechoslovakia, and during the Nazi invasion of the East, from Estonia, the Ukraine and Russia. They maintained them through the remainder of the war and facilitated the onward passage of those who wished to go on to Palestine. It was through these Zionist agents that Adolph Eichmann's offer came to the Zionist Organization to liberate the remaining Jews of Poland, after 3.5 million had already been killed, in return for war equipment and money, and it was through these same agents that the offer of S.S. officers in Budapest was passed on to the Allies to arrange for an early peace. Turkey allowed all this activity to go on despite strong and vehement opposition by Great Britain and the Vatican due to fears of Arab reaction against their nationals and interests, though a few local British officials as well as the Vatican's Istanbul representative, Angelo Roncalli, later Pope John XXIII, did secretly provide assistance to the Zionist agents on their own initiative. Britain urged the Balkan states, before they were taken over by Germany, to prevent Jewish emigration to Turkey and Palestine and it went on to pressure the governments of both Turkey and Greece to refuse landing privileges to ships carrying Jewish refugees. The most disastrous incident resulting from this situation involved the ship Struma, carrying 769 Jews fleeing from Poland, which Britain advised Turkey to refuse admission to its ports due to fears that it would go on to Palestine, after which it sank after returning to the Black Sea, with only six passengers surviving.[6] For the most part, however, in the face of all this pressure, the Turkish government allowed the Zionist agents to use its facilities to smuggle diamonds, gold coins, and currency into the Nazi occupied lands to help feed and house Jews who were not able to flee, with the Turkish ambassadors and consular representatives at times helping and even arranging for Jews to flee to Turkey. While Nazi and British pressure at times forced Turkey to overtly limit these Zionist rescue activities by closing the *Aliyah* office and limiting Jewish immigration to those who could show British permission for them to enter Palestine, the Turkish government allowed the same Zionists to maintain the unofficial *Aliyah Bet* organization to continue to bring in Jewish refugees and send them on to Palestine on an 'illegal' basis.

Moshe Shertok later stated that from the Jewish perspective, Istanbul was far more important as a base for gathering information and providing refuge for Jews fleeing from the Nazis than were the other neutral centers in Europe, Geneva, Stockholm or Lisbon, since only Istanbul provided direct connections between European Jewry and the *Yishuv* in Palestine. Zionist agents who were active in Istanbul during the war remain convinced to the present day that, in the absence of assistance from the great Jewish communities of Britain, America and South Africa, it was their activities alone, done with the full knowledge and silent support of the Turkish government, that provided European Jews with the feeling that some people still remembered them and were trying to help them.[7]

Most of this, however, was not known to Turkish Jews. The *Varlık Vergisi* disappointed many who had surrendered their special rights following the Turkish War for Independence in the expectation that they would be treated as fully equal by the Turkish Republic. As a result of this as well as a hard-sell campaign encouraging emigration by Jewish Agency agents sent from Israel immediately after the war, almost one-third of the Turkey's wartime Jewish population, particularly the poorer Jews and most of those who had come as refugees from the Nazis, emigrated to the new state of Israel, with 26,306 going in 1949 alone.[8]

In the late 1960s and early 1970s a second, much less numerous, wave of emigration of Turkish Jews to Israel took place inspired largely by desires to support the latter against the threat posed by Arab attacks during and after the Six Day War, and also by Greek attacks on Jews and Jewish property in Istanbul, Izmir, and Cyprus as part of the attacks on Turks which accompanied Greece's efforts to annex independent Cyprus following the British withdrawal in the early 1970s. For the most part, these immigrants were far more educated and prosperous than were those who left Turkey immediately after World War II.

Most likely, even had the *Varlık Vergisi* episode not occurred, such large-scale Jewish emigration from Turkey would have taken place in any case once a Jewish state was established, with the opportunities for economic advancement in a new environment being of special inducement to the poorer elements of Turkish Jewry who were strongly influenced by Zionist immigration agents in the years following the war. One has to assume from the fact that a substantial number of Jews remained in Turkey after this mass immigration, that they again began to participate actively and successfully in Turkey's economic life, and that 5,047 Turkish Jews who had gone to Israel returned to settle in Turkey between 1948 and 1965, that they were satisfied with their situation and convinced that most other Turks understood that the *Varlık Vergisi* was a mistake and were determined that such actions would never happen again. Even those Turkish Jews who emigrated to Israel and remain there today have retained close ties with Turkey. They are proud of their Turkish heritage, continue to use Turkish and Ladino in their daily lives, sing and play Turkish music and eat Turkish food, and maintain contact with Turkish friends and Jewish relatives in Turkey. The 'Union of People from Turkey' (called *Türkiyeliler Birliği* in Turkish and *Itahdut Yotse Tuyrkiye be Israel* in Hebrew) represents them on the national level, while the *Morit* (*Moreshet Yagdut Turkiya*) Foundation for Turkish Jews in Israel, which promotes their culture, is building a major museum and cultural center at Herzliya as well as promoting conferences and studies of their lives under Ottoman rule.

As a result of this mass emigration, the population of Turkish Jews in Israel rose from 10,701 in 1948 to 41,605 in 1951, remaining at approximately the same figure during the next three decades. Of course the number of Israeli Jewish children of Turkish-born fathers increased considerably during these same years to some 40,000, bringing the total of Turkish Jews and their children to about 80,000 in 1989, most of whom live along the Mediterranean coast at Bat Yam, eight miles east of Tel Aviv at Yahud, which they developed following 1948, at the Rahov Levinsky section of Tel Aviv itself, and at Holon and Herzliya. About the same number of Turkish Jews and their children live in western countries. The number of Turkish Jews, which had reached 79,424 in 1927, when the first official census was taken in the Republic, with 47,035 in Istanbul, 17,094 in Izmir and 6,098 in Edirne, and rose to an estimated 125,000 during World War II, fell from 76,965 immediately afterwards to 45,995 in 1955. This fell to 43,928 in 1960, by which time most Jews had moved away from the smaller towns to the major cities. In 1965, a total of 38,267 Jews remained in Turkey, of whom 30,831 were in Istanbul, 4,067 in Izmir, and the remaining 3,369 in small towns and villages throughout the country.[9]

The official Turkish census commission has not compiled statistics by religion since the 1960s, so it is impossible to secure an accurate count of the Jewish population in Turkey today. The Chief Rabbinate counts some 5,500 officially registered members of Turkish synagogues which, figuring an average of four persons per family, brings a total of 22,000, including 20,000 in Istanbul and 2,000 in Izmir, with smaller groups in Adana, Ankara, Çanakkale, Bursa and Kirklareli. Some suggest, however, that there could be an additional 10,000 Turks of Jewish origin who, not actively practicing their religion or registering with any synagogue, are not normally counted as being Jews. There are also several thousand Jews, and Dönmes who do not accept the leadership of the Chief Rabbinate and who are not therefore included in this total. On the other hand, others maintain that many of those registered as synagogue members do not in fact even live in Turkey so that the actual figure could be less than 20,000. Whatever the figure, however, it is only one-fourth of that when the Turkish Republic was established, but it remains the second largest Jewish community in the former Ottoman lands, exceeded only by Israel.

The Republican People's Party founded by Atatürk remained in control of the Turkish government following his death in 1938 until the elections of 1950, when it was supplanted by the Democrat Party, led by President Celal Bayar and Prime Minister Adnan Menderes, which imposed far fewer government controls and encouraged free enterprise to a much greater extent than had been possible during the forced modernization of the Atatürk years. The Democrat Party remained in power for a decade, as time went on easing many of the previous secular restrictions in order to gain the votes of religiously-minded citizens of all persuasions. As a result, restrictions on the repair and building of new synagogues, as well as mosques and churches, were relaxed, and Hebrew along with religious lessons were included in the curriculum of Jewish schools, just as Arabic and Islam were added to the programs of students in the state schools.

It was during the Democratic decade that Turkish Jewry finally felt the need for a new Chief Rabbi for the first time since the death of Haim Bejerano in 1931. On 25 January 1953 community representatives elected to the post Rabbi Rafael David Saban (1873–1960), who had years of experience in community administration, having served as a member of the Religious Council (*Meclisi Ruhani*) and of the Istanbul Religious Court (*Bet Din*) starting in 1903, as a member of the Istanbul Religious Council (*Meclisi Idare*) between 1908 and 1925, and as *Mare de Atra* (district religious chief) of Hasköy (1907–12) and then of the Galata-Beyoğlu-Şişli-Kasımpaşa district and of the Italian and Ashkenazi communities from 1912 until his appointment as Chief Rabbi, all the while serving as confidential advisor to all his predecessors since the days of Grand Rabbi Moshe Levi. Having long served with the Ashkenazi and Italian Jewish communities, he considered it his special function to restore good relations with them and to bring all the Turkish Jewish communities together, going so far as to try to end the differences with the Karaites, though in this he was not as successful. Like Bejerano, he strongly emphasized the close relationship of Turks and Jews, leading the community in joining other citizens of the Republic in celebrating the 400th anniversary of the Turkish conquest of Byzantine Constantinople and of Mehmed II's invitations to the Jews of Central Europe to come under his protection.

On 21 August 1961 a Jewish community council of sixty-one delegates elected as Saban's successor his secretary and advisor, Rabbi David Asseo, who has served with great distinction since that time. Born in Hasköy in 1914 and educated in the Rabbinical College at Rhodes, Asseo has led his community in both administration and religion, even while maintaining close ties with Turkish Muslim and Christian leaders. He is the official representative of Turkish Jewry with the central government as well as with groups and individuals outside Turkey. He is assisted by a small staff at the Chief Rabbinate, a Religious Council, which has taken over the name of the old religious court, *Bet Din*, composed of the Chief Rabbi and three other Istanbul rabbis, which cares for personal matters such as registration of births, deaths, marriages, divorces and conversions, a Lay Council (*Fahri Danişmanlar Kurulu*/Council of Honorary Advisors) consisting of 35 leading Turkish Jews nominated by the Chief

Rabbi, and an Executive Committee (*Icra Kurulu*) of fourteen members, whose President at least must be elected from among the members of the Lay Council. Together these Councils and employees supervise all synagogues and community institutions and activities, providing them with operating funds. It supports the Jewish elementary school and lycee located in Galata, the community old age home (*Ihtiyarlar Yurdu*) in Hasköy, which occupies the building of a nineteenth century Alliance school, and the 98-bed Jewish community hospital (*Or Ahayim Hastanesi*) opened in 1897 across the Golden Horn in Balat on land donated by Sultan Abdül Hamid II. In Izmir the Jewish community has since 1874 maintained the Karataş Hospital (twenty-two beds), which served also as an old age home until a new *Yaşlılar Yurdu* was built especially for this purpose in 1958, while additional rooms and medical facilities were added in 1962. Other funds are provided for the vacation house (*Tatil Evi*) for Jewish children on Burgaz island and a small *Talmud Torah* that trains religious assistants for Turkish synagogues.

Each synagogue and hospital is organized by Turkish law into a foundation (*vakıf*) with its own administrators and executive committee. By law it is legally autonomous of the Grand Rabbinate and responsible directly to the General Directorate of Foundations (*Vakıflar Genel Müdürlüğü*), to which it must report all income and expenditures of the congregation. It is difficult to imagine, however, that the Grand Rabbinate remains without influence in the institutions.

Deficits in the budgets of these synagogues and other institutions are made up by the central Jewish community budget. A substantial portion of the Jewish community's revenues come from the religious foundations, but in addition all Jews over the age of eighteen are expected to voluntarily provide contributions to the community in proportion to their incomes in addition to an informal *kisbe* tax, which finances the activities of the Chief Rabbinate and the community religious services. Additional fees also are collected in return for particular services, such as the performance of weddings, circumcisions, bar-mitzvahs, funerals, circumcisions and the like, and sale of the right to perform ritual functions during religious services.

There are sixteen synagogues operating at the present time in Istanbul, in addition to those at Izmir, Bursa, Kirklareli, Ankara, Çanakkale, Iskenderun and Antakya. The remaining Jewish communities elsewhere in Turkey for the most part are too small to provide the *minyans* of ten needed to hold religious services on a regular basis, so their synagogues are opened only for holidays and other special occasions.

The Istanbul Jewish community is now divided into eight synagogue districts (*hashgahot*), combining several of the old Ottoman *kehillas*, each administered by a communal council (*vaad ha-kehilla*): Neve Şalom (Galata-Beyoğlu-Şişli), Balat, Hasköy, Sirkeci, Ortaköy, Kuzguncuk,

Kadıköy-Caddebostan and Büyükada. It also has representatives of the Ashkenazi and Italian communities.

A survey of Istanbul Jewry carried out in February 1987, by the German Lycée, found that the bulk of Istanbul Jewry now lives in the area north of Taksim, in the Şişli (31 percent), Gayrettepe (25 percent), Nişantaşı (17 percent), and Kurtuluş (6 percent) areas, while most of the remainder live in the Anatolian suburbs of Göztepe (5 percent), Caddebostan (5 percent), and Suadiye (3 percent), and the remaining 13 percent live elsewhere.[10] The Ashkenazi community maintains its own foundation and synagogue on the Yüksek Kaldırım slope which descends precipitously from Beyoğlu to Galata, while close by on Küçük Hendek Sokak in Galata, the Italian synagogue established by separation from the Sephardim in the mid-nineteenth century also continues to hold its own services. Both, however, accept the authority of the Chief Rabbi and Chief Rabbinate and both have representatives among its Honorary Advisors.

The some eighty Karaite Jews continue to observe their own rites and traditions outside the authority and control of the Chief Rabbinate, going to Israel to perform marriages when necessary. The *dönmes* are said to maintain their own synagogue, school and social organizations, but in great secrecy, so there is little information about them except that they continue to be very prosperous. While there is no significant Jewish population in old Istanbul, there is a small synagogue in the Sirkeci quarter still holding Friday services just behind the main Istanbul railroad station. It is operated principally by and for Jewish businessmen in the area, mostly descendants of the founders who lived in the area a century or so ago when they first came to Istanbul as refugees from persecution elsewhere in Europe. Some older synagogues, such as the ancient Ahrida and Yanbol in Balat, and the Ma'alem in Hasköy, which do not hold regular services, still are used on the more important holidays, while others, like the *Mekor Haim* in Çanakkale, the Great Synagogue of Edirne, and the Samanpazarı synagogue on Birlik Sokak near the Ankara citadel,[11] are used rarely because of small communities. Outside of Istanbul, the only synagogue regularly holding Friday services is the *Bikur Holim* synagogue of Izmir, also under the supervision of the Chief Rabbinate.

Very few ancient synagogues survive intact, having been replaced or modernized during the nineteenth century. The oldest operating synagogues, such as the Ahrida and Yanbol of Balat and the Ma'alem of Hasköy were modernized last in the late nineteenth century and, on the surface, manifest little of their historic foundations. The more contemporary synagogues of Istanbul do not reflect any special Jewish architectural style, and in fact look more like Turkish churches, with two lines of pillars dividing the buildings into three rectangles, one in the center and two on either side, with some reflecting the Muslim style of the Dome of the Rock in Jerusalem, having a dome above the pillars, which are organized in a circle, dividing the sanctuary into two cylindrical spaces. Jewish art is reflected less in the buildings themselves than in the Holy Ark and other ritual articles, such as the crowns and crescents attached to the scrolls and the oil lamps surrounding them, which also invariably bear the flag of the Turkish Republic. Oddly enough, most of the Torah scrolls are covered and decorated in the style of the Ashkenazis, with some variations in the Arabic speaking Jewish communities of the southeast, where the style is more Sephardic. All the synagogues continue to retain the Orthodox tradition of separating male and female worshippers. The rabbis (*haham*) and cantors (*hazzan*) sit in a raised area (*teva*), from which they lead the services. Turkish synagogues are surrounded by high walls, with secondary walls also in their interior courts next to the gates in order to conceal the worshippers from passers-by.

Most Jewish and non-Jewish students alike prefer to attend foreign private schools or the state schools, so the number of Jewish schools in Istanbul has been reduced to two, with one in Izmir. In place of the *heder*s and *talmud torah*s of the past, Jewish education is now carried on by the Jewish Elementary School (*Musevi Karma ve Ana Ilk Okulu*), founded originally in 1890 and reorganized in 1939, and the Beyoğlu Jewish Lycée (*Beyoğlu Özel Musevi Lisesi*), both now located in the Galata/Şişhane section of Istanbul near the Neve Şalom synagogue but soon to move to new buildings in the Ulus (Etiler) section of Istanbul. Both originally followed the curriculum of the government's Galatasaray Lycée which, founded and organized with substantial contributions by the French government, emphasized instruction in French. As a result of the urgings of Minister of Education Saffet Arıkan in 1937, however, the curriculum was changed to accord with that prescribed by the Ministry of Education (*Milli Eğitim Bakanlığı*), though with the necessary addition of lessons in Hebrew, and increasingly with Turkish teachers, both Muslim and Jewish. Since 1964, English has replaced French as the primary foreign language taught at the schools. While some feel that the future of even these schools is in doubt enrollment remains reasonably high, at least in the Lycée, where an average of 200 students attend at any given time. Instruction is carried out in modern laboratories with the latest equipment for studies of language, physics and chemistry, indicating that the Jewish community is able and willing to provide its children with the best possible education.

The Izmir Jewish community also maintains an elementary school which cares for approximately 140 children at any one time. There also a traditional Jewish *heder* in Istanbul, the *Mahazike Torah*, founded by Rabbi Nissim Bahar (1912–90 in affiliation with the Chief Rabbinates of Istanbul and Izmir. It provides weekend religious classes as well as holiday and social activities for elementary school children of especially religious families and also trains rabbis and cantors. The kosher Jewish butchers, who once formed such a powerful element of the Ottoman Jewish community, no longer exist. Their role is now assumed by Muslim butchers who sell animals slaughtered by the *Shohetim* in accordance with ritual requirements. The Jewish community makes special arrangements to bake its own *matzah* and to make *kosher* wine for Passover and other religious holidays. Several major hotels in Istanbul, including the Hilton, Sheraton and Büyük Sürmeli, maintain *kosher* kitchens to provide for group meetings as well as guests.

Most Jewish cemeteries in Turkey such as those at Hasköy and at the northern edge of Balat, and at Kuzguncuk and Ortaköy in Istanbul, are ancient, except for those in Mersin and Adana, which date from the early years of the Republic. Istanbul Jewry also maintains newer cemeteries at Arnavutköy, on the European shores of the Bosporus, and in the Şişli area, to accomodate the new centers of Jewish life, and new space has been allocated for a future Jewish cemetery near Kemerburgaz/Kilyos, on the Black Sea. The Jews of Edirne bury their dead in the Jewish cemeteries of Istanbul. Seven cemeteries in Turkey are used only by Jews, at Istanbul, Izmir, Bursa, Çanakkale, Kirklareli and Tekirdağ, but in most other places Muslims, Jews and Christians use common cemeteries. Some of the older cemeteries, particularly those at Hasköy and Ortaköy, like many Muslim cemeteries, have been partially disrupted by the large highway projects which have changed Istanbul so radically during the last decade, but many still survive, at least in part, though often in decaying condition due to lack of attention.The older tombstones bear Hebrew and Ladino inscriptions, with a few written in Arabic with Hebrew letters, but since 1923 inscriptions have been written in both Ladino and Turkish, with the latter predominating in recent years. The Turkish government has been quite cooperative in providing the community with new cemetery space adjoining the old ones when needed.

Jews participate in most aspects of Turkish life. Major Jewish industrialists include Jak V. Kamhi, Chairman of the Board of Profilo Holding Company, leading manufacturer of electrical appliances, and for a number of years President of the *Iktisadi Kalkınma Vakfı*, in charge of negotiating to secure Turkey's entry into the European Common Market; Ishak Alaton, Chairman of Alarko, a major industrial holding company; Üzeyir Garih, his partner in Alarko, which he co-founded with Alaton; Remzi Pensoy, the Becerano brothers and Nedim Yahya. There are also major painters such as Yosef Habib Gerez, also Private Secretary to the Chief Rabbi; Bubi, and Margareth Maim; the poets Berta Brudo, Yusuf Algazi and Yosef Habib Gerez; the writers Naim Güleryüz, Historian and Councellor to the Chief Rabbinate; Sami Kohen, leading correspondent on International Affairs for the national newspaper *Milliyet*; Beki L. Bahar (literature and playright), Mario Levi (literature),

Jak Deleon (literature), Nesim Benbanaste, Beki Bardavit, the journalists of *Şalom* Silvyo Ovadya, Rina Eskenazi, Nana Tarablus, Yusuf Altıntas, Dalia Sayah, and Lizi Behmoaras; the well-known retailer Vitali Hakko, President of the *Vakko* department store chain, largest in Turkey; and in public relations: Eli Acıman, Chairman of Manajans/Thompson, Turkish representative of the international advertising firm J. Walter Thompson and pioneer founder of modern advertising in Turkey; Izidor Barouh, of the *Ilancılık* Agency, and Sedat Scialom, of *Grafika Ajansı*; the actors Rozet Hubes, Izzet Bana and Selim Hubes; the folk musicians of *Los Pasaros Sefardis* and the *Aroyo Chorale* as well as Jak and Janet Esin; and the photographers Izzet Keribar, Yusuf Tuvi and Albert Modiano. There also are numerous Jewish professors in the major Turkish universities such as Selim Kaneti (law), Cem Bahar (economics) Yuda Yurum (chemistry) and Norma Razon (psychology), and teachers in public and private schools. Turkish Jews are also laborers, engineers, classical Turkish and jazz musicians, attorneys, artisans, journalists, painters and sculptors, athletes, automobile racers, physicians, advertising agents, models, philatelists, and merchants and shopkeepers of all sorts. While Jews participate freely in Turkish social, cultural and sports organizations, they also maintain Jewish community groups as well in the areas where they live, including the Yıldırım Sports Club (*Yıldırım Spor Klübü*) and the Göztepe Cultural Society (*Göztepe Kültür Derneği*). Jews participated in Turkish politics during the first three decades of the Republic, but very few have done so in the last few years, most likely because of the far greater opportunities available in the areas of private enterprise except for Isak Altabev, son of Grand Rabbinate General Secretary Samuel Altabev, who served as Democrat party deputy for Istanbul in the Grand National Assembly from 1952 until 1960.

Regardless of origin most Turkish Jews remain assimilated to Sephardic culture, but Turkish rather than Ladino has become their primary language while French, Italian and English now have the status of second, foreign, languages. Younger Turkish Jews are for the most part fully integrated into Turkish society. As such, they speak only Turkish, at home as well as outside, and have difficulty communicating with their elders in either Judeo-Spanish or French. A recent survey[12] found that in the 1920s and 1930s forty percent of Jewish men and ten percent of Jewish women gave Turkish as their first language, with fifty percent of the women and ten percent of the men giving Judeo-Spanish, and twenty percent of both giving French. After the 1950s, this changed to one hundred percent of both men and women giving Turkish as their native language.

Judeo-Spanish remains the second language for most older Turkish male Jews and the first language for older females, except those living at Iskenderun and Antakya, for whom Arabic is used in addition to Turkish,

Men and women giving Turkish as their native language

	French	Turkish	Judeo-Spanish	French Turkish	French Turkish Judeo-Spanish	Judeo-Spanish French
Men to 1920	20	40	10	30		
Women to 1920	20	10	50			20
Men 1921–1940	–	40	10	40	10	
Women 1921–1940	30	10	–	40	20	
All 1941–1960		100				
All 1961	–	100				

and those at Mersin, where two-thirds speak Ladino and one-third Arabic.

Until fairly recently the general secular approach of the Turkish Republic, the ending of large-scale anti-Semitic riots as a result of the departure of most members of the Christian minorities, and emigration by wealthier Jews out of strictly Jewish quarters into more luxurious mixed suburbs, led many Turkish Jews to ignore their religious and social obligations to the community, very much like many American Jews. A strong Muslim revivalism among many Turks since the 1960s, however, has been paralleled by a similar revival among younger Jews, who are taking much more of an active role in community life and activities than did their fathers a generation ago.

Following World War II, the established Jewish newspapers that existed before 1939 were supplemented by a number of short-lived daily and weekly newspapers, which combined articles in both Judeo-Spanish and Turkish such as Şabat (The Sabbath) (1947–50), edited by Moşe Benbasat (Benbasan) (1920–86) and Izak Yaeş (1922–70), continued with La Vara, edited by Moşe Benbasat in 1950. Atikva (Hatikva), edited by Ya'kov Kıymaz and Avrom Benaroya in 1947, encouraged Istanbul's Jews to emigrate to Israel. There were also the bi-weekly Or Yehuda, edited by Izak Yaeş and Menahem Maden in 1948 and 1949; Haftanın Sesi (Voice of the Week) (1957), edited by Robert Sezer, Isak Kohen, Davit Eskenazi, Ferit Alsait and Naim Güleryüz; La Luz (The Light), edited by Elyazar Menda, Robert Bali (1899–1982) and Moşe Levi Belman from 1950 to 1953; La Boz (The Voice), edited by Moşe Levi Belman in 1952–53; La Trompeta (The Trumpet), edited by Raphael Alkaher starting in September, 1951; the La Vera Luz (The True Light), edited by Elyazar Menda from February 1953 to January 1972; the weekly La Luz de Türkiye (Light of Turkey), edited by Robert Bali, with articles by Moşe Benbasat, from February 1953 until 1955; El Tiempo (The Times), published by Moshe ha-Levi Belman and

Isaac Kohen from June 1957 until 1959; and, finally, *Şalom*, which lasted from 29 October 1947 until the retirement of its editor, Avram Leyon (1912–1985), publishing its last issue on 28 December 1983.

Şalom was revived starting in 1984 by some younger Turkish Jews under the dynamic leadership of Naim Güleryüz, Nedim Yahya, Leon Haleva, Jako Molinas, Yakup Bensusen, Suzet Sidi and others. It is now published by the Gözlem Company, whose president is Izidor Barouh. It was edited by Leon Haleva from 1984 to 1987, and subsequently by Salamon Bicirano, with Silvyo Ovadya as Publication Administrator, all of whom have transformed it into a center of Turkish-Jewish life, though sometimes in opposition to the more conservative community establishment centered in the Chief Rabbinate. Published for the most part in Turkish, with only one page presented in Judeo-Spanish, it concentrates on important social and cultural issues such as the revival of Judeo-Spanish in the community, Jewish assimilation and intermarriage and the advancement of women's rights. A weekly Judeo-Spanish newspaper formerly published in Israel and regularly available in Turkey, *La Luz de Israel*, also provided older Turkish Jews with news, but with the constant decline of its readership, it ceased publication in 1990.

What are the main problems facing the community of Turkish Jews in the modern world?

The first and foremost problem is that of assimilation, very much as in other countries throughout the world. Now that Jews really are equal with Turks of other religions, now that they participate fully in Turkish life, now that they speak primarily Turkish, now that they go to Turkish schools along with Muslim Turks, and now that a growing number of young Turkish Jews are learning about Islam in the religious lessons taught in the public schools, the old prejudices on both sides have disappeared except among the most uneducated. Jews in education and business get along with other Turks without difficulty. Without persecution, then, the bonds which held many members close to, and under the control of, the community have loosened, to the regret of some who would prefer to retain the kind of tightly knit society which persecution forced on Jews in other countries and other times. Many of the strains which continue to exist within the Jewish community come from an increasing conflict between the Chief Rabbinate, which retains highly orthodox religious traditions, and the younger generation of Jews, who would prefer to follow the more secular rituals and practices accepted by most younger Jews in the United States, Europe and Israel. Some Turkish Jews have either become Muslims or have entirely abandoned religion in order to become part of the secular way of life established in Turkey by Mustafa Kemal Atatürk. Some also have intermarried with Muslim Turks, at a rate estimated by some as high as eight to ten percent a year, inevitably lessening their connections with the community.

Emigration of younger Jews to Israel, moreover, has left an increasingly older Jewish population in Turkey, with the birth rate, and the overall Jewish population, dropping accordingly.[13] Attendance in Jewish community schools has dropped precipitously, not only because of a decreasing number of school-age children but also because most Jewish families prefer to send their children to the far-better equipped and financed foreign or free state schools. At some point Turkish Jews will have to decide whether they really wish to be integrated or whether they want to preserve some sort of separate existence, which will inevitably require some inequality.

Equality also has created other problems. Because of the desire of the Turkish government to control the Muslim religious foundations, which exercised an extremely reactionary role in Ottoman life during the nineteenth century, strict controls were established over the revenues which had been set aside in foundations for all religious leaders and their institutions, appropriating them for the state treasury if their founders and administrators died without heirs or if the objectives of the foundation were no longer being fulfilled. These laws were intended for Muslim institutions, but they apply equally to Jewish foundations, which include all the Jewish synagogues and religious schools in the country. By present regulations, therefore, the Jewish community is regarded only as the administrator of such property and not as absolute owner, so that if the Jewish population moves away from the particular areas where these institutions are located, they are forfeit to the state treasury, thus lessening community property accordingly and depriving it of the income which could be derived if the property in question were sold. On the other hand, to balance this off, Jews are allowed to will their property as foundations to the community, particularly if they choose to leave the country, so there is little chance that it will wither on the vine, at least from this situation alone.

The foundation and continued existance of the state of Israel has created new strains in relations between some Turkish Muslims and Jews, since most of the former sympathize with the desire of the Palestinians to have their own state. This feeling would not have been particularly strong in the secular Turkish state had the European Economic Community not continued use various pretexts to keep Turkey out of full membership, thus making many Turks believe, with considerable justice, that Christian Europe is refusing to accept Turkey because it is predominantly a Muslim society.

Some of the Muslim states with which Turkey has developed closer diplomatic relations in recent years as a result, particularly Libya and Iran, have openly financed anti-Semitic as well as anti-secular and anti-Kemalist publications in Turkey, including several Istanbul newspapers, in which the most blatant anti-Semitic statements have appeared in

Vahdet, Milli Gazete, and *Zaman,* though at times the left-wing, intellectual *Cumhuriyet* has published similar remarks because of its strong support for Palestinian Arabs against Israel. The most blatant publications have been closed by the government in order to preserve public order and maintain good relations among the different religious groups. There have been as a result, however, verbal attacks on Jews, especially by extreme right-wing and Islamist organizations and politicians, particularly during electoral campaigns, with anti-Jewish slogans painted on the walls and leaflets distributed in Istanbul accusing Jews of 'exploiting the Turkish economy'. Most recently the Mayor of Urfa (Şanlıurfa), Ibrahim Halil Çelik, local leader of the extreme right-wing *Refah Partisi,* praised Hitler for his elimination of Jews and added other anti-Semitic remarks [14] which were condemned by Turkish and Jewish leaders alike.[15] While educated and active Muslims and Jews in Turkey develop close business and personal relationships without a trace of anti-Muslim or anti-Semitic feelings on either side, such attitudes continue to persist among the uneducated classes on both sides. No physical violence has resulted, however, and the vast majority of Turkish politicians have refrained from using this issue, mostly likely because of knowledge that it would not be received with favor by most Turks.

Arab terrorists at times have attacked both Israeli representatives and Turkish Jews and their institutions. In 1972 the Israeli Consul General in Istanbul, Yigal Alrom, was shot and killed by Arab terrorists, and in 1973 Arab terrorist bombs damaged the Israeli Pavilion at the Trade Fair held annually in Izmir. The most recent tragedy came on 6 September 1986 when Arab terrorists massacred twenty-three Jewish worshipers during services at Istanbul's Neve Şalom synagogue in Galata during the Sabbath morning services. (The synagogue was finally re-opened for services, after extensive repairs, on 20 May 1987.) This outrage elicited an extremely strong wave of horror throughout Turkey, however, with the funeral becoming a Turkish protest demonstration involving almost all Turkish political and social groups, quieting the fears of some Turkish Jews that they would be subject to increased popular abuse. Since that time the Turkish government has found that the incident was arranged by pro-Iranian terror groups active among the thousands of Iranian refugees in Turkey, and it has gone out of its way to prevent such incidents from recurring. Pro-Arab agitation, however, remains persistent among Arabs living in Turkey, however, leading most recently to the explosion of a small bomb at the Israeli Consulate General in Istanbul during the summer of 1989. As a result, many Turkish Jews feel less comfortable than in the past and try to avoid publicity and keep out of the limelight as much as possible.

Despite Turkey's support for United Nations resolutions favoring Palestinian demands against Israel, and despite diplomatic and economic pressure from the Muslim states toward which it would like to develop better relations, it has continued to maintain diplomatic relations with Israel, which it was one of the earliest states to recognize, on 31 March 1949, the only Muslim state to do so. It also has maintained strong economic relations with Israel, in 1985 importing $34.4 million worth of Israeli goods, the latter's largest customer outside the United States and the Common Market, while exporting $12.8 million in goods to Israel, principally chemicals, medicines and foodstuffs. Turkey continues its long tradition of receiving Jewish refugees from persecution, most recently thousands coming from Iran and Irak, and the Turkish intelligentsia, including many University professors, have continued to maintain close contacts with their Israeli counterparts, often spending their sabbatical leaves doing research in Israel while receiving Israeli scholars working in the Turkish archives and libraries.

Despite the problems, then, Turkish Jewry remains extremely comfortable, secure in its Turkish patriotism, strongly loyal to the Turkish Republic, and extremely resentful of outside non-Jewish nationalist groups that have tried to disturb that relationship for their own purposes by claiming that Turkish Jewry is being persecuted to attract the support of world Jewry for their national causes. The recent offer by the King of Spain to allow Sephardic Jews to return to Spain and resume their Spanish citizenship after a five-hundred year exile has been taken up by no-one in Turkey or elsewhere. Emigration to Israel by Turkish Jews has virtually come to an end, with the few still going doing so largely because of considerations of greater economic opportunities for private commercial enterprise rather than any sort of feelings of persecution or prejudice in Turkey.

While most of those who left after the establishment of the state of Israel have remained in their new home, moreover, an increasing awareness of their Turkish heritage has not only kept them together in Israel but also has led them to join in organizations to preserve and remember that heritage as well as all that the Turks did for them and their ancestors following the Spanish expulsion, with the Judeo-Spanish Israeli newspaper *La Luz de Israel* and the director of Israel radio *Kol Israel*'s Judeo-Spanish programs Moshe Shaul leading the way in reviving and preserving their traditions. At times also some of these emigrés have applied their wealth gained abroad to benefit all the people of Turkey. The most spectacular example of this was the case of Morris Shinasi, born in Manisa in 1855, who subsequently migrated to Egypt and then the United States in 1890, making a fortune in the manufacture of cigars. Following his death in 1929 he left a substantial amount of money which his wife used to establish in his name a public hospital in Manisa, the *Moris Şinasi Çocuk Hastanesi*, which continues to operate for the benefit of all the children of that city. Some of those Turkish Jews who went to Israel often return to Turkey, if not as permanent citizens at least to carry on part of their commercial and leisure activities in the land which gave their ancestors refuge and succor as well as freedom to nourish and develop their religious and cultural heritage for so many centuries.

The *500 üncü Yılı Vakıf* (Quincentennial Foundation) was founded during the summer of 1989 to coordinate the celebrations by Turks of all religions of the emigration of Spanish Jews to the Ottoman Empire in 1492. Chaired by the distinguished industrialist Jak V. Kamhi, its members include leading Jewish and Muslim Turks. Among the former are Chief Rabbi David Asseo, the advertising pioneer Eli Acıman, industrialists Ishak Alaton and Üzeyir Garih, the artist and poet Yosef Habib Gerez; Naim Güleryüz, Historian and Councellor to the Chief Rabbinate; the journalist Sami Kohen, businessman and industrialist Nedim Yahya, and Vitali Hakko, President of the *Vakko* department store chain. Among its Muslim members are the distinguished industrialists Nejat Eczacıbaşı and Sakip Sabancı, retired Ambassadors Tevfik Saracoğlu, Fuat Bayramoğlu and Behçet Türemen (General Secretary of the Foundation), Altemur Kılıç, editor of the national newspaper *Tercüman*, son of one of the major figures of the Turkish War for Independence Kılıç Ali, and historian Şinasi Orel, former Minister of Education.

The enthusiasm and dedication in which Turkish Jews and their many friends throughout the world are entering into the planned celebrations of the five hundredth anniversary of the exile from Spain and arrival in the Ottoman Empire is a fitting testimony to this heritage.

Appendixes

APPENDIX 1: GRAND RABBIS OF ISTANBUL AND THE OTTOMAN
EMPIRE, AND CHIEF RABBIS OF REPUBLICAN TURKEY

Grand Rabbis of Istanbul and the Ottoman Empire

Moses Capsali (1453?–1495?)
Elijah Mizrahi (1495?–1535?)

Grand Rabbis of Istanbul [1]

Tam ben Yahya (d. 1542)
Elie Benjamin ha-Levi (d. sometime after 1540)
Menahim Bahar Shmuel
Elie Ben Hayim (d. sometime after 1602)
Yahiel Bassan (d. 1625)
Joseph Mitrani (1625?–1639)
Yomtov ben Yaesh (1639–1660)
Yomtov ben Hanaya Benyakar (1660?–1677)
Haim Kamhi (d. 1730)
Juda Ben Rey (d. after 1721)
Judah ben Samuel Rosanes (to 1727)
Samuel Levi (1727–?)
Abraham ben Haim Rosanes (d. 1745)
Solomon Haim Alfandari (Grand Rabbi at accession of Mustafa III) (1757–1774)
Meir Ishaki
Elie Palombo (1762–?)
Haim Jacob Benyakar (still in office in 1807)

Grand Rabbis of Istanbul and the Ottoman Empire

Abraham ha-Levi	1835–1836 [2]
Shmuel Hayim	1837–1839 [3]
Moshe Fresco	1839–1841 [4]
Jacob Behar David	1841–1854 [5]
Hayim ha-Cohen	1854–1860 [6]
Yakub Avigdor	1860–1863 [7]
Yakir Geron	1863–1872 [8]
Moshe Levi	1872–1908 [9]
Haim Nahum	1908–1920 [10]
Shabetai Levi	1918–1919 [11]
Ishak Ariel	1919–1920 [12]

Chief Rabbis of the Turkish Republic

Hayim Moshe Bejerano	1920–1931 [13]
Rafael David Saban	1940–1960
David Asseo	1961–

APPENDIX 2:   POPULATION OF THE OTTOMAN EMPIRE IN THE LATE
NINETEENTH AND EARLY TWENTIETH CENTURIES ACCORDING TO
OFFICIAL OTTOMAN CENSUS REPORTS

Table 1 details the Empire totals; tables 2–12 the European provinces; and tables
13–49 the Anatolia and Asian provinces.

1. Empire Totals

Year	Totals	Jews	Muslims	Arm.Orth	Grk.Orth
1883	17,375,225	184,139	12,585,980	988,887	2,329,776
1897	19,050,307	215,425 [14]	14,111,945	1,042,374	2,569,912
1908	20,947,617	256,003	15,518,478	1,050,513	2,822,773
1914	18,520,016	187,073	15,044,846	1,294,851	1,792,206

2. Istanbul Province (Istanbul, Islands, Beyoğlu, Bosporus, Üsküdar, Şile)

Year	Totals	Jews	Muslims	Arm.Orth	Grk.Orth
1844 [15]	331,647	24,447	170,551	77,348	70,118
1856–7	378,069	26,301	181,174	72,173	85,631
1880–1	381,376	26,595	214,753	61,605	68,006
1883	873,565	44,361	384,910	149,550	152,741
1897	903,482	45,364	520,194	158,131	161,867
1908	782,231	47,779	370,343	59,963	157,165
1914	909,978	52,126	560,434	72,962	205,375

3. Şehir Emaneti (Çekmece, Gebze, Kartal, Şile, Adalar)[16]

Year	Totals	Jews	Muslims	Arm.Orth	Grk.Orth
1883	80,699	66	40,455	2,809	35,268
1908	82,335	–	61,320	1,736	19,277

4. Çatalca Sancak (Çatalca, Büyük Çekmece, Silivri)

Year	Totals	Jews	Muslims	Arm.Orth	Grk.Orth
1883	58,822	966	15,091	899	35,848
1897	61,001	1,003	16,320	929	36,520
1908	76,529	1,766	23,128	996	44,325
1914	59,756	1,480	20,048	842	36,797

5. Edirne Province (Edirne, Kirklareli, Tekfurdağı, Gallipoli)

Year	Totals	Jews	Muslims	Arm.Orth	Grk.Orth
1831[17]	421,721	2,128	158,249	247,666[18]	
1883	836,045	13,721	434,366	16,642	267,214[19]
1897	985,962	16,357	539,031	17,978	288,968
1908	1,154,344	23,939	639,189	25,954	340,788
1914	631,094	22,515	360,417	19,725	224,459

6. Salonica Province (Salonica, Seroz, Drama)

Year	Totals	Jews	Muslims	Arm.Orth	Grk.Orth
1831[20]	240,411	5,915	100,249	127,200[21]	
1883	990,400	37,206	447,864	201	277,237
1897	1,038,953	43,423	452,175	54	294,624
1908	922,359	52,395	419,604	637	263,881

7. Monastir Province (Monastir, Debre, Elbasan)

Year	Totals	Jews	Muslims	Arm.Orth	Grk.Orth
1883	664,399	5,072	225,534	29	227,766
1897	711,466	5,914	252,962	22	272,205
1908	824,808	5,459	328,531	8	286,001

8. Yanya (Janina) Province

Year	Totals	Jews	Muslims	Arm.Orth	Grk.Orth
1883	516,467	3,677	225,416	–	286,294
1897	516,681	4,144	221,475	–	287,812
1908	516,461	3,672	226,131	–	285,624

9. Işkodra (Scutari) Province

Year	Totals	Jews	Muslims	Arm.Orth	Grk.Orth
1883	87,372	–	78,600	–	5,913
1897	87,529	–	78,999	–	5,804
1908	89,848	–	81,222	6	6,098[22,23]

10. Kosovo Province

Year	Totals	Jews	Muslims	Arm.Orth	Grk.Orth
1883	721,342	1,711	409,732	–	29,393[24]
1897	754,634	1,885	432,178	1	36,420
1908	708,163	1,668	398,814	1	30,785[25]

11. Cezire-i Bahr-i Sefid/Aegean Islands Province/Dodecanese

Year	Totals	Jews	Muslims	Arm.Orth	Grk.Orth
1883	264,374	2,956	28,483	83	226,590 [26]
1897	286,736	3,033	30,578	10	253,066
1908	364,222	4,762	37,601	131	316,841 [27]

12. Biga Sancak

Year	Totals	Jews	Muslims	Arm.Orth	Grk.Orth
1883	118,824	1,755	99,468	1,731	15,100
1908	169,622	–	138,804	2,336	23,337

13. Erzurum Province (Erzincan, Refahiye, Kemah, Bayezid, Erzurum)

Year	Totals	Jews	Muslims	Arm.Orth	Grk.Orth
1883	394,968	–	312,306	73,857	3,356
1897	637,015	3	513,446	109,817	3,296
1908	675,855	10	551,506	110,310	5,822
1914	815,432	10	673,297	125,657	4,859

14. Adana Province (Adana, Qozan, Hacin, Kars, Aleppo, Tarsus, Ceyhan)

Year	Totals	Jews	Muslims	Arm.Orth	Grk.Orth
1883	384,365	–	350,376	32,815	6,262
1897	398,764	–	335,912	32,879	5,886
1908	504,426	98	435,825	47,047	11,067
1914	411,023	66	341,903	50,139	8,537

15. Ankara Province (Ankara, Çorum, Kirşehir,Yozgat)

Year	Totals	Jews	Muslims	Arm.Orth	Grk.Orth
1883	847,482	415	735,766	67,790	23,708
1897	1,018,826	693	895,196	74,031	36,767
1908	1,157,131	1,265	1,011,566	89,780	41,776
1914	953,817	1,026	877,285	44,507	20,226

16. Aydin Province (Aydın, Bergama, Menemen,Mağnisa,Denizli,Muş)

Year	Totals	Jews	Muslims	Arm.Orth	Grk.Orth
1883	1,408,387	22,273	1,118,496	13,940	195,431
1897	1,478,424	27,701	1,203,776	14,092	229,598
1908	1,727,287	32,761	1,313,011	36,542	284,905
1914	1,608,742	35,041	1,249,067	19,395	299,096

17. Bitlis Province (Bitlis, Siirt, Genc, Muş, Sassun, Malazgird)

Year	Totals	Jews	Muslims	Arm.Orth	Grk.Orth
1883	276,998	–	167,054	101,358	–
1897	338,642	–	224,772	101,586	–
1908	301,915	–	197,906	90,176	–[28]
1914	437,479	–	309,999	119,132	–

18. Beirut Province (Beirut, Nablus, Acre, Ladikiya, Tripoli)

Year	Totals	Jews	Muslims	Arm.Orth	Grk.Orth
1883	568,014	3,541	462,034	86	54,976
1897	620,763	8,825	505,019	89	57,131
1908	561,619	8,098	459,100	18	51,731
1914	824,873	15,052	648,314	1,188	87,244

19. Aleppo Province (Aleppo, Iskenderun, Antakya, Antep, Kilis)

Year	Totals	Jews	Muslims	Arm.Orth	Grk.Orth
1883	787,714	9,913	684,599	52,407	7,552
1897	819,238	10,761	712,585	53,465	7,816
1908	877,682	11,664	750,212	64,358[30]	8,920[31,32]
1914	667,790	12,193	576,320	35,104	13,772

20. Hudavendigar (Bursa) Province (Bursa, Inegöl, Yenişehir)

Year	Totals	Jews	Muslims	Arm.Orth	Grk.Orth
1883	1,336,492	3,037	1,132,761	46,823	133,017
1897	1,454,294	3,393	1,234,304	65,777	144,138
1908	1,691,277	4,337	1,430,498	77,865	166,368
1914	616,227	4,126	474,114	58,921	74,927

21. Diyarbekir Province (Diyarbekir, Mardin, Siverek, Viranşehir)

Year	Totals	Jews	Muslims	Arm.Orth	Grk.Orth
1883	368,970	1,051	289,591	46,823	1,010
1897	414,652	16,657	329,843	46,202	1,421
1908	394,123	1,165	315,569	43,524	1,125
1914	619,825	2,085	492,101	55,890	1,822

22. Suriya Province (Ba'labek, Biqa', Hawran, Damascus, Hama)

Year	Totals	Jews	Muslims	Arm.Orth	Grk.Orth
1883	400,748	6,277	338,931	199	29,399[33]
1897	551,134	6,897	476,434	336	35,720
1908	478,775	9,535	407,999	360[34]	33,170[35,36]
1914	918,409	10,140	791,582	413	60,978

23. Trablus Garb Province

Year	Totals	Jews	Muslims	Arm.Orth	Grk.Orth
1908	444,650	12,155	431,520	60[37]	780

24. Baghdad Province[38]

Year	Totals	Jews	Muslims	Arm.Orth	Grk.Orth
1883	197,756	12,715	150,108	349	33,270[39]
1897	187,285	14,567	171,398	256	–
1908	178,178	13,715	162,943	383[40]	–[41]

25. Basra Province[42]

Year	Totals	Jews	Muslims	Arm.Orth	Grk.Orth
1883	8,853	421	8,154	35	–
1897	80,071	441	79,261	33	5
1908	10,270	440	9,460	36[43]	–

26. Musul Province[44]

Year	Totals	Jews	Muslims	Arm.Orth	Grk.Orth
1883	186,111	4,286	164,593	45	–
1897	198,288	4,568	186,818	74	13
1908	161,148	4,165	148,162	45[45]	3[46]

27. Sivas Province (Sivas, Amasya, Tokat, Qarahisarsahib, Merzifon)

Year	Totals	Jews	Muslims	Arm.Orth	Grk.Orth
1883	926,564	209	766,559	116,266	37,813
1897	980,876	253	807,651	123,204	42,123
1908	1,193,679	299	973,480	145,046	65,690
1914	1,169,443	344	939,735	143,406	75,324

28. Trabzon Province (Trabzon, Lazistan,Gümüşhane, Ordu, Of)

Year	Totals	Jews	Muslims	Arm.Orth	Grk.Orth
1883	1,056,293	5	857,343	41,780	155,039
1897	1,164,595	1	933,728	47,196	181,044
1908	1,342,778	37	1,071,988	50,055	215,474
1914	1,122,947	8	921,128	37,049	161,574

29. Kastamonu Province (Kastamonu, Kangiri, Sinop, Safranbolu)

Year	Totals	Jews	Muslims	Arm.Orth	Grk.Orth
1883	949,116	–	929,300	3,373	14,539
1897	968,884	–	945,192	6,646	17,040
1908	1,105,419	67	1,072,240	9,809	22,861
1914	767,227	8	737,302	8,959	20,958

30. Konya Province (Konya, Burdur, Isparta, Akşehir, Karaağaç)

Year	Totals	Jews	Muslims	Arm.Orth	Grk.Orth
1883	944,009	216	877,226	9,813	56,534
1897	1,022,834	258	942,932	10,587	68,101
1908	1,249,777	262	1,145,713	15,537	86,561
1914	879,308	4	750,712	12,971	25,071

31. Mamuretulaziz Province (Malatya, Harput, Dersim, Mamuretulaziz)

Year	Totals	Jews	Muslims	Arm.Orth	Grk.Orth
1883	381,346	2	300,188	73,178	543[47]
1897	466,597	1	380,092	74,204	966
1908	474,370	–	390,794	67,512	651[48]
1914	538,227	14,807	446,379	76,070	971

32. Van Province (Van, Hakkari)

Year	Totals	Jews	Muslims	Arm.Orth	Grk.Orth
1883	119,860	–	59,412	60,448	–
1897	132,007	–	55,051	–	
1908	113,964	–	54,576	59,382	
1914	259,141	1,383	189,380	67,792	1

33. Eskişehir Sancak (Eskişehir, Sivrihisar, Mihalicik)

Year	Totals	Jews	Muslims	Arm.Orth	Grk.Orth
1914	152,726	728	140,578	8,276	2,613

34. Antalya Sancak (Antalya, Elmalı, Alaiye)

Year	Totals	Jews	Muslims	Arm.Orth	Grk.Orth
1914	249,686	250	235,762	630	12,385

35. Urfa Sancak (Urfa, Birecik, Rakka, Hawran)

Year	Totals	Jews	Muslims	Arm.Orth	Grk.Orth
1914	170,988	865	149,384	15,161	2

36. Iç Il Sancak (Iç Il, Anamur, Mut)

Year	Totals	Jews	Muslims	Arm.Orth	Grk.Orth
1914	105,194	10	102,034	341	2,500

37. Izmit Sancak (Izmit, Adapazarı, Give, Iznik, Karamursel)

Year	Totals	Jews	Muslims	Arm.Orth	Grk.Orth
1883	195,659	169	132,517	37,220	23,708
1897	228,443	199	155,565	43,611	27,722
1908	290,504	341	200,660	51,145	35,866
1914	325,153	428	226,859	55,403	40,048

38. Bolu Sancak (Bolu, Eregli, Bartin, Duzce, Zonguldak)

Year	Totals	Jews	Muslims	Arm.Orth	Grk.Orth
1914	408,648	20	399,281	2,961	5,146

39. Canik Sancak (Canik, Bafra, Fatsa, Çarşanba)

Year	Totals	Jews	Muslims	Arm.Orth	Grk.Orth
1914	393,302	37	265,950	27,058	98,739

40. Zor Sancak

Year	Totals	Jews	Muslims	Arm.Orth	Grk.Orth
1883	38,652	2	33,863	83	–
1897	51,260	2	50,767	365	2
1908	60,854	3	60,373	60[49]	12[50]
1914	66,294	2	65,779	67	18

41. Kudüs Sancak (Jerusalem, Yaffa, Gaza, Halilurrrahman)

Year	Totals	Jews	Muslims	Arm.Orth	Grk.Orth
1883	234,774	8,110	199,613	939	16,706[51]
1897	258,860	11,909	217,346	825	19,070
1908	231,209	7,883	197,701	706	15,885[52]
1914	328,168	21,259	266,044	1,310	26,035

42. Kara Hisar Sahib Sancak (Karahisarsahib, Bolvadin, Aziziye)

Year	Totals	Jews	Muslims	Arm.Orth	Grk.Orth
1914	285,820	7	277,659	7,437	632

43. Kayseri Sancak

Year	Totals	Jews	Muslims	Arm.Orth	Grk.Orth
1914	263,074	0	184,292	52,192	26,590

44. Kalai Sultaniye Sancak

Year	Totals	Jews	Muslims	Arm.Orth	Grk.Orth
1914	165,815	3,642	149,303	2,541	8,550

45. Karesi Sancak

Year	Totals	Jews	Muslims	Arm.Orth	Grk.Orth
1914	472,970	362	359,804	8,704	97,497

46. Kütahya Sancak

Year	Totals	Jews	Muslims	Arm.Orth	Grk.Orth
1914	316,894	243	303,348	4,548	8,755

47. Maraş Sancak

Year	Totals	Jews	Muslims	Arm.Orth	Grk.Orth
1914	192,555	251	152,645	38,433	34

48. Menteşe Sancak

Year	Totals	Jews	Muslims	Arm.Orth	Grk.Orth
1914	210,874	1,615	188,916	12	19,923

49. Niğde Sancak

Year	Totals	Jews	Muslims	Arm.Orth	Grk.Orth
1914	291,117	0	227,100	5,705	53,312

Sources:
1883: Istanbul University Library, Manuscript TY 4807.
1897: Nezaret-i Umum-u Ticaret ve Nafia, Istatistik-i Umumi Idaresi, *Devlet-i Aliye-i Osmaniyenin 1313 senesine mahsus Istatistik-i Umumisidir* (Istanbul, 1316/1900).
1908: Istanbul University Library, Manuscript TY 947.
1914: *Tableaux indiquant le nombre des divers éléments de la population dans l'Empire Ottoman au 1er Mars 1330 (14 Mars 1914)* (Constantinople, 1919). The detailed figures forming the basis for this report can be consulted in the historical archives of the Turkish General Staff, Ankara (Genelkurmay Harb Tarih Arşivi, A 1–2, D 1016, F 2–1 to 2–25).

APPENDIX 3: JEWISH POPULATION IN THE TURKISH REPUBLIC, 1927–1965

Province	Year of Census				
	1927	1945	1955	1960	1965
TOTALS	81,872	76,965	45,995	43,928	38,267
Adana	159	n/a	n/a	218	n/a
Afyonkarahisar	11	3	0	0	4
Amasya	23	121	2	7	26
Ankara	663	1,565	578	648	671
Antalya	38	1	4	9	3
Aydın	15	8	0	5	0
Balıkesir	43	43	6	25	16
Bilecik	4	1	0	0	3
Bolu	2	0	2	0	7
Burdur	1	0	0	2	2
Bursa	1,915	1,103	382	373	331
Çanakkale	1,845	1,433	553	555	496
Diyarbekir	392	441	21	12	34
Edirne	6,098	2,441	638	438	312
Elâziğ	1	21	22	6	1
Erzincan	0	22	2	8	6
Erzurum	0	1	41	15	8
Eskişehir	25	45	33	3	7
Gaziantep	742	327	151	141	152
Giresun	6	1	0	0	1

Hakkâri	43	34	2	1	0
Hatay	Syria	263	162	158	195
İçel	0	495	106	90	44
İstanbul	47,035	49,452	36,914	35,485	30,831
İzmir	18,157	15,784	5,383	5,067	4,067
Kars	1	33	52	41	5
Kayseri	15	178	4	3	22
Kirklareli	978	378	110	156	45
Kırşehir	3	64	0	0	0
Kocaeli	5	64	7	26	52
Konya	17	148	18	4	47
Kütahya	19	2	1	0	7
Malatya	8	55	7	0	5
Manisa	278	308	26	16	23
Maraş	265	211	12	24	0
Mardin	490	17	7	12	9
Mersin	122	n/a	n/a	n/a	n/a
Muğla	291	280	31	59	36
Niğde	0	12	3	0	1
Ordu	2	4	0	0	4
Sakarya	n/a	n/a	1	18	6
Samsun	95	76	15	17	8
Seyhan	n/a	187	n/a	n/a	n/a
Sinop	0	0	2	7	11
Sıvas	6	77	31	7	21
Tekirdağ	1,481	n/a	339	239	170
Tokat	92	0	6	2	9
Trabzon	3	0	3	1	1
Urfa	318	234	11	2	14
Van	129	132	76	9	91
Yozgat	23	5	2	1	201
Zonguldak	18	6	2	0	13

Sources:
1927. Republique Turque, Presidence du Conseil, Office Central de Statistique, *Istatistik Yıllığı/Annuaire Statistique* V (1931–2) (Istanbul, 1932): '1927 Umumi Nüfus Tahriri', pp. 68–69.
1945. Republique Turque, Présidence du Conseil, Office Central de Statistique, *21 Ekim 1945 Genel Nüfus Sayımı/Recensement Général de la Population du 21 Octobre 1945* (Ankara, 1950).
1955. Republic of Turkey, Prime Ministry, General Statistical Office, *23 Ekim 1955 Genel Nüfus Sayımı/Census of Population, 23 October 1955/Türkiye Nüfusu/Population of Turkey* (Ankara, 1961).
1960. Republic of Turkey, Prime Ministry, State Institute of Statistics, *23 Ekim 1960 Genel Nüfus Sayımı: Türkiye Nüfusu/Census of Population, 23 October 1960, Population of Turkey* (Ankara, 1965).
Republic of Turkey, Prime Ministry, State Institute of Statistics, *23 Ekim 1965 Genel Nüfus Sayımı: Türkiye Nüfusu/Census of Population, 23 October 1965: Population of Turkey* (Ankara, 1970).

Note:
The Turkish Department of Census did not count people by religion starting with the 1970 census by order of the Council of Ministers.

APPENDIX 4:   POPULATION OF ISTANBUL BY RELIGION,
1883 STATISTICS AND 1927 CENSUS

	Old Istanbul	Islands	Bakırköy	Beyoğlu	Üsküdar	Total 1927	Total 1883
Muslims	191,039	4,052	9,826	145,140	98,794	447,851	384,910
Catholics	723	410	146	19,793	1,497	22,569	6,442
Protestants	384	41	36	3,384	444	4,289	819
Orthodox	19,137	6,039	1,925	63,284	8,697	99,082	152,741
Armenians	18,545	1,014	1,117	23,517	8,386	52,579	149,590
Jews	9,600	274	239	32,227	4,308	46,698	44,361
Other Chs.	6,296	464	1,101	6,059	2,027	15,957	5,396[53]
Other rel.	169	8	9	866	152	1,204	129,243[54]
Unknown*	89	8	10	470	51	628	
TOTAL						690,857	873,565

Note:
Other Chs. – Other Christians
Other rel. – Other religions
* Unknown/none.

Sources:
1883: Istanbul University Library, Manuscript TY 4807 and 1927: T.C. Istatistik Umum Müdürlüğü, *Istatistik Yıllığı, Cilt 5, 1931/32* (Ankara, 1932), pp. 80–81.

APPENDIX 5:   OFFICIAL TURKISH JEWISH COMMUNITY RENUNCIATION
OF SPECIAL PRIVILEGES PROVIDED BY THE
TREATY OF LAUSANNE, ARTICLE 42, 15 SEPTEMBER 1925.
Translation of French text in Galante, *Turcs* VIII, 31–36

Following the acceptance and proclamation of the principle separating religion from the affairs of State, the same principle as in other civilized countries, and following the decision relative to the elaboration of all laws on purely secular bases, an extraordinary session, presided over by the Grand Rabbi, and attended by members of the lay, religious and general councils as well as the notables of the community, was convoked at the Grand Rabbinate to discuss the new situation created regarding the fixing of family rights and of personal statute, and in the course of this meeting the following resolutions were taken, which we consider to be our duty to submit to our Republican government.

If it is true that in virtue of article 42 of the Treaty of Lausanne dispositions regarding ways and customs should be defined by a commission, it should be noted that when this treaty was signed, our national government, taking into consideration personal statues and family laws, which find their source in Muslim religious principles and which cannot be applied to non Muslim minorities, agreed to fix and apply special dispositions for each of the minorities. But as a result of the complete separation of religion from things of this world, and in view of the fact that all laws, without exception, are being elaborated and applied outside of all religious ideas and considerations and conforming to the needs of the country and to the progress of contemporary law, there is no longer any need to elaborate dispositions relative to the family laws of Jews; and to the contrary the elaboration of such exceptions would signify the preservation for Jews of a personal statute based on secular principles. In addition, it has been proven by experience and by historic witness that Jews not only have never been indifferent to political and social revolutionary movements of the countries in which they live but rather, to the contrary, they have taken part in them and have added their influence. From another point of view, since the political and general order of the Turkish republic is completely based on separation of religion from the things of this world, the Jews who have always considered themselves to be true children of this country cannot conceive of any incapability regarding the application, for them, of exceptions, which would be in contradiction with this principle and the obligations of patriotism. Given then that the personal statute which is now being elaborated is inspired by the principles accepted in all civilized countries and of our civil and social rights, we have no doubt that it will satisfy all the civil and social needs of all Turks inhabiting Turkey as well as Jewish Turks.

There remains only the question of marriage and divorce. Jews who want to satisfy their religious sentiments can, as is done in Europe and America, address themselves, relying on freedom of conscience proclaimed and affirmed by the organic statute of the Republic, to the Grand Rabbinates in their religious centers so as to accomplish their religious ceremonies after first conforming to the dispositions of secular law, which constitutes no legal impediment. As a result, taking into consideration what we have said, we Turkish Jews accept the vow from which we profit as well as the other civil laws and secular dispositions that the Republican government publishes relative to personal statute and family rights, and we present the sentiments of our gratitude.

Notes

DEDICATION

1. Mustafa Kemal Atatürk statement to a press conference in Izmir on 2 February 1923, reported in the newspapers *Sadayı Hak* and *Anadolu* on 3 February 1923. See Abraham Galante, *Türkler ve Yahudiler* (Istanbul, 1949), 86; and Naim Güleryüz, '1992'a doğru', *Şalom* (Istanbul), 26 September 1984.

CHAPTER 1: INGATHERING OF THE JEWS

1. Starr, 89.
2. Starr, 147.
3. Yvonne Friedman, 'Antijüdischen Polemik des 12 jahrhunderts', *Kairos* XXVI/1–2 (1984), 80–88.
4. Baron, XVII, 21.
5. Tamir, 38–39.
6. V.S. Kiselkov, *Zhitie it podvizi na nashiya prepodoben Otets Teodosi* (Sofia, 1926), 19–21, quoted in Tamir, 39.
7. The word *ta'ife* also was used, especially in the earlier centuries, but for purposes of simplicity the word *millet* will be used consistently in this study.
8. M. Lattes, *Likkutim de-Vei Eliyahu*, 7, quoted in 'Ottoman Empire', *EJ* XVI, 1532.
9. *Seder Eliyahu Zuta*, by Rabbi Eliyahu Capsali, vol. I, ed. Aryeh Shmuelevitz (Jerusalem, 1975), 81; English translation: Bowman, 315–16.
10. The brilliant Ph.D. dissertation produced in 1978 at the Hebrew University of Jerusalem by Joseph Hacker, *Ha-hevra ha-yehudit be-Saloniqi ve 'agapeha ba-me'ot ha-15 veha-16. Pereq be-toledot ha-hevra ha-yehudit ba-'imperia ha-'otmanit vihaseha im ha-siltonot* (Jewish Society at Salonica and its environs in the 15th and 16th century. A chapter of history of Jewish society in the Ottoman Empire), analyzes this famous letter and its various versions, concluding that the author in fact was the contemporary Istanbul Jewish philosopher Mordehai ben Eliezer Comtino (1430–80).
11. His family continued to lead the Jewish community of Edirne until 1722.
12. Argenti, 150–52; see also I. Loeb, 'Epistle from Salonica, 1550', REJ, XV (1887), 270–72.
13. Zinberg, 5–6.
14. Rosanes I, 60; Capsali, Seder Eliyahu Zuta, pp. 218–19; Abraham Galante, *Istanbul*, I, 123; Barnai, p. 19.
15. Franco, 37; Galante, *Istanbul* I, 123–24.
16. Zinberg, 4.
17. Repeated by Sultan Abdül Aziz on 25 July 1865, as related in Galante, *Turcs et Juifs*, pp. 29–30, and Güleryüz, 'Türkiye Yahudileri Tarihi: I. Rodos'un fethi, Mısır Isyanı ve Budin'in fethi', *Şalom*, 6 November 1875.

CHAPTER 2: THE GOLDEN AGE OF OTTOMAN JEWRY

1. The provincial census figures have been derived from the Ottoman
    Cadastal Records, as cited in Mark Epstein, *The Ottoman Jewish Com-
    munities and their role in the Fifteenth and Sixteenth Centuries* (Freiburg, K.
    Schwarz, 1980). Scholars have never determined exactly how many people
    constituted an Ottoman household (*hane*) but I calculate seven persons per
    Jewish household.
2. Goldman, *Zimra*, 86.
3. D. Grabrijan and J. Neidhardt, *Architektura Bosne i put u suvremeno* (The
    Architecture of Bosnia and the way to Modernity) (Sarajevo, 1957),
    p. 50.
4. Goldman, *Zimra*, 89–90, from the *Responsa of Rabbi David Ibn Abi Zimra*,
    vol. III (Warsaw, 1882) III, no. 518, I, no. 378.
5. Goldman,*Zimra*, 90–91, from the Manuscript of the Responsa of Rabbi
    David Ibn Abi Zimra, in the Library of the Jewish Theological Seminary,
    New York, p. 44a.
6. Goldman, *Zimra*, 87–88.
7. This discussion of Ottoman synagogue names is based on the work of
    Güleryüz, 'Sinagoglarımızın Isimleri ve Anlamları', *Şalom* (Istanbul), 9
    January 1985; additional information has been derived from Abraham
    Galante, *Istanbul*, I, 285–299 and *Les Juifs de Constantinople sous Byzance*
    (Istanbul, 1940), reprinted in Galante, *Turquie* I, 30–38.
8. Juhasz, 'Costume', Juhasz, p. 126.

CHAPTER 3: DECLINE OF OTTOMAN JEWRY IN THE SEVENTEENTH AND EIGHTEENTH CENTURIES

1. The original language remained as *Ladino*, preserved largely untouched
    to provide translations of the Holy Books of the Jewish religion, with the
    Hebrew Rashi letters increasingly used for both in place of the Latin script
    brought originally from Spain.
2. Starting in 1693, the French government sent a series of orders to
    its ambassador in Istanbul and consuls around the Ottoman Empire
    forbidding them from protecting Jews. See, for example, Archives
    Nationales (Paris), Archives de la Marine, B7 61: fol. 596v. Dispatch
    from the Bureau du Levant to sieur de Riants, Consul at Izmir, 5
    August 1693; fol. 597–597v. Dispatch of the Bureau of the Levant
    to sieur de Magy, French consul of Cairo, 5 August 1693; fol.
    597–597v. Dispatch from Bureau de Levant to M. de Castagnères,
    French ambassador to Istanbul, 2 December 1693; fol. 633. Dispatch
    from Bureau de Levant to M. de Riants, French consul at Izmir,
    2 December 1693. 'The intention of the King is that you execute
    regarding the Jews the last orders that you have received and
    that you deprive them of the protection of France ... to force
    them to increase the price of their merchandise and the customs
    taxes that they will be forced to pay, or make a lesser profit in
    their commerce ... '; fol. 643v. Dispatch from Bureau du Levant to
    M. de Castaguères, French Ambassador to Istanbul, 10 December
    1693.

CHAPTER 4: THE REVIVAL OF OTTOMAN JEWRY IN THE NINETEENTH AND TWENTIETH CENTURIES

1. The original Ottoman text is in BVA *Cevdet Adliye* 6/550 and *Gayri Muslim* 18, pp. 31–33; a French translation can be found in Galante, *Istanbul* I 375–79.
2. The relevant passages of the two Imperial Rescripts are given in Galante, *Documents* V, 6–10; Franco, 143–51.
3. Regulation of 6 August 1910: text in Galante, *Documents* V, 28–30; see also Nehama VII, 539.
4. Aron Rodrigue, 'The Alliance Israélite Universelle and the attempt to reform Jewish religious and rabbinical instruction in Turkey', *L'Alliance dans les communautés du bassin méditerranéen a la fin du 19ème siècle*, ed. Simon Schwarzfuchs (Jerusalem, 1987), pp. LIII-LXXX.
5. The *Irade* of 2 Safar 1280/20 July 1863: text in Galante, *Documents* V, 12.
6. The original manuscript text of the Grand Rabbinate Organic Statute/*Hahambaşılık Nizamnamesi*, dated 22 Şeval 1281/19 February 1865 is found in the BA, Istanbul, *Buyuruldu* register V, 132–39; It was published in *Dustur* II (1289/1873), 962–75; its French translation, dated 23 Şevval 1281/1 April 1864, is found in Galante, *Documents* V (Istanbul, 1987), 13–26; it was also published separately in Judeo-Spanish as *Statuko Organiko de la Komunidad Israelita*, and *La konstitusion para la nasion israelita de Turkia* (Istanbul, Estamparia del Jurnal Israelit, 5625/1865).
7. As opposed to 168 Greek orthodox districts, 26 and 13 bishoprics respectively for the Armenian Gregorians and Catholics.
8. For appointment *berats* of these chief rabbis, see BBA register *Gayri Muslim*, vol. 18.
9. 26 Safar 1308/29 September 1306. BA, Istanbul, *Meclisi Mahsus* 1347; *Nizamiye* V, 15.
10. Juhacz, 'Costume', Juhacz, p. 127.
11. *Etz ha-Haim*, founded in Byzantine times, *Gerush*, constructed in the fifteenth century by Iberian refugees, *Portugal*, which centered the opponents of Shabbatai Tzvi during the late seventeenth century, *Galante*, built by one of Tzvi's partisans, Rabbi Moise Galante, the first to declare that Tzvi was the true Messiah, *Mahazike Torah* (Sonsino), built in 1722 and repaired after fires in 1838 and 1850, *Shalom*, founded in the time of Rabbi Escapa, *Talmud Torah*, repaired after fires in 1839 and 1842, *Bikur Holim*, founded by a Dutch refugee Solomon de Ciaves in 1724, restored after a fire in 1800, *Algazi* (*Kal de ariva*), built in 1724, *Geveret* (*Seniora*), built by a Dutch Jewess Osbio, and *Orahim* (*Forasteros*), built by foreign Jews, both rebuilt after the great Izmir fire of 1841.
12. Juhacz, 'Costume', p. 127.
13. The text of the 1911 Organic Statutes organizing both the Central Administration and the *Bet Din* of Izmir are in Galante, *Anatolie* III, 223–248.
14. Shlomo Rozanes, *Korot Hayehudim Beturkiyah Vebeartzot Hakedem: Hadorot Haachronim* (Jerusalem, 1945), pp. 42–44, cited in Yitzchak Kerem, 'The Influence of Anti Semitism on Jewish Immigration Patterns from Greece to the Ottoman Empire in the 19th Century', pp. 2, 14.
15. Maxime Raybaud, *Memoires sur la Grece, pour servir a l'histoire de la Guerre de l'Independence* (2 vols, Paris, 1824), pp. 5–19; Galante, *Turcs et Juifs* (Istanbul, 1932), 76–77.

16. Rev. T. S. Hughes, *Travels in Greece and Albania* (2nd edn, 2 vols, London, 1830), II, 194–95.
17. Rev. John Hartley, *Researches in Greece and the Levant* (London, 1831), 207, quoted in Yitzchak Kerem, 'Jewish Immigration Patterns from Greece to the Ottoman Empire in the Nineteenth Century', published paper delivered at the *Comité International d'Etudes Pré-Ottomanes et Ottomanes, VIII Symposium, 'Decision-Making and the Transmission of Authority in the Turkic System'*, University of Minnesota, Minneapolis, Minnesota, 14–19 August 1988, p. 4.
18. Hartley, *ibid.*, pp. 206–7. William Martin Leake, *Travels in Northern Greece* (2 vols, London, 1835) II, 231–32, 609; Errikos Sevillas, *Athens-Auschwitz* (Athens, 1983), p. ix, quoted in Kerem, *ibid.*, p. 14.
19. Documented in Kerem, *ibid.*, pp. 14–19. Pearl L. Preschel, *The Jews of Corfu (Greece)*, Unpublished Ph.D. dissertation, New York University, 1984. George Finlay, *History of the Greek Revolution* (London, 1861), 172, 179–86; See also 'Greece', *EJ* VII, 876–77.
20. Yoannina Vasdraveli, *Ee Thessaloniki: Kata Ton Agona Tis Aneksantizias* (Salonica, 1946), pp. 19–35; Yitzchak Kerem, *An Outline of the History of the Jews of Salonica* (in Hebrew) (Museum of Kibbutz Lohama, Getaot, 1985), p. 21, quoted in Kerem, *ibid.*, p. 15.
21. Kerem, *ibid.*, pp. 8–12. 'The Persecution of the Jews', *Times* (London), 16 May 1891; A. Ablagon to AIU, 19 October 1898, AIU, *Grèce* VIII.B.34. Schaki (Larissa) to A.I.U., 23 August/4 September 1893, *BAIU, Grèce, Deuxième Série*, no. 18, 1er et 2e Semestre, 1893); Elia Fraggi (Larissa) to AIU, 5 June 1874, AIU Grèce, I.C.22; Larissa AIU representatives to AIU, 23 June/5 July 1897, *AIU, Grèce* II.B.16; Jewish community of Canea leaders in Samos to AIU, 3 March, 1897, AIU, *Grèce* VIII.B.35.
22. Rumanian persecution of its Jews is described in detail in Carol Iancu, *Les Juifs en Roumanie, 1866–1919* (University of Provence, France, 1978).
23. Haim Keshales, *Korot Yehudey Bulgariya* (History of Bulgaria's Jews), vol. 1 (Tel Aviv, 1971); Tamir, 93–94; FO 195/1184, no. 15, Blunt to Layard, Edirne, 7 January 1877.
24. The original of this document was found in the Başbakanlık Arşivi, Istanbul S.II, Karton 108, Dosya 27 by retired Turkish Ambassador Ilhan Akant; it later was expanded by the Secretary-General of the *AIU*, Isadore Loeb, into a major study, *La Situation des Israélites en Turquie, en Serbie et en Roumanie* (Paris, 1877).
25. *BAIU no. 29, Année 1904* (Paris, 1904), pp. 53–55.
26. Pearl L. Preschel, *The Jews of Corfu (Greece)*, Unpublished Ph.D. dissertation, New York University, 1984.
27. Leon Sciaky, *Farewell to Salonica: Portrait of an Era* (New York, 1946); Edgar Morin, *Vidal et les Siens* (Paris, Seuil, 1989), 55–67; Paul Dumont, 'The social structure of the Jewish community of Salonica at the end of the nineteenth century', *Southeastern Europe* V (1979), 33–72; Galante, *Turcs* VIII, 18–21; Rodrigue, pp. 178–80.
28. A. Cohen, Ecole Secondaire Moise Allatini, Salonica, to AIU, Paris, no. 7745/7, 4 December 1912, in AIU Archives I C 49.
29. Mizrahi, President of AIU at Salonica, to AIU (Paris), no. 2704/3, 25 July 1913. In AIU Archives (Paris) I C 51.
30. no. 2416/8, 21 December 1912 (AIU Archives II C 13)
31. to AIU (Paris) no. 2096/2 (10 May 1912) (AIU Archives II C 12)
32. AIU Archives II C 8.

33. Robert Mantran, 'La structure sociale de la communauté juive de Salonqiue a la fin du dix-neuvième siècle', *RH* no. 534 (1980), 384–89; David Kushner, 'Intercommunal Strife in Palestine during the Late Ottoman Period', *AAS* XVIII (1984), 187–204, particularly pp. 192–99.Detailed references regarding Christian attacks on Ottoman Jews can be found in S. J. Shaw, 'Christian Anti-Semitism in the Ottoman Empire', to be published in *Belleten* (1991).

34. See, for example, the reports of A. Eskenazi (Istanbul) to the AIU (Paris), 5 July 1897, 26 March 1901, 1 June 1899, and 27 June 1898, in AIU Archives (Paris) II C 7. Also the report in *El Tiempo*, 11 and 12 May and 1 June 1899. Jews were attacked in the Salonica newpaper *L'Acropolis* on May 2, 1897, with the accusation that they were profaning churches. Robert Mantran, 'La structure sociale de la communauté juive de Salonqiue a la fin du dix-neuvième siècle', *RH* no. 534 (1980), 387–88.

35. H. H. Jessup, *Fifty Three Years in Syria* (2 vols, London, 1910), II, 424–25.

36. Galante, *Documents*, V, 126–129, 172–81.

37. M. Franco, 'Les Juifs de l'Empire Ottoman au Dix Neuvième Siècle', *REJ*, XVI (1893), 126; Güleryüz, 'Türkiye Yahudileri Tarihi: 19. Yüzyıl: Tanzimat Dönemi', *Şalom*, 6 August 1986; Franco, 145.

38. M. Franco, 'Les Juifs de l'Empire Ottoman au Dix Neuvième Siècle', *REJ*, XVI (1893), 126.

39. *El Tiempo*, 28 April 1926; Galante, *Istanbul* I, 185; Galante, *Documents* V, 340–41.

40. FO 78/430, enclosed in Baring no. 207 to Lord Salisbury, Cairo, 25 June 1890, reprinted in Landau, 'Ritual Murder Accusations', p. 450.

41. Jacob Landau, 'Ritual Murder Accusations and Persecutions of Jews in Nineteenth Century Egypt', *Sefunot* V (1961), 425–27; for example see report in BAIU, first semestre 1881, pp. 66–67. Galante also reported similar difficulties with the Greek religious leaders while he was teaching in Rhodes.

42. Ashkenazi Community, Çorlu, to AIU no. 8783, 2 May 1902, in AIU Archives (Paris) II C 8, with report printed in *El Tiempo* of 1 May 1902.

43. Güleryüz, 'Türkiye Yahudileri Tarihi: 19. yüzyıl sona ererken (2)', *Şalom*, 19 November 1986.

44. Robert Mantran, 'La structure sociale de la communauté juive de Salonqiue a la fin du dix-neuvième siècle', *RH* no. 534 (1980), 388; D. Levi, Ecole des Garçons, Rodosto, to AIU, 6 May 1920 (AIU Archives I C 33) describes a typical Greek blood libel incident at Gallipoli in 1920.

45. Galanté, *Istanbul*, 134–35. *El Tiempo*, 28 May 1920; Galante, *Documents* V, 181–96; Galante, *Nouveau Recueil de Nouveaux Documents Inedits concernant l'Histoire des Juifs de Turquie* (Istanbul, 1952), reprinted in Galante, *Turquie* VI, 324.

46. The fire drove out 55,000 Jews, 10,000 Christians and 10,000 Muslims; see 'Saloniko en Flamas: el Fuego del 18–19 Agosto 1917', *Şalom*, 3 October 1984; Loni Çakon, 'Yunanistan Yahudileri', *Şalom*, 17 February 1988; and Turkmen Parlak, *Yeni Asrin Selanik Yılları, 1895–1924* (Izmir, 1989).

47. Robert Mantran, 'La structure sociale de la communauté juive de Salonqiue a la fin du dix-neuvième siècle', *RH* no. 534 (1980), 391–92; Nehama VII, 762; Joseph Nehama (Salonica) to AIU (Paris) no. 2868/2, 12 May 1903 (AIU Archives I-C-43); and no. 2775, 10 January 1900 (AIU Archives I-C-41), describing daily battles between Jewish and Greek children in the streets of Salonica. Benghiat, Director of Ecole Moise Allatini, Salonica, to AIU (Paris), no. 7784, 1 December 1909 (AIU Archives I-C-48), describing Greek

attacks on Jews, boycotts of Jewish shops and manufactures, and Greek press campaigns leading to blood libel attacks. Cohen, Ecole Secondaire Moise Allatini, Salonica, to AIU (Paris), no. 7745/4, 4 December 1912 (AIU Archives I-C-49) describes a week of terror that followed the Greek army occupation of Salonica in 1912, with the soldiers pillaging the Jewish quarters and destroying Jewish synagogues, accompanied by what he described as an 'explosion of hatred' by the local Greek population against local Jews and Muslims. Mizrahi, President of the AIU at Salonica, reported to the AIU (Paris), no. 2704/3, 25 July 1913 (AIU Archives I-C-51), that 'It was not only the irregulars (Comitadjis) that massacred, pillaged and burned. The Army soldiers, the Chief of Police, and the high civil officials also took an active part in the horrors . . . ', Moise Tovi (Salonica) to AIU (Paris) no. 3027 (20 August 1913) (AIU Archives I-C-51) describes the Greek pillage of the Jewish quarter during the night of 18–19 August 1913.

48. See the Appendix.
49. BAIU no. 18 (1893), pp. 38–39.
50. Report of Grand Rabbi Haim Nahum Efendi (Istanbul) to AIU (Paris) no. 6187/2, 15 September 1908, in AIU Archives I C 1, regarding his visit to Armenian Patriarch Izmirliyan: 'Il etait en fonctions lors des massacre des Armenians, comme le bas peuple juif de Haskeuy avait joué un role en aidant les Kurds a decouvrir la retrait des fugitifs, il reste encore dans le coeur des Armenièns une haine pour les Juifs . . . ' Also: Guéron (Hasköy) to AIU (Paris) no. 4750, 21 September 1896, and Bloch (Istanbul) to AIU no. 9479, 12 April 1887, in AIU Archives I C 7.
51. BA, *MVM* (Minutes of the Council of Ministers), 19 October 1881; *Levant Herald*, 24 November 1881.
52. For example see *BAIU no. 7, 2e Semestre 1883* (Paris, 1883), pp. 8–10.
53. D. Nabon to AIU (Paris) no. 2612, 17 December 1890, and no. 4060, 16 May 1893, both in AIU Archives (Paris), I C 7.
54. Fresco (Istanbul) to AIU (Paris), 1 August, 19 August and 30 August 1900 (AIU Archives II-C-8). *El Tiempo*, 20 May 1900.
55. See, for example, the reports of E. Benforado, AIU Boy's School, Edirne, to AIU (Paris), 14 June 1882 (in AIU Archives I C 1), of I. Dalem (Istanbul) no. 7132/2 of 23 September 1891, and of I. Behor, of the Kuzguncuk Boys School, to the AIU (Paris) no. 8347, of 17 June 1892, all in AIU Archives I C 7.
56. Friedman, *Herzl, 3*; *Herzl Year Book*, ed. Raphael Patai (New York, 1961–62) IV, 236–38.
57. *Note Verbale* from Sublime Porte to American Embassy, Istanbul, 4 October 1888; United States Department of State, *Papers on Foreign Relations* II, 1619; FO 195/1607, White to Moore, 6 October 1888; Mandel, 'Ottoman Policy', 323.
58. Dated 19 June 1896: Theodore Herzl, *Diaries*, I, 378; quoted in Mandel, 'Ottoman Policy', 317, and *Arabs*, 11; and Friedman, *Herzl*, 132.
59. BA Yıldız Esas Arşivi ÇII/35–37/54/136; Turkish Foreign Ministry Archives/*Hazinei Evrak* 332/17 no. 9550/63, 29 April 1898; and 332/17 no. 27849/21; quoted in Jacob Landau and Mim Kemal Öke, 'Ottoman Perspectives on American Interests in the Holy Land', *With Eyes Toward Zion*, ed. Moshe Davis, Boulder Colorado (1986), 265.
60. M. Nathan, AIU teacher at Galata to AIU 14 May 1935 (no. 4442/15: Archives of the AIU, Paris II C 8) and M. Fresco report to the AIU (Paris)

on 28 July 1908 (no. 6030), and on 3 August 1908 (no. 6052) (Archives of the AIU II C 8).

61. This account of the life of Haim Nahum Efendi is based on interviews conducted with him in Cairo by the author on January 15, 22 and 23 and March 3 and 5, 1956; and on the brilliant Ph.D. dissertation by Esther Benbassa (Dudonney), *Haim Nahum Efendi, dernier grand rabbin de l'Empire Ottoman (1908–1920), son role politique et diplomatique*, Paris, Université de Paris II (Sorbonne Nouvelle), Doctorat d'Etat es Lettres, 1987, partly published as *Un Grand Rabbin Sepharade en Politique, 1892–1923* (Paris, CNRS, 1990).

62. Benbassa, 112–15; Bigart to Nahum, 25 January 1909: AIU Archives, Registre de correspondance, p. 219, text in Benbassa, *Politique*, p. 202; His decree of appointment is found in the BA, Istanbul, *BEO, Adliye tezkeresi* 695, 17 January 1324/30 January 1909, confirmed by *Tezkerei Sami* of the Grand Vezir on 17 February 1324/2 March 1909. The French translation is in Galante, *Documents* V, 38–41,and Benbassa, *Politique* , pp. 204–5.

63. AIU archives, Paris, Turquie I.G. 1. I. Fernandez to J. Bigart, 6 September 1897, quoted in Benbassa, 'Le Sionisme dans l'Empire Ottoman', 73.

64. See for example the report of the dragoman to the British Consulate General in Baghdad of 27 February 1910, that 'The Turkish government fully realize that the Jews are one of the chief elements in the progress of the country. The Turks have all along regarded the Jews as very faithful subjects of the Sultan and have placed confidence in them. On the other hand the Jews of Baghdad have borne feelings of gratitude towards the Turkish government ever since the immigration of their co-religionists from Spain into Asia Minor some hundreds of years ago. The community is anxious to co-operate with the government for the improvement of the country . . . ', quoted in Elie Kedourie, *Arabic Political Memoirs and other Studies* (London, 1974), 263–72.

65. Haim Nahum to Victor Jacobson, 26 September 1913: Central Zionist Archives, Jerusalem, Z3/66, quoted in Benbassa, *Politique* 65.

66. Justin McCarthy, 'Factors in the Analysis of the Population of Anatolia, 1800–1878', *AAS* XXI (1987), 33–63.

67. There were 30 active synagogues in Istanbul in 1302/1897, according to a detailed Ottoman survey of all buildings in the city, found in the Istanbul University Library no. 80872.

68. BA, *BEO* 333983, Council of Ministers decision 156 of 26 January 1916.

69. Haim Nahum to *AIU*, 14 November 1912: *AIU* Archives, Turquie II C 8, text in Benbassa, *Politique*, pp. 223–24; Haim Nahum to *AIU*, 4 May 1914: *AIU* Archives Turquie XXX. E. Text in Benbassa, *Politique*, pp. 224–25.

70. Mordechai Eliav, *Eretz Yisrael and Its Yishuv in the Nineteenth Century, 1777–1917* (in Hebrew) (Jerusalem, 1978), 437–38.

71. Nathan (Galata) to AIU (Paris), 15 May 1935: Archives of the AIU (Paris) II C 8.

72. BA, *BEO* 328588, Council of Ministers decision 369, 21 October 1331/3 November 1915; 337018, Council of Ministers decision 417, 6 December 1917. After the initial order of 17 December 1914, 7475 Jews were expelled to Alexandria by 31 January 1915; see Benbassa, 542–43.

73. Gustav von Dobeler, 'A Jewish Republic in Palestine', in FO 371/3062; Zimmermann to Wangenheim, 1 November 1914, in German Foreign Office Archives *Türkei* 195, IV, K17611–2, Cable 1096, reproduced in Friedman, *Germany*, 71–72.

74. BA, Istanbul, *Adliye Tezkere* 60, 31 May 1332/15 June 1916, and *Şuray Devlet mazbata* 482 of 30 November 1332/15 December 1916; *BEO* 333261, Council of Ministers Decision of 23 November 1332/6 December 1916; 338821, *Şurayı Devlet mazbata* 244 of 4 June 1334/17 June 1918.
75. This discussion is based on Mordechai Eliav, *Eretz Yisrael and Its Yishuv in the Nineteenth Century, 1777–1917* (in Hebrew) (Jerusalem, 1978), and the same author's, *Under Imperial Austrian Protection: Selected Documents from the Archives of the Austrian Consulate in Jerusalem, 1849–1917* (in Hebrew) (Jerusalem, Yad Ben-Zvi, 1985)
76. See the dossier *Filistin Musevi Meselesine ait telgraflar* (telegrams regarding the problem of Palestinian Jews), in HTA, Dolap 13–113, Göz 16–4, Klasör 533, Dosya 1240–2087. In particular communication from the Military Censor (*Askeri Sansor Müfettişliği*), Istanbul, to the Intelligence Department of the Istanbul Army (*Qarargâh-ı Umumi Istihbarat Şubesi Müdüriyet-i Aliyesi*), 16 May 1333 (29 May 1917) in A 1/2, Dosya 1240, Fihrist 1–2), enclosing an intercepted undated letter from Bishop Damiyanos (Jerusalem) to the Ecumenical Patriarch (Istanbul), stating that more than one thousand Russian Jews have settled in Jerusalem, greatly harming Greek interests, and proposing that the Patriarch ask the Ottoman government to remove them from Jerusalem in return for promises for the Orthodox Church to publicly help contradict European propaganda claims against the Ottomans. Damiyanos added that Syrian Governor Cemal Pasha had in fact been providing special food rations to Greek Orthodox and Armenian Gregorian Christians in Jerusalem and had prevented destruction of their churches, but that he did not wish to acknowledge this unless the Ottomans helped them with their 'Jewish problem' in return. Also letter from Damiyanos to the Apostolic Delegate in Istanbul, Monsignor Dolci (n.d.), intercepted by the Military Censor of Istanbul, in the *Filistin Musevi Meselesine aid telgraflar* dossier of the HTA: A1–2, Dossier 1240, Fihrist 1–4, which states that Cemal Pasha had been protecting Christians in Palestine and that the evacuation of Jews from Jaffa and Gaza had been directly due to Christian influence on Cemal Pasha.
77. These intelligence reports are found in HTA, no. 1–1, Dolap 101, dossiers 158, 174, 176, 193, 203, 202, Dolap 105, 759, 762, 765, 768, 770, 772, 773; no. 1–2, Dolap 109, dossier 1361, Dolap 110, dossier 1476; and in numerous files.
78. The name consists of the first letters of the Hebrew verse *Nezzakh Yisrael Lo Yeshakker* ('The Strength of Israel will not die', from 1 Samuel 15:29).
79. Winstone, 231, 300–302; Friedman, *Germany*, 354–56, 410–11; Sazanov to Buchanan, 'Armenian agents in touch with Russian Government', 29 December 1915, in Public Record Office, London, CAB 37/139, and India Office, London, Political and Secret Records 10/525; Richard Meinertzhagen, *Middle East Diary* (London, 1959), 5, 211.
80. Winstone, 231–35; A. Engle, *The NILI Spies* (London, 1959); Alex Aaronsohn, *With the Turks in Palestine* (Bern, 1916); Richard Meinertzhagen, *Middle East Diary* (London, 1959).
81. *El Tiempo*, 10 March 1919; Isaiah Friedman, 'German Intervention on Behalf of the Yishuv, 1917', *JSS* XXXIII (1971), 23–43; Winstone, 460, explains these moves as necessary due to the British advance: 'Jamal's decision was characteristically abrupt, and both German and Allied protests were justified. But most writers on these events ignore the fact that the order was issued as the British advanced on Gaza and the Turks

C-in-C expected a full scale advance to Jerusalem.' See also Consul General Brode to German Ambassador Kühlmann in Istanbul, 5 April 1917, reporting on meeting with Cemal Pasha, in German Foreign Office Archives 195, vol. XII, K178503–8, Report 33, reproduced in Friedman, *Germany*, 341–50.

82. German Ambassador Bernstorff in Istanbul to German Foreign Office, 30 October 1917, reporting on information provided by Grand Vezir Talat Pasha; from German Foreign Office Archives, *Türkei* vol. XVI K179664, Cable 1345; reproduced in Friedman, *Germany*, 358; Jacob Thon, Zionist chief in Jerusalem, 15 November 1917, from German Foreign Office Archives, *Türkei* 195, vol. XVIII, K180161, reproduced in Friedman, *Germany*, p. 359.

83. Mark Sykes original demands to General Clayton (in Jerusalem) that information to show Ottoman persecution of Jews be sent to London for propaganda purposes is found in Sykes to Clayton, 2 January 1918, in FO 371/3383/1634; Sykes dissatisfaction with reports, including statement 'he has no idea of propaganda . . . ' is found as Minute to Wingate to Foreign Office, 15 January 1918 (FO 371/3383/9383); Wingate's subsequent report, 'Information at present available does not disclose any authentic cases of sacrilege or systematic looting. General state of Jerusalem does not appear to justify so serious a charge' as desired by Sykes is found in Wingate to Foreign Office, 9 January 1918 (FO 371/3388/6074). Sykes subsequent proposals for atrocity reports to be sent from Palestine is found in Sykes to Wingate, 14 January 1918 (FO 371/3388/6074/W/44); Wingate's reply that 'I do not think there is much solid ground for any artificial propaganda', with Sykes's continued angry insistence that propaganda reports be sent, is in Wingate to Foreign Office, 15 January 1918 (FO 371/3388/10748).

84. Report dated November, 1917, found in State Department decimal archives 867.4016/363, National Archives, Washington, D.C.

85. Report to the Ottoman Prime Minister's office by its Intelligence Department/*Şube-i Mahsusa* no. 106, dated 9 March 1334/1918, found in *BEO*, BA, Istanbul, no. 102/*Şube-i Mahsusa*; Justin McCarthy, *Muslims and Minorities* (New York, 1983), pp. 117–44.

86. Ottoman Council of Ministers Minutes/*MVM* vol. 215 no. 157, 12 April 1919, vol. 220, no. 607, 29 November 1920.

87. See, for example, the report by British Intelligence in Salonica to the Director of DMI in London, 16 December 1918, in Public Record Office FO 371/3421/209381, and in particular the Foreign Office minute stating: 'The Turkish Masonic lodges are of course the framework on which the CUP have built up their secret organization. When the CUP carried out their great coup d'état the mob marched into the Sublime Porte under the banner of the Jewish lodge of Salonica and murdered Nazim Pasha. British Freemasonry, I believe disowns the Oriental type, but I do not know what the attitude of American freemasonry is. Italian freemasonry is in the cloest touch with the CUP rite from Italy. It is probable that (Grand Rabbi Haim) Nahum's intrigues with America are largely carried out through Masonic lodges.' Also the report by Assistant British High Commissioner in Istanbul Webb to the Foreign Office, 5 December 1918, in Public Record Office, FO FO 371/3418/202011: 'I think scheme I have described must originate with Jewish members of the CUP whose affiliation are, I believe, sufficiently well known.'

88. Emmanuel Carasso and Albert Carasso (Istanbul) reported to the President

of the AIU (Paris) on 7 November 1919 (no. 7288/4, Archives of the AIU II C 8) that they had formed the *Comité de Secours aux Juifs de Russie* to assist Russian Jews suffering from pogroms at the hands of Denikin's army, but that over 120,000 Jews had been killed during the previous two months. The *Kievskov o Echo* (Kiev) of 1 October 1919 described a six day (22–28 September 1918) pogrom at Fastow, near Kiev, by members of Denikin's volunteer army, with 1,600 to 2,000 Jews killed or badly wounded and 200 houses burned during an orgy of massacres, torture and pillaging, and with the streets left full of corpses. The *Sovremenoie Slovo* of 28 October 1919 presented a series of reports of pogroms at fourteen neighboring villages between October 13 and 18.

89. Edgar Morin, *Vidal et les siens* (Paris, Seuil, 1989), 67–93. A dossier of reports on Greek atrocities against people and officials in the Izmir area is in BA, Adliye tezkere 246/2740, 18 September 1920; see also Ottoman Council of Ministers Minutes/*MVM* vol. 213 no. 457, 24 November 1334/1918; vol. 215, no. 249, 28 May 1335/1919; vol. 216 no. 263, 1 June 1335/1919, describing Greek soldiers driving the settled population out of Bergama and Izmir; vol. 216, no. 269, 1 June 1335/1919, describing the displacement of Jews and Muslims at the Dardanelles/Çanakkale by Greek settlers from the Aegean islands; vol. 216 no. 288, 9 June 1919, regarding Ayvalık; vol. 216 no. 380, 21 June 1919, describing Greek and Allied attacks on the local populations in Thrace and at Izmir, Diyarbekir and Bayezid; vol. 216 no. 323, 26 June 1919; vol. 216, no. 337, 15 July 1919; vol. 216 no. 339, 15 July 1919; and particularly vol. 216 no. 343, 16 July 1919, regarding Greek atrocities in Aydın province; vol. 217 no. 573, 29 November 1919, and vol. 221 no. 127, 30 April 1921, and no. 239, 4 August 1921, on Greek atrocities in Thrace; vol. 218 no. 9, 11 January 1920 on resettlement of Greeks from America in Anatolia; also *BEO*, 343329; The Greek atrocities in southeastern Anatolia and Thrace were condemned by an international investigation commission headed by American High Commissioner in Istanbul, Admiral Mark Bristol, leading the Allies to abandon further support for the Greek invasion. See Ottoman Council of Ministers Minutes, vol. 217 no. 481, 16 October 1919. Also Hayyim Cohen, *Jews of the Middle East*, 18.

90. Similar reports came from Nabon to the AIU on 2 July 1919 (no. 23/915), 9 July 1919 (no. 26/927), 12 July 1919 (no. 27/932) and 14 July 1919 (no. 28/933). In Nabon's report of 17 July 1919 (no. 30/935), he stated that the Greeks at Aydın had burned 200 Jewish houses and 13 shops, had despoiled all the local Jews of their money and property, and had strangled two Jews as well as driving the remainder to seek refuge in the local AIU school: 'At Aydın, Manisa, Tire and everywhere else, our Jews live in an atmosphere of suspician by the Greek inhabitants' who suspect that they favor the Turks. On 23 July 1920 Nabon reported that all the Jews had left Izmir, the synagogue had not been burned, but the Greeks had taken all its valuables as well as the property of local Jews, and that the streets were full of bodies.

91. Güleryüz, *ibid.*; Galante, *Turcs et Juifs* (1932), 54.

92. Galante, *Anatolie* (1939) II, 41.

93. Güleryüz, *ibid*; Galante, *Anatolie* II, 101–2.

94. See Güleryüz, 'Kurtuluş Savaşında Egede ve Bursada Yahudiler', *Şalom*, 30 October 1985; Galante, *Turcs et Juifs*, in *Histoire des Juifs de Turquie*, 26–28, and *El Tiempo*, 22 October 1922.

95.   *Univers Israelite,* 2 September 1921, p. 467–48, quoted in Güleryüz, *ibid;* see also Galante, *Anatolie* II (1939), 70–100; and 'Manissa', *EJ* XI, 878–79.
96.   Général Jean Bernachot, *Les Armées Françaises en Orient après l'Armistice de 1918, III: Le Corps d'Occupation de Constantinople (6 Novembre 1920–22 Octobre 1923* (Paris, 1972), 58–152.

CHAPTER 5: THE JEWS OF THE TURKISH REPUBLIC SINCE 1923

1.   For the complete text, see: J. C. Hurewitz, ed., *The Middle East and North Africa in World Politics: A Documentary Record. Second Edition, Revised and Enlarged* (2 vols, Yale University Press, New Haven and London, 1979), II, 325–37.
2.   A translation of the text of the Jewish document of renunciation can be found in Appendix 5.
3.   *JO,* 26 and 28 January 1938.
4.   Lothar Krecker, *Deutschland und die Turkei im Zweiten Weltkrieg* (Frankfurt, 1964); Fritz Neumark, *Zuflucht am Bosporus* (Frankfurt, 1980).
5.   J. Brand, *The Satan and the Soul* (in Hebrew) (Tel Aviv, 1960), 34; I. Wiesman, *Confronting the Mighty Evil* (in Hebrew) (Yavne, Tel Aviv, 1968), 44–46; Shabtai Tevet, *David's Envy, III, The Burning Soil* (in Hebrew) (Jerusalem, Schoken, 1987), 432.
6.   Turhan Aytul, 'Struma Facıası', *Milliyet,* 30 June–6 July 1985.
7.   See Barry Rubin, *Istanbul Intrigues: A True-Life Casablanca* (New York, 1989), and Tevet, 436–37.
8.   Israel, Central Bureau of Statistics, *Immigration to Israel, 1948–1972* (Jerusalem, 1978), pp. 4–7.
9.   See Appendix 3; also Shaul Tuval, 'The Jewish Community in Turkey Today' (in Hebrew), *Pe'amim,* no. 11–14 (1982), pp. 114–39, written by the Israeli Consul in Istanbul from 1975 to 1979.
10.   'Istanbul Özel Alman Lisesi Öğrencilerinin 'Türkiye Yahudileri' Üzerine Araştırması', *Şalom* (Istanbul), 11 February 1987.
11.   Ankara is said to have a Jewish population of some 30 families with approximately one hundred people. Naim Güleryüz, *Şalom,* 15 May 1990.
12.   Published by Karen Gerson, 'Judeo-Espanyol, Diğer diller ve Türkçe', *Şalom* (Istanbul), 23 and 30 December 1987
13.   *Şalom* of 13 February 1985 published the following statistics for the Turkish-Jewish community:

Year	Births	Deaths	Bar Mitzvas	Marriages
1981	125	267	60	108
1982	115	270	80	105
1983	107	320	93	103
1984	94	327	80	107

14.   Published in the national newspaper *Milliyet* on 14 May 1989.
15.   *Şalom* (Istanbul), 24 and 31 May, 14 June 1989; Coşkun Kırca in *Milliyet,* 29 May 1989.

APPENDIX 1: GRAND RABBIS OF ISTANBUL AND THE OTTOMAN EMPIRE, AND CHIEF RABBIS OF REPUBLICAN TURKEY

1. Based on Abraham Galante, *Istanbul*, in *Histoire des Juifs de Turquie* I, 237–70.
2. Appointment decree printed in *Takvimi Vekayi*, 23 Şevval 1250/22 February 1835.
3. Abraham ha-Levy was dismissed because of old age and replaced by Shmeul Hayim, of Hasköy, whose appointment *berat* was published in the *Takvimi Vekayi* of 19 Receb 1252/19 October 1837.
4. Shmuel Hayim was dismissed as Grand Rabbi when it was discovered that he was not an Ottoman national, and Moshe Fresco of Balat was appointed in his place. The original Turkish text of his appointment *berat* of 1254 is in BBA, *Gayri Muslim* 17, pp. 98–101, and that of his re-appointment following the accession of Sultan Abdül Mecid is in BBA, *Gayri Muslim* 18, pp. 7–8.
5. Appointment *berat* text is in BBA, *Gayri Muslim* 18, pp. 23–24.
6. Haim ha-Cohen was a teacher in a Jewish elementary school in Ortaköy when he was appointed. His appointment *berat* text in BBA, *Gayri Muslim* 18, pp. 31–32, and *Cevdet Adliye* 6/550.
7. Appointment *berat* text in BBA, *Gayri Muslim* 18, p. 153.
8. Text of his appointment *berat* published in *Journal Israélite*, 11 August 1863, published in Franco, 167, and Galante, *Istanbul* I, 252–53.
9. Appointment *berat* in BBA, *Gayri Muslim* 18, p. 155; French translation in Galante, *Documents* V, 37–38.
10. Appointment *berat* in BBA, *Gayri Muslim* 18, pp. 38–40; French translation is in Galante, *Documents* V, 38–41.
11. brother of Moshe Levi.
12. President of Istanbul *Bet Din*, appointed while Nahum was in Europe, and again after Nahum resigned and left for Paris in May, 1920.
13. Galante, *Documents* V, 42–44.

APPENDIX 2: POPULATION OF THE OTTOMAN EMPIRE IN THE LATE NINETEEN AND EARLY TWENTIETH CENTURIES ACCORDING TO OFFICIAL OTTOMAN CENSUS REPORTS

14. Franco, p. 1 uses Theodore Reinach, *Histoire des Israelites*, pp. 393–95 to state that there were 314,000 Jews in the Ottoman Empire, including 105,000 in European Turkey, 195,000 in Asiatic Turkey, 8,000 in Egypt and 6,000 in Tripolitania. Since the official figures exclude both Egypt and Tripolitania, and include only men for Baghdad and Basra, this estimate might well be accurate.
15. MS TY 8949 in Istanbul University Library; figures compiled by The Commission for the Census/*Komisyon-i tahrir-i nufus*, only for Istanbul Municipality, including old Istanbul and Beyoğlu, for the years 1260/1844, 1273/1856–57, and 1298/1880–1.
16. Incorporated into Istanbul province after 1883.
17. These figures are for males only, from the only partially-complete first census of 1831. See Enver Ziya Karal, *Ismanlı Imparatorluğunda ilk nüfus sayımı, 1831*, 196–201.
18. This figure is for all Christian males in Edirne province in 1831.
19. Bulgarians, 102,245.

20. These figures are for males only, from the only partially-complete first census of 1831. See Enver Ziya Karal, *Osmanlı İmparatorluğunda ilk nüfus sayımı, 1831*, 196–201.
21. This figure is for all Christian males in Salonica province.
22. And 2178 Greek Catholics
23. And 293 Latins.
24. And 274,826 Bulgarians.
25. And 272,917 Bulgars.
26. And 6,229 foreign subjects.
27. And 4,956 foreign subjects.
28. And 5,174 Armenian Catholics.
29. And 21,690 Maronites; also 16,421 Armenian Catholics.
30. And 10,623 Armenian Catholics.
31. And 7,915 Greek Catholics
32. And 3,144 Protestants.
33. And 25,240 Catholics.
34. And 192 Armenian Catholics
35. And 14,816 Greek Catholics
36. And 5,036 Maronites; also 956 Protestants and 6445 Suryanis.
37. And 28 Greek Catholics.
38. Very small percentage of women counted in Baghdad province.
39. Foreign subjects.
40. And 723 Armenian Catholics
41. And 13,715 Suryanis.
42. Few women counted in Basra province.
43. And 334 Armenian Catholics.
44. Few women counted in Musul province.
45. And 4126 Armenian Catholic men. All figures are only for men.
46. And 1,024 Yakubi.
47. And 4,971 Protestants; also 1,915 Catholics.
48. And 6,326 Armenian Catholics; also 7,284 Protestants.
49. And 233 Armenian Catholics.
50. And 26 Greek Catholics.
51. And 6,849 Latins.
52. And 6,632 Latins.

APPENDIX 4: POPULATION OF ISTANBUL BY RELIGION, 1883 STATISTICS AND 1927 CENSUS

53. Bulgarians and Latins.
54. Foreigners and other religions counted in 1883 statistics but not in 1927 census.

Select Bibliography
on Ottoman and Turkish Jewry

I. THE JEWS OF ISLAM BEFORE THE RISE OF THE OTTOMAN EMPIRE

Eliyahu Ashtor. *The Jews of Moslem Spain*, tr. A. Klein and J. M. Klein (3 vols, Philadelphia, 1973–84).

Eliyahu Strauss (Ashtor), *A History of the Jews in Egypt and Syria under the Rule of the Mamluks* (in Hebrew) (3 vols, Jerusalem, 1944–70).

Edmond Ashtor, *A Social and Economic History of the Near East in the Middle Ages* (London, 1976).

Edmond Ashtor, *Levant Trade in the Later Middle Ages* (Princeton, 1983).

Edmond Ashtor, *The Jews and the Mediterranean Economy, 10th–15th Centuries* (London, 1983).

Edmond Strauss (Ashtor), 'The Social Isolation of Ahl adh-Dhimma', *Etudes orientales a la memoire de P. Hirschler*, ed. O. Komlos (Budapest, 1950).

Edmond Ashtor-Strauss, 'Saladin and the Jews', *HUCA* XXVII (1956), 305–26.

Edmond Ashtor, 'On the Jewish Community of Egypt in Medieval Times' (in Hebrew) *Zion* XXX (1964–65), 61–78, 128–57.

Edmond Ashtor, 'The Number of Jews in Medieval Egypt', *JSS* XVIII (1967), 9–42, XIX (1968), 1–22.

Edmond Ashtor, 'New Data for the History of Levantine Jewries in the Fifteenth Century', *Bulletin of the Institute of Jewish Studies* III (1975), 67–102.

Edmond Ashtor, 'Gli Ebrei di Ancona nel periodo della repubblica. Appunti di archivio', *Le Marche e l'Adriatico orientale* (Ancona, 1978), 331–68.

Edmond Ashtor, 'The Jews in the Mediterranean Trade in the fifteenth century', *Wirtschaftskraefte und Wirtschaftswege. Festschrift für Hermann Kellenbenz* (Nürnburg, 1978), 441–54.

Edmond Ashtor, 'The Jews in the Mediterranean Trade in the Later Middle Ages', *HUCA* vol. 55 (1984), 159–78.

A. Assaf, 'Slavery and Slave Trade among the Jews during the Middle Ages' (in Hebrew) *Zion* IV (1938), 91–125, V (1940), 271–80.

Salo W. Baron, *A Social and Religious History of the Jews: Second Edition, revised and enlarged, vol. XVII, Byzantines, Mameluks, and Maghribians* (New York, Columbia University Press, 1980)

Bat Ye'or, *The Dhimmi: Jews and Christians under Islam* (London and Toronto, 1985).

C. E. Bosworth, 'The Concept of *Dhimma* in Early Islam', Braude/Lewis I, 37–51.

Sheldon Brunswick, ed., *Studies in Judaica, Karaitica and Islamica: Presented to Leon Nemoy on his Eightieth Birthday* (Ramat Gan, Israel, 1982).

Claude Cahen, 'Dhimma', *EI* II, 227–31.

Claude Cahen, 'Djizya', *EI* II, 554–67.

Mark R. Cohen, 'The Jews under Islam: From the Rise of Islam to Sabbetai Zevi', *The Study of Judaism II: Bibliographical Essay in Jewish Medieval Studies*, ed. Y. Yerushalmi *et al.* (New York, 1976), 214–29.

Mark R. Cohen, *The Origins of the Office of Head of the Jews (Ra'is al-Yahud) in the Fatimid Empire: The Period of the House of Mevorakh b. Saadya ca. 1064–1126* (Unpublished Ph.D dissertation, Jewish Theological Seminary of America, 1976).

Mark R. Cohen, *Jewish Self-Government in Medieval Egypt* (Princeton, N.J., 1980).

Alan Cutler, *The Jew as Ally of the Muslim: medieval roots of Anti-Semitism* (Notre Dame, Indiana, 1986).

Daniel Dennett, *Conversion and the Poll Tax in Early Islam* (Cambridge, Mass. 1950).

Shmuel Ettinger, ed., *Histoire des Juifs en terre d'Islam* (in Hebrew) (Jerusalem, 1981).

Walter Fischel, *Jews in the Economic and Political Life of Medieval Islam* (New York, 1969).

Walter Fischel, 'Azarbaijan in Jewish History', *Proceedings of the American Academy for Jewish Research* XXII (1953), 1–21.

Walter Fischel, 'The Jews of Central Asia (Khorasan) in Medieval Hebrew and Islamic Literature', *Historia Judaica* VII (1945), 29–50.

Walter Fischel, 'New Sources for the History of the Jewish Diaspora in Asia in the 16th Century', *JQR* XL (1950), 379–99.

Walter Fischel, 'The Region of the Persian Gulf and the Jewish Settlements in Islamic Times', *Alexander Marx Jubilee Volume* (New York, 1950), 203–30.

Abraham Galante, *Les Juifs sous la Domination des Turcs Seldjoukides* (Istanbul, 1941), reprinted in Galante, *Turquie* I, 71–88.

Jane Gerber, 'Anti-semitism and the Muslim world', *History and Hate* (1986), 73–93.

S. D. Goitein, *Jews and Arabs: Their Contacts Through the Ages* (3rd edition, New York, 1974).

S. D. Goitein, *A Mediterranean Society; The Jewish Communities of the Arab World as Portrayed in the Documents of the Cairo Geniza* (5 vols, Berkeley and Los Angeles, 1967–85).

S. D. Goitein, 'The Local Jewish Community in the Light of the Cairo Geniza Records', *JSS* XII (1961), 133–58.

S. D Goitein, 'The interplay of Jewish and Islamic laws', *Jewish Law in Legal History*, ed. B. Jackson (1980), 61–77.

S. D. Goitein, ed., *Proceedings of the Seminar on Muslim-Jewish Relations in North Africa* (New York, 1975).

S. D. Goitein, 'Jewish Society and Institutions under Islam', *Journal of World History* XI (1968), 170–84, and *Jewish Society through the Ages*, ed. H. H. Ben-Sasson (1971), 170–84.

R. J. H. Gottheil, 'A Cairo Synagogue Eleventh Century Document', *JQR* XIX (1907), 467–539.

Naim Güleryüz, 'Türkiye Yahudileri Tarihi: Ispanyada Yahudiler (History of the Jews of Turkey: the Jews in Spain)', *Şalom* (Istanbul), 18 September 1985.

W. Heyd, *Histoire du commerce du Levant au moyen age* (2 vols, 2nd edn., Leipzig, 1936).

Roger Highfield, 'Christians, Jews and Muslims in the same Society: The Fall of Convivencia in Medieval Spain, *Religious Motivation*, ed. D. Baker (1978), 121–46.

Haim Hirschberg, 'Almohade Persecutions and the Indian Trade', *Yitzhak F. Baer Jubilee volume*, ed. Salo Baron (1960), 134–53.

Shimon Khayyat, 'The Interrelationship between Jews, Christians, Moslems and others, as reflected in Arabic proverbs', *Essays, Dropsie University*, ed. Abraham Katsch (1979), 237–63.

F. Lebrecht, 'Essay on the Caliphate of Baghdad during the Later Half of the Twelfth Century' (in Hebrew), Benjamin of Tudela, *Sefer Masa'ot* (2 vols, ed. A. Asher, Berlin, 1840) II, 318–92.

Yosef Levanon, *The Jewish Travellers in the Twelfth Century* (Lanham, Md., University Press of America, 1980).

Bernard Lewis, *The Jews of Islam* (Princeton, 1985).

Bernard Lewis, *Semites and Anti-Semites: An Inquiry into Conflict and Prejudice* (New York and London, Norton, 1986).

Bernard Lewis, 'The Decline and Fall of Islamic Jewry', *Commentary* LXXVII (1984), 44–54.

Bernard Lewis, 'An Anti-Jewish Ode: the Qasida of Abu Ishaq against Joseph ibn Nagrella, *Salo Wittmayer Baron*, ed. S. Lieberman (1975), 657–68.

Bernard Lewis, 'An Apocalyptic Vision of Islamic History', *BSOAS* XIII (1949–51), 308–38.

Jacob Mann, *The Jews in Egypt and in Palestine under the Fatimid Caliphs* (2 vols, Oxford, 1920–22, reprints Oxford, 1969, New York, 1970).

Jacob Mann, 'A Second Supplement to 'The Jews in Egypt and in Palestine under the Fatimid Caliphs,' *HUCA* III (1926), 257–310.

Vera Moreen, 'The Downfall of Muhammad Beg, Grand Vizier of Shah 'Abbas II', *JQR*, LXXII (1981), 81–99.

Vera Moreen, 'The Status of Religious Minorities in Safavid Iran, 1617–1661', *Journal of Near Eastern Studies* XL (1981), 119–34.

Gordon Newby, *History of the Jews of Arabia* (Columbia, S.C., 1988).

Fausto Parente, *et al.*, eds, *Gli ebrei nell'alto medioevo* II (Spoleto, 1980).

Rudi Paret, 'Toleranz und Intoleranz in Islam', *Speculum* XXI (1970), 344–65.

Moshe Perlmann, 'Eleventh Century Andalusian Authors on the Jews of Granada', *Medieval Jewish Life*, ed. Robert Chazan (New York, Ktav, 1976), 147–268.

Stephen Ricks, 'Kinship bars to marriage in Jewish and Islamic law', *Studies in Islamic and Judaic traditions*, ed. W. Brinner and S. Ricks (1986), 123–41.

Erwin Rosenthal, *Judaism and Islam* (London, 1961).

Kurt Schubert, 'Das Judentum in der Welt des Mitteralterlichen Islam: Das Judentum in Osteuropa; Zionismus und Israel', *Das Osterreichische Judentum*, ed. N. Vielmetti (1974), 165–207.

Ezra Spicehandler, 'Persecution of the Jews of Isfahan under Shah 'Abbas (1642–1666), *HUCA* XLVI (1975), 331–56.

Norman Stillman, *The Jews of Arab Lands: A History and Source Book* (Philadelphia, 1979).

Norman Stillman, 'Aspects of Jewish Life in Islamic Spain', *Aspects of Jewish Culture*, ed. P. E. Dzarmach (1979), 51–84.

Arthur Tritton, *The Caliphs and Their Non-Muslim Subjects* (London, 1930, reprinted 1970).

Abraham Udovitch, 'The Jews and Islam in the high Middle Ages: a case of the Muslim view of differences', *Gli ebrei nell'alto medioevo*, ed. F. Parente, A. Udovitch, S. D. Goitein, *et al.* (Spoleto, 1980), 655–83.

Gustav E. von Grunebaum, 'Eastern Jewry under Islam', *Viator*, ed. Lynn White II (1971), 365–72.

W. Montgomery Watt, *Muhammed at Mecca* (Oxford, 1953).

W. Montgomery Watt, *Muhammad at Medina* (Oxford, 1956).

W. Montgomery Watt, 'Condemnation of the Jews of Banu Qurayzah', *Muslim World* XLII (1952), 160–71.

II. THE JEWS OF ROME, BYZANTIUM, AND CHRISTIAN EUROPE

Zvi Ankori, *Karaites in Byzantium: The Formative Years, 970–1100* (New York, Columbia University Press, 1957, reprint 1968).

Zvi Ankori, 'Some Aspects of the Karaite-Rabbanite Relations in Byzantium on the Eve of the First Crusade', *Medieval Jewish Life*, ed. Robert Chazan (New York, Ktav, 1976), 169–82.

Zvi Ankori, 'The Correspondence of Tobias Ben Moses the Karaite of Constantinople', *Essays of Jewish Life and Thought* (New York, 1959), 1–38.

Zvi Ankori, 'Some Aspects of the Karaite Rabbinite Relations in Byzantium on the Eve of the First Crusade', *Proceedings of the American Academy for Jewish Research* XXIV (1955), 19–25, XXV (1956), 166–73.

Zvi Ankori, 'Greek Orthodox-Jewish Relations in Historic Perspective: The Jewish View', *GOTR* XXII (1977), 17–57.

Zvi Ankori, H. Binart and H. Ben Sasson, *Bibliographical Guide to the History of the Jews in the Middle Ages* (Jerusalem, 1961).

Philip Argenti, *The Religious Minorities of Chios: Jews and Roman Catholics* (Cambridge, 1970).

Pinhas Artzi, ed., *Bar-Ilan studies in History* (Ramat-Gan, Israel, 1978).

Yitzhak Baer, *The Pogroms of 1096* (Jerusalem, 1953).

Yitzhak Baer, *History of the Jews in Christian Spain* (2 vols, Philadelphia, 1961–71, reprinted 1978).

Salo W. Baron, *A Social and Religious History of the Jews: Second Edition, revised and enlarged, vol. XVII, Byzantines, Mameluks, and Maghribians* (New York, Columbia University Press)

Benjamin of Tudela, *The Itinerary of Benjamin of Tudela*, ed. and tr. by A. Asher (2 vols, Malibu, CA, 1983).

Haim Hillel Ben-Sasson, *Reformation in Contemporary Jewish Eyes* (1970).

M. Benvenisti, *The Crusaders in the Holy Land* (Jerusalem, 1970).

Meir Benayahu, 'The sermons of Rabbi Yosef ben Meir Garson as a source for the history of the expulsion of Jews from Spain and their life in the Turkish diaspora' (in Hebrew), Michael, *On the History of the Jews in the Diaspora* VII (1981), 42–205.

B. Blumenkranz, *Juifs et Chrétiens dans le monde occidental, 430–1096* (Paris, 1960).

B. Blumenkranz, 'Les auteurs chrétiens latins du moyen age sur les Juifs et le Judaisme', *REJ* CIX (1948), 3–67, CXI (1952), 5–61, CXIII (1954), 5–36, CXIV (1955), 37–90, CXVII (1958), 5–58.

F. Bourdrel, *Histoire des Juifs en France* (Paris, 1974).

Steven Bowman, *The Jews of Byzantium, 1204–1453* (University, Alabama, University of Alabama Press, 1985).

Johannes Brosseder, 'Luther und der Leidensweg der Juden', *Die Juden und Martin Luther*, ed. H. Kremers (1985), 109–35.

M. Carmoly, *Notice historique sur Benjamin de Tudele; Nouvelle edition suivie de l'examen géographique de ses voyages, par J. Lelewel* (Brussels and Leipzig, 1852).

Demetrios J. Constantelos, 'Greek Orthodox-Jewish Relations in Historical Perspective', *GOTR* XXII (1977), 6–16.

A. Crémieux, 'Les Juifs de Marseilles au moyen age', *REJ* XLVI (1903), 1–47, 246–68, XLVII (1903), 62–86, 243–61.

Alan Cutler, *The Jew as Ally of the Muslim: medieval roots of Anti-Semitism* (Notre Dame, Indiana, 1986).

Alan Cutler, 'Innocent III and the Distinctive Clothing of Jews and Muslims', *Studies in Medieval Culture*, ed. J. Sommerfeldt III (1970), 92–116.

Claudine Dauphin, 'Jewish and Christian Communities in Roman and Byzantine Gaulanitis: A Study of Evidence from Archaological Surveys', *Palestine Exploration Quarterly* vol. 114 (1982), 129–42.

David D'Beth Hillel, *The Travels of R. David D'Beth Hillel*, ed. Walter Fischel (New York, 1973).

Ben-Zion Degani, 'Die Formulierung und Propagierung des Jüdischen Stereotyps in der Zeit vor der Reformation und Sein Einfluss auf den jungen Luther', *Die Juden und Martin Luther*, ed. H. Kremers (1985), 3–44.

E. L. Dietrich, 'Das Judentum im Zeitalter der Kreuzzüge', *Saeculum* III (1952), 94–131.

B. Dinur, 'A Study of the History of the Jews in Palestine during the First Crusade' (in Hebrew), *Zion-Measef* II (1927), 38–66.

S. M. Dubnow, *History of the Jews in Russia and Poland from the Earliest Times until the Present Day* (2 vols, New York, 1975).

Gerhard Dunnhaupt, ed., *The Martin Luther Quincentennial* (Detroit, Michigan, Wayne State University Press, 1985).

J. D. Eisenstein, ed., *A Collection of Itineraries by Jewish Travellers to Palestine, Syria, Egypt and other Countries* (Tel Aviv, 1969).

Jerome Friedman, 'Jewish conversion, the Spanish pure blood laws and Reformation: a revisionist view of racial and religious antisemitism', *Sixteenth Century Journal* XVIII (1987), 3–29.

Jerome Friedman, 'Protestants, Jews and Jewish sources', *Piety, Politics and Ethics*, ed. C. Lindberg (1984), 139–56.

Jerome Friedman, 'The Reformation in Alien Eyes: Jewish Perceptions of Christian Troubles', *Sixteenth Century Journal* XIV (1983), 23–40.

Amos Funkenstein, 'Changes in the Patterns of Christian Anti-Jewish Polemics in the 12th Century' (in Hebrew), *Zion* XXXIII (1968), 125–44.

Abraham Galante, *Les Juifs de Constantinople sous Byzance* (Istanbul, 1940), reprinted in Galante, *Turquie* I, 5–70.

A. E. Gardner, S. J. D. Cohen, H. A. Green, eds, *Proceedings of the 9th World Congress of Jewish Studies, Jerusalem, August 1985* (Jerusalem, 1985).

Günther B. Ginzel, 'Martin Luther: 'Kronzeuge des Antisemitismus', *Die Juden und Martin Luther*, ed. H. Kremers (1985), 189–210.

Patrick Girard, *Les Juifs de France de 1789 a 1860: de l'émancipation a l'égalitè* (Paris, 1976).

S. D. Goitein, 'Religion in Everyday Life as Reflected in the Documents of the Cairo Geniza', *Religion in a Religious Age*, ed. S. Goitein (1974), 3–23.

S. D. Goitein, ed., *Letters of Medieval Jewish Traders* (Princeton, N.J., 1973).

S. D. Goitein, 'New Sources on the Fate of the Jews in the Time Jerusalem was Conquered by the Crusaders', *Zion* XVII (1952), 129–47.

S. D. Goitein, 'A Letter from Ascalon during its Occupation by the Crusaders', *Tarbiz* XXXI (1962), 287–90.

N. Golb, 'New light on the persecution of the French Jews at the time of the First Crusade', *Proceedings of the American Academy for Jewish Research* XXXIV (1966), 1–45, and *Medieval Jewish Life*, ed. Robert Chazan (New York, Ktav, 1976), 289–333.

S. Grayzel, *The Church and the Jews in the XIIIth Century* (New York, 1966)

Michael Graetz, *Les Juifs de France au XIXe siècle. De la révolution française a l'Alliance israélite universelle* (Paris, 1989).

H. A. Harris, *Greek Athletics and the Jews*, ed. I. M. Barton and A. J. Brothers (University of Wales Press, 1976).

A. Hertzberg, *The French Enlightenment and the Jews* (New York, 1968).

A. Herculano de Carvalho e Araujo, *History of the Origin and Establishment of the Inquisition in Portugal* (1926).

David Jacoby, 'Les Quartiers Juifs de Constantinople a l'époque Byzantine', *Byzantion* XXXVII (1967), 167–227.

David Jacoby, 'Les Juifs Venetiens de Constantinople – leur Communauté du XIIIe au milieu du XVe siècle', *REJ* CXXXI (1972), 397–472.

J. Juster, *Les Juifs dans l'Empire Romain, leur condition juridique, économique et sociale* (2 vols, Paris, 1914).

A. Kraabel, *Judaism in Western Asia Minor under the Roman Empire* (Ph.D. dissertation, Cambridge, Mass., 1968).

H. Kremers, ed., *Die Juden und Martin Luther* (1985).

Pinchas Lapide, 'Stimmen Jüdischer Zeitgenossen zu Martin Luther', *Die Juden und Martin Luther*, ed. H. Kremers (1985), 171–85.

Pinchas Lapide, 'Die Stellung Zietgenoessischer Juden zu Luther', *Die Reformation geht weiter*, ed. L. Markert and K. Stahl (1984), 169–84.

Harry Leon, *The Jews of Ancient Rome* (Philadelphia, 1960).

I. Levi, 'Les Juifs de France du milieu du IXe siècle aux croisades', *REJ* LII (1906), 161–68.

Isaac Levitats, *The Jewish Community in Russia, 1772–1844* (New York, 1943).

Isaac Levitats, *The Jewish Community in Russia, 1844–1917* (Jerusalem, 1981).

Jack Lightstone, 'Christian anti-Judaism in its Judaic mirror: the Judaic context of early Christianity revised', *Anti Judaism in Early Christianity* (1986), ed. S. Wilson, II, 103–32.

H. Liebenschütz, 'The Crusading Movement in its Bearing on the Christian Attitude Towards Jewry', *JSS* X (1959), 97–111.

I. Loeb, 'La Controverse Religieuse entre les Chrétiens et les Juifs au Moyen Age in France et en Espagne', *Revue de l'Histoire des Religions* XVII (1888), 311–37, XVIII (1889), 133–56.

I. Loeb, 'Polémistes chrétiens et juifs en France et en Espagne', *REJ* XVIII (1889), 43–70, 219–42.

Robert Sabbatino Lopez, 'Silk Industry in the Byzantine Empire', *Speculum* XX (1945), 1–42.

Robert Macina, 'Cassiodore et l'Ecole de Nisibe: Contribution a l'étude de la culture Chretienne Orientale a l'Aube du Moyen-Age', *Le Museon* vol. 95 (1982), 131–66.

A. Milano, *Storia degli ebrei in Italia* (Turin, 1963).

Marko Mirch, 'Jevreji na Balkonskom Polustrvu i u staroj srpskoj drzhavi do dolaska Turaka' (The Jews of the Balkan Peninsula and all the Serbian States until the arrival of the Turks), *Jevrejski Almanah, 1957–1958*, pp. 49–58.

Ralph Moellering, 'Luther's Attitude toward the Jews up to 1536', *Concor* XX (1949), 45–59.

Ralph Moellering, 'Luther's Later Attitude toward the Jews, 1536–1546', *Concor* XX (1949), 194–215.

D. C. Munro, 'The Speech of Pope Urban II at Clermont, 1095', *American Historical Review* XI (1905–6), 231–42.

Renée Neher-Bernheim, 'L'assimilation linguistique des Juifs d'Alexandrie: une des sources de l'antijudaisme antique', *Hellenica et Judaica*, ed. A. Caquot, M. Hadas-Lebel and J. Riaud (1986), 313–19.

G Nickelsburg. 'Christians and Jews in first-century Alexandria', *Christians among Jews and Gentiles*, ed. George W. E. Nickelsburg and George W. MacRae (Philadelphia, Pa: 1986)

Heiko Oberman, 'Luthers Stellung zu den Juden: Ahnen und Geahndete', *Leben und Werk Martin Luthers*, ed. H. Junghans (1983), 519–30.

George C. Papademetriou, 'Judaism and Greek Orthodoxy in Historical Perspective', *GOTR* XXI (1976), 93–113.

J. Parkes, *Conflict of the Church and the Synagogue: A Study in the Origins of Antisemitism* (New York, 1934, reprint 1974).

J. Parkes, *The Jew in the Medieval Community* (London, 1938).

Moshe Perlman, 'The Medieval Polemics between Islam and Judaism', *Religion in a Religious Age*, ed. S. D. Goitein (Cambridge, Mass., 1974), 103–29.

Charles Porgès, Les Relations Hébraiques des Persécutions des Juifs pendant la Première Croisade', *REJ* XXV (1892), 181–201, XXVI (1893), 183–97.

J. Prawer, 'Jerusalem the Capital City of the Crusaders' (in Hebrew), *Yehudah Vi-Yerushalayim* (Jerusalem, 1957), 90–105.

J. Prawer, 'Jewish Resettlement in Crusader Jerusalem' (in Hebrew), *Ariel* XIX (1967), 60–66.

J. Prawer, 'The Jews in the Latin Kingdom of Jerusalem' (in Hebrew), *Zion* XI (1945–46), 38–82.

Tessa Rajak, 'Jewish Rights in the Greek Cities under Roman Rule', *Approaches to Ancient Judaism*, ed. W. Green V (1985), 19–35.

David Raphael, *The Alhambra Decree* (North Hollywood, CA, 1988).

Salomon Reinach, 'L'Accusation du Meutre Rituel', *REJ* XXB (1892), 161–80.

Cecil Roth, *The Spanish Inquisition* (London, 1937, reprint New York, 1964).

Cecil Roth, *History of the Jews of Italy* (Philadelphia, Pa., 1946).

Cecil Roth, *The Ritual Murder Libel and the Jew* (London, 1935).

Michel Rouche, 'Les Baptemes Forcés des Juifs en Gaule Merovingienne et dans l'Empire d'Orient', *De l'Antijudaisme Antique*, ed. V. Nikiprowetzky (1979), 105–24.

Steven Rowan, 'Luther, Bucer and Eck on the Jews', *Sixteenth Century Journal* XVI (1985), 79–90.

M. Samuel, *Blood Accusation* (New York, 1966)

Johann M. Schmidt, 'Martin Luther's attitude towards the Jews and its impact on the Evangelical church in Germany in the beginning of the Third Reich', *Proceedings of the 9th World Congress of Jewish Studies*, ed. J. Bleich *et al.*, III (1986), 157–64.

Stefan Schreiner, 'Was Luther vom Judentum wissen konnte', *Die Juden und Martin Luther*, ed. H. Kremers (1985), 58–71.

J. B. Segal, 'The Jews of Northern Mesopotamia before the Rise of Islam', *Studies in the Bible*, ed. J. M. Grintz and J. Liver (1964), 32–63.

Andrew Sharf, *Byzantine Jewry: From Justinian to the Fourth Crusade* (London, Routledge Kegan Paul, 1971).

Andrew Sharf, 'Jews, Armenians, and the Patriarch Athanasius I', *Bar Ilan Annual* XVI–XVII (1979), 31–48.

Leonore Siegle-Wenschkewitz, 'Wurzeln des Antisemitismus in Luthers Theologischen Antijudaismus', *Die Juden und Martin Luther*, ed. H. Kremers (1985), 351–67.

Marcel Simon, *Verus Israel: étude sur les relations entre Chrétiens et Juifs dans l'empire romain (135–425)* (2nd edn, Paris, 1964).

Joshua Starr, *Jews in the Byzantine Empire, 641–1204* (Athens, 1939).

Joshua Starr, *Romania: The Jewries of the Levant after the Fourth Crusade* (Paris, 1949).

Joshua Starr, 'Jewish Life in Crete under the Rule of Venice', *Publications of the American Academy of Jewish Research* XII (1942), 59–114, and *Medieval Jewish Life*, ed. Robert Chazan (New York, Ktav, 1976), 233–88.

Menahem Stern, *Greek and Latin Authors on Jews and Judaism* (3 vols, Jerusalem, Israel Academy of Arts and Sciences, 1980–84).

Martin Stoehr, 'Martin Luther und die Juden', *Die Juden und Martin Luther*, ed. H. Kremers (1985), 89–108.

Hermann L. Strack, *La Superstition du Sang dans l'Humanité et les Rites Sanguinaires* (Munich, 1892).

C. B. Sucher, *Luthers Stellung zu den Juden* (Nieukoop, 1977).

Victor Tcherikover, *Hellenistic Civilization and the Jews* (Philadelphia, Pa., 1959).

Nomikos Vaporis and Marc Tanenbaum, ed., *Greek Orthodox-Jewish Consultation, GOTR XXII* (1977), 1–156.

Chantal Vogler, 'Les juifs dans le Code Theodosien', *Les Chretiens devant le fait juif*, ed., J. Le Brun (1979), 35–74.

Johannes Wallmann, 'The reception of Luther's writings on the Jews from the Reformation to the end of the 19th century', *Lutheran Quarterly* n.s. I (1987), 72–97.

Robert Wilde, *The Treatment of the Jews in the Greek Christian Writers of the First three Centuries* (Washington, D.C., 1949).

Diana Wood, 'Infidels and Jews: Clement VI's Attitude to Persecution and Toleration', *Persecution and Toleration*, ed. W. Sheils (1984), 115–24.

III.   MIDDLE EASTERN SOCIETY IN ISLAMIC AND OTTOMAN TIMES

Fanny Davis, *The Ottoman Lady: A Social History from 1713 to 1918* (Westport, Conn, 1986).

Paul Fesch, *Constantinople aux derniers jours d'Abdül Hamid* (reprint, New York, 1971).

Sidney Nettleton Fisher, *The Middle East: A History: Fourth Edition*, revised by William Ochsenwald (New York, McGraw Hill, 1989)

Lucy Garnett, *Turkish Life in Town and Country* (New York and London, 1904).

Lucy Garnett, *Home Life in Turkey* (New York, 1909).

Lucy Garnett, *Turkey of the Ottomans* (New York, 1914).

Théophile Gautier, *Constantinople* (Paris, 1857; reprint Istanbul, Isis, 1990).

H. A. R. Gibb and Harold Bowen, *Islamic Society and the West* (1 vol in 2 parts, Oxford University Press, London and New York, 1950–57). I/2, 179–261.

Halil Inalcık, *The Ottoman Empire: The Classical Age, 1300–1600* (London, Widenfeld and Nicolson, 1973)

Clarence Johnson, ed., *Constantinople To-Day or the Pathfinder Survey of Constantinople: A Study in Oriental Social Life* (New York, 1922).

Bernard Lewis, *The Emergence of Modern Turkey* (2nd edn, Oxford University Press, 1968).

Raphaela Lewis, *Everyday Life in Ottoman Turkey* (London and New York, 1971).

Robert Mantran, ed., *Histoire de l'Empire ottoman* (Paris, Fayard, 1989).

Eliot G. Mears, *Modern Turkey: A Politico-Economical Interpretation, 1908–22* (New York, 1924).

Jacques Pervitich, *Istanbul: Cadastral Survey* (4 vols, Istanbul, 1922–52).

Stanford J. Shaw, *History of the Ottoman Empire and Modern Turkey, vol. 1: Empire of the Gazis* (Cambridge University Press, 1976 and six later editions).

Stanford J. Shaw and Ezel Kural Shaw, *History of the Ottoman Empire and Modern Turkey, vol. 2: Reform, Revolution and Republic: The Rise of Modern Turkey* (Cambridge University Press, 1977 and six later editions).

Stanford J. Shaw, *Between Old and New: The Ottoman Empire under Sultan Selim III* (Cambridge, Mass., 1971).
George Young, *Constantinople* (London, 1927).

IV. THE HISTORY OF OTTOMAN JEWRY

Aaron Aaronsohn, *Yoman, 1916–1918* (in Hebrew) (Tel Aviv, 1970).
Aaron Aaronsohn, 'La Colonisation Juive en Palestine', *Bulletin de la Societé Botanique de France*, 24 April 1909.
Abraham Danon (1857–1925), sa vie et ses oeuvres (Paris, 1925).
Alex Aaronsohn, *With the Turks in Palestine* (Boston, 1916).
U. D. Adam, *Judenpolitik im Dritten Reich* (Düsseldorf, 1979).
E. Adamow, ed., *Die europaeischen Maechte und die Türkei wahrend des Weltkrieges, Konstantinopel und die Meerengen. Nach des Geheimdokumenten des ehemaligen Ministeriums für Auswaertige Angelegenheiten* (2 vols, Dresden, 1930).
R. Adelson, *Mark Sykes: Portrait of an Amateur* (London, 1975).
L. Adler and R. Dalby, *The Dervish of Windsor Castle: Life of Arminius Vambéry* (London, 1979).
Feroz Ahmad, 'Unionist Relations with the Greek, Armenian and Jewish Communities of the Ottoman Empire, 1908–1914', Braude/Lewis I, 401–34.
Engin Akarlı, 'Abdül Hamid II's Attempt to Integrate Arabs into the Ottoman System', *Palestine in the Late Ottoman Period*, ed. David Kushner (Brill, Leiden, 1986), 74–92.
M. M. Alexandru-Dersca, 'Un Privilège accordé par Suleyman Ier après l'occupation de Bude (1526)', *Revue des Etudes sud est europeens* IV (1966), 377–91.
Isaac Algazi, *El Judaismo Religion de Amor* (Buenos Aires, Editorial Judaica, 1945), tr. as *Breve Historia do Povo Judeu* (2 vols, Rio de Janeiro, Ediçoes Biblos/Biblioteca de Cultura Judaica*, 1962–63).
Aron Alkalaj, 'Zhivot i obichaji u nekadashnjoj jevrejskoj mahali Beograda' (Life and customs in the old Jewish neighborhood of Belgrade), *Jevrejski Almanah 1961–62*, 82–97.
Ivo Andrich, 'Na Jevrejskom Groblju u Sarajevo','(At the Jewish Cemetery in Sarajevo), *Jevrejski Almanah 1955–56*, 256–61.
Marc Angel, *The Jews of Rhodes: the history of a Sephardic community* (New York, Sepher-Hermon Press, 1978).
Zvi Ankori, *Jews and the Jewish community in the history of mediaeval Crete* (Athens, 1968). *Reprint from Second International Congress of Cretological Studies* (Athens, 1968).
Zvi Ankori, 'Giacomo Foscarini and the Jews of Crete: A Reconsideration', *Michael, On the History of the Jews in the Diaspora* VII (1980), 9–118.
Zvi Ankori, 'From *Zudecha* to *Yahudi Mahallesi*: The Jewish Quarter of Candia in the Seventeenth Century', *Baron Jubilee Volume*, ed., S. Lieberman I (Jerusalem, 1975), 63–127.
Zvi Ankori, *Jews and the Jewish community in the history of mediaeval Crete* (Athens, 1968). *Reprint from Second International Congress of Cretological Studies* (Athens, 1968).
A. Arce, 'Espionage y ultima aventura de José Nasi (1563–1574)', *Sefarad* III (1953), 257–86.
Benjamin Arditi, *The Jews of Bulgaria during the Years of Nazi Occupation, 1940–1944* (in Hebrew) (Tel Aviv, 1962).

Philip Argenti, *The Religious Minorities of Chios: Jews and Roman Catholics* (Cambridge, England, 1970).

Philip Argenti, *Diplomatic Archive of Chios, 1577–1841* (2 vols, Cambridge, England, 1954).

Aristarchi Bey, *Législation Ottomane au recueil des lois, règlements, ordonnances, traites, capitulations et autres documents officiels de l'Empire Ottoman* (Constantinople, 1874).

Pierre Arminjon, *Etrangéres et protégés dans l'Empire Ottoman* (Paris, 1903).

A. Ascher, Tibor Halasi-Kun and Bela Kiraly, eds, *Mutual Effects of the Islamic and Judeo-Christian Worlds: The East European Pattern* (New York, Brooklyn College, 1979).

S. Assaf, 'New Material on the History of the Karaites in the Orient' (in Hebrew), *Zion* I, 208–51.

Abe Attrep, 'A State of Wretchedness and Impotence: A British View of Istanbul and Turkey, 1919', *IJMES* IX (1978).

Phyllis Auty and Richard Clogg, *British Policy towards Wartime Resistance in Yugoslavia and Greece* (London, 1975).

Ehud Avriel, *Open the Gates* (New York, 1975).

Ekrem Hakkı Ayverdi, 'Fatih Devrinde Istanbul Mahalleleri' (Istanbul Quarters in the time of the Conqueror), *Vakıflar Dergisi* IV (1958), 249–61.

Franz Babinger, 'Ja'qub Pasha, ein Leibarzt Mehmed's II', *Revista degli Studi Orientali* XXVI (1951), 82–113.

Franz Babinger, 'Fatih Sultan Mehmet ve Italya', *Belleten*, XVII (1953), 41–82.

Franz Babinger, 'Grossherrliche Schutzvorschrift gegen nutzniesslichen glaubenswechsel', *Der Orient in der Forschung*, ed. W. Hoenerbach (1967), 1–8.

R. Bachi, *The Population of Israel* (Jerusalem, 1977).

Gabriel Baer, *A History of Land Ownership in Modern Egypt, 1800–1962* (Oxford, 1962).

Gabriel Baer, 'The Administrative, Economic and Social Functions of Turkish Guilds', *IJMES* XI(1970), 28–50.

Gabriel Baer, 'Village and City in Egypt and Syria, 1500–1914', *The Islamic Middle East, 700–1900: Studies in Economic and Social History*, ed. Abraham L. Udovitch (Princeton, 1981), 595–652.

Gabriel Baer, 'Monopolies and Restrictive Practices of Turkish Guilds', *JESHO* XIII (1970), 145–65.

Ali Ihsan Bağış, *Osmanlı Ticaretinde Gayri-Müslimler* (Non Muslims in Ottoman Trade) (Ankara, 1983).

Muhammad Adnan Bakhit, *The Ottoman Province of Damascus in the Sixteenth Century* (Beirut, 1982).

P. Ballin-Greenbaum, *Joseph Nasi, Duc de Naxos* (Paris, REJ XII, 1968).

Shalom Bar-Asher, Jacob Barnai and Joseph Tobi, *History of the Jews in the Lands of Islam during Modern Times* (in Hebrew), ed. Shmuel Ettinger (Jerusalem, 1981).

Bertrand Bareilles, *Constantinople, Ses Cités Franques et Levantines (Pera-Galata-Banlieue)* (Paris, 1918).

Ömer Lütfi Barkan and Ekrem Hakkı Ayverdi, *Istanbul Vakıfları Tahrir Defteri* (Register of Istanbul Foundations) (Istanbul, 1970).

Ömer Lütfi Barkan, 'Les déportations comme méthode de peuplement et de colonisation dans l'Empire Ottoman', *Revue de la Faculté des Sciences Economiques de l'Université d'Istanbul* XI (1949–50), 67–131.

Ömer Lütfi Barkan, 'Türkiyede Imparatorluk Devirlerinin büyük nüfus ve arazi tahrirleri ve Hâkana mahsus istatistik defterleri' (The Great population and land censuses and statistical registers for the rulers of the Ottoman Empire in Turkey) *Iktisat Fakültesi Mecmuası* II (1940–41), 20–59, 214–257.

Ömer Lütfi Barkan, 'Essai sur les Données Statistiques des Registres de Recensement dans l'Empire Ottoman aux XVe et XVe Siecles', *JESHO* I (1957), 3–26.

Ömer Lütfi Barkan, 'Les Déportations comme méthode de peuplement et de colonisation dans l'Empire Ottoman', *Revue de la Faculté des Sciences Economiques de l'Université d'Istanbul* XI (1949–50), 67–131.

Ömer Lütfi Barkan, 'Research on the Ottoman Fiscal Surveys', *Studies in the Economic History of the Middle East*, ed. M. Cook (London, 1970), 163–71.

Ömer Lütfi Barkan, '894 (1488/89) yılı Cizyesinin Tahsilâtına âit Muhasebe Bilançoları', *Belgeler* I (1964), 1–117.

Ömer Lütfi Barkan, 'Quelques observations sur l'organisation économique et sociale des villes ottomanes des XVIe et XVIIe siècles', *La Ville* VII (Brussels, 1955).

Ömer Lütfi Barkan, 'The Price Revolution of the Sixteenth Century: A Turning Point in the Economic History of the Near East', *IJMES* VI (1975), 3–28.

Elisabeth Barker, *British Policy in South-East Europe in the Second World War* (London, 1976).

H. Barnai, *Portuguese Marranos in Izmit in the Seventeenth Century* (in Hebrew) (Jerusalem, 1942).

Yaakov Barnai, *Yehude Erets-Yisrael ba-me'ah ha-hasut 'Pekide Kushta/The Jews in the Land of Israel in the eighteenth century under the patronage of the Constantinople Committee Officials of Eretz Israel* (Jerusalem, 1960).

Yaakov Barnai, 'The Statute of the 'General Rabbinate' of Jerusalem in the Ottoman Age' (in Hebrew), *Cathedra* no. 13 (1980), 47–69.

Yaakov Barnai, 'Outlines of the History of the Istanbul Community in the 18th century' (in Hebrew), *From East and From West*, ed. J. Barnai *et al.* (Haifa, 1981).

Yaakov Barnai, 'The Jews in the Ottoman Empire' (in Hebrew), Ettinger II, 183–297.

Yaakov Barnai, 'The Origins of the Jewish Community in Izmir in the Ottoman Period' (in Hebrew), *Pe'amim* no. 12 (1987), 47–59.

Yaakov Barnai, 'Messianism and Leadership: the Sabbatean Movement and the Leadership in Ottoman Jewish Communities', Unpublished paper presented at *First International Congress on Turkish Jewry*, Herzlia, Israel, 18 October 1989.

Yaakov Barnai and Haim Gerber, 'Jewish guilds in Constantinople in the late 18th century' (in Hebrew), Michael, *On the History of the Jews in the Diaspora* VII (1981), 206–26.

Jacob Barnai, 'On the History of the Jews in the Ottoman Empire', *Sephardi Jews in the Ottoman Empire*, ed. Esther Juhasz (1990), pp. 19–35.

David N. Barocas, *A Study on the Meaning of Ladino, Judezmo and the Spanish Jewish Dialect* (New York, Foundtion for the Advancement of Sephardic Studies and Culture, 1976).

Deborah Baron, *The Exiles* (in Hebrew) (Tel Aviv, 1970).

Salo W. Baron, *A Social and Religious History of the Jews: Second Edition, Revised and Enlarged. Late Middle Ages and Era of European Expansion, 1200–1650, vol. XVIII, The Ottoman Empire, Persia, Ethiopia, India and China* (Columbia University Press, 1983).

Salo W. Baron, *A Social and Religious History of the Jews: Second Edition, revised and enlarged, vol. XVII, Byzantines, Mameluks, and Maghribians* (New York, Columbia University Press, 1983).

Michael Barsley, *Orient Express* (New York, 1967).

Israel Bartal, 'The Old Yishuv in Eretz Yisrael, 1777–1914' (in Hebrew), *History of the Yishuv*, ed. S. Stempler (Tel Aviv, 1983).

Elie Baruh, *From the History of the Bulgarian Jews* (in Hebrew) (Tel Aviv, 1960).

Deborah Barzilay-Yegar, 'Crisis as Turning Point: Chaim Weizmann in World War I', *Studies in Zionism* (Jerusalem) VI (1982), 241–54.

Michael Bar-Zohar, *Spies in the Promised Land*, tr. from French by Monroe Stearns (London, 1972).

Eliezer Bashan, 'Economic Life from the 16th to the 18th Century' (in Hebrew), Jacob Landau, ed., *The Jews in Ottoman Egypt (1517–1914)* (in Hebrew) (Jerusalem, 1988), 63–112.

A. Batur, A. Yücel and N. Fersan, 'Istanbulda Ondukuzuncu Yüzyıl Sıra Evleri' (Nineteenth Century Row Houses in Istanbul), *Orta Doğu Teknik Üniversitesi Mimarlık Fakültesi Dergisi*, Fall, 1979, 185–205.

Yehuda Bauer, *A History of the Holocaust* (New York, 1982).

Celal Bayar, *Celal Bayar diyorki, 1920–50* (Celal Bayar Says, 1920–50) (Ankara, 1964).

Alex Bein, ed., *Arthur Ruppin: memoirs, diaries, letters* (New York, 1972).

I. Beldiceanu-Steinherr, 'Le Règne de Selim Ier: Tournant dans la vie politique et religieuse de l'Empire Ottoman', *Turcica* VI (1975), 34–48.

Yehosha Ben Arieh, *Jerusalem in the 19th Century: The Old City* (New York, St. Martin's Press, 1984)

Avraam A. Benaroya, 'Beginnings of the Socialist movement among the Jews of Salonica' (in Hebrew), *Zikhron Saloniki*, ed. D. A. Recanati (Tel Aviv, 1972).

Nesim Benbanaste, *Örneklerle Türk Musevi Basının Tarihçesi* (History of the Turkish Jewish Press with Examples) (Istanbul, 1988).

Esther Benbassa (Dudonney), *Haim Nahum Efendi, dernier grand rabbin de l'Empire Ottoman (1908–1920), son role politique et diplomatique* (2 vols., Unpublished thèse de doctorat, Université de Paris III, Sorbonne Nouvelle, 1987. Doctorat d'Etat es Lettres).

Esther Benbassa, *Un Grand Rabbin Sepharade en Politique, 1892–1923* (Paris, CNRS, 1990).

Esther Benbassa, 'La Presse d'Istanbul et de Salonique au service du Sionisme (1908–1914): Les Motifs d'Une Allegiance', *RH* no. 276 (1986), pp. 337–65.

Esther Benbassa, 'L'Alliance israélite universelle et l'élection de Haim Nahum au grand rabbinat de l'Empire Ottoman (1908–1909)', *Proceedings of the Ninth World Congress of Jewish Studies* (Jerusalem, 1986), 83–90.

Esther Benbassa, 'Israel face a lui-même: Judaisme occidental et judaisme ottoman (XIXe–XXe siècles), *Pardès* VII (1988), 105–29.

Esther Benbassa, 'Le Sionisme dans l'Empire Ottoman a l'Aube du 20e siècle', *Vingtieme Siecle: Revue d'Histoire* no. 24 (Octobre–Decembre 1989), 69–80.

Esther Benbassa, 'Le sionisme ou la politique des alliances dans les communautés juives ottomanes (début XXe siècle), *REJ* (1990).

Esther Benbassa, 'Associational strategies in Ottoman Jewish society in the Nineteenth and Twentieth Centuries', *The Jews in the Ottoman Empire*, ed. Avigdor Levi (to be published by University Press of New England).

Esther Benbassa, 'Political Conscience-National Conscience in the Jewish-Ottoman Communities in the Early 20th Century'. Unpublished paper presented at *First International Congress on Turkish Jewry*, Herzlia, Israel, 18 October 1989.

Esther Benbassa et Aron Rodrique, 'L'artisanat juif en Turquie a la fin du 20ème siècle', *Turcica* XVII (1985), 113–26; translated as '19. Yüzyıl Sonunda

Türkiye'deki Yahudi Esnafı', *Tarih ve Toplum*, no. 66 (June 1989), 343–47.

David Ben-Gurion, *A Personal History* (London, 1972).

A. Ben-Jacob, *A History of the Jews in Iraq from the End of the Geonic Period to the Present Time* (Jerusalem, 1965).

A. Ben-Jacob, *Kehillot Yehudei Kurdistan* (Jerusalem, 1961).

H. H. Ben-Sasson, 'The Generation of the Spanish Exiles on its Fate' (in Hebrew) *Zion* XXVI (1961), 23–64.

Norman Bentwich and M. Kisch, *Brigadier Frederick Kisch: Soldier and Zionist* (London, 1966).

I. Ben Zeeb, *The Jews in Arabia* (Jerusalem, 1957).

Yitzhak Ben Zvi, 'Eretz Yisrael under Ottoman Rule, 1517–1917', Louis Finkelstein, ed., *The Jews: their history, culture and religion* (3rd edn, New York, 1960) I, 602–89; and in Louis Finkelstein, ed., *The Jews: Their History* (4th edn, New York), pp. 399–486.

Yitzhak Ben Zvi, *Eretz Israel under Ottoman Rule: Four Centuries of History* (in Hebrew) (2nd edn, Jerusalem, 1966).

Yitzhak Ben Zvi, 'Jewish Settlements in Palestine in the Seventeenth Century', (in Hebrew), *Zion* VII, 156–71, VIII, 183.

Yitzhak Ben Zvi and M. Benayahu, 'Studies and Texts on the History of the Jewish Community in Safed', *Sefunot* VI (1962), 43–59.

Charles Berlin, 'A Sixteenth Century Hebrew Chronicle of the Ottoman Empire: The Seder Iliyahu Zuta of Elijah Capsali and its Message', *Studies in Jewish Bibliography, History and Literature in honor of I. Edward Kiev* (New York, Ktav Publishing House, 1971), 21–44.

Charles Berlin, *Elijah Capsali's Seder Eliyyahu Zuta*. Unpublished Ph.D. dissertation, Harvard University (1962).

Count Johan Bernstorff, *Erinnerung und Briefe* (Zürich, 1936).

Jacques Bigart, *L'Action de l'Alliance Israélite en Turquie* (Paris, 1913).

Karl Binswanger, *Untersuchungen zum Status der Nichmuslime im Osmanischen Reich des 16. Jahrhunderts, mit einer Neudefinition des Begriffes 'Dimma,'* Beitraege zur Kenntnis Südosteuropas und des Nahen Orients, Band 23 (Munich, 1977).

Eliezer Birnbaum, 'Hekim Ya'qub, Physician to Sultan Mehemmed the Conqueror', *Hebrew Medical Journal* I (1961), 222–50.

H. W. Blood-Ryan, *Franz von Papen* (London, 1939).

Arnold Blumberg, *Zion before Zionism, 1838–1880* (Syracuse University Press, 1985).

Salvatore Bono, 'Achat d'Esclaves Turcs pour les Galères pontificales, XVe–XVIIIe siècle', *ROMM* no. 39/1 (1985), *Les Ottomans en Méditerranée* (Aix en Province, 1985), 79–92.

Morton Borden, *Jews, Turks and Infidels* (Chapel Hill, N.C., 1984).

E. Borè, *Almanach de l'Empire ottoman, années 1849 et 1850* (Constantinople, 1850).

Leah Bornstein, *The Structure of the Spiritual Leadership and the Jewish Courts of Law in the Ottoman Empire During the 16th and 17th Centuries* (in Hebrew) (Ramat Gan, Israel, 1972).

Leah Bornstein, 'The Structure of the Rabbinate in the Ottoman Empire' (in Hebrew), *East and Maghreb*, 223–58.

Leah Bornstein-Makovetzky, 'The Land of Israel in the Responsa Literature of Turkish Rabbis in the 16th, 17th and 18th centuries', Unpublished paper presented at *First International Congress on Turkish Jewry*, Herzlia, Israel, 18 October 1989.

Leah Bornstein-Makovetzky, 'The Community and its Institutions' (in Hebrew),

Jacob Landau, ed., *The Jews in Ottoman Egypt (1517–1914)* (in Hebrew) (Jerusalem, 1988), 129–216.

Eugene Borrel, 'La Musque Turque', *Revue de Musicologie* III (1922), 149–61.

Eugene Borrel, 'Contribution a la bibliographie de la musique turque au XXe siècle', *Revue des Etudes Islamiques* IV (1928), 513–27.

Gülnihal Bozkurt, *Alman-Ingiliz Belgelerinin ve Siyasi Gelişmelerin ışığı altında Gayrimüslim Osmanlı Vatandaşlarının Hukuki Durumu (1839–1914)* (Ankara, TTK, 1989).

Gülnihal Bozkurt, 'Islâm Hukukunda Zimmilerin Statüleri', *Kudret Ayiter'in Anısına Armağan, 9 Eylül Üniversitesi Hukuk Fakültesi Dergisi* III/4 (Izmir, 1987), 115–56.

Gülnihal Bozkurt, 'Islâm Hukukunda Müste'menler', *Fadıl Hakkı Sur'un Anısına Armağan* (Ankara, 1983), 361–79.

J. Braslawsky, 'The Jewish Settlement in Tiberias from Don Joseph Nasi to Ibn Yaish' (in Hebrew), *Zion* V, 45–72.

Benjamin Braude and Bernard Lewis, ed., *Christians and Jews in the Ottoman Empire* (2 vols, New York, Holmes and Meier, 1982). Abbrev: Braude/Lewis.

Benjamin Braude, 'Foundation Myths of the Millet System', Braude/Lewis I, 69–88.

E. Brauer, *Yehudei Kurdistan* (Jerusalem, 1947).

A. J. Brawer, 'Damascus Affair', *EJ* VI.

A. J. Brawer, 'The Jews of Damascus after the Blood Libel of 1840' (in Hebrew) *Zion* 11 (1946), 83–108.

S. B. Breehof, *The Responsa Literature* (Philadelphia, Pa., 1938).

William M. Brinner, 'The Egyptian Karaite Community in the Late Nineteenth Century', *Studies in Judaica, Karaitica and Islamica* (Ramat-Gan, Israel, 1982), 127–44.

Bulletin de l'Alliance Israélite Universelle Deuxième Sèrie (Paris, 1890–1911).

Bulletin de l'Hopital National Israélite Or Ahaim (Constantinople, 1921–22, 1923, 1925–26).

David M. Bunis, *The Hebrew and Aramaic Component of Judezmo: A Phonological and Morphological Analysis*, Unpublished Ph.D. dissertation, Columbia University, 1981.

Elisabeth Burgoyne, *Gertrude Bell: From Her Personal Papers* (2 vols, London, 1958–61).

Briton Cooper Busch, *Britain, India and the Arabs* (Berkeley and Los Angeles, 1971).

Briton Cooper Busch, *Mudros to Lausanne: Britain's Frontier in West Asia, 1918–1923* (Albany, N.Y., 1976).

Zvi Cahn, *The Rise of the Karaite Sect: a new light on the Halakah and Origin of the Karaites* (New York, 1937).

Neil Caplan, *Palestine Jewry and the Arab Question* (London, 1978).

Eliyahu Capsali, *Seder Eliyahu Zuta toldot ha-'Ot 'omanim u-Venitsi'ah ve-korot 'am Yisra'el be-mamlekhot Turkiyah, Sefarad u-Venitsi'ah hibro Eliyahu b.R.* by Rabbi Eliyahu Capsali vol. I, ed. Aryeh Shmuelevitz (Jerusalem, 1975).

E. Carmoly, *Don Josef, Duc de Naxos* (Brussels, 1855).

Daniel Carpi, 'The Diplomatic Negotiations over the Transfer of Jewish Children from Croatia to Turkey and Palestine in 1943', *Yad Vashem Studies on the European Jewish Catastrophe and Resistance* (Jerusalem) XII (1977), 109–24.

David Cassuto, 'The Synagogues in Cairo', Jacob Landau, ed., *The Jews in Ottoman Egypt (1517–1914)* (in Hebrew) (Jerusalem, 1988), 311–70.

Moses Cassuto, 'The Travels of Moses Cassuto', *Remember the Days*, ed. J. M. Shaftesley (London, 1966), 73–121.

Lazar Chelap, 'Jevreji u Zemunu za vreme Vojne granice' (Jews of Zemun in the time of the Frontier War), *Jevrejski Almanah 1957–1958*, 59–71.

Mustafa Cezar, 'Osmanlı Devrinde Istanbul Yapılarında Tahribat Yapan Yangınlar ve Tabii Afetler' (Destruction caused by fires and natural disasters to Istanbul buildings in the Ottoman Age), *Türk Tarih Araştırma ve Incelemeleri* I (1963), 327–414.

Frederick Chary, *The Bulgarian Jews and the Final Solution, 1940–1944* (Pittsburgh, Pa., 1972).

André Chouraqui, *Between East and West: A History of the Jews of North Africa* (Philadelphia, Pa, 1968)

André Chouraqui, *100 ans d'Histoire: L'Alliance Israélite Universelle et la renaissance juive contemporaine, 1860–1960* (Paris, 1965).

Sir Gilbert Clayton, *An Arabian Diary* (Berkeley and Los Angeles, 1969).

Haviv Cna'an, *The War of the Press: The Struggle of the Hebrew Press in Eretz Yisrael Against British Authority* (in Hebrew) (Jerusalem, Zionist Library, 1967).

Amnon Cohen, *The Jews of Jerusalem in the 16th Century according to Turkish Documents of the Shari'a Court* (in Hebrew) (Jerusalem, 1966).

Amnon Cohen, *Jewish Life under Islam: Jerusalem in the 16th Century* (Cambridge, Mass., Harvard University Press, 1984).

Amnon Cohen, *Palestine in the 18th Century: Patterns of Government and Administration* (Hebrew University, Jerusalem, 1973).

Amnon Cohen, *Ottoman Documents on the Jewish Community of Jerusalem in the Sixteenth Century* (in Hebrew) (Jerusalem, 1976).

Amnon Cohen, 'On the Jews of Gallilee (16th–18th centuries)', *International Conference on the Jewish communities of Muslim lands* (Jerusalem, 1974).

Amnon Cohen and Bernard Lewis, *Population and Revenue in the Towns of Palestine in the sixteenth Century* (Princeton, N.J., 1978).

Amnon Cohen, 'Sixteenth Century Egypt and Palestine, The Jewish Connection as reflected in the sijill of Jerusalem', *Egypt and Palestine*, ed. A. Cohen and Gabriel Baer (Jerusalem, 1984), 232–40.

Eliyahou Cohen, *L'influence intellectuelle et sociale des écoles de l'Alliance Israélite Universelle sur les Israélites du Proche-Orient.* Unpublished Ph.D. dissertation, University of Paris, 1962.

G. Cohen, 'The Story of the Four Captives', *Proceedings of the American Academy for Jewish Research* XXIX (1960–61), 55–131.

Hayyim J. Cohen, *The Jews of the Middle East, 1860–1972* (New York and Toronto, Wiley, 1973).

Hayyim J. Cohen and Zvi Yehuda, eds, *Asian and African Jews in the Middle East, 1860–1971: Annotated Bibliography* (Jerusalem, 1976).

M. R. Cohen, *The Jews under Islam from the Rise of Islam to Shabbatai Tzvi* (Princeton, 1981).

Rivka Cohen, 'Romaniotes and Sephardim: The Struggle for Hegemony in Istanbul in the late 15th and early 16th centuries'. Unpublished paper presented at *First International Congress on Turkish Jewry*, Herzliya, Israel, 18 October 1989.

Stuart Cohen, 'Israel Zangwill's Project for Jewish colonization in Mesopotamia: Its Context and Character', *MES* XVI (1980), 200–208.

A. Comen, 'Ritual Murder Accusations against the Jews during the Days of Suleiman the Magnificent', *Journal of Turkish Studies* X (1986), 73–86.

Mercado Covo, *Aperçu Historique sur la Communauté Israélite de Serres* (Tel Aviv, 1962).

G. Cozzi, ed., *Gli Ebrei a Venezia secoli XIV–XVIII* (Milano, 1987).

Bistra Cvetkova, *Vie économique de villes et ports Balkaniques aux XVe et XVIe siècles* (Paris, 1971).

Zeynep Çelik, *The Remaking of Istanbul: Portrait of an Ottoman City in the Nineteenth Century* (Seattle, Washington, 1986).

Abraham Danon, 'Recueil de romances judéo-espagnoles chantées en Turquie', *REJ* XXXII (1896), 102–23, 263–75, XXXIII (1897), 255–68.

Abraham Danon, 'La communauté juive de salonique au XVIe siècle', *REJ* XL(1900), 206–30, XLI (1900), 98–117, 250–65.

Abraham Danon, 'Alaman Family' (in Hebrew), *Yoseph Da'at* I(1888), 6–8, 18–20, 34–37, 50–53, 98–101, 115–20, 130–34, 146–47.

Abraham Danon, 'Etude Historique sur les Impots directs et indirects des Communautés Israélites en Turquie', *REJ* XXXI (1895), 52–61.

Abraham Danon, 'Documents Relating to the History of the Karaites in European Turkey', *JQR* XVII, 165–98, 239–322.

Abraham Danon, 'Karaites in European Turkey', *JQR* XV (1924–25), 285–360, XVII (1926–27), 165–98, 239–322.

Arsène Darmesteter, 'Lettres des Juifs d'Arles et de Constantinople', *JQR* n.s. XV (1924–25), 285–360, XVII (1926–27), 165–98, 239–322.

Avraham David, 'The Nassi Family and the Reconstruction of Tiberias', Unpublished paper presented at *First International Congress on Turkish Jewry*, Herzlia, Israel, 18 October 1989.

Abraham David, 'Jewish Settlements from the 16th Century to the 18th Century' (in Hebrew), Jacob Landau, ed., *The Jews in Ottoman Egypt (1517–1914)* (in Hebrew) (Jerusalem, 1988), 13–26.

Abraham David, 'Castro, Jacob ben Abraham', *EJ* V, 245.

Lucy Davidowicz, *The War Against the Jews, 1933–1945* (London, 1975).

Basil Davidson, *Special Operations Europe: Scenes from the Anti-Nazi War* (New York, 1981).

Roderic Davison, 'Turkish Attitudes concerning Christian-Muslim Equality in the Nineteenth Century', *AHR* LIX (1953–54), 844–64.

Esther Debus, *Die islamisch-rechlichen Auskünfte der Milli Gazete im Rahmen des 'Fetwa-Wesen' der Türkischen Republic* (Berlin, 1984).

Renzo De Filice, *Ebrei in un paese arabo. Gli Ebrei nella Libia contemporanea tra colonialismo, nazionalismo arabo e sionisme (1835–1970)* (Bologne, 1978).

Sergio Della-Pergola, 'Jewish Population in the 19th and 20th Centuries' (in Hebrew), Jacob Landau, ed., *The Jews in Ottoman Egypt (1517–1914)* (in Hebrew) (Jerusalem, 1988), 27–62.

Sergio Della Pergola, 'Aliya and Other Jewish Migrations: Toward an Integrated Perspective', *Studies in the Population of Israel in Honor of Roberto Bachi, Scripta Hierosolymitana*, ed. U. O.Schmelz and G. Natan, XXX (1986), 172–209.

Sergio Della Pergola, *La trasformazione demografica della diaspora ebraica* (Turin, 1983).

Simonetta Della Setta, 'La Situazione Socio-Territoriale in Palestina ed il Primo Insediamento Ebraico Precedente al Mandato Britannico', *Storia Contemporanea* XV (1984), 181–211.

John A. De Novo, *American Interests and Policies in the Middle East, 1900–1939* (Minneapolis, 1963).

Miroslav Despot, 'Zagrebachki Knijizhar Lavoslav Hartman, 1813–1881' (The Zagreb Publisher Levoslav Hartman, 1813–1881), *Jevrejski Almanah 1955–1956*, 71–85.

Miroslava Despot, 'Protuzhidovski izgredi u Zagoru i Zagrebu godina 1883', (Anti Semitic incidents in Zagreb in 1883), *Jevrejski Almanah 1957–1958*

Paul Dumont, *La Turquie Dans les Archives du Grand Orient de France* (Strasbourg, 1980).

Paul Dumont, *Mustafa Kemal* (Paris, 1983).

Paul Dumont, 'Jewish Communities in Turkey during the Last Decades of the Nineteenth Century in the Light of the Archives of the Alliance Israélite Universelle', Braude/Lewis.

Paul Dumont, 'La condition juive en Turquie a la fin du XIXème siècle', *Les nouveaux cahiers* no. 57 (summer, 1979), 25–38.

Paul Dumont, 'Une source pour l'étude des communautés juives de Turquie: les Archives de l'Alliance Israélite Universelle', *Journal Asiatique*, CCLXVII (1979), 101–35.

Paul Dumont, 'Jewish Communities in Turkey during the Last Decades of the Nineteenth Century in the Light of the Archives of the *Alliance Israélite Universelle*', Braude/Lewis I, 209–42.

Paul Dumont, 'The social structure of the Jewish community of Salonica at the end of the nineteenth century', *Southeastern Europe* V (1979), 33–72; published in French as 'La structure sociale de la communauté juive de Salonique a la fin du dix-neuvième siècle', *RH* CCLXIII/2 (1980), 351–93.

Paul Dumont, 'Une communauté en quête d'avenir. Le sionisme a Istanbul au lendemain de la Prèmiere Guerre mondiale d'apres la *Nation*, Organe de la Fédération Sioniste d'Orient, 1919–1922', *Les Juifs dans la Méditerranée médiévale et moderne*: Actes des Journés d'études, Nice, 25 et 26 Mai 1983 (Nice, Université de Nice – Centre de la Méditerranée moderne et contemporaine, 1986), 97–124.

Paul Dumont, 'Les Organisations Socialistes et la Propagande Communiste a Istanbul pendant l'Occupation Aliée, 1918–1922', *EB*, XV (1979), 31–51.

Paul Dumont, 'Bolchevisme et Orient: Le parti communiste turc de Mustafa Suphi, 1918–1921', *Cahiers du Monde Russe et Soviètique* XVIII (1977).

Divna Durich-Zamolo, 'Stara Jevrejska chetvrt i Jevrejska ulica u Beogradu', (Old Jewish neighborhoods and Streets in Belgrade) *Jevrejski Almanah 1955–1957*, 41–76.

Maurice Edelman, *Ben Gurion* (London, 1964).

Y. Eilam, *The Hebrew Battalions in World War I* (in Hebrew) (Tel Aviv, 1973).

Robert Eisenman, 'The Young Turk Legislation, 1913–1917, and Its Application in Palestine/Israel', *Palestine in the Late Ottoman Period*, ed. David Kushner (Brill, Leiden, 1986), 59–73.

Yigal Elam, *The Jewish Legion in World War I* (in Hebrew) (Tel Aviv, Ministry of Defense, 1973).

Itimar M. Elbogen, *History of Israel in the Last Century* (in Hebrew) (Tel Aviv, 1947).

Yoseph El-Gamil, 'Karaite Jews in Egypt, 1517–1798' (in Hebrew), Jacob Landau, ed., *The Jews in Ottoman Egypt (1517–1914)* (in Hebrew) (Jerusalem, 1988), 513–56.

Mordechai Eliav, *Die Juden Palaestinas in der deutschen Politik, 1842–1914* (Tel Aviv, 1973)

Mordechai Eliav, *David Wolffsohn, The Man and his times* (in Hebrew) (Tel Aviv/Jerusalem, 1977).

Mordechai Eliav, *Eretz Yisrael and Its Yishuv in the Nineteenth Century, 1777–1917* (in Hebrew) (Jerusalem, 1978)

Mordechai Eliav, *Under Imperial Austrian Protection: Selected Documents from the Archives of the Austrian Consulate in Jerusalem, 1849–1917* (in Hebrew) (Jerusalem, Yad Ben-Zvi, 1985).

Mordechai Eliav, 'German Interests and the Jewish Community in Nineteenth Century Palestine', Ma'oz, pp. 423–41.

Abraham Elmaleh, *Palestine and Syria during the World War* (in Hebrew) (2 vols, Jerusalem, 1929).

Abraham Elmaleh, 'Rabbi Haim Nahoum, sa vie, ses oeuvres', *Le Judaisme Sephardi* XX (1961), 946–48.

Amos Elon, *The Israelis: Founders and Sons* (Tel Aviv, 1981).

G.H. El-Nahal, *The Judicial Administration of Ottoman Egypt in the Seventeenth Century* (Minneapolis and Chicago, 1979).

David Elnecavé, 'Folklore musical de los Sefaradies de Turquia', *Sefarad* XXIII (1963), 121–33, 325–34, XXIV (1964), 121–36.

Isaac Samuel Emmanuel, *Histoire des Israélites de Salonique* (2 vols, Paris, 1936).

Isaac Samuel Emmanuel, *Histoire de l'industrie des tissus des Israélites de Salonique* (Paris, Lipschutz, 1935).

Franz Carl Endres, *Der Weltkrieg der Turkei* (Berlin, 1920).

A. Engle, *The NILI Spies* (London, 1959).

Mark A. Epstein, *The Ottoman Jewish Communities and their Role in the Fifteenth and Sixteenth Centuries* (Freiburg, 1980).

Mark A. Epstein, 'The Leadership of the Ottoman Jews in the Fifteenth and Sixteenth Centuries', Braude/Lewis I, 101–15.

Yavuz Ercan, 'Türkiye'de XV. ve XVI. yy.larda Gayrimüslimlerin Içtimai ve Iktisadi Durumu', *Belleten* XLVII (1983).

Leila Erder and Suraiya Faroqhi, 'Population Rise and Fall in Anatolia, 1550–1620', *MES* XV (1979), 322–45.

Leila Erder, 'The Measurement of Preindustrial Population Changes: The Ottoman Empire from the Fifteenth to the Seventeenth Centuries', *MES* XI (1975), 284–301.

Osman Ergin, *Mecelle-i Umur-u Belediye* (Journal of Municipal Affairs) (5 volumes, Istanbul, 1914–1919).

Osman Ergin, *Istanbulda Imar ve Iskan Hereketleri* (Construction and Settlement movements in Istanbul) (Istanbul, 1938).

Osman Ergin, *Türk Imar Tarihinde Vakıflar, Belediyeler, Patrikhaneler* (Foundations, Municipalities and Patriarchates in the history of Turkish construction) (Istanbul, 1944).

Osman Ergin, 'Istanbul'un nüfusu' (The population of Istanbul) *Şehremaneti Mecmuası* I (1340/1924), 129–37, 161–71.

Osman Ergin, 'Istanbulda mahalle mıntaka ve daire taksimatı' (District locations and department divisions in Istanbul) *Şehremaneti Mecmuası* IV (1928), 404–15, 559–73, 750–60.

Osman Ergin, 'Istanbul Itfaiyesi', (Istanbul fire departments) *Şehremaneti Mecmuası* V (1928), 140–65.

Celal Esat, *Eski Istanbul* (Old Istanbul) (Istanbul, 1909).

Celal Esat, *Eski Galata ve Binaları* (Old Galata and its Buildings) (Istanbul, 1911).

E. Eshkenazi, 'Evreite na Balkanskiya poluostrov prez XV i XVI vek, techniyat bit, kultura, masovi razsloeniya, pominuk i organizatsiya na obshtinite im' (Jews in the Balkan Peninsula during the 15th and 16th centuries, their customs, culture, stratification, occupations and organization of their governing bodies), *Godishnik na obshtestvenata kulturno-prosvetna organizatsiya na evreite v NR Bulgariya* (Annual of the General Cultural Educational Organization of Jews in the Peoples Republic of Bulgaria) III (1968), 127–50.

José Estrugo, *Los Sefardies* (Havana, 1958).

Akiva Etinger, *With Hebrew Agriculturalists in Our Land* (in Hebrew) (Tel Aviv, 1945).

Evliya Çelebi, *Evliya Çelebi Seyahatnamesi* (10 vols, Istanbul, 1898–1938).

Evreiski izvori za obshtestveno-ikonomicheskoto razvitiye na balkanskite zemi prez XVI i XVII vek (Jewish sources on the socio-economic development of the Balkans in the 16th and 17th centuries) (2 vols, Sofia, 1958–1960).

Cyril Falls, *Military Operations in Egypt and Palestine from June 1917 to End of War* (London, Committee of Imperial Defence, Historical Division, 1933).

M. Fargeon, *Les Juifs en Egypte depuis les origines jusqu'a ce jour* (Cairo, 1938).

David Farhi, 'Documents on the Attitude of the Ottoman Government Towards the Jewish Settlement in Palestine After the Revolution of the Young Turks, 1908–1909', Ma'oz, pp. 190–210.

David Farhi, 'The Jews of Salonica during the Young turk Revolution' (in Hebrew) *Sefunot* XV (1981), 137–52.

N. Farhi, *La Communauté Juive d'Alexandrie de l'antiquité a nos jours* (1945).

Soraya Faroqhi, 'The Early History of the Balkan Fairs', *Südost Forschungen* XXXVII (1978), 50–68.

Suraiya Faroqhi, 'Ein Günstling des osmanischen Sultans Murad III: David Passi', *Der Islam* XLVII (1971), 290–97.

Süreyya Faruki, 'The Venetian Presence in the Ottoman Empire (1600–1630)', *Journal of European Economic History* XV (1986), 345–84.

Antoine Fattal, *Le statut légal des non-Musulmans en pays d'Islam* (Beirut, 1958).

Federation of Jewish Communities in Yugoslavia, *Posslovice i Izreke Sefardkih Jevreja Bosne i Herzegovine* (Proverbs and Sayings of the Sephardi Jews of Bosnia and Herzegovina) (Beograd, 1976).

Federation of Jewish Communities in Yugoslavia, *Jevrejski Almanah* (Jewish Almanac), ed. Ivan Ivanji, Aleksandar Levi and Zdenko Levntal (Belgrade, 1955–).

Eliyahu Feldman, 'The Question of Jewish Emancipation in the Ottoman Empire and the Danubian Principalities after the Crimean War', *JSS* XLI (1979), 41–74.

W. Filchenfeld, D. Michaelis and L. Pinner, *Ha'avara Transfer nach Palastina und Einwanderung Deutschen Juden, 1933–1939* (Tübingen, 1972).

Carter V. Findley, *Bureaucratic Reform in the Ottoman Empire: The Sublime Porte, 1789–1922* (Princeton, N.J., 1980).

Carter V. Findley, *Ottoman Civil Officialdom: A Social History* (Princeton, N.J., 1989)

George Finlay, *History of the Greek Revolution* (London, 1861).

A. W. Fisher, 'The Sale of Slaves in the Ottoman Empire – Markets and Taxes on Slave Sales', *Boğaziçi Üniversitesi Dergisi* VI (1978), 149–74.

Moise Franco, *Essai sur l'histoire des Israélites de l'Empire Ottoman depuis les origines jusqu'a nos jours* (Paris, 1897; reprint, Paris, 1980)).

Moise Franco, 'Les Juifs de l'Empire Ottoman au Dix Neuvième Siècle', *REJ* XVI (1893), 220–33.

Elena Frangakis, 'The Ottoman Port of Izmir in the Eighteenth and Early Nineteenth Centuries, 1695–1820', *ROMM*, no. 39/1 (1985), 148–62.

Elena Frangakis, 'The *Raya* Communities of Izmir in the Eighteenth Century, 1690–1820: Demography and Economic Activities', *Actes du Colloque Internationale d'Histoire. La ville neohellènique. Hèritages ottomanes et état grec* I (Athens, 1985), 27–42.

Elena Frangakis-Syrett, 'Greek Mercantile Activities in the Eastern Mediterranean, 1780–1820, *Balkan Studies* XXVIII (1987), 73–86.

Helen (Elena) Frangakis, *The Commerce of Izmir in the Eighteenth Century, 1685–1820* (Unpublished Ph.D. dissertation, University of London, 1985).

Ludwig August Frankl, *The Jews in the East*, by Rev. P. Meaton . . . . , from the German of Dr. Frankl (2 vols, Westport, Conn, 1975, from original 1859 edition.)

Ludwig August Frankl, *Nach Jerusalem; ein Reisebericht aus der Mitte des neunzehnten Jahrhunderts*. (Berlin, 1935).

S. B. Freehof, *The Responsa Literature* (Philadelphia, 1955).

David Fresco, *Le Sionisme* (Istanbul, 1909).

Harriet Pass Friedenreich, *The Jews of Yugoslavia. A Quest for Community* (Philadelphia, Jewish Publication Society, 1979).

Isaiah Friedman, *The Question of Palestine, 1914–1918: British-Jewish-Arab Relations* (London, Routledge Kegan Paul, 1973).

Isaiah Friedman, *Germany, Turkey and Zionism, 1897–1918* (Oxford, Clarendon Press, 1977).

Isaiah Friedman, ed., *The Rise of Israel: Herzl's Political Activity, 1897–1904* (New York and London, 1987).

Isaiah Friedman, ed., *The Rise of Israel: Germany, Turkey and Zionism, 1914–1918* (New York and London, 1987).

Isaiah Friedman, 'German Intervention on Behalf of the Yishuv, 1917', *JSS* XXXIII (1971), 23–43.

Isaiah Friedman, 'The Hilfsverein der deutschen Juden, The German Foreign Ministry and the Controversy with the Zionists, 1901–1918', *Leo Baeck Institute Yearbook* no. 24 (London, 1979), 291–319.

Isaiah Friedman, 'The system of Capitulations and its effects on Turco-Jewish relations in Palestine, 1856–1897', *Palestine in the late Ottoman period. Political, social and economic transformation* (Jerusalem and Leyden, 1986).

E. Gabbay, 'Alexandrie', *Juifs d'Egypte: Images et textes* (Paris, 1984), 74–78.

E. Gabbay and L. Mizrahi, 'Apogée et déclin: la période moderne" *Juifs d'Egypte: Images et textes* (Paris, 1984), 33–40.

Abraham Galante, *Histoire des Juifs de Turquie* (9 vols, Istanbul, Isis, 1987).

Abraham Galante, *Les Juifs sous la Domination des Turcs Seldjoukides* (Istanbul, 1941), reprinted in Galante, *Turquie* I, 71–88.

Abraham Galante, *Les Juifs de Constantinople sous Byzance* (Istanbul, 1940), reprinted in Galante, *Turquie* I, 5–70.

Abraham Galante, *Histoire des Juifs d'Istanbul depuis la prise de cette ville en 1453 jusqu'a nos jours* (Istanbul, 2 vols, 1941–42). Reprinted in Galante, *Turquie* I, 113–396, II, 3–241.

Abraham Galante, *Les Juifs d'Istanbul sous Le Sultan Mehmet le Conquerant* (Istanbul, 1953). Reprinted in Galante, *Turquie* I, 89–112.

Abraham Galante, *Medecins Juifs au service de la Turquie* (Istanbul, Babok, 1938). Reprinted in Galante, *Turquie* IX, 77–117.

Abraham Galante, *Histoire des Juifs d'Anatolie* (2 vols, Istanbul, 1937–39). Reprinted in Galante, *Turquie* II, 243–90, III, 1–352, IV, 1–377.

Abraham Galante, *Appendice a l'Histoire des Juifs d'Anatolie* (Istanbul, Kâğit, 1948).

Abraham Galante, *Documents officiels turcs concernant les Juifs de Turquie* (Stamboul, 1931). Reprinted in Galante, *Turquie* V, 1–208.

Abraham Galante, *Appendice a l'ouvrage Documents officiels turcs concernant les Juifs de Turquie* (Istanbul, Hüsnütabiat, 1941). Reprinted in Galante, *Turquie* V, 209–53.

Abraham Galante, *Recueil de nouveaux documents inéedits concernant les Juifs de*

Turquie (Istanbul, Kâğit, 1949). Reprinted in Galante, *Turquie* V, 255–341.

Abraham Galante, *Nouveau Recueil de Nouveaux Documents Inedits Concernant l'Turquie* (Istanbul, 1952). Reprinted in Galante, *Turquie* V, 1–84.

Abraham Galante, *Encore un nouveau recueil de documents concernant l'histoire des Juifs de Turquie* (Istanbul, Fakülteler, 1953). Reprinted in Galante, *Turquie* VI, 85–174.

Abraham Galante, *Quatrième recueil de documents concernant les Juifs de Turquie. Proverbes judeo-espagnols* (Istanbul, Fakülteler, 1954). Reprinted in Galante, *Turquie* VI, 175–238.

Abraham Galante, *Cinquième recueil de documents concernant les Juifs de Turquie* (Istanbul, Cituri Biraderler, 1955). Reprinted in Galante, *Turquie* VI, 239–98.

Abraham Galante, *Sixième recueil de documents concernant les Juifs de Turquie et Divers sujets Juifs* (Istanbul, Cituri Biraderler, 1958). Reprinted in Galante, *Turquie* VI, 299–367.

Abraham Galante, *Septième recueil de documents concernant les Juifs de Turquie et Divers sujets Juifs* (Istanbul, Cituri Biraderler, 1958). Reprinted in Galante, *Turquie* VII, 1–55.

Abraham Galante, *Turcs et Juifs: Etude historique, politique* (Istanbul, Haim Rozio, 1932). Reprinted in Galante, *Turquie* VII, 321–42, VIII, 1–114.

Abraham Galante, *Appendice a l'ouvrage turcs et Juifs: étude historique, politique* (Istanbul, M. Babok, 1937). Reprinted in Galante, *Turquie* VIII, 115–50.

Abraham Galante, *Appendice a mes Ouvrages Turcs et Juifs* (Istanbul, 1954). Reprinted in Galante, *Turquie* VIII, 151–65.

Abraham Galante, *Les Synagogues d'Istanbul* (Istanbul, 1937).

Abraham Galante, *Histoire des Juifs de Rhodes, Chio, Cos, etc.* (Istanbul, 1935). Reprinted in Galante, *Turquie* VII, 57–237.

Abraham Galante, *Appendice a l'Histoire des Juifs de Rhodes, Chio, Cos, etc., et fin Tragique des Communautes Juives de Rhodes et de Cos oeuvre du Brigandate Hitlerien* (Istanbul, 1948). Reprinted in Galante, *Turquie* VII, 239–320.

Abraham Galante, *Le Juif dans le Proverbe, Le Conte, et la Chanson Orientaux* (Istanbul, 1935). Reprinted in Galante, *Turquie* IX, 133–72.

Abraham Galante, *La Presse Judeo-Espagnole Mondiale* (Istanbul, 1935). Reprinted in Galante, *Turquie* IX, 207–26.

Abraham Galante, *Les Juifs d'Istanbul sous Le Sultan Mehmet le Conquerant* (Istanbul, 1953). Reprinted in Galante, *Turquie* I, 89–112.

Abraham Galante, *Ankara Tarihi* (History of Ankara) (Istanbul, Tan, 1951).

Abraham Galante, *Bodrum Tarihi* (History of Bodrum) (Istanbul, Tan, 1945).

Abraham Galante, *Bodrum Tarihine ek* (Supplement to the History of Bodrum) (Istanbul, Tan, 1946).

Abraham Galante, *Niğde ve Bor Tarihi* (History of Niğde and Bor) (Istanbul, Tan, 1951).

Abraham Galante, 'Nouveaux documents sur Joseph Nassy, Duc de Naxos', *REJ* LXIV, 236–43. Reprinted in Galante, *Turquie* VIII, 293–323.

Abraham Galante, *Don Salomon Aben Yaeche, Duc de Metelin* (Istanbul, 1935). Reprinted in Galante, *Turquie* IX, 19–40.

Abraham Galante, *Hommes et Choses Juifs Portugais en Orient* (Istanbul, 1927), Reprinted in Galante, *Turquie* IX, 41–75.

Abraham Galante, *Esther Kyra, d'après de nouveaux documents, contribution a l'histoire des Juifs de Turquie* (Istanbul, Fratelli Haim, 1926). Reprinted in Galante, *Turquie* IX, 1–18.

Abraham Galante, *Abdül Hamid II et le Sionisme* (Istanbul, 1933). Reprinted in Galante, *Turquie* IX, 173–88.

Abraham Galante, 'The Blood Libel in Damascus and Rhodes', *Mizrah Umaarav* V (April 1930), 47–51.

Abraham Galante, *La Presse Judeo-Espagnole Mondiale* (Istanbul, 1935). Reprinted in *Turquie* IX, 207–26.

Rabbi Moshe Galante, *A Book of Questions and Answers from Rabbi Moshe Galante* (in Hebrew) (Jerusalem, 1960).

Moshe D. Gaon, *The Oriental Jews in the Land of Israel* (in Hebrew) (Jerusalem, 1938).

Moshe D. Gaon, *A Bibliography of the Judeo-Spanish Press* (in Hebrew) (Tel Aviv, 1965).

Brian Gardner, *Allenby of Arabia* (New York, 1966).

N.M. Gelber, 'Philipp Michael de Newlinski: Herzl's Diplomatic Agent', *Herzl Year Book* II (1959), 113–52.

N. M. Gelber, 'Jewish Life in Bulgaria', *JSS* VIII (1946), 13–126.

Haim Gerber, *Ottoman Rule in Jerusalem* (Berlin, 1985).

Haim Gerber and Y. Barnai, *Jewish Guilds in Istanbul at the end of the 18th Century* (in Hebrew) (Tel Aviv, 1982).

Haim Gerber and Yuval Kamrat, ed., *Yehude ha-Imperyah ha-'Otmanit bame'ot ha 16–17 kalkalah ve hevrah/Economic and Social life of the Jews in the Ottoman Empire in the 16th and 17th Centuries* (Jerusalem, 1982).

Haim Gerber and Y. Barnai, *The Jews of Izmir in the Nineteenth Century* (in Hebrew) (Jerusalem, 1984).

Haim Gerber, 'An unknown Turkish document on Abraham Di Castro', *Zion* (Jerusalem) XL (1980), 158–63.

Haim Gerber, 'Guilds in 17th Century Anatolian Bursa', *AAS* XI (1976).

Haim Gerber, 'Enterprise and international commerce in the economic activity of the Jews of the Ottoman Empire in the 16th–17th centuries' (in Hebrew), *Zion* (Jerusalem) XLIII (1978), 38–67.

Haim Gerber, 'The Jews in the Economic Life of the Anatolian City of Bursa in the Seventeenth Century: Notes and Documents' (in Hebrew), *Sefunot* XVI, 235–72.

Haim Gerber, 'Jews and Money-Lending in the Ottoman Empire', *JQR* LXXI (1981), 100–18.

Haim Gerber, 'Sharia Kanun and Custom in Ottoman Law: the Court Records of 17th Century Bursa', *International Journal of Turkish Studies* II (1981), 133–35.

Haim Gerber, 'On the History of the Jews in Istanbul in the 17th and 18th centuries' (in Hebrew), *Pe'amim* no. 12 (1982).

Haim Gerber, 'History of the Jews in Istanbul in the 17th and 18th Centuries', *Pe'amim: Studies in the Cultural Heritage of Oriental Jewry*, Ben Zvi Institute for the Study of Jewish Communities in the East, no. 12 (1982), pp. 27–45.

Haim Gerber, 'A New Look at the *Tanzimat*: The Case of the Province of Jerusalem', *Palestine in the Late Ottoman Period*, ed. David Kushner (Brill, Leiden, 1986), 30–45.

Haim Gerber, 'Jewish Tax Farmers in the Ottoman Empire in the 16th and 17th Centuries', *Journal of Turkish Studies* X (1986), 143–62.

M. Geshuri, 'The Road Pavers (On the Luminaries in the Song of the Sephardi Jews)', *Hallel* II (1930), 39–41.

H. A. R. Gibb and Harold Bowen, *Islamic Society and the West* (1 vol in 2 parts, London, Oxford University Press, 1950–57)

Dan Giladi, 'The Beginning of Agricultural Settlement in Eretz Israel in the Nineteenth Century' (in Hebrew), *History of the Yishuv*, ed. S. Stempler (Tel Aviv, 1983), 44–54.

Dan Giladi, 'The Era of the Second Aliya (1904–1914): A General View' (in Hebrew), *History of the Yishuv*, ed. S. Stempler (Tel Aviv, 1983), 85–113.

E. Gilmor, *War and Hope – A History of the Jewish Legion* (1969).

Johannes Glasneck, *Methoden der Deutsch-Faschistestchen Propagandatatigheit in der Turkei vor und Wahrend des Zweites Weltkrieges* (Halle, German Federal Republic, 1966).

S. D. Goitein, *Jews and Arabs: Their Contacts Through the Ages* (3rd edn, New York, 1974).

Ismail Göldaş, *Istanbul Ilkokul Öğretmenlerinin Grevi (1920)* (The Strike of Istanbul Elementary School Teachers in 1920) (Istanbul, 1984).

P.S. Goldberg, *Karaite Liturgy and its Relation to the Synagogue* (Manchester, England, 1957)

Israel M. Goldman, *The life and times of Rabbi David Ibn Abi Zimra; a social, economic and cultural study of Jewish life in the Ottoman Empire in the 15th and 16th centuries as reflected in the Responsa of the RDBZ* (New York, Jewish Theological Seminary of America, 1970).

Feldmarschall Colman Freiherr von der Goltz, *Denkwürdigkeiten* (Berlin, 1929).

Morris S. Goodblatt, *Jewish Life in Turkey in the 16th Century as reflected in the legal writings of Samuel de Medina* (New York, Jewish Theological Seminary of America, 1952).

Paul Goodman, *Moses Montefiore* (Philadelphia, 1925).

H. Gramel, 'Die Auswanderung der Juden aus Deutschland Zwischen 1933 und 1939', *Gutachten des Institut für Zeitgeschichte* (Munich, 1982).

Jean-Louis Bacqué-Grammont and Paul Dumont, ed., *Economie et Sociétés Dans l'Empire Ottoman (Fin du XVIIIe-Début du XXe siècle* (Paris, 1983).

(Grand Rabinato de Turkia), *La konstitusion para la nasion israelita de Turkia* (Istanbul, Estamparia del Jurnal Israelit, 5625/1865).

Grand Rabinato de Turkia, *Las eleksiones para el medjlis umumi* (Istanbul, El Korreo, 5671/1910).

(Grand Rabinato de Turkia), *Hahamhane Nizamnamesi. Estatu organiko de la komunidad israelita* (Istanbul, Imprimeria Izak Gabai, 5673/1913).

Yekutiel Y. Greenwald, *Rabbi Joseph Caro and his Time* (in Hebrew) (Jerusalem 1954).

A. Griesbach, *Reise durch Rumelien und nach Burssa im Jahre 1839* (2 vols, Göttingen, 1841).

Nathan Grinberg, *The Hitlerist Pressure for destroying the Jews of Bulgaria* (in Hebrew) (Tel Aviv, 1961).

Nathan Grinberg, *Dokumenti* (Sofia, Central Consistory of Bulgarian Jews, 1945).

Paul Grunebaum, 'Les Juifs d'Orient d'apres les Geographes et les Voyaguers', *REJ* XXVII (1893), 121–35.

H. Gross, 'La Famille juive des Hamon. Contribution a l'histoire des Juifs en Turquie', *REJ* LVI, 1–26, LVII, 55–78.

K. Grünwald, *Türkenhirsch* (London, 1966).

H. Guhr, *Als türkischer Divisions-Kommandeur in Kleinasien und Palastina* (Berlin, 1937).

H. S. Gullett, *Sinai and Palestine: Official History of Australia in the War of 1914–18* (Sydney, 1935).

Joseph Gur-Arieh, 'Istanbul as a World Center of Karaim after the Conquest', Unpublished paper presented at *First International Congress on Turkish Jewry*, Herzlia, Israel, 18 October 1989.

Nuvit Guvrim, 'The Meeting of the Jews Who were expelled from Eretz Israel with Egypt and its Jewish Community during World War I' (in Hebrew) *Pe'amim* no. 25 (1985), 73–102.

Nuvit Guvrim, *Egypt* (in Hebrew) (Haifa, 1985).

Lütfi Güçer, 'XV–XVI asırlarda Osmanlı Imparatorluğunda Tuz Inhisarı ve Tuzların Işleme Nizamı' (the Salt Monopoly in the Ottoman Empire in the 15th and 16th Centuries and regulations for operation of the salt mines', *Iktisat Fakültesi Mecmuası* XXIII (1962–63), 97–143.

Naim Güleryüz, 'Türkiye Yahudileri Tarihi (History of the Jews of Turkey)', *Şalom* (Istanbul), 17 April 1985–31 December 1986.

Naim Güleryüz, 'Osmanlı Imparatorluğu döneminde Türk Yahudi Basını (The Turkish Jewish Press during the time of the Ottoman Empire)', *Şalom*, 31 October 1984.

Naim Güleryüz, 'Sinagoglarımızın isimleri ve Anlamları (The names and meanings of our Synagogues)', *Şalom* (Istanbul), 9 January 1985.

Naim Güleryüz, 'Türkiye Yahudileri Tarihi: Hahambaşı Kaymakamı Moşe Levi (History of the Jews of Turkey: Grand Rabbi Lieutenant Moshe Levi)', *Şalom*, 29 October 1986.

Naim Güleryüz, 'Türkiye Yahudileri Tarihi: 19. yüzyıl sonlarında Sinagoglar ve Balat hastahanesi (History of the Jews of Turkey: Synagogues and the Balat hospital at the end of the 19th Century)', *Şalom*, 26 November 1986.

Naim Güleryüz, 'Kan Iftirası (The Blood Libel)', *Şalom* (Istanbul), 20 November 1985.

Naim Güleryüz, 'Hamon (Amon) Ailesi' (The Hamon Family) *Şalom* (Istanbul), 4 December 1985.

Naim Güleryüz, ' 'Alliance' Okulları' (The Alliance Schools) *Şalom*, 5 November 1986.

Naim Güleryüz, 'Istanbul Italyan Musevi Cemaatı' (The Italian Jewish Community of Istanbul) *Şalom* (Istanbul), 17 and 24 December 1986.

Naim Güleryüz, '19. yüzyıl sonunda Izmir Hahambaşı Haim Palacci' (Izmir Chief Rabbi at the end of the 19th Century Haim Palacci) *Şalom*, 7 January 1987.

Naim Güleryüz, 'Türk-Yahudi Basını'nın Duayeni: David Fresko' (The doyen of Turkish Jewish press David Fresco) *Şalom*, 31 October 1984.

Naim Güleryüz, 'Kurtuluş Savaşında Egede ve Bursada Yahudiler' (The Jews in the Aegean and at Bursa during the War for Independence) *Şalom*, 30 October 1985

Naim Güleryüz, 'Hahambaşı Haim Moşe Becerano Efendi' (Chief Rabbi Haim Moshe Bejerano Efendi) *Şalom*, 14 August 1985.

Naim Güleryüz, 'Türkiye Yahudileri Tarihi: Merhum Hahambaşı Refael David Saban' (History of the Jews of Turkey: The Late Grand Rabbi Raphael David Saban) *Şalom* (Istanbul, 10 December 1986.

Joseph A. Hacker, The 'Chief Rabbinate' in the Ottoman Empire in the 15th and 16th centuries' (in Hebrew) *Zion* (Jerusalem) XLIX (1984), 225–63.

Joseph A. Hacker, 'Ottoman Policy toward the Jews and Jewish Attitudes toward the Ottomans during the Fifteenth Century', Braude/Lewis I, 117–26.

Joseph A. Hacker, 'Spiritual and Material Links between Egyptian and Palestinian Jewry in the Sixteenth Century', *Egypt and Palestine*, Amnon Cohen and Gabriel Baer, eds. (Jerusalem, 1984), 241–50.

Joseph A. Hacker, 'The Intellectual Activity of the Jews of the Ottoman Empire during the sixteenth and seventeenth centuries', *Jewish Thought in the Seventeenth Century*, ed. I. Twersky and B. Septimer (Cambridge, Mass., Harvard University Press, 1987), 95–135.

Joseph A. Hacker, 'Istanbul Jewry: 1750–1970', *A Tale of Two Cities*, The Jewish Museum (New York, 1972).

Yosef Hacker, *The Jewish Community in Saloniki and Its Periphery in the 15th and 16th Centuries* (in Hebrew). Unpublished Ph.D. dissertation, Hebrew University, Jerusalem, 1979.

Mordechai Ben Hillel ha-Cohen, *The War of Nations: An Eretz Israel Diary, 1914–1918* (in Hebrew) (Jerusalem, 1981).

Abraham Haim, 'The Grand Rabbi of Istanbul and the Rabbinic war at Jerusalem', (in Hebrew), *Peamim* XII (1982), 105–13.

Nadav ha-Levi, 'Jewish Economy in the Era of the Yishuv' (in Hebrew), *History of the Yishuv*, ed. S. Stempler (Tel Aviv, 1983), 205–16.

Don A. Halperin, *The Old Synagogues of Turkey* (Wyndham Hall, 1987).

Alice Halphen, *Une grande dame Juive de la Renaissance: Gracia Mendesia Nasi* (Paris, 1929).

A. Hananel and E. Eshkenazi, *Evreiski Izvori za obshestveno-ikonomichesko razvitie na balkanskite zemi prez XVI vek/Fontes Hebraici ad res oeconomicus socialesque Terrarum Balcanicarum saeculo XVI Pertinentes* (2 vols, Sofia, 1958–60).

George Harris, *The Origins of Communism in Turkey* (Stanford, California, 1967).

Jacques Hassoon, *Alexandries* (Paris, 1985).

Jacques Hassoon, *Juifs du Nil* (Paris, 1981).

Jacques Hassoon, ed., *Juifs d'Egypte. Images et textes* (Paris, 1984).

Jacques Hassoun, 'The Penetration of Modernization into Jewish Life in Egypt, 1870–1918" (in Hebrew), Jacob Landau, ed., *The Jews in Ottoman Egypt (1517–1914)* (in Hebrew) (Jerusalem, 1988), 559–76.

Jacques Hassoun, 'Accusations de meurtres rituels portées par les Chrétiens contre les Juifs en Egypte entre 1870 et 1910', *REJ* CXL (1981).

Shlomo Zalman Havlin, 'Intellectual Creativity' (in Hebrew), Jacob Landau, ed., *The Jews in Ottoman Egypt (1517–1914)* (in Hebrew) (Jerusalem, 1988), 245–310.

U. R. Q. Henriques, 'Journey to Romania, 1867', *The Century of Moses Montefiore*, ed. Sonia and V. D. Lipman (Oxford, 1985).

Allan Z. Hertz, 'Muslims, Christians, and Jews in Sixteenth Century Ottoman Belgrade', *The Mutual Effects of the Islamic/Judeo-Christian worlds*, ed. A. Ascher (1979), pp. 149–64.

Theodor Herzl, *The Complete Diaries of Theodor Herzl*, ed. Raphael Patai and tr. H. Zohn (5 vols, New York and London, 1960).

Theodor Herzl, *Herzl Year Book*, ed. Raphael Patai (New York, 1961–62).

Uriel Heyd, *Ottoman Documents on Palestine, 1552–1615* (Oxford, 1960)

Uriel Heyd, *The Jews of Eretz Yisrael at the end of the 17th Century* (in Hebrew) (Jerusalem, 1953).

Uriel Heyd, *Studies in Old Ottoman Criminal Law*, ed. Victor Menage (Oxford, 1973).

Uriel Heyd, 'Blood Libels in Turkey in the 15th and 16th Centuries' (in Hebrew) *Sefunot* no. 5 (1961), pp. 135–49.

Uriel Heyd, 'Moses Hamon, Chief Physician to Sultan Süleyman', *Oriens* XVI (1963), 152–70.

Uriel Heyd, 'Turkish Documents on the Construction of Tiberius in the Sixteenth Century' (in Hebrew), *Sefunot* X (1966), 195–210.

Uriel Heyd, 'Turkish Documents on the Jews of Safed in the Sixteenth Century', (in Hebrew), *Yerushalayim* II (1956), 128–35.

Uriel Heyd, 'The Jewish Communities of Istanbul in the Seventeenth Century', *Oriens* VI (1953), 299–314.

Uriel Heyd, 'Osmanlı Tarihi İçin Ibranice kaynaklar' (Hebrew sources for Ottoman history), *VI. Türk Tarih Kongresi-Ankara 20–26 Ekim 1961* (Ankara, 1967)

Raul Hilbert, *The Destruction of the European Jews* (Chicago, 1961).

Ronald Hingley, *The Russian Secret Police* (London, 1970).

F. H. Hinsley, *British Intelligence in the Second World War* (3 vols, London, 1979–84).

H. Hirschberg, 'Udzial Josefa Nasi w pertraktaciach polsko-tureckich wr 1562', (The Participation of Joseph Nasi in the Turco-Polish Negotiations of 1562), *Miesiecznik Zydowski* IV (1934), 426–39.

H. Hirschberg, 'A Karaite Conversion Story', *Jews College Jubilee Volume* (London, 1906), 81–100.

Haim Z. Hirschberg and Y. Geller, 'Ottoman Empire', *Encyclopedia Judaica* XVI, 1530–1534.

Haim Z. Hirschberg, 'Documents from the Period of the Ottoman Conquest' (in Hebrew), *Eretz Yisrael* II (1953), 196–98.

Haim Z. Hirschberg, 'Ottoman Rule in Jerusalem in the Light of Firmans and Shari'ah Documents', *Israel Exploration Journal* II (1952), 237–48.

Haim Z. Hirschberg, 'The Oriental Jewish Communities', Arthur J. Arberry, ed., *Religion in the Middle East* I(Cambridge, 1969), 119–225.

Haim Z. Hirschberg, *A History of the Jews in North Africa* (2nd edn, 2 vols, Leiden, Brill, 1974–81).

Haim Z. Hirschberg, 'The Agreement between the Musta'ariba and the Maghribs in Cairo, 1527', *Salo Wittmayer Baron Jubilee Volume – English Section* II (Jerusalem, 1974), 577–90.

Ira Hirschmann, *Caution to the Winds* (New York, 1982).

B. Homsy, *Les capitulations et la protection des chrétiens au Proche-Orient aux XVIe, XVIIe et XVIIIe ss* (Paris, 1956).

R. Humbsch, *Beitraege zur Geschichte des Osmanischen Agyptens (nach Arabischen Sultans und Statthatlerskunden des Sinai klosters)* (Freiburg, 1976).

Albert Hyamson, *The British consulate in Jerusalem in relation to the Jews of Palestine, 1838–1914* (2 vols, London, 1939–41).

Carol Iancu, *Les Juifs en Roumanie, 1866–1919* (University of Provence, France, 1978).

Carol Iancu, 'Adolphe Crémieux, l'Alliance Israélite Universelle et les Juifs de Roumanie au début du règne de Carol Hohenzollern Sigmariengen', *REJ*, CXXXIII (1974), 481–502.

Carol Iancu, 'Benjamin Franklin Peixotto, l'Alliance israélite universelle et les Juifs de Roumanie. Correspondance inédite, 1871–1876', *REJ* CXXXVII (1978), 77–147.

A. Z. Idelsohn, *Gesaenge der orientalischen Sefaradim.* vol. 4 of *Hebraeisch-Orientalische Melodienschatz* (Jerusalem, Berlin, Vienna, 1923).

Tzvi Ilan, 'On the History of the Jewish Yishuv in Lebanon in Modern.Times', *Kardom*, no. 26–27 (Jerusalem, March, 1983).

Jon Immanuel, 'Lucky Jews', *Jerusalem Post: International Edition*, 28 October 1989, p. 11.

Halil Inalcık, *The Ottoman Empire, Conquest, Organization and Economy* (London, 1978).

Halil Inalcık, 'Bursa and the Commerce of the Levant', *JESHO* III (1960), 131–47.

Halil Inalcık, 'Capital Formation in the Ottoman Empire', *Journal of Economic History* XXIX (1969), 97–140.

Halil Inaclık, 'Istanbul', *EI* IV, 224–48.
Halil Inalcık, 'Osmanlılarda Raiyyet Rüsumu' (The Poll Tax in Ottoman Times) *Belleten* XXIII (1959), 575–610.
Halil Inalcık, 'The Policy of Mehmed II toward the Greek Population of Istanbul and the Byzantine Buildings of the City', *Dumbarton Oaks Papers* XXIII–XXIV (1969–70), 229–49.
Halil Inalcık, 'Adâletnâmeler', *Belgeler* II (1965), 49–142.
Halil Inalcık, 'Bursa and the Commerce of the Levant', *JESHO* III (1960), 131–47.
Halil Inalcık, 'Mehmet II', *Islam Ansiklopedisi* VII, 506–35.
Halil Inalcık, 'The Ottoman Economic Mind and Aspects of the Ottoman Economy', *Studies in the Economic History of the Middle East*, ed, Michael A. Cook (London, 1970), 207–18.
Halil Inalcık, 'Ottoman Methods of Conquest', *Studia Islamica* II (1954), 103–29.
Halil Inalcık, 'Süleyman the Lawgiver and Ottoman Law', *Archivum Ottomanicum* I (1969), 105–38.
Halil Inalcık, 'The Ottoman Decline and its Effects upon the Reaya', Henrik Birnbaum, ed., *Aspects of the Balkans: Continuity and Change* (The Hague, 1972), 338–54.
Halil Inalcık, 'The Heyday and Decline of the Ottoman Empire', *Cambridge History of Islam* vol. I (Cambridge, 1970), 324–53.
P.G. Inciciyan, *XVIII. Asırda Istanbul* (Istanbul in the 18th Century) (Istanbul, 1956).
Gerard Israel, *L'Alliance Israélite Universelle: 1860–1960* (Paris, 1960).
Charles Issawi, 'The Transformation of the Economic Position of the *Millet*s in the Nineteenth Century', Braude/Lewis I, 261–85.
Vladimir Jabotinsky, *The Story of the Jewish Legion* (New York, 1945).
Vladimir Jabotinsky, *Speeches, 1905–1926* (in Hebrew) (Jerusalem, 5707/1927).
Benjamin Jaffe, *A Portrait of Eretz Israel, 1840–1914* (in Hebrew) (Tel Aviv, Dvir and Carta, 1983).
Gotthard Jaeschke, *Die Türken in Den Jahren 1942–1951* (Wiesbaden, 1955).
Ronald Jennings, 'Loans and Credit in Early 17th Century Ottoman Judicial Records', *JESHO* XVI (1973), 168–215.
Ronald Jennings, 'Urban Population in Anatolia in the Sixteenth Century: A Study of Kayseri, Karaman, Amasya, Trabzon and Erzerum', *IJMES* VII (1976), 21–57.
Ronald Jennings, 'Zimmis (Non-Moslems) in Early 17th Century Ottoman Judicial Records', *JESHO* XXI (1978).
H. H. Jessup, *Fifty Three Years in Syria* (2 vols, London, 1910).
Clarence R. Johnson, *Constantinople Today: The Pathfinder Survey of Constantinople* (New York, 1922).
Judah Magnes Museum, *Embellished Lives: Customs and Costumes of the Jewish Communities of Turkey* (Berkeley, California, 1989).
Esther Juhasz, ed., *Sephardi Jews in the Ottoman Empire: Aspects of Material Culture* (Israel Museum, Jerusalem, 1990).
Esther Juhasz, 'The Custom of Serving Sweets among the Jews of Izmir', *The Israel Museum News* (1979), 72–79.
Esther Juhasz, 'Costume', Juhasz, pp. 121–71.
Esther Juhasz, 'Marriage', Juhasz, pp. 197–217
Esther Juhasz, 'Paper-cuts', Juhasz, pp. 239–53.
Esther Juhasz, 'Synagogues', Juhasz, pp. 37–59.
Esther Juhasz, 'Textiles for the Home and Synagogue', Juhasz, pp. 65–119.

Albert Kalderon, *Galante: a biography* (New York, 1983).

Hajim Kamhi, '400-ta godishnjica jevrejske opshtine u Sarajevu' (400 years of Jewish Community in Sarajevo), *Jevrejski Almanah 1961–1962*, 15–23.

Ruth Kark, 'The Contribution of the Ottoman Regime to the Development of Jerusalem and Jaffa, 1840–1917', *Palestine in the Late Ottoman Period*, ed. David Kushner (Brill, Leiden, 1986), 46–58.

Ruth Kark, 'Changing Patterns of Landownership in Nineteenth Century Palestine: The European Influence', *Journal of Historical Geography* X (1984), 357–384.

Ilan Karmi, 'Patterns of Urbanization and Modernization within Istanbul Jewry', Unpublished paper presented at *First International Congress on Turkish Jewry*, Herzlia, Israel, 18 October 1989.

Kemal Karpat, *Ottoman Population 1830–1914* (Madison, Wisconsin, 1985).

R. Kashani, *Kehiloth ha-Yehudim b'Turkhih/The Jewish Communities in Turkey* (Jerusalem, 1968)

Samuel Katz, *Battleground: Fact and Fantasy in Palestine* (London, Allen, 1973).

Yossi Katz, 'An internal Zionist dispute on Jewish settlement outside the land of Israel: the case of Turkey, 1911–12' (in Hebrew), *Zion* vol. 49 (1984), 265–88.

Dimitri Kazasov, *Burni godini, 1918–1944* (Turbulent Years, 1918–1944) (Sofia, 1949).

Haim Kechales, *History of the Jews in Bulgaria* (in Hebrew) (5 vols, Tel Aviv, 1969–73).

Elie Kedourie, *Britain and the Middle East, 1914–1921* (London, 1956).

Elie Kedourie, *The Chatham House Version and Other Middle Eastern Studies* (London, 1970).

Elie Kedourie, *Arabic Political Memoirs and other Studies* (London, 1974).

Elie Kedourie, 'Young Turks, Freemasons and Jews', *MES* VII/1 (1971), 89–104. and Elie Kedourie, *Arab Political Memoirs and other Studies* (London, 1974), 243–52.

Elie Kedourie, 'The Jews of Baghdad in 1910', *MES* VII (1971), 355–61.

Yitzchak Kerem, 'Jewish Immigration Patterns from Greece to the Ottoman Empire in the Nineteenth Century', unpublished paper delivered at the *Comité International d'Etudes Pré-Ottomanes et Ottomanes, VIII Symposium, 'Decision-Making and the Transmission of Authority in the Turkic System'*, University of Minnesota, Minneapolis, Minnesota, 14–19 August 1988.

R. Khoury, 'Note sur les foires et pélerinages juifs d'Egypte', *Hommages a la mémoire de Serge Sauneron II: Egypte post-pharaonique* (Cairo, 1979), 459–69.

Franz Kobler, ed., *A Treasury of Jewish Letters* (2 vols, Philadelphia, 1953)

Abraham Kolban, 'The Jews in Central Asia' (in Hebrew), *Yalkut Moreshet* (Jerusalem) XXV (1978), 181–85.

Zhak Konfino, 'Bibliographia Judaio Jugoslavia 1945–1955' (Bibliography of Yugoslav Judaism) *Jevrejski Amanah, 1955–1956*, pp. 395–96.

Bozhidar Kovachevic, 'O Jevrejima i Srbiji' (Of the Jews in Serbia) *Jevrejski Almanah, 1959–1960*, pp. 105–12.

Maria Kowalska, *Ukraina w polowie XVII Wieku w Relacji Arabskiego Podroznika Pawla, Syna Makarego z Aleppo. The Ukraine in the Middle of the 17th Century. Account by Bulus Ibn Makariyus al-Halabi, an Arab Traveller* (Warsaw, Polska Akademia Nauk Komitet Nauk Orientalistycznych. Prace Orientalistyczne tom XXXIII, 1986).

A. Kraabel, *Judaism in Western Asia Minor under the Roman Empire* (Ph.D. dissertation, Cambridge, Mass., 1968).

Gudrun Kraemer, *Minderheit, Millet, Nation? Die Juden in Aegypten 1914–1956*

(Wiesbaden, Harrassowitz, 1982).

Lothar Krecker, *Deutschland und die Turkei im Zweiten Weltkrieg* (Frankfurt, 1964)

H. Kresevljakovic, *Esnafi i obrti u starom Sarajevu* (Guilds and crafts in Sarajevo) (Sarajevo, 1958).

H. Kresevljakovic, *Esnafi i obrti u Bosni i Hercegovini* (Guilds and crafts in Bosnia and Herzegovina) (Sarajevo, 1961).

General Friederich Freiherr Kress von Kressenstein, *Mit den Türken zum Suezkanal* (Berlin, 1938).

Richard Kühlmann, *Erinnerung* (Heidelberg, 1948).

A. Kuhn, *Hitlers Aussenpolitisches Programm: Entstehung und Entwicklung, 1919–1939* (Stuttgart, 1970).

Bruce Kuniholm, *The Origins of the Cold War in the Near East: Great Power Conflict and Diplomacy in Iran, Turkey and Greece* (Princeton, New Jersey, 1980).

Yuluğ Tekin Kurat, *Ikinci Dunya Savaşında Türk-Alman ticaretindeki iktisadi siyaset* (Ankara, 1961).

David Kushner, ed., *Palestine in the Late Ottoman Period: Political, Social and Economic Transformation* (Brill, Leiden, 1986).

David Kushner, 'Intercommunal Strife in Palestine during the Late Ottoman Period', *AAS* XVIII/2 (1984), 187–204.

Abdürrahman Küçük, *Dönmeler ve Dönmelik tarihi* (The Dönmes and the History of Dönme-ism) (Istanbul, 1979).

Jacob Landau, *Ha-Yehudim be-Mizrayim* (The Jews in Egypt) (Jerusalem, 1967).

Jacob Landau, *Jews in Nineteenth Century Egypt* (New York, New York University Press, 1969).

Jacob Landau, *Radical Politics in Modern Turkey* (Leiden, 1974).

Jacob Landau, *Pan Turkism in Turkey: A Study of Irredentism* (London, 1981).

Jacob Landau, *Tekinalp, Turkish Patriot, 1883–1961* (Istanbul, Netherlands Archaeological Institute, 1984).

Jacob Landau, ed., *The Jews in Ottoman Egypt (1517–1914)* (in Hebrew) (Jerusalem, 1988).

Jacob Landau, 'Un tentativo di colonizzazione ebraica nella regione di Akaba negli anni 1890–1892: Da documenti tratti degli Archivi inglesi', *Rassegna Mensile di Israel* XIX/11 (Citta di Castello, 1953).

Jacob Landau, 'Abu Naddâra – An Egyptian Jewish nationalist', *JSS* III (1952), 30–44, V (1954), 179–80.

Jacob Landau, 'The Beginnings of Modernization in Education: The Jewish Community in Egypt as a Case Study', *Beginnings of Modernization in the Middle East: The Nineteenth Century*, ed. W. R. Polk and R. L. Chambers (Chicago, 1968), 299–312.

Jacob Landau, 'Hebrew Sources for the Socio-Economic History of the Ottoman Empire', *Der Islam* LIV (1977), 205–12.

Jacob Landau and Mim Kemal Öke, 'Ottoman Perspectives on American Interests in the Holy Land', *With Eyes Toward Zion*, ed. Moshe Davis, Boulder, Colorado (1986), 261–302.

Jacob Landau, 'Muslim Turkish Attitudes Towards Jews, Zionism and Israel', *Die Welt des Islams* XXVIII (1988), 291–300.

Jacob Landau, 'Jews in Nineteenth Century Egypt – Some Socio-Economic Aspects', *Political and Social Change in Modern Egypt*, ed. P. M. Holt (London, 1968), 196–208.

Jacob Landau, 'The National Salvation Party in Turkey', *AAS* II/1 (1976), 1–57.

Jacob Landau, 'Ritual Murder Accusations and Persecutions of Jews in 19th Century Egypt' (in Hebrew) *Sefunot* V (1961), 417–60.

Jacob Landau, 'Sources on the History of the Jews of Egypt and Turkey in Recent Times', *Pe'amim*, no. 23 (Tel Aviv, 1985), pp. 99–110.

Jacob Landau, 'The Young Turks and Zionism: Some comments', *Studies in Honor of Raphael Patai*, ed. V. D. Sanua (Rutherford, N.J., Farleigh Dickinson University, 1983), 197–205.

Jacob Landau, 'The Jews and their Neighbours: The Destruction of the Cairo Community, 1735' (in Hebrew), Jacob Landau, ed., *The Jews in Ottoman Egypt (1517–1914)* (in Hebrew) (Jerusalem, 1988), 471–512.

Maurice Larcher, *La Guerre turque dans la guerre mondiale* (Paris, 1926).

Nelly Las, *Les Juifs de France et le Sionisme. De l'affaire Dreyfus a la Second Guerre mondiale (1896–1939)*. Unpublished Ph.D. dissertation, Université de la Sorbonne Nouvelle-Paris III, 1985.

M. Lascaris, *Salonique a la fin du XVIIIe siècle* (Athens, 1939).

Michael M. Laskier, *The Alliance Israélite Universelle and the Jewish Communities of Morocco, 1862–1962* (Albany, New York, 1983).

Michael M. Laskier, 'Abraham Antebi, aspects of his activities in the years 1879–1914', *Peamim* XXI (1984), 50–82.

Moshe Lazar, ed., *The Sephardic Tradition: Ladino and Spanish Jewish Literature* (New York, 1972).

Lucien Lazare, 'L'Alliance Israélite Universelle en Palestine a l'époque de la Révolution des 'Jeunes Turcs' et sa mission en Orient du 29 Octobre 1908 au 19 Janvier 1909', *REJ* CXXXVIII (1979), 307–35.

Alfred LeMaitre, *Musulmans et Chretiens. Notes sur la guerre de l'Independence Grecque* (Paris, 1895).

Zdenko Levntal, 'Josef Ibn Danon iz Beograda' (Joseph Ibn Danon of Belgrade), *Jevrejski Almanah, 1959–1960*, pp. 59–62.

Uzi Lev, 'From "Bar-Giora" to "Hashomer"' (in Hebrew), *History of the Yishuv*, ed. S. Stempler (Tel Aviv, 1983), 135–51.

Isak Levi and Joseph Konforti, 'Jedan Stari statut jevrejski sefaradske opshtine u Sarajevo', *Jevrejski Almanah, 1968–1970*, pp. 86–97.

Narcisse Leven, *Cinquante ans d'histoire: L'Alliance Israélite Universelle (1860–1910)* (Paris, 2 vols, 1911–1920).

Avner Levy, 'Jewish journals in Izmir' (in Hebrew), *Pe'amim* XII (1982), 87–104.

Avner Levy, 'The Jews of Turkey on the Eve of the Second World War and During the War' (in Hebrew) *Pe'amim*, no. 26–29 (Tel Aviv, 1986), pp. 32–47.

Avner Levy, 'El Jurnalismo djudio en Izmir', *Aki Yerushalayim* IV/16 (1983).

Avner Levy, 'Status and Self Identity Changes in Turkish Jewry and the issue of Citizenship', Unpublished paper presented at *First International Congress on Turkish Jewry*, Herzlia, Israel, 18 October 1989.

Isaac Levy, *Chants judéo-espagnols* (4 vols, London and Jerusalem, 1959–73).

Isaac Levy, *Antologia de liturgia judeo-espanola* (10 vols, Jerusalem, Division de Cultura del Ministerio de Education y Cultura, 1964–80).

Moritz Levy, *Die Sephardim im Bosnien. Ein Beitrag zur Geschichte der Juden auf der Balkanhalbinsel* (Sarajevo, 1911).

M. A. Levy, *Don Joseph Nasi, Herzog von Naxos, seine Familie, und zwei jüdische Diplomaten seiner Zeit* (Breslau, 1859).

Bernard Lewis, *The Jews of Islam* (Princeton, 1984).

Bernard Lewis, *Semites and Anti-Semites: An Inquiry into Conflict and Prejudice* (New York and London, Norton, 1986).

Bernard Lewis, *Notes and Documents from the Turkish Archives: A Contribution to the History of the Jews in the Ottoman Empire* (Jerusalem, Oriental Notes and Studies, 1952).

Bernard Lewis, 'The Privilege granted by Mehmed II to His Physician', *Bulletin of the School of Oriental and African Studies* XXI (1954), 469–501.

Bernard Lewis, 'Studies in the Ottoman Archives I', *Bulletin of the School of Oriental and African Studies* XVI (1954), 469–501.

Bernard Lewis, 'The Privilege granted by Mehmed II to His Physician', *Bulletin of the School of Oriental and African Studies* XXI (1954), 469–501.

Bernard Lewis, 'A Jewish Source on Damascus just after the Ottoman Conquest', *Bulletin of the School of Oriental and Africa Studies* X (1940–41), 179–84.

Bernard Lewis, 'Jaffa in the Sixteenth Century, According to the Ottoman Tahrir Registers', *Necati Lugal Armağanı* (1968), 435–46.

Bernard Lewis, 'Population and Tax Revenues in Palestine in the Sixteenth Century according to Turkish Documents' (in Hebrew), *Yerushalayim* IV (1952), 133–37.

Bernard Lewis, 'Ottoman Observers of Ottoman Decline', *Islamic Studies* I (1962), 71–87.

Bernard Lewis, 'Eretz Israel in the First Fifty Years of Ottoman Rule according to the Registers of the Ottoman Cadaster', *Eretz Israel* IV (1956), 170–87.

Bernard Lewis, 'Islamic Revival in Turkey', *International Affairs* (London), XXVIII/1 (1952), 38–48.

Adina Weiss Liberles, 'The Jewish Community of Turkey', *The Balkan Jewish Communities: Yugoslavia, Bulgaria, Greece and Turkey*, by Daniel J. Elazar *et al.*, (New York, 1984).

Adina Weiss Liberles, 'The Jewish Community of Greece', *The Balkan Jewish Communities: Yugoslavia, Bulgaria, Greece and Turkey*, by Daniel J. Elazar *et al.*, (University Press of America, New York, 1984).

Richard Lichtheim, *Rückkehr* (Stuttgart, 1970).

Michael Littman, 'The Jewish Family in Egypt' (in Hebrew), Jacob Landau, ed., *The Jews in Ottoman Egypt (1517–1914)* (in Hebrew) (Jerusalem, 1988), 217–44.

John Livingston, 'Ali Bey al-Kabir and the Jews', *MES* VII (1971), 221–28.

Eliezer Livneh, ed., *Nili. Toledoteha shel He'azah Medinut* (Jerusalem, 1961).

Eliezer Livneh, *Aaron Aaronsohn, ha-Ish u-Zemanno* (Tel Aviv, 1969).

J. de V. Loder, *The Truth about Mesopotamia, Palestine and Syria* (London, 1923).

Isidore Loeb, *La Situation des Israélites en Turquie, en Serbie et en Roumanie* (Paris, 1877).

Dr L. Loewe, ed., *Diaries of Sir Moses and Lady Montefiore* (2 vols, Chicago, 1890).

Robyn Kay Loewenthal, 'Elia Carmona's Autobiography: Judeo-Spanish Popular Press and Novel Publishing milieu in Constantinople, Ottoman Empire, circa 1860–1932 (Unpublished Ph.D. dissertation, University of Nebraska-Lincoln, University Microfilms, 1984).

John Lord, *'Duty, Honour, Empire': The Life and Times of Colonel Richard Meinertzhagen* (London, 1971).

David Lotz, 'Luther: From Alpha to Omera', *Sixteenth Century Journal* XVI (1985), 135–38.

Heath W. Lowry, 'Portrait of a City: The Population and Topgraphy of Ottoman Selânik (Thessaloniki) in the year 1478', *Diptykha* (Athens) II (1980–81), 254–92.

A. Lowy, *The Jews of Constantinople: A Study of their Communal and Educational Status* (London, 1890).

B. MacGowan, *Economic Life in Ottoman Europe – Taxation, Trade and the Struggle for Land, 1600–1800* (Cambridge, 1981).

G. MacMunn and Cyril Falls, *Military Operations in Egypt and Palestine from the Outbreak of War to June 1917* (London, Committee of Imperial Defence, Historical Division, 1924).

E. Malcov, *From Egypt until now, very interesting article concerning what happened to the Jews after the beginning of World War I* (in Hebrew) (Jaffa, 1924).

Neville Mandel, *The Arabs and Zionism before World War I* (Berkeley and Los Angeles, University of California Press, 1976).

Neville Mandel, 'Turks, Arabs and Jewish Emigration into Palestine, 1882–1914', *St. Antony's Papers*, XVII, *Middle Eastern Affairs, No. 4*, ed. Albert Hourani (Oxford, 1965), 77–108.

Neville Mandel, 'Ottoman Policy and Restrictions on Jewish Settlement in Palestine, 1881–1908" *MES* X/3 (1974), 312–32.

Neville Mandel, 'Ottoman Practice as regards Jewish settlement in Palestine, 1881–1908', *MES* XI/1 (1975), 33–46.

Neville Mandel, 'Attempts at an Arab-Zionist Entente: 1913–1914', *MES* I/3 (1965), 238–67.

Andrew Mango, 'Remembering the Minorities', *MES* XXI (1985).

Robert Mantran, *Istanbul dans la Second Moitié du XVIIe Siècle* (Paris, 1962).

Robert Mantran, 'L'Empire Ottoman et le commerce Asiatique aux 16e et 17e siècles', *Islam and the Trade of Asia*, ed. S. R. Richards (Oxford, 1970), 169–79.

Robert Mantran, 'Le milieu urbain et social a Istanbul--les gens des corporations', *L'Empire Ottoman du 15e au 18e siècle* (London, 1984), III, 118–313.

Robert Mantran, 'La transformation du commerce dans l'empire Ottoman au 18e siècle', *L'Empire Ottoman du 15e au 18e siècle* (London, 1984) VI, 220–35.

Robert Mantran, 'La structure sociale de la communauté juive de Salonique a la fin de dix-neuvième siecle', RH no. 534 (1980), 384–89.

Moshe Ma'oz, ed, *Ottoman Reforms in Syria and Palestine, 1840–1861* (Oxford, 1968).

Moshe Ma'oz, ed., *Studies on Palestine during the Ottoman Period* (Jerusalem, 1975).

Moshe Ma'oz, 'Changes in the Position of the Jewish Communities of Palestine and Syria in the Mid-Nineteenth Century', *Studies on Palestine during the Ottoman Period*, ed. Moshe Ma'oz (Jerusalem, 1975), 142–63.

Moshe Ma'oz, 'Communal Conflicts in Ottoman Syria during the Reform Era: The Role of Political and Economic Factors', Braude/Lewis II, 91–105

Moshe Ma'oz, 'Muslim Ethnic Communities in Nineteenth-Century Syria and Palestine: Trends of Conflict and Integration', *AAS*, XIX (1985), 283–307.

S. Marcus, 'The History of the Jews of Cyprus in the Days of the Turks and Greeks' (in Hebrew), *Osar Yehude Safarad* VI, 84–101.

Israel Margalith, *Le Baron Edmond de Rothschild et la colonisation juive en Palestine, 1882–1899* (Paris, 1957).

Isaac Markon, 'Solomon Mazal Tov' (in Hebrew), *Alexander Marx Jubilee Volume, Hebrew Section* (New York, Jewish Theological Seminary of America, 1950).

Marko Markovich, 'Pripovjedachki Lik Isaka Samokovlije' (Narrative Personality of Isaac Samokovlija) *Jevrejski Almanah, 1955–1956*, pp. 225–36.

Emile Marmorstein, 'European Jews in Muslim Palestine', *MES* XI (1975), 74–87.

John Mason, *Three Years in Turkey: The Journal of a Medical Mission to the Jews* (London, 1890).

Paul Masson, *Histoire du Commerce français dans le Levant au XVIIème siècle* (Paris, 1896).

Alexander Matkovski, *A History of the Jews in Macedonia* (Skopje, Yugoslavia, 1982).

Alexander Matkovski, *Tragediyata na Evreita od Mekedonija* (Skopje, 1962).

Alexander Matkovski, 'The Destruction of Macedonian Jewry', *Yad WaShem Studies on the European Jewish Catastrophe and Resistance* III (1959), 222–58.

Nathan Mayer, *The Jews of Turkey* (London, 1913).

Justin McCarthy, *Muslims and Minorities: The Population of Ottoman Anatolia and the End of the Empire* (New York and London, New York University Press, 1983).

Justin McCarthy, *The Arab World, Turkey and the Balkans: A Handbook of Historical Statistics* (Boston, G. K. Hall, 1982).

Justin McCarthy and Carolyn McCarthy, *Turks and Armenians* (Washington, D.C., 1989).

Justin McCarthy, 'Factors in the Analysis of the Population of Anatolia, 1800–1878', *AAS* XXI (1987), 33–63.

Justin McCarthy, 'Foundations of the Turkish Republic: Social and Economic Change', *MES* XIX (1983).

L. Meignen, 'Esquisse sur le commerce français du café dans le Levant au 18 siècle', *Dossiers sur le commerce français en Méditerranée Orientale au 18e siècle*, ed. J. P. Filippini *et al.* (Paris, 1976), 102–50.

Richard Meinertzhagen, *Middle East Diary, 1917–1956* (London, 1959).

Richard Meinertzhagen, *Army Diary* (London, 1960).

Richard Meinertzhagen, *Diary of a Black Sheep* (London, 1964).

J. B.Menkes, 'Indexing the Responsa in the New York Public Library', *Bulletin of the New York Public Library* XL (1936), 9–11.

M. Meyerhof, *Medieval Jewish Physicians in the Near East from Arabic Sources* (Bruges, 1938).

Saul Mezan, *Les Juifs espagnols en Bulgarie* (Sofia, 1925).

Michael, *On the History of the Jews in the Diaspora* (in Hebrew) ed. Daniel Carpi and Shlomo Simonsohn (9 vols, Tel Aviv, Diaspora Research Institute, 1980–1985).

A. Milano, *Storia degli ebrei italiani nel Levante* (Firenze, 1949).

Maurice Mizrahi, *L'Egypte et ses Juifs. Le Temps Révolu (XIX et XX Siècles)* (Lausanne, 1977).

Isaac Molho, *Histoire des Israélites de Castoria* (Salonica, 1938).

Isaac Molho, 'The Falsification of the Picture of Don Joseph Nasi' (in Hebrew), *Behair haMizrah* (Jerusalem, 1944).

M. Molcho, *Essai d'une Monographie sur la Famille Perahia a Thessaloniki* (Salonica, 1938).

Michael Molho, *Literatura Sefardita de Oriente* (Madrid, 1960).

Michael Molho, *Usos y costumbres de los sefardies de Salonica* (Madrid, 1950).

Michael Molho, *In Memoriam, Hommage aux victimes juives des nazis en Grèce* (Salonica, 1948).

Y. R. Molho, 'Rabbi Moshe Almosnino, Procurer of Independence for the Salonika community in the Sixteenth Century' (in Hebrew), *Sinai* IV (1941), 245–56.

J. H. Mordtmann, 'Die Jüdischen Kira im Serai der Sultane', *Mitteilungen des Seminars für Orientalische Sprachen, Westasiastische Studien* XXXII (1929), 1–38.

Arieh Morgenstern, 'Pekidei Eretz Israel Organization in Istanbul in the 18th and 19th centuries', Unpublished paper presented at *First International Congress on Turkish Jewry*, Herzlia, Israel, 18 October 1989.

Edgar Morin, *Vidal et les Siens* (Paris, 1989).

John Morley, *Vatican Diplomacy and the Jews during the Holocaust* (New York,

1980).

J. Mosseri, 'The Synagogues of Egypt–Past and Present', *The Jewish Review* V (1913–14), no. 25, pp. 31–44.

H. Motzki, *Dimma und Egalité: Die nichtmuslimischen Minderheiten Aegyptens in der zweiten Haelfte des 18. Jahrhunderts und die Expedition Bonapartes (1798–1801)* (Bonn, 1979).

Vera Mutafchieva, *Le Vakif – un aspect de la structure socio-économique de l'empire ottoman, XVe–XVIIe siecles* (Sofia, 1981).

Carl Mühlmann, *Die Deutsch-Türkische Waffenbündniss im Weltkrieg* (Leipzig, 1940).

Gérard Nahon, 'Les Marranes espagnols et portugais et les communautés juives issues du marranisme dans l'historiographie récent (1960–75)', *REJ* CXXXVI (1977), 297–367.

Haim Nahoum, ed., *Recueil de firmans impériaux Ottomans adressés aux valis et aux khédives d'Egypte, 1006 H.-1322 H (1597–1904)* (Cairo, 1934).

Haim Nahoum, 'Jews', *Modern Turkey*, ed. Eliot Mears (New York, 1924), 86–97.

A. Namdar, 'On the Interpretation of Community Ordinances by R. Samuel de Medina' (in Hebrew), *East and Maghreb*, 295–331.

J. G. Nanninga, ed., *Bronnen tot de Geschiedenis van den Levantschen Handel. Vierde deel, 1765–1826* (S-Gravenhage, 1966).

Gad Nassi, 'The Sabbatean Movement and the Ottoman Mystical Tradition', Unpublished paper presented at *First International Congress on Turkish Jewry*, Herzlia, Israel, 18 October 1989.

Naphtali Nathan, 'Notes on the Jews of Turkey', *Jewish Journal of Sociology* VI (1964), 172–89.

S. Naum-Duhani, *Vielles gens, vielles demeures, topographie sociale de Beyoğlu au XIXème siècle* (Istanbul, 1947).

Isaac Navon, 'Music among the Near Eastern Jews', *Hallel* III (1930), 55–57.

Ülker Necim, *The Rise of Izmit, 1688–1740*, Unpublished Ph.D. Dissertation, University of Michigan (1974).

Yossef Nadava, 'Nili--with the end of the Yossef Lishansky Affair' (in Hebrew), *History of the Yishuv*, ed. S. Stempler (Tel Aviv, 1983), 157–63.

Boris Nedkoff, *Die Gizya (Koptsteuer) im Osmanischen Reich* (Leipzig, 1942). Turkish version: 'Osmanlı Imparatorluğunda Cizye (Baş Vergisi)', *Belleten* VIII (1944), 599–652.

Joseph Nehama, *Histoire des Israelites de Salonique* (7 vols, Salonica, 1935–78).

Joseph Nehama, *Dictionnaire du judeo-espagnol* (Madrid, 1976).

Oded Neumann, 'The Jewish Community in Palestine During World War I, 1914–1918', Unpublished research paper for Near Eastern Seminar, University of California, Los Angeles, December 1988.

Fritz Neumark, *Zuflucht am Bosporus* (Frankfurt, 1980).

Julius Newman, *Semikhah (Ordination): A Study of Its Origin, History and Function in Rabbinic Literature* (Manchester, England, 1950).

Catherine Nicault-Lèvigne, *La France et le sionisme, 1869–1914* (Unpublished thèse de doctorat, Université de Paris I, 2 vols, 1986).

Catherine Nicault-Lèvigne, 'Les Juifs français et le sionisme de 1896 a 1920', *Yod* III/2 (1978), 30–41.

Francis Nicosia, *The Third Reich and the Palestine Question* (Austin, Texas, 1985).

Robert Olson, 'Jews in the Ottoman Empire and their Role in the Light of New Documents', *JSS* vol. 41/1 (1979), 75–88; *Tarih Enstitusu Dergisi* (Istanbul) VII–VIII (1976–77), 119–44.

Robert Olson, 'The Young Turks and the Jews: A Historiographical Revision', *Turkica* XVIII (1986), 219–25.

Robert Olson, 'Jews, Janissaries, Esnaf and the Revolt of 1740 in Istanbul: Social Upheaval and Political Realignment in the Ottoman Empire', *JESHO* XX/2 (1977), 185–207.

Robert Olson, 'The Sixteenth Century 'Price Revolution' and its Effect on the Ottoman Empire and the Ottoman Safavid Relations', *Acta Orientalia* XXXVII (1976), 45–54.

Robert Olson, 'The Patrona Halil Rebellion of 1730 in Istanbul: Political Realignment in the Ottoman Empire', *JESHO* XVII (1973), 329–44.

Or Ahayim Musevi Hastantesi/Hospital Israelite Or Ahaim (Istanbul, 1930).

Nachum Orland, 'Reichsregierung und Zionismus im Ersten Weltkrieg', *Saeculum* XXV (1974), 56–87.

Dietrich Orlow, *The Nazis in the Balkans* (Pittsburg, Pa., 1968).

Ilber Ortaylı, *Tanzimattan Sonra Mahalli Idareler, 1840–1878* (Local Administrations following (declaration of) the Tanzimat, 1840–1878) (Ankara, 1974).

Ilber Ortaylı, 'The Sabbatean Enlightenment in Turkish Cultural and Social Life', Unpublished paper presented at *First International Congress on Turkish Jewry*, Herzlia, Israel, 18 October 1989.

A. Ovadiah, 'Rabbi Eliyahu Mizrahi' (in Hebrew), *Sinai* III (1939), 393–413, III (1939–40), 73–80, 230–41, 412–19, 510–16, III (1940), 99–110, 367–76, IV (1941), 122–28.

A. Ovadiah, *Ketavim Nivharim* I (1942), 63–108.

Mim Kemal Öke, *Osmanlı Imparatorluğu, Siyonizm ve Filistin Sorunu, 1880–1914* (Zionism and the Palestine Question, 1880–1914) (Istanbul, 1982).

Mim Kemal Öke, *II. Abdül Hamid, Siyonistler ve Filistin Meselesi* (Abdül Hamid II, the Zionists, and the Palestine Question) (Istanbul, 1981).

Mim Kemal Öke, *Ingiliz Casusu Prof. Arminius Vambery'nin gizli raporlarında II. Abdül Hamid ve Dönemi* (Abdül Hamid II and his time in the secret reports of the English spy Professor Arminius Vambery) (Istanbul, 1983).

Mim Kemal Öke, 'Zionists and the Ottoman Foreign Ministry during the Reign of Abdül-Hamid II, 1876–1909', *Arab Studies Quarterly* II/4 (1980), 364–74.

Mim Kemal Öke, 'The Ottoman Empire, Zionism and the question of Palestine (1880–1908), *IJMES* XIV (1982), 329–41.

Mim Kemal Öke, 'Young Turks, Freemasons, Jews and the Question of Zionism in the Ottoman Empire (1908–1913), *Studies on Zionism* VII (1986), 199–218.

Faik Ökte, *The Tragedy of the Turkish Capital Tax* (London, 1987).

Rifat Önsoy, '19. Yüzyılın Ikinci Yarısında Suriyenin Sanayi ve Ticareti', *Belleten* L (1986), 825–32.

Snedzka K. Panova, *Stopanskata dejnost na Evreite na Balkanite prez XVI-XVII v* (Economic Activity of the Jews of the Balkans in the 16th and 17th Centuries) (Sofia, 1967).

Snedzka K. Panova, 'Turgovskata i finansova deinost na evreite na Balkanite prez XVI–XVII v.' (Trade and financial activity of the Jews in the Balkans during the 16th and 17th centuries), *Istoricheski pregled* XXIII/3 (1967), 30–60.

Daniel Panzac, *La peste dans l'Empire Ottoman, 1700–1850* (Louvain, 1985).

Tudor Parfitt, "The Year of the Pride of Israel' Montefiore and the Damascus Blood Libel of 1840', *The Century of Moses Montefiore*, ed. Sonia and V. D. Lipman (Oxford, 1985), 131–70.

R. Paris, *Histoire du commerce de Marseille, V: de 1660 a 1789, Le Levant* (Paris, 1957).

Türkmen Parlak, *Yeni Asırın Selanik Yılları, 1895–1924* (The Salonica Years of *Yeni Asır*) (Izmir, 1989).

J. H. Patterson, *With the Zionists in Gallipoli* (London, 1916).

J. H. Patterson, *With the Judeans in the Palestine Campaign* (London, 1922)

B. Penanovic, *Stanovnistvo Bosne i Hercegovine* (The Population of Bosnia and Herzegovina) (Belgrade, 1955).

Marina Penava, 'Garments of the Jews in the Balkan Provinces of the Ottoman Empire', *Annual* XX (1985).

Moshe Perlmann, 'Dönme', *EI* II, 615–17.

Thomas Philipp, 'The Farhi Family and the Changing Position of the Jews in Syria, 1750–1860', MES XX (1984), 37–52.

A. Pingaud, *Histoire diplomatique de la France pendant la Grande Guerre* (Paris, 1938).

Samuel Pinto, 'Prosvijetna Prilike Bosanskih Jevreja za Turske Vladavine', (Educational Opportunities for Bosnian Jews during the period of Turkish Rule), *Jevrejski Almanah, 1955–1956*, pp. 64–70.

Stephen M. Poppel, *Zionism in Germany, 1897–1933. The shaping of a Jewish identity* (Philadelphia, 1977).

Dina Porat, *An Entangled Leadership: The Yishuv and the Holocaust. 1942–1945* (in Hebrew) (Tel Aviv, Am Oved, 1986).

S. Posener, *Adolphe Crémieux* (2 vols, Paris, 1933)

H. Rabinowicz, 'Joseph Colon and Moses Capsali', *JQR*, n.s. XLVII (1956–57), 336–44.

André Raymond, *Artisans et commerçants au Caire au XVIIIe siècle* (2 vols, Damascus, 1973–74).

André Raymond, 'The Economic Crisis of Egypt in the Eighteenth Century', *The Islamic Middle East, 700–1900*, ed. A. Udovitch (Princeton, 1981), 687–707.

André Raymond, 'Une liste de corporations de métiers au Caire en 1801', *Arabica* IV (1957), 150–63.

André Raymond, 'Quartiers et mouvements populaires au Caire au XVIIIe siècle', *Political and Social Change in Modern Egypt*, ed. P. M. Holt (London, 1968), 104–16.

Avraam S. Recanati, 'The Maccabi, the heroic period of the Zionist movement in Salonica' (in Hebrew) *Zikhron Saloniki*, ed. David Recanati (Tel Aviv, 1972).

David A. Recanati, ed., *Zikhron Saloniki: Grandeza i Destruyicion de Yeruchalayim del Balkan. I. Salonique* (Tel Aviv, 1971–72).

David A. Recanati, 'Sacred poetry and its singing in Salonica' (in Hebrew), *Zikhron Saloniki: Grandezi i Destruyicion de Yeruchalaim del Balkan*, ed. David A. Racanati (Tel Aviv, El Comitato por la Edition del Livro Sovre la Communita de Salonique, 5746), 337–47.

Ahmed Refik, *Onuçuncu asr-ı hicride Istanbul hayatı* (Life in Istanbul in the 13th Century of the Hicra) (Istanbul, 1914–15).

Anshel Reis, 'Chapters on the Aid and Rescue Activities', *Pages for the Research of the Holocaust and Revolt*, Series II (Hakibbutz Hameuhad, Israel, 1970).

Gerald Reitlinger, *The Final Solution: The Attempt to Exterminate the Jews of Europe, 1939–1945* (New York, 1953).

Nessim Rejwan, *The Jews of Iraq* (Boulder, Colorado, Westview Press, 1985).

Raymond Robert Renard, *Sepharad. Le monde et la langue judéo-espagnole des Séphardim* (Mons, Belgium, 1966).

Sir G. W. Rendel, *The Sword and the Olive: Recollections of Foreign Diplomacy, 1913–1957* (London, Murray, 1957).

J. Reznik, *Le Duc Joseph de Naxos: contribution a l'histoire juive du XVIe siècle* (Paris, 1936).

Vitoro Ugo Righi, *Papa Giovanni sulle rive del Bosforo* (Padua, Italia, 1971).

Moshe Rinott, 'Capitulations: The case of the German-Jewish Hilfsverein Schools in Palestine, 1901–1914', *Palestine in the Late Ottoman Period*, ed. David Kushner (Jerusalem, 1986), 294–302.

Aron Rodrigue, *De l'Instruction a l'Emancipation: Les enseignants de l'Alliance Israélite Universelle et les Juifs d'Orient, 1860–1939* (Paris, Calmann-Lèvy, 1989).

Aron Rodrigue, *French Jews, Turkish Jews: The Alliance Israélite Universelle and the Politics of Jewish Schooling in Turkey, 1860–1925* (Bloomington, Indiana, Indiana University Press, 1990).

Aron Rodrigue, 'Jewish Society and Schooling in a Thracian Town: The Alliance Israelite Universelle in Demotica, 1897–1924', *JSS* vol. 45/3–4 (1983), 263–86.

Yaacov Ro'i, 'The Zionist Attitude to the Arabs, 1908–1914', *MES* IV/3 (1968), 198–242.

A. Romano, Joseph Ben, and Nisim Levi, *The Jews of Bulgaria* (in Hebrew) (Jerusalem, 1968).

Elena Romero, *El teatro entre los sefardies orientales* (3 vols, Madrid, 1979).

Elena Romero, 'Las Coplas Sefardies: Categorias y Estado de la Cuestion', *Actas de las Jornadas Sefaradies*, Caceres (1980), 69–98.

Elena Romero, 'El Teatro Sefardi en Turquia', *5th World Congress of Jewish Studies* ed. A. Shinan, IV (1973), 191–94.

Solomon Rosanes (Rozanes), *Korot ha-Yehudim be Turkyah ve Arzot ha-Kedem* (History of the Jews in Turkey and in the Orient) (6 vols, Jerusalem and Sofia, 1930–45), also published in part as *Divrei Yemei Yisrael be-Togarmah* (1907–14).

C. H. Rose, 'New Information on the Life of Joseph Nasi Duke of Naxos: the Venetian Phase', *JQR* LX, 330–44.

G. Rosental, *Banking and Finance among Jews in Renaissance Italy – A Critical Edition of the Eternal Life (Haye Olam) by Yehiel Nissim da Pisa (Florence 1507– ca. 1574)* (New York, 1962).

M. Rossen, *The Patonia, A Chapter in the History of Mediterranean Trade in the Sixteenth and Seventeenth Centuries* (Haifa, 1981).

Mordecai Roshwald, 'Marginal Jewish Sects in Israel', *IJMES* IV (1973), 219–73, 328–54.

Cecil Roth, *The House of Nasi: Dona Gracia* (Jewish Publication Society of America, Philadelphia Pa. 1948).

Cecil Roth, *Dona Gracia of the House of Nasi* (Jewish Publication Society of America, Philadelphia Pa. 1977).

Cecil Roth, *The House of Nasi: The Duke of Naxos* (Jewish Publication Society of America, Philadelphia Pa. 1949).

Cecil Roth, *A History of the Marranos* (Philadelphia, 1947).

Cecil Roth, *History of the Jews in Venice* (Philadelphia, Pa., 1930).

Cecil Roth, 'The Jews of Malta', *Transactions* of the Jewish Historical Society of England, XII, 187–251.

J. Rothschild, *The Communist Party of Bulgaria: Origins and Development, 1883–1936* (New York, 1959).

Minna Rozen, 'Influential Jews in the Sultan's court in Istanbul in support of the Jewish community of Jerusalem in the 17th century' (in Hebrew), Michael, *On the History of the Jews in the Diaspora* VII (1981), 394–430.

Minna Rozen, 'The Relations Between Egyptian Jewry and the Jewish Community of Jerusalem in the Seventeenth Century', *Egypt and Palestine – A Millenium of Association (868–1948)*, ed. Amnon Cohen and Gabriel Baer (Jerusalem, 1984), 251–68.

Minna Rozen, 'The Naqib al-ashraf Rebellion in Jerusalem and its repercussions on the city's Dhimmis', *AAS* XVIII/3 (1984), 249–70.

Minna Rozen, 'Les marchands juifs livournais a Tunis et le commerce avec Marseilles a la fin du XVIIe siècle', *Michael* IX (1985), 87–129.

Minna Rozen, 'France and the Jews of Egypt: An Anatomy of Relations, 1683–1801' (in Hebrew), Jacob Landau, ed., *The Jews in Ottoman Egypt (1517–1914)* (in Hebrew) (Jerusalem, 1988), 421–70.

Minna Rozen, 'Contest and Rivalry in Mediterranean Commerce in the First Half of the Eighteenth Century – The Jews of Salonica and the European Presence', *REJ* (forthcoming).

Barry Rubin, *Istanbul Intrigues: A True-Life Casablanca* (New York, 1989).

Barry Rubin, 'Ambassador Laurence A. Steinhardt: the Perils of a Jewish Diplomat, 1940–1945', *American Jewish History* LXX (1981).

Sir Stephen Runciman, *The Great Church in Captivity* (Cambridge, 1971)

Arthur Ruppin, *The Agricultural Colonization of the Zionist Organization in Palestine* (London, 1926).

Miriam Russo-Katz, 'Childbirth', Juhasz, pp. 255–70.

Miriam Russo-Katz, 'Jewelry', Juhasz, pp. 173–95.

Giacomo Saban, *Ebrei di Turchia* (Rome, 1983).

Shalom Sabar, 'Decorated *Ketubbot*', Juhasz, pp. 219–37.

Ahmed Sabri Bey, *When I Was a Boy in Turkey* (Boston, 1924).

Howard Sachar, *History of Israel from the Rise of Zionism to Our Time* (New York, 1976).

Halil Sahıllıoğlu, 'Bir mültezim zimem Defterine göre XV. yüzyıl sonunda Osmanlı Darphane Mukataaları' (Ottoman Mint tax farms at the end of the 15th century awarding to the account register of a tax farmer), *Iktisat Fakültesi Mecmuası*, XXIII (1962–63), 145–218.

Halil Sahıllıoğlu, 'XVIII Yüzyıl Ortalarında Sanayı Bölgelerimiz ve Ticari Imkânları' (Our Industrial Districts and Commercial Possibilities in the mid 18th century), *BTTD* no. 11 (August 1968), 61–67.

I. Sakuzov, 'Turgoviyata na Bulgariya s Ankona prez XVI i XVII v. ponovi izvori' (Trade between Bulgaria and Ancona in the 16th and 17th centuries according to new sources), *Izvestiya na Bulgarsko istorichesko druzhestvo* IX (1929), 1–44.

Jeremy Salt, 'A Precarious Symbiosis: Ottoman Christians and Foreign Missionaries in the Nineteenth Century', *International Journal of Turkish Studies* III/2 (Winter 1985–86), 59–64.

Isak Samokovlija, 'Sarajevska Megila' (The Sarajevo Megila), *Jevrejski Almanah, 1955–1956*, pp. 245–46.

Avedis Sanjian, *The Armenian Communities in Syria under Ottoman Dominion* (Cambridge, Mass., 1965).

Marc Saperstein, 'Martyrs, Merchants and Rabbis: Jewish Communal Conflict as Reflected in the Responsa on the Boycott of Ancona', *JSS* LXIII (1981), 215–28.

D. S. Sassoon, 'The History of the Jews in Basra', *JQR* XVII, 407–69.

S. Schechter, 'Safed in the Sixteenth Century: A City of Legists and Mystics', in S. Schechter, *Studies in Judaism*, 2nd series (1908), 202–36.

Joseph B. Schechtman, *Rebel and Statesman: The Vladimir Jabotinsky Story* (2 vols, New York, 1956).

340   Select Bibliography on Ottoman and Turkish Jewry

Alexander Scheiber, 'Jewish Tombstones of Buda from the Period of Turkish Rule', *Journal of Semitic Studies* I (1956), 269–78.
U. O. Schmelz, 'Some Demographic Peculiarities of the Jews in Jerusalem in the Nineteenth Century', M. Ma'oz, ed, *Studies on Palestine during the Ottoman Period*, pp. 119–41.
A. B. Schneider, 'XV. Yüzyılda Istanbul Nüfusu' (The Population of Istanbul in the 15th Century) *Belleten* XVI (1952), 35–48.
Marijana Schneider, 'Predmeti zhidovskog verskog karaktera u Povejisnom muzeju Hrvatske u Zagrebu' (Jewish religious artifacts in the Historical Museum of Croatia in Zagreb), *Jevrejski Almanah, 1957–1958*, pp. 86–93.
Gershom Scholem, *Shabbatai Tzvi: The Mystical Messiah 1626–1676* (Princeton, N.J., Bollingen, 1973).
Gershom Scholem, 'Shabbatai Zevi', *EJ* XIV (1971), 1219–54.
Gershom Scholem, 'Doenme', *EJ* VI, 148–52.
Gershom Scholem, 'Kabbalah', *EJ* X, 489–653.
Gershom Scholem, 'Zohar', *EJ* XVI, 1193–2015.
B. P. Schroeder, *Deutschland und der Mittlere Osten im Zweiten Weltkrieg* (Göttingen, 1975).
Emil Schultheiss, 'A Short History of Epidemics in Hungary until the Great Cholera Epidemic of 1831', *Centaurus* (Denmark) XI (1966), 279–301.
S. Schwarzfuchs, 'La Décadence de la Galilée Juive de XVIe siècle et la Crise du Textile au Proche Orient', *REJ*, CXXI (1962), 169–79.
S. Schwarzfuchs, 'La 'Nazione Ebrea' Livournaise au Levant', *La Rassegna Mensile di Israel VI* (1984), 707–24; and *Les Juifs de France* (Paris, 1975).
Leon Sciaky, *Farewell to Salonica: Portrait of an Era* (New York, 1946).
Tom Segev, *The First Israelis* (New York, 1986).
Haim Vidal Sephiha, *L'Agonie du Judeo-Espagnol* (Paris, 1977).
Haim Vidal Sephiha, *Le Ladino, judeo-espagnol calque: structure et evolution d'une langue liturgique* (2 vols, Paris, 1986).
Edwin Seroussi, *Mizimrat Qedem: The Life and Music of R. Isaac Algazi from Turkey* (Jerusalem, Renanot Institute for Jewish Music, 1989).
Zekeriya Sertel, *Hatirladiklarım* (My memories) (Istanbul, 1977).
Midhat Sertoğlu, 'Osmanlı Imparatorluğunda Azınlık Meselesi' (The Minority Problem in the Ottoman Empire), *BTTD* no. 25 (1947).
Moshe Sevilla-Sharon, *Türkiye Yahudileri Tarihsel Bakış* (A Short History of the Jews of Turkey) (Jerusalem, 1984).
Shimon Shamir, 'Muslim-Arab Attitudes toward Jews in the Ottoman and Modern Periods', *Violence and Defense in the Jewish Experience*, ed. S. Baron, George Wise and Lenn Goodman (Philadelphia, Pa., 1977), 191–203.
Rachel Sharaby, 'The Grand Rabbinate of Jerusalem, conflicts and personalities, 1906–1914' (in Hebrew) *Cathedra* XXXVII (1985), 95–121.
Stanford J. Shaw, 'The Ottoman Census System and Population, 1831–1914', *IJMES* XI (1978), 325–38.
Stanford J. Shaw, 'The Population of Istanbul in the Nineteenth Century', *Tarih Dergisi* XXXII (1979), 403–14.
Stanford J. Shaw, 'Christian anti-Semitism in the Ottoman Empire', *Belleten* (1991).
Aryeh Shmuelevitz, *The Jews of the Ottoman Empire in the Late Fifteenth and the Sixteenth Centuries: Administrative, Economic, Legal and Social Relations as Reflected in the Responsa* (Leiden, Brill, 1984).
Aryah Shmuelevitz, 'Capsali as a Source for Ottoman History, 1450–1523', *IJMES* IX (1978), 339–44.

Nathan Shur, 'The Jews of Lebanon in the Ottoman period in the light of travellers' literature' (in Hebrew) *Pe'amim*, 1988, pp. 117–35.

Nathan Shur, *History of Safad* (in Hebrew) (Tel Aviv, 1983).

Karl L. Signell, *Makam. Modal Practice in Turkish Art Music* (Seattle, Asian Music Publications, University of Washington, 1977).

Karl L. Signell, 'Hebrew Poetry in the East after the Spanish Expulsion' (in Hebrew), *Pe'amim* XXVI (1986), 29–45.

Shlomo Simonsohn, 'A Christian Report from Constantinople Regarding Shabbetai Zebi', *JSS* XII (1961), 33–85.

Shlomo Simonsohn, 'Marranos in Ancona under Papal Protection' (in Hebrew), in Michael, *On the History of the Jews in the Diaspora* (Jerusalem, 1985), 234–67.

Dushan Sindik, 'Muzej Saveza Jevrejskih Opshtina Jugoslavije' (The Museum of the Federation of Jewish Communities of Yugoslavia), *Jevrejski Almanah, 1959–1960*, pp. 194–200.

Dushan Sindik, 'O Jevrejskim shkolama u Beograd u XIX veku','(Jewish Schools in Belgrade in the XIXth Century), *Jevrejski Almanah, 1961–1962*, pp. 98–109.

Barukh Sivi, 'The Po'ali Zion/Workers of Zion movement at Salonica' (in Hebrew), *Zikhron Saloniki*, ed. D. A. Recanati (Tel Aviv, 1972).

David Slinas, 'The Relations between the Ottoman Empire and Spain in the Context of the Expulsion', Unpublished paper presented at *First International Congress on Turkish Jewry*, Herzlia, Israel, 18 October 1989.

M. Sokoloski, 'Aperçu sur l'Evolution de Certaines Villes plus importantes de la partie meridionale des Balkans au XVe et au XVIe siecles', *Istanbul a la Jonction des Cultures Balkaniques, Mediterraneennes, Slaves et Orientales aux XVIe–XIXe Siècles* (Bucharest, 1973), 81–89.

Salomon Stambouli, 'The Economic Activity of Egyptian Jews, 1798–1918' (in Hebrew), Jacob Landau, ed., *The Jews in Ottoman Egypt (1517–1914)* (in Hebrew) (Jerusalem, 1988), 113–28.

Edvard Stankijevich, 'Balkanski i slovenski elementi u Judeo-shpanskom jeziku Jugoslavije' (Balkan and Slavic elements in Judeo-Spanish spoken in Yugoslavia), *Jevrejski Almanah, 1965–1967*, pp. 84–91.

Joshua Starr, 'The Socialist Federation of Saloniki', *JSS* VII/4 (October 1945).

Leonard Stein, *The Balfour Declaration* (London, 1961).

M. Steinschneider, 'Jüdische Aerzte', *Zeitschrift für hebraeische Bibliographie* XVII (1914), 63–96, 121–67.

Shmuel Stempler, ed., *History of the Yishuv: Landmarks before Statehood* (Tel Aviv, Ministry of Defense, 1983).

Eliahu Stern, 'The relations of the Istanbul delegation with Polish Jewry" (in Hebrew), *Yalkut Moreshet* (Israel), no. 39 (1985), 135–52.

Selma Stern, *The Court Jew* (Philadelphia, 1950).

Desmond Stewart, *Theodor Herzl, Artist and Politician* (London, 1974).

Norman Stillman, *The Jews of Arab Lands: A History and Source Book* (Philadelphia, 1979).

Ntalija Strunjash, 'Jevreju u Jugoslovenskoj Leteraturi' (Jews in Yugoslav Literature), *Jevrejski Almanah 1965–1967*, pp. 115–28.

N. Svoronos, *Le Commerce de Salonique au XVIIIe siècle* (Paris, 1956).

Zosa Szajkowski, 'Jewish Emigration Policy in the Period of the Rumanian 'Exodus' 1899–1903', *JSS* XIII/1 (1951), 47–70.

Zosa Szajkowski, 'Conflicts in the Alliance israélite universelle and the Founding of the Anglo-Jewish Association, the Vienna Allianz and the *Hilfsverein*', *JSS* XIX (1957), 21–40.

Jorjo Tadich, *Jevreji u Dubrovniku do polovine XVII stoleca* (Jews in Dubrovnik until the mid 17th century) (Sarajevo, 1937).

Jorjo Tadich, 'Iz Istorije Jevreja u Jugoistochnoj Evropi' (From the History of the Jews of Southeastern Europe), *Jevrejski Almanah, 1959–1960,* pp. 29–53.

Vicki Tamir, *Bulgaria and Her Jews: The History of a Dubious Symbiosis* (New York, Sepher-Hermon Press, 1979).

B. Taragan, *Les Communautés Israelites d'Alexandrie: Aperçu historique depuis les temps des Ptolémés jusqu'a nos jours* (Alexandria, 1932).

Jacques Thobie, *Intérets et impérialisme française dans l'Empire ottoman (1895–1914)* (Paris, Sorbonne, 1977).

Robert L. Tignor, 'Egyptian Jewry, Communal Tension, and Zionism' *Egypt and Palestine: A Millenium of Association (868–1948),* ed. Amnon Cohen and Gabriel Baer (Jerusalem and New York, 1984), 332–47.

Nicolai Todorov, *La Ville Balkanique, XVe–XIXe Siècles* (Sofia, 1970); translated as *The Balkan City, 1400–1900* (Seattle and London, 1983).

Rabbi Daniel Tsion, *Spomeni: Pet godini pod fashistki gneg* (Memoirs: Five Years under fascist terror) (Sofia, 1945).

Cemal Tukin, 'Osmanlı Imparatorluğunda Girit Isyanları: 1821 Yılına kadar Girit', *Belleten* IX (1945), 164–206.

Tarik Tunaya, *Türkiyede Siyasal Partileri* (Political Parties in Turkey) (3 vols, Istanbul, 1984–1989)

Mete Tunçay, *Türkiyede Sol Akımlar (1908–1925)* (Leftist Movements in Turkey) (3rd edition, Istanbul, 1978).

Şerafettin Turan, 'Rodos ve 12 Adanın Türk Hakimiyetinden Çıkışı', *Belleten* XXIX (1965), 77–119.

Shaul Tuval, 'The Jewish Community in Turkey Today' (in Hebrew), *Pe'amim,* Ben Zvi Institute, Hebrew University Jerusalem, no. 11–14 (1982), pp. 114–39.

Isadore Twersky, 'The *Shulhan Aruch*: Enduring Code of Jewish Law', *Judaism* XVI (1967).

N. Ülker, *The Rise of Izmir, 1688–1740* (Unpublished Ph.D. dissertation, Ann Arbor, Michigan, 1975).

A.E. Vacalopoulos, *A History of Thessaloniki* (1963).

Lucette Valensi, 'La tour de Babel: groupes et relations ethniques au Moyen-Orient et en Afrique du Nord', *Annales* IV (1986), 817–35.

Armenius Vambéry, *Freiheitliche Bestrebung im Moslimischen Asien* (Berlin, 1893).

Armenius Vambéry, 'Personal Recollections of Abdül Hamid II and his court', *The Nineteenth Century and After* LXV/388 (1909), 980–83, LXVI/389 (1909), 69–88.

Marie-Christine Varol, *Balat: Faubourg Juif d'Istanbul* (Istanbul, Isis, 1989).

I. K. Vasdravellis, *Historica archeia Macedonias I, Archeion Thessalonikis, 1695–1912* (Historical Archives of Macedonia, vol. I, Archives of Salonica, 1695–1912) (Thessaloniki, 1952).

Gilles Veinstein, 'Une communauté ottomane: les Juifs d'Avlonya (Valona) dans la deuxième moitié du XVIe siècle', *Gli Ebrei a Venezia secoli XIV–XVIII,* ed. G. Cozzi (Milano, 1987), 781–828.

Gilles Veinstein, 'Ayan de la région d'Izmir et le commerce du Levant (deuxième moitié du XVIIIe siècle)', *Revue de l'Occident Musulman et de la Mediterranée,* 1975.

Stefan Velikov, 'Sur le mouvement ouvrier et socialiste en Turquie après la révolution jeune-turque de 1908', *EB* (Sofia), 1964/1.

Nikolaus Vielmetti, 'Der Wiener Judische Publizist Ludwig August Frankl und die Begrundung der Lamelschule in Jerusalem, 1856', *Jahrbuch des Institut für Deutsche Geschichte* (Jerusalem) IV (1975), 167–204.

Vuk Vinaver, 'Jevreji u Srbiji Pochetkom XX Veka' (Jews in Serbia at the Beginning of the 20th Century), *Jevrejski Almanah, 1955–1956*, pp. 28–34.

Vuk Vinaver, 'O Jevrejima u Dubrovniku u XVIII Veku' (Jews in Dubrovnik in the Eighteenth Century), *Jevrejski Almanah, 1959–1960*, pp. 65–78.

David Vital, *The Origins of Zionism* (Oxford, 1980).

David Vital, *Zionism: the formative years* (Oxford, 1982).

David Vital, *Zionism: The Crucial Phase* (Oxford, 1987).

Franz von Papen, *Memoirs* (New York, 1968, London, 1972).

Franz von Papen, *Der Wahrheit eine Gasse* (Munich, 1952).

E. Vourazeli-Marinakou, *Hai en Thrake syntechniae ton Hellenon kata ten Tourkokratian* (The guilds of the Greeks in Thrace under Turkish rule) (Salonica, 1959).

M. L. Wagner, *Caracteres generales del judeo-espanol de Oriente* (Madrid, 1930).

Walter Weiker, *The Unseen Israelis: The Jews from Turkey in Israel* (Lanham, Md., University Presses of America, 1989).

Walter Weiker, 'Turkish-Jewish Relations and the Development of Turkish Nationalism', Unpublished paper presented at *First International Congress on Turkish Jewry*, Herzlia, Israel, 18 October 1989.

Edward Weisband, *Turkish Foreign Policy, 1943–1945* (Princeton, New Jersey, 1973).

Chaim Weizmann, *Trial and Error* (London, 1949).

Chaim Weizmann, *The Letters and Papers* (New Brunswick/Jerusalem, 1968).

Saadia E. Weltmann, 'Germany, Turkey and the Zionist Movement, 1914–1918', *Review of Politics* XXIII (1961), 246–69.

R. J. Z. Werblowsky, *Joseph Caro: Lawyer and Mystic* (1962).

S. Werses, 'From the Life of the Jewish Community in Izmir' (in Hebrew), *Yavneh* III, 93–111.

Jonas Weyl, 'Les Juifs protégés français aux échelles du Levant et en Barbarie', *REJ* XII (1886), 267–82.

Horst Widmann, *Exil und Bildungshilfe* (Frankfurt, 1973).

J. Blow Williams, *British Commercial Policy and Trade Expansion, 1750–1850* (Oxford, 1972).

H. V. F. Winstone, *The Illicit Adventure: The Story of Political and Military Intelligence in the Middle East from 1898 to 1926* (London, Cape, 1982).

Michael Winter, *Society and Religion in Early Ottoman Egypt: Studies in the Writings of 'Abd al-Wahhâb al-Sha'râni* (New Brunswick, N.J., 1982).

Michael Winter, 'The Islamic profile and the religious policy of the ruling class in Ottoman Egypt', *Religion and Government in the World of Islam, Israel Oriental Studies* X (1980), 132–45.

Michael Winter, 'Egyptian Jews in the Ottoman Period according to Turkish and Arab Sources' (in Hebrew) *Pe'amim*, 1984–85, pp. 5–17.

Michael Winter, 'The Relations of Egyptian Jews with the Authorities and with the Non-Jewish Society' (in Hebrew), Jacob Landau, ed., *The Jews in Ottoman Egypt (1517–1914)* (in Hebrew) (Jerusalem, 1988), 371–420.

M. Wischnitzer, *A History of Jewish Crafts and Guilds* (New York, 1965).

Lucien Wolf, *The Life of Sir Moses Montefiore* (New York, 1881).

I. Wolfson, 'Ali Bey al-Kabir and the Jews' (in Hebrew), *Zion* III (1939), 237–49.

E. J. Worman, 'Notes on the Jews in Fustat from the Cambridge Genizah Documents', *JQR* XVIII (1906), 1–39.

E. J. Worman, 'Un document concernant Isaac Louria', *REJ* LVII (1909), 281–82.

William Yale, 'Ambassador Henry Morgenthau's Special Mission of 1917', *World Politics* I/3 (1949), 308–20.

Raouf Yekta Bey, 'La Musique Turque', *Encyclopédie de la Musique et Dictionnaire du Conservatoire*, ed. Albert Lavignac (Paris, 1922) V, 2945–3064.

Rabbi Yishaq Yerushalmi, *Kanun Name de Penas: Letras de Muestro Sinyor el Rey, Y" H sigun lo escrito se deve de afirmar 5620* (1860) (Cincinnati, Ohio, 1975).

D. Yudelevitz, 'The Eretz Israel deportees in Egypt (during World War I)', *Miyamim Rishomim* (Jerusalem), vol. I, no. 7 (1934), 177–85, no. 8 (Jan. 1935), pp. 209–20, no. 9 (Feb. 1935), pp. 265–77, no. 11 (April 1935), pp. 305–17, no. 12 (May 1935), pp. 337–48; vol. II, no. 1 (June–July 1935), pp. 24–40.

E. Zechlin, *Die deutsche Politik und die Juden im Ersten Weltkrieg* (Göttingen, 1969).

H. J. Zimmels, *Magicians, Theologians and Doctors – Studies in Folk Medicine and Folklore as Reflected in the Rabbinical Responsa (12th–19th Centuries)* (London, 1952).

H. J. Zimmels, *Ashkenazim and Sephardim: Their Relations, Differences, and Problems as Reflected in the Rabbinical Responsa* (London, 1958)

H. J. Zimmels, *Rabbi David Abi Simra: Ein Beitrag zur Kulturgeschichte der Juden in der Türkei im 16. Jahrhundert auf Grund seiner Gutachten* (Breslau, Bericht des Jüdisch-Theologischen Seminars-Hochschule für jüdische Theologie für das Jahr 1932, 1933).

Israel Zinberg, *A History of Jewish Literature. vol. V. The Jewish Center of Culture in the Ottoman Empire* (Hebrew Union College Press, Ktav Publishers, New York, 1974).

Zvi Zohar, 'Halakhic Reactions to Modernization, 1882–1918' (in Hebrew), Jacob Landau, ed., *The Jews in Ottoman Egypt (1517–1914)* (in Hebrew) (Jerusalem, 1988), 577–608.

Index

Principal page references are in *italics*. The numerous divergent spellings of Jewish Turkish names have been standardized, with alternate spellings given in parentheses. Turkish words, and those relating to Jews in the Turkish Republic, have been spelled according to modern Turkish orthography, in which ç, in particular, is pronounced 'ch' and ş as 'sh'.

Cohn, Albert (1814–77, Rothschild agent in Istanbul), 155, 159
coinage, currency, 111
communications, 112–13
community control, 64–5
community organization, Jewish, *see millet* and *kahal*
Comtino, Mordehai ben Eliezer (1420–87), *101–2*, 289
conscription of non-Muslims, 156, 211, 226, 228, 231
Constantinople, Byzantine, 4, 15, 25
Persecution of Jews at, *15–23*
Jewish settlements and population at, *17–18*, 37
Ottoman conquest of, 26, 27, 41
see also Istanbul
Constitutional era in Ottoman Empire (1908–12), 180, 182, 220, 226
consuls, European consular powers in Ottoman Empire, consular courts, 110, 116–18, 120, 125
see also Capitulations
contracts, 96, 229
conversos, 12, 13, 88
copper, coppersmiths, Jews as, 17, 29, 97, 113
coral trade, 95
Cordova (Spain), 12, 69
Cordovero, Jacob, 101
Corfu, 24, 35, 94, 190, 191, 194–5
corporal punishment, 46, 60
cortijo (multiple Jewish dwelling bungalow surrounding courtyard), 56
corvée (forced labor), 120, 232
Cossacks, attacks against Jews by, 74, 107, 124, 133, 189, 192
cotton, cotton trade, 80, 95, 141
Counter-Reformation (16th century), effect of, on Jews, 7
Courrier d'Orient (Istanbul), 224
courts, *see* Justice
Covo, Chief Rabbi Asher (Salonica), 163, 170
Crémieux, Isaac Adolphe (1796–1880), 199–200
Crespin, Elia, 181
Crete, 24, 89, 191
Crimea, Tatar kingdom of, 25
Crimean War, 159–60, 169, 192
Crusades and Crusaders, Crusading orders, role in persecuting and

attacking Jews, *4–5*, 8, 12, 15, 17–18, 22, 73, 114
Culi, Jacob ben Meir (1690–1732), 144
cultivators, 112, 140
Cumhuriyet (Republic), 255, 269
currency exchange, international, 64, 94
custom, Jewish (*haggadah*), 64
customs duties and houses, 55, 75, 87, 91, 95, 115, 141, 155
Cyprus, 34
Jewish migration to, 35
Ottoman conquest of (1570), *89*, 90
Cycliad islands (Andros, Paris, Antiparos, Milo, Sira and Santorin), 89
Çakacı ('clothiers') synagogue (Balat), 66
Çanakkale, 67, 259, 261, 262, 264, 285, 298
Çatalca (Istanbul), 240, 274
Çelebi, 34
Çelik, Ibrahim Halil, 269
Çorapcı Han synagogue (Istanbul), 66
Çorlu, 195–6, 204

Dalem, Jules (teacher in Camondo school), 160
Dalmatia, Dalmatian coast, 53, 118, 191
Dalmedico, Moise (1848–1937), 181, 186, 248
Dalmedico, Dr. Rafael, 159
Damascus, 26, 33, 45, *55*, 95, 121, 143, 164, 168, 199, 201–2, 203, 278
Damascus Pogrom (1840), *199–200*
Damiyanus (Greek Orthodox Bishop in Jerusalem), 233, 296
Damietta, 55
Danon, Abraham (1857–1925), 184, 219, 220, 221
Danon, Samuel, 146, 174–5
David, Yako Jacob Behar (Ottoman Grand Rabbi, 1841–54), 152, 272
dayyan (Heb: judge, pl. *dayyanim*), 42, 59, 60, *see also* Justice
deaths, registration of, 260
de Fonseca, Daniel (1672–1740), 142
Deleon, Jak, 265
de Medina, Samuel ben Moses (1506–89), 52, 99, 102, *104–5*
Democrat Party, 259–60, 265
de Vidas, Elijah ben Moses, 101

Uziel, Jacob, 183
Üsküdar (Scutari), 113, 114, 129, 273, 287, 210, 241, 246
Üsküp synagogue (Istanbul), 66

Va'ad Pekidim (Committee of Functionaries), 161
vaad ha-kehilla (Heb: Jewish district communal council), 261–2
Van, 281, 286
Vahdet (Unity), 269
vakıf, 75, see also foundation
Vakko department stores, 265, 271
Valencia, 12, 13
Valero, Izak, 146
Valide Sultan (Turk: Sultan's mother, head of Palace Harem), 148
Valona (Avlonya, Albmieux), 38, 94
Varlık Vergisi (World War II Turkish Capital Tax, introduced 11 November 1942, annulled 17 September 1943, collections abandoned 15 March 1944), 255–6, 258
Varna, 39, 186
Varon, Gelibolulu Ishak (1882–1962), 250
Vatican, opposition to admitting Jewish refugees from Nazis into Turkey, 257
vegetable trade, 97, 140
Venice, 24, 74, 87, 89, 90, 91, 94, 95, 103, 114, 116, 119, 122, 123, 141, 190
  colonies of, in Constantinople, 18, 115
Ventura, Jak, 184
Ventura, Mishon, 243
Ventura, Moshe (Moşe), 252
Verya synagogue (Balat), 66
Vidin, 38, 190, 192
  migration of European Jews to, 33
Vienna
  Ottoman sieges of (1529, 1683), 25, 118, 125
Vilna, 15
vineyards, 54
Virane synagogue (Kuzguncuk), 67
Vital, Hayyim ben Joseph (1542–1620), 104, 105

Wallachia, 89, 118, 188–9, 190
war taxes, 75, 120, 122

water supplies, 111
weaving, weavers, 92–3, 124, 140, 164
weddings, 65, 105, 172, 261
weights and measures regulation, 57, 92
Weizmann, Chaim (1874–1952), 234
widows, 60
wheat, wheat trade, 88, 141
wheelwrights, 92
Wilhelm II (1858–1941), German Kaiser (1888–1918), support for Zionism by, 212–13
wine, manufacture and trade, 65, 89, 95, 126, 130, 140, 172, 174, 264
Winterstein, Hans (1879–1963), 253
women
  position of, in Ottoman Jewish communities, 46, 69, 74, 90–1, 137–8, 162, 164, 169–70, 229–30, 263
wood, woodworkers, 53, 93, 95
wool industry, trade, 54, 88, 95, 97, 141
World War I (1914–18), 3, 147
  in Ottoman Empire, 229–38, 297
  in Eretz Israel, 232–7
  Jewish contribution to Ottoman war effort during, 3, 230–1
  massacres and deaths in Ottoman Empire during, 238
  Allied propaganda against Ottomans during, 236–7, 297
World War II (1939–45), 3
  in Turkey, 255–8
Wrangel, White Russian General, 240

Yaesh (Yaeş), Isak (1922–70), 266
Yaesh, Soloman Aben (Abanaes, 1520–1603), 91–2
Yaesh, Yomtov ben (Istanbul Grand Rabbi, 1639–60), 272
yahudhâne (Turk: Jewish tenament), 129, 130, 140
Ya'akoviyim (dönme followers of Jacob Querido), 178
Yahya, Nedim (b. 1925), ix, 264, 267, 271
Yakub Efendi (Maestro Jacobo, physician to Mehmed II), 86
Yanbol synagogue (Balat), 50, 66, 230, 247, 248, 262, Plate 5
yasak (Turk: prohibition), 81–2, 127
yaşamak (Turk: overcoat), 80